Discourses of Weakness in Modern China

Discourses of Weakness and Resource Regimes

Edited by Iwo Amelung, Moritz Epple, Hartmut Leppin, and Susanne Schröter

Volume 2

Iwo Amelung is Professor for Sinology at Goethe-University Frankfurt

Iwo Amelung (ed.)

Discourses of Weakness in Modern China

Historical Diagnoses of the "Sick Man of East Asia"

Campus Verlag
Frankfurt/New York

The Collaborative Research Center 1095 is funded by the German Research Foundation.

ISBN 978-3-593-50902-0 Print
ISBN 978-3-593-43895-5 E-Book (PDF)

All rights reserved. No part of this book may be reproduced or transmitted in any form or by any means, electronic or mechanical, including photocopying, recording, or by any information storage and retrieval system, without permission in writing from the publishers.
Despite careful control of the content Campus Verlag GmbH cannot be held liable for the content of external links. The content of the linked pages is the sole responsibility of their operators.
Copyright © 2020 Campus Verlag GmbH, Frankfurt-on-Main
Cover design: Campus Verlag GmbH, Frankfurt-on-Main
Printing office and bookbinder: CPI buchbücher.de, Birkach
Printed on acid free paper.
Printed in Germany

www.campus.de
www.press.uchicago.edu

Contents

Introduction 9
Iwo Amelung

Part I: Examining the Sick Man—Describing Symptoms of Weakness

From Discourse of Weakness to Discourse of Empowerment:
The Topos of the "Sick Man of East Asia" in Modern China 25
Jui-sung Yang

A Two Step Transition 1895–1900. Discourses of Weakness as
basso continuo of Chinese Modernity 79
Daniel Hausmann

Records from a Defeated Country: Different Chinese Narratives about the
First Sino-Japanese War (1894/95) and their Spreading during the
Last Period of the Qing Dynasty 109
Sun Qing

"Lack of Nation" and "Lack of History": The Emergence of a Discourse
of Weakness in Late Qing China 137
Zhang Qing

Part II: Diagnosing the Sick Man—Divided, Imperilled, Humiliated

The Privileges of the Powerful and the Discourses of the Weak:
The Dissemination and Application of the Concept of
"Extraterritoriality" in Modern China 161
Huang Xingtao

Discourses on "National Humiliation" and "National Ruin" as Reflected
in Late Qing and Early Republican Era History Textbooks 223
Li Fan

The Discourse on "National Humiliation" during the Early
Period of the Chinese Communist Party—The
Case of *The Guide Weekly* (1922–1927) 245
Li Lifeng

The Boundaries of the Chinese Nation: Racism and Militarism
in the 1911 Revolution 283
Clemens Büttner

The Idea of "Intellectual Warfare" and the Dispersion of Social Darwinism
in Late Qing China (1897–1906) 335
Sebastian Riebold

Part III: Prognosis for the Sick Man—Ruin, Resistance and Restauration

Evolution of the Late Qing Historical Writing on the
Decline of Poland 379
Zou Zhenhuan

Selfish Faint Hearts, Ardent Fighters, and Gallant Heroines?—Characters
in Plays about the Taiwan Republic 411
Mirjam Tröster

Progress or Decline: China's Two Images of India during the
Nineteenth Century 465
Zhang Ke

Part IV: Treating the Sick Man—Co-existence, Science and Profit

Nationalism, Human-Co-Existentialism, Pan-Asianism: The Weakness Discourse and Wang Jingwei's Intellectual Transformation 489
Zhiyi Yang

Science and National Salvation in Early Twentieth Century China 519
Iwo Amelung

Capitalising on Crisis: The Expansion of the Late Qing Newspaper Market 565
Tze-ki Hon

Acknowledgements 583

Authors 585

Introduction

Iwo Amelung

China's (forced) integration into the global society during the 19th century, especially after her defeat in the First Opium War, was accompanied by the emergence of concepts and descriptive devices which, in one way or another, aimed at describing and evaluating China's position in an ever changing world. Some of these concepts quickly evolved into powerful images, such as, for example, the common reference to China as the county of the "Four hundred million"[1]—pointing to China's population—or the reference to a China which was asleep, but would be "awakened" sooner or later.[2] Such ascriptions had a comparative element, one which could have either a positive or a negative connotation. Other ascriptions, which became equally or even more powerful, such as the "dividing up of the melon",[3] or the ubiquitously employed image of the "sick man of East Asia", were less merciful at first sight, and, as such, quite successful in depicting a weak and almost helpless country. If no remedy was attempted or possible, China's descent into becoming a mere plaything of the Powers of the West (and Japan) seemed inevitable. While some writers and commentators were at least willing to pity the helpless giant, there were also those who conceptionalised this development as the inevitable result of the Darwinian forces of international politics. It it is clear in any case that such ascriptions of weakness soon became an indispensable component of Western attempts to evaluate and classify both the international order and the situation in the world, which became increasingly complex and indispensable when a shrinking world encountered the rise of high-imperialism during the second half of the 19th century.

It is, indeed, remarkable how fast China was removed from a position of adoration, which it had enjoyed in the minds of many thinkers of the enlightenment period and which had been related to an almost universal *Chinoiserie* in the crafts and even in architecture.[4] In fact, to some extent, China was written out

---

1 Bréard (2019), "Four Hundred Million".
2 Wagner (2011), "China 'Asleep' and 'Awakening'".
3 Wagner (2017), "'Dividing up the [Chinese] Melon, guafen 瓜分'".
4 Hertel (2019), *Siting China in Germany*.

of history, as, for example, occurred with Hegel.[5] For Herder, it had already been an "embalmed mummy",[6] while Ranke made China into "a people of perpetual stagnation", which "virtually subjects itself to the European Spirit".[7] Quite often, such ascriptions did not really aim to describe the situation in China, but were rather a means of self-assertion with a view of the dynamical development of the West, which was brought about by the development of capitalism and the industrial revolution from the early 19th century onwards. This does not mean, however, that they did not exert a lasting impact on the Western image of China.

Ascriptions of weakness within Western discourse could serve other purposes as well. In their extreme form, such as the "Sick Man of East Asia", they were certainly capable of embodying a rather triumphant attitude, which considered China's weakness as a well-deserved punishment for supposedly arrogant Chinese claims of superiority. To some extent, this is already visible in the writings of Robert Fortune (1812–1880), who, in 1847, noted that China was "retrograding" and "in decay", which he relished given that "they [the Chinese], from the highest Mandarin down to the meanest beggar, are filled with the most conceited notions of their own importance and power; and fancy that no people however civilised, and no country however powerful, are for one moment to be compared with them".[8] Similar ideas can easily be found with other Western writers of the period, such as the American consul, Gideon Nye (1812–1888), who claimed that China's weakness until the Opium War had been hidden "behind a wall of exclusiveness" and that now "the assumption of superiority and universal Empire" must "be relinquished".[9]

Putting glee aside, however, Western ascriptions of weakness served other goals as well. During the 19th century, they were certainly an important basis for missionary activities. It was much easier to justify Christian missions as an indispensable remedy for a society that was somehow deficient and weak, and diagnosed as suffering from serious problems.[10] At the same time, supposed racial weaknesses and deficits began to serve as a basis for racial segregation and discrimination against Chinese people in Australia and the US in particular, where the adoption of exclusion acts became possible because the Chinese state was indeed too weak to counter such discriminatory legislation. Racial prejudice, ascriptions of weakness and China's geopolitical situation, thus went hand in hand. It was also at this time—since the beginning of the 1870s—that the idea

---

5 Franke (1970), "Hegel und die Geschichte Chinas".

6 Lee (2003), *"Anti–Europa": Die Geschichte der Rezeption des Konfuzianismus*, p. 248.

7 Pigulla (1996), *China in der deutschen Weltgeschichtsschreibung*, pp. 220–221.

8 Fortune (1847), *Three Years of Wandering*, p. 9, p. 2.

9 Nye (1857), *The Rationale of the Chinese Question*, p. 25, p. 9.

10 Schoppa (2002), *Revolution and its Past*, p. 62.

of the "Yellow Peril" gained currency, which, on the one hand, pointed at a large number of Chinese with "weak" and "decrepit" intellect, but, on the other, also reflected a China which suddenly appeared surprisingly strong—able to suppress its internal rebellions and trying to "strengthen itself". [11] Nonetheless, for Western observers, the ascription of weakness was a way of defining (and defending) hierarchies. The weakness of a state or a particular historical formation implied a lower position in the civilisational order, and could thus be used to legitimatise such an international order, which, during the late 19th century, seemed to be increasingly subject to the rules of social Darwinism. This weakness was—allegedly—often based upon racial features and deficiencies.

At the same time, such ascriptions of weakness constituted the point of departure for a "civilising mission" on the part of the countries of the West (of which Japan tried to become a part by breaking away from Asia), which, as Osterhammel has correctly pointed out, not only aimed at "palliatively doing away with grievances, but at a transformative change of societal structures". [12]

Not surprisingly, it was China's defeat in the war against Japan in 1894/95, which put the last brushstroke on the picture of an extremely weak China, an image which was to endure for a long time. China had now become a "dying whale", surrounded by a "set of hungry sharks", [13] or even—as Mahan (1840–1914) implicitly suggested—a "carcass" to be dissected or devoured by the "eagles" of the developed world. [14] In the eyes of Western beholders, it was not only the sick man of East Asia, but was also, in fact, already dead, "in a pitiable state of weakness and decay…[it is] the Empire of the Dead". [15] Japanese nationalists used this as a starting-point for their own version of the "civilising mission", as, for example, can be seen from Tokutomi Sohō 徳富蘇峰 1863–1957), who, in 1896, stated that "East Asia becoming a mire of disorder is something that our nation will not tolerate. … We have a duty to radiate the light of civilization beyond our shores and bring the benefits of civilization to our neighbors". [16] In 1900, however, another Japanese observer was more pessimistic:

The Sick Man of the Far East is much nearer dissolution than the Ottoman Empire is, or ever has been. China's malady is mortal. Japan sincerely wishes to see the independence and the integrity of the Middle Kingdom maintained; but the trend of events serves

---

11 Scott (2008), *China and the International System*, p. 70.
12 Osterhammel (2005), "The Great Work of Uplifting Mankind", p. 371.
13 Senex, "Our Future Empire in the Far East", p. 163.
14 Mahan (1900), *The Problem of Asia*, pp. 15–16.
15 Scott (2008), *China and the International System*, p. 151.
16 De Bary et al. (2005), *Sources of Japanese Tradition*, p. 805.

to indicate only too clearly that this is impossible, and that the sand in the hour-glass is running down apace.[17]

The Boxer Rising and the siege of the legations in Beijing in the year 1900 served to reinforce further the impression that China had distanced itself from "civilisation" (in Western terms). The allied victory again showed China's weakness, and when allied troops entered the Forbidden City, quite a few of them commented on the alleged "decay" of the palaces and the "absolutely shocking condition", both of which were considered as a physical corroboration of China's weakness.[18]

The examples given here, which could easily be greatly expanded, make clear that late 19th and early 20th century Western discourses of depicting China as weak—or even at death's door—could serve for multiple, and at times even contradictory, purposes.

In any case, it is important to realise that many of the conceptionalisations and metaphors which were employed in such discourses of weakness were transcultural in nature. This even holds true for caricatures—quite a number of which were popular both in China and in the West, as Rudolf G. Wagner has demonstrated.[19] Indeed, the Western ascriptions of weakness to China were matched by an incalculable amount of Chinese self-ascriptions of being weak and on the verge of perishing both as a state and as a nation.

Many historians have, of course, noted that references regarding the weakness of China during the late 19th and early 20thcenturies constituted a common feature in the writings of Chinese scholars and officials.[20] However, one of the few scholars who has tried to approach the phenomenon in a more systematic way is Rebecca Karl. She correctly points out that the "central concepts that came to constitute a discourse of nationalism" were linked to the world around China. A nationalist discourse only becomes possible if the existence of other nations is acknowledged, and if the situation and the fate of one's own nation, in one way or another, is compared with them. Nationalism is thus part of a "global historical problematic". Karl explicitly takes up the issue of the weakness of China, showing to what extent, during the late Qing period, other nations—such as Poland—were transformed into tropes which could be used to highlight certain aspects of China's weakness.[21]

---

17 Ozaki (1900), "Misunderstood Japan", p. 574.

18 Hevia (2003), *English Lessons*, p. 207.

19 Wagner (2011), "China "Asleep" and "Awakening".

20 This already begins with Levenson (1959), *Liang Ch'i–ch'ao*, and Schwartz (1964), *In Search of Wealth and Power*, and continues until today, in, for example, Tang Xiaobing (1996), *Global Discourse*, Pye (1992), *The Spirit of Chinese Politics*, pp. 7 and 71, and, in particular, Tsu (2005), *Failure, Nationalism, and Literature* (2005).

21 Karl (2002), *Staging the World*.

INTRODUCTION

The present volume begins from this starting-point, and develops this approach one step further. It collects the contributions to a conference, which was held in Frankfurt am Main in December 2015, and which aimed at investigating the Chinese "Discourses of Weakness" of the late 19th and early 20th century. The definition of the term "discourse" proposed at the conference was a rather simple one, namely, "statements that organise themselves systematically with regard to a certain topic and are characterised by a uniform (not identical) repetition from a discourse".[22] In order to accommodate the clearly visible impact of some of the historical actors on the development of these discourses—such as the famous translator Yan Fu 嚴復 (1853–1921), the reformer Liang Qichao 梁啟超 (1873–1929) and others—we take our lead from Pocock, who has pointed out that individual actors have the potential, through "utterance and response", to change "language"—by which he means discourse.[23] Discourse itself—"language" in the usage of Peter Burke—not only has the power to control others, but is also actually, as Burke holds, "an active force in society" and can be used "to change society or to prevent others from changing it".[24] And, indeed, it is quite clear that some of the discourses of weakness which emerged from the late 19th century were highly consequential in changing Chinese society. One rather prominent example is the discourse on the Chinese national character, which was based upon the quite racist ideas of Arthur Smith, and became an important component of the writings of the famous author Lu Xun 魯迅 (1881–1936),[25] and, in a transformed way, again re-emerged in the cultural critic Bo Yang's 柏楊 (1920–2008) famous *The Ugly Chinaman*.[26]

Even more important, however, both then and now is another discourse also embodying a kind of "negative nationalism",[27] namely, the idea of national humiliation, which can be considered as a congealed and even canonized discourse of weakness, a "handy catalogue of infamy" as Bickers characterised the thick *Dictionary of National Humiliation* published in 1992.[28] The preface of the book—written by the ultra-orthodox historian Dai Yi 戴逸—does indeed, and not surprisingly, hint at the Darwinian law of the jungle (*ruorou qiangshi* 弱肉強食, literally, the weak meat will be eaten by the strong), and complains that the invaders saw the Chinese nation as an "inferior nation" (*liedeng minzu* 劣等民族) and the "sick man of East Asia" (*dongya bingfu* 東亞病夫). It also takes up the legend of the famous (and incorrect) story of a park in the Shanghai interna-

---

22 Landwehr (2008), *Historische Diskursanalyse*, pp. 92–93.
23 Pocock (1989), "The Concept of a Language", p. 100.
24 Burke (1987), "Introduction", p. 13.
25 Liu (1996), *Translingual Practice*, pp. 45–76.
26 Mitter (2004), *A Bitter Revolution*, pp. 262–272.
27 Gilley (2004), *China's Democratic Future*, p. 218.
28 Bickers (2011), *The Scramble for China*, p. 5.

tional concession that allegedly put up a sign which read "Chinese and Dogs not allowed" (*Huaren yu gou budei runei* 華人與狗不得入內)[29] and also cites the often used passage from the *Shiji* 史記 stating that "others are the knife and cutting board, while we are the fish and the meat" (*ren wei dao zu wo wei yu rou* 人為刀俎我為魚肉).[30] Callahan has convincingly characterised "national humiliation" as a narrative which "produces nation-states out of empire and civil war".[31]

Every Chinese school child today knows, that "national humiliation" should never be forgotten (*wuwang guochi* 毋忘國恥), but the question of whether it has been completely "cleansed away" is, somehow, left open and remains undecided. Such vacillating between desperation and pride in Chinese agency in order to overcome all odds (or, at least, the latent ability for it) is actually part and parcel of late 19th and early 20th century discourses of weakness as well. As this volume also shows, these discourses rarely serve as a means of (national) self-flagellation, but rather serve as a medium for mobilisation, legitimation, and, at times, as a resource for celebrating triumph.

Late 19th and early 20th century Chinese discourses of weakness are thus a highly interesting phenomenon. There is a clear need for documentation and systematic research, not only due to their ubiquitousness at the time in question, but also because they are still around, and, as such, one of the most important means for "producing" nationalism, which, in its coagulated form (the ruins of the Yuanmingyuan 圓明園, for example), can be consumed and maybe even enjoyed.[32]

It is not easy to establish clear functional differentiations between the Chinese discourses which are the subject matter of this volume. In many cases, different aspects were intertwined and referred to each other, and could, furthermore, evolve and change over time. Moreover, not all the discourses dealt with here work with the metaphor of the "Sick Man". Nonetheless, we have decided to adhere to it, and even apply it in the organisation of the book. It will become clear that the historical actors, considered the metaphor—even if not explicitly mentioned—as both important and very powerful, so that it is crucial to document the phenomenon. The analysis undertaken in the individual chapters aims to provide a new framework for the problem, and will corroborate the usefulness—and the actual indispensability—of the concept of "dis-

---

29 Bickers, Wasserstrom (1995), "Shanghai's 'Dogs and Chinese not admitted' Sign".

30 Bickers does not explicitly say which book he refers to, I assume that he points at the most voluminous (almost 900 pages) of a large number of similar books, which, moreover, was produced by the Academy of Social Sciences Zhongguo shehuikexueyuan jindaishi yanjiusuo jindai ziliao bianjishi (1992), *Guochi shidian* , The quotations are on p. 2.

31 Callahan (2004), "National Insecurities", p. 207.

32 Callahan (2007), "History, Identity, and Security"; Lee (2009), "The Ruins of Yuanmingyuan".

INTRODUCTION 15

courses of weakness", when researching into many areas of China's history since the late 19th century.

The first part, "Examining the Sick Man—Describing Symptoms of Weakness", begins by looking into the origins and the development of the metaphor of the "Sick Man" in China. Jui-sung Yang shows that the metaphor was originally used to describe the situation of the state and the nation. It was a Chinese tendency of self-victimisation, which transformed the metaphor into the supposed humiliation of the inferiority and sickness of the bodies of the individual Chinese people. Similar to the famous "Chinese and dogs not allowed" sign, the supposed "sick body" of the Chinese became one of the *leitmotifs* of Chinese nationalist discourse, and has—as suggested above—remained as such. The idea that Westerners used it in order to slight individual Chinese people has persisted, as became clear again in February 2020 during the Corona-virus outbreak in China—completely independent of the origins of the discourse. In his essay on "Discourses of Weakness as a *basso continuo* of Chinese Modernity", Daniel Hausmann suggests that Chinese discourses of weakness can be associated with certain features of modernity, in particular, with the growing importance of the concept of nation and the notion of linear time. They are thus related to the emergence of a Chinese modernity which can be dated to the period of the last years of the 19th and the beginning of the 20th century. The state's weakness, which became manifest for all to see during the Sino-Japanese war of 1894/95, made new discourses possible. Hausmann demonstrates how the main contents of the discourses shifted—namely, from a fixation mainly on the state (and thus on the ruling élites) to one which addressed the nation, which implied focusing on those who would form the nation and those who should be worshipped for their heroic dedication. In her "Records from a Defeated Country", Sun Qing shows how the traumatic experience of the Sino-Japanese War opened the way for the formation of very different narratives of the war, namely, one which narrated China's defeat in the war as a result of China's supposed "civilisational backwardness"—understood, of course, in terms of Western civilisation—and another which considered the defeat as an accidental misfortune for which China's general deficits could not be blamed, but for which those in charge of the war effort were responsible. In the chapter "'Lack of Nation' and 'Lack of History'", Zhang Qing also deals with the "unprecedented crisis" which China experienced during the last years of the 19th century, and links it to a "deficit discourse" which focused on the supposedly lacking "nation state" and the efforts to establish such a modern entity during this historical period. Zhang shows how these supposed "deficits" are in line with the Levenson thesis, that is, the shift from culturalism to nationalism and the identity crisis produced by it. In particular, he highlights the role of Liang Qichao in this process, who postulated that it was the confrontation between nations which was to result in the emergence of a Chinese nation. All four essays make clear to what extent discourses of weakness were related to ideas of a global modernity, or—maybe more precisely—how discourses of weakness contributed to the definition of China as a political entity which was fitted into global structures which are a characteristic of modernity, and how it needed to define and revise its position in emerging global hierarchies.

The second part of the volume "Diagnosing the Sick Man—Divided, Imperilled, Humiliated" opens with a chapter by Huang Xingtao on the "Dissemination and Application of the Concept of 'Extraterritoriality'", which takes up the arguably most powerful symbol of China's weakness after the Opium War. Applying a perspective informed by considerations of conceptual history, Huang shows how "extraterritoriality" was originally shrouded by misunderstandings, and how—related to the successive loss of real power—"extraterritoriality" not only became a symbol for China being mistreated by the Western powers and by Japan, but was also intricately linked to China's legal reform and—equally important—increasingly became a powerful tool of political mobilisation especially during the 1920s and was thus important to legitimise the "anti-imperialist national revolution" in China. In his essay on historical textbooks, Li Fan points out how, in correspondence to the discourse on "national ruin" in China's history textbooks, a powerful discourse on national humiliation emerged, which, however, was not presented as inevitable, but rather as a challenge which needed to be faced. Li Lifeng takes these ideas further into the 1920s and analyses them as they appear in the Communist journal *The Guide Weekly* between 1923 and 1927. Li stresses that this crucial period of the construction of historical memory was influenced by a discourse of weakness or even of collective trauma. This again makes clear to what extent the construction of the modern Chinese nation-state is intimately interwoven with the sense of national humiliation. Li convincingly shows that, for the Communist Party, the so-called "anti-imperialist" movement was more important than the fight against the warlords, and that national humiliation was an important resource for communist mobilisation during the time in question. These intensive discussions also resulted in a hierarchy of imperialist enemies, quite similar to the establishment of the civilisational order during the 19th century mentioned above: not surprisingly, England was enemy number one, while Germany, Austria and Russia—defeated in World War I—were no longer considered as belonging to the Imperialist camp.

In his contribution "The Boundaries of the Chinese Nation", Clemens Büttner stresses the great importance of social Darwinist thought from 1895 onwards for the emergence of discourses of weakness which would bring about the creation of a "Chinese nation". He shows that, in the eyes of many revolutionaries, the piteous state of China was due to ethnic problems, especially the supposed racial deficiency of the ruling Manchu. At the same time, the look towards Japan revealed a deficiency on the part of China with regard to martial qualities, which needed to be addressed in order to make China competitive. Büttner argues that, partially due to the danger of the disintegration of the Chinese state following the 1911 Revolution, militaristic behaviour became the main vehicle for obtaining the qualities deemed necessary for a modern state in a world conceptionalised along Darwinian lines. These insights are illustrative for the methodological advantage which can be gained from the systematic application of the concept of discourses of weakness when researching modern Chinese history. Büttner's interpretation is corroborated and supplemented by Sebastian Riebold's chapter on the "Idea of 'Intellectual Warfare'", which also shows how much late Qing discourses of weakness were dominated by a Darwinian worldview, in which warfare was ubiquitous and penetrated deeply into the world of learning. In this way, education became an important issue for discourses of weakness, and, as the chapter suggests, an instrumental view of education—that is to say, as a means to enhance one's position in global competition—evolved as a result.

Part Three of the volume deals with "Prognosis for the Sick Man—Ruin, Resistance and Restoration". Since the Chinese discourses of weakness dealt with in this volume were closely related to the Chinese appropriation of new knowledge from the world at large, these discourses attained a strikingly international outlook, as Rebecca Karl has pointed out, too. History was still seen as providing insights and guidance for one's own action. However, the subject matter of history was now greatly expanded to cover the whole world, in particular those countries which were perceived as having been—or still being—in a situation comparable to that of China. The prime example was, as already suggested by Daniel Hausmann, the tragic fate of Poland. In his contribution on the "Evolution of late Qing Historical Writing on the Decline of Poland", Zou Zhenhuan provides a comprehensive and careful analysis of how the "national ruin"—in particular, the partitioning of Poland—was received and disseminated in the Chinese discourse. Zou makes it clear that it was not just the reformers, who used the example of Poland, but that, after the turn of the century, when, after the Boxer Rising, China's situation appeared to be even more threatening, translations from Japanese sources which transformed Poland into a "nationalist symbol", as he calls it, also had a considerable impact. The importance of this discourse cannot only be ascertained by looking into the prominence of the contributors—such as the comprador and reformer Zheng Guanying and the poet and revolutionary Liu Yazi—but into the recipients and readers as well. Lu Xun's brother Zhou Zuoren, for instance, noted in his diary how moved he became upon learning of the fate of Poland. One alternative to the envisioned imminent spectre of ruin was resistance, which is highlighted in MirjamTröster's article on "Plays about the Taiwan Republic". Here, she draws attention to the strange but brief history of the first Asian Republic, which, by proclaiming itself independent from China, tried to escape Japanese dominance, and then goes on to stress the importance of theatre as a means of popularising discourses of weakness among the wider population. In particular, Tröster highlights the role and agency of women in the plays she cites, since, in many fictional works of the late Qing and the Republic, women epitomize the weak and the oppressed. In her analysis, she shows that the two plays she focuses on both suggest resistance as the means to overcome weakness—albeit resistance in different ways—collaborative resistance in one play, and resistance fed by physical prowess and mental strength—the "heroic" solution—in the second, which was staged during the war against Japan in 1942, and which sought to inspire a mental frame of resisting the enemy against all odds. Finally, Zhang Ke deals with the "Two Images of India in China during the Nineteenth Century", and shows that the assumption of India as being a fellow sufferer from Imperialist incursions and of the existence of a "sympathy narrative" is seriously flawed, and that, although India was often used as an example of what could happen to China, a feeling of cultural superiority dominated the view of most Chinese intellectuals. As noted above, Chinese discourses of weakness did contribute to the establishment of a rank-based view of civilisation—unquestionably assigning the higher ranks to the Western powers and Japan—but there were differentiations among the "victims" of civilisation as well. India had been completely colonised, as many Chinese scholar officials and scholars clearly thought, and thus occupied a lower place than China in civilisational hierarchy.

The fourth part of the book is entitled "Treating the Sick Man—Coexistence, Science and Profit". We have seen that, in almost all cases, late 19th and early 20th century discourses of weakness aimed at generating consternation or shock, and, in this way, aimed at mobilising a larger number of people for the common cause to overcome the perceived deadly peril. There were, however, discourses of weakness which called for providing much more specific remedies, such as legal reform in order to overcome "extraterritoriality", as seen in the contribution of Huang Xingtao introduced above, or militarism as analysed by Clemens Büttner. In her article on "Wang Jingwei's Intellectual Transformation", Zhiyi Yang suggests that Wang Jingwei's political actions, which go from assassin, establishment politician, to collaborator (or traitor), can be explained by looking into Wang's *leitmotif*, namely, his concern with China's perceived national weakness. Like Hausmann, in his contribution to this volume, Yang points out that martyrdom—Wang's real goal of his assassinist phase—served as an important resource for mobilisation in order to overcome China's weakness, which Wang, like many others, associated with the Manchu rule. Later on, Wang changed his stance and became a propagandist of "human co-

INTRODUCTION 19

existentialism" as a means of dealing with China's weakness in the international realm. From here, it was only a short way to Pan-Asianism, which was one of the ideological fundaments of his collaborative regime, and which he could depict as saving the Chinese nation. After the end of World War II, Wang Jingwei and his regime were considered as traitors. Furthermore, the idea of Pan-Asianism never took root in China. Very much in contrast with this, the idea that science would be able to save China has remained of great importance right up to the present day, as Iwo Amelung shows in his contribution to the book. Amelung traces the origins of this idea and suggests that there was a close link to social Darwinist thinking. He shows that the science discourse greatly contributed to efforts to popularise science during the 1920s and the 1930s, which, in fact, can be linked to tangible progress in the development of the sciences in China. It also contributed, however, to the further popularisation of the supposed scientific origins of social Darwinian theories, which were used to establish civilisational rankings and a highly utilitarian approach to science, which, in fact, has remained important to this very today. The final contribution to the volume is Tze-ki Hon's chapter on "Capitalising on Crisis", which, on the one hand, shows to what extent China's fledgling newspaper market at the beginning of the 20th century was indebted to the need to report constantly on the national crisis—and thus fed into the different discourses of weakness of that time. Hon makes clear, on the other hand, that, among these newspapers, there were publications which were fully conscious of the fact that they also had the function of integrating China's society, both vertically and horizontally, and thus had an impact on the success or failure of those reforms which were considered to be indispensable in order to overcome China's weaknesses.

The contributions collected in this volume provide a historical analysis of the development of discourses of weakness in modern China. In fact, it seems justified to go one step further: in the same way in which China's weakness during the 19th and early 20th century has shaped the development of modern China, speaking (or writing) about weakness is an almost indispensable feature of contemporary China's discourses. Many of the topics addressed in this volume thus appear eerily present today—the Chinese government's obsession with sovereignty and the apprehension of foreigners interfering in China's so-called "internal affairs" can certainly be linked to the issue of "extraterritoriality". The militarist streak in modern Chinese politics was recently celebrated during the megalomanic military parade on the occasion of the 70th anniversary of the founding of the People's Republic of China. Intellectual competitiveness is clearly of great concern for the Party and government leaders, as is the focus on the development and application of science and technology, including the intensive attempts to popularise them.

Nonetheless, dealing with Chinese discourses of weakness of the late Qing and early Republican period today—in 2019/20—is not without irony. The discourses of weakness analysed in this volume almost all entail an idea of "hope", or the expectation that China (at least, China proper)—however serious the Chinese situation may have appeared at the end of the 19th and the beginning of the 20th century—was able to provide the basic conditions that would enable it to overcome the multitude of problems that it was facing at the time. Today, we have to acknowledge the surprising correctness of these assertions. Whether this will lead to the disappearance of Chinese discourses of weakness, however, is a completely different question. In the end, it is politically useful for the rulers of a country to have at their disposal the idea of a "threat to the country, which can be updated almost at will" as Joachim Kurtz has fittingly framed it.[33] It seems even more ironic that, during the last few years, the idea of the China-threat has re-surfaced. It is now Europe that leads a veritable discourse of weakness *vis-à-vis* China's perceived innovativeness and economic power. For better or for worse? For the moment, it is too early to tell.

Bibliography

Bickers, Robert (2011), *The Scramble for China. Foreign Devils in the Qing Empire, 1832–1914*, London: Allen Lane.

Bickers, Robert A., Jeffrey N. Wasserstrom (1995), "Shanghai's 'Dogs and Chinese Not Admitted' Sign: Legend, History and Contemporary Symbol", *The China Quarterly*, 142, pp. 444–466.

Bréard, Andrea (2019), "400 Millionen. Globale Wirkungen einer mächtigen Zahl", in: Haas, Stefan, Michael Schneider and Nicolas Bilo (eds.), *Die Zählung der Welt. Kulturgeschichte der Statistik vom 18. bis 20. Jahrhundert*, Stuttgart: Franz Steiner Verlag, pp. 219–234.

Burke, Peter, "Introduction: Concepts of Continuity and Change in History" in: Burke, Peter (ed.). *The New Cambridge Modern History*, vol. XIII: Companion Volume, Cambridge, London: Cambridge University Press 1979, pp. 1–14.

Callahan, William A. (2004), "National Insecurities: Humiliation, Salvation, and Chinese Nationalism", *Alternatives*, 29, pp. 199–218.

— (2007), "History, Identity, and Security: Producing and Consuming Nationalism in China", *Critical Asian Studies*, 38:2, pp. 179–208.

De Bary, Wm. Theordore, Carol Gluck and Arthur E. Tiedemann (comps.) (2005), *Sources of Japanese Tradition* (2nd ed.), volume II: 1600 to 2000, New York: Columbia University Press.

Franke, Wolfgang (1970), "Hegel und die Geschichte Chinas", *Verfassung und Recht in Übersee / Law and Politics in Africa, Asia and Latin America*, 3:3, pp. 279–283.

---

33 Kurtz (2003), "Selbstbehauptung mit geliehener Stimme", p. 227.

Fortune, Robert (1847), *Three Years of Wandering in the Northern Provinces of China. Including a Visit to the Tea, Silk, and Cotton Countries*, London: John Murray, 1847.

Gilley, Bruce (2004), *China's Democratic Future: How it will Happen and Where it will Lead*, New York: Columbia University Press.

Hertel, Christiane, *Siting China in Germany. Eighteenth Century Chinoiserie and its Modern Legacy*, University Park: Pennsylvania State University Press 2019

Hevia, James L. (2003), *English Lessons: The Pedagogy of Imperialism*, Durham NC: Duke University Press.

Karl, Rebecca (2002), *Staging the Word. Chinese Nationalism at the Turn of the Twentieth Century*, Durham NC: Duke University Press.

Kurtz, Joachim (2003), "Selbstbehauptung mit geliehener Stimme: J.G. Fichte als Redner an die chinesisische Nation", in: Iwo Amelung, Matthias Koch, Joachim Kurtz, Eun-Jeung Lee and Sven Saaler (eds.), *Selbstbehauptungsdiskurse in Asien: China—Japan—Korea* (Monographie aus dem Deutschen Institut für Japanstudien 34), Munich: Judicium , pp. 219–242.

Landwehr, Achim (2008), *Historische Diskursanalyse*, Frankfurt, New York: Campus.

Lee, Eun–Jeung (2003), *"Anti-Europa". Die Geschichte der Rezeption des Konfuzianismus und der konfuzianischen Gesellschaft seit der frühen Aufklärung* (Politica et Ars 6), Münster: Lit-Verlag.

Lee, Haiyan (2009), "The Ruins of Yuanmingyuan. Or, How to Enjoy a National Wound", *Modern China*, 35:2, pp. 155–190.

Levenson, Joseph R. (1959), *Liang Ch'i-ch'ao and the Mind of Modern China*, Cambridge MA: Harvard University Press.

Liu, Lydia (1996), *Translingual Practice. Literature, National Culture, and Translated Modernity—China, 1900–1937*, Stanford CA: Stanford University Press 1995.

Mahan, Alfred Thayer, *The Problem of Asia and its Effect upon International Policies*, Boston MA: Little, Brown and Company 1900.

Mitter, Rana (2004), *A Bitter Revolution: China's Struggle with the Modern World*, Oxford: Oxford University Press.

Nye, Gideon (1857), *The Rationale of the Chinese Question*, Macao: Friend of China Office.

Osterhammel, Jürgen (2005), "The Great Work of Uplifting Mankind. Zivilisierungsmission und Moderne" in: Boris Barth and Jürgen Osterhammel (eds.), *Zivilisierungsmissionen. Imperiale Weltverbesserung seit dem 18. Jahrhundert*, Konstanz: UVK Verlagsanstalt, pp. 363–426.

Ozaki, Y. (1900), "Misunderstood Japan", *The North American Review*, 171 (Oct. 1900), pp. 566–576.

Pigulla, Andreas (1996), *China in der deutschen Weltgeschichtsschreibung vom 18. bis zum 20. Jahrhundert* (Veröffentlichungen des Ostasien-Instituts der Ruhr-Universität Bochum 43), Wiesbaden: Harrassowitz.

Pocock, J.G.A. (1989), "The Concept of a Language and the metier d'historien: Some Considerations on Practice", in: J.G.A. Pocock, *Politics, Language, and Time. Essays on Political Thought and History*, (2nd ed.) London, Chicago IL: University of Chicago Press, pp. 87–105.

Schoppa, R. Keith (2002), *Revolution and its Past: Identities and Change in Modern Chinese History*, Upper Saddler River NJ: Prentice Hall.

Schwartz, Benjamin (1964), *In Search of Wealth and Power. Yen Fu and the West*, Cambridge MA: Harvard University Press.

Scott, David (2008), *China and the International System, 1840–1949. Power, Presence, and Perceptions in a Century of Humiliation*, Albany NY: State University of New York.

Senex (1898), "Our Future Empire in the Far East", *Contemporary Review* 74 (August), pp. 153–166.

Tang, Xiaobing (1996), *Global Space and the Nationalist Discourse of Modernity. The Historical Thinking of Liang Qichao*, Stanford CA: Stanford University Press.

Tsu Jing Yuen (2005), *Failure, Nationalism, and Literature. The Making of Modern Chinese Identity, 1895–1937*, Stanford CA: Stanford University Press.

Wagner, Rudolf G. (2011), "China 'Asleep' and 'Awakening'. A Study in Conceptualizing Asymmetry and Coping with it", *Transcultural Studies*, 2011:1, pp. 4–139.

– (2017), "Dividing up the [Chinese] Melon, guafen 瓜分": The Fate of a Transcultural Metaphor in the Formation of National Myth", *Transcultural Studies*, 2017:1, pp. 9–122.

Zhongguo shehuikexueyuan jindaishi yanjiusuo jindai ziliao bianjishi 中國社會科學院近代史研究所近代資料編輯室 (ed.) (1992), *Guochi shidian* 國恥事典 (Encyclopedia of National Humiliation), Chengdu: Chengdu chubanshe.

Part I:
Examining the Sick Man—Describing Symptoms of Weakness

From Discourse of Weakness to Discourse of Empowerment: The Topos of the "Sick Man of East Asia" in Modern China

*Jui-sung Yang**

> I spoke just now of having suffered together indeed, suffering in common unifies more than joy does. Where national memories are concerned, grief is of more value than triumph, for it imposes duties, and requires a common effort.[1]
>
> Ernest Renan

> It is noteworthy that, in seeking to incite passion, Chinese political leaders have not turned spontaneously to charismatic appeals and themes of heroic glory that characterise the nationalism of most transitional societies. *Instead, to a large degree they have sought to detail the real and imagined ways in which China has been humiliated by others.*[2]
>
> Lucian W. Pye

I. Introduction: The Origin of the Problem

In a critical discussion of American scholarship on modern Chinese history, the well-known American historian of China, Paul A. Cohen (*1934), argued that Western scholars ought to examine closely certain blind spots created by Western scholarship's long-standing practice of adopting a Euro-centric point of view which treats historical developments in the West as universal principles. He appealed to his colleagues to be wary of the possible fallacies of Western chauvinism: these include the belief that those historical developments in modern Chinese history which (at first glance, at least) bear no or only tenuous relation to the West are not worthy of investigation, as well as the tendency, be it intentional or unintentional, to exaggerate unduly the role of the West and its power of influence concerning various historical issues. In his opinion, there ought to be a new reflective and progressive orientation in research that approaches modern Chinese history impartially and with an open mind, and that attempts to re-assess the actual role played by the West in this history; then,

---

* The author has previously published Chinese versions of this article in the *Zhengzhi daxue lishi xuebao* 政治大學歷史學報 (2005), as well as in Chapter 2 of his 2010 book entitled *Sick Man, Yellow Peril, and Sleeping Lion (Bingfu, huanghuo yu shuishi* 病夫、黃禍與睡獅). See Yang Ruisong (2005), "Xiangxiang minzu chiru", pp. 1–44; Yang Ruisong (2010), *Bingfu, huanghuo, shuishi*, pp. 17–67.

1 Renan (1990), "What is a Nation?", p. 19.

2 Pye (1992), *The Spirit of Chinese Politics*, p. 71; author's emphasis.

and only then, would it be possible to "discover history in China", as Cohen had hoped to do.[3] In this work, which primarily aimed to introduce an element of self-reflection into Western research on Chinese history, Cohen made the following interesting observation: one of the main reasons why Western scholars find it difficult to escape their own Western biases is that contemporary Chinese scholars themselves widely accept Western viewpoints and analytical frameworks in their treatment of Chinese history, and, in similar fashion, stress the key role that the West has played in modern China. Thus, it is quite problematic for Western historians of China to challenge their positions by adopting the so-called "insider perspective" and engaging in a critical dialogue between the two research cultures.[4]

But what role did the West actually play in modern Chinese history? Anyone with some knowledge about history will not be able to deny that it was an important one, but many of the details are still very much contended. As a Western specialist in the field of history, Cohen's views regarding the importance of self-examination, along with his attempts to put the long overemphasised role of the West on the stage of modern Chinese history into perspective, certainly reflect a larger recent trend in Western scholarship towards greater critical self-reflection when engaging with other cultures.[5] Aside from this, however, it is his central goal and wish to come to an accurate evaluation of the role of the West in modern Chinese history and to determine the true scope of its influence. However, we must ask ourselves whether academic and cultural circles in China are willing to adopt a similar spirit of introspection and re-address the question of how the role of the West in modern Chinese history may be characterised accurately? Especially when it comes to certain historical topics, the historical role of the West has long been firmly established as that of a merciless brutaliser. And this view has been perpetuated by political manip-

---

3 Cohen, it is worth noting, did not at all imagine that it would be possible to avoid ethnocentric distortion altogether. Instead, he cautiously hoped that one could substantially reduce its adverse effects through careful and critical self–scrutiny. He phrased his aim thusly: "The great challenge for Western historians is not the impossible one of eliminating all ethnocentric distortion; it is the possible one of reducing such distortion to a minimum and, in the process, freeing ourselves in order to see Chinese history in new, less Western–centred ways." Cohen (1984), *Discovering History in China*, p. 1. For a detailed discussion, refer to ibid., pp. 1–7.

4 Ibid., p. 1.

5 This trend is famously represented in the work of Edward Said, who has long criticised that the West's interpretations of non–Western cultures are typically full of distortions due to the former's egocentric mentality and its desire to exercise hegemony over the cultural discourse in question: They are the product of a reductive essentialism. The true aim of such interpretations is thus not actually to understand and value the other culture's rich inner life, but to reduce it by claiming the existence of a binary opposition between the West and its opposite, thereby consolidating existing prejudices and exerting discursive dominance over the other culture. His views are detailed in Said (1994), *Orientalism*.

ulation, cultural propaganda and handed-down misconceptions based upon other misconceptions. Can Cohen's appeal to re-examine the precise role of the West find resonance within the Chinese intellectual and cultural sphere? To put it even more unequivocally, the historical role assigned to the West in modern Chinese history is the role of the main or principal antagonist. In the national collective memory, this image is fraught with emotion, and constitutes, together with other, closely-related interpretations of history that have already become firmly established in the public psyche, an indispensable part of the Chinese collective identity. Considering this, re-evaluating the "true historical role of the West" is no longer purely an issue of historical research. The kind of rational, sober re-examination that Cohen proposes, I fear, faces challenges not just from academic circles.

This article puts the arguments outlined above at the forefront of the present investigation mainly because they have sharpened my own awareness concerning these issues in my inquiries into the history of the cultural discourse on the body in modern China. This body, especially when one takes the conglomeration of the physical bodies of every individual citizen as the object of research, is undoubtedly a key component in the reform of modern China. Whether in physical education, various areas of everyday life, or public health, from the late Qing period onwards, there is no aspect concerning the remaking of the said body that has not become a major target of reform.[6] When one studies historical documents and other sources from the last century relating to the topic, especially when it comes to those concerning the discourse on the remaking of the body, one often comes across strongly emotionalised language. And among the relevant verbal tropes, none is more well-known than the ever-present expression "Sick Man of the East" (*dongfang bingfu* 東方病夫) or "Sick Man of East Asia" (*Dongya bingfu* 東亞病夫). Through a careful critical comparison of Chinese and Western documents, I discovered a critical gap in the way these two cultures have understood and discussed the "Sick Man of East Asia" over the course of the last 100 years. What is even more important, seen from the perspective of intellectual and cultural history, is that we can see, from the development of the meaning of the term "Sick Man of East Asia" in modern Chinese public discourse, the decisive role that the West played in the nation-building process of modern China—a role that was far more decisive than the West itself had anticipated at the time or is even aware of today.

For a long time, the "Sick Man of East Asia" has been a well-known and recurring topic in the study of Chinese body culture and can be found in political propaganda, public discourses, or products of mass consumption, not only in China proper but also in Chinese cultural products world-wide. When Bruce

---

6 Relevant works on the subject include Huang Jinlin (2000), *Lishi, shenti, guojia*; Xu Yixiong *et al.* (1996), *Zhongguo jindai tiyu sixiang*; and Brownell (1995), *Training the Body for China.*

Lee (Li Xiaolong 李小龍), in the film *Fist of Fury* (*Jingwu Men* 精武門; also known as *The Chinese Connection*) of 1972, with his fierce look, intimidating physique, and impeccable martial arts skills (quite literally) smashes the image of China as the "Sick Man of East Asia", he has arguably carried the imperative that the national disgrace symbolised by the "Sick Man" must be totally eradicated to the extreme. This kind of collective sense of humiliation, which is derived from the physical body, can, with some justification, be seen as a collective psychological trauma that is deeply imprinted in the hearts of the Chinese people, whether they live on the mainland or in overseas Chinese communities.

In a 1987 talk, Deng Xiaoping 鄧小平 (1904–1997) touched upon the question of how to use history in the education of China's youths. He said:

Since the Opium Wars, China had been reduced to a semi-colonial, semi-feudal society and the Chinese people had become the famous "Sick Men of East Asia" in the eyes of the world.[7]

Similarly, Dr. Li Yuanzhe 李遠哲 (Yuan Tseh Lee, president of the Academia Sinica from 1994–2006) clearly stated in a 1986 interview (the year he was awarded the Nobel Prize in Chemistry):

The image of the "Sick Man of East Asia" and similar issues with which the Chinese people have had to deal, has had a great impact on my youthful spirit [and] henceforth I came to understand that it was only by assiduousness and hard work that one might improve the state of the country's poverty and backwardness. At the same time, I also realised that it would not at all be impossible to transform China from the "Sick Man of East Asia" into one of the strongest countries in the world.[8]

We can see from the two paragraphs cited above that the "Sick Man of East Asia" is a negative epithet with a double referent: it points to both China as a country and to the Chinese as a people.

A recent introductory work on the history of the development of physical education in China during the last century used the "Sick Man of East Asia" even more prominently in its title *From "Sick Man of East Asia" to Stronghold of Athleticism* (*Cong "Dongya bingfu" dao tiyu qiangguo* 從 "東亞病夫" 到體育強國). Appealingly written and illustrated, it depicts how the Chinese people were reduced to the "Sick Men of East Asia" due to the opium epidemic, but eventually, step-by-step, developed into a strong nation that was (at the time of publication) about to realise its dream of hosting the Olympics.[9] Moreover, the official Chinese website of the 2008 Olympics featured a special article with the

---

7 For Deng Xiaoping's words, see Yang Yingxiong (ed.) (1994), *Deng Xiaoping wenxuan*, vol. 3, p. 225.

8 Li Yuanzhe's speech can be found online. See Li Yuanzhe (1986), "Wo de chengzhang licheng".

9 Gao Cui (2002), *"Dongya bingfu"*.

FROM DISCOURSE OF WEAKNESS TO DISCOURSE OF EMPOWERMENT

similar title "From Sick Man of East Asia to Powerhouse of Competitive Sports" (*Cong Dongya bingfu dao jingji daguo* 從東亞病夫到競技大國) that equally emphasised how the Chinese had realised a century long dream in hosting the Olympics.[10]

Aside from official materials and specialist works such as these, the "Sick Man of East Asia" is also to be encountered innumerable times in discussions in a myriad of other publications such as various forms of news reports from China, Hong Kong, and Taiwan, and on websites and Internet message boards. This number only increased in the years leading up to the Beijing Olympics.[11] Among these, there are a lot of publications that make use of affective diction such as "cleansing humiliation" (*xuechi* 雪恥) or "removing the label which the foreigners have forcibly pinned on the Chinese people" (*zhaidiao yangren qiangjia zai Zhongguoren de maozi* 摘掉洋人強加在中國人的帽子), and give voice to the conviction that hosting the Olympics in Beijing, along with the anticipated outstanding results of the Chinese team, as a grand historical moment and a significant step towards ridding China and of the slanderous tag the "Sick Man of East Asia" which the Westerners, or so the saying goes, have been imposing and deliberately continue to do so on the country and its people for the last 100 years.

Whether in academic literature or public discourse, the "Sick Man of East Asia" is a truly ubiquitous trope with which both the older and younger generations are all too familiar. It is no wonder than that one American scholar used the expression "original sin" to describe the status of the "Sick Man of East Asia" in the collective consciousness of modern China.[12]

Just as one might have expected, after the 2008 Beijing Olympics, there was a veritable explosion of articles that referred to the "Sick Man of East Asia". The Beijing-friendly Hong Kong daily newspaper *Wen Wei Po* (*Wenhuibao* 文滙 報), for instance, published an article entitled "Purge the Sick Man of East Asia,

---

10 For the whole content of the article refer to "Cong Dongya bingfu dao jingji daguo".

11 Examples for this are legion. The most commonly encountered assertion is that the "Sick Man of East Asia" has to be regarded as a label that was attached to the Chinese people a long time ago. The *Wen Wei Po* (cited on the following page), for instance, once described the significance of holding the Olympics in China in the following terms: "In China, sports cannot possibly be divorced from national glory and national dishonour (*minzu de rongru* 民族的榮辱), so much so that all of China's people will become inspired by the winning of a gold medal, and the entire country will become disheartened over losing a soccer match. But one must not, upon this basis, deduce a supposed frailty of the Chinese national spirit (*Zhongguo minzu jingshen zhi cuiruo* 中國民族精神之脆弱). As a matter of fact, this rather goes to show that the label of the 'Sick Man of East Asia' has been weighing heavily on the Chinese people for a long, long time; and that their long–cherished wish to be free of their humiliation has seeped deeply into their soul." Available at: http://www.wenweipo.com/special/WWP-50/china50/part2u.htm (18 July 2004). (The article is, as of July 2018, no longer found in the paper's online database.)

12 Heinrich (2002), "The Pathological Body", p. 2.

Ascend to the Rank of Stronghold of Athleticism" (*Xituo Dongya bingfu, jishen tiyu qiangguo* 洗脫東亞病夫，躋身體育強國) which, having praised the success of the 2008 Chinese Olympic team, detailed how their athletic achievements could "cleanse national humiliation" (*xishua guochi* 洗刷國恥) from history:

Let us here look back on the series of extraordinary performances of China's top athletes in their struggle for the glory of our country. But even more so, *let us look back on the illustrious names [of the people who] purged the shame of the "Sick Man of East Asia" from new China.*[13]

There was naturally a good deal of excitement in the Chinese language news media regarding the relationship between the "Sick Man of East Asia", the remarkable performance of the Chinese athletes, and China's national humiliation. This atmosphere electrified mainstream Western media outlets as well. For examples, Reuters, reporting on the Beijing Olympics, bore an article entitled "China's 100-Year Dream, a Cure for the Sick Man of Asia" in which the special significance of hosting the Olympics for contemporary China was analysed.[14]

How are we to interpret the historical and cultural significance of these emotionally-laden statements? In the discussions outlined above, the "Sick Man of East Asia" seems to be an extremely negative image. At the same time, however, the "original sin" of the people of modern China, that is, considering the bodies of the entirety of Chinese people as a matter of shame, appears to serve the function of condensing the mass of diverging popular emotions into general hatred for a common enemy.[15] Of even greater significance is that these collective negative characteristics that modern China is imagined to possess fostered a deeply felt sense of collective suffering and humiliation. The "Sick Man of East Asia" is therefore no longer merely a negative characterisation of the "Chinese body". It has also time and time again been stressed that it is a slanderous label of Western origin. In other words, the "Sick Man" is not usually recognised today as a largely self-given epithet that was supposed to encourage self-criticism and self-reproach among the Chinese people. Rather, it supposedly stems from a vision of the Orient (and a rather grim and insulting vision at that) held by China's "Other", that is, the West. Simply put, it possesses a pecu-

---

13 See "Xituo Dongya bingfu, jishen tiyu qiangguo", for the entire article. Translator's note: The phrases containing "sick man" (or similar expressions) is always highlighted (using italics), as was done by Jui–sung Yang in the original Chinese version of this text.

14 See Mulvenney (2008), "China's 100–Year Dream", for the entire article.

15 In other words, the collective shame over one's imagined communal body becomes a driving force in the process of "imagining the nation" and thus occupies an important place in the formation of the modern nation, as analysed by political scientist and historian Benedict Anderson. See Anderson (1991), *Imagined Communities*.

liar and complex dual nature—the "Sick Man of East Asia" belongs to the East as much as it belongs to the West.[16]

What strikes one as rather bizarre is that, in marked contrast to the outright "fascination" with the "Sick Man of East Asia" betrayed by Chinese academia and the Chinese cultural sphere, very little has been written on the so-called "Sick Man of East Asia" by contemporary Western scholars in their discussions on the body culture of modern China. In a good number of publications concerning modern Chinese history, there are precious few that touch upon this term (and if they do, they mention it only briefly) and the same is true for monographs on physical education and body culture in modern China. The important thing to note is that there is a clear and crucial discrepancy between our understanding of the true historical and cultural significance of this term and its current usage, as detailed above.

To give an example, Susan Brownell, in a major work on modern Chinese body culture, explained the expression thus: the "Sick Man of East Asia" was an "insult that the Chinese believed was applied to them by Japan and the West",[17] and "gained mythic proportions in [the Chinese] people's minds".[18] Another scholar, in a study on modern Chinese masculinity, even more explicitly stated that the "Sick Man of East Asia" became a mode of self-identification, as the people of modern China saw themselves as lacking the strength to fend-off Western incursions.[19]

Western scholars have voiced their mystification and astonishment at the fact that the people of modern China show such a considerable degree of fascination for this "negative label". Furthermore, and more importantly, they all emphasise that the considerable cultural significance of this term in modern China was the result of the Chinese people's strong affirmation and adoption of this characterisation. However, it has been apparently of little to no concern for them to investigate whether the expression really stems from the West and, if so, whether it is rightfully deemed a malicious slander by the West against the people of China. Why is there such a wide discrepancy between the ways in which scholars and political commentators in China and the West respectively understand and interpret the "Sick Man of East Asia"? Could it be that Western

---

16 Said points out that it is an almost universal phenomenon in the process of understanding another culture to construct "opposites and 'others'" to distinguish one's own culture and to encourage the growth of one's own cultural identity. It is worth noting that this identity construction, according to him, "is a much worked–over historical, social, intellectual, and political process that takes place as a contest involving individuals and institutions in all societies". The identities of "Self" and "Other" are therefore not at all inalterable, but are constantly re–created and re–interpreted. Said (1994), *Orientalism*, pp. 331–332.

17 Brownell (1995), *Training the Body for China*, p.327.

18 Ibid., p. 22.

19 Louie (2003), "Chinese, Japanese and Global Masculine Identities", p. 9.

scholars wilfully downplay the actual physical harm that the West had, for a long time, inflicted upon the Chinese people? Could it be that the expression in question, which has long since been regarded as a matter of great shame and humiliation in China's cultural memory, is nothing but a mode of self-identification on the part of the Chinese people and not at all a label forced upon them by the West?

These points of contention bring into plain view how important it is to be aware of the crucial issues in the study of modern Chinese history raised by Cohen and summarised at the beginning of this article. To interpret the role of the West on the stage of modern Chinese history accurately is, I believe, not just a matter of self-reflection on the part of Western scholars. Is it not equally the task of scholars within the Chinese cultural and academic sphere to examine anew some of their established historical interpretations and even parts of their historical imagination concerning the major impact (both positive and negative) that the West has had on China?

In order to reach an understanding of the precise historical and cultural significance of the "Sick Man of the East", and its particular impact on the construction of modern China's national imagination as well as the ways in which the mutual understanding of Chinese and Western civilisation developed, this article seeks to historicise the meaning of this trope and delineate its development through history. I shall delve into the myth of the trope's Western origin and furthermore analyse how its meaning in modern Chinese cultural discourse changed over time, so as to reveal the function that it served in China's evolving national imagination and the ways in which modern China defined itself and imagined its "Other". As this article will show, the present understanding of the so-called "Sick Man of East Asia" is the result of a tortuous historical process. But, as this process has largely been forgotten, the vast majority of people, including scholars and experts, commit the fallacy of "presentism" when evaluating its meaning and historical significance. That is, they rely on an ahistorical interpretation and read the current understanding of the trope into the past, and, in so doing, obtain a naïve and erroneous picture of the past that misses all the nuances.

Modern China's conviction that the "Sick Man of East Asia" is constitutive for the West's image of the Chinese people not only oversimplifies the many-sidedness and complexity of the cultural entanglements of China and the West, but has also obstructed and misled the endeavours in China's cultural sphere to understand properly how the rest of the world actually perceives and imagines Chinese culture and the Chinese people.

We shall see how the manipulation of the meaning of the trope in the course of the last century has engendered all too many emotional impulses and created a number of avoidable mistaken beliefs. In this way, tracing the history of the

"Sick Man of East Asia" may offer some insights into the complex of shifting emotions, ranging from adoration to hatred, that helped shape modern China as it faced the challenges of Western culture.

II. Returning to the Starting Point of the Story: The Birth of the "Sick Man"

22nd year of the *Guangxu* 光緒 reign period (1896)
On the 11th day of the 9th month (17 October), an English language newspaper in the foreign concession (in Shanghai) reprinted a special article from the London *Xuexiao suibao* 學校歲報 [that contained the following line]: "for China is a sick man of the East" (*fu Zhongguo yi dongfang zhi bingfu* ye 夫中國一東方之病夫也). Henceforth, the Chinese were often disparagingly referred to as the "sick men of East Asia" by the Westerners.[20]

The lines concerning the origin of the "Sick Man of East Asia" quoted above are not from a historical document, but can instead be found in a modern-day official account of the Shanghai Administration of Sports (*Shanghai shi tiyuju* 上海市體育局) listing 500 years of sporting events. This official website contains a searchable item-by-item list of records concerning traditional martial arts and modern sports competitions relevant to the city of Shanghai from 1514 (*i.e.*, during the Ming dynasty) until 1997. What is interesting to note is that the item in question mentioning the "Sick Man of East Asia" bears absolutely no relation to any sporting event and does not actually seem to fit with the other items listed on the page that (naturally) relate to sports activities of all kinds. However, the page's web master evidently correctly anticipated that to his broad readership, being well-versed in sports and some of the discussions surrounding it, coming across accounts about the "Sick Man of East Asia" would not come as any surprise at all. In this cultural context, the record mentioned is not very "natural" at all and merits some explanation. Yet, there are not even two lines of text dedicated to providing the reader with some historical context concerning the origins of the 100-year-old familiar term the "Sick Man of East Asia".

But what does it tell us when a government-sanctioned website relates and propagates the history behind the "humiliating label" "Sick Man of East Asia" in this manner? At the surface, the database entry offers the typical information of a reliable source: time (*i.e.*, 12 October 1896), place(s) (*i.e.*, from London to Shanghai), source (a certain London paper; an English language concession paper), and a (seemingly) quite unambiguous quotation: "for China is a sick

---

20 Seems to have been taken offline as of July 2018: http://tyj.sh.gov.cn/dashiji.jsp, last accessed 18 July 2004.

man of the East". It even provides some historical analysis: "Henceforth, the Chinese were often disparagingly referred to as 'sick men of East Asia' by the Westerners." Be that as it may, it merits attention that the narrative on this official website omits a few things. Some additional explanations are therefore in order.

The original English language article as it had appeared in London was first republished in the *North China Daily News* (Chinese: *Zilin xi bao* 字林西報; founded as the weekly newspaper *North-China Herald*) in 1896 and subsequently translated into Chinese by the *Shiwubao* 時務報 (also known as *Chinese Progress*). The article in question bore the title "China's Actual Situation" (*Zhongguo shiqing* 中國實情) and appeared in November of the same year.[21] The sentence "for China is a sick man of the East" quoted above thus stems from a Chinese language translation However, we must leave the question of whether these omissions are due to negligence unanswered for now. The curious thing is that this historical narrative, seemingly based upon good evidence, in its (overly) simple and clear explanation of the start and development of China's "One Hundred Years of Shame", affirms an already existing bias in the minds of the general readership; namely, that this case of national humiliation came from the West.[22]

If we subject this apparently "concise and comprehensive" story behind the origins of the "Sick Man of East Asia" to a more careful scrutiny, however, we discover that there remain at least three layers of context to this interpretation that need to be uncovered, clarified, and analysed.[23] (1) First, what is the textual

---

21 *Shiwubao* 10, pp. 650–652.

22 The interpretation promulgated by the Shanghai Sports Administration and the arguments made in other studies on related topics are basically identical. For example, Xiong and others, in a relevant periodical article, although they mention that Yan Fu in his essay "On Strength" published in March of 1895 had already used the term "Sick Man" to describe the situation of contemporary China, are nevertheless convinced that the saying of the "Sick Man of East Asia" certainly stems from an 1896 article in a London paper. It has to be pointed out that Xiong *et al.* contradict themselves even further when they state that, after the article had been translated and re-published in Chinese, "the Sick Man of East Asia immediately became a rallying cry to urge the paralysed Chinese people into action" (*bianchi mamuburen de Zhongguoren de jingyu* 鞭笞麻木不仁的中國人的警語). See Xiong Xiaozheng *et al.* (1997), "20 shiji Zhongguoren tiyu renzhi de guiji", 21–24. Gao Cui makes a similar argument. Gao Cui (2002), *"Dongya bingfu"*, p. 9.

23 In my analysis, I am indebted to US historian Herman Ooms' thoughts on "historical origin theories". In his study on the relationship between politics and Neo-Confucian teachings in the political regime of Tokugawa Japan, Ooms argues that many historians unthinkingly accept the traditional view that, after Tokugawa Ieyasu 德川家康 (1543–1616) had achieved military victory in 1600, he, in his desire to bring about a long period of peace and order in the realm, elevated the Neo-Confucian doctrines to the status of official ideology and that this marked the starting point of Neo-Confucianism as state philosophy. This, from the very beginning, rendered many historians unable to analyse and question a lot of the presuppositions underlying this theory of historical origins that actually still warrant confirmation, as well as to put to scrutiny the specific mentalities reflected in these assumptions. Ooms thus reminds us as his-

context of the sentence "for China is a sick man of the East"? That is to say, what is the whole content of the original English language article as it appeared in the *Shiwubao*? (2) Second, what is the historical context underlying the article? Or to phrase it differently, what are the historical circumstances under which the article was produced in 1896? (3) Lastly, and most importantly, what does the term "Sick Man" (*bingfu* 病夫) refer to in the context of contemporary Western discourse, and especially in discussions on international relations?

When it comes to the textual context, the astonishing discovery is that the article entitled "China's Actual Situation" in its Chinese version is, in actuality, a political commentary specifically written in admonition of the failing reform movement and not at all an exposition on the general characteristics of the Chinese nation. The reason why "Sick Man" is used to describe China in the beginning of the article is because, as the author opines:

[China] has been apathetic for a long time and the root cause of her illness goes deep. Since the war between China and Japan, every country in the world has known perfectly well in what kind of shape (China) is.[24]

Aside from the rather histrionic introduction, the appellation "Sick Man" does not appear again. The article's harsh criticism is mainly directed against corruption in the Qing bureaucracy, and the fact that Chinese officialdom is too set in its ways. This, it is argued, led to multiple deplorable failings in military and political reform. And although severely critical in their assessment, the author states at the end of the article that, as the various nations are currently locked in a stalemate, China still has the opportunity to carry out modernisation reforms. Consequently, they strongly urge the Chinese government that "late is better than never":

In conclusion, provided that the power holders in Beijing get rid of their old maladies, and make it a matter of urgency to make new plans, it is not yet too late [to turn the tide in China's favour] even though the situation is indeed precarious![25]

It should be especially noted that the Chinese government is the sole target of criticism, and that there is not even a word directed against the Chinese common people. The kind of political reform advocated by the article does not contain a single measure that would relate to the remaking of the physical bodies of the people. Simply put, the gist of the article is quite clear: the country

---

torians to be sure to call into question any and all seemingly "objective" or "natural" origin stories. Thereby, we will be able to understand more clearly the complex historical phenomena hiding behind these discourses that have—intentionally or unintentionally—fallen from sight. For Ooms' full thoughts on the subject, see Ooms (1989), *Tokugawa Ideology*, pp. 3–17 (especially p. 6).

24 *Shiwubao* 10, p. 652.

25 Ibid.

"China" is called a "Sick Man" because its government has long proven itself to be unable to carry out meaningful reforms. In all fairness, considering the sincere, well-intended advice offered at the end of the article, it would seem that this text hardly qualifies as a slander of the Chinese people by the English press.

Regarding the historical context underlying the production of the article, the statement (cited in the first quotation above) which appeared at the beginning of the text, provides an important clue. That is to say, the fact that China is seen as a "Sick Man" in the eyes of the West is a manifestation of the international shock, in view of China's crushing defeat in the war of 1894–95 which had revealed that the long years of reform efforts during the Self-Strengthening Movement had done little in terms of addressing China's fundamental weaknesses in order to restore the country's internal stability and external prestige.

Prior to the war against Japan, the Western powers had already realised that China was no longer a match for the West, but, even so, the fact that China had, contrary to all expectations, actually been defeated at the hands of the "upstart" Japan proved, once and for all, that the internal problems hindering the Chinese reforms were, in fact, much graver than popular perception in the West had previously believed.

As a matter of fact, as early as December of 1894, that is, while the war was still in progress, the journal *A Review of the Times* (*Wanguo gongbao* 萬國公報; henceforth: *WGGB*), carried an article drawn from a French paper, *Faguo shibao* 法國時報 (probably referring to the daily newspaper *Le Temps*). It was one among a series of similar opinion pieces on the Sino-Japanese War republished from papers of various Western countries. The article clearly stated that:

there is now *yet another sick man in the East*. Japan, small though she may be, will shake his roots and destroy his leaves and branches.[26]

Moreover, the British journalist, writer, and diplomat Ignatius Valentine Chirol (1852–1929), working for the English paper *The Times*, launched a severe attack directed against the Chinese government's performance both during the war and in the post-war reforms. In his collection of essays entitled *The Far Eastern Question*, published in 1896, we find the following characterisation in his analysis of the so-called Triple Intervention by Germany, France, and Russia after the conclusion of the war, which prevented Japan from annexing Port Arthur:

---

26 *Wanguo gongbao* 71, p. 14885. In addition, an analytical report entitled "China and Japan" that appeared in the English *The Times* quotes an article from the French *Le Temps* on its views on Japan's chief aims in the Treaty of Shimonoseki: "Japan has obtained for herself a position so favourable as to be sure of being the first to appropriate the spoils and to receive the inheritance of the new 'sick man' of the Far East". "China and Japan" (1895), p. 5. We can see from this evidence that the "Sick Man" was used metaphorically in the contemporary English and French press to describe how "the sun had set" on Qing China.

FROM DISCOURSE OF WEAKNESS TO DISCOURSE OF EMPOWERMENT

Their action was practically a notice served upon Japan that, even though the *Sick Man of the Far East* was lying on her deathbed, she was to have no share in his future inheritance. This notice she was obliged to accept, and under the present conditions, she must, for some time to come, acquiesce in its consequences. From the moment, therefore, that she finds herself excluded from all further participation in the spoils of the *Sick Man*, her interests are transferred from the side of those who aim, more or less openly, at the dismemberment of the Chinese Empire to that which makes for the maintenance of the *status quo*.[27]

We can clearly discern from the passage quoted above that Chirol used the image of the "Sick Man" who is at death's door specifically to describe the precarious international status of Qing China in the wake of the First Sino-Japanese War.[28]

It can be inferred from these examples that the new regional balance in East Asia created by the First Sino-Japanese War is likely to have been the key historical element driving the increasing popularity of the term "Sick Man" in the Western media used to describe the "ancient oriental Empire" of China.[29] Another *Shiwubao* article entitled "The World's Four Sick Men" (*Tianxia si bingren* 天下四病人), also a translation piece taken from the *North China Daily News* (this time from the 30 November issue), used the epithet "The World's Four Sick Men" summarily to refer to China, Turkey (*i.e.*, the Ottoman Empire), Persia, and Morocco. When discussing the weakness of China, the article stated:

In former times, when China and Japan did battle—provided that no one interfered and things were allowed to take their own course—it was seldom the case that China was not the one that perished (*mie* 滅).[30]

---

27 Chirol (1896), *The Far Eastern Question*, pp.150–151.

28 It needs to be pointed out that, according to the relevant lemma in the *Oxford English Dictionary*, Chirol has been identified as the initiator behind the "Sick Man's" usage in Western public discourse to describe China's dire situation after the First Sino-Japanese War. "Sick man" in: *Oxford English Dictionary* (1989), 2nd ed., vol 15, p. 410. Himself a contributor to *The Times*, Chirol repeatedly wrote reports and commentaries on China during and after the war. In the preface to his abovementioned *The Far Eastern Question*, he explicitly states that he had worked a number of views concerning the political situation in the Far East into the book which he had previously expressed in *The Times*. Chirol also related some of his personal experiences in Tianjin and his conversation with the Chinese diplomat Li Hongzhang 李鴻章 (1823–1901).

29 A search in *The Time*'s full-text online database conducted by the author has revealed that Qing China has been described as a "Sick Man" as early as 31 October 1876. The original article reads: "If affairs in East of Europe were less exciting, we should be more often remember [sic] that the East of Asia has also its 'sick man'. Whether China is sick unto death we may not know for a good many years." We can thus surmise that more than 20 years lie between this first instance of a metaphorical usage of "sick man"(meaning China) and the point in time it gained widespread currency and was introduced into China.

30 *Shiwubao* 14, pp. 918–919.

It is worth noting that, according to the article, China had been able to preserve its sovereignty despite its glaring weaknesses precisely because:

[her] people are fierce and bold in temperament and rely only on slaughter and rebellion. Among the countries [of the world], there are none that are willing to exert their minds and impose good order on all of (China's) 300 million people.[31]

From the contrast between these two conflicting characterisations, we can clearly see that there is no necessary conceptual relationship between the "Sick Man" China and both its waning political power and the physical condition of the Chinese people who are, in said article, nonetheless described as a "ferocious and brutal mass that is difficult to govern" (*xionghan canbao er nanzhi zhi zhong* 凶悍殘暴而難治之眾). It needs to be made perfectly clear that this kind of usage can hardly be reconciled with the long-standing, commonly held interpretation of the "Sick Man of East Asia" in the Chinese-speaking world. But why is that the case?

A comprehensive analysis of this phenomenon requires us, first of all, to reach a proper understanding of how the term "Sick Man" was used in Western political discourse and especially in the context of international relations. To anyone who is well-versed in the history of European international relations, "Sick Man" ought not to be an altogether unfamiliar expression. The predecessor of modern Turkey, that is, the Ottoman Empire (c. 1299–1922/1923), had been in a state of decline from the middle of the nineteenth century. Repeatedly browbeaten by the Western powers, the Empire responded by initiating a series of profound internal reforms (known as the Tanzimat) which helped significantly to strengthen the Ottoman central state, although its international position remained precarious. According to the traditional account, it was the ruler of its strong neighbour Russia, Tsar Nicholas I (r. 1825–1855) who first mockingly called Turkey the "Sick Man of Europe" in 1853. This appellation henceforth circulated widely in all of Europe. In other words, before "Sick Man" was used in Western public discourse to describe the waning national strength of ultra-conservative China at the end of the nineteenth century, the Ottoman Empire, having found itself in a similar situation, had already been conventionally referred to in this manner for some time. This is precisely why the previously mentioned *Faguo shibao* article, as it appeared reprinted in the *WGGB*, featured the phrase "there is now yet another sick man in the East". And the editors of the *WGGB* even added a special explanation relating the historical background behind the term and how it had been used by the countries of Europe to speak about Turkey.[32] As a matter of fact, usage of "Sick Man" in modern Western public discourse to describe a country's waning national power

---

31 Ibid.

32 *Wanguo gongbao*, 71, p. 14885.

FROM DISCOURSE OF WEAKNESS TO DISCOURSE OF EMPOWERMENT   39

and lack of concerted action was by no means restricted to discussions of Turkey or China. Apart from the previously cited example of the "The World's Four Sick Men", we have United States congressman Samuel S. Cox (1824–1889), who incidentally served as ambassador to the Ottoman Empire for a brief period, describing the Mexico of his time as a "Sick Man".[33] Moreover, in recent years, the weakness (in certain respects) and failing reform efforts of countries including Great Britain, Italy, Germany, Austria, Russia, and Japan, among others, have led various Western media outlets to liken their respective predicaments to those of a "Sick Man" in their headlines.[34] In summary, "Sick Man" has been—and, indeed, still is—a sort of stock phrase in Euro-American political discourse.

From the comprehensive analysis provided in this section, we can see how "Sick Man"—a political term (to describe a country's waning political power and its disconcerting inability to carry out reforms) which the Western media had long been in the habit of using—began to be applied in discussing China's political situation at the end of the nineteenth century in the wake of the First Sino-Japanese War.[35] And this phenomenon, that is, this new usage of the term, was disseminated in the intellectual and literary circles of contemporary China, among other routes, via articles translated from Western publications that appeared in the Chinese reform press.

We are hard-pressed to find any references to the condition of the Chinese people in the relevant Western source materials. Specifically, "Sick Man" was, to the best of my knowledge, never used when talking about the physical characteristics of the Chinese people or in discussing questions of what would later be

---

33 For examples of the usage of the "Sick Man" in modern European political discourse, refer to the lemma "sick man" in the *Oxford English Dictionary*.

34 We can see this practice in the following articles and online sources. For describing Germany in this way, see Bertram (1997), "Germany: The Sick Man of Europe?"; Japan: Friedman (2004), "Asia's Sick Man Jumps Out of Bed"; Britain: "Is Britain Europe's New Sick Man?" (2004); Italy: Hutton (2003), "The New Sick Man of Europe"; Russia: Menon (2003), "The Sick Man of Asia: Russia's Endangered Far East". The *Wall Street Journal* even featured an article calling all of Europe a "Sick Man": "All of Europe is the Sick Man Now" (2002).

35 It has to be pointed out, however, that judging from the available English-language sources, even though an article might make use of the specific term "Sick Man" to describe contemporary China, it is usually mentioned only in passing and not sensationally proclaimed in big letters in the headline. The book by Chirol cited above (which is almost 200 pages long) mentions the Chinese "Sick Man", aside from the quotation above, only in one additional paragraph: "By her intervention Russia openly proclaimed her determination to assume henceforth the guardianship of the Chinese Empire until such time as by the laws of nature, assisted or unassisted, the sick man of the Far East should pass away and his inheritance be formally appropriated." Chirol (1896), *The Far Eastern Question*, p. 66. In the remainder of the book, the Middle Realm is simply referred to as "China".

known as "physical education" (*tiyu* 體育).[36] In addition, in translated articles that appeared in publications such as the *Shiwubao* or the *WGGB*, "Sick Man" (*bingfu* or *bingren* 病人) was similarly used exclusively to criticise the government of Qing China, and, again, these articles draw no connection whatsoever between the "Sick Man" and the common Chinese people. This usage completely reflects Western attitudes regarding China's waning national strength and the Qing government's inability or unwillingness to reform the country's political institutions.

But is this not strange? For, if this is the case, how come that we find assertions such as that of the Shanghai Administration of Sports proclaiming that "the Chinese were henceforth often disparagingly referred to as 'sick men of East Asia' by the Westerners"? Or how are we to explain the ubiquity of statements—to be heard *ad nauseam*—such as: "We shall clear the Chinese people's disgraceful reputation as 'Sick Men of East Asia', which has been forced upon them by the foreigners, with trophies won in international athletic contests." It needs to be pointed out that the infamous expression "Sick Man of East Asia", as it is presently commonly used in the Chinese-language media, is hardly ever encountered outside of China's cultural sphere. Strictly speaking there exists—at most—an awareness of the existence of the saying "Sick Man of East Asia". But, if this is the case, then what historical developments were responsible for the "Sick Man", as it emerged in the West, and took on the features that it has today? Even more importantly, we have to answer the questions regarding which factors facilitated these developments, whether these factors originate from the West or from China itself, and, if they do stem from China, then how are we to re-evaluate the claim that the "Sick Man of East Asia" constitutes a case of "Western humiliation". I will delve more deeply into these questions in the following section.

---

36 Translator's note: Even the infamous *Chinese Characteristics* (1890) by Arthur H. Smith, which contains more than a few ill-founded generalisations about the Chinese people, summarises the gist of the chapter "Physical Vitality" in the following words: "If a people with such physical endowments as the Chinese were to be preserved from the effects of war, famines, pestilence, and opium, and if they were to pay some attention to the laws of physiology and of hygiene, and to be uniformly nourished with suitable food, *there is reason to think that they alone would be adequate to occupy the principal part of the planet and more.*" Smith (1890), *Chinese Characteristics*, p. 192.

III. The "Sick Man" Grows and Transforms: From "China is the Sick Man of the East" to "China is the Country of the Sick Men of the East"

1. "Sick Man": A Concept Takes Root

In the previous analysis, we examined three layers of context that aided us in our understanding of the definitive meaning of the "Sick Man" trope in both Western and Chinese popular discourse around the turn of the nineteenth century. Apart from these, there is yet one more contextual dimension to the topic to be explored in this article that warrants clarification and it is a rather important one: How did intellectual and literary circles in Qing China regard this "Western" idea of the "Sick Man" at the time? What kind of response did it elicit in China?

As many scholars have pointed out, the First Sino-Japanese War had a profound effect on Chinese intellectuals, an effect greater by far than any other military loss against a Western power that Qing China had had to suffer prior to 1895. The fact that the Great Qing Empire had, contrary to all expectations, suffered a crushing defeat at the hands of Japan, a country China had long looked down upon, left intellectuals concerned with national affairs disheartened, indignant, disoriented, and harbouring a host of similar complicated emotions.[37] This intellectual atmosphere characterised by a surging sense of crisis and a craving for self-inspection and change, expedited the general eagerness to understand Western learning, brought about the emergence of a large number of new-style newspapers, and led many to start to advocate vociferously for the spreading of Western knowledge. The most eminent publication in this spirit was undoubtedly the *Shiwubao*, launched in 1896 under the devoted leadership of Liang Qichao 梁啟超 (1873–1929)[38] who, in an article entitled "On the Benefits of the Press in National Affairs" (*Lun baoguan youyi yu guoshi* 論報館有益於國事) frankly stated that, when running a paper one ought

to translate extensively [texts concerning] recent events in the five continents so that the readers may gain an understanding of the general situation in all places [of the world] as well as insights into the reasons behind strength, prosperity, weakness, and ruin, instead of remaining trapped in ignorance and self-delusion and discussing heaven and earth while sitting in a dry well [*i.e.*, without having any information].[39]

---

37 There is a host of popular works on the profound influence of the First Sino-Japanese War on the contemporary Chinese intellectual sphere. Studies to be consulted include: Tang Zhijun (2003), *Wuxu bianfa shi*, pp. 1–347; Ge Zhaoguang (2002), "1895 nian de Zhongguo", pp. 530–550; Zhang Hao (1982), "Wan Qing sixiang fazhan shilun", pp. 19–33.

38 Zhang Hao (1982), "Wan Qing sixiang fazhan shilun", p. 29.

39 Liang Qichao (1941 [1896]), "Lun baoguan youyi yu guoshi", p. 102.

We can see how this call to translate a wide variety of foreign texts to supply China's intellectuals with knowledge about the outside world and its vicissitudes was put into actual practice by the *Shiwubao*, as the journal remained true to its word and indeed published a large number of articles and commentaries translated from foreign languages. Seen from this perspective, translation pieces such as "China's Actual Situation" (which featured the infamous provocative statement "for China is a sick man of the East") or "The World's Four Sick Men", give proof to the *Shiwubao*'s conviction that one should not hesitate to use foreign knowledge to eradicate one's domestic shortcomings. The people behind the publication hoped that, in this manner, the readers would learn about the attitudes and opinions of foreign observers about the Chinese reforms. It was not at all their intention to report specifically on the ways that foreigners insulted and humiliated China and the Chinese people.

What is even more noteworthy is that Gilbert Reid (Li Jiabai 李佳白, 1857–1927), a missionary in China at the time, who energetically tried to persuade the Chinese government to reform and pursue national strengthening, published an article in the *WGGB* entitled "Tracing the Origins of Poverty" (*Tanben qiong yuan lun* 探本窮源論), in which he wrote, several months prior to the *Shiwubao*'s "China's Actual Situation", that "the situation of China may be likened to a giant sick man" (*Zhongguo zhi qingxing piru yi da bingren* 中國之情形譬如一大病人). He believed that:

Under the present circumstances, nothing is more important than sending for a doctor and choosing a [proper] method of treatment. [One has to] drain the endogenous causes of the sickness (from the body) and remove them energetically one by one to the degree that neither root nor trunk remains. Only then can one go about developing (the patient's) vitality.[40]

Reid further elaborated on his views concerning the Qing bureaucracy and the government's financial and education policies in similarly themed articles such as "On the Nature of Illness" (*Lun bibing zhi qingxing* 論弊病之情形), "On the Source and Course of Illness" (*Lun bibing zhi yuanliu* 論弊病之源流), "On Removing the External Factors of Illness"(*Lun chu bibing zhi waigan* 論除弊病之外感), or "On Removing the Root of Illness" (*Lun chu bibing zhi gen* 論除弊病之根. It is interesting to note that he adopted a noticeable "consoling" tone when discussing the state of China's illness: "It is not the case that only China alone is sick and the Western countries are not. This is only a matter of degree."[41]

He wrote that, if one were to rank the countries of the world according to the gravity of their sickness on a scale of 1 to 10, then Turkey would be situated

---

40 Li Jiabai (Reid) (1896), "Tanben qiong yuan lun", pp. 16075–16084.
41 Ibid.

between seven and eight, Russia between five and six, and England between one and two. In short, the main idea behind these and like-minded texts seems to be that being a "sick man" is not at all a matter of great shame, and certainly not incurable. Reid believed that the crucial thing was to confront the illness, understand its causes and where it was located, and, after that, choose the medicine best suited to combat the illness. Only if one proceeded in this manner would China be able to "wake up quickly to reality and vigorously bounce back; if China is truly happy, the world is truly happy" (*fanran xingwu li zi zhenba, Zhongguo xingshen tianxia xingshen* 翻然醒悟力自振拔中國幸甚天下幸甚).[42]

We can thus see that the habit of using the term "Sick Man" to describe the plight of contemporary China in arguments proposing political reform measures stemmed, on the one hand, from Western public discourse, but can also be observed in the writings of those Westerners who had observed and experienced China's situation first hand. Moreover, many Chinese intellectuals including Yan Fu 嚴復 (1854–1921), Kang Youwei 康有為 (1858–1927), and Liang Qichao, likened China's difficult circumstances to a "Sick Man" in their own works discussing the state and prospects of the country's reforms. In his famous essay entitled "On Strength" (*Yuan qiang* 原強; published in March 1895), Yan Fu wrote:

The affairs of a state, are like (the affairs of) the human body. It is the general consent today that the body becomes weak when idle and strong when it labours. However, if a sick man were, day in, day out, to try to surpass everyone and excel at everything, in a quest to become strong, this person would quickly die. *Is today's China not indeed like a sick man?*[43]

Yan Fu here used the term "sick man" as a metaphor to describe the China of his time, in order to argue that political reform and the pursuit of strength would only lead to the sick man's (China's) quick and sure demise if reform efforts did not commence at the root—by which he meant his three key proposals to "encourage the people's force" (*gu minli* 鼓民力), "broaden the people's intelligence" (*kai minzhi* 開民智), and "renovate the people's virtue" (*xin minde* 新民德). One has to point out that, although Yan Fu emphasised the importance of developing the physical skills and physical strength of the people in this text, and although he expressed his dismay concerning the harmful effects of opium and the practice of foot binding, at no point did he use the term "sick man" to describe the physical characteristics of the Chinese people.

One can easily imagine that Liang Qichao, who, in his capacity as editor-in-chief of the *Shiwubao*, cultivated personal relationships and intellectual exchanges with many other proponents of social and political reform such as Yan

---

42 Ibid.
43 Yan Fu (1962 [1895]), "Yuan qiang", p. 369.

Fu and Gilbert Reid, was equally no stranger to the "Sick Man" metaphor or to the fact that it was commonly employed in contemporary Chinese and Western political discourse to describe China's current situation.[44] In an 1897 article on reform, he forcefully rejected the idea that, in order for China to become strong, the country had to emulate the West in its emphasis on "training troops" (*lianbing* 練兵). In his view, China's reform had to start at the root, by which he meant establishing schools, revamping the bureaucracy, subsidising agriculture, and encouraging business enterprises. This, according to him, was because:

When they train troops in the West, they fit strong men with armour and weaponry. *Today's China, being the sick man that she is*, does not do much to treat the illness [first] but instead does what [only] strong men are supposed to do. Therefore, I say: That which will destroy everything under heaven is surely this proposal [to give priority to the training of troops].[45]

Liang is very similar to Yan Fu (quoted above) in his view that China, as a "sick man", first had to address its most fundamental issues, and that the reforms must not be hurried. In addition, the opening remark in Liang's "Preface to [Tang Rui's 湯叡 translation of] *(Records of the war between Russia and Turkey)*" (*E-Tu zhanji xu* 俄土戰紀敍), published in 1898, is even more clear-cut:

The people of Western Europe have a common saying: *"There are two countries in the east that are like sick men. These are China and Turkey."* Turkey has been crippled for two reasons. One, its internal affairs are not in order, the social order is lax, its government officials are greedy and wanton, and it cruelly oppresses its people. Turkey slavishly sticks to established methods, unwilling to change even the slightest bit. [The country] is fettered by (tradition), yet [often] acts rashly, which causes popular uprisings. Two, [the Turkish] are unwary in foreign affairs, are arrogant and act self-importantly [when dealing with other countries]. They do not abide by international law and incidents involving missionaries occur frequently. This gives others a basis for gossip and brings upon them the resentment of every other country, which jointly scheme against them. Alas! How similar this is to the situation of today's China![46]

From this quotation, we can clearly see that Liang Qichao not only readily adopted the expression "sick man" as it was used in contemporary Western

---

44 Liang Qichao, in a 1897 text, commemorated the Academy of the Exaltation of the Worthy (*Shangxian tang* 尚賢堂) founded by Reid (probably on his request). Here, he mentions that he and Reid had become acquainted via the Strengthening Learning Society (*Qiangxuehui* 強學會). See Liang (1999 [1897]), "Ji Shangxian tang", p. 112. Kang Youwei and Liang Qichao were both deeply influenced by the Western knowledge that missionaries had introduced to China, especially by members of the Extension of Learning Society (*Guangxuehui* 廣學會) like Timothy Richard (1845–1919). For a detailed discussion, see Wang(1980), *Wairen yu Wuxu bianfa*, pp. 99–112.

45 Liang Qichao (1941 [1896–1897]), "Lun bianfa buzhi benyuan zhi hai", p. 11.

46 Liang Qichao (1941 [1898]), "E-Tu zhanji xu", p. 33.

discourse, but also skilfully used his analysis of the "pathogenesis" of Turkey's degeneration (*i.e.*, the country's turning into a sick man) to illustrate indirectly the domestic and international factors underlying China's own transformation into a "sick man": "Alas! How similar this is to the situation of today's China!" Comparable to the other articles already discussed, Liang's sole target of his criticism were the failings of the government; he did not include any factors pertaining to the people or their physical constitution among the causes of the "illness" of China that he identified. This marks a point of difference to his later views. Below, I will explore this shift more thoroughly.

We may surmise from the examples given above that speaking about China as a "Sick Man" at the end of the nineteenth century, and especially in the context of the changed intellectual *milieu* that had emerged after the First Sino-Japanese War, cannot be understood and, indeed, was not understood as a malicious Western defamation of China. Rather, in the hands of China's advocates of change, it became an efficient rhetorical tool in their efforts to "save the country from extinction". In the concluding paragraph to the preface to his *Record of the Degeneration of Turkey for Presentation to the Imperial Throne (Jincheng Tujue xiaoruo ji* 進呈突厥削弱記), submitted to the Guangxu Emperor in June 1898, Kang Youwei bluntly stated:

The *Book of Documents* says: "Walk on the same path as order and nothing will not flourish. Walk on the same path as chaos and nothing will not perish." *China and Turkey (Tujue* 突厥) *have long been reproachfully referred to as the two sick men of the east by Western Europe*, by which they seem to mean that one does not know which one of the two will die first. At present, China's condition is the same as Turkey's, and China's sickness is equally the same as Turkey's. Your humble servant has translated and compiled this (work on the) situation of Turkey and he shudders, seeing the [similar] dangers [facing China], and is restless and tearful. Thankfully, we are blessed with Your Majesty's sageness and valour, [Your willingness to] reform and modernise, and Your decision to establish a constitution. We thus have the means to alleviate the weakness should a sickness arise and this alone distinguishes us from Turkey. China is not ruined and the Chinese people are not enslaved. This is only because we can rely on Your Majesty. The *Book of Documents* says: "When the One Man [*i.e.*, the ruler] shows aptitude, millions of people may [confidently] depend on him." This is the fortune of the 400 million people of China.

I have, with all solemnity, translated and compiled (this text) and submitted it to Your Majesty to serve as a lesson.

Preface written by Your humble servant Kang Youwei.[47]

There are a few points of note in this paragraph of Kang Youwei's: the expression "sick man", as it is used here, does not purely describe China's staunch conservatism and inability to carry out reforms, but also serves as a kind of prophecy that predicts "death" (*i.e.*, the destruction of the country). In other

---

47 Kang (1981 [1898]), "*Jincheng Tujue xiaoruo ji* xu", p. 300.

words, should the "sick man" fail to decisively carry out reforms decisively, he will not only face defeat again, but will, in all likelihood, end up a ruined nation. Second, Kang Youwei and Liang Qichao both acknowledge that China and Turkey were faced with similar ailments. Guided by this premise, Kang encourages the emperor by assuring him that China still "has the means to alleviate the weakness should a sickness arise" and commends him for his sincere devotion to the reformist cause.

The analysis above reveals that, seen from the perspective of the proponents of political reform, the "sick man" had, in the wake of the First Sino-Japanese War and the growing sense of crisis in China's cultural and intellectual sphere, become a vehicle for unvarnished but earnest criticism meant to inspire the nation to reflect on its shortcomings.[48] The trope not only vividly described the rigid conservatism and prolonged state of "poor health" of Qing China, but also became a rallying call in the mouths of the advocates of reform to convey their conviction that China would surely degenerate into a moribund ruined country if it failed to undertake radical reforms. Therefore, faced with the basically Western characterisation of China as a "sick man", China's intellectual circles at the end of the nineteenth century essentially adopted an attitude of profound introspection and self-criticism and even began to cite the expression so as to strengthen reformist determination. To phrase it differently, at the time in question, evoking the "Sick Man of East Asia" was not a matter of Westerners mocking the Chinese in general, or their physiques in particular. It would be inaccurate to liken the idea to a label that was forced upon the people of China, and it was not part of a discourse that argued in favour of cleansing the national shame of the "Sick Man of East Asia" by athletic contests, either. In order to understand the subsequent historical development that led to the dramatic transformation and re-interpretation of the expression "sick man", and why it became part of a veritable collective humiliation complex among the people of China, we have to go one step further and analyse some important trends in the development of modern Chinese thought after the failure of the reform movement of 1898.

---

48 In 1901, the *Qingyibao* 清議報 (Journal of Pure Critique) carried a commentary entitled "China after the Peace Negotiations" (*Lun yihe hou zhi Zhongguo* 論議和後之中國) which clearly stated that, by being seen as a "Sick Man" in their eyes, Turkey had become a plaything in the hands of the powers, who constantly plotted against it. The author warned that "the sick men of east and west have now become yoked and tied by these six countries and are unable to break free from their grasp. If we want to counteract this technique and deal with the [label of the] Sick Man of the Far East (*Taidong bingfu* 泰東病夫), we will also have to employ their old tricks". Judging from this, it is evidently the case that the "Sick Man" had been commonly understood as a political metaphor in the public discourse at that time. For the article, see "Lun yihe hou zhi Zhongguo" (1901), pp. 4481–4486.

FROM DISCOURSE OF WEAKNESS TO DISCOURSE OF EMPOWERMENT 47

2. "Sick Man": Modification and Transformation of a Concept

Aside from the reform efforts and the accompanying sense of crisis discussed above, the post-war intellectual and cultural landscape of China witnessed a second profound and far-reaching transformation, namely, the emergence of modern Chinese nationalism. In addition, Social Darwinism, as introduced by Yan Fu, brought with it a new "objective truth"—the existence of a struggle for survival among states, or, more precisely, a struggle to decide the survival or demise of races. This became a basic conviction in all contemporary thought that concerned itself with the current state and future fate of the country. In Yan's view, the key point of Darwin's theory lay in the following:

All people and all animals vie for survival. In the beginning, race vied with race, and when they formed groups and states, groups vied with groups and states vied with states. The weak were liable to become the meat of the strong, and the ignorant were liable to become the servants of the intelligent. If there is [a species] that was able to survive and to ensure the continuation of its kind [over a long period of time], this means that it [has proven itself to be] the fittest regarding [characteristics such as] strength, endurance, eminence, and ruthlessness or vigour, agility, cunning, and wisdom, given the climatic, geographical, or other external conditions at hand.[49]

In other words, the competition between countries is no longer a competition between its leaders or governments, but rather a total war between the people who make up these countries. The strength and weakness of a country is therefore not only decided by a government's leadership and the merits of its policies, but depends, above all, on the quality of its people who, after all, form the basis of a country's wealth and strength: a strong country has to begin with a strong race. This is exactly the reason why Yan Fu believed that the foundation of the reformation of Qing China was to "encourage the people's force, to broaden the people's virtue, and to raise the people's intelligence".[50]

The move to equate the nation's (*zu* 族) strength with the both country's (*guo* 國) strength and the demand that political reforms needed to commence with the remodelling of the people, arguably constituted a major shift in the thinking of the Chinese reform movement, and this conviction was only deepened by the Qing court's continuing failure to follow through with political reforms. It is generally held that Liang Qichao's *Xinmin shuo* 新民說 (*Treatise on the Renewal of the People*), published (in multiple instalments over a period of several years) at the beginning of the twentieth century, was particularly representative for this new mode of thought. However, a close reading of Liang's "A Discussion of the Causes Underlying China's Long-Standing Weakness" (*Zhongguo jiruo suyuan lun* 中國積弱溯源論 (written in 1900, the 26th year of the

---

49 For Yan Fu's whole argument, see Yan Fu (1962 [1895]), "Yuan qiang", pp. 357–377.
50 Ibid.

reign of the Guangxu-Emperor) reveals that this earlier work already emphasised the point that political reform had to start by reforming the people. In this rather long article, Liang argues that China's situation was just like that of a person who has long suffered from an illness to the point where he is no longer aware of it and that "the government as well as the people are to blame" (*gai zhengfu yu renmin ge jie youzui yan* 蓋政府與人民各皆有罪焉) for China's sickness. He holds that, while China's government officials could hardly escape the charge that they had plunged the country into disaster and grievously harmed the people, one nevertheless had to remember that:

officials come from among the people, as the fruit comes from the roots. When the tree is sweet, its fruit will always be sweet; when the tree is acrid, its fruit will always be acrid.[51]

In accordance with this argument that sought to trace the problem to its root cause, Liang related, in painful detail, the collective maladies of the Chinese people, maladies which had grown over hundreds and thousands of years: their servility had instilled in them a kind of slave-mentality. They were ignorant and selfish, only considering their own individual well-being and having no sense of community or the greater good. In addition, they were mendacious, cowardly, and loathed change. On top of that, his fellow countrymen neither understood the difference between the country and (civilised) world (*tianxia* 天下), nor the distinction between the country and the court, nor the relationship between the country and its citizens. This, as Liang termed it, "threefold ignorance" (*san bu zhi* 三不知) of the people was also one of the main causes behind China's sickness and weakness. In this article, which might be characterised as a "medical report" on the physical and mental condition of early twentieth century China, Liang adopts a tone that bespeaks a deeply rooted bitterness. He minutely enumerates all of China's "pathogens", as he sees them, and states outright that:

China, after the Kangxi reign, became more corrupted by the day, and more spoiled by the month, and gradually turned into the world's foremost defunct country.[52]

Granted, Liang labelled contemporary Qing China as a "sick country" (*bingguo* 病國) rather than a "sick man" in this text. However, in his diagnosis of the various items on his list of pathogens, he nonetheless expressed in very clear language his deep concern and anxiety for a country that had not seen much improvement in its national strength following the war with Japan. We should, however, pay attention to the fact that, when Liang attacked the people of his country as being cowardly, weakness-loving, and lacking a martial spirit, he did

---

51 Refer to Liang Qichao (1941 [1901]), "Zhongguo jiruo suyuan lun", pp. 14–42 for the detailed argument.

52 Ibid.

not waste much ink on the topic of their physical condition, and rather focused on their ideological attitudes and system of values. Regarding the former aspect, Liang further developed his thoughts on the issue in his *Xinmin shuo*, mentioned above. As this shift is of some relevance to the angle of inquiry of the present article, we therefore need to delve more deeply into Liang's famous treatise for some new arguments concerning the physical body and the physical strength of the Chinese people.

In the essay entitled "On Esteeming Martiality" (*Lun shangwu* 論尚武), which appeared in 1903 as part of his serialised *Xinmin shuo*, Liang not only continued his prior criticism of what he regarded as the effeminate character of the Chinese nation and its lack of a martial spirit, but also stressed that what the country needed was a national military education akin to that of ancient Sparta, which would foster bravery and ferocity in its citizens from childhood.[53] The text touches on the "Sick Man" numerous times:

We are known in the world as a sick man. Our hands and feet are palsied and we have utterly lost the capability to protect ourselves. Among all the countries of the east and the west, there are none which do not sharpen their weapons to be ready to cow and oppress us. If we fail to pull out the evil root of effeminacy quickly and to wash away the shame that has mounted due to our lack of martial qualities, how could there still be a way for the Chinese race to gain a foothold on the battle field of the twentieth century?[54]

From the context, it is evident that the "we" in the above sentence "We are known in the world as a sick man", still refers to feeble, conservative Qing China. But, in another paragraph, "Sick Man" evidently carries a different meaning:

Two thousand years of corruption and failure have penetrated deeply into the brains of the citizens. *This has caused the people of the entire country to wheeze and pant like sick men now,* become limp and saggy like weak women, mild-mannered like Bodhisattvas, and meek and docile like tame lambs.[55]

Here, Liang quite obviously uses the term "Sick Man" to describe all the people of the country. And herein lies the true root cause for China's sickness, as Liang explains in more detail:

---

53 Liang's thoughts on national military education undoubtedly reflect earlier ideas of the Movement to Militarize the Citizens (*Jun guomin yundong* 軍國民運動) initiated by Cai E 蔡鍔 (1882–1916) and Jiang Baili 蔣百里 (Jiang Fangzhen 蔣方震; 1882–1938) and their conviction that "all citizens ought to be soldiers" (*quanmin jie bing* 全民皆兵). For an analysis of the intellectual and cultural milieu of this movement, see Huang Jinlin (2000), *Lishi, shenti, guojia*, pp. 55–69. The relationship between national military education and physical education is discussed in Xu Yixiong (1996), "Jun guomin jiaoyu zhi tiyu sixiang", pp. 37–121.

54 Liang Qichao (1999 [1902–1906]), "Xinmin shuo", p. 712.

55 Ibid., p. 711.

The Chinese people pay no heed to hygiene and they marry too young. To pass on one's seed under these circumstances, creates a race that is already frail and weak. [But as if this were not enough,] after they have learned to emulate their teachers, they spend the whole day bent over their desks and shut themselves away in their rooms. They remain completely sedentary, exhaust their eyesight [reading] and become blind, and become hunchbacked even though they are not yet withered and old. Furthermore, they have got into the habit of being frail and lazy and show no inclination to be industrious or active. Be it clothing, food, or any other daily activity, they always need someone else [to do it for them]. Effeminacy is taken to be a praiseworthy trait; frailty and timidity are taken to be signs of grace and nobility. A delicate prettyboy, too weak to withstand a gust of wind, is called a man (*zhangfu* 丈夫). [Already] weaker than a girl, he [eventually] enters (full) adulthood only to wrap himself in silk and sleep in a mansion thus, consuming his energy and he starts smoking opium, thus harming his body. He becomes emaciated and pallid, his gait becomes wobbly, and his blood stops flowing. His face looks like he is near to death, his body flaccid, and his breathing feeble. And if one were to gather all of (China's) 400 million people, one would not be able to assemble even a single whole and healthy body [from their parts]. *Alas! If its people are all sick men, how can the country possibly be something other than a sick country?* To encounter a different nation that is ferocious, fearsome, valiant, and fierce in such a condition, is like sending a dwarf to battle an invincible giant. Even if the (other nation does not hold a weapon, it would take but a wave of their hand and we would collapse immediately. Alas! [In the face of] the struggle for survival and the survival of the fittest, I hope that our compatriots will train their muscles and bones, and learn to be brave and powerful, lest they become dilapidated and exhausted and fall incurably ill.[56]

On the one hand, Liang here clearly reiterates the view that China inescapably finds itself in a reality in which the international system is dominated by the Social Darwinist maxim of the survival of the fittest. But what is even more important, is that Liang, under the premise that a strong country required first of all a strong race, makes it even more explicit, compared with his earlier arguments, that the people of the entire country (*i.e.*, China's 400 million) are all "Sick Men" and that this is the reason behind China's sickness. We may say that, at this point, Liang transmutes the meaning of the original "Sick Man" trope, which, as we have seen, after the First Sino-Japanese War, had been used exclusively to describe China's waning power and its lack of willingness to carry out reforms. "Sick Man" is no longer used to refer only to China as a country. Its meaning has evolved to describe all of China's 400 million people which, in Liang's eyes, appeared, without exception, as people whose "blood has stopped flowing, with faces that look like they are near death, their bodies flaccid, and their breathing feeble". Although we cannot be one hundred per cent certain that Liang was really the first person to have expanded the meaning of the term "Sick Man" in this influential manner, it is clear that, in writings by people participating in the political discourse surrounding the "Sick Man", including that

---

56 Ibid., p. 713.

FROM DISCOURSE OF WEAKNESS TO DISCOURSE OF EMPOWERMENT

of Liang himself, that were published prior to *Xinmin shuo*, "Sick Man" never appears in the meaning it carries in the lengthy quotation above.[57] But, at a time when surging nationalist thought and a growing sense of crisis mandated to "protect the country and protect the race" (*baoguo baozhong* 保國保種), Liang's idea that the fate of the state was closely tied to the fate of the individuals out of which the community was composed, was fairly widespread.

Liang's criticism manifested in the sentence that his "400 million compatriots are all sick men" had already been quite harsh, but, in his text entitled "Journey to the New World" (*Xin Dalu youji* 新大陸游記), published in 1904, he was even more merciless and compared the people of China very unfavourably with the strong and healthy American people he had observed during his travels. He believed that "the character (*xingzhi* 性質) of the Chinese people was in many ways inferior to that of the Westerners" and provided an item by item list of what were, in his view, some of the key differences regarding everyday life, work and leisure, and the physical characteristics between "our race" and "their race":

---

57 One should pay attention to the fact that Zhang Zhidong 張之洞 (1837–1909), in an 1897 text concerning the movement to prohibit foot binding, argued as follows: "Presently, [we find ourselves in a situation where] weakness stemming from Western opium has already arisen, but weakness stemming from a lack in moral character has not yet emerged. Within a few decades or a few hundred years [at most], how can it not be the case that the people of our China will have degenerated into a state where everyone is a sick man and every family is a family of midgets? [At this point,] we will not be able to resist being trampled by [people] from strange lands (yifang 殊方) and being oppressed by foreign nations (*yizu* 異族)." See Yuan et al. (1998), *Zhang Zhidong quanji*, p. 10061. Although Zhang's fear that "everyone will be a sick man" echoes the article of Liang Qichao's quoted above, he is only describing a possible future scenario for the people of China that might become a reality "a few decades or a few hundred years" from now and does not actually refer to the present situation. Furthermore, expressions like "everyone will be a sick man" appear only once in Zhang's entire article, in stark contrast to Liang's *Xinmin shuo*, where he argues at length and with great conviction how present-day China had already turned into a sick country created by 400 million sick men. We can thus surmise that the two discussions are very different in content and purpose. Tang Caichang 唐才常 (1867–1900), in a text of his also discussing the prohibition of foot binding, quotes Zhang's opinions in support of his own argument. The interesting thing is that Tang slightly changes Zhang's formulation, which in his rendition becomes: "[...] how can it not be the case that the people of our China will have degenerated into a state where every family is a family of sick men and everyone is a midget? [At this point,] we will not be able to resist being trampled by [people] from strange lands and being oppressed by foreign nations." (*I.e.*, "jiajia wei bingfu, renren wei zhuru" 家家為病夫人人為侏儒, instead of "renren wei bingfu, jiajia wei zhuru" 人人為病夫家家為侏儒.) See Hunan sheng zhexue shehui kexue yanjiusuo (ed.) (1982), *Tang Caichang ji*, p. 146. From the fact that Tang seemingly unconcernedly replaced "every family" with "everyone", we can deduce that Zhang's expression "everyone will be a sick man" might perhaps have been a warning cast into a metaphor, but was nowhere near as striking as Liang's usage. The latter's closely argued judgement that the "400 million" had, without exception, already become sick men betrays the deeply felt sense in those years that China's existence as a country as a well as a nation was in dire peril.

Let us assume that we were to gather some 100 Chinamen in a meeting hall. Although [the occasion] would be exceedingly solemn and calling for silence, there would surely be four kinds of noise: the most frequent sound would be coughing; followed by yawning; then sneezing; and finally the sound of people wiping their noses. I have heard this happening before during speeches. These four types of noise are like linked pearls, that is, they will never cease. But when one listens to Westerners during a speech or a theatrical performance, one will not hear a sound, even if thousands of people are present. In East Asia (*Dongyang* 東洋),[58] there are always spittoons placed in trains and streetcars because people there spit notoriously and incessantly. In America, there are very few spittoons on trains and, if there are some, they are almost never used. In East Asia, people nap for most of the journey, even if it takes no more than two or three hours. In America, even though the trains run all day long, there has never been a person who has made (a train) their domicile. *[From this] we can see how very different east and west are with respect to strength and weakness, and superiority and inferiority.*[59]

In San Francisco, there is no spitting allowed on the two pedestrian paths on either side of the road—while the middle is for vehicles. It is also not allowed to throw away wastepaper or other trash, and offenders are fined five dollars. In New York, spitting is not allowed on streetcars, and offenders are fined five hundred dollars. Such is the value that they place on cleanliness. Their interference [in other people's affairs] can be just as rigorous, and their restrictions of liberties can be just as severe. *It is no wonder, then, that they are disgusted by Chinamen being the disorderly and vile people that they are.*[60]

When Westerners walk on the road, there are none whose posture is not upright and there are none whose head is not held high. In our China, on the other hand, people of the (lowest) first rank hunch, people of the second rank stoop, and people of the third rank bow their heads. In comparison, I feel that we are truly inferior. When Westerners walk on the road, their pace is never leisurely. At a glance, one realises that, in a bustling city, all people follow a trade, and it is as if they can never manage to do all they have to do. Chinese people, on the other hand, walk at a measured pace, dignified and poised and one can hear the clinking sound of their jade ornaments. How perfectly disgusting. If you see, some dozen yards in the distance, a Chinese person on the street as they approach head on, you will immediately be able to identify them, not only by their short stature but also by their yellow faces. When several Westerners walk together, they are (orderly) like a flock of geese; when several Chinese people walk together, they are like scattered ducks.[61]

In this depiction of the "400 million sick men" in *Xinmin shuo*, Liang Qichao is showing us the physical characteristics of the Chinese people in a big close-up. He puts the "diseased Chinese people" in juxtaposition with their "Other", an "Other" that is, according to Liang, characterised by a strong country and a strong race. In this way, he amplifies his criticism of the bodily weakness and

---

58 Translator's note: *Dongyang* often refers specifically to Japan. However, in this context, the translation "East Asia" seemed more appropriate, as Liang is not discussing Japan's national characteristics but rather China's.

59 Liang Qichao (1999 [1904]), "Xin Dalu youji", p. 1187.

60 Ibid., p. 1189.

61 Ibid.

FROM DISCOURSE OF WEAKNESS TO DISCOURSE OF EMPOWERMENT

inferior lifestyle of the Chinese people. The Westerners play, for him, the role of the "superior race" that he admires and this ideal is contrasted with the "inferior nation" embodied by the Chinese people.

Liang Qichao's *Xinmin shuo* was of great influence in China's intellectual sphere and drew a huge response that went far beyond the immediate readership of the *New Citizen Miscellany* (*Xinmin congbao* 新民叢報).[62] His interpretation of the weakness and physical condition of the Chinese people as resembling that of "Sick Men" was subsequently further fermented in the popular media. The most interesting example of this is probably the best-selling 1905 novel entitled *A Flower in a Sea of Degradation* (*Niehai hua* 孽海花) which was published under the pseudonym the "Sick Man of East Asia" (*Dongya bingfu* 東亞病夫). *A Flower in a Sea of Degradation* was initially written by Jin Songcen 金松岑 (Jin Yi 金一, 1873–1947). Later, Zeng Pu 曾樸 (1872–1935) took over and reworked the story into a major novel. Zeng cultivated close ties with the reformers of his day, supported political change, and was infatuated with French literature. In 1905, together with a friend, he founded the Grove of Fiction Press (*Xiaoshuo lin chubanshe* 小說林出版社) in Shanghai, and promoted the publication of translated as well as original works of fiction. Zeng Pu had originally used the pseudonym "Sick Man of Sick Man Country" (*Bingfuguo zhi bingfu* 病夫國之病夫), which appeared in an advertisement for the publication of *A Flower in a Sea of Degradation*. When the novel was officially released, he changed his *nom de plume* to "Sick Man of East Asia" and did not alter it until the end of his life.[63] Judging from the timing of this name change and the fact that Zeng was deeply familiar with current intellectual and cultural trends, it seems likely that his decision and choice of pseudonym was influenced by the "Sick Man" metaphor as used in *Xinmin shuo*. However, one also has to take into account that Zeng had only recently started to recover from a three-year long illness which had plagued him from 1900 to 1903. And this personal life experience was probably also a factor in Zeng seeing himself as a "Sick Man". It is quite ironic, then, that, following the commercial success of *A Flower in a Sea of Degradation*—the novel was reprinted multiple times in its first and second year and reached over 50,000

---

62 On the broad impact of *Xinmin shuo* during the twentieth century, see Huang Kewu (1994), *Yi ge bei fangqi de xuanze*, pp. 52–60.

63 On Zeng changing his pseudonym, see Wei Ruhui (1984), "Niehai hua zahua", pp. 457–462. It has not yet been fully explained why Zeng changed his pseudonym. However, in 1905, the Grove of Fiction Press bought its own print shop which was named *Dongya yinshuguan* 東亞印書館 (The East Asia Publishing Company) and he might have got the inspiration to use the two words "East Asia" from this name. As for the reasons why Zeng published under a pseudonym at all: first, there are some parts of the novel that are based upon anecdotes involving family members or friends. His father-in-law actually obstructed the publication of the novel. Second, the book includes anti-Manchu and revolutionary ideas. For these two reasons, Zeng Pu probably preferred to use a pseudonym in order to remain anonymous. See Li (1977), *Zeng Mengpu de wenxue lücheng*, pp. 93–94.

copies, the "Sick Man of East Asia"(both the pseudonym and the trope in general) gained considerable fame while the readership remained unaware that Zeng Pu was actually the original author. As a result, the "Sick Man" not only acquired a new layer of meaning in the cultural and intellectual sphere of early twentieth century China and gained an actual real and living spokesperson— namely, Zeng's alter ego as the "Sick Man of East Asia". From this point on, the "Sick Man of East Asia" itself undoubtedly gained currency in Chinese public discourse and would eventually become a phrase that was all but universally known even a hundred years later. Be that as it may, how many people are there today who, as they pledge to take off the so-called "label forcefully put on the Chinese by the Westerners", are able to imagine that, amidst the idyllic scenery in Changshu city's 常熟 Jiangnan Park, where Zeng's last resting place is located, we find a stone tablet marking the "Grave of Mr. Zeng Pu, the Sick Man of East Asia"? The other "Sick Man", however, has not been laid to rest to date.[64]

Liang Qichao's argument tying the destiny of the Chinese nation to the physical build of its citizens and his expanded interpretation of the "Sick Man" is also reflected in a 1906 article in *L'Impartial* (*Dagongbao* 大公報; today internationally called *Ta Kung Pao*) entitled "Report on the Sports Meeting at Imperial Peking University" (*Jingshi daxuetang yundonghui ji* 京師大學堂運動會記). Here, the author asserts that when foreigners insult China "as a dotard and a sick man" (*wei laoda, wei bingfu* 為老大為病夫), their charge is not wholly unfounded. Those among China's 400 million people who practice such things as foot binding or opium smoking, who indulge in women and drink, and are fond of quietude and inaction, are indeed equal to "dotards and sick men". And for those very few Chinese who are "neither geriatric, nor sick men" it would be impossible to create a strong and great country on their own:

Alas! When more than 1.6 billion people [*i.e.*, the world's population around 1900] not only have to provide for themselves but additionally have to provide for 382 million of their number [who are old and sick], how can this country become strong? Is it then possible to realise our wish that other people will not treat us as dotards and sick men?[65]

In the article, the author not only reiterates Liang Qichao's opinion that the Chinese people are sick men, he also thinks that the reason why China is now ridiculed as a "Sick Man" by foreigners is the result of the physical weakness and frailty of its citizens, and that only by enhancing their physical fitness would it be possible to avoid being continually reduced to a "geriatric, sick man". Accordingly, "Sick Man", as used in the article, is targeted at both the country as well as its people.

---

64 See Shen Qian (2004), "Banshi fengliu *Niehai hua*", p. 111.

65 *Dagongbao*, 6 May 1905, p. 3.

FROM DISCOURSE OF WEAKNESS TO DISCOURSE OF EMPOWERMENT

In addition, in the article entitled "National Hygienics" (*Guomin weishengxue* 國民衛生學), published in 1903 in the journal *Student Body of Hubei* (*Hubei xueshengjie* 湖北學生界), it is made clear from the outset that the survival of the fittest race is a general rule of evolution. Immediately after this assertion, it continues by launching an attack on the "Chinese race" (*Zhina zhongzu* 支那種族) that has allegedly degenerated into a race that is:

at its last breath, and close to its demise. Now [epithets like] the "Chinese sick man" or the "Chinese inferior race" are on the verge of becoming stereotypes in each and every country. Although these are slanderous words by foreigners, considering the present condition of our nation and how it serves to verify the rules of evolution, there is nothing wrong with them.[66]

Here, the two words "Sick Man" emphasise the general sickness and weakness of the entire citizenry. And although the author expresses their indignation that "these are slanderous words by foreigners", they nevertheless concede that there is some truth to this characterisation.

Another piece, on the subject of medicine, "Promoting Medical Knowledge" (*Xing yixue tong* 興醫學通), reads:

Nowadays, people of learning are pained by the fact that ours is a country of sick men. There are none who do not have their eyes and minds set on doing everything to work towards a cure, to remove the pathogens, and to write about the symptoms.[67]

In the introduction, the text emphasises how the promotion of medicine might sharpen awareness concerning hygiene and help to make the people healthier and stronger physically. At the end, the author articulates their exasperation that medical science is not valued as highly as it should be:

For some decades now, key figures and outstanding people have made it their chief occupation to talk about nothing but politics. This science (*i.e.*, medicine) which has gradually led to the entire country turning into a sick man, has been completely ignored. What a frightful disappointment![68]

In this, the article echoes the new usage of the term "Sick Man" put forth by Liang Qichao as referring not only to the country but also to the bodies of the entire people.

We thus see that, although Liang Qichao's veneration for the martial spirit and his advocacy of a national military education received approval as well as opposition at the beginning of the twentieth century, his way of problematising the body of the "400 million compatriots" was without a doubt a major current in contemporary thought. That is to say, even if someone did not approve of

---

66 "Guomin weishengxue", (1903), p. 79.
67 "Xing yixue tong", (1903), pp. 61, 72.
68 Ibid.

his proposal to employ military methods to drill the bodies of the citizens, they nevertheless tended to agree that likening the physical state of the Chinese people to that of "Sick Men" was not actually far off the mark and that it needed a set of appropriate measures to improve this condition. Xu Yibing 徐一冰 (1881–1922), for example, who was a famous callisthenics instructor of the early Republican Era, even though he was vehemently opposed to the idea of basing physical education on the militaristic "esteeming martiality" ideal, nevertheless made it the school motto to "strengthen the physique of the Chinese nation and wash off the disgrace of the Sick Man of East Asia" (*zengqiang Zhonghua minzu tizhi, xishua Dongya bingfu chiru* 增強中華民族體質洗刷東亞病夫恥辱) when the first modern institution dedicated to physical education in China was opened in Shanghai in 1908.[69] We can thus see that "Sick Man of East Asia" had, by that time, already come to be understood as an insult against the Chinese nation by its contemporaries. In a similar vein, Chen Duxiu 陳獨秀 (1879–1942), who was strongly opposed to the use of traditional martial arts and military callisthenics in physical education for young people, also conducted a "physical examination" of China along the lines laid out by Liang. He stated:

Finding, in a huge crowd of young people, someone who is physically strong, a powerful and brawny fellow like those [to be found among] European and American youths, is actually akin to [finding] a phoenix feather or a unicorn horn. *People have styled us the country of the "Sick Men of the East"* (*Dongya bingfu guo* 東亞病夫國). *How can it possibly be that, among all our children and youths, there is no one who is not to be counted among the ranks of sick men? And if this is the case, how can the nation hope to survive?*[70]

Although Chen Duxiu did not, as Liang Qichao had done, extend his criticism to include all "400 million compatriots", the two overlap in their belief that there exists a causal relationship between the physical weakness of the individual (or even the collective) and the survival or perdition of the nation. Moreover, Chen, like Liang, took the Westerners as the ideal when it came to the body so as to reinforce the distinct contrast between them and China, where "there is no one who is not to be counted among the ranks of sick men". In another paragraph, Chen Duxiu drew on the physical ideal of Western people in order to express his disdain for the physical body of the Chinese people even more strongly:

Tan Sitong 譚嗣同 (1865–1898) once said: "Considering the physical state of the Chinese people, we are indeed doomed! If we compare the Chinese to the Westerners, we see their listlessness, we see their wretchedness, we see their vulgarity, and we see their boorishness. Some are thin and sallow, some are fat and soft, and some are withered and hunchbacked. Those who are impressive, beautiful, and promising are but one

---

69 Cf. Xu Yuanmin (1999), *Zhongguo jindai zhishi fenzi dui tiyu sixiang zhi chuanbo*, pp. 99–121; Gao (2002), *"Dongya bingfu"*, p. 9.

70 Chen Duxiu (1996 [1915]), "Xin qingnian", p. 58.

or two in ten million!" But what is the reason for this? The reason is that Chinese education places the greatest emphasis on memorisation in the hindbrain as well as a little emphasis on thinking in the forebrain. Education that trains the entire body, on the other hand, has never enjoyed much attention. Those who have never received any instruction are therefore actually a bit more robust physically. Only the bookworms eventually know only studying, the sound of recitation, and the shaking of heads. If they find themselves in front of other people, they dully and stupidly incline their heads, hunch their backs, and bend at the waist. They have slanting shoulders, sallow and skeletal faces, and their ears and eyes, hands and feet are neither nimble nor useful. Such people, although they have hands, feet, ears, and eyes, how much better are they really than lame, deaf, blind, mute, maimed, crippled, or useless people? Education in the occident entails drilling the whole body and does not solely focus on the brain. It includes callisthenics to develop the strength of the whole body as well as painting and various games to improve one's agility and skill in using one's ears and eyes, and hands and feet. Therefore, all of them, be they men or women, old or young, are, without exception, energetic and awe-inspiring no matter what they do and wherever they go. *How can they ever think highly of us, those disgusting Chinese people?*[71]

This text, with its sharp contrast between Chinese and Western bodies, and the description from Liang Qichao's "Journey to the New World" cited above, arguably use different approaches with the same outcome. Chen Duxiu shows even less reservation in his assertions and goes so far as to allege that Chinese people cannot but feel inferior and begin to view themselves critically when faced with Western people.

Regarding the main argument of the present article, we may surmise from the ease in which Chen speaks of China as the "Sick Man of the Orient" and declares the physical bodies of every single person there to belong to "the ranks of sick men", that the expanded interpretation of the term "Sick Man" had already impressed itself deeply upon everyone's mind. In this light, it is hardly surprising that a certain Zhu Liang 朱亮 (fl. 1918), in his preface to Guo Xifen's 郭希汾 (1893–1984) *History of Physical Education in China* (*Zhongguo tiyu shi* 中國體育史), a pioneering inquiry into the subject which was finished in 1918, unambiguously stated:

A nation's rise and decline, strength and weakness can always be judged by the spirit and physique of its citizens. In our country, it had been the tradition for thousands of years to favour civility and disdain martiality, thus resulting in our long-standing weakness. *This resulted in China being called the country of the "Sick Men of the East"* (*Dongya bingfu zhi guo* 東亞病夫之國). (*The whole country*) *was* [*naturally*] *outraged and felt greatly humiliated!* In the last decades, our citizens have gradually awoken from their pipe dream and started to forsake the habit of placing too much emphasis on civility. However, as a cure, this has

---

71 The text was published in 1917. Chen Duxiu (1996 [1917]), "Jindai xiyang jiaoyu", pp. 109–110.

58 JUI-SUNG YANG

proved to be insufficient and consequently they have formed associations and clubs and have begun to study physical education.[72]

The analysis above lets us see the historical process that transformed "China as the sick man of East Asia" into "China as the country of the sick men of East Asia": a metaphorical verbal expression from Western political discourse was, in the course of China's evolving intellectual landscape and value system, modified and transformed in the public sphere of modern China to be turned into a significant element in the discourse regarding China's characteristics as a modern nation and its collective imagination over the last hundred years. In this process, the "Sick Man" trope took on a new meaning as well as a new function as its discursive context changed during the construction of modern China's national imagination: it helped the individual mindsets of the people of China to "coalescence" into a national consciousness. This transformation of the "Sick Man" is not an altogether unparalleled phenomenon. The most typical example for this ought to be the symbol of the Yellow Emperor that was recast in the nationalist discourse from the late Qing period onward and evolved from the common ancestor to which the beginning of the imperial lineage was traced in order to be regarded as the common ancestor of the Chinese nation. Through this new identity, the Yellow Emperor helped to create a collective consciousness in which the individual people of China were seen as "related by blood, and sharing weal and woe" (*xuemai xianglian, xiuqiyugong* 血脈相連休戚與共).[73] Seen from this perspective, and quite different from the positive role of the Yellow Emperor in forging a collective Chinese identity, the "Sick Man" can be considered to symbolise China's collective social flaws or even—to borrow the formula of the American scholar quoted in the introduction—its collective "original sin". The question of how this collective "original sin" might be surmounted and finally cast off turned into one of the most influential issues in China's national imagination during the course of the last century. Therefore, regardless of whether we consider Liang Qichao's or Chen Duxiu's description of the "pathological state" of the Chinese body, the "Sick Man" trope can be characterised as a discursive strategy to set off and legitimise reform measures and to highlight the necessity of political change. This move to "defame" rhetorically the very thing one aims to reform is arguably a very common occurrence in modern China's pursuit of modernisation. *The True Story of Ah Q* (*A Q zhengzhuan* 阿Q正傳) penned by Lu Xun 魯迅 (1881–1936), Bo Yang's 柏楊 (1920–2008) *The Ugly Chinaman* (*Choulou de Zhongguoren* 醜陋的中國人), and the New Life Movement (*Xin shenghuo yundong* 新生活運動) initiated by Chiang Kai-shek (Jiang Jieshi 蔣介石; 1887–1975), count among the most famous

---

72 Guo Xifeng (1967), *Zhongguo tiyushi*, p. 1.

73 For a detailed analysis of this phenomenon, see Shen Songqiao (1997), "Wo yi wo xue jian Xuanyuan", pp. 1–77.

examples. All of these take one or more aspects of the lives of the Chinese people at the time and denounce this characteristic as downright "savage" (*ye-man* 野蠻) or "akin to cattle, horses, pigs, and sheep" (*he niu ma zhu yang yiban* 和牛馬豬羊一般).[74] However, when we conduct a more thorough analysis, we discover that, when we compare the "Sick Man of East Asia" to Ah Q or the "Ugly Chinaman", the former appears to occupy a particularly prominent place in the collective identity of modern China, even though it could be argued that the latter two characterisations greatly exceed the "Sick Man" in the degree of "ugliness" that they ascribe to the Chinese people. In its later development, the "Sick Man of East Asia" came to arouse ever stronger emotions that eventually snowballed into an almost all-pervasive sense of humiliation. Why was this the case?

Undoubtedly, people like Liang Qichao, Chen Duxiu, and others engaged with the "Sick Man" as a means of offering earnest advice through harsh words (regardless of whether it was understood as a description or a criticism of the individual body, the nation, or the relative strength of the Chinese state) and of creating a mentality of self-examination that could serve as the basis of reform. Or we can take the example of Zeng Pu, who adopted the pseudonym "Sick Man of East Asia" almost in an act of self-mockery. Yet, all of these do not fully do justice to the intricate web of emotions surrounding the "Sick Man" in modern China. For, faced with this label of Western origin—and especially the two-pronged way it was later used to criticise the "deformed" bodies of each and every Chinese person, as well as the country as a whole—the national discourse in modern China saw itself unable to look on the "Sick Man" calmly and dispassionately. It increasingly came to be understood as a vicious act of humiliation by a supercilious "Other" against the dignity of the Chinese nation in order to stress feelings of hostility towards this "Other" and to strengthen China's own national consciousness. These hostile emotions were rationalised by painting "our nation" as an innocent victim, whereas its opposite was stylised as a ruthless victimiser. Coming from this point of departure, determining how reasonable this negative critique of China and the Chinese people actually is, is not very high on the agenda. Instead, it was the fact that the epithet in question had originally come from the West and it was the occidental nature itself that became the linchpin of the discourse. Within the confines of this interpretation, the most important function of the term "Sick Man" lies in its ability to help in the fostering a collective sense of humiliation. During the analysis in this article, it has become clear that, even though it had been the West who had "given birth" to the "Sick Man", it essentially played only an outsider

---

74 On the ways in which Chiang Kai-shek used a rhetoric of "defamation" to legitimise the control that his state apparatus exerted over Chinese society, see Huang Jinlin (1998), "Chouguai de zhuangban", pp. 163–203.

role in the modification and transformation of the trope in the Chinese context. It is therefore rather bizarre that the West is nonetheless far from absent in the Chinese discourse on the "Sick Man". Indeed, it was particularly in discourses which emphasise that the "Sick Man" constituted a most grave insult that the West was not be permitted to be absent. But before we analyse this question in more detail, we first have to learn more about the discourses that stress the humiliating nature of the "Sick Man".

Chen Tianhua 陳天華 (1875–1905) mentions the "Sick Man" metaphor in his famous text *An Alarm to Awaken the Age* (*Jingshi zhong* 警世鐘), written in 1903:

> Shame! Shame! Shame! Look at this great country China. Has she not been called the Great Celestial Empire by the four barbarian tribes and [all] the small states ever since antiquity and up to the present? How can it be that today she has fallen from [the rank of] a first-class country to that of a fourth-class country? *When foreigners do not insult us as Sick Man of the East, they insult us as an uncivilised and inferior race.* When Chinese people arrive in a foreign country, they are treated worse than oxen or horses.[75]

The immediate context for this statement is Chen's discussion on why the Chinese have been reduced to the lackeys of foreigners and have become an inferior race in their eyes. He juxtaposes the "Sick Man of East Asia" with the "uncivilised and inferior race" to characterise the alleged low status of the Chinese. It might be said that, according to Chen, the fate of China was inextricably wedded to the fate of the Chinese people, thus giving full expression to the aforementioned pronounced sense of crisis informed by Social Darwinism and the mandate to protect both the nation and the race.[76] Even more importantly, in this piece, brimming with sentimental diction and violent attitudes, the "Sick Man of East Asia" does not serve as an admonition that is geared to engender critical self-reflection about China's national power or the ways to improve the physical fitness of its citizens. Rather, the text adopts the mood set by the agitating opening line "Shame! Shame! Shame!" and fixes the expression's meaning to be nothing but an insult against China and the Chinese people, placing it on the same level as other highly offensive words of insult such as "uncivilised/savage" and "racially inferior". This technique of stoking a reader's sense of humiliation so as to incite them to feel hate for a common enemy is nothing short of nationalist populism.

Ironically, Chen Tianhua—not at all dissimilar to the reformist texts discussed above—equally bitterly attacks the Qing government for its unwillingness to carry out reforms, thus leading China to the brink of national ruin and racial extinction. When we compare his *An Alarm to Awaken the Age* to texts like

---

75 Chen Tianhua (1962 [1903]), "Jingshi zhong", p. 527.

76 It needs to be explained that what Chen here defines as "Chinese people" are ethnically Han Chinese. He rejects Manchus, among others.

"China's Actual Situation", the views expressed in them regarding the incompetence and corruption of the Qing regime are all but unanimous. They only differ in their interpretations of the "Sick Man of East Asia": a mere insult for the former, the latter text uses the expression in its opening remarks to describe the predicament of Qing China and the extent of its illness. It should also be pointed out that Chen himself verbally assails the Chinese people on multiple occasions and the savagery of his diction goes far beyond any possible connotation that the "Sick Man of East Asia" could possibly carry. For instance, Chen expresses his sorrow over the fact that there are numerous cases in Chinese history of Chinese killing Chinese (*i.e.*, Han killing Han) in order to gain favour in the eyes of foreigners. He summarises these accounts of fratricide in the following words:

All these [foreign] countries did not have to deploy a single soldier or lose a single arrow. The Chinese people were pretty good at killing each other. Dear heaven! Dear Earth! Dear compatriots! Among all the nations of the world, there are none where such an inferior race exists! And if such an inferior race existed, how could it not become extinct? I do not know what the character and the five organs of our Chinese people are made of. Why are we so utterly savage and ruthless? Oh, it just breaks my heart.[77]

Moreover, Chen Tianhua expressly scolded the Chinese people for being contented to "serve as lackeys" (*zuo nucai* 作奴才) (similar to Liang Qichao). And, during the crisis when China faced the danger of partition, he stated: *"How pitiful that the Chinese seem to behave like corpses (siren* 死人*) and are not aware of anything at all."* [78] Sharp and uncompromising expressions such as "inferior race" (*jianzhong* 賤種) or "lackey/slave", and especially the "corpse" analogy, are severely self-critical if not self-abusive, no less so than the label "Sick Man". In other words, despite the fact that Chen Tianhua insists that the "Sick Man of East Asia" is a foreign insult—a move intended to foment a sense of national disgrace in his readership—if we take the entire article into account, Chen's skill in using "defamation" as a rhetorical tool is second to neither Liang Qichao nor to Chen Duxiu.

However, defining the "Sick Man of East Asia" as a humiliating slur by foreigners against the people of China fits into the aforementioned trend to modify the usage of the "Sick Man" metaphor into a characterisation of the physical weakness of the Chinese people. The final result was that the "Sick Man of East Asia" was gradually seen as a sneering remark of the people of the West against the physical constitution of the Chinese within the Chinese public sphere at the beginning of the twentieth century. In sources such as Xu Yibing's motto for the sports academy—"strengthen the physique of the Chinese nation and wash

---

77 Chen Tianhua (1962 [1903]), "Jingshi zhong", p. 526.
78 Ibid., p. 522.

off the disgrace of the Sick Man of East Asia"—or the previously cited *L'Impartial* editorial, it becomes evident that the interpretation of the "Sick Man of East Asia" as an act of foreign verbal aggression had gained widespread currency by that time. And similar ideas can be found in contemporary government propaganda, discourses on education, and popular debates. Take, for example, the sports educator Cheng Dengke 程登科 (1902–1991), who studied in Germany and strongly endorsed the idea of militarising physical education, who said:

At present, it has become a widespread phenomenon among the people of our country to be short of stature and emaciated. As for national characteristics such as determination and courage, we must remedy this growing tide of degeneration, realise the ancient maxim [to paraphrase the anti-Manchu activist Gu Yanwu 顧炎武 (1613–1682)] that "the rise and fall of the country is the responsibility of the ordinary man" (*guojiaxingwang, pifuyouze* 國家興亡匹夫有責), and *cast off insulting labels such as the Western "Sick Man of East Asia" and the Japanese "inferior race"*.[79]

In a similar vein, Chiang Kai-shek emphasised how foreigners used the "Sick Man of East Asia" to insult China and its people in a speech of encouragement in front of the youth cadre:

At present, it is all too common for violent invaders to dare to despise our China and to humiliate our China. The chief cause for this is that they scorn the physique of us, the Chinese people, and the fact that we cannot match them physically. The bodies of our ordinary compatriots are usually weak and frail, which is indeed the greatest shame for a nation. From this day forward, we have to strengthen ourselves actively. Lest others will slight us, we have, first of all, to stress physical education and to promote physical education. [...] In this way, it will take but 30 years of time for the physique of our nation gradually to regain its health and strength and to *wash away completely the insulting label of the "Sick Men of East Asia"*.[80]

This sort of emphasis on the "foreign and insulting" nature of the epithet is developed particularly grandiosely and eloquently in the popular 1920s novel *Modern Legends of Chivalry and Heroism* (*Jindai xiayi yingxiong zhuan* 近代俠義英雄傳). In the text, the novelist gave voice to this notion in the words of a Russian strongman who had come to Tianjin to make a living as a performer. In a deliberately provocative tone, he declares to the Chinese spectators in the audience:

When your humble servant was still in his home country, he once heard people say that *China was the country of the "Sick Men of East Asia". All the people of the country are like sick men and do not pay any attention to physical education.* At the time, your humble servant did not really believe it. *Later, I travelled to many countries in Europe and America and what I heard there was about the same.* When I came to China, I carefully scrutinised the social situation here

---

79 Cheng Dengke (1988 [1935]), "Zenyang liyong junjing quanli", p. 422.

80 Jiang Jieshi (1988 [1941]), "Dui Sanminzhuyi qingniantuan quanguo ganbu gongzuo huiyi yunci", p. 421.

and was thus able to ascertain that what your humble servant had heard before was actually not inaccurate at all.[81]

We can clearly see that the novelist greatly exaggerates here. Via a Westerner (the Russian strongman), who plays the role of witness, the author "reports" on the "fact" that the saying "China is the country of the 'Sick Men of East Asia'" had already become everyday street gossip and common knowledge within the countries of Europe and America. In the novelist's rendition, a phrase which was originally nothing more than a description of the (lack of) power of Qing China in Western discourse becomes a common stereotype of the people of Euro-America to express their disdain for China and especially to mock the physique of the Chinese people. The Western strongman is, of course, more than a mere "witness". Within the plot of the novel, he speaks on behalf of the countless "arrogant Westerners" who otherwise feature in the story only as abstractions. Inside of Chinese territory, and in front of numerous Chinese people, he brazenly and publicly shames the audience in front of the stage by using the vicious label of the "Sick Man". (Naturally, the actual desired outcome was to shame the Chinese readership of this bestselling novel.) These opening remarks prepare the stage for the hero of the novel, Huo Yuanjia 霍元甲 (who is based upon a real martial artist of the same name that lived 1868–1910) who sets out to avenge China's national humiliation by responding:

He says, China is the country of the "Sick Men of East Asia" and that all our fellow countrymen are like sick men. He is the world's strongest man, so what does he fear that a sick man from the country of sick men like me might do? May I trouble you to ask him to please come here? *I, Huo Yuanjia, am a sick man from the country of sick men and possess no reputation among the world's strongmen.* Neither have I ever studied physical education, nor have I ever received praise from all the people of the country. Tell him that he needs to have no fear, and that I simply have to pit myself against him in a trial of strength![82]

Does this brief exchange of words not read like a digest version of one of those stories of modern national heroes in which the protagonist's heroic deeds wash away the nation's humiliation?[83] Productions that loudly applaud the "cleansing of humiliation" and that are brimming with satisfaction for having overcome foreign injustice—such as when film-goers enjoy watching Bruce Lee smashing the "Sick Man of East Asia" sign on the silver screen, or when the news media excitedly headlines stories about outstanding displays by Chinese athletes in

---

81 See Xiang (as Pingjiang buxiao sheng) (1984), *Jindai xiayi yingxiong zhuan*, p. 160.
82 Ibid., p. 168.
83 In the novel, when the Russian strongman learns about Huo Yuanjia's prowess, he does not dare to meet this challenge and promptly flees to Japan and no longer has the courage to talk big or to insult the Chinese people. For an analysis of how martial arts heroes became the paragons of cleansing national humiliation during the cultural history of modern China, see my own previous article on the subject. Yang Ruisong (2000), "Shenti, guojia yu xia", pp. 87–106.

international sports competitions with phrases such as "cleansing the national humiliation of the Sick Man of East Asia"—have become a common occurrence. This just goes to prove that the original features of the "Sick Man"—a self-critical, metaphorical portrayal of China as a "sick country" used by reformers to encourage their peers—are no longer commonly known. These original features have been replaced by new ones in a historical process exacerbated by the ever growing tide of nationalism and have turned the "Sick Man of East Asia" into an emblem of national humiliation and a symbol for China's merciless and malicious mockery by its "Other". In short, it has become a symbol of ill will. The "Sick Man of East Asia" has already lived a very long life. Its original version was somewhat superficially altered in the intellectual and cultural milieu of early twentieth century China, but its present form was nurtured into existence only by modern Chinese nationalism and has now become deeply ingrained in the collective consciousness and identity of modern China. I will return to the current image of the "Sick Man of East Asia" in the concluding section.

IV. Long Live the "Sick Man"?—A Reflection on China's Obsession with the "Sick Man of East Asia" during the Last Century

This article has made a sustained attempt to establish the root of the "Sick Man of East Asia" motif. I have detailed the different connotations of the trope in different historical settings and upon this basis explored the role that it played in the imagination of the modern Chinese nation. We can say with some certainty that the First Sino-Japanese War at the end of the nineteenth century prepared the ground for the subsequent popularity of the "Sick Man of East Asia" in the Western media. Certain Western observers, having closely and personally experienced how ineffective the late-Qing reforms up to 1895 had been and how serious China's internal problems were, drew on the commonly used simile of the Ottoman Empire (Turkey) as a "sick man" to convey their impressions regarding the current predicament of Qing China. To be sure, characterising a country in this manner can hardly count as a compliment, but neither was it an act of spiteful defamation or some random, racially motivated insult. Accordingly, it was the immediate reaction of the Chinese media and especially those publications dedicated to reform and renovation, to understand the epithet in the spirit of a piece of advice that might grate on the ear but was earnestly meant. Furthermore, it is equally evident that this "report on the physical state of Qing China", albeit Western in origin, was actually congruent with the general views of China's reformers concerning the national crisis at that time. And progressive Chinese thinkers also cited similar analogies to emphasise the necessity, urgency, and legitimacy of change in contemporary China. However, with the dawn of the twentieth century, the "remaking of the people" became an essential part of many new currents in political and social reform. In particular, the idea that a strong country had to start with a strong race made critical evaluations of the citizens' physical characteristics into a staple intellectual exercise. In this new intellectual *milieu*, the meaning of the "Sick Man" was significantly altered and modified into a descriptive term aimed at an alleged literal bodily weakness of the Chinese people. It even became a style used by at least one Chinese writer—Zeng Pu—to refer metaphorically to himself (as we have seen in Section III.2). On the other hand, however, with China's surging national consciousness, the "foreign quality" of the notion of the "Sick Man" began to be highlighted as well. Under the impact of these new historical factors, the original historical background of the birth of the "Sick Man of East Asia" along with its original, unadorned meaning was gradually lost to the public. Nourished and fostered by modern Chinese nationalism, the "Sick Man of East Asia" became what it has been to the Chinese collective memory for the last 100 years, that is, a derogatory term which Westerners are supposedly only too quick to wield in order to mock China and the Chinese people. Briefly put, this "Sick Man" that grew into maturity (and was modified) during the course of Chinese intellectual and cultural history of the last century, is nothing less than an "execration by the other" created in the imagination of the Chinese people. Conversely, it became an "original sin" of sorts to China's collective identity: it requires the glory gained by one's physical ability to prove continuously to oneself and others that it has been purged and washed away.

But how might the lasting appeal of the "Sick Man of East Asia" be explained? What has led modern Chinese nationalists constantly to call upon it to urge the people to action? These are complex questions and not easily answered, but the present article will propose a few preliminary thoughts regarding two aspects. First, after the foreign quality of the "Sick Man" had become the main focus of attention in the wake of the gradual rise of modern Chinese nationalism, it was now interpreted as yet another manifestation of Western imperialism's oppression of China. It was taken as a historical fact that the white race, imbued as they were with feelings of superiority, resorted to forms of discursive violence to humiliate the people of China. When the Chinese people came to see the "Sick Man of East Asia" in this light and were instilled with new convictions concerning the role of the West, the four characters in question came to signify a device to debase the physique of the Chinese and to humiliate the dignity of the Chinese so as to continue the imperialist oppression of China with other means. With this mindset and its new presuppositions, the expression the "Sick Man of East Asia" gained an infamy similar to the official signpost reading "Chinese and Dogs not Admitted" which was reportedly located in Shanghai's foreign-administered Huangpu Park. Within modern Chinese nationalist discourse, the authenticity and true meaning of these phrases are not to be called into question and are not to be analysed. They have taken on a fixed function not unlike the musical *leitmotifs* in a Wagner opera that cue the appearance of the villain on stage. To wit, they are supposed to arouse negative emotions toward the play's "villain" in the audience: one must never fail to remember who the evil operators behind the "Sick Man of East Asia" and the "Chinese and Dogs not Admitted" sign were or are— Western imperialists.[84]

Approached from another perspective which moves beyond rigidly defining the "Sick Man of East Asia" as an emblem of Western imperialist discursive violence, the reason why the "Sick Man of East Asia" stands out so prominently in the collective national memory of modern China is that—along with additional "roles" and "plots"—it readily fits into the "victimisation narrative" of Chinese nationalism; a narrative around which much of modern Chinese history is constructed.[85] How well the trope fits conventional Chinese historiography becomes particularly evident in explanations of the role of opium in modern Chinese history. Although most discourses that have a bearing on the "Sick Man of East Asia" pass censure on its use as a verbal insult by Westerners against Chinese people, there are nonetheless some that conform to the view that the Chinese are inherently physically frail and weak. Consequently, these analyses, when they tackle the question of the reasons behind China's weakness, often suggest a causal relationship between the fact that opium indisputably harmed the Chinese physically and the so-called "Sick Man of East Asia" phenomenon. This leads to explanations of the following type:

The physical health of China's people went into a precipitous decline because the Western powers, in their efforts to open the gate to China, callously smuggled opium into the country's interior. Concurrently, they used military force to coerce the Qing government to sign unequal treaties in which it consented to forfeit certain sovereign rights. The opium trade was thereby legitimised and led to an epidemic that extended from the emperor's relatives above, via the high officials, people of eminence, Eight Banners and ordinary Chinese soldiers, down to the mass of common people. They all became drug addicts and were unable to extricate themselves from their affliction. The prospects of

---

84 On the authenticity of the "Dogs and Chinese Not Admitted" sign and discussions on its bearing on modern Chinese nationalism, see Ishikawa (2002), "'Huaren yu gou bude runei' gaoshipai wenti kao", pp. 137–156; Bickers and Wasserstrom (1995), "Shanghai's 'Dogs and Chinese not Admitted' Sign", pp. 444–466.

85 On the impact of this "victimisation narrative" on the writing of modern Chinese history, see Gries (2004), *China's New Nationalism*, pp. 43–53; Cohen (2002), "Remembering and Forgetting", pp. 1–39.

the nation thus fell into an abyss deeper than the tallest mountain. The drug wreaked havoc among the people and destroyed their physical health to the point that their vital organs were consumed, even though no blood was spilt. Ever since then, we have been tagged with the humiliating label of the "Sick Men of East Asia".[86]

Although late Qing thinkers such as Liang Qichao and Yan Fu had equally been convinced that opium had contributed to both bodily harm and deteriorating health, they did not locate the main cause for the opium epidemic in Western interference. (See note 51 above for Liang Qichao's views on opium and physical health.) However, they nevertheless unequivocally identified Western imperialism as the chief culprit behind the opium trade, as was emphasised in the nationalist discourse outlined above. In other words, opium and physical frailty, in the context of historical interpretations of this kind, serve as important pieces of evidence in arguments to expose Western aggression.[87]

Within the aforementioned nationalist view of history, it was impossible to discuss the idea of the "Sick Man of the East" without the key role of the West: if it was not, in fact, the case that the people of modern China were afflicted with physical frailty, then the "Sick Man of East Asia" would demonstrably be a label forced on the Chinese by arrogant Westerners and the West would undoubtedly intentionally injure China (via discursive violence). In the opposite case, that is, if the people of modern China actually were hopelessly weak, this would also have been chiefly caused by the Westerners (via opium poisoning). What is even more critical, in the second scenario, the Westerners would actually use the rhetoric of the "Sick Man of East Asia" as a secondary means to injure further the already damaged dignity of the Chinese people who would thereby fall prey to a two-fold victimisation. And the West would accordingly appear as a victimiser who harms in two complementary ways. In the modern Chinese discourse on the "Sick Man of East Asia", the West is therefore unable to shake off the role of the injuring party. This is not only because of the firmly established, unbreakable conceptual relationship between the West and the

---

86 Gao Cui (2002), *"Dongya bingfu"*, p. 9. For additional more detailed discussions and illustrations, see ibid., pp. 9–17. Similar arguments are made by numerous other people. For example: Fu Juan (1996), "Shijiu shiji Zhong Ying yapian maoyi hefahua tanxi", pp. 126–132; Zheng Zhilin (1999), "Shi 'Dongya bingfu'", pp. 50–54.

87 In recent years, scholars in both China and abroad have begun to discuss a new actual relationship between opium consumption and the so-called physical constitution of the nation. In opposition to the previous view that regarded opium consumers simply as drug addicts, this new research stresses the roles of opium as medicine, commodity, and consumer good in order to re-evaluate its true societal role and to gage the full extent of its socio-cultural impact. It has thus moved away from a research perspective that judged the historical role of opium in China exclusively and too narrowly from the standpoint and prejudices of the opium oppositionists. For relevant discussions refer to Newman (1995), "Opium Smoking in Late Imperial China", pp. 165–794; Laamann (2002), "Pain and Pleasure", pp. 1–20; Lin (1999), "Caijing anwen yu Guomin jiankang zhi jian", pp. 501–551.

"Sick Man of the East", but also because the "Sick Man of East Asia" has already become an indispensable part of modern China's victimisation narrative that begins with the First Opium War.

If we contrast the analysis above with the previous analysis of the various aspects of the idea of the "Sick Man" during the late Qing period undertaken in the present article, we will be surprised to discover that the "Sick Man", when it was first introduced to Qing China in the late nineteenth century, did not cause an uproar, nor, indeed, did it cause much of an emotional response at all. Rather, it was readily accepted and cited to advance the reformist cause during those years. Even after its meaning had evolved into a rather unflattering remark aimed at the physical constitution of the Chinese, we can still see how reformers used it to bring to light China's various shortcomings and to exhort the Chinese people to engage in critical self-examination. However, beginning in the recent past, in the wake of the development of modern Chinese nationalism, the "Sick Man" was no longer solely a companion to proponents of reform and could no longer be used by writers and scholars to deliver a dose of self-mockery.[88] This is because, in the context of nationalist discourse, the "Sick Man" represents a hundred years of national oppression and humiliation and has become a weapon wielded by nationalists to mobilise the masses and to summon the spectre of national humiliation. During the historical developments of those hundred years, a trope that once played a supporting role in the reformist rhetoric at the turn of the century, had actually been twisted into a major figure in the discourse to oppose Western hegemony and had become a symbol meant to evoke feelings of hostility towards the West in the hearts of millions upon millions of Chinese people. The "Sick Man" has thus taken on features completely different from its Western "home" since it was introduced into China's intellectual and cultural environment a hundred years ago. In all likelihood, the Western political commentators who originally conceived it—without giving it much thought, no doubt—could not have foreseen what kind of career this notion would eventually make.

However, it is precisely this "dazzling" "Sick Man of East Asia" of the here and now that has nowadays robbed many Chinese (unless they happen to be very well-versed in its history) of their ability to discern that the expression had actually been fairly bland and featureless a century ago. In other words, there

---

88 When I was writing this article in June of 2016, an online news report said that there was a gamer from mainland China who used the ID "Sick Man of East Asia" (*Dongya bingfu* 東亞病夫). This gamer actually triggered a mighty uproar with his chosen ID and was at once denounced both orally and in writing. There was even someone who claimed that said gamer must have been Japanese and that he was intentionally provoking the Chinese online community. What might the author of *Sea of Degeneration*, Zeng Pu, the self-styled "Sick Man of East Asia" have to say about this modern-day "Sick Man of East Asia"? For the relevant news item refer to "Shu wan wanjia shengtao 'Dongya bingfu'" (2004).

are precious few modern Chinese scholars (or sinologists in general) who, when they parse historical source materials and come across the "Sick Man of East Asia", will not immediately jump to the conclusion that the original author must have intended it as an insult against the Chinese, especially if it was mentioned by a foreigner. Let me illustrate this bias by way of example: the famous editor-in-chief of the *WGGB*, the American missionary Young John Allen (1836–1907), came from the United States to China at the age of 23 and died in Shanghai in 1907, having lived in the country for 47 years. During his time in China, he not only did missionary work and introduced Western knowledge, but also frequently wrote texts in support of the domestic reform movement. In a recently published study on the *WWGB* and the Western missionaries involved in its publication, the author Wang Lin 王林 passes the following judgement in his discussion of Allen:

[Young John Allen] said of the Chinese that they were the sick men of East Asia. [He wrote:] "Those who presently discuss current events, commonly call China a great sick man in East Asia (*Yadong yi da bingfu* 亞東一大病夫), just as they have formerly called Turkey a great sick man of eastern Europe. The way I see it, this appraisal is truly irrefutable." The *WGGB*'s aim, in crassly slandering the Chinese people in this way, was to show that the Chinese, fettered and confined by Confucianism as they were, and having lost their way and fallen into moral decadence, had to convert to Christianity as the only way to bring them back from the brink of death and to get them out of harm's way and to safety.[89]

From Allen's statement that "those who presently discuss current events, commonly call China a great sick man in East Asia", quoted by Wang Lin, it is evident that Allen was aware that China being the "Sick Man of East Asia" was a common stereotype among the people of his day. And as he himself had observed first-hand how the Chinese reforms had failed again and again, he was bound to agree with this evaluation. Allen's words here are, in fact, no more than an expression of his disappointment about how little the Chinese reform movement had achieved.[90] Wang Lin, however, from the start, takes them very

---

89 Wang Lin (2004), *Xixue yu bianfa*, p. 259.

90 For the entire article, see Lin Lezhi (Allen) (1902), "Lun Zhonghua shiju", pp. 20737–20744. Here, Allen explicitly states that he had already been living in China for over 40 years and sincerely hoped that the country would soon regain its vigour. In a critical manner but nonetheless having China's best interests in mind, he thus put forward his ideas concerning reform. His text offers harsh criticism, yet, just as often, his words betray his good intentions. Nowadays, one still finds Chinese scholars who, because they have misinterpreted the meaning of the "Sick Man of East Asia", have stood the intentions behind the expression almost completely on its head (thus making a travesty out of its "lifelong efforts"). By comparison, the 1906 *Dagongbao* commentary cited above actually contains one paragraph that is enough to set people thinking. Nevertheless, based on the analysis of the present study, one would still have to conclude that the article in question also mistakenly holds that the Western "Sick Man" is a term of mockery directed against the physical characteristics of the Chinese people:

much at face value and categorically asserts that "Young John Allen said of the Chinese that they were the sick men of East Asia". He continues by claiming that Allen had thereby "crassly slandered the Chinese people". This kind of misreading that sticks slavishly to the surface meaning makes evident how influential nationalist historiography has actually been. Modern researchers have essentially been "pre-programmed" to read a derived meaning into the "Sick Man of East Asia", even if the expression as encountered in the relevant source materials does not, in fact, carry any such historical baggage. In so doing, they distort the original intention of the author. Considering that even someone who spent two-thirds of his life in China and devoted all of his time and money to further the Chinese reformist enterprise was overshadowed as he was by the "Sick Man of East Asia", not spared from such harsh criticism, how can the thousands and tens of thousands of faceless Westerners, who exist only as abstractions and are frequently imagined to harbour ill-intentions towards China, possibly hope to do so?

Finally, having taken stock of the history of the "Sick Man of East Asia" and its role in the transformation of modern China, and having understood its changing meanings, and the tasks to which it was put at different times, how are we now to respond to Paul Cohen's challenge in his *Discovering History in China* cited in the introduction? Based upon the results of the present study in which I explored the topic of the "Sick Man of East Asia", and seeing how the West has already been branded as the chief instigator behind 100 years of humiliation and how this interpretation of history has long since become deeply ingrained in the

---

"Alas! The countries of east and west [alike] curse our country as a dotard and a sick man. When I first heard these expressions, I was first angry, then anguished, but finally touched (*gan* 感). Why was I angry? I was angry about the impertinence in these words. Why was I anguished? Things first have to rot, only then do the vermin emerge. If we were not really dotards, who could turn us into dotards? If we were not really sick men, who could turn us into sick men? Since the foreigners already consider us to be dotards and think us sick men, it must be that we, prior to this, have considered ourselves to be dotards and sick men. Undoubtedly so! Why was I moved? The foreigners are completely frank and already consider us to be dotards and think us sick men. When I heard this, [I thought] it would be right to [conceive ways] to make us repent, and that it would be right to [conceive ways] to encourage us. [Furthermore,] it would be right to [conceive ways] to get rid of the dotard and turn (China) into a youthful guy, and to get rid of the sick man and turn (China) into an able-bodied man. Let us assume that the foreigners, on the inside [kept] thinking of us as dotards and sick men, but on the outside, contrariwise, flattered us with 'you youthful guys, you able-bodied men', we would hear it and not understand at all [what deplorable state we were in], [but instead] happily and proudly say: 'us youthful guys, us able-bodied men'. Alas! [If this were the case, then,] in the end, we would really be dotards, we would really be sick, and there would be no hope to redeem this situation. [Therefore,] when I first heard these expressions, how could I not have been angry, and anguished, and touched?" *Dagongbao* (6 May 1906), pp. 2–3. These critical remarks on the "Sick Man" from a century ago, which arguably reveal a high degree of self-examination, can help us shed light on the bustling fervour created by the mandate to "cleanse national humiliation" we can presently observe online and elsewhere.

collective psyche through political propaganda and various forms of cultural production, how much room is there actually left for efforts to—as Cohen had hoped—dispassionately and rationally re-evaluate the proper place of the West in Chinese history? Or, to phrase it more clearly, can these efforts hope to exert any kind of influence on such deeply entrenched "mythological" historiography that is guided by brazenly nationalist sentimentalities? Perhaps Cohen's research into the conventional interpretation of the Boxer Rebellion in modern China provides a few pointers to help us ponder this question and address the doubts expressed above.

There are essentially two extreme positions among modern evaluations of the Boxer Rebellion in Chinese scholarship. The first views the Boxers as representatives of old China: backward, superstitious, ignorant, and conceited. According to this interpretation, the savagery displayed by the Boxers and their agitation against everything foreign, formed a great obstacle to China's pursuit of modernisation. By contrast, the other extremist interpretation holds that the Boxers were Chinese heroes who patriotically resisted foreign invaders. Their movement thus represents a determined act of collective resistance by an oppressed people and constitutes a glorious feat in the history of the fight against imperialism. Cohen is of the opinion that, since the nineteenth century, China has maintained two diametrically opposed images of the West which have led to ambivalent responses. The two extreme interpretations delineated above correspond closely to this idea: the West opposed by the Boxers was, on the one hand, venerated as a "blessing angel". It was regarded as the epitome of progress, modernity, and civilisation and an ideal to be diligently emulated and closely studied. On the other hand, the West was also the "devil incarnate", an imperialist who had relentlessly encroached on China's sovereignty and territory, an arch-criminal who had poisoned the bodies and minds of the Chinese people, and a destructive force that impeded China in becoming a dignified and sovereign nation-state.[91] Naturally, these two attitudes towards the West did, in reality, not exist in clear separation, but rather should be seen as two major forces in the construction of the Chinese national identity that engendered complicated feelings in every Chinese person's heart regarding their self-image and the ways they understand the "Other".

The different faces of the "Sick Man of East Asia" in Chinese intellectual and cultural history, in fact, also reflect these two contradicting, complex emotions of the Chinese people regarding this "Other", which is the West, as I have argued above. From the point of view of those reformers who saw in the West a model to be studied, the "Sick Man", in its original meaning or the broader meaning that it acquired during its later development, generally represented the

---

91 Cohen (1997), *History in Three Keys*, pp. 287–288.

outcome of a "diagnosis", informed by Western norms of "progress" and "civilisation", of the actual conditions of China and the Chinese. Therefore, as long as China was courageous enough to face this reality and undertake the appropriate reform measures, it would, before long, get rid of its "pathologic condition" and gain admission to the circle of strong countries. And its people would, accordingly, gain an "angelic" physical appearance, just like the Westerners. Correspondingly, in the eyes of radical nationalists who saw the West as an "incarnation of the devil", the "Sick Man of East Asia" was a vicious insult or (at least) a false accusation and a concrete manifestation of Western imperialist discursive violence. For them, the "Sick Man of East Asia" bears testimony to the pernicious nature of Western imperialism and, in concert with the import of opium, constitutes the paragon of the West's two-fold—material and spiritual—oppression of China.[92] If one defines the historical significance of the trope in this way, it is hardly surprising that this "devil's execration" has become an indispensable part of history education in China, as the statement by Deng Xiaoping reveals. Considering the career of the "Sick Man of East Asia" during the course of modern Chinese history, the latter interpretation seems to have become the dominant view. For this particular reason, taking into consideration that the "victimisation narrative" is still a fundamental premise in mainstream modern Chinese history, and adding to this the epic furore surrounding the 2008 Olympics in Beijing, it is probably safe to say that the "Sick Man of East Asia", laden as it is with a ton of historical baggage, and despite its respectable old age of more than a hundred years, is not going to die a natural death and withdraw from the stage of history any time soon.[93] Indeed, a rational analysis would suggest that the birth, growth, and transformation of the "Sick Man of East Asia" are all brimming with instances of faulty reasoning and unnecessary emotional manipulation. However, precisely because of this, following its century-long historical trajectory allows us to gain insights into the ways in which people in modern China comprehend both themselves and the rest of the world. Its history is also a page in the history of the vicissitudes of the ambiva-

---

92 What is interesting is the fact that, as mentioned above, these two attitudes towards the West, in reality, interact and influence each other. Even though firmly guided by nationalist ideas, this camp nonetheless for the most part advocates the use of "angelic skill" to counteract the "devil's execrations" in the context of international athletic competitions. This amply demonstrates that the physical ideal advertised by modern Western sports and the nationalist emotions stirred by winning an Olympic gold medal, as a matter of fact, constitute important factors in the present-day discourse to cleanse the national disgrace of the "Sick Man of East Asia".

93 If present-day China, in its continuing attempts to understand different cultures, nevertheless cannot overcome, as Edward Said criticises, reductionist tendencies like binary oppositions and essentialisms, then instances of misunderstanding the "Other" will occur again and again in the future. And this analysis of the tortuous history of the "Sick Man of East Asia" has revealed exactly what kind of absurdities can emerge from such misreadings.

lent emotions—from admiration to loathing—that the Chinese have felt (and continue to feel) towards the West and its people.

(Translated by Sebastian Riebold)

Bibliography

"All of Europe Is the Sick Man Now" (2002). http//www.freedomand prosperity.org/Articles/wsj10-14-02/wsj10-14-02.shtml (18 July 2004).

Anderson, Benedict (1991), *Imagined Communities: Reflections on the Origin and Spread of Nationalism*, London: Verso Books.

Bertram, Christoph (1997). "Germany: The Sick Man of Europe?", available at: http://www.project-syndicate.org/commentaries/commentary_text.php4 ? id=83&lang=1&m=contributor (18 July 2004).

Bickers, Robert A., and Jeffrey N. Wasserstrom (1995). "Shanghai's 'Dogs and Chinese not Admitted' Sign: Legend, History and Contemporary Symbol", *The China Quarterly*, 142, pp. 444–466.

Brownell, Susan (1995). *Training the Body for China: Sports in the Moral Order of the People's Republic*, Chicago IL: University of Chicago Press.

Chen Duxiu 陳獨秀 (1996 [1917]). "Jindai xiyang jiaoyu" 近代西洋教育 (Modern Western Education) in: Chen Duxiu, *Duxiu wencun* 獨秀文存 (Preserve of the Writings of Chen Duxiu), Hefei: Renmin chubanshe, pp. 109–110.

— (1996 [1915]), "Xin qingnian" 新青年 (New Youth), in: Chen Duxiu, *Duxiu wencun* 獨秀文存 (Preserve of the Writings of Chen Duxiu), Hefei: Renmin chubanshe, pp. 57–62.

Chen Tianhua 陳天華 (1962 [1903]), "Jingshi zhong" 警世鐘 (An Alarm to Awaken the Age), in: Zhongguo Kexueyuan zhexue yanjiusuo Zhongguo zhexueshi zu 中國科學院哲學研究所中國哲學史組 (ed.), *Zhongguo zhexueshi ziliao xuanji—jindai zhi bu xia* 中國哲學史資料選集——近代之部下 (Selection of Documents from the History of Chinese Philosophy—The Modern Period, Part 2), Beijing: Zhonghua shuju, pp. 520–613.

Cheng Dengke 程登科 (1988 [1935]), "Zenyang liyong junjing quanli fuzhu minzhong tiyu shi quanmin tiyuhua" 怎樣利用軍警權力輔助民眾體育使全民體育化 (How to Use the Power of the Military and the Police to Assist the Physical Education of the Masses and to Help the entire People to Become Physically Fit), in: Chengdu tiyu xueyuan tiyu shi yanjiusuo 成都體育學院體育史研究所 (ed.), *Zhongguo jindai tiyushi ziliao* 中國近代體育史資料 (Materials in the Modern History of Chinese Physical Education), Chengdu: Sichuan jiaoyu chubanshe, p. 422.

"China and Japan" (1895), *The Times*, 23 April 1895, p. 5.

Chirol, Ignatius V. (1896), *The Far Eastern Question*, New York: Macmillan and Co.

Cohen, Paul A. (1984), *Discovering History in China: American Historical Writing on the Recent Chinese Past*, New York: Columbia University Press.

— (1997), *History in Three Keys: The Boxers as Event, Experience, and Myth*, New York: Columbia University Press.

- (2002), "Remembering and Forgetting: National Humiliation in Twentieth Century China", *Twentieth-Century China*, 27.2, pp.1–39.

"Cong Dongya bingfu dao jingji daguo" 從東亞病夫到競技大國 (From Sick Man of East Asia to Powerhouse of Competitive Sports), available at: http:// www.beijing-2008.org/51/81/article211618151.shtml (July 18 2004).

Dagongbao 大公報, 6 May 1905, p. 3.

Dagongbao 大公報, 6 May 1906, pp. 2–3.

Friedman, Thomas L. (2004), "Asia's Sick Man Jumps Out of Bed", *The International Herald Tribune*, 18 May 2004, available at: http://www.iht.com/articles/ 517763.html (18 July 2004).

Fu Juan 傅娟 (1996),"Shijiu shiji Zhong Ying yapian maoyi hefahua tanxi" 十九世紀中英鴉片貿易合法化探析 (An Inquiry into the Legitimisation of the Opium Trade between China and Britain during the Nineteenth Century), *Sichuan shifan daxue xuebao* 23.2, pp. 126–132.

Gao Cui 高翠 (ed.) (2002), *Cong "Dongya bingfu" dao tiyu qiangguo* 從 "東亞病夫" 到體育強國 (From "Sick Man of East Asia" to Stronghold of Athleticism), Chengdu: Sichuan renmin chubanshe.

Ge Zhaoguang 葛兆光 (2002), "1895 nian de Zhongguo: Sixiangshi shang de xianzheng yiyi" 1895 年的中國：思想史上的象徵意義 (China in 1895: The Symbolic Signif-icance of that Year in Intellectual History) in: Ge Zhaoguang, *Zhongguo sixiangshi*, Shanghai: Fudan daxue chubanshe, vol. 2, pp. 530–550.

Gries, Peter H. (2004), *China's New Nationalism: Pride Politics, and Diplomacy*, Berkeley CA: University of California Press.

Guo Xifen 郭希汾 (1967), *Zhongguo tiyushi* 中國體育史 (History of Physical Education in China), Taibei: Shangwu.

"Guomin weishengxue" 國民衛生學 (National Hygienics) (1903), *Hubei xueshengjie*, 5, p. 79.

Heinrich, Larissa N. (2002), "The Pathological Body: Science, Race, Literary Realism in China 1770–1930", Ph.D. dissertation, University of California, Berkeley.

Huang Jinlin 黃金麟 (1998), "Chouguai de zhuangban: Xinshenghuo yundong de zhengl üe fenxi" 醜怪的裝扮：新生活運動的政略分析 (The Power of the Grotesque and the New Life Movement, 1934–1937), *Taiwan shehui yanjiu jikan*, 30, pp. 163–203.

- (2000), *Lishi, shenti, guojia* 歷史、身體、國家 (History, Body, Nation), Taibei: Lianjing.

Huang Kewu 黃克武 (1994), *Yi ge bei fangqi de xuanze: Liang Qichao tiaoshi sixiang zhi yanjiu* 一個被放棄的選擇：梁啟超調適思想之研究 (An Abandoned Choice: A Study of Liang Qichao's Adjustment Theory), Taibei: Zhongyang Yanjiuyuan jindaishi yan-jiusuo.

Hunan sheng zhexue shehui kexue yanjiusuo 湖南省哲學社會科學研究所 (ed.) (1982), *Tang Caichang ji* 唐才常集 (Collected Writings of Tang Caichang), Beijing: Zhonghua shuju.

Hutton, Will (2003), "The New Sick Man of Europe", available at: https://www.theguardian.com/world/2003/dec/28/italy.eu (2 July 2018).

"Is Britain Europe's New Sick Man?", available at: http://www. businessweek.com/ magazine/content/02_50/b3812068.htm (18 July 2004).

Ishikawa Yoshihiro 石川禎浩 (2002), "'Huaren yu gou bude runei' gaoshipai wenti kao" 「華人與狗不得入內」告示牌問題考 (Investigating the Issue of the 'Dogs and

Chinese not Admitted' Sign) in: Huang Kewu (ed.), *Sixiang, zhengquan yu shehui liliang*, Taibei: Zhongyanyuan shisuo, pp. 137–156.

Jiang Jieshi 蔣介石 (Chiang Kai-shek) (1988 [1941]), "Dui Sanminzhuyi qingniantuan quanguo ganbu gongzuo huiyi yunci" 對三民主義青年團全國幹部工作會議訓詞 (Instructions for the Working Conference of the Three People's Principles National Youth Cadre), in: Chengdu tiyu xueyuan tiyu shi yanjiusuo 成都體育學院體育史研究所 (ed.), *Zhongguo jindai tiyushi ziliao* 中國近代體育史資料 (Materials in the Modern History of Chinese Physical Education), Chengdu: Sichuan jiaoyu chubanshe, p. 421.

Kang Youwei 康有為 (1981 [1898]), "*Jincheng Tujue xiaoruo ji xu*" 進呈突厥削弱記序 (Preface to *Record of the Degeneration of Turkey for Presentation to the Imperial Throne*) in: Tang Zhijun 湯志鈞 (ed.), *Kang Youwei zhenglun ji* 康有為爭論集 (Collection of the Political Writings of Kang Youwei), Beijing: Zhonghua shuju, vol. 1, p. 300.

Laamann, Lars P. (2002), "Pain and Pleasure: Opium as Medicine in Late Imperial China", *Twentieth-Century China*, 28.1, pp.1–20.

Li Jiabai 李佳白 (Gilbert Reid) (1896), "Tanben qiong yuan lun" 探本窮源論 (Tracing the Origins of Poverty), *Wanguo gongbao*, 89, pp. 16075–16084.

Li Peide 李培德 (1977), *Zeng Mengpu de wenxue lücheng* 曾孟樸的文學旅程 (Zeng Mengpu's Literary Journey), Taibei: Zhuanji wenxue chubanshe.

Li Yuanzhe 李遠哲 (1986), "Wo de chengzhang licheng" 我的成長歷程 (How I Grew up), available at: http://www.sinica.edu.tw/as/person/ytlee/37.html (18 July 2004).

Liang Qichao 梁啟超 (1941 [1896]), "Lun baoguan youyi yu guoshi" 論報館有益於國事 (On the Benefits of the Press in National Affairs) in: Liang Qichao, *Yinbingshi wenji* 飲冰室文集 (Collected Works from the Ice Drinker's Studio), Shanghai: Zhonghua shuju, vol. 1, p. 100–102.

— (1941 [1896–1897], "Lun bianfa buzhi benyuan zhi hai" 論變法不知本原之害 (The Dangers of not Understanding the Principles of Reform) in: Liang Qichao, *Yinbingshi wenji* 飲冰室文集 (Collected Works from the Ice Drinker's Studio), Shanghai: Zhonghua shuju, vol. 1, p. 8–13.

— (1941 [1898]), "*E-Tu zhanji* xu" 俄土戰紀敘 (Preface to [Tang Huan's translation of] *Records of the war between Russia and Turkey*), in: Liang Qichao, *Yinbingshi wenji* 飲冰室文集 (Collected Works from the Ice Drinker's Studio), Shanghai: Zhonghua shuju, vol. 3, p. 33.

— (1941 [1901]), "Zhongguo jiruo suyuan lun" 中國積弱溯源論 (A Discussion of the Causes Underlying China's Long-standing Weakness), in: Liang Qichao, *Yinbingshi wenji* 飲冰室文集 (Collected Works from the Ice Drinker's Studio), Shanghai: Zhonghua shuju, vol. 5, pp. 12–42.

— (1999 [1897]), "Ji Shangxian tang" 記尚賢堂 (Commemorating the Academy of the Exaltation of the Worthy), in: Liang Qichao (author), Zhang Pinxing 張品興, Yang Gang 楊鋼, Wang Xiangyi 王相宜 (eds.), *Liang Qichao quanji* 梁啟超全集 (Complete Works of Liang Qichao), Beijing: Beijing chubanshe, vol. 1, p. 112.

— (1999 [1902–1906]), "Xinmin shuo" 新民說 (Treatise on the Renewal of the People), in: Liang Qichao (author), Zhang Pinxing 張品興, Yang Gang 楊鋼, Wang Xiangyi 王相宜 (eds.), *Liang Qichao quanji* 梁啟超全集 (Complete Works of Liang Qichao), Beijing: Beijing chubanshe, vol. 3, 655–735.

— (1999 [1904]), "Xin Dalu youji" 新大陸游記 (Journey to the New World), in: Liang Qichao (author), Zhang Pinxing 張品興, Yang Gang 楊鋼, Wang Xiangyi 王相宜

(eds.), *Liang Qichao quanji* 梁啟超全集 (Complete Works of Liang Qichao), Beijing: Beijing chubanshe, vol. 4, pp. 1125–1230.

Lin Lezhi 林樂知 (Young John Allen) (1902), "Lun Zhonghua shiju" 論中華時局 (On China's Current Political Situation), *Wangguo gongbao*, 157, pp. 20737–20744.

Lin Manhong 林滿紅 (1999), "Caijing anwen yu guomin jiankang zhi jian: Wan Qing de tuchan yapian lunyi (1833–1905)" 財經安穩與國民健康之間：晚清的土產鴉片論議（1833–1905）(Between Economic Security and National Health: A Discussion of Late Qing Local Opium Production (1833–1905)), in: Zhongyang Yanjiuyuan jindaishi yanjiusuo shehui jingji shi zu 中央研究院近代史研究所社會經濟史組 (ed.), *Caizheng yu jindai lishi lunwenji* 財政與近代歷史論文集 (Essays on Finance and Modern History), Taibei: Zhongyang Yanjiuyuan jindaishi yanjiusuo, pp. 501–551.

Louie, Kam (2003), "Chinese, Japanese and Global Masculine Identities", in: Kam Louie, Morris Low (eds.), *Asia Masculinities: The Meaning and Practice of Manhood in China and Japan*, London: Routledge Curzon, pp. 1–15.

"Lun yihe hou zhi Zhongguo" 論議和後之中國 (China after the peace negotiations) (1901), *Qingyibao*, 70, pp. 4481–4486.

Menon, Rajan (2003), "The Sick Man of Asia: Russia's Endangered Far East", *The National Interest* 73, pp. 93–105.

Mulvenney, Nick (2008), "China's 100-Year Dream, a Cure for the Sick Man of Asia", available at: https://www.reuters.com/article/us-olympics-china/chinas-100-year-dream-a-cure-for-the-sick-man-of-asia-idUSPEK33620320080807 (15 June 2018).

Newman, Richard K. (1995), "Opium Smoking in Late Imperial China: A Reconsideration", *Modern Asia Studies*, 29.4, pp.765–794.

Ooms, Herman (1989), *Tokugawa Ideology*, Princeton NJ: Princeton University Press.

Pye, Lucian W. (1992), *The Spirit of Chinese Politics*, Cambridge MA: Harvard University Press.

Renan, Ernest (1990), "What is a Nation?" in: Homi K. Bhabha (ed.), *Nation and Narration*, London: Routledge, pp. 8–22.

Said, Edward (1994), *Orientalism*, London: Vintage Books.

Shen Qian 沈潛 (2004), "Banshi fengliu *Niehai hua*—jindai wenxuejia Zeng Pu zhuanlüe -"半世風流孽海花——近代文學家曾樸傳略 (Made Popular by Sea of Degeneration—A Short Biography of the Modern Writer Zeng Pu), *Zhuanji wenxue* 84.1, pp. 101–111.

Shen Songqiao 沈松僑 (Sung-chiao Shen) (1997), "Wo yi wo xue jian Xuanyuan—Huangdi shenhua yu wan Qing de guozu jiangou" 我以我血薦軒轅——黃帝神話與晚清的國族建構 (I Present my Blood to Xuanyuan—The Myth of the Yellow Emperor and the Construction of Chinese Nationhood in the Late Qing), *Taiwan shehui yanjiu jikan*, 28, pp. 1–77.

Shiwubao 時務報 10 (5 November 1896), pp. 650–652.

"Shu wan wanjia shengtao 'Dongya bingfu' ru Hua zhuolang" 數萬玩家聲討 "東亞病夫" 辱華濁浪 (Tens of Thousands of Gamers Denounce the 'Sick Man of East Asia' for Insulting China) (2004), available at: http://bbs.comefromchina.com/threads/252248 (18 June 2018).

"Sick Man" in: *Oxford English Dictionary* (1989), 2nd ed., vol 15, p. 410.

Smith, Arthur H. (1890), *Chinese Characteristics*, Shanghai: North China Herald.

Tang Zhijun 湯志鈞 (2003), *Wuxu bianfa shi* 戊戌變法史 (History of the 1898 Reform Movement), Shanghai: Shanghai shehui kexueyuan chubanshe.

"Tianxia si bingren" 天下四病人 (The World's Four Sick Men) (1896), *Shiwubao* 14, pp. 918–919.

Wang Lin 王林 (2004), *Xixue yu bianfa*—Wanguo gongbao *yanjiu* 西學與變法——《萬國公報》研究 (Western Learning and Political Reform—A Study of the *Wanguo gongbao*), Jinan: Qilu shushe.

Wang Shuhuai 王樹槐 (1980), *Wairen yu Wuxu bianfa* 外人與戊戌變法 (Foreigners and the Reforms of 1898), Tabei: Zhongyanyuan jinshisuo jikan.

Wanguo gongbao 萬國公報 71 (December 1894), p. 14885.

Wei Ruhui 魏如晦 (1984), "Niehai hua zahua" 孽海花雜話 (Miscellaneous Ideas on Flower in a Sea of Degradation) in: Zeng Pu 曾朴, *Niehai hua—Lunanzi* 孽海花·魯男子 (Flower in a Sea of Regret—The Man from Lu) Taibei: Guiguan, pp. 457–462.

Xiang Kairan 向愷然 (as Pingjiang buxiao sheng 平江不肖生) (1984), *Jindai xiayi yingxiong zhuan* 近代俠義英雄傳 (Modern Legends of Chivalry and Heroism), Taibei: Lianjing chubanshe.

"Xing yixue tong" 興醫學通 (Promoting Medical Knowledge) (1903), *Hubei xueshengjie*, 2, pp. 61, 72.

Xiong Xiaozheng 熊曉正, Cao Shouhe 曹守訴, Lin Dengyuan 林登轅 (1997). "20 shiji Zhongguoren tiyu renzhi de guiji" 20世紀中國人體育認知的軌迹 (The Trajectory of the Chinese People's Understanding of Physical Education in the Twentieth Century), *Tiyu wenshi*, 1, pp. 21–24.

"Xituo Dongya bingfu, jishen tiyu qiangguo" 洗脫東亞病夫，躋身體育強國 (Purge the Sick Man of East Asia, ascend to the rank of stronghold of athleticism) (2009). Available at: http://paper.wenweipo.com/2009/09/29/CH0909290069.htm (29 November 2009).

Xu Yixiong 許義雄 (1996), "Jun guomin jiaoyu zhi tiyu sixiang (1880–1918)" 軍國民教育之體育思想 (1880–1918) (Thoughts on Physical Education in National Military Education (1880–1918)), in: Xu Yixiong et al. (eds.), *Zhongguo jindai tiyu sixiang* 中國近代體育思想 (Modern Chinese Thought on Physical Education), Taibei: Qiying wenhua gongsi, pp. 37–121.

Xu Yixiong 許義雄 et al. (eds.) (1996), *Zhongguo jindai tiyu sixiang* 中國近代體育思想 (Modern Chinese Thought on the Body), Taibei: Qiying wenhua gongsi.

Xu Yuanmin 徐元民 (1999), *Zhongguo jindai zhishi fenzi dui tiyu sixiang zhi chuanbo* 中國近代知識份子對體育思想之傳播 (Modern Chinese Intellectuals and the Spread of Ideas about Physical Education), Taibei: Shida shuyuan.

Yan Fu 嚴復 (1962 [1895]), "Yuan qiang" 原強 (On Strength), in: Zhongguo Kexueyuan zhexue yanjiusuo Zhongguo zhexueshi zu 中國科學院哲學研究所中國哲學史組 (ed.), *Zhongguo zhexueshi ziliao xuanji—jindai zhi bu xia* 中國哲學史資料選集——近代之部下 (Selection of Documents from the History of Chinese Philosophy—The Modern Period, Part 2), Beijing: Zhonghua shuju, p. 369.

Yang Ruisong 楊瑞松 (Jui-sung Yang) (2000), "Shenti, guojia yu xia—qianlun jindai Zhongguo minzuzhuyi de shentiguan he yingxiong chongbai" 身體、國家與俠——淺論近代中國民族主義的身體觀和英雄崇拜 (Body, Nation, and Knights—A Preliminary Investigation of Views on the Body and Hero Worship in Modern Chinese Nationalism), *Zhongguo wen-zhe yanjiu tongxun*, 10.3, pp. 87–106.

— (2005), "Xiangxiang minzu chiru: Jindai Zhongguo sixiang wenhuashi shang de 'Dongya bingfu'" 想像民族恥辱：近代中國思想文化史上的「東亞病夫」

(Imagining National Humiliation: The "Sick Man of East Asia" in Modern Chinese Intellectual and Cultural History), *Zhengzhi daxue lishi xuebao*, 23, pp. 1–44.

– (2010), *Bingfu, huanghuo, shuishi—"Xifang" shiye de Zhongguo xingxiang yu jindai Zhongguo guozu lunshu xiangxiang* 病夫、黃禍與睡獅——「西方」視野的中國形象與近代中國國族論述想像 (Sick Man, Yellow Peril, Sleeping Lion—"Western" Visions of China and the National Imagination of Modern China), Taibei: Zhengda chubanshe.

Yang Yingying 楊英英 (ed.) (1994), *Deng Xiaoping wenxuan* 鄧小平文選 (Selected Works of Deng Xiaoping), vol. 3, Taibei: Diqiu chubanshe.

Yuan Shuyi 苑書義, Sun Huafeng 孫華峰, Li Bingxin 李秉新 (eds.) (1998), *Zhang Zhidong quanji* 張之洞全集 (Complete Works of Zhang Zhidong), 12 vols., Shijiazhuang: Hebei renmin chubanshe.

Zhang Hao 張灝 (1982), "Wan Qing sixiang fazhan shilun—ji ge jiben lundian de tichu yu jiantao" 晚清思想發展試論——幾個基本論點的提出與檢討 (On the Development of Late Qing Thought—A Few Basic Arguments and their Discussion), in: Zhou Yangshan 周陽山, Yang Suxian 楊肅獻 (eds.), *Jindai Zhongguo sixiang renwu lun: Wan Qing sixiang* 近代中國思想人物論 (Modern Chinese Thinkers: Late Qing Thought), Taibei: Shibao, pp. 19–33.

Zheng Zhilin 鄭志林 (1999), "Shi 'Dongya bingfu'" 識 "東亞病夫" (Knowing the "Sick Man of East Asia"), *Zhejiang tiyu kexue*, 21.2, pp. 50–55.

A Two Step Transition 1895-1900. Discourses of Weakness as *basso continuo* of Chinese Modernity

Daniel Hausmann

Before a *coup d'état* ended the Reform of a Hundred Days, the Guangxu 光緒 emperor (1871-1908) had granted scholars the right to submit their opinions to the court freely.[1] It was, allegedly, Kang Youwei's 康有為 (1858–1927) *Record of the Partition and Destruction of Poland (Bolan fenmie ji* 波蘭分滅記) which moved the emperor so deeply to implement such a policy.[2] This tract was a thinly veiled critique of the current situation, the powerlessness of the emperor, the intrigues by high officials, and the rampant conservatism which clamorously muted the voices of reform.[3] A few years later, Liang Qichao 梁啟超 (1873–1929) commented on this episode, "[Kang] drastically shows [in the *Record of the Partition and Destruction of Poland*] that conservatism and the suppression of the people necessarily lead to demise. His presentation is both sad and striking. The emperor was moved and took more courage for reform".[4] Here, Liang shared Kang's belief in the power of discourse, in particular, those about weakness and break-up.[5] Such discourses allegedly changed men fundamentally; they could even destroy deeply held convictions such as the relation between father and son, and they could make men sacrifice their lives for a higher cause.[6]

In fact, stories about the demise of Poland circulated widely. The first reports about it appeared in the 1830s, but they gained currency with the much feared "division of the Chinese melon" (*guafen* 瓜分), especially after the ratification of the Treaty of Shimonoseki in 1895.[7] Yan Fu 嚴復 (1853–1921),[8]

---

1 Mao Haijian (2005), *Wuxu bianfa shishi kao*, pp. 219–221, 229–237.

2 Critiqual about this Kwong, Luke (1984), *Mosaic*, p. 194.

3 Compare Hsiao Kung-chuan (1975), *A Modern China and a New World: K'ang Yu-wei, Reformer and Utopian*, p. 203 Fn. 35. On the influence of Kang Youwei see Kwong (2000), "Chinese Politics at the Crossroads: Reflections on the Hundred Days Reform of 1898". Note also that Kang's discourse differs most from Liang Qichao's "Bolan miewang ji", which was published two years earlier in the *Shiwubao*, in highlighting the situation at court, whereas Liang emphasized the role of the *shi* 士 (see in particular Liang Qichao, "Bolan miewang ji", 4a.

4 Liang, Qichao (1898f), *Wuxu zhengbian ji*, p. 19.

5 This is also clear from Zou Zhenhuan (2016), "Wan Qing Bolan wangguoshi shuxie de yanbian xipu", pp. 85–86.

6 This is spelled out very clearly already in Kang, Youwei (1886), *Kangzi neiwai pian*.

7 Wagner (2017), "Dividing up the [Chinese] Melon, *guafen* 瓜分' The Fate of a Transcultural Metaphor in the Formation of National Myth".

Tang Caichang 唐才常 (1868–1900),[9] and later also Chen Tianhua 陳天華 (1875–1905),[10] Song Jiaoren 宋教仁 (1882–1913)[11] and Zou Rong 鄒容 (1885–1905)[12] referred to the division and demise of Poland.[13]

Such discourses about the demise of Poland are but one example out of a variety which pertain to what is called here a "discourse of weakness", that is, a historical and comparative tract about China's role and situation in the world, in which past, present and future are all seen through the lens of weakness. These discourses characterised late Qing modernity and possessed a high degree of tenacity and flexibility. Similar discourses were promoted by individuals of different political or ideological orientations and persisted in similar form through the succeeding decades even though the persons in question had seen fundamental ideological changes of heart. The main questions of this essay are thus: When did such historical discourses of weakness, generically, not necessarily just that of Poland, become an important political force in nineteenth and twentieth century history? What were their main features? And finally, why and how did they persist?

I. A Transition in Two Steps

This essay discusses a transition in two temporally close steps: on the semantic level of discourse, beginning with Kang Youwei, Yan Fu and others, historical comparison with other nations entered discourses of policy-making on a large scale. Before 1895, Kang Youwei appears to be searching for his political vision and he, in many ways, continued the tradition of an upright and critical official (*jianchen* 諫臣) and scholar-celebrity (*mingshi* 名士) dating back to the Jiaqing 嘉慶 period (1796–1820). After 1895, however, he based many of his policy proposals upon a historical discourse of weakness which centred on the Chinese nation. He, as Luke Kwong pointed out, performed "the shift in Chinese perspective from unique Sinocentric history to comparative world history".[14] Kang

---

8 Yan Fu (1895), "Yuan qiang", p. 12; compare also Huters (2005), *Bringing the World Back Home*, pp. 43–72; Schwartz (1964), *In Search of Wealth and Power*, pp. 42–90 in particular pp. 42–43, 80–81.

9 Tang Caichang (1899), "Da ke wen Zhina jinshi", p. 192.

10 Chen Tianhua (1903b), *Menghui tou*, p. 16; Chen Tianhua (1903a), *Jingshi zhong*, pp. 74–75; on Chen Tianhua see Rhoads (2000), *Manchus and Han. Ethnic Relations and Political Power in Late Qing and Early Republican China, 1861–1928*, pp. 12–18.

11 Song Jiaoren (1905), "Wuhu Hunan yu Duan Fang", pp. 10–11.

12 Zou Rong (1903), *Gemingjun*, p. 185.

13 For an overview of the breakup of Poland after 1898 see in particular Zou Zhenhuan (2016), "Wan Qing Bolan wangguoshi shuxie de yanbian xipu", see also Zou's article in this volume.

14 Kwong (1984), *Mosaic*, p. 227.

developed a notion of linear progress along which China had to evolve in order to prevail.[15] In short, his shift in perspective is a shift of discursive rules from those associated with an upright and critical official to an all encompassing, comparative and linear historical discourse of weakness.

These historical discourses of weakness profoundly shaped modernity both in the late Qing China and in Republican China. In his controversial engagement with the Chinese past, Lucian Pye, for instance, repeatedly stressed that the perception of weakness was deeply imprinted in Chinese modernity.[16] William A. Callahan remarked that it were the maps of national humiliation that made the transition from an imperial perception of the realm to a modern nation possible. Perceptions of shame and weakness were imprinted in these maps.[17] Wang Zhen holds that discourses of national humiliation shape modernity to this very day,[18] and Rudolf Wagner's studies of the role of metaphor in the late nineteenth century Qing are teeming with images of weakness.[19] Yang Ruisong 楊瑞松 has convincingly shown how depictions of the sick man of Asia (*Dongya bingfu* 東亞病夫) or of the sleeping lion (*shuishi* 睡獅) imbued China's modernity with a sense of weakness.[20] This is, of course, not to say that there is no sense of greatness. To the contrary, the idea of having been great in the past, having a potential to greatness at that time, and being great again soon, fundamentally underpins all these discourses of weakness.

The second transitional step concerns commemoration, or, more to the point, a deliberate blurring of boundaries between history and remembering. A quite remarkable feature of the discourses at that time was their appeal to the

---

15 Luke Kwong has convincingly shown that a linear notion of time seems to have begun to emerge already in the 1860s (Kwong (2001), "The Rise of the Linear Perspective on History in Late Qing China, c. 1860–1911"). A completely different but less convincing reading of Kang Youwei's historical writing is presented by Roland Felber (1997), "The Use of Analogy by Kang Youwei in His Writings on European History." Most research on historiography, however, dates the emerges of linear time in China to the early 20th century (Huang Kewu (2003), "Liang Qichao yu Zhongguo xiandai shixue zhi zhuixun"; Mittag (2003), "Die Konstruktion der Neuzeit in China. Selbstvergewisserung und die Suche nach Anschluß an die moderne Staatengemeinschaft").

16 Pye (1992), *The Spirit of Chinese Politics*, pp. 6, 71. In contrast, see Wang Ermin's 王爾敏 catalogue of criteria for the Chinese modernity. Idem (1969), "'Xiandaihua' de shidai yiyi ji qi jingshen jichu", pp. 277–282.

17 Callahan (2009), "The Cartography of National Humiliation and the Emergence of China's Geobody".

18 Wang (2008), "National Humiliation, History Education, and the Politics of Historical Memory".

19 Wagner (2011), "China 'Asleep' and 'Awakening'. A Study in Conceptualizing Asymmetry and Coping with it"; Idem (2017), "'Dividing up the [Chinese] Melon, *guafen* 瓜分': The Fate of a Transcultural Metaphor in the Formation of National Myth".

20 Yang Ruisong (2010), *Bingfu, Huanghuo yu Shuishi: 'Xifang' shiye de Zhongguo xingxiang yu jindai Zhongguo minzu lunshu xiangxiang*, see also Jui-sung Yang's article in this volume.

duty of remembering, that is, to the people not "to forget one's country" (*wang guo* 忘國). For instance, the philanthropist Xie Jiafu 謝家福 (1847–1897) feared that relief for the Great North China Famine (1876–78) would be instrumental in shifting the loyalty of the people to "the West", and that it would be imperative to provide relief for them so that they would not forget (*wang* 忘) China (*Zhongguo* 中國).[21] Zhang Zhidong 張之洞 (1837–1909) articulates a similar warning in his *Exhortation to Learning* (*Quanxue pian* 勸學篇): the West presented an unprecedented challenge, and it was imperative to focus on "Chinese" learning in order not to forget one's ancestors[22] or the country.[23] Liang Qichao reflected on the failure of the 1898 Reform and commemorated the six martyrs, sentenced to death for allegedly instigating the assassination of the empress dowager. One of the lessons drawn by him was that the mindset of all the Chinese had to be changed before any reform would be possible: they would have to be awakened to the importance of the nation to their lives. An idealised notion of willingness to make sacrifices, such as the six martyrs, and commemoration thus merged. However, Liang still continued to produce these historical, comparative and linear discourses of weakness, introduced, among others, by Kang Youwei. They bestowed a sense of significance upon calls for awakening and commemoration. In brief, discourses of weakness should, in Liang's view, become part of the memory culture, that is to say, of the personal recollection of every citizen, a fact which is clearly articulated in his biographies of the six martyrs of the Hundred Days Reform.

In the Republican Period, such memory politics were neatly associated with "spiritual education" (*jingshen jiaoyu* 精神教育) and "national humiliation" (*guochi* 國恥), both of which aimed at moulding a nation through a sense of shame and weakness in comparison with other countries.[24] Similar worries shape public discourses in China today. Political and, in particular, patriotic, education were on the rise from the 1990s when memory of defeat and humiliation took pride of place, in particular, the second Sino-Japanese war (1937–1945).[25] On the occasion of annual commemorations of nine-one-eight (*jiuyiba* 九一八), the Japanese assault on Manchuria on September 18 in 1931, the CCP's official organ *Qiushi* 求實 published an article in 2015 in which it wrote, "history is inscribed in the heart of the people; it is intolerable to delete it it is impossible

---

21 Xie Jiafu (late 19th century), *Qi dong riji*, pp. 86–87.

22 Zhang Zhidong (1898), *Quanxue pian*, preface, pp. 2a–b.

23 Ibid., pp. 3a–b.

24 Cohen (2002), "Remembering and Forgetting. National Humiliation in Twentieth Century China".

25 Wang (2008), "National Humiliation, History Education, and the Politics of Historical Memory: Patriotic Education Campaign in China".

A Two Step Transition

to delete it", and "to forget history is to commit treason".[26] *Qiushi* thus conflates the imperative to remember history and personal experience. In this case, historical events allegedly displaying the weakness of the Chinese nation are transformed into personal experiences, namely, recollections.

Some rough criteria about the nature of modern discourses of weakness may be derived from these brief remarks about weakness and historical memory. Such a discourse is historical and comparative in nature, its historical narrative is shaped by a linear notion of time, contains the idea of progress and the situation of many nations competing with each other, and finally, is inseparably connected to a politics of remembering which demands every national to commemorate the events narrated. Such a historical discourse appears on the stage of the policy debates that were contemporary with Kang Youwei, who was one of its most vociferous proponents, but its connection with commemoration was only made after 1898 by, among others, Liang Qichao.

This shift unfolded along two lines, one reaching back to changes in the early nineteenth century, and the other beginning at the immediate aftermath of the 1898 *coup d'état*. The first following section, Section Two, briefly describes the rather rigid hierarchies in the later period of the Qianlong 乾隆 reign (r. 1735–1796) and serves as a foil for Section Three. It, in turn, sketches an intellectual transition of policy debates in the 1870s and 1880s and examines Kang Youwei's writings in the mid-1890s. After 1895, Kang's discourses of weakness entered debates about policy-making and shaped subsequent discussions about the fate of the Qing. This essay closes with an analysis of Liang Qichao's commemorations of the events of 1898 which highlight heroism and martyrdom against the backdrop of national weakness and failure. The purpose of this arrangement is to highlight two historical breaks, one of which is the emergence of discourses of weakness in the mid-1890s which still inherited some of the features of older nineteenth century debates. As the example of Kang Youwei shows, such discourses suspended the political language of the dynasty and replaced it with a comparative historical discourse which conceived the Qing as one country among others which faced an uncertain fate, possibly its own demise. The other emphasises the influence of discourses of weakness on memory culture and, in particular, on the need to commemorate heroic deeds. Among other things, this is a shift from state to nation and from officialdom to the mind (*jingshen* 精神) of the nationals. Together they form a typical pair how modern nations imagined their weakness, as weak states in the concert of nations and as consisting of citizens forgetful of their past and thus of their identity.

---

26 Topic group for social sciences of the journal *Qiushi* (2015), "Mingji weida lishi, zhangxian xueshu huayu", p. 7.

II. *Shengshi* 聖世 ("Sagely World") and Critique

The Qianlong reign was a period of prosperity (*sheng* 盛), but also one of bureaucratic rule[27] and intellectual repression.[28] This common, but rather simplified view of the reign, however, imposes a uniform picture onto a reality. The early period was, in fact, not so repressive, the Qianlong emperor (1711–1799) frequently showed lenience towards censors,[29] the emperor and the bureaucrats did not pursue intellectual deviance on such a large scale as would be the case in the 1770s and successive decades.[30] However, by and large factual, that is, *shi* 實 , policies and discussion were at the centre of attention, officials were not to address larger problems, and scholars or officials from the lower strata of society or the bureaucracy were largely prevented from voicing their opinions at court.[31]

Around the 1770s, in particular with the editing of the *Siku quanshu* 四庫全書, public opinion began to be repressed further.[32] This repression or censorship was, of course, never total, and, simply due to the understaffed and underfinanced bureaucracy, such a policy could never attain the levels of state control achieved by the totalitarian regimes in the twentieth century.[33] But their consequences were sometimes severe for individual scholars. In any event, the major point here is that such repression was more about status than about content, and that those without the right to address the court were muzzled, such as common students (*shengyuan* 生員) who would voice their discontent at the end of the nineteenth century.

The sixty-year-old student Wu Ying 吳英 may serve as an example. He begged the Guangxi treasurer, Zhu Chun 朱春 (1709–1784), to forward his policy proposals to the throne. Zhu, however, had Wu arrested, notified governor Yao Chenglie 姚成烈 (1716–1786), and complained that Wu's proposal, which was, in fact, rather conventional, would infringe taboos for written language, an issue that the young Qianlong emperor proclaimed to hold a lenient attitude on, and finally that Wu's writing would contain many absurdities. Wu was accused of presenting "insane speech", not quietly performing his role in society (*bu anfen* 不安分), and treason. He was sentenced to the death by a

---

27 Bartlett (1991), *Monarchs and Ministers: The Great Council in Mid-Ch'ing China, 1723–1820*; Will (1997), "The 1744 Annual Audits of Magistrate Activity and their Fate".

28 Guy (1987), *The Emperor's Four Treasuries*, pp. 197 ff.

29 See for instance Ginggun (1827), *Qinding taigui*, 3/1a ff.; Guy (1987), *The Emperor's Four Treasuries*, pp. 31–33.

30 Guy (1987), *The Emperor's Four Treasuries*, pp. 33–34.

31 On *jingshi* 經世 in the Qianlong reign see Yang Nianqun (2010), *Hechu shi 'Jiangnan': Qingchao zhengtongguan de queli yu shilin jingshen shijie de bianyi*, pp. 318–365.

32 Guy (1987), *The Emperor's Four Treasuries*, pp. 33–34, 34 ff.

33 See for instance Will (1997), "The 1744 Annual Audits of Magistrate Activity and their Fate".

thousand cuts (*lingchi* 凌遲). His male descendants were sentenced to death and his female descendants and family were enslaved.[34] "Insane speech" and critique by an ordinary student were, in a "sagely world", identical to treason, and, as such, a threat to social order.[35] Even though it is hard to say whether Wu Ying's fate was representative, several others, such as the student (*shengyuan*) Liu Zhenyu 劉震宇 were given the same sentence, mainly on account of their low social position.[36] In short, the main "crime" of Liu Zhengyu and of Wu Ying was to infringe the social hierarchies. One major feature, however, of nineteenth century policy debates, which peaked in the reform movement of the so-called "Hundred Days", was to overturn this taboo.

III. Critique in Transition until the 1880s

Such a transformation did not take place over night. In the late Qianlong reign, Yao Nai 姚鼐 (1731–1815) and Hong Liangji 洪亮吉(1746–1809) had already come to represent a new strata of moral engaged officials and scholars.[37] Heshen's 和珅 (1750–1799) racketeering resulted, among other things, in a more liberal attitude towards criticism voiced by Han *literati*.[38] The power and influence of the local élites, who were, in the long run, crucial to national policy-making, grew in the Jiaqing 嘉慶 (1796–1820) and, in particular, in the Daoguang 道光 (1821–1850) periods.[39] One may or may not share the full set of assumptions associated with the revisionist scholars who proposed that the Jiaqing period was the *de facto* transition to modern China,[40] but it is certainly true that some features crucial to late Qing reform debates originated in this period, such as the slightly more liberal attitude towards deviant or critical opinions at court.[41] This essay builds on the continuities from the early nineteenth century to the early 1890s, but, in contrast to the revisionist scholarship on the

---

34 Beiping gugong bowuyuan wenxianguan (eds.) (1931–34), *Wenziyudang*, pp. 493–501.

35 See for instance Guy (1987), *The Emperor's Four Treasuries*, pp. 176–179; 186–187.

36 Beiping gugong bowuyuan wenxianguan (eds.) (1931–34), *Wenziyudang*, pp. 41–46.

37 On Yao Nai see Guy (1987), *The Emperor's Four Treasuries*, pp. 140 ff.; on Hong Liangji see Mann (1971), *Huang Liang-chi 1746–1809*.

38 Susan Mann first advanced a similar view in her PhD dissertation on Hong Liangji, see Mann (1971), *Hung Liang-chi 1746–1809*. See also Kuhn (1995), "Ideas behind China's modern State"; Mosca (2011), "The Literati Rewriting of China in the Qianlong-Jiaqing Transition".

39 Han Seunghyun (2016), *After the Prosperous Age*, pp. 14–17.

40 For a synthesis see Rowe (2011), "Introduction: The Significance of the Qianlong-Jiaqing Transition in Qing History"; for an earlier provocative formulation of such a thesis see Philip A. Kuhn (2002), *Origins of the Modern Chinese State*.

41 Wang Wensheng (2014), *White Lotus Rebels and South China Pirates: Crisis and Reform in the Qing Empire*. Cambridge, Mass.: Harvard University Press, pp. 162–63.

Jiaqing reforms, it argues that the evidence from the "discourses of weakness" suggests a break with the early nineteenth century debates and problems after the conclusion of the Sino-Japanese War (1894–95).[42]

Most relevant to the argument pursued here is Yao Nai's writing "On the Hanlin" (*Hanlin lun* 翰林論), in which he sketched the demise of the Hanlin Academy and demanded the restoration of its original function of providing policy advice based upon the classics.[43] His influence covered the whole nineteenth century and he ranks among the progenitors of the so-called "moralistic school" (*yili pai* 義理派), as opposed to the Gongyang school (*gongyang pai* 公羊派) to which Kang Youwei belonged.[44] Famous representatives of the moralistic school were the "four Hanlin critics" (*Hanlin sijian* 翰林四諫), namely, Baoting 寶廷 (1840–1890), Zhang Peilun 張佩綸 (1848–1903), Huang Tifang 黃體芳 (1832–1899) and Zhang Zhidong.[45]

After the Tongzhi emperor suddenly died from smallpox in January 1875, the Guangxu emperor ascended the throne. The edict on the ascent formulated by the empress dowagers in combination with the raging Great North China Famine (1876–78) thus triggered boiling dissatisfaction which lifted the lid on critique at court. The four Hanlin critiques began to submit a series of reform memorials. Most importantly, they adamantly demanded that the so-called "thoroughfare for speech" (*yanlu* 言路) should be kept wide open so that criticism would not only be received tolerantly, but also that the voice of lower officials without the right (or duty) to present their opinions to the court (*yanze* 言責) would be heard. Their reform proposals were, however, in terms of content, not very imaginative.

Although Kang Youwei belonged to the Gongyang party and ideologically opposed the moralistic party of the four Hanlin critics, his first memorials written in the late-1880s still continued the moralist tradition.[46] In particular, lan-

---

42 See Philip A. Kuhn's argument for a "consitutionalist agenda" (Kuhn (2002), *Origins of the Modern Chinese State*, pp. 8–24, 114–135), and more recently William T. Rowe's suggestions in his analysis of Bao Shichen's 包世臣 (1775–1855) thought (Rowe (2018), *Speaking of Profit. Bao Shichen and Reform in Nineteenth-Century China*). The timeline defended here builds on insights originally formulated in the albeit dated work of Benjamin Schwartz (1964), *In Search for Wealth and Power. Yan Fu and the West*, pp. 10–18.

43 Yao Nai (1798), "Hanlin lun", pp. 1/4a–5a.

44 Ōtani Toshio (1991), "Shindai keisei shisō ni okeru ni dai chōryū—kakyo, gakkō seido, keisei bunhen to no kanren ni oite".

45 The concept of *qingliu* 清流 has frequently been used to analyze this period (for affirmative treatments see Eastman (1965), "Ch'ing-i and Chinese Policy Formation during the Nineteenth Century"; Edgerton-Tarpley (2008), *Tears from Iron Cultural Responses to Famine in Nineteenth-Century China*; Rankin (1982), "'Public Opinion' and Political Power: Qingyi in Late Nineteenth Century China"), but it seems to me of doubtful usefulness (see Kwong (1984), *Mosaic*, pp. 70–71, 305 n. 16, 305–306 n. 20).

46 Here I agree with Luke Kwong and not with Wong Young-tsu (Wong (1992), "Revisionism Reconsidered", p. 516; Kwong (1984), *Mosaic*, pp. 85–86).

guage and logic were very similar.[47] For instance, he submitted a memorial in December 1888, reacting to the retreat of the empress-dowager Cixi 慈禧 (1835–1908) from power. There Kang employed the rhetoric of the four Hanlin critics: he alluded to the external danger, which would only be harmful if the realm was internally weak; he mentioned that an earthquake, floods in Shandong and a drought were bad omens, and would, as such, call for reform; and he criticised the conduct of high officials, demanded the promotion of talent and the opening of the "thoroughfare of speech".[48]

IV. Kang Youwei's Discourses of Weakness in 1895

The end of the first Sino-Japanese War and the Treaty of Shimonoseki also terminated Kang's rather aimless search for his political vision, and discourses of weakness became an essential part of his thinking. During the peace negotiations with Japan, an opposition movement against the treaty was being formed. The terms were harsh and humiliating, despite Japan's fear of foreign intervention. The Treaty of Shimonoseki rang in the so-called "scramble for concessions" in China, a dynamic which was already shaping imperialist politics elsewhere, in particular in Africa.[49] One tangible consequence of this scramble was Germany's occupation of Jiaozhou 膠州 Bay in 1898, which was, next to the Treaty of Shimonoseki, among the major catalysts for the reform movement of 1898.[50]

These events caused the dissatisfied scholar-celebrities (*mingshi*) to erupt in patriotic fervour.[51] In May 1895, the petition of the examination candidates (*gongche shangshu* 公車上書) was submitted to the court and a flood of other memorials and petitions reached the emperor.[52] The examination candidates,

---

47 His private writings at that time differ considerably from his memorials but are also inconsistent. In some he copied the *more geometrico* trying to deduce the rules for society (See in particular Kang Youwei (1888d), *Shili gongfa quanshu*; Idem (1888ab, "Lun shiwu"). In others he focused on infrastructure and resources (See for instance Kang Youwei (1888b), "Lun shiwu"; Idem (ca. 1888a), *Biji*), while authoritarian reform from above never seems to have escaped his attention (Kang Youwei (1886), "Kangzi neiwaipian", pp. 97, 99).

48 Kang Youwei (1888c), "Shang Qingdi diyi shu"; Idem (1889b), "Wei Zongshe yanzhong guoshi youwei qi ci miandui yi jie yucheng zhe"; Idem (1889a), "Menzai gaijing qing xing shizheng er da tianjie zhe".

49 Paine (2005), *The Sino-Japanese War of 1894–1895: Perceptions, Power, and Primacy*, pp. 247 ff.

50 Liang Qichao (1898f), *Wuxu zhengbian ji*, p. 1.

51 Kwong (1984), *Mosaic*, pp. 71–73; Hu Sijing (1913), *Wuxu lüshuang lu*, p. 1/5a.

52 Mao Haijian (2005c), "'Gongche shangshu' kaozheng bu yi", 7 ff. On this event see Kwong (1984), *Mosaic*, pp. 90–93; Fang Delin (2007b), "Kang Youwei yu gongche shangshu – du "'Gongche shangsh' kaozheng bu" xianyi yi"; Fang Delin (2007a), "Kang Youwei yu gongche

who had recently travelled to the capital, reacted angrily against the conclusion of the First Sino-Japanese War. They filed a petition and rang in three years of reform-thinking which culminated in the so-called Hundred Days' Reform (*wuxu bianfa* 戊戌變法). However, the precise course of events seems to be anything but clear. Contemporary scholars debate whether the petition was a movement supported by the students below or orchestrated from above, and question what Kang Youwei's role was in this movement. The academic community is divided on these questions: Huang Zhangjian 黃彰健, Luke Kwong and Mao Haijian 矛海建 among others doubt that Kang Youwei played the crucial part in orchestrating this movement and drafting the petition in question.[53] Wong Young-tsu 汪榮祖 and Fang Delin 房德鄰 believe he did.[54] Such disputes, in fact, date back to the Hundred Days' Reform and, as Liang Qichao aptly grasped, "it is essential that regardless of how [people] slander him, accuse him or oppose him, all eyes are surely upon him".[55] Many different interpretations of Kang's role have been advanced in the secondary literature. He was a utopian reformer for some,[56] a pioneer awakening China,[57] one of the last Confucians for others,[58] even a Confucian radical,[59] or delusional traditionalist who failed to grasp the consequences of global capitalism.[60] Still others believe him to be a traitor,[61] a charlatan,[62] or a conceited manipulator.[63] However, no one disputes Kang's importance.[64]

Despite this variety of opinion, all seem to agree that Kang held onto the firm belief in his destiny, his role as the "uncrowned king" (*suwang* 素王) like Confucius,[65] that his thinking was highly eclectic and that later perceptions of

---

shangshu – du "'Gongche shangsh' kaozheng bu" xianyi er"; Mao Haijian (2005c), "'Gongche shangshu' kaozheng bu yi"; Mao Haijian (2005b), "'Gongche shangshu' kaozheng bu er".

53 Huang Zhangjian (1970), *Wuxu bianfa shi yanjiu*; Mao Haijian (2005), *Wuxu bianfa shishi kao*; Kwong (1984), *Mosaic*.

54 Fang Delin (2007a), "Kang Youwei yu gongche shangshu"; Wong Young-Tsu (1992), "Revisionism Reconsidered: Kang Youwei and the Reform Movement of 1898".

55 Liang Qichao (1901), "Nanhai Kang xiansheng zhuan", p. 88.

56 Hsiao Kung-chuan (1975), *A Modern China and a New World*.

57 Fitzgerald (1996), *Awakening China: Politics, Culture, and Class in the Nationalist Revolution*; Yü Ying-shih (1993), "The Radicalization of China in the Twentieth Century".

58 Zarrow (2012), *After Empire*; Levenson (1968), *Confucian China and its Modern Fate*.

59 Chang Hao (1987), *Chinese Intellectuals in Crisis*.

60 Zarrow and Karl (2002), "Introduction".

61 Lei Jiasheng (2015), "Kang Youwei shi maiguozei ma? Zai lun Wuxu Bianfa de yuanyin".

62 Huang Zhangjian (1970), *Wuxu bianfa shi yanjiu*. See also Wong Young-Tsu (1992), "Revisionism Reconsidered: Kang Youwei and the Reform Movement of 1898".

63 Kwong (1984), *A Mosaic of the Hundred Days: Personalities, Politics, and Ideas of 1898*; Hsiao (1975), *A Modern China and a New World*, pp. 18–21, 54 ff.

64 See Kwong and Wong (1993), "Communications to the Editor".

65 Chang Hao (1987), *Chinese Intellectuals in Crisis*, 24–25; Fitzgerald (1996), *Awakening China*, pp. 69–70; Hsiao Kung-chuan (1975), *A Modern China and a New World*, pp. 18–28.

his *persona* were, to a non-negligible extent, shaped by Kang's own vision of his earlier self.[66] Although this essay has nothing fundamentally new to add to this debate, it is clear that the authorship and origin of the petition in question are not really important for the argument pursued here. Authorship, after radical announcements such as "the author is dead", does not, in any way, exhaust the significance of the documents in question, and the following is solely concerned with the latter.

Whatever the case, original or counterfeit, the discourses of weakness articulated by Kang Youwei were widely shared. In May 1895, he and other examination candidates in the capital submitted a collectively-signed memorial to the court. It was signed by roughly 1,500 examination candidates.[67] The petitionists anticipated the division and demise of China should it not change. Reforms were necessary, that is to say, modernisation of the railway network, a currency reform, the tapping of natural resources and so forth,[68] a set of rather widespread policy proposals at the time.[69] This reform's main aims were to enrich (*fu* 富) the state and thus enable it to perform its duties again, and to make it strong (*qiang* 強) by educating the people and making them contribute to the state's wealth. As a necessary condition for this agenda to enrich and strengthen the state, the petitioners envisioned a new role and new opportunities for the political élite, that is to say, for themselves. Classical examinations should be abolished, talented officials should be promoted, and the "thoroughfare for speech" should be opened widely.[70] This set of proposals in many ways resembled the landscape of opinions dominant throughout the 1870s and 1880s.[71]

The petition of the examination candidates set the tone for the debates in the following months, and, as a response, the Guangxu emperor promulgated an edict opening the "thoroughfare for speech" widely. But the emperor also reacted to a flood of other critical memorials and not just to the aforementioned petition.[72] He thus legitimated an established practice. Kang still used this opportunity to submit other memorials, one on 29 May and another on 30 June the same year, in which he put the main stress on other themes. It is here that Kang Youwei fully develops a historical discourse of weakness for the first time.

---

66 Hsiao Kung-chuan (1975), *A Modern China and a New World*, pp. 15–21; Kwong (1984), *Mosaic*, pp. 6–9.

67 Mao Haijian (2005c), "'Gongche shangshu' kaozheng yi".

68 Hsiao Kung-chuan (1975), *A Modern China and a New World*, chapter eight.

69 Kwong (1984), *Mosaic*, pp. 101–102, 111–113.

70 Kang Youwei (1895b), "Shang Qingdi di'er shu".

71 Mao Haijian (2005c), "'Gongche shangshu' kaozheng yi", pp. 26 ff.

72 Ibid., pp. 7 ff.

Kang observed that recent history suggested that the demise of China was only a matter of less than three or four years away. The Qing had lost territories, had been forced to open trade ports, the capital Beijing had been invaded, and the dynasty had lost vassal states such as Vietnam, Myanmar, the Ryūkyū islands, and recently Korea. Foreign countries were cutting off the Qing's extremities and their knife sometimes even reached the heart of the realm. Kang compared this situation to a disease, in which the dynasty had become empty and rotten in the interior making its vital *qi* (*yuanqi* 元氣) weak which increased the possibility and success of foreign invasions.[73] But, Kang asked, how could this be? How could such a populous country as China, which dominated such a huge territory and had access to unfathomably rich resources, actually end up weak?[74]

In China, all under Heaven has, for two thousand years, been governed by statutes (*fa* 法). But today's poverty and weakness, which gave rise to peril, is, in fact, a result of ruined statutes.[75] The system of statutes (*fa*) has been in place for a long time and thus began to rot. There are plenty of inept and disloyal officials, education is bad and unpractical, knowledge is scarce and shallow, the military are old and weak, agriculture is underdeveloped and inefficient, commerce and crafts wither. Officials can't fulfill their duties and governance thus declines. Foreign attractions, oddities and illicit goods enter the realm, the people grow poorer, form bands of beggars or robbers, and the realm would collapse even without a foreign invasion.[76]

Today more than ten countries wolfishly look [at China]. This is a [unique] emergency in four thousand years. The sweltering summer heat is already at its peak, and if [we] don't remove [our] heavy fur coats, the disease will already have changed and we will still be using old methods. Then, we will die from sunstroke and be at great risk.[77]

The history of the Chinese nation, Kang further elaborated, was shaped by periods of unity (*yitong* 一 統) and periods of disunity (*lieguo* 列國). In times of unity, the nation was often militarily threatened by the so-called "barbarians", but its civilisation remained unchallenged.[78] Kang stated, for instance,

I believe that today's governance should be creatively (*kaichuang* 開創) governing all under heaven, but not conservatively (*shoujiu* 守舊). It should govern all under heaven while various countries oppose each other, but not in unity and ritual. To be creative means to change and renew the rules, but to be conservative means to follow the old

---

73 Kang Youwei (1895c), "Shang Qingdi disan shu", p. 68.
74 Ibid., pp. 69, 78.
75 Ibid., p. 69.
76 Ibid., p. 69.
77 Ibid., p. 69.
78 Kang Youwei (1895d), "Shang Qingdi disi shu", p. 82.

precedents. Heroes struggle and knowledge competes when various countries oppose each other. Kowtow and passivity rule in times of unity and ritual.[79]

Commerce was most important in times of various countries opposing each other, even more important than the military, and thus it should take the place of agriculture.[80] Another period of many nations (*lieguo*) competing for supremacy had dawned again bearing some similarities to the Spring and Autumn (771–476 BC) or the Warring States (475–222 BC) periods. This all conformed, Kang argued, to an eternal law originally formulated in the *Book of Changes*, "accomplishment after change, durability after accomplishment" (*bian ze tong tong ze jiu* 變則通通則久). It was now time to act in accordance with the times and change in order not to be doomed to oblivion.[81]

This historical discourse about the logic of Chinese history which forms the centre of Kang's argument thus consists of three interrelated propositions. Kang had a sharp and probably exaggerated sense of crisis since he forecasted the Qing's demise within four years if nothing changed. The causes for this current weakness had to be historical, since the Qing was strong in terms of the extent of its domain, its access to resources and its population. The main cause for this historical decline was the tradition of governance, which went back to the Qin empire (221–206 BC). It established its rule upon the basis of statutes (*fa*) and reigned autocratically without virtue. This spirit, according to Kang, infected every domain of life and state, such as the quality of officials, a poetic, rather than a pragmatic, intellectual culture, a static agriculture, and a disregard of trade and artisanship. On a deeper layer, Kang sought the reason for such a standstill in unification (*yitong*). A unified empire would not innovate, he argued. It would rely on ritual, statutes, promote, but not reform, agriculture, and it would impede commerce. Now, the Qing dynasty faced again, as in the Warring States period, challenges from other countries and its history entered the stage of *lieguo* again.

To strengthen his view, Kang narrated similar transitions in Europe, advancing from a unified but autocratical realm under the "king of teachings" (*jiaowang* 教王), that is to say, the pope, to a historical situation shaped by different nations (*lieguo*) competing with each other. If the governments of their states were just slightly inferior to others, these states would be eliminated. Thus, Kang argued, every one in these states, that is, the common people and the ruling élites, would exert themselves to the utmost in order to promote good governance, advance talent, and foster virtue.[82] The rise began with Francis Bacon (1561–1626) and an epistemic revolution. Kang placed this event in the

---

79 Kang Youwei (1895c), "Shang Qingdi disan shu", p. 69.
80 Ibid., p. 72.
81 Kang Youwei (1895d), "Shang Qingdi disi shu", pp. 81, 82, 86.
82 Ibid., p. 81.

Yongle period (1402–1424), and claimed that it gave rise to new knowledge, innovation and the spread of education to the people. Craftsmen built new machines, others explored new territories, tapped new resources, and some even reached Asia. Innovations in recent years were many, such as telegraphs and railways, and they allowed these Westerners to occupy parts of the Qing, India, Myanmar, Vietnam, Siberia and the territories east of it. Rule and railways were forming a close liaison.[83] The Northeast of the Qing escaped a cut off by railways as in eighteenth century Poland.[84] Thus, "[these] people fear the power of the Westerners appearance and their marvellous machines. But if one traces their origin, it all comes from rank and compensation to encourage learning and knowledge".[85]

Several countries close to the Qing fared less well. India did not encourage education and knowledge, and it was thus doomed. "India cherishes the way [*dao* 道], but is passive and thus met with demise".[86] It fell because it could not adapt to the new challenges of a period in which many countries competed. Vietnam and Myanmar suffered a similar fate. They were conservative (*shoujiu*), did not change, their rulers were elevated and there was no contact between ruler and the common people.[87] Only Japan succeeded in adapting to modern times, and it even realised its colonial ambitions.[88] Even more, "the West needed 500 years to strive for this, but Japan only 20 years to achieve it".[89] The Qing should thus emulate Japan, which would be even easier since the Qing was bigger, more powerful and not feudalistic (*fengjian* 封建). Kang dreamt, "if China, with its extensive territory and large population, was to learn from Japan, then a grand model would be established after three years, specific regulations after five, this plan would be effective after eight years, and after ten years [China's] hegemony".[90] However, Kang by no means took pity on the fallen countries such as India, Vietnam or others.[91] They were just warning examples to avoid.

Even so, like India, Vietnam, Poland, the Ottoman Empire or Myanmar, China had remained static for hundreds or thousands of years. Westerners held the Chinese, according to Kang, to be like "African slaves" (*Feizhou nu* 非洲奴)

---

83 Ibid., pp. 81–82.

84 Cited in Zou Zhenhuan (2016), "WanQing Bolan wangguoshi shuxie de yanbian xipu", p. 85.

85 Kang Youwei (1895d), "Shang Qingdi disi shu", p. 82.

86 Ibid., p. 74.

87 Kang Youwei (1895a), "Jingshi qiangxuehui xu", pp. 89

88 Kang Youwei (1898c), *Riben bianzheng kao*, p. 103; Kang Youwei (1895d), "Shang Qingdi disi shu", p. 83.

89 Kang Youwei (1898c), *Riben bianzheng kao*, p. 103.

90 Ibid., p. 105.

91 Kang Youwei is very explicit on this point in 1902, "I don't pity India, but I worry that our nation will be like India" (Kang Youwei (1902), "Yu tongxue zhuzi Liang Qichao deng lun Yindu wangguo youyu gesheng zili shu", p. 339).

and to be "deaf, blind, stupid and dim witted" (*long gu chun ming* 聾瞽蠢冥).[92]
To protect (*baohu* 保護) such a country meant destruction (*wangguo* 亡國).[93]

Some [countries] perish by being carved up immediately, as happened to all countries in Africa; some perish by being carved up into multiple slices, as Russia, Germany and Austria did to Poland; some lose their sovereignty and perish immediately, this was what France did to Vietnam; the territory and waters of some countries are occupied and they perish step by step, as England did to India. [...] as the West partitions Asia. They flock together, but being jealous of each other, their military valor is very weak. They repeatedly cut out one of Turkey's provinces so that it still continues to moan. They removed sovereignty in Persia completely and only the old nobility remains. The territory of China is wide. They leisurely partition it and slowly dominate it. This can take several years.[94]

It was the sole aim of unity, not fertile competition, that shaped Chinese history. Science could not develop, talent was wasted, infrastructure was abandoned, and a strict hierarchy separating rulers from ruled shaped society not only in China but also in India, Vietnam and Myanmar.[95] This, according to Kang, led to a huge waste of resources and to endemic corruption. While India, Vietnam and Myammar had already fallen, China was now awakened from its slumber to a world shaped by mutual competition among countries (*lieguo bingzheng* 列國並爭).[96] Were China not to adapt, it would certainly meet the fate of India, Vietnam or Myanmar.

India had formerly been a famous country in Asia. For Kang, it was conservative and did not change.

In the Qianlong period, the English came with a company of 120.000 gold pieces in order to trade and settled in India. Turkey was formerly a great *hui* country. Its territory covered Asia, Europe and Africa, but it was conservative and did not change, and six countries curbed its politics. They carved up its territory and unseated its ruler. The other countries similar to Vietnam, Myanmar, Korea, Ryukyu, Thailand, Persia, Afghanistan, Pakistan, and all the islands in the Pacific and Africa, are today either curbed or have perished. All these conservative countries exist aimlessly in shame.[97]

The fate of the "conservative" (*shoujiu*) Ottoman Empire in the nineteenth century was thus but one of many countries, but it still caught Kang's attention more than others. In a letter about the demise of India in 1902, Kang stressed that historical comparison should focus on sufficiently similar cases. At that time, India appeared to him to be the country most similar to China, a country

---

92 Kang Youwei (1898d), "Shang Qingdi diwu shu", p. 2.
93 Kang Youwei (1895), "Zhong Ri heyueshu hou", p. 99.
94 Kang Youwei (1898d), "Shang Qingdi diwu shu", pp. 4–5.
95 Kang Youwei (1895), "Shang Qingdi di'er shu", p. 36.
96 Ibid., pp. 32–33.
97 Kang Youwei (1895a), "Jingshi qiangxuehui xu", p. 89.

whose fate was thus most revealing about the decisions to be taken in China in 1902.[98] The situation in the 1890s was, of course, different, but there is no evidence that Kang Youwei paid more attention to the fall of India rather than to the demise other countries. Also, his pan-Asianist outlook of 1902, when he adamantly claimed that some aspects of Turkish (*tujue* 突厥)[99] culture and Persian culture were so similar to China that they formed a common cultural sphere,[100] is hard to detect in his earlier writing. Nonetheless, certain cultural, geographic and social similarities, be they imagined or real, were important to Kang even in the 1890s, in particular those to Japan.[101] Furthermore, comparisons with Japan, India or the Ottoman Empire worked on a slightly different plane than those of Russia and Poland. The former relate to the fate of countries while the latter more narrowly focus on the virtues of the emperor or the court, and were thus tacitly but directly addressed to the Guangxu emperor in person.[102] The similarities to the Qing period that Kang saw in the Ottoman Empire were its size, its population, its conservatism, and mainly its recent history of territorial losses.

Its dominion extended over a wide space covering two continents. It possessed the biggest army and navy, at least according to Kang, but it did not promote knowledge and talents.[103] Russia defeated the empire, or, as Kang put it, Russia shamed the Ottoman Empire, once in 1828–29 and then in 1877–78. Uprisings were endemic in Bulgaria (1875–76), Romania (1848), Montenegro (1858) and Serbia (1804–13) of the period, which became independent as a consequence. Later, the Ottoman Empire had to cede the Black Sea to Russia in 1878, Bosnia and Herzegowina to Austria in the same year, Cyprus to Great Britain, and the "White Sea" (Akdeniz or Aegean Sea) to Greece.[104] All these countries overthrew their traditional rulers and installed parliaments. The main reason for this decay was, Kang stressed, the conservatism of the Ottoman Empire.[105] Despite, or even because of, Kang Youwei's obvious historical igno-

---

98 Kang Youwei (1902), "Yu tongxue zhuzi Liang Qichao deng lun Yindu wangguo youyu gesheng zili shu", pp. 334–335.

99 Kang Youwei clearly but incorrectly uses *tujue* it in the sense of Turkey, Kang Youwei (1898c), *Riben bianzheng kao*, p. 104..

100 Kang Youwei (1902), "Yu tongxue zhuzi Liang Qichao deng lun Yindu wangguo youyu gesheng zili shu", p. 343.

101 Kang Youwei (1898c), *Riben bianzheng kao*, pp. 103, 104, 105; Idem (1902), "Yu tongxue zhuzi Liang Qichao deng lun Yindu wangguo youyu gesheng zili shu", p. 345.

102 For the relevant passage on Poland see Kang Youwei (1898a), *Bolan fenmie ji*, pp. 397–398; for Russia see Kang Youwei (1898b), *E Bide bianzheng ji*, p. 35.

103 Kang Youwei (1895c), "Shang Qingdi disan shu", p. 74.

104 In fact, the quarrel concerned the border between Epierius and Thessalian, the latter fell to Greece in 1881.

105 Kang Youwei (1895d), "Shang Qingdi disi shu", p. 83.

A Two Step Transition   95

rance,[106] the Ottoman Empire served as a useful foil to imagine how vast conservative empires could fall, how partition of a huge territory such as that of the Qing's could be carried out gradually.

Kang placed historical comparison at the centre of his argument. In this vein, three years after the *coup d'état*, Liang Qichao concluded that Kang's thinking was based upon history.[107] Thus, Kang not only returned to such patterns of thought time and time again, but also composed several historical tracts which allegedly uncovered the historical dynamics underlying reform and downfall, such as his tract about Russia under Peter the Great, the reforms in Meiji Japan, and the tract about the demise of Poland. Kang thus replaced his earlier experiments with the *more geometrico*,[108] ecological explanations for the rise and fall of nations,[109] and his use of imperial rhetoric with an essentially historical narrative. He believed that the European countries rose because of incessant struggle, and that China stagnated because of its unending unity. Whether Kang was a convinced Social Darwinist is highly doubtful,[110] but his faith in the experience of struggle as a necessary step on the ladder of progress seems to have been unwavering. Nevertheless, he couched this new narrative in a tradition of critique reaching back to the 1870s. By addressing the court and appealing for an opening of the "thoroughfare for speech" (*yanlu*), Kang and the other examination students inherited this tradition.

V. Liang Qichao Commemorates Heroic Deeds

In the immediate aftermath of the crackdown on the 1898 reform movement until the early 1900s, Liang Qichao was arguably the most influential public intellectual in the Chinese speaking world.[111] Among his many writings from this period, the *Records of the Coup d'état 1898* (*wuxu zhengbian ji* 戊戌政變紀) and his commemorations of the six martyrs of the reform constitute his most explicit reaction to this unfortunate turn of events. Among other things, these writings outline how Liang connected discourses of weakness to commemora-

---

106 Kwong (1984), *Mosaic*, pp. 102–3.
107 Liang Qichao (1901), "Nanhai Kang xiansheng zhuan", p. 88.
108 In his *Shili gongfa quanshu* Kang Youwei clearly imitates a deductive approach from so-called "self-evident" principles which is in philosophy often associated with René Descartes or in morals with Immanuel Kant.
109 Kang Youwei (1888), "Lun shiwu", p. 164; Idem (1886), "Kangzi neiwai pian", pp. 109–10.
110 Pusey (1983), *China and Charles Darwin*, pp. 89–90; Chang Hao (1987), *Chinese Intellectuals in Crisis*, p. 62.
111 Cf. Levenson (1968), *Confucian China and its Modern Fate*; Zhang Pengyuan (1964), *Liang Qichao yu Qingji geming*.

tion, thus preserving the spirit (*jingshen* 精神) of the reform. One means to do this were obituaries.

There, Liang constantly refers to the weakness of China and the importance of international threats.[112] China was weak like India,[113] Poland[114] or Egypt,[115] but could only be rescued through heroic sacrifice. He composed several biographies of revolutionary heroes underscoring the intimate relation of weakness and heroism, such as Lajos Kosshut (1802–1894) or Giuseppe Mazzini (1805–1872). Both were heroes who, according to Liang, guided their countries out of a dark period of autocratic conservative rule while threatened by outside powers.[116]

However, actual reform in the late 1890s seemed rather unrealistic to Liang, and he diagnosed that China would enter a transitional period (*guodu shidai* 過度時代).[117] The reformers initiated the age of destruction.[118] Individuals such as Kang Guangren 康廣仁 (1867–1898), Kang Youwei and Tan Sitong 譚嗣同 (1865–1898) were simply living at the wrong time.[119] This meant, among other things, that the spirit (*jingshen*) but not the practice of the six martyrs should be retained.[120] It was, of course, Liang's task to preserve that spirit and to spread it to the people in the hope that they would thus be transformed.

The six martyrs displayed, according to Liang, similar virtues. These honest, courageous and upright *shi* (士), known since the Ming Dynasty and, in particular, the Donglin 東林 movement,[121] were "infuriated by national humiliation"[122] (*fafen guochi* 發憤國恥), allegedly the driving force for any kind of political and social change at that time.[123] However, they fell victim to one of the sources of China's weakness, namely, a cabal orchestrated by high court officials motivated by greed and selfishness.[124]

According to Liang, one of these six martyrs, Yang Rui 楊銳 (1855–1898), was an upright personality motivated by "righteous fury" (*yifen* 義憤) who mod-

---

112 This is especially clear in Liang, Qichao (1898f), *Wuxu zhengbian ji*, p. 26. See also Liang, Qichao (1898f), *Wuxu zhengbian ji*, p. 74; Liang, Qichao (1898e), "Renxue xu".

113 Liang Qichao (1901b), "Mieguo xinfa lun", pp. 35–36.

114 Ibid., p. 35.

115 Ibid., p. 33.

116 Levenson (1968), Liang Ch'i-chao, 123 ff.; Tang Xiaobing (1996), *Global Space and the Nationalist Discourse*, pp. 80–116.

117 Liang Qichao (1901a), "Guodu shidai lun", pp. 27–32.

118 Liang Qichao (1899c), *Ziyoushu*, p. 84.

119 Liang Qichao (1901a), "Guodu shidai lun".

120 Liang Qichao (1904), "Yu zhi shengsiguan".

121 Liang Qichao (1898f), *Wuxu zhengbian ji*, pp. 75, 92–93.

122 Ibid., p. 81.

123 Ibid., pp. 25–26.

124 Ibid., pp. 69–70.

elled his behaviour on the Donglin faction.[125] Yang Shenxiu 楊深秀 (1849–1898) was born into a poor family, and an upright and talented scholar who, in his youth, adored *wuxia* 武俠 stories.[126] Liu Guangdi 劉光第 (1861–1898) also came from poor circumstances. He was serious, knowledgeable, upright, lived in seclusion and rarely spoke. In Liang's judgement he "really was a man of ancient times, ah!"[127] Unsurprisingly, Lin Xu 林旭 (1875–1898) was also an upright, talented and courageous scholar who sacrificed himself for the reform. Lin wanted to save the country, abandoned his beloved poetry, but eventually succumbed to court intrigues.[128]

Liang put most emphasis on the obituaries of Tan Sitong and Kang Guangren. The former is well known,[129] and I will thus focus on the latter only. Kang was the younger brother of Kang Youwei, a courageous, intelligent, understanding and serious character. He served briefly in Zhejiang as a clerk, but learned only to detest officialdom. According to Liang, he was the main engine behind the initiative to abandon the "eight legged essay" (*baguwen* 八股文) which would open the path to real talent. It prevented the élites from opening their minds to the world and to the pitiful situation in which the country found itself.[130] Kang firmly believed in his sacrifice for the country and thus displayed his righteousness.[131] His resolve, however, was also strengthened by a firm belief in Buddhist rebirth.[132]

Liang did, without doubt, paint a highly idealised and partly distorted picture of these reformers,[133] but he certainly succeeded in establishing this image as commonsensical. His idealised commemoration concurred with two other claims. After the reform had failed, Liang dismissed all reform through the institutions of the dynasty as it was. He gained the insight that the people (*min* 民) had to be changed first before reform could be effected. The people lacked knowledge and, in particular, lacked national consciousness.[134] The weakness of China could only be cured if "the grey matter of 400 million Chinese was altered",[135] a grey matter into which thousand years of greed and decadence were inscribed and which was shaped by a "slave mentality" (*nuxing* 奴性).[136] Even if the reform failed, it was nevertheless a stepping-stone which would

---

125 Liang Qichao (1898g), "Yang Rui zhuan", pp. 393–94.
126 Liang Qichao (1898h), "Yang Shenxiu zhuan", pp. 389–92.
127 Liang Qichao (1898c), "Liu Guangdi zhuan", p. 458.
128 Liang Qichao (1898b), "Lin Xu zhuan", pp. 455–457.
129 Liang Qichao (1904), "Yu zhi shengsiguan".
130 Liang Qichao (1898a), "Kang Guangren zhuan", pp. 325–26.
131 Ibid., pp. 329–30.
132 Liang Qichao (1904), "Yu zhi shengsiguan".
133 Kwong (1984), *Mosaic*, p. 184.
134 Liang Qichao (1899a), "Guomin shida yuanqi lun", p. 77.
135 Liang Qichao (1900b), "Zhongguo jiruo suyuan lun", p. 17.
136 Liang Qichao (1899a), "Guomin shida yuanqi lun", pp. 65, 73.

establish a historical process of change.[137] The reformer's main contribution was the discovery of patriotism and patriotic sacrifice.[138] Stories about this spread in newspapers and made an impression on the public.[139] Liang's main instrument to achieve such a historical change thus was the discourse.[140] In short, it was important for him to commemorate and discursively promulgate the deeds of the six martyrs.[141]

Liang clearly felt that he was witnessing a transition (*guodu* 過度) between the old and the new. The dynasties of China were old and doomed to fail, while the nation was young and showed future promise.[142] Partly spurred by the fake reform (*wei weixin* 偽維新) orchestrated by the imperial court, Liang wanted to instill vigour into progressive movements and newspapers.[143] His output in form of articles during the years 1900 to 1901 reached hitherto unknown heights. Most texts address the accumulated weakness (*jiruo* 積弱), the partition (*guafen*) of China, the danger of national annihilation (*mieguo* 滅國), and, above all, the national conscience.[144] Here, Liang frequently refers to the fate suffered by Egypt, India, Poland or South Asian states such as Vietnam or Myanmar echoing Kang Youwei's remarks about those countries.[145] He developed a notion of heroism in relation to their times.[146] That is, Liang juxtaposed, among other things, discourses of weakness such as those of Kang Youwei to commemoration of heroic deeds. It is in this sense that the fate of the nation took a human shape for others to remember and emulate. Such a development is by no means surprising since, as many scholars have already remarked, it was precisely this period in which Liang turned to the mind of every Chinese national which he then found to be of superior importance in comparison to the integrity of the territory or constitutional reform (*bianfa* 變法).[147]

---

137 Liang Qichao (1899c), *Ziyoushu*, p. 59.

138 Liang Qichao (1899a), "Guomin shida yuanqi lun", p. 67.

139 Liang Qichao (1899c), *Ziyoushu*, p. 55.

140 On the power of discourse see Liang Qichao (1900), "Zhongguo jiruo suyuan lun", p. 17.

141 Liang Qichao (1898f), *Wuxu zhengbian ji*, pp. 95–112; Liang Qichao (1898), "*Renxue* xu"; Liang Qichao (1898d), "Qingyibao xuli".

142 Liang Qichao (1900a), "Shaonian Zhongguo shuo", p. 9–10.

143 Liang Qichao (1901d), "Qingyibao yibai ce zhuci bing lun baoguan zhi zeren ji benguan zhi jingli", p. 57.

144 See in particular Liang Qichao (1900b), "Zhongguo jiruo suyuan lun"; Idem (1901), "Mieguo xinfa lun"

145 See in particular Liang Qichao (1901b), "Mieguo xinfa lun"; Idem (1899b), "Lun jinshi guomin jingzheng zhi dashi ji Zhongguo qiantu", p. 57–58.

146 On Mazzini see Liang Qichao (1900a), "Shaonian Zhongguo shuo", p. 10; on Liang's notion of heroism see Idem (1901a), "Guodu shidai lun", pp. 30–32, Idem (1901), "Nanhai Kang xiansheng zhuan", pp. 58–59.

147 Liang Qichao (1901b), "Mieguo xinfa lun", pp. 43–44. See also Zou Zhenhuan (2016), "Wan-Qing Bolan wangguoshi shuxie de yanbian xipu", p. 89; Lin Yingyu (2016), "Minqi keyong: cong geming guafen lunzhan kan wan Qing de minqi lunshu".

In sum, Liang cherished the ideal of sacrifice for the nation as embodied by the six martyrs which was transported by a discourse for the people to remember. He thus "democratised", albeit in a limited sense, the ideals of the 1898. This change surely reflected his flight to Japan, the apparent impossibility of achieving reform through traditional officialdom, and his role as editor of the *Qingyibao* 清議報. It is, however, important to see that Liang clearly couched this urge in a discourse of weakness first articulated by Kang Youwei. The urgency of sacrifice and the need to preserve the memory of such sacrifices were justified by China's weakness in comparison to other nations. Liang's writings teem with references to the demise of Poland, Turkey, India and other countries. But he addressed another audience and drew entirely different conclusions from such a discourse of weakness than those of Kang Youwei. Instead of urging for a reform through the institutions of the dynasty as a critical official (*jianchen*), which Kang Youwei and others had envisaged after 1895, Liang promoted a reform of the spirit (*jingshen*) of every Chinese after 1898. In this sense, Liang translated a historical story into a personal narrative in order to transform the identity of every national.

VI. From Dynasty to State to Nation, Two Aspects of Talking about Weakness

In 1898, Kang Youwei and Liang Qichao were confident that the *Record of the Partition and Destruction of Poland* could move the emperor and thus promote reform. After the *coup d'état*, stories about the demise of Poland continued to proliferate, but their meaning had changed significantly. Several articles argued that the situation of China was just like that of Poland in the eighteenth century.[148] Signs for an upheaval seemed to been brewing, the people sought independence, and Poland seemed to revive, in contrast to India, which some observers believed to be irredeemably lost.[149] One newspaper article in 1901 pointed out that the country of Poland might have been destroyed, but the Polish people still resisted and formed a strong identity, which, among else, was strengthened by commemorating fallen heroes. But the Chinese, the article continues, would "live drunk and die dreaming" completely oblivious to their situation, and their national vigour could thus not be compared to that of the

---

148 *Shaoxing baihua bao* 紹興白話報, 1900, 105, p. 4; *Beijing xinwen huibao* 北京新聞匯報, 1901, 2nd month, pp. 2–6; *Jinghua bao* 京話報, 1903, 1, pp. 1–8; *Fubao* 复報, 1906, 1, pp. 42–44; Liang Qichao (1901b), "Mieguo xinfa lun", pp. 42–43.

149 *Cuixin bao* 萃新報, 1904, 5, p. 11; *Zhenguang yuebao* 真光月報, 1904, 7 (3), p. 19; *Fubao*, 1906, 1, pp. 42–44.

Poles.[150] In particular, the Polish intellectuals (*zhishi* 志士) engraved their Polish identity in their hearts and never forgot (*wang* 忘) it. They succeeded in grinding "one Poland" into the brains of the people.[151] Another article finally stressed that the Poles, in contrast to the Chinese, who were allegedly living in oblivion and behaved like slaves (*nuli benfen* 奴隸本分), would never forget (*wang*) the shame inflicted upon them by the foreign powers.[152] A few years after Kang Youwei had submitted his tract on Poland to the emperor, these discourses about Poland had changed, among other things, from a historical narrative about the fate of nations to commemorating and worshiping the vigour of individuals or national conscience of the people.[153] Nation replaced state, a refashioning of the people's hearts took the place of constitutional reform (*bianfa*), territorial concerns gave way to a concern about the individual national, at least on paper, and, I might add, upon the basis of the preceding discussions, the importance of memory and commemoration for historical discourses began to grow.

However, beneath this shift, weakness, its perception and articulation, was ubiquitous in the Chinese-speaking community in the early twentieth century. The same stories about the demise of other countries and the weakness of China still circulated widely, but their meaning changed after 1898. These bemoaned China's weakness, fully conscious that "China" was, in reality, strong because it was populous and rich in resource endowments.[154] Discourses about weakness were like a *basso continuo* underlying a cacophony of various opinions, and they fit smoothly into various architectures of thought. Despite this proliferation, no historical work has yet addressed this phenomenon systematically, and this essay has tried to fill a tiny bit of this lacuna by tackling some of the basic conceptual issues. None of this breaks new empirical ground, but, by asking what discourses of weakness were, when they appeared, and how they persisted and changed, something meaningful might be added to the field of late Qing history.

The short response to what such an answer could be is that discourses of weakness were a persistent and flexible feature characteristic of Chinese modernity. As such, discourses of weakness were, of course, shaped by, and help to shape, modernity. The discourses of Kang Youwei focus on the nation, project it far into the past, unfold its history along a one dimensional historical line, and place it into a concert of nations. Key features of it are thus typical of

---

150 *Shaoxing baihua bao* 紹興白話報, 1900, 119, p.6.
151 *Dongfang zazhi* 東方雜誌, 1904, 4, pp. 9–10.
152 *Fubao*, 1906, 1, pp. 42–44; *Dongfang zazhi*, 1904, 2, pp. 133–141.
153 This shift is largely confirmed by Zou Zhenhuan, "Wan Qing Bolan wangguoshi shuxie de yanbian xipu", p. 90.
154 Liang Qichao (1903), "Lun Zhongguo guoren zhi pinge", p. 5.

modernity in a more general sense, in particular the growing importance of the nation and the increasing dominance of linear time.[155] According to the term "discourse of weakness", as it is used here, it would probably only be this period and after, when it is sensible to postulate the existence of discourses of weakness in the Chinese-speaking world.

Having dealt with the place of discourses of weakness in Chinese history, now let me turn to their significance. In my view, it seems that their most important feature was their indeterminacy and flexibility. They did not imply a certain ideology or world view, and many lessons could be drawn from them. Clearly, such an indeterminacy made them flexible, since they could serve to justify many ideologically-opposed views. The section on Liang Qichao serves to highlight this. 1898 is commonly seen as a break in his intellectual biography, but this section shows, I hope, that he formulated his new prescriptions for the "sick man of Asia" against the background of a discourses of weakness which dates back to the immediate aftermath of the Sino-Japanese War. In sum, a sense of national fate, unending but stereotypical comparison, implicit or explicit heroism, and a nearly unconstrained ideological flexibility, all serve to shape the nature of the discourses of weakness in Chinese modernity. Their value might lie in making pertinent features of modern Chinese history a little bit more intelligible, such as the radicalisation of intellectuals, the high degree of intellectual inconsistency, the frequency of change in opinion, and, finally, the high emotionality typical of these debates. Most works on Chinese modernity in intellectual history focus on biographies, ideologies or systems of thought, but less so on common themes, which is a hindrance to grasping commonalities or shared assumptions. The recent work of Rudolf Wagner gives us a certain sense of what it means to focus on certain themes,[156] and examining discourses of weakness certainly explores this territory further. Its value for research, to repeat a phrase just used, may thus be to uncover a *basso continuo* among the cacophony of opinions in the last decade of the nineteenth century. This in turn may help to better understand the forces of cohesion and identification.

Bibliography

Bartlett, Beatrice (1991), *Monarchs and Ministers: The Great Council in Mid-Ch'ing China, 1723–1820*, Stanford CA: University of California Press.

---

155 Compare for instance some introductory remarks in Giddens (1990), *The Consequences of Modernity*, pp. 14–15, 17–21.

156 Fitzgerald (1996), *Awakening China*; Yü Ying-shih (1993), "The Radicalization of China in the Twentieth Century".

Beiping gugong bowuyuan wenxianguan 北平故宮博物院文獻館 (eds.) (1931–1934), *Wenziyudang* 文字獄檔 (Archives of the Literary Inquistion). Shanghai: Shanghai shudian chuban.

Callahan, William A. (2004), "National Insecurities: Humiliation, Salvation and Chinese Nationalism", *Alternatives*, 29:2, pp. 199–218.

– (2009), "The Cartography of National Humiliation and the Emergence of China's Geobody", *Public Culture*, 21:1, pp. 141–173.

Chang Hao (1987), *Chinese Intellectuals in Crisis: Search for Order and Meaning (1890–1911)*, Berkeley CA: University of California Press.

Chen Tianhua 陳天華 (1903a), "Jingshi Zhong" 警示鍾 (Clarion Gong to Warn the People), in: Zhi Zhi (ed.) (1994), *Chen Tianhua Zou Rong ji*, Shenyang: Liaoning renmin chubanshe, pp. 41–85.

– (1903b), "Menghui tou" 猛回頭 (Ferociously Looking Back), in: Zhi Zhi (ed.) (1994), *Chen Tianhua Zou Rong ji*, Shenyang: Liaoning renmin chubanshe, pp. 1–40.

Cohen, Paul A. (2002), "Remembering and Forgetting. National Humiliation in Twentieth Century China", *Twentieth Century China*, 27:2, pp. 1–39.

Eastman, Lloyd (1965), "Ch'ing-i and Chinese Policy Formation during the Nineteenth Century", *Journal of Asian Studies*, 24:4, pp. 595–611.

Edgerton-Tarpley, Kathryn (2008), *Tears from Iron: Cultural Responses to Famine in Nineteenth-Century China*, Berkeley CA: University of California Press.

Fang Delin 房德鄰 (2007a), "Kang Youwei yu gongche shangshu—du '"Gongche shangshu'kaozheng bu" xianyi er" 康有為與公車上書 – 讀 " '公車上書' 考證補" 獻疑二 (Kang Youwei and the Petition of the Examination Candidates—Reading "Further Remarks on Examining the 'Petition by the Examination Candidates'", Articulating Doubts two), *Jindaishi yanjiu*, 2007:2, pp. 111–131.

– (2007b), "Kang Youwei yu gongche shangshu—du '"Gongche shangshu' kaozheng bu" xianyi yi" 康有為與公車上書 – 讀 " '公車上書' 考證補" 獻疑一 (Kang Youwei and the Petition of the Examination Candidates—Reading "Further Remarks on Examining the 'Petition by the Examination Candidates'", Articulating Doubts one), *Jindaishi yanjiu*, 2007:1, pp. 116–132.

Felber, Roland (1997), "The Use of Analogy by Kang Youwei in His Writings on European History", *Oriens Extremus*, 40:1, pp. 64–77.

Fitzgerald, John (1996), *Awakening China: Politics, Culture, and Class in the Nationalist Revolution*, Stanford CA: Stanford University Press.

Giddens, Anthony (1990), *The Consequences of Modernity*, Cambridge: Polity Press.

Ginggun 景文 (1827), *Qinding taigui* 欽定台規 (Imperially Mandated Rules for the Censorate). National Library of China.

Guy, Kent (1987), *The Emperor's Four Treasuries: Scholars and the State in the late Ch'ien-lung Era*, Cambridge MA: Harvard University Press.

Han Seunghyun (2016), *After the Prosperous Age: State and Elites in Early Nineteenth Century Suzhou*, Harvard MA: Harvard University Press.

Hsiao Kung-chuan (1975), *A Modern China and a New World: K'ang Yu-wei, Reformer and Utopian*, Seattle WA: University of Washington Press.

Hu Sijing 胡思敬 (1913), Wuxu lüshuang lu 戊戌履霜錄 (A Record of Treading on Frozen Ground in 1898), in: Gu Tinglong (ed.) (1995–2002), *Xuxiu siku quanshu*, Shanghai: Guji chubanshe, vo. 446.

Huang Kewu 黃克武 (2003), "Liang Qichao yu Zhongguo xiandai shixue zhi zhuixun" 梁啟超與中國現代史學之追尋 (Pursuing Liang Qichao and Chinese Modern History), *Jindaishi yanjiu suo jikan*, 41, pp. 181–213.

Huang Zhangjian 黃彰健 (1970), *Wuxu bianfa shi yanjiu* 戊戌變法史研究 (A Research into the Reform of 1898). Nangang: Zhongyang yanjiu yuan lishi yuyan yan yanjiu suo.

Huters, Theodore (2005), *Bringing the World Back Home: Appropriating the West in Late Qing and Early Republican China*, Honolulu HI: University of Hawai'i Press.

Kang Youwei 康有為(1886), *Kangzi neiwai pian* 康子內外篇 (Inner and Outer Works of Kang Youwei), in: Jiang Yihua, Wu Genliang (eds.) (1987), *Kang Youwei quanji*, Shanghai: Shanghai guji chubanshe, vol. 1, pp. 95–112.

– (ca. 1888a), Biji 筆記 (Notes), in: Jiang Yihua, Wu Genliang (eds.) (1987), *Kang Youwei quanji*, Shanghai: Shanghai guji chubanshe, vol. 1, pp. 193–219.

– (1888b), "Lun shiwu" 論時務 (On Contemporary Duties), in Jiang Yihua, Wu Genliang (eds.) (1987), *Kang Youwei quanji*, Shanghai: Shanghai guji chubanshe, vol. 1, pp. 164–167.

– (1888c), "Shang Qingdi diyi shu" 上清帝第一書 (First Memorial to the Qing Emperor), in: Jiang Yihua, Wu Genliang (eds.) (1987), *Kang Youwei quanji*, Shanghai: Shanghai guji chubanshe, vol. 1, pp. 180–184.

– (1888d), *Shili gongfa quanshu* 實理公法全書 (A Complete Book on Practical Principles and Universal Law), in: Jiang Yihua, Wu Genliang (eds.) (1987), *Kang Youwei quanji*, Shanghai: Shanghai guji chubanshe, vol. 1, pp. 146–160.

– (1889a), "Menzai gaijing qing xing shizheng er da tianjie zhe" 門災告警請行實政而答天戒摺 (A Memorial on a Warning by a Disaster at the Palace Gates, to Request Pragmatic Policies and to Answer a Heavenly Warning), in: Jiang Yihua, Wu Genliang (eds.) (1987), *Kang Youwei quanji*, Shanghai: Shanghai guji chubanshe, vol. 1, pp. 227–229.

– (1889b) "Wei Zongshe yanzhong guoshi youwei qi ci miandui yi jie yucheng zhe" 為宗社嚴重國勢憂危乞賜面對以竭愚誠折 (A Memorial Requesting an Audience to Present my Sincerity because the Dynasty is at Risk and the National Condition is Alarming), in: Jiang Yihua, Wu Genliang (eds.) (1987), *Kang Youwei quanji*, Shanghai: Shanghai guji chubanshe, vol. 1, pp. 225–226.

– (1895a), "Jingshi qiangxuehui xu" 京師強學會序 (Preface to the Strengthening Society in the Capital), in: Jiang Yihua, Wu Genliang (eds.) (1987), *Kang Youwei quanji*, Shanghai: Shanghai guji chubanshe, vol. 2, p. 89.

– (1895b), "Shang Qingdi shu" 上清帝第二書 (SecondMemorial to the Qing Emperor), in: Jiang Yihua, Wu Genliang (eds.) (1987), *Kang Youwei quanji*, Shanghai: Shanghai guji chubanshe, vol. 2, pp. 32–45.

– (1895c), "Shang Qingdi disan shu" 上清帝第三書 (Third Memorial to the Qing Emperor), in: Jiang Yihua, Wu Genliang (eds.) (1987), *Kang Youwei quanji*, Shanghai: Shanghai guji chubanshe, vol. 2, pp. 68–80.

– (1895d), "Shang Qingdi disi shu" 上清帝第四書 (Fourth Memorial to the Qing Emperor), in: Jiang Yihua, Wu Genliang (eds.) (1987), *Kang Youwei quanji*, Shanghai: Shanghai guji chubanshe, vol. 2, pp. 81–88.

– (1895d), "Zhong Ri heyueshu hou" 中日和約書後 (Postface to the Peace Treaty of China and Japan), in: Jiang Yihua, Wu Genliang (eds.) (1987), *Kang Youwei quanji*, Shanghai: Shanghai guji chubanshe, vol. 2, p. 99.

- (1898a), *Bolan fenmie ji* 波蘭分滅記 (Record of the Partition and Destruction of Poland), in: Jiang Yihua, Wu Genliang (eds.) (1987), *Kang Youwei quanji*, Shanghai: Shanghai guji chubanshe, vol. 4, pp. 395–423.
- (1898b), "E Bide bianzheng ji" 俄彼得變政記 (Account of Russians Peter's Reforms), in: Jiang Yihua, Wu Genliang (eds.) (1987), *Kang Youwei quanji*, Shanghai: Shanghai guji chubanshe, vol. 4, pp. 33–41.
- (1898c), "Riben bianzheng kao" 日本變政考 (Examination of Japanese Reforms), in: Jiang Yihua, Wu Genliang (eds.) (1987), *Kang Youwei quanji*, Shanghai: Shanghai guji chubanshe, vol. 4, pp. 101–294.
- (1898d), "Shang Qingdi diwu shu" 上清帝第五書 (Fifth Memorial to the Qing Emperor), in: Jiang Yihua, Wu Genliang (eds.) (1987), *Kang Youwei quanji*, Shanghai: Shanghai guji chubanshe, vol. 4, pp. 2–7.
- (1902),"Yu tongxue zhuzi Liang Qichao deng lun Yindu wangguo youyu gesheng zili shu" 與同學諸子梁啟超等論印度亡國由於各省自立書 (A Letter Discussing with Classmates, Disciples and Liang Qichao about the Demise of India Brought about by each Province's Self-Governance), in: Jiang Yihua, Wu Genliang (eds.) (1987), *Kang Youwei quanji*, Shanghai: Shanghai guji chubanshe, vol. 6, pp. 334–349.

Kuhn, Philip A. (1995), "Ideas behind China's Modern State", *Harvard Journal of Asiatic Studies*, 55:2 (1995), pp. 295–337.
- (2002), *Origins of the Modern Chinese State*, Stanford CA: Stanford University Press.

Kwong, Luke S.K. (1984), *A Mosaic of the Hundred Days. Personalities, Politics, and Ideas of 1898*, Cambridge MA: Harvard University Press.
- (2000), "Chinese Politics at the Crossroads: Reflections on the Hundred Days Reform of 1898", *Modern Asian Studies*, 34:3, pp. 663–695.
- (2001), "The Rise of the Linear Perspective on History and Time in Late Qing China c. 1860–1911", *Past and Present*, 173, pp. 157–190.

Kwong, Luke S.K., Wong Young-tsu (1993), "Communications to the Editor", *The Journal of Asian Studies*, 52:2, pp. 401–412.

Lei Jiasheng 雷家聖 (2015), "Kang Youwei shi maiguozei ma? Zai lun Wuxu Bianfa de yuanyin" 康有為是賣國賊嗎？再論戊戌變法的原因 (Is Kang Youwei a Traitor Selling out the Country? A New Discussion of the Reasons for the 1898 Reforms), *Shijian boya xuebao* 25, pp. 1–18.

Levenson, Joseph R. (1968), *Confucian China and its Modern Fate: A Trilogy. Volume 3: The Problem of Historical Significance*, Berkeley CA: University of California Press.

Liang Qichao 梁启超 (1896), "Bolan miewang ji" 波蘭滅亡記 (Records of the Demise of Poland), *Shiwu bao*, 3, 2b–4a.
- (1898a), "Kang Guangren zhuan" 康廣仁傳 (Biography of Kang Guangren), *Qingyibao*, 6, pp. 325–26.
- (1898b), "Lin Xu zhuan" 林旭傳 (Biography of Lin Xu), *Qingyibao*, 8 (1898), pp. 455–457.
- (1898c), "Liu Guangdi zhuan" 劉光第傳 (Biography of Liu Guangdi), *Qingyibao*, 8, p. 458.
- (1898d), "Qingyibao xuli" 清議報敘例 (Preface and Rules for the Qingyibao), in: Lin Zhijun (ed.) (1936/1989), *Yinbingshi heji: Wenji*, vol. 3, pp. 29–30.
- (1898e), "Renxue xu" 仁學敘 (Preface to Renxue), in: Lin Zhijun (ed.) (1936/1989), *Yinbingshi heji: Wenji*, vol. 3, pp. 31–33.

- (1898f), *Wuxu zhengbian ji* 戊戌政變記 (Account of the 1898 Coup d'État), in Lin Zhijun (ed.) (1936/1989), *Yinbingshi heji: Zhuanji*, vol. 1.
- (1898g), "Yang Rui zhuan" 楊銳傳 (Biography of Yang Rui), *Qingyibao*, 7, pp. 393–94.
- (1898h), "Yang Shenxiu zhuan" 楊深秀傳 (Biography of Yang Shenxiu), *Qingyibao*, 7, pp. 389–392.
- (1899a), "Guomin shida yuanqi lun" 國民十大元氣論 (On the Ten Primordial Qi of the Chinese People), in: Lin Zhijun (ed.) (1936/1989), *Yinbingshi heji: Wenji* vol. 3, pp. 61–64.
- (1899b), "Lun jinshi guomin jingzheng zhi dashi ji Zhongguo qiantu" 論近世國民競爭之大勢及中國前途 (On the Progression of the Struggle among the National People in Modernity and China's Future), in: Lin Zhijun (ed.) (1936/1989), *Yinbingshi heji: Wenji*, vol. 4, pp. 56–59.
- (1899c), Ziyoushu 自由書 (A Book on Freedom), in: Lin Zhijun (ed.) (1936/1989), *Yinbingshi heji: Zhuanji*, vol. 1, pp. 1–123.
- (1900a), "Shaonian Zhongguo shuo" 少年中國說 (On the Young China), in: Lin Zhijun (ed.) (1936/1989), *Yinbingshi heji: Wenji*, vol. 5, pp. 7–12.
- (1900b), "Zhongguo jiruo suyuan lun" 中國積弱溯源論 (On Pursuing China's Accumulated Weakness), in: Lin Zhijun (ed.) (1936/1989), *Yinbingshi heji: Wenji*, vol. 5, pp. 12–42.
- (1901a), "Guodu shidai lun" 過度時代論 (On Transition Periods), in: Lin Zhijun (ed.) (1936/1989), *Yinbingshi heji: Wenji*, vol. 6, pp. 27–32.
- (1901b)"Mieguo xinfa lun" 滅國新法論 (On New Practices to Annihilate Countries), in: Lin Zhijun (ed.) (1936/1989), *Yinbingshi heji: Wenji*, vol. 6, pp. 32–46.
- (1901c), "Nanhai Kang xianshen zhuan" 南海康先生傳 (Biography of Mister Kang Nanhai), in: Lin Zhijun (ed.) (1936/1989), *Yinbingshi heji: Wenji*, vol. 6, pp. 57–89.
- (1901d), "Qingyibao yibai ce zhuci bing lun baoguan zhi zeren ji benguan zhi jingli" 清議報一百冊祝辭並論報館之責任及本館之經歷 (Laudatio for the Hundredth Volume of the Qingyibao and a Discussion of the Responsibilities of Newspaper Houses and this House's History), in: Lin Zhijun (ed.) (1936/1989), *Yinbingshi heji: Wenji*, vol. 6, pp. 47–56.
- (1903), "Lun Zhongguo guoren zhi pinge" 論中國國人之品格 (On the Character of the Chinese People), in: Lin Zhijun (ed.) (1936/1989), *Yinbingshi heji: Wenji*, vol. 14, pp. 1–5.
- (1904), "Yu zhi shengsiguan" 余之生死觀 (My Views on Life and Death), in: Lin Zhijun (ed.) (1936/1989), *Yinbingshi heji: Wenji*, vol. 17, pp. 1–12.

Lin Yingyu 林穎鈺 (2016), "Minqi keyong: cong geming guafen lunzhan kan wanQing de minqi lunshu" 民氣可用：從革命瓜分論戰看晚清的民氣論述 (The People's Qi can be Used: Looking at late Qing Writings on the People's Qi from the Debate on Revolution and Partition), *Chengda lishi xuebao*, 52, pp. 209–238.

Mann, Susan (1971), *Huang Liang-chi (1746–1809): The Perception and Articulation of Political Problems in late Eighteenth Century China*, Ph.D thesis Stanford University.

Mittag, Achim (2003), "Die Konstruktion der Neuzeit in China. Selbstvergewisserung und die Suche nach Anschluß an die moderne Staatengemeinschaft", *Historische Zeitschrift. Beihefte, Neue Serie*, 35, "Eigene und fremde Frühe Neuzeiten. Genese und Geltung eines Epochenbegriffes", pp. 139–164.

Mao Haijian 茅海建 (2005a), *Wuxu bianfa shishi kao* 戊戌變法史事考 (Examination of the Facts of the 1898 Reform). Beijing: Sanlian shudian.

— (2005b), "'Gongche shangshu' kaozheng bu er" 公車上書'考證補二 (Further Remarks on Examining the 'Petition by the Examination Candidates', two), *Jindaishi yanjiu*, 2005:4, pp. 85–147.

— (2005c), "'Gongche shangshu' kaozheng bu yi" 公車上書'考證補 一 (Further Remarks on Examining the 'Petition by the Examination Candidates', one), *Jindaishi yanjiu*, 2005:3, pp. 1–43.

Mokros, Emily (2012), "Reconstructing the Imperial Retreat: Politics, Communications, and the Yuanming Yuan under the Tongzhi Emperor, 1873–4", *Late Imperial China*, 33:2, pp. 76–118.

Mosca, Matthew W. (2011), "The Literati Rewriting of China in the Qianlong-Jiaqing Transition", *Late Imperial China*, 32:2, pp. 89–132.

Ōtani Toshio 大谷敏夫 (1991) "Shindai keisei shisō ni okeru ni dai chōryū – kakyo, gakkō seido, keisei bunhen to no kanren ni oite" 清末経世思想における二大潮流：科舉、学校制度、経世文編との関連において (Two Trends in Ordering the World Thought at the End of the Qing: Examinations, Schooling System, Collected Writings about Ordering the World and their Relations), *Tōyōshi kenkyū*, 50:2, pp. 199–230.

Paine, Sarah CM (2005), *The Sino-Japanese War of 1894–1895: Perceptions, Power, and Primacy*, Cambridge: Cambridge University Press,

Pusey, James Reeve (1983), *China and Charles Darwin*, Cambridge MA: Harvard University Press.

Pye, Lucian W. (1992), *The Spirit of Chinese Politics*, 2nd edition, Cambridge, MA: Harvard University Press.

Rankin, Mary Backus (1982), "'Public Opinion' and Political Power: Qingyi in Late Nineteenth Century China", *The Journal of Asian Studies*, 41:3, pp. 453–484.

Rhoads, Edward J.M. (2000), *Manchus and Han. Ethnic Relations and Political Power in Late Qing and Early Republican China, 1861–1928*, Seattle WA, London: University of Washington Press.

Rowe, William T. (2011), "Introduction: The Significance of the Qianlong-Jiaqing Transition in Qing History", *Late Imperial China*, 32:2, pp. 74–88.

— (2018), *Speaking of Profit. Bao Shichen and Reform in Nineteenth-Century China*, Cambridge MA: Harvard University Press.

Schiffrin, Harold Z. (1970), *Sun Yat-sen and the Origins of the Chinese Revolution*, Berkeley CA-Los Angeles CA-London: Berkeley University Press.

Schwartz, Benjamin (1964), *In Search for Wealth and Power. Yan Fu and the West*, Cambridge MA: Harvard University Press.

Song Jiaoren 宋教仁 (1905), "Wuhu Hunan yu Duan Fang" 嗚呼湖南與端方 (Alas! Hunan and Duan Fang), in: Chen Xulu (ed.), *Song Jiaoren ji*, Beijing: Zhonghua shuju, pp. 10–11.

Tang Caichang 唐才常 (1899), "Da ke wen Zhina jinshi" 答客問支那近事 (Answering Question about China's Recent Situation Asked by a Guest) Hunansheng zhexue shehui kexue yanjiusuo (eds.) (1980), *Tang Caichang ji* 唐才常集, 185–192.

Tang Xiaobing (1996), *Global Space and the Nationalist Discourse. The Historical Thinking of Liang Qichao*, Stanford CA: Stanford University Press.

Topic group for social sciences of the journal Qiushi 求是雜誌社課題組 (2015), "Mingji weida lishi, zhangxian xueshu huayu – jinian Zhongguo renmin kang Ri zhanzheng ji shijie fan Faxisi zhanzheng shengli qishi zhounian lilun yanjiu chengguo zongshu" 銘記偉大歷史，彰顯學術話語 – 紀念中國人民抗日戰爭暨世界反法西斯戰爭勝利七十週年理論研究成果綜述 (Engrave [Our] Great History in [Our] Minds, Remarks Displaying Scholarship – A Summary of Theories and Research Results on the 70th Year Commemorating the War Against Japan Fought by the Chinese People and the Victory in the Global Anti-Fascist War), *Qiushi*, 12, pp. 4–32.

Schwartz, Benjamin (1964), *In Search of Wealth and Power. Yan Fu and the West*, Cambridge MA: Harvard University Press.

Wagner, Rudolf (2011), "China 'Asleep' and 'Awakening.' A Study in Conceptualizing Asymmetry and Coping with it", *Transcultural Studies*, 2011:1, pp. 4–139.

– (2017), "'Dividing up the [Chinese] Melon, *guafen* 瓜分': The Fate of a Transcultural Metaphor in the Formation of National Myth", *Transcultural Studies*, 2017:1, pp. 9–122.

Wang Ermin 王爾敏, "'Xiandaihua' de shidai yiyi ji qi jingshen jichu" 現代化的時代意義及其精神基礎 (The Contemporary Meaning of Modernity and its Spiritual Basis), in: Idem (ed.), *Wan Qing zhengzhi sixiang shilun*, Taibei: Huashi chubanshe, pp. 277–282.

Wang Wensheng (2014), *White Lotus Rebels and South China Pirates: Crisis and Reform in the Qing Empire*, Cambridge MA: Harvard University Press

Wang Zheng (2008), "National Humiliation, History Education, and the Politics of Historical Memory: Patriotic Education Campaign in China", *International Studies Quarterly*, 52, pp. 783–806.

Will, Pierre-Étienne (1997), "The 1744 Annual Audits of Magistrate Activity and their Fate", *Late Imperial China*, 18:2, pp. 1–50.

Wong Young-Tsu (1992), "Revisionism Reconsidered: Kang Youwei and the Reform Movement of 1898", *The Journal of Asian Studies*, 51:3, pp. 513–544.

Xie Jiafu 謝家福 (late 19th century), "Qi dong riji" 齊東日記 (Shandong Diary), in Suzhou bowuguan (ed.) (2013), *Xie Jiafu riji*. Beijing: Wenwu chubanshe.

Yan Fu 嚴復 (1895), "Yuan qiang" 原強 (Unearthing the Origin of Strength), in Hu Weixi 胡偉希 (ed.), *Yan Fu ji* 嚴復集 (Liaoning: Liaoning renmin chubanshe, 1994), 7–20.

Yang Nianqun 楊念群 (2010), Hechu shi 'Jiangnan': Qingchao zhengtongguan de queli yu shilin jingshen shijie de bianyi 何處是' 江南' ：清朝正統觀的確立與士林精神世界的變異 (Where is 'Jiangnan': The Establishment of the Qing Dynasty Orthodoxy and Changes of the Spiritual World of Scholars). Beijing: Sanlian Chubanshe.

Yang Ruisong 楊瑞宋 (2010), *Bingfu, Huanghuo yu Shuishi: 'Xifang' shiye de Zhongguo xingxiang yu jindai Zhongguo minzu lunshu xiangxiang* 病夫，黃禍與睡獅：' 西方' 視野的中國形象近代中國民族論述想像 (Sick Man, Yellow Peril, and Sleeping Lion: The Shape of China in a 'Western' Field of Vision and Imagining the Modern Chinese Nation in Writing). Taibei: Zhengda chubanshe.

Yao Nai 姚鼐 (1798), "Hanlin lun" 翰林論 (On the Hanlin), in: Idem (1798). *Xibaoxuan wenji*, in: Gu Tinglong (ed.) (1995–2002), *Xuxiu siku quanshu*, Shanghai: Guji chubanshe, vol. 1453.

Yü Ying-shih (1993), "The Radicalization of China in the Twentieth Century", *Daedalus*, 122:2, pp. 125–150.

Zhang Pengyuan 張朋園 (1964), *Liang Qichao yu Qingji geming* 梁啟超與清季革命 (Liang Qichao and the Revolution in the Qing), Taibei: Zhongyang yanjiuyuan jindaishi yanjiusuo.

Zhang Zhidong (1898), *Quanxue pian* 勸學篇 (An Exhortation to Learning).

Zarrow, Peter (2012), *After Empire: The Conceptual Transformation of the Chinese State, 1885–1924*, Stanford CA: Stanford University Press.

Zarrow, Peter, and Rebecca Karl (2002), "Introduction", in: Peter Zarrow and Rebecca Karl (eds.), *Rethinking the 1898 Reform Period. Political and Cultural Change in Late Qing China*, Cambridge MA: Harvard University Press, pp. 1–16.

Zou Rong 鄒容 (1903), Gemingjun 革命軍 (A Revolutionary Army), in: Zhi Zhi (ed.) (1994), *Chen Tianhua Zou Rong ji*, Shenyang: Liaoning renmin chubanshe, pp. 179–220.

Zou Zhenhuan 鄒振環 (2016), "Wan Qing Bolan wangguoshi shuxie de yanbian xipu" 晚清波蘭亡國史書寫的演變系譜 (Pedigree about the Change of late Qing Historical Writing about Poland's Demise), *Nanjing zhengzhi xueyuan xuebao*, 32 (4), pp. 81–91.

Records from a Defeated Country: Different Chinese Narratives about the First Sino-Japanese War (1894/95) and their Spreading during the Last Period of the Qing Dynasty

Sun Qing

The First Sino-Japanese War (1 August 1894–17 April 1895) exerted a profound influence on China. The result of this war not only transformed the domestic and the international political environment, it also had a series of interrelated effects on the intellectual situation in China. When the hostilities came to an end, different people gradually developed a different understanding of the war. At least three development tendencies are worth noticing here. First of all, the result of the Sino-Japanese War made it clear that the self-strengthening movement, which had, for thirty years, tried to make the country rich and strong, had failed disastrously. Secondly, it provided proof for those arguments for institutional reform, which, at the time, gained in importance both at central and at provincial level. The most important ideological consequence, finally, was that, because of the defeat, both the Chinese élites and public opinion, including the gentry, began to accept the assumption of modern cultural determinism, namely, the theory that the political order needed to be based upon the universal values of the Christian world.

Such opinions about the war and its outcome became so influential later that they affected Chinese perceptions of their own history as well as their understanding of their self-identity. These perspectives are closely related to the narratives of the war, which emerged during the two or three years directly following the war, and their specific forms of compilation and expression. It is therefore necessary to re-examine these narratives of the history of the war, discuss their modes of expression and look at the links between them. We need to understand the similarities and differences of their viewpoints regarding this disastrous defeat, and we also need to investigate the processes of how these viewpoints were established, and how they spread as well. Only when we are able to re-construct how the determinism of modern culture and the related "universal order" as a specific historical construct were related to each other during the last phase of Imperial China will we be able to understand this war in a more specific way as well as its far-reaching impact on modern Chinese history and Chinese historical understanding in general.[1]

It is easy to find differences in some basic judgements about the Chinese defeat in the war as narrated in the Chinese language in the years directly following the war. For example, was the defeat inevitable or avoidable? Was it, in other words, a symptom of an "epochal change" (世變), as it was called at the time, or only the result of an "accidental misfortune" (*qibian* 奇變)? By whom was China defeated? By Japanese pirates from the Eastern neighbourhood commonly called Wokou (倭寇) or by a Westernised Meiji Japan? To what should the defeat be compared? To the defeat suffered by the Wu kingdom in the famous war with the Yue kingdom during the Spring and Autumn period, or rather to France during the Franco-Prussian war of modern Europe? Which format should be used for compiling a history of the war? Should the form of a collection of documents with comments and appendices be used or should the tidy traditional historical genre of a chronicle of events (*jishi benmo* 紀事本末) with its clear-cut cause and effect relations be employed, instead? Generally speaking, it is possible to divide these different opinions into two relative.y clear-cut sources and genealogies.

Moreover, these narratives of the war manifested different forms when they came into circulation; they were, for example, serialised in newspapers and journals, they were published as monographs, subsequently put together as bound volumes and, later on, included in *collectanea*, some of which were even transformed into historical novels in colloquial speech or into illustrated books. Between these different forms, different prefaces were added, as well as appendices, which formed different kinds of symbiosis with the original text. When transformed into historical novels in colloquial speech and illustrated books, the

---

1 There has been some former research on the war narratives which became popular after the war. With regard to source material, A Ying's (1958) *Jiawu Zhong-Ri zhanzheng wenxueji* is the most concentrated. The seven volume collection on the Sino-Japanese War of 1894/95, which was compiled by the Chinese historical association and Shao Dunheng and published in 1956 also quoted some parts of the war-literature which had appeared directly after the war. Sporadic research basically remained at the stage of bibliographic description or introductions to the background of the translations and introductions to single works, and analysis of contents is often limited to the angle of literary history. Since research into the matter has more or less unfolded in the form of revolutionary history or modernisation history, the immediate sources which formed the fundamental ideas of people directly after the war have not been subjected to systematic specialised research. With regard to the question with which this article is concerned, the following works provide a useful basis, but leave enough room for entering deeper into the discussion. Cf. Wang Lin (2009), "'Zhongdong zhanji benmo' yu jiawu zhongri zhangzheng", Zhao Shaofeng (2009), "'Lüelun 'Zhongdong zhanji benmo'", Sun Wan (2013), "Lin Lezhi yu 'Zhongdong zhanji benmo'", Shu Xilong (2006), "Yao Xiguang yu 'Dongfang bingshi jilüe', Zhai Wendong (2007), "Qingmo minchu wenxue zuopin zhong de jiawu zhanzheng – yi lishi xiaoshuo wei zhongxin", and Zhu Hongjuan (2013), "Wan Qing guonan xiaoshuo yanjiu".

RECORDS FROM A DEFEATED COUNTRY

boundaries of loyalty and the differences between good and evil were strengthened, the main characters were portrayed in a clearer way, the angle of the narrative was changed from the newspaper commentator or eyewitness account into that of the omniscient storyteller, *etc.* All these phenomena are worth discussing in greater detail.

I. War Documents Compilations (*zhanji* 戰輯) and War Chronicles (*zhanji* 戰紀)

The first records about the Sino-Japanese war were produced while the war was still continuing. At the time, newspapers from China, England, Japan and many other countries had correspondents who observed the war in a number of ways and continuously published reports. These included the *Wanguo gongbao* 萬國公報 (A Review of the Times), published by the Guangxuehui 廣學會 (The Society for the Diffusion of Christian and General Knowledge among the Chinese), which was the Chinese newspaper which covered the war in the most comprehensive way. Not only did it have reporters but it also paid attention to the collection of important war-related documents, such as imperial edicts, memorials to the throne, and signed treaties, as soon as the war was over. It also published related reports from other Western newspapers and continuously published commentaries which were entitled "Public Opinion" (*gonglun* 公論). It was during this time that the newspaper's view on the war began to exert influence. There were also some war veterans and important battlefield officers such as Nie Shicheng 聶士誠 (1836–1900), the author of *The Eastern Expedition Diary* (*Dongzheng riji* 東征日記), and Li Yuanhong 黎元洪 (1864–1928), who was on duty as the third captain of naval vessel Guangjia 廣甲 during the war, both of whom left battle-field diaries in which they related their opinions and feelings about the war.

In 1895, as soon as Treaty of Shimonoseki (Maguan tiaoyue 馬關條約) which concluded the war had been signed, a man from Dongguan in the Guangdong province named Wang Bingyao 王炳耀 compiled a collection of war documents, which was arranged in chronological order, which he entitled *War Documents of the Sino-Japanese War* (*Zhong Ri zhanji* 中日戰輯), which also provided a narrative based upon cause and effect, and was published by the Wenyu tang 文裕堂 publishing house in Hong Kong.[2] The book was divided

---

2 As the preface of the books itself notes, 90 per cent of this book consists of excerpts from *Wanguo gongbao*, *Huazi ribao* 華字日報 (The Chinese Mail), and *Gongbao* 公報 while the remaining 10 per cent comes from other newspapers. Cf. Wang Bingyao (1895) *Zhong Ri zhanji* (War documents of the Sino-Japanese War), Hong Kong: Wenyu tang 1895. While the cover

into six volumes, the first one covering the background of the war, Volume Two discussed the beginning of the war, Volume Three assigned responsibility, Volume Four was on the battle of Mukden, Volume Five on dispatching envoys in order to discuss peace, while, in Volume Six, the peace negotiations by Li Hongzhang 李鴻章 (1823–1901), the resistance and independence of Taiwan, the Japanese attack of Tainan, the retreat of Commander in Chief Liu, and the return of Liaodong, *etc.*, were covered. This book collected the edicts, memorials, telegraphic communication, newspaper commentaries and articles, which had been published by *Wanguo gongbao*. They included a number of Chinese memorials, which—because direct access was lacking—were translated from Western newspapers, and, because of this, did not have their original appearance.[3]

During the same year, several other collections about the war were published. All of these collections were almost exclusively compiled from Imperial edicts, memorials to the throne, or consulted reports from high-ranking officials' diplomatic correspondence from the peace negotiations in Shimonoseki, questions and answers to newspapers, as well as literary works produced after the war. In general, a traditional pattern of compilation was applied, following the sequence of events or looking into the causal clues regarding the battles. In the same year, a number of other eye-witness accounts of the war were produced and published, such as *Narrative of the Injustice on the Sea* (*Yuanhai shuwen* 冤海述聞), *Diary of the Campaigns in the East* (*Dongzheng riji* 東征日記) and others, which described the course of specific battles, clarified details and precisely named responsible persons. In 1895, Chen Yaoqing 陳耀卿 also published his *Initial Collection of a New Compilation of Current Affairs* (*Shishi xinbian chunji* 时事新編初集), which constituted a collection of documents and related writings about the war. The book was classified in the following way: "The Situation of the Various Countries" (*geguo xingshi* 各國形勢), "Politics and Armament" (*zhengzhi wubei* 政治武備), "Diplomacy and Foreign Affairs" (*jiaoshe* 交涉), "Customs and Mores" (*fengsu* 風俗), "The Rise and Decline [of States]" (*xingshuai* 興衰), "Manufacturing" (*zhizao* 製造), and "Commerce" (*shangwu* 商務). This means that these newly created categories were to be considered as part of the *shiwu* 時務 ("practical administrative affairs") which were integrated into the canon of so-called "current practical affairs". There were also accounts by war participants. such as the *Battleground Notes Collection* (*Dunmo shiyu* 盾墨拾余) by Yi Shunding 易順鼎 (1858–1920), who had been a member of the private staff of Liu Kunyi 劉坤一 (1830–1902) general governor of the Liangjiang provinces during the time of the war. This work, which comprises 14 volumes,

---

of the book notes that it contained maps, in fact no copy including maps has been retrieved to date.

3 Cf. Wang Bingyao (1895), *Zhong Rii zhanji*, p. 12.

contains two volumes of memorials to the throne, policy advice, document drafts, and telegraphic communication. Two volumes entitled "Hunbei hundong zaji" 魂北魂東雜記 and "Hunnan ji" 魂南記 describe the different battles as well as the assistance given to Liu Yongfu 劉永福 (1837–1917) on the island of Taiwan in order to resist the Japanese forces. In 1896, Young John Allen (Lin Lezhi 林樂知 1836–1907), the chief editor of the *Wanguo gongbao* 萬國公報 and his Chinese co-operator and translator Cai Erkang 蔡爾康 (1852–1920) published the *The Whole Course the War between China and Japan* (*Zhongdong zhanji benmo* 中東戰紀本末), which will be discussed in more detail below. In addition, the *Yishu gonghuibao* 譯書公會報 (*The Translation Society Weekly Edition*) also published a war history by a Russian author, which was translated by Hu Junmo 胡濬謨 under the title *Chronicle of the War between China and Japan* (*Zhong Ri goubingji* 中日構兵記). Apparently, a monograph version in three volumes had been ready for publication but eventually did not appear. The East Asia Publishing Company (*Dongya shuju* 東亞書局) had also translated the Japanese *War between the Qing-Empire and Japan* (*Qingri Zhanzheng* 清日戰爭) and the *Diary of the Naval War between China and Japan* (*Riji Zhong Ri haizhanji* 日記中日海戰記), but they were not published.[4] In addition, there was an illustrated handbook entitled *First Collection of the Illustrated Essentials of the Mopping up of the Japanese Bandits* (*Huitu saodang wokou jiyao chuji* 繪圖掃蕩倭寇紀要初集) by Chen Yaoqing 陳耀卿. In 1897, Yao Xiguang 姚錫光 (1857–1921) compiled a new war history, which he entitled a *Brief Record of the Military Events in the East* (*Dongfang bingshi jilüe* 東方兵事紀略), which was published in Wuchang, Hubei province. Yao's book employed a traditional historical narrative and did not constitute a collection of documents. The narrative was not limited to certain battles, either. This was the reason why it had a far-reaching influence on the war histories of the Sino-Japanese war that were published later, such as the book entitled a *Complete Account of the Military Events between China and Japan* (*Zhongri Bingshi Benmo* 中日兵事本末) by Luo Dunrong 羅惇曧 (1872–1924), which was serialised in the Magazine *Yongyan* 庸言 in 1913 as historical source material (*shiliao* 史料) and then compiled into the *Sources of Chinese History during the Recent Hundred Years Zhongguo jinbainianshi ziliao* 中國近百年史資料, which were selected by Zuo Shunsheng 左舜生 (1893–1969) and published by Zhonghua book company （*Zhonghua shuju* 中華書局） in 1926. It was also compiled into the *Sino-Japanese War* (*Zhongri zhanzheng* 中日戰爭) in 1930 by Wang Zhonglin 王鐘麟 (1884–1966). Moreover, it formed the basis of the relevant chapters of *China and Japan during the Last Sixty Years* (*Liushinianlai Zhongguo yu Riben* 六十年來中國與日本) by Wang Yunsheng 王芸生 (1901–1980). The chapters related to the First Sino-Japanese war of the popular works on Chinese

---

4 Xu Weize, Gu Xieguang (1902), *Zhengban Dong Xi xueshu lu.*

modern history included in the narratives of Fan Wenlan 範文瀾 (1893–1969), Guo Moruo 郭沫若 (1892–1978) and Jian Bozan 翦伯贊 (1898–1968) were simply copied from Yao's book as whole chapters.

The collections of war documents mentioned above had appeared very early, when the war still was going on or had just been concluded. They were extracts from collections or were based upon the personal experiences of persons involved. The basic impression that people later had about the war, all had their origins in this limited number of works.[5]

2. Creation

A careful examination reveals that the narratives of the Sino-Japanese war which appeared after 1894/95 were based upon two kinds of sources of information: one was Chinese and Western newspapers, especially *Wanguo gongbao*, which published reports and commentaries, as well as edicts, memorials, letters, diplomatic communication, treaty texts, *etc.* These even include documents which had been translated from Western reports into Western languages and were then re-translated into Chinese. The other channel was that of transcripts or oral records by war veterans. There were mutual influences between these war narratives, but they all had their own sources and genealogies. However, in respect of concrete questions such as the "reasons for the defeat", "solutions for national survival", *etc.*, they had different points of view.

The *Document Collection of the Sino-Japanese War* (*Zhong Ri zhanji*) by Wang Bingyao, which was published in 1895, and the *Complete Records on Offence and Defence during China's War with the Dwarfs* (Zhongwo zhanzhou shimoji 中倭戰守始末記) explicitly stated that they were based upon *Wanguo gongbao* and other Chinese and foreign newspaper reports. Actually, the "Society for the Diffusion of Christian and General Knowledge Among the Chinese"(*Guangxuehui* 廣學會) was not happy about the fact that other people publicly pirated its material in order to compile their own monographs. It claimed:

---

5 There was also a manuscript compiled by Wen Tingshi 文廷式 (1856–1904) of 1896 entitled *Wen chen ou ji* 聞塵偶記 (Jottings of Hearing Dust), which contained political anecdotes related to the war. This manuscript, however, was not published during the late Qing period. Because of the chaos brought about by the war, it only was published in serialized form in the *Qinghe* journal in 1933. In 1955, Ye Gongzhuo 葉恭綽 (1881–1968) was entrusted by the heirs of Mr. Wen to hand the manuscript over to the Institute for Modern History, by which it was published in *Sources of Modern Chinese History* (*Jindaishi ziliao*) in 1981, and it was only in this way that it became known to the world. For this reason, it was not taken into consideration in preparing for this article.

[they] extracted and pirated thirteen parts of our 'Records of a Dynasty in Chaos' and from several of our commentaries.... but not more than thirty to forty per cent, and they absolutely did not understand the implications [of our reporting].

For this reason, Young J. Allen and Cai Erkang "made a painstaking effort of twenty full months" in order to compile their own *Zhongdong zhanji benmo* and to offer "help to bring forward China's revitalisation" (qu wei zhenxing Zhongguo zhi yi zhu 取為振興中國之一助).[6]

The reason why the Society for the Diffusion of Christian and General Knowledge Among the Chinese could say that the *Zhongri zhanji* and the *Zhongwou zhanshou shimo ji* were not in accordance with its own intentions was actually due to the fact that the above-mentioned two works were compiled according to the natural progress of the war events, so that they could not reflect the "public opinion", which the *Wanguo gongbao* had always wanted to reveal and which transcended the state-based narrative, namely, a universal order based upon the idea of civilisation. But how could such a universal order be reflected in a monograph through a suitable arrangement?

In April 1896, *Zhongdong zhanji benmo* was published. Young J. Allen and Cai Erkang had compiled it from war reports and official files such as imperial edicts, memorials to the throne, the lateral communication of ranking officials, official letters and their own commentaries, along with translated digests from other newspapers into what were, originally, eight chapters. It included a detailed exposition of all the major campaigns of the war, such as the battle of Pyongyang, the battles in the Yellow Sea, as well as the Liaodong battles. This book was in very high demand. In February 1897, a sequel of four chapters was published, and, in 1900, a second sequel was released, consisting of another four chapters. At the same time, the compilation also contained Young J. Allen's personal comments on the Chinese people, China's civilisation and his proposals for reform (as *Zhi'an xin ce* 治安新策, in eight chapters). This sort of compilation form already clearly displays a Western universalist "civilisation"-order. Having consulted the whole book, readers could get the following feeling: although the defeat in the war was due the fact that officers and men did not obey orders and also due to corruption and timidness of officers and men, the basic reason, however, was China's backwardness and degeneration, as well as the conservatism of her system. The way to resolve these problems was to learn from Japan and to strive for a Western-style enlightened civilisation. Thus, *Zhongdong zhanji benmo* explained the defeat in the war by a fatalist determinism.

---

6 "Guangxuehui xin zhu 'Zongdong zhanji benmo' bu ri chushu tuo Shenbaoguan daishou fanke biyan" 廣學會新著《中東戰紀本末》不日出書托申報館代售翻刻必究 (The newly written *The Whole Course the War between China and Japan* will be published shortly, the Shenbao publishing house has been entrusted with the circulation, pirating will be prosecuted), *Shenbao*, 3 April 1896.

This point could be easily accepted by Li Hongzhang and others, who had direct responsibility in the war. For this reason, the reaction to it was very positive, and even the Guangxu-Emperor was provided with a copy by Sun Jianai 孙家鼐 (1827–1909) and it thus reached the Emperor's eyes and obtained his recognition.[7] Against the backdrop of the growing popularity of Western learning during the late Qing period and the reform of the examination system, it was included in the various catalogues of "New Learning" and included in a number of *collectanea*. In this way, it became one of the most popular histories of the First Sino-Japanese War during the late Qing period.

However, there were also people who were not happy at all with the explanations provided in the style of the Society for the Diffusion of Christian and General Knowledge Among the Chinese.

The secretary of the Grand Secretariat, Yao Xiguang, had originally been a member of Li Hongzhang's private staff. He had been recommended by Li to He Ruzhang 何如璋 (1838–1891), the Chinese envoy to Japan, and had served in Japan as consul. In 1895, he was transferred to the private staff of the Shandong governor, Li Bingheng. In 1896, he received an appointment from Zhang Zhidong 張之洞 (1833–1909), governor-general of Hu-Guang, to serve as the general manager of the Self-Strengthening academy. In 1897, he was appointed as the general manager of the Hubei military academy (*Hubei wubei xuedang* 湖北 武備學堂). When he served in Shandong, he had personally witnessed the war events and felt personally affected by the war and by the peace treaty. When he was working at the Self-Strengthening academy, he frequently consulted his own records, which he had compiled when serving in the military in order to reflect on the war:

I checked several drafts which I compiled when I was stationed in the barracks at the mouth of the River during the winter of 1894 and in the headquarters of the governor in Laizhou during the spring of 1895. In being exposed to these vestiges of the past, I became deeply moved. And it is like this, that everywhere one encounters the difficulties of a nation, and this is not just the wandering around without a fixed abode, which is almost unbearable to recall.[8]

Yao also frequently discussed with other high-ranking military officers who had taken part in the war and also paid attention to the reports published in newspapers. Li Yuanhong, who had survived the battle field by luck, gave Yao his wartime notes, entitled *A Brief Account Regarding the Events of Naval Wwarfare between China and Japan between 1884 (1894) and 1895 Jiashen (wu), yiwei jin Zhong ri haizhan shilüe* 甲申（午）、乙未間中日海戰事略. From the records of Yao's diary, we know that, between March and October 1896, he had eleven inter-

---

7 *Guangxuehui di shi ci nianbao, Guangxuehui di shiyi ci nianbao.*

8 Yao Xiguang (2010), *Jiang E riji*, p. 75.

views with war witnesses. He clearly did this because he was making preparations for writing his own history of the war. The direct stimulation for Yao's writing of a history of the war was that he had read his friend, Ye Han's 葉瀚 (1861–1936), copy of the *Zhongdong zhanji benmo* on 22 May 1896. He felt angry and "profoundly depressed and discontented". Yao was of the opinion that this book was nothing more than:

miscellaneous records which were bound together to form a book. It, by no means, incorporates the form of a *benmo* history; it is just like a house full of scattered pieces of coins loosened from their cash strings; by no means is it focussed. Moreover, it is called 'war-records' but only has a very limited amount of information on the actual situation of the war. Every article is full with dots for highlighting; it looks like an examination essay, or as if somebody has punctuated a novel. Its writing is in the style of newspapers, it is absolutely inacceptable!

Yao not only considered the style as heterogenous, it als was the Western style of employing comments by onlookers like in a newspaper, which was very hard for him to swallow.

Yao Xiguang's castigating of *Zhongdong zhanji benmo* was actually quite similar to the criticism of *Zhongri zhanji* and *Zhongwo zhanshou shimi ji* by the Society of the Diffusion of Christian and General Knowledge Among the Chinese. They all mainly concentrated on layout and style, that is to say, on the aspect of the outer form.

If one traces the origins of this dispute, the crux of the matter was whether the format of a collection of historical material with commentaries and notes as well as appendices should be employed, or rather the traditional historical genre as a chronicle of events based upon the actual temporal sequence, taking the cause and effect relationships into account. Yao was clearly of the opinion that the *benmo* form should be employed in order to make manifest clearly those who were responsible for the Chinese-Japanese enmity. By means of recounting the course of events of the war, those responsible for the defeat in the war should be clearly named as well as the concrete reasons for the defeat. For the Society of the Diffusion of Christian and General Knowledge Among the Chinese, however, since it firmly believed that the basic reason for the defeat was the civilisational "backwardness" of the country, the question of direct guilt and personal responsibility for the defeat was of no great importance. Its main focus was the diagnosis of civilisational backwardness and the indication of a road to a solution.

Although Yao Xiguang was not satisfied with the system of the compilation of the war history by the Society for the Diffusion of Christian and General Knowledge Among the Chinese, he still asked Ye Han to help him to obtain a copy, which he used as reference. Because the source material for *Zhongdong zhanji* was the *Wanguo gongbao* Yao borrowed three months of issues of the paper from Ye Han and Yao Wenfu 姚文甫 in order to look into it in some detail. For him, the result was that "if one examines its comments and sees how it ridicules China to the extreme, even going so far as not to consider China as a country, this will leave people resentful and hopeless".

Thus, on 5 August 1896, Yao Xiguang noted the following into his diary:

I decided to write a *Brief Chronological History of the War between China and Japan* (*Zhong Dong bingshi jilüe*). I decided to divide it into eight chapters: 1. "Reasons for the Military Affairs in the East"; 2. "Brief Account of the Military Affairs Because of Giving Support in the East", this chapter describes our troops' military events in Korea; 3. "Brief Account of the Military Affairs in Liaodong", which describes the military affairs regarding our navy, 4. "A Brief Account of the Negotiations in the East", which describes the things done by our officials after they had arrived in Japan", 5. "Military Affairs on Taiwan, Part One", which describes the defence of Taiwan, the fall of Taiwan and other things; and 6. "Military Affairs on Taiwan, Part Two", which describes the defence and war about Taizhong and Tainan and other things. Comments and maps will be attached to all chapters.[9]

On the same day Yao completed 60 per cent of the chapter "The Military Affairs on Taiwan, Part One". This was different from Young J. Allen's account with its civilisatory determinism.

Yao did not think that the war constituted an "important item of China's luck", but that it constituted an "accidental misfortune" with "consequences on the situation in Europe and the whole of Asia".

If one combs through Yao's 1896 diary, one can discover that this war history mainly made use of three kinds of sources: one is his own official and private records, which he wrote when he was working in the headquarters. Second is the diaries, written notes as well as oral recollections of the participants of the war, which had been given to him. His third source was the *Zhongdong zhanji benmo* compiled by Allen and Cai Erkang and, as the author claims, *An Illustrated Investigation into the Traces of the Sino-Japanese War* (*Zhongri zhanji tukao* 中日戰跡圖 考), which had been lithographically printed in Shanghai.[10]

In his diary, Yao Xiguang relates that he, together with a student of the self-strengthening academy, Wang Songchen 王松臣, "translated" *Zhongdong zhanji* every evening and only returned home at the second hour. This was a regular schedule showing up 26 times between 5 August when he started to write his war history until October of the same year, when the diary stops. It is unclear, however, for what reason Yao employed the word "translate" (*yi* 譯); one possible reason is that many memorials included in the *Zhanji* were re-translated from English newspapers and that they were looking for the original material. If

---

9 Ibid., p. 139.
10 This most likely actually referred to Wang Bingyao (1896), *Zhong Ri zhanji tukao*.

they really consulted a Western *Account of the Sino-Japanese War*, it remains unclear which book this might have been.

If one examines the war-history and collections of war-related material that appeared in the years directly following the war, it is possible to trace them back to two different sources.

One strand of sources reaches from the *Wanguo gongbao* to the *Zhongri zhanji* by Wang Bingyao, the *Zhongwo zhanshou shimoji* by Si Huifusheng and the *Zhongdong zhanji benmo* by Young J. Allen and Cai Erkang. These mainly include collected reports and commentaries from newspapers. In respect of the war defeat, they employ the "civilisatory" perspective, which holds that China was not defeated by a smaller Eastern neighbour, but rather by a Japan, which, after the Meiji-reforms, had become more civilised. The solution of the problems was thus reform which aimed at the standards provided by Western civilisation. The model to be followed was Japan, the very enemy of the war just fought. Other lessons could be learned from history, such as from the war between the kingdoms of Wu and Yue during the Spring-and Autumn period, as well as the more recent Franco-Prussian war in Europe.

The other strand is related to Yao Xiguang's *Dongzhong bingshi jilüe*. As already mentioned, this, later on, became the most important framework and material source for a considerable number of works. They are all of the opinion that the main responsibility for the defeat in the war rests with Li Hongzhang, Sun Yuwen 孫毓汶 (1833–1899), and other crucial high officials, who feared a war and thus quickly lost control of the situation. For this reason, it was a singular "accidental misfortune" (*qibian* 奇變), the war constituted a war between two nation states, and the party responsible for the unjustified hostilities had been Japan. Their main goals of transformation were to illustrate the humiliation brought about by the defeat and to carry out reforms in respect of strengthening the military, and promoting education and other measures on the technical level. They by no means focused on a complete transformation of the political and cultural system. It is also worth keeping in mind that Zhang Luocheng 張羅澄, one of the most important authors of the *Collection of Loyalty and Anger* (*Putian zhongfen ji* 普天忠憤集) by Kong Guangde (孔廣德), was also—like Yao Xiguang—a member of Zhang Zhidong's private staff and thus belonged into the camp of one of Li Hongzhang's most powerful political rivals.

3. Interpretations

1. Wang Bingyao's *Zhongri zhanji* and *Zhongdong zhanji benmo* by the Society for the Diffusion of Christian and General Knowledge Among the Chinese—The *Wanguo gongbao* System

In his preface to *Zhong Ri zhanji*, Wang Bingkun 王炳堃 (1846–1907), the younger brother of Wang Bingyao, expressed his fundamental opinions regarding the defeat against Japan. He held that the key for victory and defeat in the Sino-Japanese relationship was the script system. Japan had abandoned the Chinese script, which was laden with trifling details, and had, from the beginning of the "Meiji rise", started to study "Western learning" and had, in this way, attained "Wealth and Power". China, in contrast, had not been willing "to reform", and thus had become weak.

In the past, Japan had read Chinese books and had studied the Chinese script, and thus, for a long time, had been utterly weak. Since the beginning of the Meiji-rise, it had become aware of how cumbersome the Chinese script was. This indeed was the reason for tying up persons of talent. It really became envious of the simplicity of Western script and its learning, which was of real help. It resolutely gave up Chinese script and studied Western learning, and in less than twenty years was able to attain wealth and power. China is a country burdened by written culture and not willing to reform. This is the key to understand the strength and weakness of these two countries.[11]

This view is quite clearly coloured by universalist cultural determinism and it directly linked the reasons for victory and defeat in the war with the Meiji-reform, the question of script, and Western learning. Judged from the later development of China's history, this view possessed a considerable amount of representativeness. The origins of this universalist view can be clearly traced to the *Wanguo gongbao* of the Society for the Diffusion of Christian and General knowledge Among the Chinese.

The Society for the Diffusion of Christian and General Knowledge Among the Chinese also hoped to spread this basic idea of China's defeat, which was related to a civilisation-determinism based upon an understanding of biological evolution with the help of the compilation in the style of the *Zhongdong zhanji benmo*. On 3 April 1896, the Society for the Diffusion of Christian and General Knowledge Among the Chinese published an announcement in the *Shenbao*. Aiming at Wang Bingyao's *Zhongdong zhanji*, which had already appeared as a typographical edition at Wenyutang in Hong Kong, the Society for the Diffusion of Christian and General Knowledge Among the Chinese claimed that its own news-clippings and records were even more complete. The supposed key was that their own layout principles were more rational, so that it was possible

---

11 Wang Bingyao (1896), *Zhong Ri zhanji*, p. 7.

to "plant meaning, which is stable, to select words without fear". In front of the text, which consists of six chapters, they added a "Record of the Meeting for Ending the War", whose meaning was "to shine through virtue and not to look for weapons" (*yao de bu guan bing* 耀德不觀兵).[12] Compiling a history of the war was thus not to promote war, but instead aimed to highlight the "virtue" which is inherent in a process. At the end of the book was an appendix which was entitled, "A New Policy for Establishing Peace", which was actually Young J. Allen's comment on the war. In order to "remove evil practices" (*chubi* 除弊), it contained a critique of some features of the Chinese national character, and, in order to "obtain benefits" (*xing li* 興利), it made suggestions for renewal and reform. According to the announcement in the *Shenbao*, the biggest problem of Wang Bingyao's *Zhong Ri zhanji*, which had been published earlier, was that, apart from the fact that it was not complete, it considered the Korean problem ("The Records of the Alarming Situation in Korea") as the core around which the cause and effect narrative revolved. This form of compilation, however, did "not at all meet the expectations of the Society for the Diffusion of Christian and General knowledge Among the Chinese.[13]

Later on, as pointed out above, Yao Xiguang castigated the fact that the war history of the Society for the Diffusion of Christian Knowledge put its emphasis on opinion and neglected the situation in the battlefield, but was still called *Records of the War*. In fact, however, the Society for the Diffusion of Christian and General Knowledge Among the Chinese employed this style intentionally and saw it as crucial for displaying "the meaning implied by this Society", because, for the Society "weapons" were not important, as the important part was virtue.

If one scans the complete *Zhongdong zhanji benmo*, it becomes clear that it explained the war and comments on it from the so-called "public opinion" point of view. Except for the fact that, in respect to content it puts emphasis on debate and less on the situation of the war, in regard to form it also uses the collection of documents, news and comments in order to narrate the situation of the war and, in this way, waters down the real sequence of events and the cause and effect relationship.

Zhongdong zhanji benmo holds that, seen from the viewpoint of civilisation, from the moment in which post-Meiji-reform Japan came into contact with Western Christian civilisation, "the population of the whole country has become enlightened by education".[14] During the later phase of the war, the *Wanguo gongbao* commented that the Meiji reform could "show military accomplishments, provided efficient instruments, could make the national prestige

---

12 Quotation from the *Guoyu* 國語, "Zhouyu" 周語 pt 1.

13 *Shenbao*, 3 April 1896.

14 Allen, Cai Erkang (1896) *Zhongdong zhanji benmo*, p. 7.

shine, bring new policies to work, educate the thought of the people, avoid killing, and make kind-heartedness known all over the Earth".[15] They thus put the blame for the defeat in the war on the institutions, the political system, the national character, and even on Chinese culture itself. They clearly understood the Sino-Japanese War as a war between modernity and tradition, civilisation and barbarity, and democratic and autocratic forms of government, and not, as former comments had claimed, a war between two national states. From the standpoint of "Collecting Private Meaning in Order to Spread 'common Opinion' Widely", it is easy to discover that only those who had attained level of being able to distinguish between civilisation and barbarity were able to attain 'common opinion' and thus to understand the real reason for China's defeat and find the way to reform as means of rescue. This real reason was that China had been defeated by post-Meiji-reform Japan, which had indeed gone through an "epochal transformation". The only method for providing relief was, therefore, a reform towards a Westernised system, as Japan had undertaken, and, in this way, ridding itself of "ignorance", which had led to "backwardness" and ultimately to defeat.

2. *Dongfang bingshi jilüe*—The System of the War Witnesses

The most important information source for Yao Xiguang's work *Dongfang bingshi jilüe* were people who had been personally involved in the war. Most of them came together after the war in Wuchang, which belonged to the jurisdiction of the governor-general of Huguang Zhang Zhidong. They were working for military and educational institutions which had been newly founded by Zhang Zhidong, such as the Military Academy or the Self-Strengthening Academy. With the exception of those who had compiled histories or notes, such as Li Yuanhong's *Jiashen (wu), yiwei jin Zhong ri haizhan shilüe*, Wu Zhiqing's 吳质卿 *Taiwan diary Taiwan riji* 台灣日記, Jiang Yushu's 蔣玉書 *Navy diary Haijun riji* 海軍日記, Chen Shengsan's 陈省三 *Random Notes from Taiwan Taiwan zaji* 台灣雜記, *etc.*, there was a total of seventeen war-participants with whom Yao conducted interviews: These were Wang Yadong 王雅東, Zhang Junhan 張君漢, Li Yuanhong, Fan Zhongmu 範仲木, Wu Tihe 吳體和, Yang Youhe 楊佑之, Xiao Yunong 蕭雨農, Wu Junqing 吳俊卿, Luo Liuqin 羅六琴, Chen Shengsan, an officer of the Xiang army, a certain Mr. Hong 洪, the county magistrate in training Mr. Yang 楊 from Sichuan, Shen Dunshi 沈敦士, Shang Zhigao 尚志高, Shang Dezheng 商德正, Wu Xiaoying 吳孝英 and the Zhili county magistrate of Bofu 伯茀.

---

15 *Wanguo gongbao.*

Their focus of attention regarding the war was widely different from that employed by the Society for the Diffusion of Christian and General Knowledge Among the Chinese.

First, they wanted to make the public aware that "the reason for losing the war was that the other side spread malicious news about our side". The *Dongfang bingshi jilüe* was of the opinion that the responsibility for the defeat rested with "the officers in the field as well as with the commanders". They were of the opinion that they "in regard to priorities of domestic policies did not have any plan about how to build up and strengthen the military, and, regarding the foreign policy, they did not have the ideal to sacrifice their lives in order to attain the goals". Secondly, for them, looking back at the war and writing war histories had the basic goal—as for the well known defeated monarchs and officials of the Spring and Autumn period—of "displaying the principle of humiliation in teaching men to fight" (*ming chi jiao zhan* 明恥教戰), in order to strengthen the country and revenge the humiliation suffered. Defeat in a war was no humiliation; the humiliation was *not* to revenge defeat.[16] Based upon such a strong statist/nationalist view as to the reasons for triumph and defeat of a war, they were of the opinion that there is no such thing as an absolute weak country, and there was also no epochal change which necessarily would result in defeat. Everything was "accidental misfortune" and, as such, could be changed by "displaying the principle of humiliation in teaching men to fight", In history, King Zhuang of Chu 楚莊王, Fuchai of Wu 吳夫差 and Goujian of Yue 越勾踐 and France which had recently been defeated by Prussia, were all models of how weakness could be quickly transformed into strength.

In 1895, Kong Guangde from Qufu collected 29 memorials, 99 discussions, 226 poems, one eulogy, one rhapsody and 7 *ci*-poems, and, in a second volume, another 32 memorials and compiled his above-cited *Collection of Loyalty and Anger* (*Putian zhongfen ji* 普天忠憤集), which was printed lithographically in 1896 by the Liuyi publishing house and distributed in Shanghai and other treaty ports. At that time, Kong lived in Shanghai. He had been student of the Fuzhou general, Qingyun 慶裕 (?–1894). Zhang Luocheng, another important author, had also been a member of Zhang Zhidong's private staff. Their standpoints were clearly different from those of the missionary societies. By extending the scope of the war history to include poems, and by employing a compilation structure which classified according to the sort of text, and not by the sequence of time, the focus of attention was clearly shifted to arouse the "feeling" and the "loyalty and anger" of the population. The preface stated: "If there is a great change in the coming age, there are also people predestined to appear and to come to the rescue in these times." It was thus of the opinion that the Sino-Japanese War

---

16 Yao Xiguang, "*Dongfang bingshi jilüe zixu*".

constituted a "great change", but that it did not constitute an inevitable defeat or a demise of civilisation. For this reason, it was possible to wait for a "talented person" to appear and to bring about a reversal. It hoped that the readers, "because of the humiliation, are aroused in anger, and, because they are angry, will be encouraged [to do something about it]". This was still similar to the ideas of Yao Xiguang, namely, the idea to "displaying the principle of humiliation in teaching men to fight".[17]

4. Circulation, Influence and New Forms

1. Circulation and Sales—Commercialisation

The main channel of distribution of the war histories mentioned above were publishing houses and presses located in the port city of Shanghai, such as the *Shenbao* publishing house, *Gezhi shushi*, *Meihua* publisher, the *Sino-Western academy*, *Weiwen Pavillon*, *Ten-thousand Volume House*, *Shenchang* publisher, *Baoshanzhai* publisher, *Jigen* publisher, *Liuyi* publisher, *Yuanji* publisher, *Tushu jicheng* publisher, etc..[18]

It is clear that the newly-emerging book-market played a major role in the success of some of the books. Pirating, clearly, was an issue. Kong Guangde's *Putian zhongfen ji*, for example, was pirated in May 1896 by the *Cishutang* publishing house, which printed 3,000 copies and also advertised it in the *Shenbao* newspaper. In 1898, the other main author of this book, Zhang Luocheng (Zhang Shanmin) 張羅澄 （山民）, had an advertisement published in the newspapers in which he accused the head of the Cishutang publishing house, Rong Wenbin 戎文彬, of pirating and pointed out that the book suffered from a large number of mistakes and omissions, so that it was impossible to understand.[19] The case was later brought before the mixed court of the International Settlement, which ruled that the Cishutang had to pay compensation of one hundred foreign dollars to Zhang Luocheng. In 1899, after the *coup d'état* which ended the 1898 reforms, and because the political atmosphere had changed, "the old politics were re-instated" and the book-market reacted to this; even the *Zhongfen ji* became unmarketable. Although the publishing houses made a great effort to advertise their books in the newspapers, they still had several hundred copies in stock, which were impossible to sell. We can observe how the price

---

17 Kong Guangde (1895), *Putian zhongfen ji*, "zi xue" (author's preface).

18 Zhou Zhenhe (2005), *Wan Qing yingye shumu*.

19 "Chajiu fanban wu ren" 查究翻板誤人 (Investigating a case of pirating, which misleads people), *Shenbao*, 2 November 1898.

for the book dropped from the initial 2 silver dollars in 1895 to 60 cents in 1902.

During the last years of the Qing period from the Sino-Japanese war until the transformation of the examination system and the establishment of a new school system in 1902, document collections and war records narrating the Sino-Japanese War, such as *Putian zhongfen ji*, which had seen the Reform of 1898, the Boxer Rebellion and other important changes of the political situation, which influenced the book-market, still continued to be reprinted and sold. Except for the local booksellers in Shanghai, Japanese and English booksellers also participated in the dissemination of these works. The reduction of the price, in fact, also shows—except for the fact that bookseller wanted to promote sales—how these works were not only read by literati-officials, concerned about the situation and full of loyalty and anger, but that they were also consumed by a much broader readership as well. Among the factors which accelerated this tendency was the transformation of the examination system.

In 1896 Chen Yaoqing's 陳耀卿 *Shishi xinbian* 時事新編 (A New Compilation on Current Affairs)—six books in a set—was sold for 80 cents at the Liwenxuan bookshop in Shanghai, at the Shenchang and Gezhi bookstore, at Qianqintang books, and at many other bookstores. In 1897, it was re-carved and sold at several bookstores for 50 cents. Until 1902, the book was also sold by another bookseller.

On 5 May 1896, the Society for the Diffusion of Christian and General Knowledge Among Chinese published its *Zhongdong zhanji benmo* and it entrusted the Shenbaoguan, the Shenchang book and painting company, the *Gezhi shushi*, the *Zhongxi shuyuan* in Hongkou, with selling the work. Outside of Shanghai, the book was sold by the retail stores of the *Shenbao* and at Missionary bookstores. The book was sold for one dollar and 50 cents.[20] Apart from using its own retail outlets in Shanghai and outside of Shanghai in order to sell its *Zhongdong zhanji benmo*, the Society for the Diffusion of Christian and General Knowledge Among Chinese also used a series of measures such as distributing complimentary copies in order to widen circulation of the book. In this way, the 4,000 volumes of the first edition were sold out within a short time.[21]

In 1897, the Society for the Diffusion of Christian and General Knowledge Among Chinese bound the *Wenxue xingguo ce* 文學興國策 (Strategies of

---

20 "Guangxue hui xin zhu *Zhongdong zhanji benmo* san yue ershisan ri chu shu" 廣學會新著《中東戰紀本末》三月廿三日出書 (The new work *Zhongdong zhanji benbmo* by the Society for the Diffusion of Christian and General Knowledge Among Chinese was published on 23 of March), *Shenbao*, 4 May 1896.

21 "Qian ri Guangxuehui yi *Zhongdong zhanji benmo* yi shu jianzeng" 前日廣學會以《中東戰紀本末》一書見贈 (The day before yesterday the Society for the Diffusion of Christian and General Knowledge Among Chinese provided a complimentary copy of their *Zhongdong zhanji benmo*), *Shenbao*, 7 May 1896.

Strengthening the Country through Literature), which had been written by Japan's ambassador to the US, Mori Arinori, 森有礼 (1847–1889) together with *Zhongdong zhanji benmo* into a ten volume edition and asked the Tushu jicheng ju to do the printing and distributing of it. It also published the *Sequel to the Zhongdong zhanji benmo* in two volumes. Probably because the market situation was so good and the book was highly valued in the examination compounds, there was a large number of pirated copies by booksellers, which finally resulted in a request by the Society for the Diffusion of Christian and General Knowledge Among Chinese and submitted to the Susongtai Daotai to issue a writ to ban it.[22] Except for this the Society for the Diffusion of Christian and General Knowledge Among Chinese had its own channels for giving the book away freely. *Zhongdong zhanji bemo* was given to the cabinet ministers of the Korean court, to the secretary of the Zongli yamen and to the personal tutor of the Guangxu Emperor Sun Jianai. Moreover, it quickly spread to Japan and, in 1898, it was published in Japanese translated by Fujino Fojiro 藤野房次郎.

2. Symbiosis of Meanings: Prefaces, Postfaces, Appendices and the Integration into Bibliographies and *Collectanea*

The narratives of the war, which appeared shortly after the war not only employed their main texts as a source of information, but created symbiotic meaning by the way of paratexts. [23] The common understanding of many Chinese about this war was also shaped by these forms of symbiotic meaning.

It at first needs to be stated that the war document collections and war chronicles which appeared after the war, were almost all selections from reports and commentaries of Chinese and foreign newspapers. Again, the stylistic forms were quite different and they embodied quite different views of the war. They were either compiled with a focus on specific subjects, which weakened the view of the process of the war and strengthened the view on the principles underlying success and defeat, or they ordered the material according to the natural course of events of the war, and thus in the *benmo* form, emphasising cause and effect as well as the question of responsibility in order to "display the principle of humiliation in teaching men to fight". Apart from this, prefaces, postfaces and appendices are also forms of "intertextuality" to be considered when reading the main-text, and it is possible to go so far as to claim that they contributed to the formation of a "symbiotic meaning". For example, when Wang Bingyao's *Zhong Ri zhanji* was first published in Hong Kong, it already

---

22 Cf. *Shenbao*, GX23/1/8 (9 February 1897).

23 I here refer to Genette's paratext as part of Kristeva's coined intertextuality; cf. Genette (1982), *Palimpsestes*, Genette (1997), *Paratexts*.

contained, as an appendix, Hu Shaofen's 胡燏棻 (1840–1906) memorials on reform and self-strengthening (*Hu Yumei lianfang (Shaofen) zou bianfa ziqiang tiaochen shu* 胡雲楣廉訪（燏芬）奏變法自強條陳疏), as well as a memorandum of Ye Yaoyuan 葉耀元 (1864–?) to Zhang Zhidong about "Preparing the Defence against the Eastern Pirates" (*Jielu Ye Jun Yaoyuan shang Zhang Xiang shuai shu chou yu Wo ce di shiyi tiao bing tagang ershiliu tiao* fu 節錄葉君耀元上張香帥書籌御倭策十一條並大綱二十六條附). During the war, Hu had received the order to act as field paymaster. Ye Yaoyuan was one of the best graduates of the Tongwenguan in Beijing and the Guangfangyan guan in Shanghai, especially proficient in mathematics and "New learning". Thus, Wang Bingyao, apart from employing a compilation layout which described the changes that occurred during the war upon the basis of the natural course of events, and also employing words taken from *Wanguo gongbao* at the end of his compilation, added two memorials which stressed the "tasks of the time" and "Rising new Learning". In this way, with the exception of the exposition of the universalist civilisation view in Wang Bingkun's preface to the book, *Zhong Ri zhanji* was rather traditional in its basic themes. It was of the opinion that the defeat by Japan in the war was related to a very concrete sequence of cause and effect, and that, by employing concrete technical improvements in the future, the weakness-strength relationship between China and Japan could be reversed. It was for this reason the Society for the Diffusion of Christian and General Knowledge Among Chinese expressed its dissatisfaction with this form of compilation and the appendices, and its claim that this form "absolutely failed to understand the intentions of this society" was not without justification.

Actually, a rather similar situation can be observed with regard to the Society for the Diffusion of Christian and General Knowledge Among Chinese's own *Zhongdong zhanji benmo*. When *Zhongdong zhanji benmo* had not been published for a long time, the Society for the Diffusion of Christian and General Knowledge Among Chinese published a Chinese translation of a book on education reform, which, during the 1870s, had been written by the former Japanese envoy to the USA, Mori Arinori as *Wenxue xingguo ce* (Strategies of Strengthening the Country through Literature), as cited above. When it was published as a monograph, it sold bound together with *Zhongdong zhanji benmo* as a package. In advertisements, the society stressed that the two books together achieved "integrity". A little bit later, *Wenxue xingguo ce* was, as mentioned above, published together with *Zhongdong zhanji benmo* as an appendix. The Society stressed the point that defeat and victory in the war had been determined by the quality of civilisation, that the new measurement for the cultural standard was the Christian civilisation, and that reform needed to be based upon educational reform.

We have already pointed out above that the war chronicles which were compiled after the Sino-Japanese war sold particularly well because of the changes of the examination system, which contributed to the fact that they became part of the satchels of normal readers all over the empire. The fact that they were put onto the book-buying lists of normal readers was also related to the publishing of popular bibliographies of New Learning during the late Qing period. In respect to their classification and to introducing them, these bibliographies completed one more step in creating symbiotic meaning. Except for the Society's own Catalogue *General Catalogue of Newly Translated and Compiled Books of the Society for the Diffusion of Christian and General Knowledge Among Chinese*, which listed *Zhongdong zhanji benmo*, Xu Weize's 徐維則 (1866–1922) *Extended Catalogue of Chinese and Western Works*, which had been supplemented and amended by Gu Xieguang 顧燮光 (1875–1949), and was published lithographically in 1902, listed the *Benmo* in eight volumes, the *Sequel* in four volumes, and the *Second Sequel* in four volumes. Moreover, in a brief comment, it noted that these books, with regard to the form of their compilation, constituted a problem, and that their main value was in recording historical truth and preserving historical material. "One can rely on it in order to understand the sequence of events of the war, and those who, some other day, will write about the events between China and Japan, can use it as source."[24] Apart from this, Zhao Weixi 趙惟熙 (1859–1917), the commissioner for education of Guizhou province included *Zhongdong zhanji benmo* in eight volumes and the *Sequel* in four volumes into the category *Politics One: History and Records* (*zhengxue diyi shizhixue* 政學第一史志學) of his *Questions and Answer to Western Books* (*Xixue shumu dawen* 西學書目答問), which was published in 1901. His comment was: "This book is chaotic and uncouth but it contains some points regarding the view of the times."[25] He was also of the opinion that its worth was greater in terms of contents than in stylistic rules and layout.

To date, three editions of the *Dongfang bingshi jilüe* have been identified. These are the Wuchang woodblock edition, the Jiangxi Tongxuezhai edition, and the lithographic edition. Zheng Lingyuan's *Tongxuezhai congshu*, a *collecteana* of Western knowledge included it in full. The *Extended Catalogue of Chinese and Western Learning* listed it in the section History and Records among the books "Compiled or written by Chinese".

In 1904, Shen Zhaowei 沈兆禕 compiled his *Annotated Bibliography of New Learning* (*Xinxue shumu tiyao* 新学书目提要), in which he provided abstracts outlining the core of books related to the Western learning popular at the time, and also added his comments. He included Yao's book into the category "history" and he was of the opinion that Yao Xiguang' *Dongfang bingshi jilüe* in respect of recording the events of the war was more trustworthy than *Zhongdong zhanji benmo* of the Society for the Diffusion of Christian and General

---

24 Xu Weize, Gu Xieguang (1902), *Zengban Dong Xi xueshu shulu*.
25 Zhao Weixi, (1901[1997], "Xixue shumu dawen".

RECORDS FROM A DEFEATED COUNTRY

Knowledge Among Chinese because the form of a compilation of records did not enable the people to understand "the outward signs of success and failure" of this war.[26] This, also from another perspective, reflects the fact that the focal point of *Zhongdong zhanji benmo* is not on narrating history but on "knowing the future" – upon the basis of a universal "civilisational" view in order to point out the direction and concrete measures of reform in China.

As to the narratives which appeared after the Sino-Japanese War in the form of compilations of war records or chronicles, the text, together with their prefaces, postfaces, appendices and the bibliographies which appeared later, created new forms of symbiotic meaning. There is another tendency here which is worth noting: by going through a process of classification by the late Qing élites, the war narratives underwent a process of "historiographisation" (史志化). They were slowly extricated from the standpoint of judging about victory and defeat and the strength and weakness of different nations, so that it became possible calmly, objectively and rationally to consult the records and documents which were left by the British, Japanese and German participants and observers of the war in order to accomplish a common description.

In his *Bibliography of Translated Books Yishu Jingyan lu* 譯書經眼錄 of 1934, which Gu Xieguang compiled in 1934, he recorded translated books relating to "New Learning", which he had himself included in his original bibliography between 1902 and 1904. Among them, were a considerable number of books which came from Japan and constituted "Eastern learning". In his *Bibliography*, Gu has a section on history and records (*shizhi* 史志), in which he lists Tamura Korenori's *Zhondong zhanshi* in two volumes, which deals with the Sino-Japanese War among a considerable number of books dealing with developments in other parts of the world. Such a classification implies that, in the late 1930s, the Sino-Japanese War had begun to become part of normal universal historiography.

Gu, among others, mentioned Tamura Korenori's *History of the Sino-Japanese War (Zhongdong zhanshi)* in two volumes, Matsui Hirokichi's *History of the Independence of Italy (Yidali dushi shi* 意大利独立史), which was translated by the Nanyang public school, Matsui Hirokichi's *History of the American Civil War (Meiguo nanbei shizhang* 美国南北战史章)), which was translated by Mao Naiyong and Luo Zhenchang, Sibue Tamotsu's, *History of the Revolutionary War in England (Yingguo geming zhanshi* 英國革命戰史), translated by the Anji publishing house, Sibue Tamotsu's *History of the Greco-Persian Wars (Xila Bosi zhanshi* 希腊波斯战史) and others, which were all listed in the category history and records" (*shizhi*). Such a classification clearly implied that the narrative of the Sino-Japanese War had a tendency to become part of "normal" historiography.

---

26 Shen Zhaowei, *Xinxue shumu tiyao*, J. 2.

Coincidentally, *The Third Sequel to the Complete Record of the Chinese-Japanese War* mainly was based upon *A True Account of the War in the East*, which had been compiled under the supervision of an English artillerist, the records of war-observers from different major countries serving as an appendix. Compiled together with the telegrams of the US legation in Beijing and the telegraphs of the Chinese legation in London related to the war defence, the posthumous letters of Ding Ruchang 丁汝昌 (1836–1895), which were reproduced lithographically, and, finally, Li Hongzhang's memorials to the throne as well as 18 poems related to the so-called Taiwan affair, Gu Xieguang called it "reliable history".

Independently of whether it is related to the traditional Chinese view of victory and defeat, according to which one should learn from the enemy in order "to defend the national honour", or related the determinist position of a Christian universalist civilisation persistently found in the publications of the Society for the Diffusion of Christian and General Knowledge Among Chinese, the narratives appearing after the Sino-Japanese War, with the help of pre- and postfixes, appendices, bibliographies and other paratextual devices, successively abandoned a biased "the enemy and us" standpoint and adopted a broader "objective" or detached perspective in order to discuss the war. Together with the main texts, which appeared during the last period of the war, they gradually formed a symbiotic meaning and, in this way, brought about the integration into the "history" class and thus entered the knowledge area of the élites, or what Antonio Gramsci has called the "grand tradition", a trend which is well worth noting.

3. Literalisation and Visualistion

Except for being integrated into the so-called "grand tradition", by means of historical novels in colloquial language, folk literature and legends as well as by means of visualisation, the narrative of the Sino-Japanese War entered the common historical knowledge of the normal masses, or, to use Gramsci's term, the "small tradition". Luo Dunrong, for example, who would later become a scriptwriter for the Peking-Opera actor Cheng Yanqiu 程硯秋 (1904–1958) and who, during the Sino-Japanese War, was still working in the function of privately employed staff within the armed forces, took Yao Xiguang's *Dongfang bingshi jilüe* as a basis, corroborated it with the information that he had obtained when working in the army and put this in his brief, but comprehensive, *Complete Record of the Armed Confrontation between China and Japan* (*Zhong Ri bingshi benmo* 中日兵事本末). It was written in an immaculate and elegant style, made use of a wide range of material, had a very clear exposition and argumentation, and was located in between the literary and historical genres, somehow near to a personally noted sketch. This book later on by a certain "Pingqingke" 平情客 was transformed into a colloquial historical novel with the title *Zhongdong hezhan benmo jilüe* 中東和戰本末紀略 (Brief Complete Record of the Sino-Japanese War and the Peace [Treaty]) and appeared, split into 31 issues, in the *Hangzhou baihua bao* in 1902. In this way, through the link with Luo Dunrong's work, Yao Xiguang's *Dongfang bingshi jilüe* was transformed into a colloquial historical novel which, with regard to its content and form, resembled war literature. It portrayed a number of personalities, opposed to each other as traitors and loyalists, stressing a Manichaean ethic based upon good and evil, loyalty and treachery, and the inversion and opposition of victory and defeat and strength and weakness in respect to morality and justice. When, in 1908, an office for public announcements was opened in Wuhan, for the first time, a speech regarding the "national humiliation" was given. When the *Zhongdong zhanji* was read, the atmosphere became "extremely forthright", to the extent that the audience began to weep. The extent to which the popular feeling was stirred up finally made the British consul intervene during the oration.[27]

Apart from the text, the narrative of the Sino-Japanese War also appeared in the form of images. Wang Bingyao´s *Zhong Ri zhanji* of 1895 was also entitled *Zhong Ri zhanji tukao*, which originally had an appendix with illustrations of the naval battles, maps of the land battles, maps of the 18 provinces, a complete map of Taiwan, a complete map of the globe, a map of China during the Spring-and Autumn period, and other maps. This was material which was necessary in order to understand the battles, but it also had the function of making the spatial aspect of the war apparent for the readers. Apart from this, the compiler of the *Shishi xinbian* (First Collection on Current Affairs), Chen Yaoqing, also compiled the above-cited *First Collection of the Illustrated Essentials of the Mopping up of the Japanese Bandits* (*Huitu saodang wokou jiyao juji* 繪圖掃蕩倭寇紀要初集). In 1895, Guan Sijun 管斯駿 (1849–1906) wrote *An Illustrated Account of Marshall Liu's Hundred Victories in Hundred Battles when Pacifying the Japanese* (*Liu dashui (ping Wo) baizhan baisheng tushuo* 劉大帥（平倭）百戰百勝圖說) which was published lithographically by the Cishutang. The book collected material on how Liu Yongfu, at that time defended Taiwan and attacked the Japanese intruders, and compiled it into a popular question and answer style book, which resembled a picture-story-book. The front part contained ten portraits of Liu Yongfu, Wu Guanliang 吳光亮 (1834–1898), Lin Yintang 林蔭堂 (1879–1966) and others, the draft memorials relating to the events of the resistance against Japan and the military affairs, war bulletins, *etc.*, a total of 50 documents. The back part was divided into 32 illustrations praising the military accomplishments

---

27 "Ying lingshi ganyu xuanjiang zhi yuanyin" 英領事干預宣講之原因 (The Reasons for the English Consul's Intervention in the Public Orations), *Shenbao*, GX23/5/22 (20 June 1908).

of Liu Yongfu's resistance against Japan in Taizhong and Tainan. These included the descriptions of Jilong Mountain in Xinzhu and the war at Penghukou, and were comparatively concrete. The book was published in 1895.[28]

5. Conclusion

Early on, while the war was still going on, the newspapers of all countries began to form the narrative of the war in the form of reports and commentaries. War witnesses, too, left their private recollections in the form of diaries, *etc.* Later on, these war narratives were collected in the form of war-document collections or war-records, and they were published and printed in Wuchang, Shanghai and other places, and were distributed throughout the whole country with the help of the book-publishing network. The narratives which developed, one based upon the book by the Society for the Diffusion of Christian and General Knowledge Among Chinese, the other one based upon the ideas and opinions of a number of war-witnesses, many of whom were based in Wuhan after the war, differed fundamentally.

The former, for example, held that China's defeat by Japan had been inevitable, determined largely by the degree of civilisation, and treated China as a defeated nation. The latter narrative forwards the point of view that the defeat by Japan in the Sino-Japanese War was still an "accidental misfortune", and that those responsible were the commanders and generals in the field as well as the grand ministers at court responsible for directing the war effort and trying to come to a solution. Correspondingly, the view about how to respond in order to reverse the situation also differed. Although both sides endorsed the view of using the enemy-country, Japan, as a teacher, the point of departure was different. The proposal brought forward by the Society for the Diffusion of Christian and General Knowledge Among Chinese was to copy Japan in order to carry out a transformation in civilisational education. The war witnesses from Wuchang, however, progressed from the traditional view of a lost battle with a view to "displaying the principle of humiliation in teaching men to fight" and appealed to the people to understand the real course of events of the war and to stimulate the nationalist feeling of "loyalty and anger" in order to transform weakness into strength.

An important difference between the two war narratives described above is the style of compiling the war histories. The publications related to the Society

---

28 A Ying (1958), *Jiawu Zhong Ri zhanzheng wenxue ji*, p. 17.

for the Diffusion of Christian and General Knowledge Among Chinese genealogy put particular emphasis on a layout of the war history in topical form. It assembled the "private opinions" of the newspapers of the different countries and then in the form of "public opinion" spread its universalist view. At the same time, it put less emphasis on the course of the battles and magnified the importance of international conventions and wartime ethics such as the virtue of having a truce. The narrative first provided by the Wuchang war witnesses was not satisfied with form of compilation of the Society for the Diffusion of Christian and General knowledge Among Chinese, thinking that it resembled a house full of scattered coins and was not able to describe clearly the sequence of cause and effect of the war and trace the reasons for victory and defeat. This clearly had a close relationship with the fundamental different feelings and positions of both sides towards the war.

After their publication, the war narratives which appeared after the Sino-Japanese War saw a period of substantial historical change, brought about by the reform of the contents of the examination system, the 100 Days' Reform, the Boxer catastrophe, the 1902 transformation of the education system, etc. With regard to commercial circulation, they were subjected to the influence of the book market. They thus were not limited to the level of "loyal and angry literati", but they were perused by "normal" readers as well, since they were required reading for passing the examinations. Among these publications of the war witnesses and the missionary societies, some entertained very strong subjective views. And, because of the commercialisation and the popularisation, they gradually formed the common knowledge understanding of the war of the ordinary Chinese.

In the process of circulation, the narratives of the Sino-Japanese War were included into different bibliographies of New Learning. Their pre-and postfixes as well as some popular catalogues of "New Learning" together with their abstracts and classification began, together with the original text, to form a symbiosis of meaning. In the process of this mutual textual influence, the work was gradually incorporated into the class of regular "history" and thus entered the élite knowledge field, becoming "reliable history", establishing the so-called historical objectivity. On the other hand, through the means of "historical romance" written in colloquial language, folk literature myths and illustrations, they became part of the common knowledge of the history of "normal people", or—to put it differently—they became Gramsci's "small tradition". Those responsible for the discrepancies which appeared in the process of transforming élite knowledge into the common knowledge of the people, mainly came from the Wuhan camp of war witnesses, such as Luo Dunrong.

With regard to another important aspect of the war narratives, namely, illustrations and especially how illustrations employed the form of space and fiction in order to present the idea of strength and weakness and victory and defeat, I cannot discuss this here because of limitations of space but will subsequently present it in another article.

(Translated by Iwo Amelung)

Bibliography

A Ying 阿英 (ed.) (1958), *Jiawu Zhong Ri zhanzheng wenxue ji* 甲午中日戰爭文學集 (Collected Literary Records of the Sino-Japanese War of 1894/95), Beijing: Zhonghua shuju.

Allen, Young J. 林樂知, Cai Erkang 蔡爾康 (1896), *Zhongdong zhanji benmo* 中東戰紀本末 (The Whole Course of the War between China and Japan), Shanghai: Guangxuehui.

Genette, Gérard (1982), *Palimpsestes, la littérature au second degré*, Paris: Seuil.

— (1997), *Paratexts: Thresholds of Interpretation*, Cambridge: Cambridge University Press.

Guangxuehui di shi ci nianbao 廣學會第十次年報 (Tenth Annual Report of the Society for the Diffusion of Christian Knowledge) and *Guangxuehui di shiyi ci nianbao* 廣學會第十一次年報 (Eleventh Annual Report of the Society for the Diffusion of Christian Knowledge), *Chuban shiliao*, 1992:1, pp. 44–45.

Kong Guangde 孔廣德 (1895), *Putian zhongfen ji* 普天忠憤集 (Collection of Loyalty and Anger) Shanghai.

Shao Dunzheng 邵循正 (ed.) (1956), *Zhongguo jindai shiliao congkan – jiawu zhanzheng* 中國近代史資料叢刊·中日戰爭 (Source Material for the Modern History of China – The Sino-Japanese War of 1894/95), Beijing: Xin zhishi chubanshe, 7 vols.

Shenbao 申報, Shanghai 1872 ff.

Shu Xilong 舒習龍 (2006), "Yao Xiguang yu 'Dongfang bingshi jilüe'" 姚錫光與《東方兵事紀略》 (Yao Xiguang and the *Brief Record of the Military Events in the East*), *Lishi dang'an* 2006:3, pp. 81–86.

Sun Wan 孫玥 (2013), 'Lin Lezhi yu 'Zhongdong zhanji benmo'" 林樂知與《中東戰紀本末》 (Young J. Allen and the Whole Course of the War between China and Japan, MA-thesis, Shanghai Academy of Social Sciences.

Wang Bingyao 王炳耀 (1895) *Zhong Ri zhanji* 中日戰輯 (War Documents of the Sino-Japanese war), Hong Kong: Wenyu tang.

— (1896), *Zhong Ri zhanji tukao* 中日戰輯圖考 An Investigation into Documents and Illustrations Related to the Sino-Japanese War), Shanghai: Shanghai shuju.

Wang Lin, 王林 (2009), "Zhongdong zhanji benmo' yu jiawu Zhong Ri zhang" 《中東戰紀本末》與甲午中日戰爭 (*The Whole Course of the War between China and Japan and the Sino-Japanese War of 1894/95*) *Fujian luntan – renwen shehui kexue ban* 2009:4, pp. 59–63.

Xiong Yuezhi 熊月之 (2007), *Wan Qing xinxue shumu tiyao* 晚清新学书目提要 (Abstract of Late Qing Bibliographies on New Learning), Shanghai: Shanghai shudian.

— (2011), *Xixue dongjian yu wan Qing shehui* 西學東漸與晚清社會 (The Spread of Western Learning and Society during the Late Qing Period), Revised version: Beijing: Zhongguo renmin daxue chubanshe, pp. 497–502.

Xu Weize 徐維則, Gu Xieguang 顧燮光 (1902) *Zhengban Dong Xi xueshu lu* 增版東西學書錄 (Expanded Catalogue of Books [translated from] Japanese and Western Languages).

Yao Xiguang 姚錫光 (1898), "Dongfang bingshi jilüe zixu" 東方兵事紀略自序 (Author's Preface to the Brief Record of the Military Events in the East), *Shiwubao* 53.

– (2010), *Jiang E riji* 江鄂日記 (Jiangnan and Hubei diary), Beijing: Zhonghua shuju.

Zhai Wendong 翟文棟 (2007), "Qingmo minchu wenxue zuopin zhong de jiawu zhanzheng – yi lishi xiaoshuo wei zhongxin" 清末民初文學作品中的甲午戰爭– 以歷史小說為中心 (The Sino-Japanese War in Literary Works during the Late Qing Period and the Early Republican Era – With a Focus on Historical Novels), MA-thesis, Zhejiang University.

Zhao Shaofeng 趙少峰, (2009), "Lüelun 'Zhongdong zhanji benmo'" 略論《中東戰紀本末》(A Brief Discussion of the *Whole Course of the War between China and Japan*), *Huaibei meitan shifan xueyuan xuebao (zhexue shehui kexue ban)*, 12, pp. 8–13.

Zhao Weixi 趙惟熙 (1997 [1901]), "Xixue shumu dawen" 西學書目答問 (Questions and Answers Relating to Western Bibliography) in: Xiong Yuezhi (2007) *Wan Qing xinxue shumu tiyao,* Shanghai: Shanghai shudian, pp. 569–602.

Zhou Zhenhe 周振鶴 (ed.) (2005), *Wan Qing yingye shumu* 晚清營業書目 (Catalogues of the book business during the late Qing), Shanghai: Shanghai shudian chubanshe.

Zhu Hongjuan 朱紅娟 (2013), "Wan Qing guonan xiashuo yanjiu" 晚清國難小說研究 (Research on Novels on the National Crisis during the Late Qing Period), MA-thesis, Shanghai Normal University.

"Lack of Nation" and "Lack of History": The Emergence of a Discourse of Weakness in Late Qing China

Zhang Qing

Facing a so-called "crisis that has been unprecedented in the past three thousand years", one widespread discussion to understand China was based upon the concept of "lacking". Consequently, discussions relating to the supposed "lack of nation" (*wuguo* 無國) and "lack of history" (*wu shi* 無史) commanded much attention.

These discourses clearly emerged in a particular context. Not only were they products of the appropriation of new concepts, but they also made possible an unprecedented way to understand China anew. The switch from the arrogant "Celestial Empire" (*Tianchao shangguo* 天朝上國) to concepts emphasising "lack" also formed the concrete expression of a late Qing "discourse of weakness". The key issue here is that no matter what the discourses of "lack of nation" and "lack of history" were based upon, they not only aimed at the then present situation but they also had implications for China's past, and attempted to provide a new explanation of it.

Naturally, the antonym of "not having" or "lacking" is *you* 有 "to have". The concrete presentation of "having" implies that late Qing China had a new understanding of "nation" and of "history". In this, the birth of "society" as a concept was a most typical presentation of "having". Not only did the understanding of "nation" emphasise "society" as a segment, it also implied the expectation that, by establishing the level of "society", a transformation would be brought about. And "society" also set the keynote for the "New Historiography" (*xin shixue* 新史學). The introduction of "new terms" into historiography related to this makes this aspect particularly clearly visible.

I. Manifestations of the Discourse of "Lack of Nation"

Seen from its implications, the so-called "lack of nation" has different dimensions. They are either related to the designation of the state or they are related to a "nation-state", which corresponds to the "all under heaven" concept. This is the basic background against which the discourse of "lack of nation" emerged during the late Qing period. It is concerned with a new understanding of past intellectual resources. It was just these reflections, which gave rise to the new understanding of "national state", which deserves a brief explanation.

In the *Mencius*, it is stated that: "The lords have three treasures: land, people, and policies."(Mencius, *Jinxin xia*). While Chinese traditional intellectual resources also contain arrangements related to the political order, the Chinese people of the past nevertheless mainly regarded China "as a cultural system instead of consisting of a clearly defined stretch of political territory".[1] This point is clearly explained in the famous argument concerning the "loss of the country" (*wang guo* 亡國) and the perishing of the Empire (*wang tianxia* 亡天下) by Gu Yanwu 顧炎武 (1613–1682).[2] Precisely because of the epistemological centrality formed by the "All under Heaven" idea, the "lack of nation" provided other hinges. The ideal of "Great Harmony" (*datong* 大同) described by Kang Youwei 康有為 (1858–1927) had the goal of "removing national boundaries and uniting the whole Earth", seeking to get rid of "the harm of having nations" and then later on "combining nations, races and religions until finally there are no more races, no more nations and no more religion".[3] Tan Sitong 譚嗣同 (1865–1898) also employed it as a concrete revelation of the ideal *tianxia datong* 天下大同, great harmony under heaven, "The globe is perfectly governed when there is *tianxia* but no nation."[4]

From which point forth did the "lack of nation" become the central point of anxiety among scholars? Combining different statements given by Liang Qichao 梁啟超 (1873–1929) may help us to understand the basic line of argumentation. His thoughts emerged against a background in which "combining as a group" *hequn* 合群 was a goal which was striven for with great energy. At the beginning, this was also based upon a conception of "all under heaven". In an 1897 article, Liang explained his views clearly: "Under the heavens there are all the various countries. It is one's own group and the other's group, which divides them." The distinction between China and the West lay exactly in the fact that China employs "selfish interests in order to control the group", whereas Western nation-states' adoption of democracy almost a century earlier shows that they employ the "art of good grouping" (*shanqunshu* 善群術).[5] Liang, at that time, was still, however, burdened with the concept of "all under heaven", and thus "nation" consisting of "big groups" (*daqun* 大群) might not have been his ultimate goal: "There is the state-group and there is the All-under-heaven-group. The political rule of the West is to apply it to the group of the state and

---

1 Xing Yitian (1981), "Tianxia yi jia", p. 452.
2 Huang Rucheng (1994), "Zheng shi", p. 471.
3 Kang Youwei (1935), *Datong shu*, p. 134.
4 Tan Sitong (1981), "Ren xue, xia" p. 367.
5 Liang Qichao (1897), "Shuo qun", p. 1.

"LACK OF NATION" AND "LACK OF HISTORY"

that is all. There has never been anybody who has applied it to the All-under-heaven-group."[6] From this, it becomes clear that, at this time, Liang had not freed himself from the influence of the "Three-ages-theory" (*san shi shuo* 三世說) of his teacher Kang Youwei. What is important in our respect is that Liang employed a view according to which, if the "art of good grouping" could not be realised, then "this is called lack of nation".

It was only in exile that Liang Qichao finally shed himself of the concept of "all under heaven". Against the background of having left the home-country (*quguo* 去國), he began to ponder the question of the "national state" (*guojia* 國家). The *Qingyi Newspaper* 清議報 (*The China Discussion*), which had been founded in December 1898, contains a collection of Liang's essays on this question. Liang summarised China's problem as follows:

It is not that we Chinese people do not have a patriotic nature. We do not love the nation simply because we do not know that there is something called a nation.

Therefore, "knowing what a nation-state is" became an issue with which China had to come to terms.[7] In his article entitled "On the Origins of our Accumulated Weaknesses" ("Jiruo suyuan lun" 積弱溯源論), Liang Qichao emphasised that "the weakness of patriotic feeling is, in fact, the most important origin of our accumulated weaknesses". This found its expression, first, in "not knowing the difference between nation and *tianxia*", and second, in "not knowing the boundary between nation and dynasty".[8] Moreover, in an article entitled "On the Similarities and Differences of the Changes of National Thought" ("Guojia sixiang bianqian yitong lun" 國家思想變遷異同論) Liang clearly considered the nation as a product of the modern era. He thereupon pointed out that, if "the idea of nation" (*guojia sixiang* 國家思想) was widely accepted, "then the founding of our nation would be soon realised."[9] In an article which was published later in the *Xinmin congbao* 新民叢報 (*New Citizen Journal*), Liang Qichao also described a related view and gave his answer to the question of "what is the idea of nation?":

First, knowing that there is a nation with regard to individuals; second, knowing that there is a nation with regard to a dynastic reign; third, knowing that there is a nation with regard to alien races; fourth, knowing that there is a nation with regard to the world.

In particular, he accepted the viewpoint that "only when there is confrontation between nations will our nation come into existence".[10]

---

6 Luo Zhitian (2007), "Tianxia yu shijie", p. 192.

7 Liang Qichao (1899), "Aiguo lun".

8 Liang Qichao (1901b), "Jiruo suyuan lun", p. 3.

9 Liang Qichao (1901a), "Guojia sixiang bianqian yitong lun.", p. 1

10 Liang Qichao (1902). "Xinmin shuo. Di liu jie: lun guojia sixiang.", p. 1

Liang Qichao divested himself of the constraints of "All under heaven" and began to discuss "nation" in a related context. "China's name includes the word for nation, but the shape of the nation does not exist, and, for this, it is similar to the 'lack of nation'".[11] This was a viewpoint widely shared by his contemporaries. Worrying about the "lack of nation" commanded much attention, as, for example, Zhang Shizhao 章士釗 (1881–1973) says: "The people feel sorry for themselves because of the lack of the nation. They come together and exchange their unbridled views."[12] An article published in *Zhejiang Tide Zhejiang chao* 浙江潮 in 1903 expressed it this way: "Today is a time in which nationalism has become developed. And China suffers from its onrush. For this reason, our China will really perish if we still refrain from promoting nationalism in our China". The article also stresses that a "nation state without a nationality cannot be called nation".[13] An article entitled "Lack of Nation-state" (*wu guojia* 無國家), which was published in the journal *Jiangsu* 江蘇 says, "The Japanese scholar Tokutomi Sohō says: 'Japan has a nation-state but not individuals, China has individuals but no nation-state.' I am deeply anguished by these words."[14] An article published the same year in the Shanghainese journal *Jingshi wenchao* 經世文潮 says: "Oh, what tragic fate suffer the people that lack a nation. In the East of Asia, there are the *Zhina* 支那-people who, from the earliest time on, never had a nation."[15]

Clearly, regarding the discourse of "lack of nation", different perspectives could be taken. One started from a racist view considering the Manchu dynasty as an alien race intruding in the Central Plains. Another considered the modern nation state as standard and stressed that China had only had "dynasties", but no nation. The former called for a racial revolution, whereas the latter hoped for national construction.[16] It should be acknowledged that both positions found their expressions. According to Liu Yazi 柳亞子 (1887–1958), "lack of nation" and "lack of history" both fall into the former category. He laments: "Alas, now my race has already lacked a nation for 261 years; my race has also lacked history for 261 years."[17] On the other hand, Liang Qichao's opinion shows that he had accepted the theory of the nation-state which was prevalent at the time. It is reflected in his ardent admiration of Johann Caspar Bluntschli's (1887–1958) ideas. "If Rousseau is the father [original mother] of the nineteenth century, then Bluntschli is the father of the twentieth century".[18] In this respect,

---

11 Liang Qichao (1903), "Zhengzhixue dajia Bolunzhili zhi xueshuo", p. 4.
12 Zhang Shizhao (1981), "Shu 'Huangdi hun'", p. 221.
13 Yu Yi (1903), "Minzuzhuyi lun", p. 20.
14 "Wu guojia" (1903), p. 3.
15 "Ai zai wuguo zhi min" (1903), pp. 17.
16 Wang Fansen (2001), "Wan Qing de zhengzhi gainian yu 'xin shixue'".
17 Qijizi (1904), "'Qing mishi' xu", p. 1.
18 Liang Qichao (1903). "Zhengzhixue dajia Bolunzhili zhi xueshuo", p. 35.

"LACK OF NATION" AND "LACK OF HISTORY"

Zhang Taiyan's 章太炎 (1869–1936) experience was also quite representative. He originally held a viewpoint based upon racist thought and only later was his view of the modern nation state formed.[19]

In other words, modern China's anxiety to describe the state probably also needs to take into consideration the process of maturation of the modern world. Eric Hobsbawm (1917–2012) has discussed the importance of the "dual revolution"—the French Revolution and the British Revolution—for the world. According to him, the two revolutions are not historical events which merely belong to these two countries; rather, they should be seen as a "the twin craters of a rather larger regional volcano".[20] The emergence of a modern "national consciousness" is also the central issue to an understanding of modern China's landscape of transformations. One opinion, which possesses a certain degree of representativeness, is: "In large part, the intellectual history of modern China has been the process of making *kuo-chia* [*guojia*] of *t'ien-hsia* [*tianxia*]."[21] Other scholars have described this pattern as the "culturalism to nationalism thesis".[22] Regardless of how it is expressed, the fundamental point remains, namely, that giving up the idea of "All under heaven" implies accepting the existence of rival political entities—"one nation versus another". For this reason, in late Qing China, adopting the standpoint of "lack of nation" constituted an important starting-point in order to re-consider what kind of nation China should construct.

II. The Prevalence of the Discourse of "Lack of History"

The discourse on the "lack of nation" was both accompanied by and merged with the prevalence of the discourse on "the lack of history". Compared to the expositions on "lack of nation", the emergence of the discourse of "lack of history" was more striking, given the fact that China had both a long history and a long tradition of history writing. Nevertheless, such a discourse did prevail in China during the first years of the twentieth-century. When the discourse of the "lack of history" was related to that of "lack of nation" this was often done in order to argue that the "lack of history" would result in the "lack of nation". Chen Yinke 陳寅恪 (1890–1969) provided an important explanation and pointed out that this concern had a special meaning. Every time dynastic change took place, the scholars who were affected by this "experienced failure

---

19 Zhang Taiyan (1906), "Yanshuo lu". , p. 1.
20 Hobsbawm (1962), *The Age of Revolution*, p. 5.
21 Levenson (1958), *Confucian China and Its Modern Fate, Volume One*, p. 103.
22 Townsend (1996), "Chinese Nationalism", p. 1.

and success in terms of moral conduct", and "differences in scholarship developed, which could not easily be reconciled", but, the scholars "in their heart, had one common concept: even if the country perished, history could not be destroyed."[23] It was precisely because "history" had more significance than nation that the idea of "lack of history" became so popular, was an exceptionally clear aspect of the "discourse of weakness" in late Qing China, and also, because of this, had an influence on the understanding of the past.

An article published in *Tiannan xinbao* 天南新報 in 1902 contains a comparison between "public history" (*gongshi* 公史) and "private history" (*sishi* 私史) and argues that China has no history. It points out that "private history" is the "history of one family and is not the history of a complete nation. It is the history of one particular point in time and is not the history of ten thousand generations. It is the chronological history of princes and nobility; it is not the history of the powers of the world. If one takes this as history, one can also call it 'lack of history'." This implies that "lack of history" means a "lack of public history".[24] In *Four Thousand Years' of History of Chinese Civilisation (Zhina siqian nian kaihua shi* 支那四千年開化史) published in 1903, the author also explained in the preface that the goal of translating this book was to learn from it so as to "get rid of the facts relating to the 24 dynastic families and use that which relates to civilisational progress" in order to "feed our scholars who lack history".[25]

It is particularly worth noting that the discourse of the "lack of history" also prevailed in the works of those authors who upheld the "national essence" *guocui* 國粹. The *Zhengyi tongbao* 政藝通報 established by Deng Shi 鄧實 (1877–1951) and Huang Jie 黃節 (1873–1935) in February 1902 strove for "making known to all in the Empire our learning, in order to love our country, so that, in this way, the learning will be preserved and the nation will not perish".[26] From related articles published in the journal, it can be easily seen that the authors consider the question of historiography (*shixue* 史學) against the background of national ruin 亡國. In "A General Introduction to History" (*Shixue tonglun* 史學通論) written by Deng Shi, the author questioned the statement that "China has a history". According to Deng, reading through works on history which spanned across three thousand years, he had to sigh, "Is history really like this? Does China really have a history?" He not only held the view that China was "lacking history", but also stated that the "lack of history" led to the lack of nation". "If the tide of the revolution of the Chinese historical world does not rise, then China will lack history forever. Lack of history will lead to the lack of

---

23 Chen Yinke (2001), "Wuguo xueshu zhi xianzhuang ji Qinghua zhi zhize", pp. 361–362.

24 Huang Shizhong (1902), "Sishi.", p. 1

25 Zhina shaonian (1903), Zhina siqian nian kaihua shi, p. 1.

26 Deng Shi (1908), "Diqi nian 'Zhengyi tongbao' tiji" p. 1.

"LACK OF NATION" AND "LACK OF HISTORY"

nation."[27] Upon this basis, Deng Shi and his fellows also actively promoted the establishment of scholarly associations and, in January 1905, they founded the Association for the Preservation of National Learning (*Guoxue baochu hui* 國學保存會) in Shanghai which published the *Academic Journal of National Essence* (*Guocui xuebao* 國粹學報). Discussions about "national learning" (*guoxue* 國學) were often carried out by combining the "lack of nation" and the "lack of history". In the first issue of *Academic Journal of National Essence*, Huang Jie explained his opinion "Mr. Yellow History has suffered through reading 4,000 years of Chinese history. He then had to sigh: 'Oh, how long is it that China has been 'lacking a nation', and how could [this] history be enough to speak about'"?[28]

As pointed out by Wang Fansen 王汎森, in order to understand how the issue of "having a history" versus "lack of history" emerged during the late Qing period, it may be necessary to have a grasp of the political concepts which developed at the time. However, debating on such an issue in a country with a deep-rooted tradition of historical learning means that the people's understanding of history had developed beyond traditional categories and that the question of "what is history?" was put forward again.[29] Indeed, the birth of "New Historiography" 新史學 in the early years of the twentieth century was closely related to a new definition of history as an academic discipline, as becomes apparent in Liang Qichao's discussion regarding the "New Historiography": "If one wants to establish a new historiography, it is first necessary to provide a clear definition of historiography. If one wants to know how to define historiography, it is first necessary to know clearly the scope of history."[30] Liang is, by no means, a unique example.

In his translation of *The Study of Sociology* (*Qunxue yiyan* 群學肄言), Yan Fu 嚴復 (1854–1921) not only suggested that, when examining the past, one should pay attention to "the reasons for strength and weakness, order and chaos, rise and fall of a group", but he also pointed out that the traditional form of history writing "focused on the acts of emperors and aristocrats, no matter how trivial they were; ignored issues related to people's livelihood, no matter how major they were".[31] When Deng Shi pointed to China's "lack of history", he was, in fact, expressing his hope that China would produce new historians and new historical knowledge. "There is no lack of history, but there is a lack of historians; there is no lack of historians, but there is a lack of historical

---

27 Deng Shi (1902), "Shixue tonglun yi" p. 1.
28 Huang Jie (1905), "Huang shi". p. 1.
29 Wang Fansen (2001), "Wan Qing de zhengzhi gainian yu 'xin shixue'".
30 Liang Qichao (1989). "Xin shixue", p. 7.
31 Spencer (1981), *Qunxue yiyan*, p.8.

knowledge."[32] Ma Xulun's 馬敘倫 (1885–1970) analysis of "the lack of history" is also concerned about extending the scope of history: "If one holds history in high esteem, why must the 24 dynastic histories be taken as history? Why must the *Three Comprehensives,* the *Six Comprehensives* and the *Nine Comprehensives* be considered as history? And even more, why must the *Six Canons* be considered as the model of history?"[33] These opinions became a consensus of the era. Lecturing on the "General History of China" (*Zhongguo tongshi* 中國通史) at the Metropolitan University (*Jingshi daxuetang* 京師大學堂), Wang Zhouyao 王舟瑤 (1858–1925) also held a sympathetic attitude towards "the lack of history". He said that "although these words go too far, this is not without reason", and stressed that:

When Western people research history, their most important concern is to look into the politics, customs, society, religion, learning, education, economy and industry [of a country]. It is this which pushes forward the progress of the world; it strengthens the ambition of the citizens. The history of China puts emphasis on the sovereign and neglects the people. It emphasises the past and only briefly deals with the present. Correctness and mistakes compete with each other. It has nothing to do with the facts; biographies extend over many volumes, at times resembling epitaphs, they only rarely are able to express any special spirit and thus, hinder the progress of the people. As a result, it is inevitable that [this kind of history] is blamed by those engaging in new learning and that it is ridiculed by young scholars. The scholars need to establish their own ideals and read the old histories with a high degree of sensitivity, so that they are not fooled by the ancients.[34]

It is not specifically necessary to point out that the Late Qing dynasty's forceful attempts to extend the scope of history were the result of the confluence of Western and Chinese historical learning. We can see this point from the various compilations of Western scholarly works. The *Xixue santong* 西學三通 (Three Comprehensive Collections of Western Learning) published in 1902 was a rather influential compilation of Western scholarly works, among which *Xishi tongzhi* 西史通志 (Comprehensive Record of Western History) strove to "provide records on all great countries according to the order of the five continents."[35] The second volume of the book *Bibliography of New Learning with Abstracts* (*Xinxue shumu tiyao* 新學書目提要), compiled by the Shanghai Tongya Press 上海通雅書局 in 1903, is on history. It combines works by both Chinese and foreign historians.[36] It may be worth noting here that the Late Qing intelligentsia made a distinction between "new studies" *xinxue* 新學, and "old studies" *jiuxue* 舊學, to which a distinction between "Western historiography"

---

32 Deng Shi (1902). "Shixue tonglun yi". p. 1.
33 Ma Xulun (1903), "Shijie datong shuo."; p.
34 Jingshi daxuetang Zhongguo tongshi jiangyi (1904). pp. 1–3.
35 "Xishi tongzhi" (1902), p.1.
36 "Lishilei zongxu" (1903), p. 1.

(*xishi* 西史) and "Chinese historiography" *zhongshi* 中史 corresponded. In other words, in the process of introducing the West into China, history as an academic discipline and as an important component of Western learning was also discussed. Against this backdrop, the integration of Chinese and Western historical learning directly caused an extension of the "scope of history" and also influenced the transformation of history as an academic discipline in China. It was through these episodes that questions such as the meaning and the scope of history and the like, which are clearly disciplinary in nature, started to attract attention from historians.[37]

To put it differently, the extension of the scope of history was a result of accepting a new understanding of history. Such a new understanding is reflected not only in an extension of the contents of this, which was covered by historical writing, but also reflected in a new understanding of the status of history as an academic discipline. When criticising the old history and elaborating the prospect of the new historiography, Liang Qichao, Zhang Taiyan and others had already clearly adopted a new understanding of the discipline. Liang even began his piece on "New Historiography" with comments on Chinese historical learning by connecting it to modern academic disciplines. However, this, too, can also only be considered as an important sign of the communication between Chinese and Western academic learning and should not overshadow the differences which existed between the two. The establishment of history as a modern academic discipline in China was also an issue faced by China's history field in the first years of the twentieth-century. It is indeed necessary to take a disciplinary perspective to analyze this issue further. The point is that the argument about China's "lack of history" was based upon the extension of the scope of history. Correspondingly, we should be concerned about which segments formed the main axle of historical writing.

III. "Others" in the Discourse about "Lack of nation" and "Lack of history"

The discourses of nation and history based upon a lack of the two are, without any doubt, the concrete expression of a late Qing discourse of weakness. The existence of an "other" in these discourses is the main source for the transformation of late Qing China's self-understanding. The "others" not only include "weak nations" but also "strong nations", and especially the examples

---

37 For discussion in this regard, see Zhang Qing (2003), "Pubian lishi yu Zhongguoshi zhi shuxie", see also Zhang Qing（2005）, "Zhong Xi lishi zhi 'huitong' yu Zhongguo shixue de zhuanxiang"

of nations which had managed to transform themselves from "weak" nations into "strong" ones.

Xiao Yongshi 蕭庸士 (*i.e.*, Xiao Yingchun 蕭應椿, 1856–1922), in the "Reading Instructions" to the book *Brief Description of the Five Continents* (*Wuzhou shulüe* 五洲述略), which he had compiled, pointed out how he had made his choice among the nations of the five continents. "In respect to the strong countries of Europe and Japan in Asia as well as the United States in America, I have made rather detailed descriptions and pointed out the means by which they rose. As to the other weak and small countries, I only classified them and made some notes on them.". However, "Korea in Asia and Turkey in Europe, although they are nothing more than small and weak countries, in describing them, I did not include them in those countries which are only classified and briefly mentioned; instead, I made it clear how they had declined."[38] In 1902, Ma Junwu 馬君武 (1881–1940) wrote in the "Introduction by the Translator" (*yixu* 譯序) of his *Modern French History* (*Falanxi jin shi shi* 法蘭西今世史) that "Our middle Kingdom has existed in this world for 4,000 years [and still exists]. however, it only has an imperial court and no state; it has a tyrannical government and not one that carries out its duties correctly." Ma explained in particular that his interest in France was not only because it was "the land in which European civilisation reached fruition first," but also because "up to Louis XVI's execution in 1793, France was also trapped in an autocratic rule by despots. The miserable life of the French people was no different from the situation in China today."[39]

Within East Asia, Japan and Korea were also typical "others" that contrasted greatly with each other, one being strong and the other weak. This also caused similar discussions. In volume 91 of the *Xixue santong* (Three Comprehensive Collections of Western Learning) mentioned above, the part entitled "Comprehensive Western History" in its "Records of the Course of Development, Part 1" (*Yange zhi yi* 沿革志一), includes an "Overview of the Asian Continent", (*Yaxixya zhou zongshuo* 亞細亞洲總說), which emphasises that "drawing lessons from other countries should start from countries on the same continent", and thus making it clear why Japan and Korea constituted two so important "others".[40] The importance of the two examples surely does not end there. Tao Jun 陶鈞 also wrote in the "Preface to the Comprehensive Record of Western History" ("Xishi tongzhi xu" 西史通志序) that "Asia has the vastest expanse among the four continents", and that "the West of Asia is the locality of the earliest ancestors of all humanity, rationality, skills and religions

---

38 "Fanli" (1902), p. 1

39 Ma Junwu (2000 [1902]), "Yixu", pp. 46–47.

40 "Xishi tongzhi" (1902), p.1.

"LACK OF NATION" AND "LACK OF HISTORY" 147

all originate from Asia. For this reason, from time immemorial to this very day, it is considered as an important place".

Here, the reference to Asia is clearly related to the matter of self-respect. An example which corroborates this point can be found in the *Most Recent Textbook of the National Language (Edition for Elementary Schools) (Zuixin guowen jiaokeshu [chudeng xiaoxuetang keben]* 最新國文教科書[初等小學堂課本]), which was published by The Commercial Press in 1904. Lesson 5 and Lesson 6 of the book introduce Japan and Korea respectively. Especially noteworthy is the perspective provided by the book, which points out that: "If we observe the Japanese example, then the people of our country can be encouraged." This does nothing other than to stress that Japan, which belongs to the same Asia as China, can serve as inspiration for China's revitalisation. At the same time, it emphasises that Korea "will, in the end, not be able to rise again", which means that Korea, which belongs to the self-same Asia is treated as a negative example.[41] In fact, this way of examining problems is central to the Late Qing discourse of Asia. With regard to the topic of this article, we can observe that the existence of such "others" played an important role in the emergence of the discourses on the "lack of nation" and "the lack of history".[42] It thus reflects that one's self-understanding is bound by "vertical" and "horizontal" factors. The former refers to past historical experiences of "managing barbarian affairs" (*yiwu* 夷務), while the latter refers to the Chinese-foreign exchange "felt" in the world at the time. It is not possible to deny that, when trying to understand the time in which they lived, late Qing intellectuals were hardly able to rid themselves of imaginations based upon history. It was very natural for them to drag history into the framework of the Spring and Autumn and Warring states periods, whereas it was very difficult for them to penetrate the unprecedented pattern in order to understand the construction of the modern world. The Late Qing catchphrase of the "emergency that had been unprecedented in the past three thousand years" is, in itself, proof of how difficult it was for China's understanding of the external world to get rid of the restrictions brought about by the vertical direction. The appearance of the "others", on the other hand, provided a basis for breaking out of such a cage and for re-understanding both "nation" and "history".

---

41 Zuixin guowen jiaokeshu (chudeng xiaoxuetang keben) (1904), vol. 9, pp. 4–5.
42 Zhang Qing (2010), "Zhongguo shanshu Yazhou suo yanxu de lishi jiyi".

IV. The Importance of the Emergence of the Concept of "Society"

Discussing the concepts related to "the lack of" (*wu*) is only one aspect of the problem. The corresponding question of "having" (*you*), of course, also is worth being noting. It is also is important segment of late Qing discourses related to the construction of the nation, history, *etc.* The discussion of these discourses also provides some food for thought. Most important among them is the emergence of the concept of "society", which constitutes a concrete example for the construction of "having". We should briefly note here that getting rid of the ideas of the "lack of nation" and the "lack of history" and the new construction of "having a nation" and "having history", was premised on acquiring a new understanding of "nation" and "history". And it was also necessary that the concept of "society" emerged.

"Society" as a concept emerged against the background of "uniting as a group" (*hequn* 合群). This implied the formation of collecting power by forming associations. Looking into the descriptions of late Qing scholars, it is not difficult to understand how "uniting as a community" could become the focus of attention. In his 1895 article entitled "Whence Strength" ("Yuanqiang" 原強), Yan Fu brings the Darwinian "struggle for existence" into play. He made the following remark with regard to social transformation: "At the beginning, race competes against race. Since they form groups in order to form the state, it is competition between groups and then competition between countries." In particular, he stressed that "if one masters sociology, then one can govern the nation and bring peace to the world. One uses it in order to guarantee peace and protect the people and gradually to arrive at the zenith of good government".[43] In his self-compiled chronological biography, Kang Youwei also wrote about why the focus of "uniting as group" *hequn* should be on organising gatherings (*kaihui* 開會).

It has always been common practice in China [that the people] persisted to be scattered. The scholar officials are wary because of the banning of 'societies' (*shehui* 社會)during the Ming-Dynasty, and, because of this, they do not dare to assemble and speak out. For this reason, bringing about change is extremely complicated. When one thinks about opening up common practices and increasing knowledge, this will not be possible if one does not form a large group. Moreover, it is imperative to form a large group because only then will the force increase.[44]

Regarding the question of how to "form groups," in the beginning, late Qing intellectuals usually suggested three factors, namely, the school, study associ-

---

43 Yan Fu (1986), "Yuan Qiang", pp. 5, 7.
44 "Kang Nanhai zibian nianpu" (1953), p. 133.

ations, and newspaper agencies. Their discussions often cover these three in combination rather than focusing on only one of them, in order to try to get the group's voice heard by employing these "media". The fact that "forming groups" was a sensitive issue at the time can be easily imagined. Wang Xianqian 王先謙 (1842–1917) regarded "forming groups" as a major danger for all under heaven. At the beginning of his work, *On Groups* (*qun lun* 群論), he remarked that the "biggest disaster for all under heaven is called 'group'". [45] In the wake of the Hundred Days' Reform (*wuxu bianfa* 戊戌維新), when Kang Youwei's "crimes" were named, one often-mentioned item was the "forming of illegal associations" (*shehui*), and, based upon this, the Qing government also imposed a ban on associations. This shows how difficult it was for Chinese intellectuals, carrying the burden of "Gentlemen don't form parties", to gather and form collective power.

However, the complications were that understanding society and nation based upon "forming groups" had one main tendency, namely, that a "national consciousness"—in a modern sense—gradually allowed a clear understanding of "society" (*shehui*) to emerge. In this process, the Japanese factor played an important role in both the acceptance of the translated term "*shehui*" 社會 and the definition of the concept. Newspapers established by Late Qing intellectuals usually included a column called "Japanese Newspapers Translated" (*Dongwen baoyi* 東文報譯). In a considerable number of articles published in this column, the word *shehui* for 'society' is directly used. An article entitled "On Society" (*Lun shehui* 論社會) in the "Japanese Newspaper Translated" section of the *Shiwu bao* 時務報 states that, "In the areas of the barbarians there is no society. But when civilisation is gradually unfolded, minuscule sprouts appear and in the long run a 'society' is formed". [46] Articles translated and introduced by Japanese-based newspapers also put "society", "forming groups" and "nation" together for discussion. In an article entitled "A New Meaning of Sociology", published in the *Dongya bao* 東亞報 in 1898, and which actually introduced the Japanese translation of a book by Herbert Spencer, the relationship between "society", "nation" and "people of a nation/citizens" was made explicit:

Citizens is the term given to those who have a clearly defined piece of land and live under a clearly defined political body. The nation, then, is a clearly defined piece of land which is spoken about together with the people. Its rights are better than the rights of one person, its force is superior to the force of one person. For this reason, it can restrict the rights of one person. But the meaning of society is even broader than this. No matter whether the territory, the people or the political body is fixed, in all cases in

---

45 Wang Xianqian (2008), "Qun lun", p. 14.
46 "Lun shehui" (1897).

which there is a larger number of people and they assemble in order to live in the form of one group, this can be called 'society'.[47]

This shows that the emergence of "society" as a concept became prevalent at the same time as "nation", "citizen" and other concepts, and that together they constructed a particular discourse. Alluding to the "group" (*qun*) and "society" at the same time shows that "forming a group" not only had the function of promoting "society", but also the goal of heading further towards "society" and "nation". A 1902 article in the *Nanyang qiri bao* 南洋七日報 pointed out that "to form a group is a doctrine, which should exist within a society. When the society is transformed and one arrives at the nation, its nature is still similar but its aim is the opposite." In order to make this clearer, it also stressed that:

Today, if, in our China, one speaks about the nation when it is not convenient to mention the topic, then one goes down one step and speaks about society. This is not far from the 'group'. As the proverb goes: Men group with those to whom they are similar. It is imperative to employ society as a doctrine; all people should abide it. And when they are numerous [enough], then there will be the day in which we can proceed to the nation.[48]

The book *New Erya* 新爾雅 compiled by Wang Rongbao 汪榮寶 (1878–1933) and Ye Lan 葉瀾 (1875–?) in 1903 includes a section entitled "Explaining the Group" (*shi qun* 釋群), which clearly describes the relationship between the "group" and "society": "When more than two persons together form a common body in order to assist each other in life, this is called 'group'; there are also those who call it 'society'." It specifically points out that "Modern humanity cannot exist isolated and on its own. [The people] thus must rely on each other and must assemble together and form a nation".[49]

The implication here is that, after entering the twentieth-century, Chinese scholars who were influenced by the Western theory of the "nation-state" tended to ponder about the complicated issues according to an "individual—society—nation" framework. The article entitled "Reforming China" (*Zhongguo zhi gaizao* 中國之改造) published in the *Dalu*-magazine 大陸 in 1903 provided clear definitions: "The state is a compound structure of assembled individuals. Society is also a compound structure of assembled individuals." "In all cases, healthy individuals, who have a developed mind, and who are similar with regard to attaining benefits and suffering harm can form a political group and these will form the state."[50]

---

47 "Xin shu yilu: shehuixue xinyi" (1898), p. 1.
48 "Lun guojia yu shehui zhi bianbie" (1902), pp. 22–23.
49 Wang Rongbao, Ye Lan (1903). *Xin Erya*, pp. 63–63, p. 51.
50 "Zhongguo zhi gaizao" (1903), No. 3, p. 10 and 4, p.1.

"LACK OF NATION" AND "LACK OF HISTORY" 151

Such a definition of nation is, of course, not clear enough, but it does show that intellectuals were quite concerned about finding a new arrangement between the nation and the individual, and between the nation and society, only that they might hold different standpoints. An article entitled "Respectful Information for my Fellow Provincials" (*jinggao wo xiangren* 敬告我鄉人) published in *Zhejiang Tide* (*Zhejiang chao* 浙江潮) in 1903 discusses the issue from a perspective of the division of power in the following way: the administrative organs of the modern state can roughly be divided into "official authorities" (*guanfu* 官府) and "self-governing bodies" (*zizhi ti* 自治體). The former refers to the administrative organs directly under the control of the state, which directly have the goal of preserving national sovereignty, while the latter refers to the indirect governing organs of the state. Local personnel are used in order to administer local affairs, and in order to achieve the goal of governing the state indirectly.[51] This article is concerned with the division of the state powers. In direct contrast to this, an understanding of the state based upon the description of the "citizens" also commanded attention. In 1907, Yang Du 楊度 (1875–1932) wrote in his "Introduction" to the *New Journal of China* (*Zhongguo xinbao xu* 中國新報敘) that, "Described in one sentence, present day China's government is not a responsible government". This clearly puts responsibility for the nation on the citizens: "That what those who plan the country advocate is only the discourse on the responsibility of the citizens and that is all."[52]

No matter whether they are based upon the "citizens" or upon "self-governing bodies", both arguments have their flaws, but the suggestion of the two concepts *per se* is worth noting. It shows that, upon entering the twentieth-century, as the national consciousness in a modern sense gradually emerged, intellectuals now not only tried to explore the issue of the division of state power, but also started to think about the new status of the individual under a state regime, or, in other words, to what extent the new forces of society should take part in the construction of state power.

Such ideas were expressed in an article entitled "On the Phenomenon of the Chinese Society and on the Ideas of How to Make it Thrive". ("Lun Zhongguo shehui zhi xianxiang jiqi zhenxing zhi yaozhi" 論中國社會之現象及其振興之要旨) published in *The Eastern Miscellany* (*Dongfang zazhi* 東方雜誌). The article also quoted the proverb: "With the skin gone, what can the hair adhere to?" in order to stress the importance of "society". "Society" thus was likened to the "skin", which would replace "government".[53]

It can be claimed that advancing the idea of "forming groups" helped to push forward a better understanding of society and nation. It was not sufficient,

---

51 Gongfazi (1903), "Jinggao wo xiangren.", p. 3.
52 Yang Du (1907), "Zhongguo xinbao xu".
53 Peiqing (1905), "Lun Zhongguo shehui zhi xianxiang jiqi chenxing zhi yaozhi.", p. 281.

however, to reveal the real meaning of a mature, grown-up society. How then, did the "having" of a society find its concrete expression? It is certain that the idea of "forming groups" promoted the re-organisation of society, especially the emergence of the concept of "trade", of which "professional field" (*yejie* 業界) is an important expression. This means that "trades" or "professional fields" formed a portrait of the force of society and also constituted its basic element.

This may be seen as the meaning of "having" a society, but it can also be claimed that the emergence of "society" as a concept encouraged intellectuals at that time to think about how to organise Chinese society. In other words, understanding "society" based upon a modern notion of "nation" and differentiating between "nation" and "society" is only one side of the story. On the other hand, after having acquired the concept of "society", what attracted most attention was the meaning of "society", *i.e.*, how a society should be organised. It was these considerations that pushed society forward and made it a substantial concept. Its transformation from "abstract" to "concrete" can also be considered as a symbol for the profound dynamics in Chinese society.[54]

V. "Society" as the Fundamental Key for the Establishment of "New History"

The emergence of "society" as a concept not only influenced the understanding of "nation", but the so-called "having a nation" reflected even more so the confirmation of the position of society and emphasised that the maturing of society was the main focus of the modern nation. What is equally remarkable is that the expectations regarding "New History" also mainly revolved around the dealing with "society". It even could be said that "society" was the fundamental key for "New Historiography"

In his translation of Herbert Spencer's *A Study of Sociology* (*Qunxue yiyan* 群學肄言), Yan Fu pointed out that the system of old history writing "focused on the acts of emperors and aristocrats, no matter how trivial they were and ignored issues related to people's livelihood, no matter how major they were." He suggested that, when examining the past, one should focus on the "reasons for strength and weaknesses, order and chaos, and the rise and fall of a group".[55] Although Yan Fu did not explicitly demand the writing of a history of society, his intention is not difficult to read. In fact, there was no lack of voices pointing out that China's "lack of history" was due to the fact that there was no

---

54 I can here only briefly touch the issue. For more details see Zhang Qing (forthcoming), "Shehui de xu yu shi – lüelun wan Qing Zhongguo gainian fuxian de yiyi."

55 Spencer, Herbert (1981), *Qunxue yiyan*, p. 8.

"LACK OF NATION" AND "LACK OF HISTORY"

history of "society". Moreover, in an article, Liang Qichao pointed out that China's history writing in the past was aware that "there was an Imperial court, but did not know that there was a society, was aware that there was power, but did not know that there was civilisation/enlightenment (*wenming* 文明)". He therefore considered "society" as the core of the history writing of the new historiography.[56] Zhang Taiyan's opinion on this issue is also quite representative. In a letter to Liang Qichao in 1902, Zhang wrote that, when compiling a *General History of China* (*Zhongguo tongshi* 中國通史), it was important to "discover the principles for the progress and decline of society and politics."[57] In his *Yellow History* (*huang shi* 黃史), Huang Jie also clearly stated that, with regard to what constituted history, it was "putting together the past, present and future of society and that which was born of this", and he pointed out that, "Our historiographers of 4,000 years, have [written] biographies of individuals but no history of the society". Not only did he put special emphasis on "society" but, in particular, he also noted that new academic disciplines, including "sociology", would be very beneficial to the writing of history.[58]

It was precisely the maturing of the notion of "society" which influenced the direction of history writing. More concretely, the re-definition of the "scope of history" by Late Qing historians largely revolved around putting stress on "society". When the scope of history was extended to cover "history as a whole body", it became clearly apparent that society became the axis of history writing. And once society was put in the centre, it was inevitable to employ knowledge borrowed from other academic disciplines for a better understanding of 'society'. The reason is that, guided by the modern national consciousness, the construction of "society" became a major concern. The mission of explaining "society" was shared by different disciplines. Correspondingly, history writing now was closely combined with knowledge from other academic disciplines and widely adopted the technical terminology of these disciplines. This, in fact, also played a major role for including newly coined technical terminology in history writing. In his *Textbook of Chinese History* (*Zhongguo lishi jiaokeshu* 中國歷史教科書) written by Liu Shipei 劉師培 (1884–1919) between 1905 and 1906, the author, who attached much importance to the written language, also widely adopted new terms. Section titles in the book include new terms such as *zhengzhi* 政治 for "politics", *zongjiao* 宗教 for "religion", *quanli* 權利 for "rights", *yiwu* 義務 for "obligation", *caizheng* 財政 for "finance", *gongyi* 工藝 for "handicraft" and *meishu* 美術 for the "fine arts", many of which related to academic disciplines.[59] In other words, the new concepts that emerged in

---

56 Liang Qichao (1902b), "Dongji yuedan".

57 Zhang Taiyan (1902), "Zhang Taiyan laijian", p. 4

58 Huang Jie (1905), "Huang shi". p. 2.

59 Liu Shipei (1997),"Zhonggu lishi jiaokeshu—Fanli."

modern China also became a symbol of its "transformation"; it is even possible to claim that they remoulded Chinese society and China's history.[60]

Discussions related to the "lack of" during the late Qing period not only extended to "nation" and "history" but, in fact, also became visible in many more topics. In his *Yellow history*, Huang Jie points out that: "As long as the different kinds of learning in our country are not clear, there are no names for the academic disciplines; as long as the nation has not been founded, there is no designation for the nation."[61] Except for discussions on the lack of "learning" and the lack of "society" many other "lacks" stood out. The *Zhengyi tongbao* 政藝通報 and *Academic Journal of National Essence* (*Guocui xuebao* 國粹學報) both wrote about the "lack of academic learning" and stressed that "The last two-hundred years of our all under heaven empire could be aptly called an epoch lacking in learning".[62] In addition, the emergence of the concept of "society" was also based upon the "lack of". The aforementioned article "On Society" in the "Japanese Newspapers translated" column in the *Shiwu bao* points out that, "In the areas of the barbarians, there is no society". Moreover, during the May Fourth Movement, the discourse on the "lack of society" was still prevalent. A short article by Fu Sinian 傅斯年 (1896–1950) entitled "Society—the Mass" ("Shehui—qunzhong" 社會——群眾) made a differentiation between "society" and "the mass", and emphasised that, in China, there was still a situation in which "it was named society, but in fact was mass", and, in this way, he tried to point out that China was still in the stage of the "lack of society".[63]

Zhuangzi said that, "The system of the Dao was about to be torn into fragments all under the sky"(*Zhuangzi - tianxia pian*). Late Qing intellectuals often mentioned a "crisis unprecedented in the past three thousand years". Their opinions regarding "the lack of nation" and the "lack of history" can be considered as reflecting precisely this idea. The process in which "nation", "history" and "society" were transformed from "lacking" to "existing" demonstrates, without any doubt, the location where late Qing concepts were maturing. To some extent, this is an issues which one encounters when engaging in an analysis from a perspective of conceptual history. The reason why this transformative process from "lacking" to "existing" is worth analysing is also that the so-called "existing" is related to questions pointing in different directions. In fact, it reflects the transformation of a whole discourse. It is related to the emergence of a language environment revolving around the emergence of a national consciousness in a modern sense. In 1913, the American Presbyterian Mission Press in Shanghai 上海美華書館 published a small volume which

---

60 Zhang Qing (2014) , "'Wenming' yu 'shehui' zunding de lishi jidiao.."
61 Huang Jie (1905), "Huang shi", pp. 8–9.
62 Deng Shi (1904), "Guoxue baocun lun, p. 6.
63 Fu Sinian (1919), "Shehui – qunzhong", p. 345.

directly showed how new terms contributed to the reception of "new ideas".[64] Studies of the new terms and new concepts of the Late Qing period also reveal that, when analysing the cultural and temporal asepcts of the knowledge transfer that took place, we "must consider a wide range of economic, social and ideological aspects that are inevitably involved in the process of transmission and reception".[65] It is clear that understanding China upon the basis of the assumption of a "lack", which became the prevalent form of discussion, is the concrete expression of a discourse of weakness. It can, of course, also be considered as an early example that shows China's involvement in the modern world. It was against such a background that China's discourse of "modernity" began to emerge and that the question of national construction and other problems were re-considered in a global context.

(Translated by Mei Chen and Iwo Amelung)

Bibliography

"Ai zai wuguo zhi min" 哀哉無國之民 (Oh How Pathetic are the People without a Nation), *Jingshi wenchao*, 4, (8 August 1903), pp. 17–19.

Amelung, Iwo, Joachim Kurtz and Michael Lackner (2001), "Introduction", in: Michael Lackner, Iwo Amelung, Joachim Kurtz (eds), *New Terms for New Ideas. Western Knowledge and Lexical Change in Late Imperial China*, Leiden: Brill.

Chen Yinke 陳寅恪 (2001), "Wuguo xueshu zhi xianzhuang ji Qinghua zhi zhize" 吾國學術之現狀及清華之職責 (The Current State of our Nation's Academic Scholarship and the Responsibility of Qinghua [University]), in: Chen Yinke, *Chen Yinke ji – Jin Mingguan conggao er bian*, Beijing: Sanlian shudian. pp. 361–363.

Deng Shi 鄧實 (1902), "Shixue tonglun yi" 史學通論一 (A General Introduction to Historiography, first part), *Zhengyi tongbao*, 1902:12 (18 August 1902), p. 1.

– (1904), "Guoxue baocun lun" 國學保存論 (On the Preservation of National Learning), *Zhengyi tongbao*, 1904:3 (31 March 1904). p. 6.

– (1908), "Diqi nian 'Zhengyi tongbao' tiji" 第七年〈政藝通報〉題記 (Guiding Inscription for the 7th Year of the Publication of the Zhengyi tongbao), *Zhengyi tongbao*, 1908: 1 (16 February 1908), pp. 1–3.

"Fanli" 凡例 (Editorial Guide) (1902), in: Xiao Yongshi (ed.), *Wuzhou shulüe* (A Brief Introduction of the Five Continents). Ziteng shuguan, p. 1.

Fu Sinian 傅斯年 (1919), "Shehui—qunzhong" 社會——群眾 (Society – The Mass), *Xinchao*, 1:2 (1 February 1919).

Gongfazi 攻法子 (1903), "Jinggao wo xiangren" 敬告我鄉人 (An Admonition to my Fellow Provincials) *Zhejiang chao*, 2 (18 March 1903), pp. 1–12.

---

64 Mateer (1913), *New Terms for New Ideas: A Study of the Chinese Newspaper.* The book by Lackner et al (see below) also adopted such an opinion and uses it as the book title.

65 Amelung, Kurtz, Lackner (2001), "Introduction".

Hobsbawm, Eric (1962), *The Age of Revolution: Europe: 1789–1848*, London: Weidenfeld & Nicolson.

Huang Jie 黃節 (1905), "Huang shi" 黃史 (Yellow History), *Guocui xuebao*, 1 (23 February 1905).

Huang Rucheng 黃汝成 (1994), "Zhengshi" 正始 (The Real Beginning), in: *Rizhilu ji shi*, Changsha: Yuelu shushe.

Huang Shizhong 黃世仲 (1902), "Sishi" 私史 (Private History). Originally published in: *Tiannan xinbao* (12 September 1902). Quoted from *Xinmin congbao*, 19 (31 October 1902), pp. 7–8.

*Jingshi daxuetang Zhongguo tongshi jianyi (daxuetang jiaoxi Wang Zhouyao jiangshu)*京師大學堂中國通史講義 （大學堂教習王舟瑤講述） (Lecture Notes for the General History of China at Jingshi University (by Wang Zhouyao, Lecturer of the University)) (1904), Jingshi xuewu, (1904). pp. 1–3.

"Kang Nanhai zibian nianpu" 康南海自編年譜 (1953) (Self compiled chronological autobiography of Kang Youwei), *Zhongguo jindai shizhi ziliao congkan. Wuxu bianfa*, Shanghai: Shenzhou guoguangshe.

Kang Youwei 康有為 (1935), *Da tong shu* 大同書 (The Book of Great Harmony). Shanghai: Zhonghua shuju.

Levenson, Joseph R. (1958), *Confucian China and its Modern Fate, Volume One: The Problem of Intellectual Continuity*, Berkeley CA: University of California Press.

Liang Qichao 梁啟超 (1897). "Shuo qun, zixu" 說群自序 （On groups, authors preface), *Shiwubao*, 26 (12 May 1897), p. 1.

– (1899), "Aiguo lun" 愛國論 (On Patriotism), *Qingyi bao*, 6, (20 February 1899), p. 1.

– (1901a), "Guojia sixiang bianqian yitong lun" 國家思想變遷異同論 (On the Similarities and Differences of the Changes of National Thought), *Qingyi bao*, 94, (1 September 1901), pp. 1–4.

– (1901b), "Jiruo suyuan lun" 積弱溯源論 (On the Origins of our Accumulated Weaknesses), *Qingyi bao*, 77, (29 April 1901), p. 3.

– (1902a), "Dongji yuedan" 東籍月旦 (Notes on Japanese Books), *Xinmin congbao*, 13.

– (1902b), "Xinmin shuo. Di liu jie: lun guojia sixiang" 新民說四·第六節：論國家思想 (On the New Citizen, 4–6: On the Idea of the Nation), *Xinmin congbao*, 4, (24 March 1902), pp. 1–3.

– (1903), "Zhengzhixue dajia Bolunzhili zhi xueshuo" 政治學大家伯倫知理之學說 (The Great Political Scientist Bluntschli's Theory), *Xinmin congbao*, 38–39, (4 October 1903).

– (1989), "Xin shixue" 新史學 (New Historiography), in: Liang Qichao, *Yinbingshi heji – wenji zhi 9*, Beijing. Beijing: Zhonghua shuju, pp. 1–32.

"Lishilei zongxu" 歷史類總敘 (1903), (General Preface to the Category History), in: *Xinxue shumu tiyao*, vol. 2. Shanghai tongya shuju.

Liu Shipei 劉師培 (1997), "Zhonggu lishi jiaokeshu—Fanli" 中國歷史教科書·凡例 (Editorial Guide to Textbook of Chinese History), in: *Liu Shenshu yishu*, Nanjing: Jiangsu guji chubanshe, vol. 2, p. 2177.

"Lun guojia yu shehui zhi bianbie" 論國家與社會之辨別 (On the Difference between Nation and Society), *Nanyan qiri bao* 18 (12 January 1902), pp. 22–23.

"Lun shehui" 論社會 (1897)(On Society), *Shiwu bao*, 17 (13 January 1897, pp. 23–24) and 18 (22 February 1897, p. 28) column "Dongwen baoyi", pp. 23–24 (translated from Osaka Asahi Shimbum, 10 December 1896).

Luo Zhitian 羅志田 (2007), "Tianxia yu shijie: Qingmo shiren guanyu renlei shehui zhishi de zhuanbian—zezhong Liang Qichao de guannnian" 天下與世界：清末士人關於人類社會認知的轉變——側重梁啟超的觀念 (Tianxia and the World: Transformations in the Understanding of Human Society by Late Qing Scholars—Focusing on the Thoughts of Liang Qichao). *Zhongguo shehui kexue*, 5, pp. 191–204.

Ma Junwu 馬君武 (2000 [1902]), "Yixu" 譯序 (Preface of the translator), in: Zeng Degui (ed.), *Ma Junwu wenxuan*, Guilin: Guangxi shifan daxue chubanshe, (2000), pp. 46–47.

Ma Xulun 馬敘倫 (1903), "Shixue datong shuo" 史學大同說 (On Great Harmony in Historiography), *Zhengyi tongbao*, 16, (21 September 1903).

Mateer, Ada Haven (1913), *New Terms for New Ideas: A Study of the Chinese Newspaper*, Shanghai: American Presbyterian Mission Press.

Peiqing 培卿 (1905), "Lun Zhongguo shehui zhi xianxiang jiqi chenxing zhi yaozhi" 論中國社會之現象及其振興之要旨 (On the phenomenon of the Chinese Society and on the Ideas of How to Make it Thrive), *Dongfang zazhi*, 1:12, (30 January 1905), pp. 279–284.

Qijizi 棄疾子 (1904), " ´Qing mishi´ xu" 清秘史敘 (Preface to the Secret History of the Qing-[dynasty], in: Yougui, Xueyin, *Qing mishi*, Luchen congshu she.

Spencer, Herbert 斯賓塞 (1981), *Qunxue yiyan* 群學肄言 (The Study of Sociology), translated by Yan Fu 嚴復, Beijing: Shangwu yinshuguan.

Tan Sitong 譚嗣同 (1981), "Renxue xia" 仁學（下）(A Study of Humanity, Second Part), in: Cai Shangsi, Fang Xing (eds.), *Tan Sitong*, Beijing: Zhonghua shuju, vol. 2. p. 367.

Townsend, James (1996), "Chinese Nationalism", in: Jonathan Unger (ed.), *Chinese Nationalism*, (Armonk NY: M.E. Sharpe), pp. 1–30.

Wang Fansen 王汎森 (2001), "Wan Qing de zhengzhi gainian yu 'xin shixue'" 晚晴的政治概念與'新史學'(Late Qing Political Concepts and 'New Historiography'), in: Wang Fansen, *Zhongguo jindai sixang yu xueshu de xipu*, Shijiazhuang: Hebei jiaoyu chubanshe, pp. 165–196.

Wang Rongbao 汪榮寶, Ye Lan 葉瀾 (1903). *Xin Erya* 新爾雅 (New Erya), Shanghai: Mingquanshe.

Wang Xianqian 王先謙 (2008), "Qun lun" 群論 (On Groups), in: Wang Xianqin, *Wang Xianqian shiwen ji*, Changsha: Yuelu shushe, p. 14.

"Wu guojia" 無國家 (Lacking a Nation-state), *Jiangsu*, 3 (25 June 1903).

Xing Yitian 邢義田 (1981), "Tianxia yijia—Zhonguoren de tianxia guan" 天下一家——中國人的天下觀 (All under the Heaven is a Family: The Chinese View of Tianxia), in: Liu Dai (ed.), *Zhongguo wenhua xin lun. Genyuan pian*, Taipei: Lianjing chuban gongsi, p. 452.

"Xishi tongzhi" 西史通志 (1902)(Comprehensive Record of Western History), in Yuan Qingfang, Yan Hailan (eds.), *Xixue santong*, Shanghai: Wenshengtang, pp. 1–4.

"Xin shu yilu: shehuixue xinyi" 新書譯錄：社會學新義 (1898) (Notes on a Newly Translated Book: The New Meaning of Sociology), *Dongyabao* 1 (29 June 1898), p. 1.

Yan Fu (1986), "Yuan Qiang", 原強 (Whence Strength?), in: *Yan Fu ji*. Beijing: Zhonghua shuju, pp. 5–15.

Yang Du 楊度 (1907), "Zhongguo xinbao xu" 中國新報敘 (Introduction to New Journal of China), *Zhongguo xinbao* 1: 1 (2 January 1907), pp. 1–2.

Yu Yi 余一 (1903), "Minzuzhuyi lun" 民族主義論 (On Nationalism), *Zhejiang chao* 1, (17 February 1903); 2 (18 March 1903).

Zhang Qing 章清 (2003), "Pubian lishi yu Zhongguoshi zhi shuxie" 普遍歷史與中國史之書 (Universal History and the Writing of Chinese History), in: Yang Nianqun et al. (eds), *Xin shixue—duo xueke duihua de tujing*, part 1, Beijing: Zhongguo renmin daxue chubanshe, pp. 236–264.

– (2005), "Zhong Xi lishi zhi 'huitong' yu Zhongguo shixue de zhuanxiang" 中西歷史之 '會通' 與中國史學的轉向 (The Confluence of Chinese and Western Histories and the Transformation of Chinese Historical Learning), *Lishi yanjiu*, 2005: 2, pp. 75–95.

– (2010), "Zhongguo shanshu Yazhou suo yanxu de lishi jiyi—jian lun zuo wei 'tazhe' de Riben yu Chaoxian" 中國闡述 '亞洲' 所延續的 '歷史記憶' ——兼論作為 '他者' 的日本與朝鮮 (The Continuing Historical Commemoration of Asia in Chinese Descriptions—also Discussing Japan and Korea as an 'Other'), in: *Yazhou: Wenhua jiaoliu yu jiazhi shanshi*, Shanghai: Fudan daxue chubanshe, pp. 3–23.

– (2014), "'Wenming' yu 'shehui' zunding de lishi jidiao—lüelun wan Qing yijiang 'xin mingci' de fuxian dui Zhongguo lishi de chongsu" "'文明' 與 '社會' 奠定的歷史基調——略論晚晴以降 '新名詞' 的浮現對 '中國歷史' 的重塑" ("The Fundamental Topic of History Set by 'Civilisation' and 'Society': A Brief Discussion on the Emergence of 'New Terms' since Late Qing and its remoulding of the 'Chinese History'"]. *Yazhou gainian shi yanjiu*, 2, pp. 187–228.

– (forthcoming), "Shehui de xu yu shi—lüelun wan Qing Zhongguo gainian fuxian de yiyi" 社會' 的虛與實——略論晚清中國概念浮現的意義 ('Society' in Theory and Practice—A Brief Study on the Meaning of the Emergence of Concepts during the Late Qing).

Zhang Shizhao 章士釗 (1981). "Shu 'Huangdi hun'" 疏 '黃帝魂 (Commentary to 'The Soul of Huangdi'"), in: *Xinhai geming huiyi lu* Beijing: Wenshi ziliao chubanshe, vol. 1, p. 221.

Zhang Taiyan 章太炎 (1902), "Zhang Taiyan laijian" 章太炎來簡 (Letter from Zhang Taiyan), *Xinmin congbao*, 13. (4 August 1902).

– (1906), "Yanshuo lu" 演說錄 (Record of a Speech), *Minbao*, 6 (25 July 1906), pp. 1–15.

Zhina shaonian 支那少年 (ed. and trans.) (1903), *Zhina siqian nian kaihua shi* 支那四千年開化史 (A History of 4000 Years Civilisation in China), Shanghai: Zhina fanyi huishe.

"Zhongguo zhi gaizao" 中國之改造 (China's Reform) (1903), *Dalu* 3 (7 February 1903), p. 10, and 4 (8 March 1903), p. 1.

Zuixin guowen jiaokeshu (chudeng xiaoxuetang keben) 最新國文教科書 （初等小學堂課本） (1904), (Most Recent Textbook of the National Language (Edition for Elementary Schools)), Shanghai: The Commercial Press.

Part II:
Diagnosing the Sick Man—Divided, Imperilled, Humiliated

The Privileges of the Powerful and the Discourses of the Weak: The Dissemination and Application of the Concept of "Extraterritoriality" in Modern China

Huang Xingtao

The political discourse of weak countries in modern Asia has quite often been subjected to the complicated influences of modern international law, which was first established by the countries of the West, as well as by the knowledge and concepts related to it. It has become a prominent feature of the discourse of the weak state in Modern China to express demands with regard to domestic affairs and foreign relations in order to promote domestic reforms and to safeguard the sovereignty and dignity of the state through the understanding and application of the knowledge, concepts and spirit of international law, which bears a special stamp of the times.

In China of the late Qing and the Republican period, the emergence and the early use of the notion of "rights" (*quanli* 權利), and a group of concepts related to it, is the most concentrated reflection of the discourse of a weak nation. Exploring its early forms, its modes of application and its function has thus become an efficient path to highlight the historical discourse of the weak country. "Rights", "sovereignty" (*zhuquan* 主權), "national sovereignty" (*guoquan* 國權) and "privileges/prerogatives" (*tequan* 特權), in their modern sense, were first produced in a translated work which had been organised by the American missionary W.A.P. Martin (Ding Weiliang 丁韙良, 1827–1916), and which was published in Beijing in 1864 as *Wanguo gongfa* 萬國公法 and constituted an early translation of modern Western International Law. The formation and the application of new Chinese terms relating to "power", which appeared after this, such as "civil rights/liberties" (*minquan* 民權), "human rights" (*renquan* 人權), "women's rights" (*nuquan* 女權), "legal rights", as well as "extraterritoriality" (*zhiwai faquan* 治外法權), "consular jurisdiction" (*lingshi caipan quan* 領事裁判權), "educational rights" (*jiaoyuquan* 教育權), "copyright" (*banquan* 版權), "tariff autonomy" (*guanshui zizhuquan* 關稅自主權), "railway rights" (*luquan* 路權), "mineral rights" (*kuangquan* 礦權), *etc.*, not only became an important focus of research in conceptual history,[1] but also has a special function for understand-

---

1 Huang Xingtao (2012), "Gainianshi fangfa yu Zhongguo jindaishi yanjiu".

ing "discourses of weakness" and "discourses of national weakness". Extraterritoriality symbolises the partial loss of sovereignty in modern China. Its being put into practice in China symbolised China's weakness and, at the same time, also pushed forward and strengthened the Chinese self-perception of being weak.[2]

This article does not intend to come to grips with the whole new terminological group related to "power/rights", but limits itself to the concept of "extraterritoriality" and provides a historical examination of the question of how it was disseminated, appropriated and used in modern China. I believe that this approach may be of some use in order to understand the bigger picture of the modes of expression of "discourses of national weakness", the peculiarity of how they were used, and how they exerted external and internal influence.

1. On Research and the Definition of "Extraterritoriality" in Modern China

There is already some Chinese historical research on the question of extraterritoriality in China. This is concentrated on the aspect of how the Qing rulers and the Republican government dealt with the problem of extraterritoriality in concrete, and on the process of the abolition of extraterritoriality. Legal scholars have focused on the connotations of the concept of "extraterritoriality", pointing out the difference to "consular jurisdiction" and its relation with it. These two aspects are both related to the questions that I will be addressing here, and the research contributions of Li Yang, Gao Hancheng and others are especially worth mentioning.[3] However, with regard to the origins of the Chinese word

---

2 This article is based upon a contribution to the international conference "Discourses of Weakness in Late Imperial and Early Republican China" at the Goethe-University, Frankfurt am Main, Germany in December 2015. During the conference and after, the discussions with Iwo Amelung, Zhang Ke, Sun Qing and others were of considerable importance. I would like to take this opportunity to thank them for their input. In the two years following the conference, I presented the paper at Nankai University, Nanjing University and other places and obtained important insights which allowed me to make revisions and additions for this publication.

3 Representative historical research was done by Yang Tianhong, Wu Yixiong and Li Yumin; cf. Yang Tianhong (2005), "Beiyang waijiao yu 'zhiwai faqun' de chefei", Wu Yixiong (2006), "Yapian zhanzheng yiqian Yingguo zai Hua zhiwai faquan zhi yunxiang yu changshi," and Li Yumin (2009), "Wan Qing gaijin, shouhui lingshi caipanquan de mouhua ji nuli". In legal studies, it was Li Qicheng and Zhao Xiaogeng who, at first, again brought up the problem and did research on the problem of conceptual discrepancies; cf. Li Qicheng (2003), "Lingshi caipanquan zhidu yu wan Qing sifa gaige zhi zhaoduan", and Zhao Xiaogeng, "Shixi zhiwai faquan yu lingshi caipanquan". Li Yang's achievements are particularly noteworthy. In recent

EXTRATERRITORIALITY IN MODERN CHINA

for "extraterritoriality" and the concept, the question of how the Chinese understood the term early on, the peculiarities of how it was used and what effect it had on Chinese society, as well as with regard to source material and analysis, there is still room for providing further excavations and discussion.

The concept of "extraterritoriality", which belongs to the realm of International Law, which originated in the West, was formed during the seventeenth century, and became more common at the end of the eighteenth century. The original English corresponding terms were "exterritoriality" and "extraterritoriality".[4] Its most fundamental contents or literal meaning is that a certain group of persons or an organisation which resides in another country has the right not to be subject—or subjected—to that country's jurisdiction, or, to put it in the words of the *Dongfang zazhi* 東方雜誌 (*Eastern Miscellany*), "having the meaning of enjoying legal rights outside one's own area of jurisdiction".[5] In Western usage, there was originally no difference between "exterritoriality", and "extraterritoriality", and it is only today that "extraterritoriality" (or its abbreviation "extrality") is much more common in modern English usage. Thus, the difference between the two emerged very late.

In the unequal intercourse between the West and the countries of the East, the concept and practice of extraterritoriality had an impact on both China and Japan. In their interaction with the West and the contest between the two countries, China and Japan, could also help to develop their own understanding of the concept and employ it selectively in order to express their own internal and external political demands. This resulted in the internationalisation of the concept, and contributed both to its complexity and to the problems of modern observers to define it.

Even today, there are clear differences among academics in understanding the concept. The *Encyclopedia Britannica* equals "extraterritoriality" with "diplomatic immunity",[6] and this is the same in the newest edition of the Chinese encyclopaedic dictionary *Cihai* 辭海,[7] while the *Encyclopedia Americana* situates "consular jurisdiction" in the category of "extraterritoriality". The latter is of the

---

years, he has published several articles which delve ever deeper into the matter; cf. Li Yang (2013), "Zhiwai faquan haishi lingshi caipanquan", "Cong ciyi dao yujing: Zhiwai faquan wudu, wuyong ji wuhui". See, also, Gao Hancheng (2017) in his new work "Zhiwai faquan, lingshi caipanquan ji qita—ji yu yuyuxue shijiao de lishi fenxi", and his "Zhongguo jindai 'zhiwai faquan' gainian de cihuishi" (2018), which provided new material and new vistas which are worth noting. One important English language contribution is Wang Dong (2005), *China's Unequal Treaties*.

4 At times also related expressions such as "extra-territorial rights" or "extraterritorial jurisdiction" are employed.

5 Zhou Gengsheng 周鯁生 (1923), "Lingshi caipanquan wenti" 領事裁判權問題 (The Problem of Consular Jurisdiction), *Dongfang zazhi*, 13: 8, pp. 9–10.

6 *Bulitun baikequanshu* (2007), vol. 6, pp. 198–199.

7 Xia Zhengnong (1989), *Cihai*, p. 1039.

opinion that, apart from the main meaning of diplomatic immunity in modern times, it also has an exceptional form, which is, that some strong countries, especially Western countries, by means of treaties, extend the meaning of the term by which diplomatic immunity is accorded to heads of states, members of the foreign office, the diplomatic corps and other special groups, to *all* their citizens living abroad in some Asian and African countries, so that their nationals are neither constrained by the laws of the foreign countries in which they reside nor by the legal judgments of the states in which they are resident.[8]

Some scholars think it is possible to distinguish between a broad and a narrow understanding of these concepts.

In a narrow sense, it relates to diplomatic immunity as a common provision of International Law; in a broader sense, it includes consular jurisdiction and other "legal rights outside one's own area of jurisdiction", which some refer to as "jurisdiction abroad" (*yuwai guanxiaquan* 域外管轄權). With regard to "extraterritoriality", the renowned Chinese international law scholar Wang Tieya 王鐵崖 basically maintains an understanding which distinguishes between a broad *and* a narrow definition of the term.[9]

In addition, there is another view that treats the concepts of "extraterritoriality" and "consular jurisdiction" as identical, and believes that their implications and usage in modern China are basically the same. The scholar Kang Dashou 康大壽, for example, believes that judged from the use of the concept of extraterritoriality in modern Chinese texts, especially when combined with the reality of modern Chinese history, the extraterritoriality enjoyed by foreigners in modern China already does not any longer have the meaning of a diplomatic privilege or an [diplomatic] exemption as in normal international law. We are dealing with a specific historical concept, which contains the idea of illegal aggression in the guise of consular jurisdiction.[10]

Some of the above-mentioned understandings and definitions are purely based upon the principles of jurisprudence of International Law. Some claim that they are arguing in terms of the practical usage of the term in the modern Chinese language. Others try to balance and reconcile the two. However, the kind of definition which is more in line with the modern practice of Chinese-foreign diplomatic interactions, how it existed and how, in the end, the exchange between the two sides worked, as well as the implications that it finally had, all of this awaits more thorough historical research.

---

8 *Encyclopedia Americana* (1985), vol. 10, pp. 806–807.

9 Wang Tieya (1996), *Zhonghua faxue da cidian – guoji faxue juan*, p. 676.

10 Kang Dashou (2000), "Jindai wairen zai Hua 'zhiwai faquan' shiyi".

2. The Early Dissemination of the Concept of "Extraterritoriality" and the Earliest Misunderstandings (1843–1894).

As is widely known, by using the form of the unequal treaties, the Western powers in China practised extraterritoriality in the sense of consular jurisdiction. The excuse for this was the alleged cruelty and brutality of Chinese law, the filthiness of Chinese prisons, the unfairness of trials, *etc.* This began during the Opium War period (1839–42). In the years 1843 and 1844, the Chinese-British "General Regulations under which the British Trade is to be Conducted at the Five Ports of Canton, Amoy, Foochow, Ningpo, and Shanghai" ("Wukou tongshang zhangcheng" 五口通商章程), the Chinese-American "Wangxia Treaty" (Wangxia tiaoyue 望厦條約), the Chinese-French "Whampoa Treaty" (Huangpu tiaoyue 黃埔條約) and other unequal treaties, all contained paragraphs on lawsuits in which English, American and French persons in Chinese treaty ports were involved, which were to be adjudicated by the consuls and the administrative personnel. In the Chinese and foreign versions of the relevant treaties, however, neither the term "consular jurisdiction" nor "extraterritoriality" were mentioned. At the time, the foreign diplomats taking part in the negotiations were scheming incessantly, while the Chinese officials were muddleheaded and completely ignorant, and only wanted to use these provisions in order to restrain the Westerners and to extricate themselves from managing the many inconveniences which these demanding foreigners were causing. How then could they have tried to obtain equal rights with the Western powers? They hardly realised the fact that, in their helplessness and carelessness, they had lost the sovereignty of their country.

Later on, by way of the "Treaty of Tianjin" (Tianjin tiaoyue 天津條約) and the "Convention of Peking" (Beijing tiaoyue 北京條約) and other regulations, extraterritoriality, in the sense of the consular jurisdiction of all Western powers, was extended to a larger area beyond that of the treaty ports. After the Zongli Yamen, which was responsible for foreign relations, had been established, in order to make foreign relations more convenient, the first batch of publications relating to International Law was translated and published under the direction of the American missionary W.A.P. Martin, who later served as professor of international law at the Tongwenguan. These books, which included the *Wanguo gongfa*, *Xingyao zhizhang* 星軺指掌 (*Guide diplomatique*), *etc.*, all, albeit to different degrees, touched upon knowledge of the concepts and systems of state legal power. Among these was the book entitled *Wanguo gongfa*, which was a translation of the volume by the American scholar of international law, Henry Wheaton, entitled *Elements of International Law* (1836), which was published in 1864 and had considerable influence. In this book, *zhuquan*, as a translation for "sovereignty", was mentioned for the first time. It stressed that, among "sovereign states", there is none "which does not have the power to order its internal affairs", that all could promulgate laws and would have jurisdiction over *all* the people residing on its territory (its own people *and* foreigners), and could "adjudicate and punish all criminal cases committed on its territory", stressing that this is a "common practice" (*changli* 常例) or "fundamental practice" (*dali* 大例), which means a legal principle, which needs to be observed. But, at the same time "special cases" (*teli* 特例) or "exceptional cases" (*liwai* 例外) existed, which, in the original book, were termed as "the municipal laws [which] operate beyond its territorial jurisdiction". The phrase "laws are applied in outside territories" (*fa xing yu jiangwaizhe* 法行於疆外者) was a translation of the phrase "laws operate extra-territorially" in the original.

Among the "laws applied in outside territories" introduced by the *Wanguo gongfa*, there are those which are "due to official business", and those because of "personal status", and there are "laws applied in outside territories because of a treaty", in which other concrete situations are introduced. These include "laws applied in outside territories because of personal status", which are related to a sovereign, to envoys and towards naval vessels leaving their own country and entering other countries and enjoying the right not to be subject to another country's jurisdiction. They are also concerned with the privilege of diplomatic personnel being exempt from paying taxes. "Laws applied in outside territories because of a treaty" relate to "consular jurisdiction" and its special power, which is formed because of a treaty. The book says:

The municipal laws and institutions of any state may operate beyond its own territory, and within the territory of another state by special compact between two states. Such are the treaties by which the consuls and other commercial agents of one nation are authorized to exercise over their own countrymen, a jurisdiction with the territory of the state where they reside. The nature and extent of this peculiar jurisdiction depends upon the stipulations of the treaties between the two states.[11]

It explicitly stresses:

Every sovereign state is independent of every other in the exercise of its judicial power. This general position must, of course, be qualified by the exceptions to its application arising out of express compact, such as conventions with foreign states and acts of confederation, by which the state bay be united in a league with other states for some common purpose. By the stipulations of these compacts it may part with certain portions of its judicial power. [Original Chinese text "this power may be reduced"].[12]

This acknowledges that consular jurisdiction as a treaty privilege does, in fact, constitute an injury towards the sovereignty of a sovereign country. There is a

---

11 Note by translator: I use the original wording of Wheaton's book here; cf. Wheaton (1836), *Elements*, p. 109.

12 Ibid., pp. 109–110.

EXTRATERRITORIALITY IN MODERN CHINA

clear difference between this kind of conditionally-limited right and diplomatic immunity, which belongs to the "great principles" of international law, which clearly is based upon the principle of equality, and does not harm national sovereignty.

In the section in which "consular jurisdiction" is explained, the *Wanguo gongfa* also makes clear that "consuls are not entitled to the privileges of a public minister bestowed to them by International Law". With the exception of "whatever special privileges may be conferred upon them by international compact",[13] they are no different from normal foreign persons. However, the prerogative stipulated by these kinds of treaties, namely, that consuls were not to be subject to local jurisdiction, still belongs to the privileges possible, according to International Law, which need to be observed. Even though it is a "forced treaty", the rule still applies. Or to use W.A.P. Martin's words: "Even if it is forced, it still needs to be meticulously applied."[14]

In discussing these contents, the *Wanguo gongfa* points, in particular, to paragraphs 21 and 25 of the Chinese-American Wangxia-Treaty, which deal with the American privilege of consular jurisdiction.[15] This, of course, is not part of the original English edition of 1836, but was specifically added by Wheaton in the third edition of 1846. In doing so, the author had a clear and easily visible purpose. In the book, the term used for "diplomatic immunity" is "extraterritoriality", while the word used for *lingshi caipanquan* is "consular jurisdiction", but the translator is quite indistinct about the meaning of both, and was not able to express the original meaning accurately.

Through the above-described contents of the *Wanguo gongfa*, one can observe that "laws, which are applied outside of the territory", including the contents of extraterritoriality in its wide sense, as outlined above, become clearly visible, or, as has been pointed out by one scholar, "are already absolutely obvious".[16] In other words, in the earliest translation and dissemination of the *Wanguo gongfa*, diplomatic immunity and consular jurisdiction, which are quite different in nature, are both included within the privilege of extraterritoriality, and then, in this bundled way, imparted to the Chinese.

Wheaton, the author of the book, was clearly aware that "consular jurisdiction", as a treaty right, was not compatible with the general line of International Law. Without any doubt, however, it embodied the logic of the stronger.

After its publication, the *Wanguo gongfa* was quickly transmitted to Japan and received a high degree of attention from the court personnel and was copied

---

13 Ibid., p. 181.

14 Ding Weiliang (2002), *Wanguo gongfa*, p. 90.

15 See ibid., pp. 44, 57–58, 85.

16 Gao Xiaocheng (2017), "Zhiwai faquan, lingshi caipan yu qita". See, also, Yang Chao, (2015), *Ding yi* Wanguo gongfa *yanjiu*, appendix Chinese-English comparative table.

time and again. The formation of "extraterritoriality" and other terms in Japanese was also influenced by the diffusion of this book. In China, however, it merely functioned as a manual for officials working for the government's foreign service. Only very rarely were there persons researching the legal principles behind extraterritoriality. The book *Xingyao zhizhang* (*Guide diplomatique*), which had been chosen for translation by Martin in 1876 and whose translation he had organised met with a similarly complicated fate.

The book was originally published in French, the author being the Swiss scholar Charles de Martens. In the book, diplomatic immunity was touched upon, the contents on consular jurisdiction were particularly rich, including parts on its origins, privileges and working rules, *etc.*, at times translating it as *lingshiguan shenduan zhi quan* 領事館審斷之權 (lit. "the right of consuls to pass judgments after examination"). In its sequel chapter, there is a long translation of selected passages of the "Guidelines for American Consuls" which includes two chapters on "The Rights Enjoyed by Consuls According to Treaties" and "The Right of Consuls to Provide Judgments in the Countries of the East". And it did not stop there: the book openly praised consular jurisdiction, stressing: "consuls exercise the right to administer and to adjudicate. This is not only beneficial for the people of the country, it is also of benefit for the people of the other country."[17] Translated knowledge, selectively chosen under Western guidance, of course, could not directly incite the Chinese of that time to reflect upon consular jurisdiction or extraterritoriality used in this way, or let them hope to abolish it in order to remove national humiliation. It could only guide a concept of comparing the reasonability of Western privileges in China, and, for later Chinese generations, serve as a kind of intellectual resource for reflection.

Beginning with the second half of the 1860s, there were persons at the Qing court who gradually began to realise some of the dangers and inequalities brought about by actual extraterritoriality in the guise of consular jurisdiction.

In negotiations with Western countries on the opening of the interior and on missionary problems, the abolition of this right became for a time one of the most important controversial issues.[18] As can be seen, for example, in 1868, when the Minister of the *Zongli yamen*, Wen Xiang 文祥 (1818–1876), who was well versed in foreign affairs, in negotiating the Alcock Convention, complained to the Englishmen by stating: "Do away with your extra-territoriality clause, and merchant and missionary may settle anywhere and everywhere; but retain it, and we must do our best to confine you and our trouble to the treaty ports."[19]

---

17 Charles de Martens (2006), *Xingyao zhizhang*, pp. 125, 122, 159–161, 208–210.

18 Aoki Hiroyu (2008), "Wan Qing guanyu zengshe zhu nanyang lingshi de zhenglun", p. 614.

19 Hart 2005, *Zhexie cong Qinguo lai*, p. 45. Translator's note: here, I quote from the original, Hart (1903), *These from the Land of Sinim*, p. 69.

The fact that extraterritoriality gave the Chinese an ever stronger feeling of dissatisfaction and left them with the impression of being deeply humiliated was related to the first group of diplomatic envoys, which was sent to Japan and the West by the Qing court in 1875/76. It was able to make clearer contrasts and actually experienced the inequality with regard to diplomatic privileges and the inferior position of their own state. It was exactly as the Inspector General of the Imperial Customs Robert Hart pointed out: "its [extraterritoriality's] humiliating effect was more and more felt as intercourse grew and Chinese representatives abroad became better acquainted with procedure elsewhere."[20]

To say that, even prior to this, the Chinese were disgusted by extraterritoriality in the sense of consular jurisdiction, as such, is not correct, however; rather, it should be said that the Chinese were disgusted by its one-sidedness and inequality, which means the irrationality that the Chinese could not enjoy this privilege in the same way as the Western powers were able to. In the "Revised Treaty with Japan" (*Zhong Ri xiuhao tiaoyue* 中日修好條約) of 1871, it was acknowledged that both sides enjoyed consular jurisdiction. In 1875, when negotiating with the envoys of Spain and other countries on the issue of Chinese workers in Cuba, the *Zongli yamen* still demanded consular jurisdiction for both sides in Cuba.[21] In January 1876, Hart made the following note:

On more than one occasion, a high official has said: 'give up exterritoriality and you may go where you like'; and the last time the subject came up, he asked: 'will you even let *our* people in *your* ports have the standing we give *yours* in *ours*?'[22]

From this, one can see the real attitude of the Chinese Imperial court towards consular jurisdiction, but it also constitutes a reflection of its political naïvety.

After the middle of the 1870s, in the process of understanding the real nature and the dangers of Western extraterritoriality towards China better, the Chinese began to experience the influence of Japan. This was especially so because of the great stimulation of the Japanese negotiations with the European and American powers in order to revise the treaties, and Japan's persisting efforts to attain the goal of the abolition of extraterritoriality. *Zhiwai faquan* is the Chinese expression which, at this time, also began to become known by the small number of Chinese who joined the diplomatic missions or went to Japan. In short, this term came to China from Japan at first. In Japanese, the word is pronounced *Chigaihoken* and originally used the character 権, and not 權, as in Chinese. It constituted the Japanese translation of "exterritoriality" and "extra-

---

20 Ibid., p. 101, original quotation in Hart (1903), *These from the Land of Sinim*, p. 158.

21 Cf. Aoki Hiroyu (2008), "Wan Qing guanyu zhengshe zhu nanyang lingshi de zhenglun", pp. 614–615. The Japanese scholar Shin Kawashima in 2018 in Guilin orally pointed out that the word may have been formed even earlier. I intend to deal with this problem in the future.

22 Hart (2005), *Zhexie cong Qinguo lai*, p. 179, original quotation in Hart (1903), *These from the Land of Sinim*, p. 230.

territoriality", and was also influenced by the diffusion of the *Wanguo gongfa* to Japan, where it had already been published during the late 1870s, and began to be disseminated in the earlier period of the 1880s. On 7 August 1878, for example, the *Tokyo nichi nichi shimbum* (Tokyo Daily News) employed it in the following way: "With regard to treaty revision, the Japanese government for the time being considers the obligations of extraterritoriality in its current form as not having been changed."[23]

In 1881, the renowned scholar Inoue Tetsujirô 井上哲次郎 (1855–1944) in his *Tetsugaku jii* (哲學字彙 Dictionary of Philosophy) explicitly employed *Chigaihoken* as translation for "extraterritoriality", pointing out that it belonged to the legal language, and this was actually the only translation that he proposed.[24] The early English-Chinese dictionaries compiled by missionaries either did not mention "exterritoriality" and "extraterritoriality", or as Lobscheid's English-Chinese dictionary from the 1860s translated "extra-territorial" as *difang waikai* 地方外嘅 – meaning "beyond one's own territory"—which, however, did not leave any traces in Chinese discourse. However, this dictionary influenced many Japanese including Inoue Tetsujirô. In 1884, when Inoue specifically revised Lobscheid's English-Chinese dictionary, apart from copying "extra-territorial" as *difang waikai*, he also added the word "exterritoriality" and translated it as "outside of jurisdiction, not belonging to a jurisdiction" (*guanxia zhiwai, bu gui guanxia* 管轄之外、不歸管轄), which means having the right to exceed the parameters governed by the law of a country. From this, it becomes clear that, when Inoue translated "extraterritoriality" as *zhiwai faquan*, he had understood the implication that it was going beyond the territorial boundaries of the jurisdiction of one country. But the English-Chinese dictionary that he compiled still lacked clarity with regard to its explanation of the legal term.

It needs to be pointed out that, in China prior to the 1880s and up to the eve of the first Sino-Japanese war (1894–1895), in the Chinese translations related to Western modern international law, no matter whether it was with regard to extraterritoriality or to consular jurisdiction or to the privilege of diplomatic immunity and other concepts, no real or exact, distinct or concise Chinese technical terminology had emerged. This not only influenced the dissemination of the related knowledge, but also offered an opportunity for the successive introduction of Japanese-coined technical terms.

From the historical sources available now, it seems that the first Chinese minister to Japan, He Ruzhang 何如璋 (1838–1891) and his attachés, such as Huang Zunxian 黃遵憲 (1848–1905) and others, may have been the first members of the Chinese élite to come into contact with the term *zhiwai faquan*, the Japanese-coined Chinese term. They realised that the privilege of Westerners in

---

23 Sato Tooru (2007), *Gendai ni ikiru Bakumatsu Meiji shoki kango jten*, p. 596.
24 Inoue Tetsujiro (1881), *Tetsugaku ji*, p. 33.

China not being subject to Chinese legal sanctions in Japan was called *zhiwai faquan* and they started to employ this legal term consciously. The historian Dai Dongyang 戴東陽, who has studied the Chinese-Japanese relations, has revealed that He Ruzhang, who had gone to Japan as an envoy in 1877, was moved to observe how, after the year 1880, the forces of the whole Japanese nation were mobilised in order to revise the existing treaties with the Western powers. In particular, he observed the importance of the questions of tariff autonomy and legal rights, and, in this respect, wrote earnest letters to the *Zongli yamen* and to persons who had influence on diplomatic relations, such as Liu Kunyi 劉坤一 (1830–1902), Zuo Zongtang 左宗棠 (1812–1885), Zeng Jize 曾紀澤 (1839–1890) and others, hoping that China would emulate Japan and take the question of revising the unequal treaties with the Western powers seriously. At the end of the year 1880, in a letter to Liu Kunyi, the Governor-general of Liangjiang and superintendent of trade for the southern ports, he not only used the word *zhiwai faquan* several times, but also concisely introduced the history, the implications, and the harm of the issue of extraterritoriality.[25] However, it seems that Liu Kunyi's answer was neither active nor constructive; he was merely of the opinion that the only solution lay in China's self-strengthening. Dai Dongyang has compared this letter with Huang Zunxian's (styled "Master, foreign history says" *waishishi yue* 外史氏曰) comment on extraterritoriality appended to Chapter Seven, "Exchange with Neighbouring Countries", of Huang's *Treatise on Japan* (*Riben guozhi* 日本國志), and discovered that from the basic views to the written expression, the two almost do not have any difference. Her conclusion is that the aforementioned letter had been drafted by Huang Zunxian.[26] It is clear that this research is of great importance in order to come to grips with the question of how *zhiwai faquan* as concept and sign first entered China.

I am of the opinion that, no matter what contributions He Ruzhang made to the early compilation of the *Treatise on Japan*, it is at least clear that He Ruzhang and Huang Zunxian had already, in 1880, repeatedly exchanged their opinions on questions relating to extraterritoriality and had arrived at a high degree of common understanding. This means that the discussion on the influence of the *Treatise on Japan* on the adoption of the concept of extraterritoriality should not be restricted to the year 1887 when the book was finished for publication.

---

25 He Ruzhang (1966), "Yu Liu Xianzhuang zhifu lun Riben yi gai tiaoyue shu" 與劉峴莊制府論日本議改條約書 (Letter to Liu Kunyi on Japan's Treaty Revisions); Cf. Dai Dongyang (2004), "Riben xiugai tiaoyue jiaoshe yu He Ruzhang tiaoyue renshi", p. 175.

26 Dai Dongyang (2007), "Shilun Huang Zhuxian dui bu pingdeng tiaoyue de renshi". I would like to thank Dai Dongyang for providing the material. Up to now most researchers have neglected Dai's efforts.

Wang Tao 王韜 (1828–1897) and Xue Fucheng 薛福成 (1838–1894) were also forerunners of reformist ideas, and had paid attention to the "extraterritoriality" question from quite early on. They also began to observe the seriousness of the problem and openly expressed their ideas at the beginning of the 1880s. Xue Fucheng published his *Humble Discussion of Foreign Affairs* (*Chou Yang chuyi* 籌洋芻議 in 1881. In the chapter entitled "Concluding Treaties" (*yue zhang* 約章), he clearly stated:

I have recently heard that the US and Japan are discussing concluding a new treaty. It will allow [Japan] to regain its rights in internal affairs. Foreigners all come under the jurisdiction of the local administration. China should also use this and conclude treaties with the countries it is engaging in trade with.[27]

Quite clearly, the Japanese treaty revision influenced him as well. However, the terminology he used in his texts was still mainly based upon the *Wanguo gongfa*. The same holds true for Wang Tao.

In about 1882, Wang Tao published his article "Abolishing Additional Privileges" ("Chu ewai quanli" 除額外權利), which is probably the first specialised article on extraterritoriality. The article pointed out: "Additional [legal] privileges are not used in Europe, they are only practised in Turkey, Japan and in our China … this is something which must be fought by our officials and people." And he continued:

Among those things, which we need to contest with the Western powers, the paragraph on additional privileges is of greatest importance. This is because it relates to the power of the country. Henceforth, compassionate and outstanding persons should be attentive to it.

He also stressed: "This contests something which needs to be contested, it is fair and impartial."[28] Prior to this, in 1879, Wang Tao had made a four-month trip to Japan. He Ruzhang, the Chinese envoy to Japan, acted as his intermediary. During his trip to Japan, he often had banquets and friendly gatherings with He and Huang Zunxian, and, even more often, he had "enthusiastic conversations" with Huang Zunxian, and, in this way, the two began to know each other very well.[29] However, in this text, Wang Tao did not use the term *zhiwai faquan*, but used the term "additional privileges", in which more traces of the "consular privileges" of the *Wanguo gongfa* had been preserved. Whether it was because he did not like the Japanese expressions and deliberately coined this

---

27 Xue Fucheng (1987), "Chou yang quyi – yuezhang", pp. 527–529.
28 Wang Tao (1959), *Taoyuan wenlu waibian*, j. 3, pp. 89–90.
29 Wang Tao (1987), *Manyou suilu – Fusang youji*, pp. 197–212.

EXTRATERRITORIALITY IN MODERN CHINA 173

term is unclear.[30] However, the term "additional privileges" was not disseminated in China.

In the past, the academic community, when addressing the dissemination of the concept of extraterritoriality and its usage, had for a long time started with Huang Zunxian's *Treatise on Japan*, which had been completed in 1887, and was officially published in 1895. It tended to fail to consider the knowledge which had been available beforehand, and how this had spread. Although this is not satisfying, it is not completely without reason. Only because it was used in the seventh chapter of the book did the Chinese begin to employ the term *zhiwai faquan*, and it was specifically upon this basis that the public discussion began. Huang pointed out that the literal meaning was "to have judicial power outside the territory governed", and that the real meaning was that consuls could "use the law of their own country in order to judge their own people" so that they had consular jurisdiction. He also briefly pointed out its origins, its harm, and the different opinions about how to deal with such problems. It should be stressed that Huang Zunxian's essential understanding and communication of the concept of extraterritoriality, which, at that time, was becoming more and more popular in Japan, was basically correct. After the shock of the Sino-Japanese war of 1894–95, this had a major impact on the Chinese scholarly élite.[31] For this reason, Huang Zunxian's book deserves to be called the first monograph which gave the Chinese a correct and profound enlightenment on the concept of "extraterritoriality". Later on, this had a defining and foundational effect for the formation and dissemination of the concept of "extraterritoriality" which became very popular in China.

It is worth noting that, before the Chinese introduced extraterritoriality from Japan, what made them unhappy in the first place was the part of the privilege in the sense of unequal consular jurisdiction. Extraterritoriality in a wider sense, as in the *Wanguo gongfa* with the meaning of "overstepping the jurisdiction of Chinese laws", had actually already been narrowed down. Here, consular jurisdiction, agreed upon as an "exceptional right" in treaties, became dominant and the aspect of diplomatic immunity was basically no longer mentioned. This was a common phenomenon in both China and Japan during the early period. The reason, of course, was that it was not properly understood in the first place. For a weak country, both it and the, on the surface, equally applied diplomatic immunity had little substantive meaning. They were considered as a mere formality or of being of little consequence. At the same time, in modern China, in

---

30 It is possible that it was actually not Wang Tao who coined the term *ewai quanli*. It has recently been pointed out that it was used in the *Shenbao* of 5 May 1872 in an article on the Arrow Incident of 1856, which quoted from the *Xianggang xinbao*; Cf. Gao Hancheng (2018), "Zhongguo jindai 'zhiwai faquan gainian de cihuishi'", p. 118.

31 Huang Zunxian (2001), *Riben guozhi*, pp. 88–89.

respect to extraterritoriality, there was still the phenomenon of its application, which has only recently been the subject of research. This is to say that, from the beginning of the 1880s, when the Chinese for the first time started using the term *zhiwai faquan*, which had come from Japan, it had a meaning which was completely different from the usage of the Japanese concept: *Zhiwai faquan* did not indicate that foreigners coming to China had the privilege of not being subject to Chinese legislation, but meant that the Chinese themselves governed foreigners who came to China, or applied their legislation to foreigners in China. As far as the principles of international law were concerned, *zhiwai faquan*, in this sense, was not only not illegal, but, to the contrary, appeared to be a legitimate right that was entirely justifiable. In 1886, for example, the Shanghai newspaper *Shenbao* carried the following report:

Henceforth, Korea will treat Russia exceptionally generously. As long as they are not familiar with the legal terms and an agreement has been attained, all Russians who come to Korea will not be judged according to the right to use the law towards others.[32]

It is very clear that here *Zhiwai faquan* indicates the "right to supervise foreigners". Such examples are not rare during the late nineteenth and early twentieth centuries, but rather frequent and thus need to be taken into account when researching the concept of extraterritoriality.

If one takes the *Shenbao* as an example, then prior to 1903 there are 37 mentions of the term *zhiwai faquan*, and, of these, 26 times it means the "right to supervise foreigners", which means in 70 per cent of all cases. And the other 11 cases point to the "rights beyond one's own rule or jurisdiction (borders of territory)", the so-called "consular jurisdiction" and "diplomatic immunity". If one looks into the *Shenbao* prior to 1898, there are ten cases in which the term *zhiwai faquan* is used, and, of these, eight cases (80%) are used in the sense of the "right to supervise foreigners".

In 1903, in the *New Erya* (*Xin Erya* 新尔雅), China's first encyclopedia in a modern sense, which was compiled by Wang Rongbao 汪榮寶 (1878–1933) and Ye Lan 葉瀾 (1875–?) and which, for the first time, included *zhiwai faquan* as a dictionary entry, we find the following explanation: "The persons who are on the territory of state A must follow the laws of state A. This is called *zhiwai faquan*."[33] In fact, not only prior to 1903, but also throughout the whole Republican period, in journals, newspapers and in the normal life of the people, such a usage can be observed, and it continued for a considerable time. This can be easily ascertained by looking into journal databases, such as those of *Dagong bao* 大公報 and *Eastern Miscellany* (*Dongfang zazhi*). On the whole, however, propor-

---

32 "Gao E fuyue" 高俄附約 (Addendum to Treaty between Korea and Russia), *Shenbao*, 6 June 1886.

33 Wang Rongbao (1903), *Xin Erya*, p. 29.

tionally speaking, after 1903, the number of such examples successively decreased and became even less after the beginning of the Republican period.

Li Yang 李洋 is of the opinion that this usage of *zhiwai faquan*, which is different from that of Japan, is an obvious misunderstanding of Japanese, which was brought about by "Learning Japanese through Chinese" (*Hewen han dufa* 和文漢讀法). This is because there are clear differences in word-building methods between Japanese *Kanji* and Chinese words. Actually, as early as 1914, the linguist Hu Yilu 胡以魯 had pointed this out:

> If we understand [the word] *zhiwai faquan* [extraterritoriality], according to structural patterns of Chinese, then *zhi* is an often used transitive verb. The noun is the word *wai*, which can be understood as hinting at 'foreign country' or 'foreigner'. If one wants to employ *wai* as an adverb, this is not possible without having a noun before.[34]

According to Chinese grammatical norms, *zhi* (to rule) is a transitive verb, which requires a noun as object. But, in Japanese, *zhi* is an attributive modifier, and thus *zhiwai* has the meaning of "outside of administering". Thus, the literal meaning of *zhiwai faquan* is "legal rights beyond the administered territory". Li Yang, moreover, is of the opinion that, because of this misunderstanding, since the late Qing, the ubiquitous phrase "to *regain* extraterritorial rights" (*shouhui zhiwai faquan* 收回治外法權) is actually incorrect, and it should be "to *abolish*" (*quxiao* 取消 or *feichu* 廢除) in order to be correct.[35]

However, very recently, Gao Hancheng has written an article advancing a different opinion. He firmly believes that the *zhiwai faquan*, which was mentioned in the *Shenbao* in 1886, was the earliest public propagation of the word. "Stubbornly calling *zhiwai faquan* a loanword seems to be biased." And, seen from this meaning, this usage embodies precisely the principle that a territory controls another sovereign entity, so that there is no misreading or misinterpretation. And, naturally, it also cannot be said that the phrase "to regain extraterritorial rights" is not correct.[36] However, I do not share Gao Hancheng's opinion for the following reason: first, it needs to be pointed out that the article in which the term *zhiwai faquan* was employed in the *Shenbao* of 1886 actually comes from the Japanese press. Beginning with 1882, the *Shenbao* had sent out so-called "information seekers", who checked Japanese newspapers for all kinds of reports. The usage of the term *zhiwai faquan* was thus clearly related to Japan, and the term "legal power" (*faquan*) is also generally acknowledged as being coined in Japan and had not existed in China previously. In Japanese, the term *zhiwai faquan* was used as a translation of "exterritoriality" or "extraterri-

---

34 Hu Yilu (1923), "Lun yiming", pp. 134–135; the article was first published in the journal *Yongyan* 庸言.

35 Li Yang (2015), "Cong ciyi dao yujing: 'Zhiwai faquan' wudu, wuyong, ji wuhui".

36 Cf. Gao Hancheng (2017), "Zhiwai faquan, lingshi caipanquan ji qita—ji yu yuyixue shijiao de lishi fenxi".

toriality"; it is also clearly contrasted with "legal power to control one's own territory", and, for this reason, it is correct to consider the *Shenbao*'s explanation as "China's right to supervise foreigners" as a misreading. Second, the transmission of an accurate understanding of the Japanese translated word to China was earlier than 1886. Both prior to and after the Sino-Japanese war of 1894–95, the usage of Huang Zunxian was still most influential. Moreover, the meaning of the term *zhiwai faquan*, as it became popular in China later, did, on the whole, retain the meaning which had come from Japan. For this reason, it is correct to consider *zhiwai faquan* as a "loan word". Even if *zhiwai faquan* is based upon a misreading, and is considered by the Chinese to constitute a legitimate right, it is at least based upon foreign borrowing with regard to the form of the word. However, the connotation underwent some changes during the process of its diffusion to China. To make it clear: the subject of extraterritoriality is the foreigner who enjoys privileges. With regard to China, there can only be the principle of cancelling or abolishing them, but not of "recovering" privileges. The only thing which China can recover is its sovereignty, which has been lost because of "extraterritoriality". Thus, strictly speaking, precisely as Li Yang has stressed, "recovering extraterritoriality" does not make sense as a statement, although it clearly expresses the standpoint of Chinese national sovereignty and the increasingly strong nationalist mentality of the times. What is regrettable, however, is that, not only during the late Qing and the Republican period was this expression popular, but academics still cling to it even today. This, to some extent, is related to the question of whether they have or have not correctly understood the real meaning of extraterritoriality, although this is not absolute, either. There are some who have understood the real meaning of extraterritoriality, but who, at the same time, resign themselves to muddleheadedly following such a usage. This situation was particular frequent during the late Qing period. What people wanted to recover at the time was not "extraterritoriality", as such, but, rather, that part of Chinese sovereignty which, due to the extraterritoriality enjoyed by foreigners, had been lost to foreign powers, but which had originally belonged to China.[37] The usage by Yan Fu 嚴復 (1854–

---

37 Liang Qichao may have understood that *zhiwai faquan* constituted a foreign privilege, but he was also the initiator of the expression "recovering extraterritoriality". Liang, who was very familiar with *Riben guozhi* in 1899, in his article "On Mixed Residency in the Interior and its Relationship to Commerce" ("Lun neidi zaju yu shangwu guanxi" 論內地雜居與商務關係), used it in this way: "The Japanese government recovered extraterritoriality, all foreigners were subject to the Japanese law" (*Qingyi bao*, 19, p. 1200). In 1905, in the *Zhongwai ribao*, Yan Fu published an article entitled "On Important Politics which the Country Prior to the Establishment of a Constitution could Follow and on those which it should Follow" ("Lun guojia yu wei lixian yiqian you keyi xing biyi xing zhi yaozheng" 論國家於未立憲以前有可以行必宜行之要政), which also—to quite some extent—touched upon "extraterritoriality", and he certainly completely understood the correct meaning of "extraterritoriality". For this reason, he said: "Comment: The term *zhiwai faquan* comes from Japan. The term *zhiwai* is similar to the

1921), Wu Tingfang 伍廷芳 (1842–1922) and others at the beginning of the twentieth century are classical instances of this. The list of such examples is endless and not necessarily restricted to the term *zhiwai faquan*. For example, statements such as "to recover consular jurisdiction" at that time could be observed often, and are quite frequent even today.

Although I do not agree with Gao Hancheng's view, his considerations remind us that, when the Chinese first misunderstood the Japanese-coined term *zhiwai faquan* as the right to govern and adjudicate foreigners who came to China, this was not only a direct effect of the difference in word-formation in Japanese and Chinese, but also reflected the Chinese natural and naïve understanding of the principal idea of international law as being equal and fair. This actually has some cognitive peculiarities related to natural law, in contrast to legal positivism. And this kind of misreading is often, albeit not necessarily, linked to the expression of "recovering extraterritoriality" (*shouhui zhiwai faquan*). The fact that this expression could be coined and circulated is precisely because it coincides with the fundamental principle of territorialist sovereignty inherent in international law. What has been lost is the originally existing sovereignty, which needed to be recovered. At the same time, it is necessary to realise that, in the two different understandings of extraterritoriality, the subject of rights is actually the exact opposite. Based upon this misreading of extraterritoriality, the subject of the rights are the Chinese, while the subject of the rights in Western and Japanese texts is the foreigner who has come to China. Or, to put it differently, after the Sino-Japanese war of 1894–95, for the Western powers and the Japanese government, it was an underlying assumption that the Chinese were not recognised as the equal subjects of legal rights. For this reason, they should not command extraterritoriality in the sense of consular jurisdiction.

---

expression *huawai* 化外 ("beyond the pale of the Chinese civilisation"), when speaking about 'legal power', this is similar to 'power' … With regard to those who enjoy 'extraterritoriality', there aren't any except for the envoys of a country." But, at the same time, he stressed that, according to the principle of the territorialism of International Law, "If there is a country which has a territory and has a people, then there is nothing on which it does not have the sovereignty to govern. If people from other countries enter its territory, then they are subject to the control of this country", this is "the innate sovereignty of the state". "In International Law, this is called complete correspondence of territory and laws" and it "belongs to the sovereignty over the complete correspondence of law and territory"; Yan Fu (2004), "Lun guojia yu wei lixian yiqian", p. 46.

3. "Consular jurisdiction" or "diplomatic immunity"? Circulation and discrimination of the concept of "extraterritoriality" and China's claims for reform and change (1895–1918).

The term and the concept of "extraterritoriality" really began to spread in China after the Sino-Japanese war of 1894/95 and China's defeat by Japan. If we use the *Shenbao*, which publicly used the term rather early on, prior to 1894/95, we can only find the occurrence of 1886 mentioned above, as all other occurrences were later. It was precisely the defeat in the Sino-Japanese war and the humiliations inflicted by Japan and the Western powers which led to a gradually increasing usage of both the term and the concept of "extraterritoriality". The intellectual élite used it to stimulate the patriotic enthusiasm of the people and consciously promote the reform of 1898 and the "New policy reform" initiated by the Qing-government later. This made it into one of the most effective conceptual tools in the related propaganda and in public opinion.

Huang Zunxian, who, in 1895, officially published his *Treatise on Japan*, was not only the true founder of the term *zhiwai faquan* and the concept of "extraterritoriality" in the sense of consular jurisdiction, but was also the most influential tune-setter for the main argument of the extraterritoriality discourse, which, during the late Qing period, was used to cast blame on the West, to propagate studying from Japan, to carry out legal reforms, and, in particular, to push forward China's quest to compile a new legal code. At the end of Chapter Seven, entitled "Records of Diplomatic Relations", Huang Zunxian, under the guise of the "Master of foreign history", commented in particular on extraterritoriality and used the term *zhiwai faquan* six times. I am of the opinion that this is a very important event in the history of modern Chinese political concepts. Huang Zunxian at first stresses the particularly humiliating nature of extraterritoriality for the Asian peoples, pointing out:

When the Western countries have intercourse with each other in all cases in which the people and the merchants of one country reside in the other country, they are subject to the jurisdiction of that country. Their consuls do not have any other function than, restricted by contracts, to take care of them and that is it. But, in Asia, the consuls employ the law of their own country and pass judgments for their own people. The Westerners call this 'extraterritoriality', it denominates to exert power of jurisdiction outside one's own territory.

Subsequently, Huang briefly describes the origins of extraterritoriality, stressing the unequal nature of this treaty-based privilege and the harm brought about by it. In his opinion, extraterritoriality originated in Turkey. When the Turks eliminated the Holy Roman Empire and when the borders were drawn and trade with the Europeans began, the Turks detested the confusion brought about by foreign policy, so they ordered the administrators of the different peoples to take care of their own people, it was absolutely not that they were forced to conclude the treaties, for this reason there only were minor problems.

But now the Great Powers forced treaties on the countries of Asia and it was because of this that "the poison of extraterritoriality spread through the whole of Asia". Huang was by no means of the opinion that extraterritoriality corresponded to the spirit of international law, but held firmly to the existence of the principle that, "among the myriad countries of the world, no matter whether they are strong or weak, large or small, they are their own masters, thus those who step onto one other's territory should abide to its rules". This is the starting-point of his extraterritoriality-related thought.

Beginning from this, Huang Zunxian clearly criticised extraterritoriality as "unequal and unfair politics". He condemned the "arrogance and wantonness" of the foreign consuls, stating that, even in the case that they were "not partial" towards the foreigners who had come to China, a very unfair situation had emerged in which "the foreigners profit greatly", while "for us it is very inconvenient". "Different penalties for the same crime" and "different treatment for the same thing" have become possible on the pretext that "penal law is strict here and light there, there are prohibitions, which exist here, but they don't exist there and the difference that they obtain the profit there, which is lost here". Especially in the foreign concessions, even if "Chinese engage in a law case with Chinese", the foreign consuls will be involved in the joint trial. This was even more absurd and went beyond the provisions of the Chinese-Western treaties, leading to the unfavourable outcome of "applying a law outside of the law, using power beyond the legal power". Huang Zunxian went on to stress that, because of this situation, it was not accidental at all that, towards foreigners who came to China, the Chinese were "resentful" and "jealous and suspicious".[38] For this reason, he was of the opinion that the "treaties currently in use" could no longer be "patiently endured without change" and continue to be allowed to spread their poison unceasingly. But he also realised:

the foreigners have been accustomed to deriving profit [from the current situation] and stick to the old. They must be unwilling [to change]. Moreover, this is because human feelings and the customs of the countries are different, and religion and politics differ from each other. Once, one is forced to be like me, the situation necessarily becomes complicated.

But how, then, should this be dealt with? Huang explicitly stated: "In the current situation, it is impossible to force the others to be like us. Thus, we must first change ourselves to be like the others." China should thus begin to "com-

---

38 Huang Zunxian (2001), *Riben guozhi*, pp. 88–89.

ply" with the West and initiate legal reforms. He proposed at first to consider the translation of the legal codes of the different countries "currently in use", and, from these, to choose the appropriate contents and "include an additional paragraph on litigation between parties from different countries" and, at the same time, socialise with foreigners, "adopt the law of the others in dealing with one's own people" and, later on, slowly plan to reform. It was necessary to wait until "our country is powerful" and only then should it be attempted to abolish completely all the legal privileges of foreigners in China.[39]

Huang Zunxian's thinking about extraterritoriality embodies the typical features of a discourse of weakness. It not only served as guidance for later discussions on legal reform, it also laid the foundations for the form of the public discussion on this question between members of the gentry and officials. Some years later, the candidates of the Imperial examination system were quite familiar with it, and would, to some extent, copy it when composing related policy essays. In 1896, the "Japan-China Treaty on Commerce and Navigation" was signed. This resulted in an ever wider reception of the concept by Chinese officials and the gentry, and advanced the spreading of the concept in China. In these negotiations, Japan, which had just freed itself from Western extraterritoriality, assumed the Western position of a "civilised country" and forced China to accept the unilateral privilege that Japan would enjoy consular jurisdiction in China. The third paragraph of the treaty clearly postulated: Japanese consuls of all levels who reside in China enjoy the privilege of consular jurisdiction in China while Chinese consuls sent to Japan do not enjoy any similar privilege. To the contrary, it postulated: "The administration and jurisdiction over Chinese nationals and Chinese property rests with the Japanese authorities." This was tantamount to depriving China of its consular jurisdiction as stipulated upon a reciprocal basis in the original 1871 agreement. After 1886, the Japanese government had always hoped for such a result in negotiations with China on the revision of the "Sino-Japanese Friendship Treaty", but each time the Qing-government had rejected this.

The "right to make judgments" in Japan mentioned in the treaty is, to judge from its contents, similar to the popular concept of "consular jurisdiction". During the late Qing period, a rather influential dictionary of Japanese legal terminology contained the following explanation:

The right to make judgments mentioned in international treaties refers to a consul who has been dispatched and resides in the country of the treaty-partner. He has the power to make legal judgments on the people of his country in the guest countries by employing the home-country's laws.[40]

---

39 Huang Zunxian (2001), *Riben guozhi*, p. 89.
40 Qian Xun, Dong Hongyi (1907), *Riben fagui jiezhi*, p. 40.

Two years prior to the conclusion of the Japan-China Treaty, in 1894, England and Japan had agreed to abolish Britain's extraterritorial rights in Japan. In the "Anglo-Japanese Treaty of Commerce and Navigation", in the Japanese text "extraterritoriality" and "consular jurisdiction" were both used with a similar meaning (at that time, the treaty inserted "consular jurisdiction" after the expression "extraterritoriality", with the intention of limiting the scope of extraterritoriality). This time, it was intentionally changed to the more ambivalent "right to make judgments", which, at first glance, was less insulting towards China (and thus also had the advantage that it was more easily accepted by the Chinese representatives). From this, one can also imagine the deliberative nature of the Japanese representatives. The Chinese plenipotentiary Zhang Yinhuan 張蔭桓 (1837–1900) argued against the Japanese arrogance in a reasonable way and attempted to maintain the equal status of both China and Japan. In an internal edict in the form of a letter to Zhang Yinhuan, the Guangxu emperor also stated that the sentence "The administration and jurisdiction over Chinese nationals and Chinese property rests with the Japanese authorities" was "really ugly".[41] The Japanese government, however, insisted, and the defeated Chinese government was finally forced to accept this clause.

From the process of the negotiation of the "Anglo-Japanese Treaty of Commerce and Navigation" and from its actual contents, it also becomes clear that the Japanese official in the Ministry of Foreign Affairs, Hayashi Tadasu 林董 (1850–1913), clearly understood the difference between diplomatic immunity and consular jurisdiction, which were both part of the concept of "extraterritoriality" in the wider sense of the word. For this reason, their contents were deliberately described separately in the treaty. Except for using the term "the power to make judgments" in order to state clearly the privileges of Japanese consuls in the third paragraph, the second paragraph of the treaty contains a special regulation, to wit, that both countries send consuls and diplomats who reside abroad and who, "according to international law should enjoy all rights and privileges and the benefit of exemption". What was ruled hereby was, in fact, the question of diplomatic immunity practised between equal countries.

The paragraphs related to consular jurisdiction in the "Japan-China Treaty on Commerce and Navigation" of August 1896 were reported on and diffused by the *Shiwubao* 時務報, the newly-established mouthpiece of the reform movement. This report had been translated from the English-language *North China Herald*. It did not employ the term "consular jurisdiction", but used the term "extraterritoriality" instead, in order to express similar content. The report reads: "The Japanese consuls living in China, should, in accordance with the rule of 'extraterritoriality' have jurisdiction over those Japanese nationals living

---

41 Aoyama, Zhu Lin (2013), "Jindai Zhongguo he Riben de jiaocuo yu fenqi", p. 169.

on Chinese Soil."[42] The *Shenbao* also had reports on this and used the word "extraterritoriality" several times. This happened in 1895 and the news came directly from Japan. Based upon the misunderstanding of the Japanese-coined word, it repeatedly refuted and misunderstood the meaning of the so-called "'extraterritoriality' in Japan", believing that it

> means that, with regard to foreigners living in Japan, Japan has the authority to govern then. When it comes to disputes between Chinese and Japanese, one, of course, will let the Japanese official make the judgments. When there is a case in which two Chinese sue each other, the judgment should also be made by a Japanese official.[43]

The impression which was generated in this way was that, in the Japan of the times, there was also—apparently—a usage of the concept of "extraterritoriality", which was similar to that misunderstood by the Chinese in the sense of "judicial power to govern and adjudicate foreigners who live abroad". The authors were unaware that this kind of internal and external extraterritoriality, in respect of the application of the concept, was inconsistent and contradictory. At that time, what the Japanese called "complete extraterritoriality" (*zhiwai faquan quanyou* 治外法權全有)—this is the term used in the context of the negotiations with China, which may hint at the fact that Japan already considered itself being on a par with the Great Powers—meant that, in China (and not in its own country, Japan), it enjoyed "complete extraterritoriality" (speaking with regard to Japan, it had extraterritorial judicial jurisdiction), but, since China at this time was by no means in a comparable international position, its consular jurisdiction in Japan no longer existed. For this reason, the Chinese in Japan were subject to the Japanese jurisdiction, which exerted complete sovereignty. It was for this reason that Kang Youwei 康有為 (1858–1927) sighed emotionally that, on the international stage, "we and Japan are not equal. What can I say?"[44]

In June 1898, the leader of the reforms, Kang Youwei, was already quite familiar with the concept of "extraterritoriality". When he forwarded his *Researches into the Reforms of Japan* to the Emperor, he not only used the concept in the meaning of consular jurisdiction several times, he, moreover, in a comment, also arrived at a simple definition, and vividly described the hard work and tortuous course that the Japanese government had taken during the Meiji-restoration in order to obtain the abolition of extraterritorial rights.[45] He used

---

42 "Zhong Ri tongshang tiaoyue", p. 51. The *Shiwubao* used the term "extraterritoriality" rather frequently, as, for example, in no. 34, in an article on "Eguo dui wai zhengce shi" 俄國【對】 外政策史 (History of Russia's Foreign Relations), *Qiangxue bao, Shiwubao*, vol. 3, p. 2320.

43 *Shenbao*, 29 September 1895; Cf. also *Shenbao*, 1 October 1895 and *Shenbao*, 5 October 1896.

44 Jiang Yihua, Zhang Ronghua (2018), *Kang Youwei quanji*, vol. 4, p. 239.

45 Cf. Kang Youwei (2018), "Riben bianzheng kao", p. 211, 237–239, 257, 272. With regard to its usage in "Qing kai zhiduju xixing xin zheng zhe" 請開制度局議行新政摺 and other material, which is included in the *Wuxu zougao* 戊戌奏稿, they were forged by Kang later.

EXTRATERRITORIALITY IN MODERN CHINA
183

this in order to encourage and persuade the Guangxu emperor to study the case of Japan, and carry out reforms, and thus he displayed the sensibility of the political thought of a reform leader. It is particularly worth mentioning that Kang Youwei also took the lead in using the term "consular jurisdiction" in the *Research into the Reforms of Japan* and, at the same time, used the concept of "consular judges", "consular privileges" and other terms several times, which shows that he had a general understanding of the correlation between the two.

The spreading of the concept of "extraterritoriality" in China during the 1898 reform period was closely related to the further loss of power and the humiliation that followed the Sino-Japanese war of 1894–95, the deepening of the consciousness of a national crisis and the comprehensive awakening of the consciousness of sovereignty in the Chinese élite. At that time, China's loss of national power or sovereignty went far beyond that of judicial sovereignty. When Liang Qichao 梁啟超 (1873–1929) in 1899 wrote his "Note of Warning on the Partition of China" ("Guafen weiyan" 瓜分危言), which was serialised in the *Qingyi bao* 清議報 and had a tremendous impact. It included an extensive treatment of the grief caused by China's loss of various parts of its sovereignty. In Liang's view, the "invisible partition" (*wuxing zhi guafen* 無形之瓜分), which the Imperialist powers had inflicted on China, went further than the "visible partition" (*youxing zhi guafen* 有形之瓜分) because it employed the form of "seizing rights and not seizing territory" (*duo qi quan er bu duo qi tu* 奪其權而不奪其土). If one says that the "visible partition" means "to gobble up meat and bones" (*tunshi gurou* 吞噬骨肉), the "invisible partition" means to "suck up the blood" (*xi qi jingxue* 吸其精血). The article discusses, in different paragraphs, how China lost its "national rights" (*guoquan* 國權) to the imperialist powers, including "railway rights" (*tieluquan* 鐵路權), "rights of inland navigation" (*neihe xiaolunquan* 內河小輪權), "fiscal rights" (*caiquan* 財權), the "right to impose tariffs throughout the whole country" (*quanguo haiguan shui quan* 全國海關稅權), "mineral rights" (*kuangwuquan* 礦物權), "right to employ people" (*yongren quan* 用人權), the "right to train soldiers" (*lian bing quan* 練兵權), and other ingredients of national sovereignty.[46] Compared with the designations of these ingredients of national sovereignty, extraterritoriality, without doubt, has a more

---

46 Cf. Ai shi ke 哀時客 (Liang Qichao 梁啟超), "Guafen weiyan" 瓜分危言 (A Note of Warning on the Partition of China) serialised in *Qingyi bao*, 15, 16, 17, 23, (pp. 907–914, 977–1985, 1947,1054, 1455–1466). In 1899, Liang Qichao was, moreover, influenced by "rights consciousness" and evolutionary ideas. To the relevant works of the Japanese scholar Katō Hiroyuki (1836–1916), he appended an "extension" and published it as "Qiangquan lun" (On strong powers) in *Qingyi bao*. He expounded the so-called "right of the strongest" (*qiangzhe zhi quanli* 強者之權力) in order to summon the Chinese to "self-strengthening" (*ziqiang* 自強). He sighed, in the world at this time "power means privileges". In his "Guafen weiyan", he introduced Mahan's concept of "sea power" (*Haiquan lun* 海權論) and, in this way, was the first to familiarise the Chinese with "sea power".

distinct symbolic significance expressing the status of the country. For this reason, this concept very quickly entered the consciousness of the Chinese élites. In fact, even the misunderstood concept of "extraterritoriality" derived from the Japanese language also reflects the overall and profound consciousness of the value of sovereignty.

It was also at the time of the 1898 reform that other new terms and new concepts which were related to extraterritoriality and embodied the foreign invasion and China's tragic fate were disseminated for the first time, such as "imperialist powers" (*lieqiang* 列強), "imperialism" (*diguozhuyi* 帝國主義), "colonial policy" (*zhimin zhengce* 殖民政策), "colony" (*zhimindi* 殖民地), "sphere of interest" (*shili fanwei* 勢力範圍)[47] as well as "consular jurisdiction", "most favoured nation treatment" (*zui hui guo deiyu* 最惠國待遇), "sick man of East Asia" (*Dongya bingfu* 東亞病夫), *etc.* It was at this time that some of these words first appeared, while others became popular. This is helpful to allow us to understand the way in which both the concept and the term "extraterritoriality" began to spread at this time.

The spreading of the concept of "extraterritoriality" is still a joint effect of the great number of new terms composed from Chinese characters, which came into China from Japan and attained widely recognised results. It was precisely as the *Zhongwai ribao* 中外日報 stated in an article on extraterritoriality published at the beginning of the twentieth century. "The four characters of *zhiwai faquan* only spread to the mouths and ears of our people when Japanese books began to thrive in China."[48]

If we claim that the sovereignty consciousness of the reform period promoted, in a powerful way, the dissemination and the understanding of the concept of "sovereignty" among the Chinese, then the outbreak of the Boxer rebellion provided a new opportunity for the people to think about the real dangers of extraterritoriality in the sense of consular jurisdiction or guided by it, and to think actively about how to abolish it.

Around the year 1901, Ku Hung-ming (Gu Hongming 辜鴻銘 1857–1928), who, in the private secretariat of the governor general of Hunan and Hubei Zhang Zhidong 張之洞 (1837–1909), was responsible for foreign documents, as well as the Irishman Robert Hart (1835–1911), the Director General of the Imperial Custom Service and others, published books and articles in the English language, which, with their views on the Western world, reflected and criticised

---

47 In 1899, the draft of a translated text appeared in *Qingyi bao* under the title "Kuozhang guoshi ji lieqian xiexhang lun" 擴張國勢及列強協商論 (On Expanding State Powers and the Co-operation of the Imperial Powers), *Qingyi bao*, 17 (pp. 1065–1070), stressing the co-operation of the imperialist powers in partitioning China. It used terms such as "imperialist powers" (*lieqiang*), "spheres of interest" (*shili fanwei*), "imperialism" (*diguozhuyi*) and so on several times.

48 "Lun zhiwai faquan zhi jieshi" 論治外法權之解釋 (An Explanation of Extraterritoriality), *Zhongwai ribao*, 10 January 1905.

extraterritoriality and received the attention of international public opinion. In a rather typical way, they reflected a new impression of the international world towards the extraterritoriality imposed by the Western powers on China, and thus created a favourable public atmosphere for negotiations on treaty revision and law reform. In a book entitled *Papers from a Viceroy's Yamen* (Chinese subtitle *Zun wang pian* 尊王篇), Gu Hongming criticised, in an incisive way, the encroachment of the imperialist powers on Chinese sovereignty and their meddling in China's internal affairs (including missionary societies which meddled in law cases in which Chinese converts were involved). He pungently wrote:

The problem of maintaining good government among foreign subjects is not, it must be admitted, easy, for ex-territoriality is an anomaly in the law of nations.

And:

Ex-territoriality is an anomaly—infuriating already in its moral effect to the cause of good government in China. But instead of minimising the evils of this anomaly, the agents of the foreign powers are allowed to introduce a still worse anomaly, namely, *in*-territoriality. Not content that the Imperial government in China should have no jurisdiction over foreigners, the foreign powers have allowed their agents to deny jurisdiction to the Chinese government over Chinese subjects.[49]

This is the voice of a Chinese who, writing in English, made his resistance against extraterritoriality as applied by Western powers in China public and condemned it.

In his book, *These from the Land of Sinim: Essays on the Chinese Question*, the Irishman Robert Hart, based upon a position created by a special identity and complex emotions, called upon the powers to face up to the Chinese people's legal rights and understand the deeply hurt national feelings of the Chinese. He admitted:

The sting of such an exacted concession as 'extraterritoriality' is not one of those which time will deaden: on the contrary, every continued year of its existence, every advance in power or knowledge, intensifies it. It is a gift which sooner or later must be returned or withdrawn.[50]

Hart, however, also pointed out that "in no case could foreigners expect to maintain forever their extra-territorialized status and the various commercial stipulations that China had conceded to force".[51] He stressed that extraterritoriality was a "treaty privilege" which has gradually grown to be recognized as

---

49 Ku Hung-Ming (1901), *Papers from a Viceroy's Yamen*, p. 74, 57–58. Another Chinese writing in English, Lin Wenqing 林文慶, also mentions it but writes of "extraterritoriality"; Cf. Wen Ching (1901), *The Chinese Crisis from Within*, p. 288.

50 Hart (1903), *These from the Land of Sinim*, p. 277.

51 Ibid., p. 59.

an objectionable limitation of national rights on national soil", and constituted an intrusion into Chinese sovereignty.

Extraterritoriality, as long as it operates, the Government conceding it is entitled, on the one hand, to assurances that the adoption of appropriate measures will eventually procure its cancellation, and, on the other, to the fullest protection against any abuse of it while it lasts.

Only in this way might the Chinese government be able to strengthen its understanding of the necessity to protect foreigners when coming to China. But Hart also acknowledged that, for foreigners, "extraterritoriality is an invaluable benefit", which, once one had obtained it, would not be given up lightly unless the Chinese government revised its own laws in accordance with modern Western standards, and established legal institutions capable of effectively exercising jurisdiction. To this end, Hart specifically recommended to the Western powers that they should consciously create favourable conditions for the reforms of the Qing government.[52]

In 1902, the Chinese and the British governments signed the Mackay Treaty. In response to the active efforts of Zhang Zhidong and others, the United Kingdom finally promised conditionally to abandon extraterritoriality in China in the near future. The relative content was included into the twelfth paragraph of the treaty. This was also the first time that both the term and the concept of *zhiwai faquan* appeared in a foreign-Chinese treaty. The exact wording is as follows:

China, having expressed a strong desire to reform her judicial system and to bring it into accord with that of the Western nations, Great Britain agrees to give every assistance to such reform, and she will also be prepared to relinquish her extra-territorial rights when she is satisfied that the state of the Chinese laws, the arrangement for their administration, and other considerations warrant her in so doing.[53]

Commercial treaties concluded between China and the US and between China and Japan in 1903 had almost identical paragraphs. With regard to the Chinese-German and Chinese-Italian commercial treaties, although, in the end, they were not concluded, the drafts nonetheless included similar clauses. Moreover, the Chinese versions of the treaties all used the term *zhiwai faquan*.[54] From this, it can be seen that *zhiwai faquan* (the corresponding English term was "extrater-

---

52 Ibid., pp. 275–277.

53 Zhongguo jindai jingjishi ziliao congkan bianji weiyuanhui, Zhonghua renmin gongheguo haiguan zongshu yanjiushi (tr. and eds.) (1994), *Xinchou tiaoyue liding hou de shangyue tanpan*, p. 139.

54 Ibid., p. 326; the attitude of the German negotiating representative is worth mentioning: he believed that China was "eager to be on an equal footing with foreigners to soon. China's internal affairs and the narrow policy of the Chinese government do not merit the making of such a request"; Ibid., p. 333.

EXTRATERRITORIALITY IN MODERN CHINA

ritorial rights") was, at that time, a publicly-acknowledged choice by the governments of Great Britain, the US, Japan, German, Italy, and other countries. Even the Japanese government, since it had already joined the ranks of the Great Powers, did not create any controversies in this regard.

In 1906, when a Chinese legal scholar mentioned the treaties of three years earlier, he pointed out that "the 'extraterritoriality' mentioned in the treaties also includes 'consular jurisdiction'". If it refers to "diplomatic immunity", "even if the legal system of our country is reformed and clear and can proceed on the same levels as that of England, when the US and other countries conclude treaties with us, they will certainly not be happy to give this up".[55] It needs to be acknowledged that the concept of "extraterritoriality", in the sense of consular jurisdiction, as it was subsequently disseminated in China, was closely related to the existence and influence of this batch of treaties.

Since both the West's and Japan's assertion to abandon extraterritoriality was conditional on China's commitment to reform its own laws, it is not surprising at all that the concept was later on often used by enlightened scholars in order to promote the codification of new laws and the related "new policies" and "constitutional government" activities. Between 1902 and 1905, apart from the fact that Chinese newspapers and journals increasingly used the term "extraterritoriality", the reformed examination system also became a powerful way to promote the concept of "extraterritoriality". The combined regular and grace provincial examinations of 1902 in Jiangnan and Zhejiang and other places all contained questions related to extraterritoriality. By way of examining the "policy essays" (*celun* 策論) of the examination candidates, a new momentum for reform and revision of the existing laws was created.

The Jiangnan provincial examination of 1902 contained a policy question which ran:

Chinese and Foreign Penal law have their similarities and their differences. Since the opening of the ports, trade flourishes more almost daily. In respect of international relations, how should we deliberate on gains and losses and, in an appropriate way, fix a statute in order to regain extraterritorial rights?

The Zhejiang provincial examination of the same year contained the following question:

The Western laws derive from Rome. How did they evolve? Today, how many different disciplines does the study of law have? Since the rules of extraterritoriality have been used in the treaty ports, there really are great ills. Which good strategy should be employed in order to regain sovereignty?

---

55 "Lun zhiwai faquan yu lingshi caipanquan xingzhi zhi qubie" 論治外法權與領事裁判權性質 之區別 (On the Differences in Nature between Extraterritoriality and Consular Jurisidiction (abbreviated reprint from *Beiyang guanbao* 12 October 1906, *Dongfang zazhi*, 3: 13 (1906).

Among the questions of the provincial examination in Shandong of 1902 was a question which, although it did not explicitly employ the term *zhiwai faquan*, did, in fact, also discuss the related contents directly. The question runs:

In international law, there is a clause according to which people who are sojourning in a foreign country ought to be protected. This should be made clear in a realistic way in order to soothe guests.[56]

In the 1903 provincial examinations, there were still questions on similar topics.

I have examined 37 examination papers of the 1902 Jiangnan provincial examination, as included into the *Complete Collection of Vermillion Examination Essays in the Qing Dynasty*, in some detail. Apart from ascertaining that most had been influenced by the *Treatise on Japan*, their knowledge on international law originated from a number of *collectanea* on Western knowledge, which were popular at the time of the 1898 reform. Some examination papers explicitly mentioned the earlier edict of the Guangxu emperor to revise the legal codes and the paragraph of the Mackay Treaty on the abolition of extraterritoriality. While the quality of these examination papers is anything but uniform, most, to a different extent, describe and stress the unjust nature of extraterritoriality towards China, and the danger of incursions into China's sovereignty (explicitly referred to by some as "national humiliation"); they were of the opinion that following Japan's revision of criminal law and the realisation of the legal reform with Western reference and standards were the key pre-requisites for the abolition of extraterritoriality and the achieving of self-strengthening.

In respect of the understanding of the contents of the concept of "extraterritoriality", most of the examinees who wrote the above-mentioned 37 examination records understood that it was a special privilege given to foreigners who came to China and who were neither subject to Chinese law nor to the jurisdiction of the Chinese local administration; this accounts for 24 persons, 65 per cent of the complete sample; six persons clearly did not understand it and saw it as the normal legal power of China to control and adjudicate foreigners who came to China; this accounts for 16 per cent of the total sample. The other seven persons employed unclear knowledge, which was quite difficult to distinguish.[57] They included those who were not in favour of making Chinese and

---

56 *Renyin ke bianfa zhisheng weiyi* (1903); Cf. also, Song Fangqing (2009), "Keju gefei yu qingmo zhengfa jiaoyu".

57 Such as Li Guodi 李國棣, the grandson of Li Yunzhang 李蘊章, the fourth brother of Li Hongzhang, who misunderstood extraterritoriality as Chinese administering and having jurisdiction over foreigners coming to China; for another example, see Fei Yugui 費毓桂, an examination candidate from Changzhou, Suzhou prefecture. He wrote: "Since the beginning of commercial transactions between China and the West, the most relevant thing, which belongs to the universal principles of all countries, which, up to now, has not been applied in China, is nothing other than 'extraterritoriality'"; Gu Tinglong (1992), *Qingdai zhujuan jicheng*, vol. 202, pp. 89–93, vol. 203, p. 91.

EXTRATERRITORIALITY IN MODERN CHINA

Western law uniform. The examination candidate Xu Shize 徐世澤 from Suzhou in Jiangsu, for example, wrote:

> Our law certainly needs to be changed, and, moreover, we, on the sixth of the fourth month, have received an Imperial edict to this effect. This, however, is like that by which the English want to cheat us, stating that the law should be like that of the West. But what actually is a law? Is it really possible to give oneself up and follow others?

He stressed that, in respect of the Imperial powers, "to be too subservient and follow in a crooked way, to make too many compromises, is not that by which it is possible to fight extraterritoriality".[58]

In the 1902 Jiangnan provincial examinations, a number of persons participated who would later on become very well known, such as Liu Shipei 劉師培 (1884–1919), Huang Yanpei 黃炎培 (1878–1965), *etc.* While Liu Shipei's examination papers have not been included into the *Complete Collection of Vermillion Examination Essays in the Qing Dynasty*, they are representative of a comparatively high level of understanding of "extraterritoriality" among the Chinese of the times. For Liu Shipei, extraterritoriality, in respect of China at that time, had three major defects: 1. "Losing the power of the state"; 2. "Violating the principle of parity"; and 3. "Violating the equality of the law". For these reasons, it would become a "gigantic disaster" for China. He was of the opinion that, only by establishing a law-university in which law was taught, by actively engaging in code-revision, abolishing all kinds of torture instruments, abolishing forced confessions, establishing "clean jails", *etc.*, would it be possible in the end to abolish extraterritoriality. Liu Shipei was completely aware of the current practice to confuse the concept of "extraterritoriality" with "consular jurisdiction". He called extraterritoriality, which was formed by means of a treaty, as "consular power to act arbitrarily" (*lingshi zhuanduan zhi quan* 領事專斷之權) and, at the same time, spoke of a "system of consular jurisdiction". He also mentioned "public power" and "private power", and, from this, constructed an argument that it was not appropriate to "practice extraterritoriality in China".[59]

Later on, the Qing court, with Shen Jiaben 沈家本 (1840–1913) and Wu Tingfang in charge, carried out comparatively efficient code-revision work, and, in respect of the modernisation of law, made a big stride forward. This work was closely related to the abolition of extraterritoriality and the appeal against consular jurisdiction. The court was quite conscious of this, and said, in the words of the memorials and the edicts of the time, "the revision of the law in the first place aims at recovering (*shouhui*) 'extraterritoriality', and is actually of pivotal importance for reform and self-strengthening", "reform and self-

---

58 Ibid., vol. 203, pp. 19–20.
59 Guo Yuanlin (2012), *Fanghuang yu mitu*, pp. 101–103.

strengthening are based upon this", *etc*.[60] This has already been shown by previous research, and thus there is no need to explore it further here.[61]

It is noteworthy, however, that, at the end of the Qing period, there was not just the phenomenon of confusing "extraterritoriality" and "consular jurisdiction", although mixing the two was the dominant aspect, especially at the level of societal mobilisation and circulation. At the same time, there was also a clear differentiation between the two, which even went so far as to analyse their fundamental difference and usage. This epistemological situation was also closely connected to the fate of the modern Chinese state and also reflected modern China's sensitive nationalist mentality. During the last few years, the academic community has begun to look into this phenomenon, but, in most cases, it only discusses it starting from 1906;[62] however, as a point of fact, the beginning of this discussion can be pushed further back.

I have discovered that, early on during the reform period, there were already Chinese periodicals which, based upon the principles of international law, were using the concepts of "extraterritoriality" and "consular jurisdiction" differentially. They tried to show that the exact meaning of extraterritoriality in international law was actually that of "diplomatic immunity" and not that of "consular jurisdiction".

In June 1898, Jian Jingke 簡敬可, a Guangdong-born Chinese, who was temporarily living in Japan, together with Han Tanshou 韓曇首 and Han Wenju 韓文舉, disciples of Kang Youwei and others in Kobe founded the Chinese-language magazine *East-Asia Daily* (*Dongya bao* 東亞報), which was sold in large cities in the Chinese interior as an response to the reform efforts in China. In the fifth issue of the magazine, which was published in the eighth month of that year, a serialised translation from the Japanese of the part entitled "The Subject of International Law" of the book *Recent Discussions of International*

---

60 "Xingbu zou biantong zhong fa shu duan zhe" 刑部奏變通重法數端摺 (Memorial by the Board of Punishment on some Aspects of Flexible Handling Strict Laws", *Shenbao*, 3 May 1905. In a memorial, the commissioner for code revision, Wu Tingfang, also stated: "This code revision was originally embarked u[on with a view to regaining extraterritoriality. For this reason, arriving at a uniform legal system, adopting that which is good from the others in order to mend what is poor on our side is, in fact, the most important intention when starting our work"; Cf. "Xiulü dachen waiwubu you shilang Wu Xingbu zuo shilang Shen zou he yue Liu Pengnian zou tinghi xingxun qing jia xiangshen zhe" 修律大臣外務部右侍郎伍刑部左侍郎沈奏覆御史劉彭年奏停止刑訊請加詳慎摺 (The Commissioner for Revising the Legal Code and Vice-minister to the Right of Foreign Affairs and the Vice-minister to the Left for the Board of Punishments, Shen Responds in a Memorial to a Memorial of the Censor Liu Pengnian, who Asks for Additional Careful Deliberation before Stopping Torture in Legal Cases", *Dongfang zazhi*, 2: 8 (1905).

61 Cf. Li Guilian (1990), "Qingji falü gaige lingshi caipanquan", and Zhang Shiming (2013), "Zailun Qing mo bianfa xiulü gaige zhaoduan yu feichu lingshi caipan".

62 Cf. the publications of Li Yang and Gao Hancheng mentioned above.

Law appeared, which consciously differentiated between the two concepts of "extraterritoriality" and "consular jurisdiction". The translator of this text was the Japanese Daizo Kakutani 角谷大三郎. He was the full-time translator of the *East Asia Daily* and was both fluent in Chinese and familiar with the modern knowledge of International Law and willing to enlighten the Chinese in the realm of International Law. In this text, Daizo Kakutani stressed that the period of "personal authority" was already over and "territorial sovereignty had become the great principle of International Law, which cannot be shaken". In both cases, exceptions can only be made for "special reasons", one for extraterritoriality, and the other for consular jurisdiction.

What is extraterritoriality? Even if one is on foreign soil, one is treated as being on one's own soil and does not obey the sovereignty of the country in which one resides. Let us try to identify those who possess extraterritoriality: Heads of state (Emperors and kings, presidents, etc.), ministers and family servants, as well as the army of a country. When they are abroad, they are not subject to foreign sovereignty. Now the sovereignty of all countries is equal and is mutually-respected and one does not dare to destroy this important principle of International Law. The practice of extraterritoriality does not go beyond this. That which is called 'extraterritoriality' is to apply one's own legal code outside one's own control.

The article discusses other aspects of diplomatic immunity. To my knowledge, this is probably the first instance in which the designation "extraterritoriality" is used in Chinese articles or translations to discuss the content of "diplomatic immunity", or, it can be said that, for the first time, "extraterritoriality" is completely distinguished from "consular jurisdiction", and its connotations are fully explained, although the translator still does not use the technical term "diplomatic immunity". With regard to consular jurisdiction, the article not only clearly borrowed the term from Japanese very early on, but also describes its content even more clearly than Kang Youwei. The article points out that consular jurisdiction applies when the people of a civilised country reside in a "place, which has not escaped from barbarian domain and whose legal system does not conform to the principles of the world". Because of an unwillingness to obey barbaric laws, by means of a "special treaty", a "treaty privilege" is created, and, for this reason, it is also called a "treaty system of consular jurisdiction" (*tiaoyue lingshi caipan zhi zhi* 條約領事裁判之制):

The treaty item mandates that one is not subject to the jurisdiction of the country in which one resides: this is called consular jurisdiction. A treaty which agrees to 'consular jurisdiction' means relinquishing parts of one country's sovereignty, and this, inevitably, is a national humiliation.

The article laments the fact that all East Asian countries have been subject to this humiliation, and that only Japan has succeeded in obtaining a treaty revision by means of reform and thus, in the end, has washed away the humiliation.

Although China has such a vast territory and such a large population, it is still subject to this humiliation. The reason is that it is stuck with an ancient law and does not look at the general development of the world. From very early on, this was "a pipe dream". The translated text complains that China, as a subject of International Law, frequently faces the danger of its own territory being occupied by the European powers, but that it does not fight for the rights which are inherent to its position of being a subject of International Law.

If one is afraid of the intimidations of the powers, and once allows them to conspire to commit a crime, then it becomes unclear where the rights of International Law are. This is insulting one's own national sovereignty and its damage extends to the whole of the Far East. [...] Therefore, persons of ideals and integrity do not know how to deal with their sorrows [...] they unconsciously break into tears, throw away their brushes and sigh repeatedly.[63]

We do not know what feelings the Chinese had when they read these words written by a Japanese in the *East Asia News*. It should be pointed out that such a concept of "extraterritoriality", with its clear distinction from "consular jurisdiction", which was only used in the sense of "diplomatic immunity", was a translation from Japanese publications on International Law. Since it had itself proclaimed to constitute the "most recent discussions of International Law", at the time, even in Japan, it constituted a relatively new doctrine. And, of course, in China, prior to 1903, such an understanding and usage of the concept of "extraterritoriality" was very rare.

Articles on the fundamental differences between extraterritoriality and consular jurisdiction in China markedly increased after 1903. The *Diplomatic Review* (*Waijiaobao* 外交報), modern China's first journal to comment on international questions, began, in the third issue of 1903, to serialise a long article "On Extraterritoriality" ("Lun zhiwai faquan" 論治外法權), which ran over seven numbers. In quite some detail, this article discussed all the problems of diplomatic immunity, but did not touch upon consular jurisdiction at all. It becomes clear that the so-called "extraterritoriality" as a practice of International Law still meant diplomatic immunity. At the beginning, the article especially stressed: "This is an abridged translation of paragraphs 48 to 65 of Chapter Four of the book *A Treatise of International Law* written by the Englishman W.E. Hall."[64] It is clear that this legal knowledge had foreign origins. However, at the time, most

---

63 Daizo Kakutani 角谷大三郎 (tr.), "Guoji gongfa zhi zhuti" 國際公法之主體 (The Subject of International Law), *Dongya bao*, No. 5 1898, pp. 17–19. Further research is needed in order to find out from which work on law this point of view comes. According to Li Yang's research, the book *Kokusai kōhō* 國際公法 of Sadatarō Hiraoka 平岡定太郎 (1898) already employs a similar view (see pp. 72–73 of this book); Cf. Li Yang (2015), "Cong ciyi dao yujing".

64 "Lun zhiwai faquan" 論治外法權 (On Extraterritoriality), *Wajiaobao*, nos, 2, 3, 5, 8, 9, 10, 11, quotation no 2, p. 6.

EXTRATERRITORIALITY IN MODERN CHINA

193

of the translated knowledge did not come from the International Legal community in Europe, but, for the most part, came from Japan.

This kind of popular understanding quickly attracted the attention of the Qing dynasty officials. At the beginning of 1905, the examinations of the Imperial court for students returning from abroad contained a question on "what is the difference between 'exterritoriality' and 'consular jurisdiction', list the items and analyse them". There were some examination papers which were considered as so outstanding that they were published in newspapers. For example, the examination paper of the Guangdong student Tang Bao'e 唐寶鍔 (1878–1953) received much attention. Tang had graduated from Waseda University. After he had returned to China in 1905, he took part in the "palace examination" and was awarded the *jinshi*-rang of the first grade. His examination paper was published in the *Sichuan official news* (*Sichuan guanbao* 四川官報) that year.

Tang Bao'e clearly pointed out that, although there was a connection between extra-territoriality and consular jurisdiction, the difference was even larger and the two should not be confused. He was of the opinion that extraterritoriality belonged to a "principle of International Law, a general rule of all countries". It was a form of "special immunity", which constituted a mix between territorial law and personal law. Although it constituted an exception to legal territorialism, in principle it did not violate the spirit of territorial law. "Consular jurisdiction", however "cannot be mentioned in the same breath", since it completely belongs to the category of "personal law", which wrecks the sovereignty of the state. Tang wrote excitedly:

In the past, China had combined consular jurisdiction and extraterritoriality into one, and it propagated to 'recover extraterritoriality'. Apparently, it was not at all aware that extraterritoriality was the normal case in most countries, so that it is not necessary to recover it, and, moreover, it could not be recovered. Only consular jurisdiction hinders sovereignty to a great deal. If it is like this in one country, it will lose the qualification for international equality. If it is not immediately withdrawn, it will not be able to attain wealth and power.[65]

In the years after 1906, the *Beiyang guanbao* 北洋官報, the *Dongfang zazhi*, the *Guangyi congbao* 廣益叢報, the *Nanfang bao* 南方報, the *Dagongbao*, the *Shenzhou ribao* 神州日報, the *Shuntian shibao* 順天時報 and other journals all published similar articles. From many different angles, they analysed the difference between "extraterritoriality" and "consular jurisdiction", in the firm belief that the correct meaning of *zhiwai faquan* was "diplomatic immunity". In this year, for example, the *Dongfang zazhi* published a widely distributed article with the title "On the Difference of the Nature of 'Extraterritoriality' and 'Consular Jurisdiction'" ("Lun zhiwai faquan yu lingshi caipanquan xingzhi zhi qubie" 論

---

65 Tang Bao'e (1905), "Lun zhiwai faquan yu lingshi caipanquan zhi yitong".

治外法權與領事裁判權性質之區別), which stressed that the correct meaning of "extraterritoriality" was "diplomatic immunity", and not "consular jurisdiction". Both seem "to be similar but are not the same". "The misuse of the term in China stems from Japan. In Japanese texts ten years ago, they followed each other in constantly mixing it up." The author also states that the terminological problem is by no means a small issue, but a large question related to national sovereignty. "When the names are not correct, they are easily mixed up, when looking at them."

For those who today speak about politics, verbs, predicates and subjects are trifling; why should one ponder on their importance? They are not aware, that, if [a word] has been in use for a long time, it becomes a 'technical term' of politics and scholarship. One basket full of earth can block a river, the fire of one star can incite an Imperial palace. Is it not so, that, since the past, the loss of power has started from the most trifling detail?[66]

In 1907, the *Dongfang zazhi* published an article entitled "An Explanation of Extraterritoriality" ("Zhiwai faquan shiyi" 治外法權釋義), which not only stressed that extraterritoriality was diplomatic immunity, but also made four concrete points in order to distinguish it from consular jurisdiction in a general way. The former had been formed "for the convenience of etiquette", the latter for "fixing the difference of the degree of civilisation". The former was "a principle of International Law", the latter was an "exception to International Law". The former "absolutely disobeyed the sovereignty of the host country", the latter was "partially not following the sovereignty of the host country". The former was enjoyed "by specifically named men and things", the latter "not limited to specifically named persons and things".[67]

This way of contrasting the concepts of "extraterritoriality" and "consular jurisdiction" after 1907 even influenced Shen Jiaben, who was in charge of code revision, and core personalities such as Dong Kang 董康 (1867–1947) and others. It not only reached a small climax in the diffusion of newspapers and magazines, but was also strengthened by the definitions found in dictionaries from Japan. The *Japanese Dictionary of Law and Economics Translated into Chinese* published by the Commercial Press in 1908, for example, offered explanations for "extraterritoriality" as well as for "consular jurisdiction":

The right not to be governed by the country in which one resides in, but one's original country is called 'extraterritoriality'. Monarchs, envoys and the officials affiliated to them, regardless of the country to which they go, are governed by the law of their own

---

66 "Lun zhiwai faquan yu lingshi caipanquan xingzhi zhi qubie" 論治外法權與領事裁判權性質之區別 (On the Difference of the Nature of Extraterritoriality and Consular Jurisdiction), *Dongfang zazhi*, 3:13 (1906).
67 "Zhiwai faquan shiyi" 治外法權釋義 (An Explanation of Extraterritoriality), *Dongfang zazhi*, 4:11 (1907).

EXTRATERRITORIALITY IN MODERN CHINA

countries. This is a general rule of International Law. It is these people who enjoy 'extraterritoriality'. 'Consular jurisdiction' designates that an official or ordinary person of another country is not subject to the laws of the country in which they live. They are subject to the consular juridical power of those sent from their original country. Thus, it is different from 'extraterritoriality' and the result of a treaty.[68]

This kind of explanation is quite representative of Japanese social science dictionaries of the time. It even went so far as to state that those who did not understand the difference between consular jurisdiction and extraterritoriality and spoke about them "together" would be ridiculed as showing "political knowledge" but "not having legal knowledge".[69] After the beginning of the Republican period, the knowledge on the distinction between the two was further strengthened. For example, Chen Qitian 陳啓天 (1893–1984), who later became the leader of the China Youth Party, published an article in *Dongfang zazhi* in 1915 in which he criticised the ignorance of Qing officials who "had not been able to distinguish between 'extraterritoriality' and 'consular jurisdiction'". And, in the Republican era, "the mistakes of the former Qing dynasty are continued and 'consular jurisdiction' is translated as 'extraterritoriality'".[70] From this, we can infer that mixing up the two was rather common.

It is worth noting that, in response to Chen Qitian's rigorous distinction, the journalist of the *Dongfang zazhi* provided a specific answer and clearly pointed out that, not only in Chinese were these two concepts often intermingled in this way, but that also in Japanese these two concepts were often mixed and not clearly distinguished from each other, as occurred in both England and America. This situation was rather different from the standardised and rigorous academic language that was used in the norms of International Law. The journalist wrote:

The word *zhiwai faquan* follows the Japanese usage. And Japan, in respect of designating 'consular jurisdiction', also often employs the word 'extraterritoriality'. In common usage, a strict distinction is lacking. It is my intention, here, to explain *zhiwai faquan* by employing that which the four characters express. This is not more than that a person residing abroad is not subject to the legal control of the country in which he or she resides. It does not matter whether we are dealing with head of state, an envoy, a missionary or a merchant, they all enjoy it and are included into it. As far as the contents of the explanation is concerned, that which is enjoyed by a head of state or an envoy in a strict sense needs to be differentiated from that enjoyed by missionary and merchants. Academically speaking, only heads of states and envoys enjoy extraterritoriality. That

---

68 Tanabe Keiya, Wang Wozang (1911), *Hanyi Riben falü jingji cidian*, p. 55, 126.

69 "Lai gao lun lingshi caipanquan yu zhiwai faquan bu tong" 來稿論領事裁判權與治外法權不同 (Received Contribution, on the Difference between Consular Jurisdiction and Extraterritoriality), *Dagong bao* (Tianjin), 1 January 1908.

70 Chen Qitian 陳啓天, "Zhiwai faqaun yu lingshi caipanquan bian" 治外法權與領事裁判權辨 (Differentiating Extraterritoriality and Consular Jurisdiction), *Dongfang zazhi*, 12:7 (1915).

which missionaries, merchants, *etc.*, enjoy is called 'consular jurisdiction'. In a popular understanding, heads of states and envoys should enjoy this right naturally, when they specifically speak about 'extraterritoriality', they point at that which missionaries and merchants enjoy and call it in this way. The academic meaning has been defined by scholars, while the 'popular meaning' takes the societal usage as standard.[71]

While this journalist stresses that he appreciated Chen Qitian's proposal "from the point view of correcting the names", he adds that, "if one wants to make the term *zhiwai faquan* rely on an academic meaning, one must change the 'popular' meaning' so that both explanations are clarified and clear in the hearts of the people". At the same time, however, he reminds the people that, in the usual daily use of English, the two are not strictly distinguished from each other.

In order to corroborate the correctness of the words of the journalist, I specifically checked the Proquest database of historical journals, which includes twelve English journals and newspapers which were published in China. I discovered that, when, from the 1850s on, these journals used the terms "exterritoriality" or "extraterritoriality", this was, in fact, done in the sense of consular jurisdiction or in the sense of a concept of extraterritoriality which was based upon consular jurisdiction in the sense of "not being subject to the laws of the country one resides in". This is different from the situation in China, where the two are mixed up. However, the Westerners using these concepts either stress the necessity of this privilege in order to protect the "citizens of the Christian countries", or they refute China's or Japan's related denunciations and defend its continuing existence by stressing the legitimacy, normalcy and fairness of the Westerners enjoying these privileges,[72] and thus, in almost all cases, pointed out something which was completely different from the value judgement of excited Chinese nationalists. Naturally, they also often expressed this publicly: as soon as China can adopt efficient guarantees based upon European judicial principles in respect of the civil and penal code, "extraterritoriality" can be abolished.[73]

To put it differently, from the perspective of the increasingly mature and increasingly rigorous principles of International Law, it is without any doubt correct to point out the difference between consular jurisdiction and extraterritoriality in the sense of normal "diplomatic immunity". At the same time, we must also observe its use in daily societal life, a discursive reality, in which both are used in an intermingled way and not clearly distinguished form each other. This is helpful in order to understand that the English and American governments in the treaties with China were always willing to use "extraterritoriality" and did not change that. In fact, it was precisely because of this that

---

71 Ibid.

72 *The North-China Herald*, 23 February 1856, 22 January 1859, 5 December 1879, 9 April 1884.

73 Cf. *The North China Herald*, 5 April 1870.

consular jurisdiction seen as "extraterritoriality based upon treaty relations" or at least as a kind of special extraterritoriality was not unfounded. In 1905, Liang Qichao called "consular jurisdiction" a "special extraterritoriality". He was even of the opinion that, under the autocratic rulership of the Qing, those "criminals persecuted] by imperial order" residing in the concessions enjoyed this privilege. Actually, this situation had the real advantage that it allowed creative thinking, which certainly had a positive effect even though a new form of autocracy was formed in the concessions.[74] Later on, upon this basis, the Republican scholar Zhou Yusheng 周鯁生 (1889–1971) and others were of the opinion that, in respect of this "judicial power beyond one's own territory" in a wider sense, "consular jurisdiction is specifically one kind of extraterritoriality".[75]

Because the two concepts were originally ambiguous and contradictory in the English language, beginning in the late Qing period, the Chinese, based upon their sensibility towards victimisation, were always of the opinion that the Western powers exploited the Chinese ignorance towards the outside world, and that there existed a form of behaviour which "cheated", which "disguised the practice of consular jurisdiction behind the word 'extraterritoriality'".[76] In itself, this kind of ambiguous language clearly does not harm the interest of the strong, and one may even may so far as to claim that it is the embodiment of discursive privilege and the feeling of civilisational superiority. Even if there is no subjective motivation for deceiving the weak, objectively speaking, it can easily produce some kind of deceptive cognitive consequences. For this reason, this kind of sensitivity on the part of the injured party is both natural and reasonable. In order to limit both the scope of the aggression and the privilege of the Western powers and deny them legal justification, some Chinese, when discussing the concept of extraterritoriality not in the sense of diplomatic immunity, chose to employ the term "consular jurisdiction" in order to replace it. This directly influenced the result of the dissemination of those two terms of political vocabulary in China. I have used the databases and conducted a preliminary count of the use of the terms "extraterritoriality" and "consular jurisdiction" in the *Shenbao*, the *Dagongbao* of Tianjin and the *Dongfang zazhi*, and have discovered that, in the *Dagongbao* from 1908 onwards and in the *Shenbao* from 1909 onwards, the term "consular jurisdiction" was employed more frequently than "extraterritoriality". In the *Dongfang zazhi*—an academic journal—between 1907 and 1910, "consular jurisdiction" was also used more often than "extra-

---

74 Yinbing 饮冰 (Liang Qichao), "Zhiwai faquan yu guomin sixiang nengli zhi guanxi" 治外法權 與國民思想能力之關係 (Extraterritorialy and its Relationship to the Ability to Think of our Citizens", *Xinmin congbao*, 1905: 16.

75 Zhou Yusheng 周鯁生, "Lingshi caipanquan wenti" 领事裁判权问题 (The Problem of Consular Jurisdiction), *Dongfang zazhi*, 19:8 (1922).

76 "Zhiwai faquan zhi shiyi" (lu *Shibao*) twentieth day of twelfth month, quoted from Li Xinrong (2018), *Zichuang liangfa: Qingji xin xinglü de bianxiu yu fenzheng*, p. 59.

territoriality". Between 1911 and 1917, the trend was reversed, but, from 1918 to 1921, "consular jurisdiction" again surpassed "extraterritoriality" in the number of usages. This also provides us with a glimpse of the inside story.

4. "Illegal extraterritoriality"—Symbol of imperialism, reason for revolution and tool of mobilising for an "anti-imperialist patriotic movement" (1919–1949)

The year 1919 brought a major change in the Chinese's attitude towards extraterritoriality, in the sense of consular jurisdiction, as enjoyed by both the Western powers and Japan in China. On the one hand, China, after the end of the First World War, took part in the Paris Peace Conference as a victorious nation, and, publicly and explicitly, demanded the abolition of the foreign privileges. Although this wish was not fulfilled, it was agreed that, after the conference, China's legal situation would be investigated, and, it was promised that, based upon this, the process would advance further. China's government and general public, feeling further deeply humiliated because of this, strengthened their research and understanding of the question of extraterritoriality and consular jurisdiction. A large number of related publications came out, especially popularising books.[77] On the other hand, at the same time, the diplomatic determination and intensity to abolish this privilege became stronger daily, especially after the establishment of a national government, which called itself "revolutionary".

As a result of the May Fourth Movement, the anti-imperialist movement grew and the concepts of "extraterritoriality", "consular jurisdiction", and that of the "unequal treaties" were widely disseminated. As an emblem with symbolic meaning, they were not only regarded as the concentrated embodiment of the imperialist countries' joint-tyrannizing of weak and small nation states, they also became an important conceptual tool for all political parties and societal groups for denouncing imperialism and mobilising the Chinese for an anti-imperialistic, patriotic movement. During the process of actual application and

---

77 See Cheng Guangming (1919), *Lingshi caipanquan chehui zhi yanjiu*, and Gu Weijun (1925), *Waiguo zai Hua zhi diwei*. This was a new edition of Gu's Columbia University doctoral dissertation of 1911, which was first translated into Chinese in 1912, Diao Minqian (1919), *Zhongguo guoji tiayue yiwu lun* (first published by Commercial Press in English in 1917), and Hao Liyu (1925), *Lingshi caipanquan wenti*. After the May Thirtieth Movement of 1925, at Commercial Press alone the following books were published: Wu Songgao (1929), *Zhiwai faquan*, Liang Mindui (1930), *Zai Hua lingshi caipanquan lun* and Sun Xiaolou, Zhao Yinian (1937), *Lingshi caipanquan wenti*. The number of articles in journals and newspapers is impossible to count.

EXTRATERRITORIALITY IN MODERN CHINA 199

struggle, the Chinese people were, in many cases, able to understand further the damage inflicted on Chinese sovereignty and governance by the Western powers and Japan, and they attacked it in even more vigorously. Let us take the May Thirtieth Movement as an example: when the massacre had been committed, the Guomindang stressed, in a public telegram to the British House of Commons, that the existence of extraterritoriality was the main culprit of this tragedy:

The recent tragedy is only one of the countless examples of foreigners who made use of extraterritoriality in various parts of China and carried out cruel acts. This is the natural result of the existence of the unequal treaties that our country was forced to conclude.[78]

Zhu Maocheng 朱懋澄, who had studied engineering in Europe and then returned to China, personally accused the British Foreign Minister Austen Chamberlain for defending the May Thirtieth tragedy. He also—incisively and thoroughly—blamed extraterritoriality for the tragedy:

Foreigners enjoy extraterritoriality. This not only harms China's sovereignty, but moreover allows foreign vagrants to commit crimes arbitrarily. The Chinese and foreigners are not treated equally. The foreigners assume an arrogant position, so that the gap between Westerners and Chinese becomes even wider. For this reason, as long as extraterritoriality is not abolished, it will be very hard to attain peace.[79]

It is thus not difficult to understand for what reason the organisers of the May Thirtieth Movement, the Shanghai Joint Committee of Workers, Merchants and Students stressed that its main postulate in the struggle was to abrogate extraterritoriality:

The cancellation of extraterritoriality as well as the recovery of the municipal policy in the concession are really the centre of the fight of this federation. Our federation is of the opinion that if, in respect of the negotiations on the May Thirtieth tragedy, the conditions set by our federation are not followed, then our Shanghainese compatriots will be suppressed even more and more tragedies will happen.[80]

In their long-term protest and negotiations with foreign nations to abolish this privilege and their constant setbacks, the Chinese people felt strongly that extraterritoriality or consular jurisdiction were "weapons used by imperialism in

---

78 "Guomindang zhi Yinguo xiayi yuan dian" 國民黨致英國下議院電 (Telegram of the Guomindang to the British House of Commons), *Dongfang zazhi*, 22 (1925) *Extra Issue on the Occasion of the May Thirtieth Incident.*

79 Zhu Maocheng 朱懋澄, "Bo Ying waixiang Zhang Bolun dui hu an zhi yanshuo ci" 駁英外相 張伯倫對滬案之演說詞 (Refuting British Foreign Minister Chamberlain's speech on the Shanghai case), *Dongfang zazhi*, 22: 16 (1925).

80 "Shanghai gongshang xue lianhehui xuanyan" 上海工商學聯合會宣言 (Manifesto of the Shanghai Federation of Workers, Merchants and Students), *Dongfang zazhi*, 22 (1925), *Extra Issue on the Occasion of the May Thirtieth Incident.*

order to invade China".[81] Thus, the abolition of this foreign privilege must, of course, be an important task in China's anti-imperialist revolution. Only be resorting to revolutionary means or by being backed by the revolution would it be truly possible to achieve the goal of abolishing this foreign privilege. If, otherwise, one was only to rely on negotiations, this would be tantamount to going against one's own interest. In the year of the May Thirtieth Movement, Wang Jingwei 汪精衛 (1883–1944) declared in a written pronouncement:

In respect of the abolition of extraterritoriality, we not only need to make the necessary preparations regarding judicial reform and the cultivation of judicial personnel, it is also particularly important to double the focus on revolution ... this is the fundamental way to attain the abolition of consular jurisdiction.[82]

In the 1930s, a widely-read book with the title *A History of Imperialism's Invasion of China* (*Diguozhuyi qin Hua shi* 帝國主義侵華史) also stressed that the excuse that the laws were different and that there were discrepancies in the level of civilisation

is no more than a pretext for imperialism to invade weak and small countries. In fact, differences in law or differences in the civilisational development originally cannot be used as an excuse for the existence of powerful consular jurisdiction. If the power of a state is strong, then the national revolution can be achieved and then such excuses will naturally no longer exist.[83]

From this, we can also learn how the discourse on extraterritoriality and consular jurisdiction served to provide the legitimacy and rationality of the revolution, especially the anti-imperialist national revolution, thus becoming an integral part of the political revolutionary propaganda. After the May Fourth Movement, the Chinese understanding of consular jurisdiction or extraterritoriality in this sense, compared with that of the late Qing period, has a quite distinctive feature: the broader and more straightforward indication and condemnation of its illegitimate nature. At the end of the Qing dynasty, some people in the country began to realise that extraterritoriality was "not compatible with the principles of international law",[84] and that it constituted "private international law" and not "universal international law".[85] But even more people

---

81 Wang Jingwei (1925), *Guoji wenti jueyi an bing liyou shu*, p. 83.
82 Ibid., p. 101.
83 Wu Jintang (1934), *Diguozhuyi qin Hua shi*, p. 210.
84 "Lun zhiwai faquan bu he yu guoji fali" 論治外法權不合於國際法理 (On the Incompatibility of Extraterritoriality with the Principles of International Law), *Dongfang zazhi*, 3: 9 (1906).
85 Sun Baoxuan (2015), *Sun Baoxuan riji*, p. 844: "International Law can be divided into 'Private International Law' and 'Universal International Law'. 'Universal International Law' is the International Law of all countries, 'Private International Law' denotes the extraterritoriality of countries."

were of the opinion that it was the price of the country's backwardness, which had to be tolerated. As one person pointed out:

If there are two strong rivals competing with each other, both of them will not use this right; if a strong and a weak person confront each other, then the strong one has it, and the weak has to endure it.[86]

However, at the time, there were Chinese people who had changed their political stance and were no longer willing to tolerate such "illegal" foreign privileges. They publicly stated that:

If foreigners propose judicial reform in China as a pre-condition, this is totally unreasonable. If we look into the principles of International Law and its fundamental principle of independent countries and the internal situation of our country, then there is no excuse for 'consular jurisdiction' to exist. Reforming the administration of justice is a matter for China's own exclusively. We, of course, strive to improve it; we do not need foreigners to meddle in it. How could this be taken as a pre-condition for changing it? This is a very clear principle, it is the same 'we' that the foreigners cannot ask for the abolition of the Likin-transit tax as a pre-condition for tariff autonomy.[87]

This is to say that extraterritoriality as a privilege for the aggressor, even if it is granted by treaty, does not have legitimacy, and, even less, any moral justification. The Chinese should not care about it at all and needed to abolish it. In 1929, Wu Songhao 吳頌皋, in a book entitled *Extraterritoriality*, stressed that extraterritoriality in the sense of consular jurisdiction, "cannot be called legitimate extraterritoriality". In the *Great Diplomatic Dictionary* (*Waijiao da cidian* 外交大辭典), which had been compiled by the Diplomatic Research Association in 1937, the entry on "Extraterritoriality" also adopted the idea of its "illegitimacy":

This kind of unlawful right infringes on the Chinese sovereignty over its territory, it goes beyond the limits of 'extraterritoriality'. Even if it is based upon a treaty, it cannot be considered as being legitimate. Such a basis is by no means compatible with legal principles and needs to be changed fast. This also is the basis for the Chinese postulate to abolish 'extraterritoriality' since the Paris Peace Conference.[88]

The *Great Diplomatic Dictionary* also directly calls "consular jurisdiction" "a perverse aspect of International Law", which "only can be perceived as a perverse and temporary item".[89]

---

86 "Lun zhiwai faquan yu lingshi caipanquan xingzhi zhi qubie" 論治外法權與領事裁判權性質之區別 (On the Differences in Nature between Extraterritoriality and Consular Jurisidiction (abbreviated reprint from *Beiyang guanbao* 12 October 1906, *Dongfang zazhi*, 3: 13 (1906).

87 Chen Tingrui 陳霆銳, "Zhiwai faquan" 治外發權 (Extraterritoriality), speech recorded by Jun Kuang 俊狂 in: Chen Lihu (2015), *Dong Wu faxue xianxian wenlu*, p. 266.

88 Waijiao xuehui (1937), *Waijiao da cidian*, pp. 506–509. The first reference book listed in the entry is Wu Songhao's book *Extraterritoriality*.

89 Ibid., pp. 993–994.

This kind of understanding of the Chinese also received the sympathy and support of some foreign friends and people of insight.[90] But in the West and in Japan, based upon considerations related to the actual interest of national states or individuals in China, there were also those who openly opposed such proposals. After the May Thirtieth Movement, persons such as the American journalist Rodney Gilbert (1889–1968), who was considered to be an "old China hand", and the English journalist H.G.W. Woodhead (1883–1959) both wrote books forcefully opposing the abolition of extraterritoriality. Gilbert made clear that extraterritoriality, "the most cumbersome word in the Anglo-Chinese dictionary", was formed in the process of establishing relations with China, which lacked civilised legal guarantees, and that extraterritoriality was established "by virtue of actual experience with Chinese courts and not because of any initial prejudice".[91] He was extremely disgusted with the growing Chinese nationalism during the National Revolution and was hostile to the Chinese people's demands for the abolition of extraterritoriality, which he slammed, saying that, if extraterritoriality were abolished, all foreign troops would be withdrawn from China. "There can be no respect for foreign life and property in China"; for this reason, there "will also not be real security".[92] It is not difficult to discover that this kind of legal game about political justice and state interests not only runs through the entire extraterritorial legal system, but persisted to the very time that the system finally was abolished and even into its historical evaluation afterwards.

In modern China, especially under the impetus of the May Fourth Movement, the May Thirtieth Movement and the successive anti-imperialist movements, political concepts such as "extraterritoriality" and "consular jurisdiction" spread widely and were both used and understood by more and more intellectuals and scholars. Examining the databases of *Shenbao*, the *Dagong bao*[93] and the *Dongfang zazhi* helps to corroborate this point. The use of "extraterritoriality" and "consular jurisdiction" after the May Fourth Movement greatly increased in these three newspapers. During the May Thirtieth Movement in 1925, in 1929,

---

90 A typical case is that of Arthur Ransome (1884–1967), who had lived in Soviet Russia and came to China as a journalist for the *Manchester Guardian*. He was full of sympathy for the Chinese revolution and blamed the extraterritoriality existing in China not only for wrecking China's sovereignty, but also for consolidating foreign interest and its dominating position in China; See Ransome (1927), *The Chinese Puzzle*, p. 140.

91 Gilbert (1926), *What's Wrong with China?*, p. 265.

92 Gilbert (1929), *The Unequal Treaties*, p. 235. The Englishman H.G.W. Woodhead listed the reasons why extraterritoriality could not been withdrawn in ten large paragraphs; See Woodhead (1925), *The Truth about the Chinese Republic*, pp. 222–223.

93 Included into the database which we examined are the following editions of the *Dagong bao*: Tianjin (1902–1937, 1945–1949), Shanghai (1936–1937, 1945–1949), Hankou (1937–1938), Chongqing (1938–1949), Guilin (1941–1944) sowie die *Dagong Evening News* 大公晚報, Chongqing 1944–1949.

EXTRATERRITORIALITY IN MODERN CHINA 203

due to the declaration by the Nanjing national government insisting on negotiating the issue with the Western powers, and, in 1943, when China signed treaties with the US, Britain, France and Japan abrogating extraterritoriality, they respectively gained their peaks in usage.

More specifically, "extraterritoriality" was used in the *Shenbao* in 1925 226 times, which was a very high number of instances. 1929 was also a peak with 108 instances, while 1943 saw the absolute peak with 357 instances. In the *Dagongbao*, it was used 77 times in 1925, 109 times in both 1929 and 1943, when the Tianjin *Dagongbao* had already been suspended, and the Hong Kong and Chongqing *Dagongbao* used it 108 times. As a scholarly journal, the usage in the *Eastern Miscellany* was less frequent, but, for "extraterritoriality", it also had its first peak in 1925 with 22 instances, in 1927 with 25 instances, and in 1929 with 22 instances. On the whole, it can be observed that the usage corresponds to the great political changes taking place.

The usage of the word "consular jurisdiction" also increased, more or less in a similar way to "extraterritoriality". However, between 1919 and 1937, the usage of the former became more frequent than that of the latter. I have already mentioned that this happened in the *Shenbao*, beginning in 1909, and in the *Dagongbao*, in 1908. In 1925, the term was used 255 times in the *Shenbao*, reaching its peak with a usage of 408 times in 1929, and until 1937 its usage remained very high (176 instances). In the *Dagongbao*, there were 127 instances in 1925, 253 instances in 1929, and it was used 108 times in 1937. The situation was slightly different in the *Dongfang zazhi*, in which the usage decreased between 1921 and 1924, although the usage of "consular jurisdiction" was always higher than that of "extraterritoriality" between 1925 and 1937. During this period, when expressing the same concept, the Beiyang government, the Guomindang-government and the Chinese people preferred to use the term "consular jurisdiction" instead of "extraterritoriality". They did this in order to prevent the Western powers from using the "legality" of this right as a pretext. There was also the goal of limiting the arbitrarily expanding scope of the privilege in order to provide grounds for its abolition. This occurred from the end of the Qing dynasty, although there was a change in terms of the extent to which these arguments were used.[94] During the Republican period, observers remarked that: "In our countr‚y scholars, writers and others have tried to limit the privileges

---

94 At the Paris Peace Conference, the Beiyang government demanded the abolition of the extraterritoriality that the foreign powers enjoyed in China; the Chinese text used the term *lingshi caipan quan*—"consular jurisdiction". The Chinese-German treaty was signed on 20 May 1921. In announcing the abolition of extraterritoriality, the Chinese version also employed the term *lingshi caipanquan*.

enjoyed by these outsiders as much as possible; for this reason, most people call it 'consular jurisdiction'."[95]

Corresponding to this, there were people during this time who were very willing to distinguish between "extraterritoriality" and "consular jurisdiction", stressing the fundamental difference between the two concepts. This is reflected in many books on diplomatic history and in writings on the history of imperial aggression against China.[96] There were also people who condemned the Western powers for mixing the illegal privilege in the sense of consular jurisdiction with extraterritoriality in the sense of diplomatic immunity, suggesting that this was the ulterior motive for such a usage of the terms: "They take the different privileges, which their common people enjoy in China, and the different immunity obligations and draw an analogy to extraterritoriality in International Law with the intention of expanding its scope. In the end, it is for this reason that they call it 'extraterritoriality'."[97] There were also some who claimed that the foreign powers used the concept of "extraterritoriality", "which did not possess a clear-cut scope, and relied on its ambiguous meaning in order to transform it into a tool which encroached on China's rights.[98] The famous diplomatic historian Liu Yan 劉彥 (1880–1941) specifically reminded the Chinese people that, when speaking about this issue, it was best to use "consular jurisdiction", which was "legally clearly-defined and had an exact scope and less use 'extraterritoriality'":

In all cases in which a weak country and a strong country conclude a treaty, it is advisable to avoid words which do not have any definite explanation in order not to be fooled. The Chinese authorities, however, do not have this awareness. The different Imperialist powers use the four characters of the word 'extraterritoriality' because it does not have a clear-cut explanation and is not clearly limited in scope. When they negotiate treaties with China or exchange official documents, they often use this term, and they employ its vagueness in order to have a tool to encroach upon China's rights. As, for example, in 1916, when the Japanese demanded to establish Japanese police forces in Zhengjiatun and other places. At that time, the Japanese minister plenipotentiary Hayashi Gonsuke [1860–1939] sent an official communication to the Foreign minister Wu Tingfang: 'Establishing police forces is a normal method of extraterritoriality and it does not encroach on China's sovereignty'. The mentioning of 'extraterritoriality' by the

---

95 He Xiangming (1943), "Feizhi tiaoyue zhiwai faquan ying xun de tujing".

96 Wu Junru, for example, stresses: "'Consular jurisdiction' and 'extraterritoriality' by many normal people is confused as denoting the same. In fact, the two are two different things and, in International Law, clearly have different meanings and cannot be mixed"; Wu Junru (1929), *Diguozhuyi dui Hua sanda qinlüe*, p. 15, 16, 19. The situation in the books of Jiang Jianren and Jiang Gongsheng is the same. Cf. Jiang Jianren (1930) *Riben diguozhuyi qinlüe*, pp. 297–297. "All newspapers call 'consular jurisdiction' 'extraterritoriality', this creates misunderstandings, it is urgently necessary to correct that." Jiang Gongsheng (1932), *Guozhi shi*, p. 296.

97 He Xiangming (1943), "Feizhi tiaoyue zhiwai faquan ying xun de tujing", pp. 22–23.

98 Wu Jintang (1934), *Diguozhuyi qin Hua shi*, p. 209.

EXTRATERRITORIALITY IN MODERN CHINA   205

Japanese plenipotentiary refers to Japan's jurisdiction in China and is completely unclear. This is clear evidence of how foreigners apply the concept of 'extraterritoriality' in order to encroach on China's rights.[99]

In 1928, the Foreign Affairs Committee of the Ministry of Foreign Affairs of the Guomindang government specifically provided a "correct" differentiation between consular jurisdiction and extraterritoriality, and required people not to make the mistake of calling "consular jurisdiction" "extraterritoriality", and made an announcement to the people of the whole nation:

European and Americans, in respect of consular jurisdiction, hold that, even though they are in a foreign country, the judicial system is the same as in the home-country. They think that the treatment is the same as extraterritoriality for heads of state, diplomats, *etc.* Although it is also called 'extraterritoriality', it is, in fact, the result of the one-sidedness of a treaty. Seen from the perspective of its future abolition, the countries which are subject to the duty of consular jurisdiction should do their utmost to avoid using the term 'extraterritoriality' for consular jurisdiction. If, in a process of strained interpretation, consular jurisdiction is considered as a kind of extraterritoriality or is even called 'extraterritoriality'. This will cause many problems for the campaign for its abolition. In respect of foreign countries, this may create the false impression that one wants to abolish extraterritoriality as part of International Law, and thus will not enjoy sympathy in respect of the internal developments. It will make it more difficult to make the people understood the nature of consular jurisdiction, and will make it more difficult to obtain understanding.[100]

On 30 December 1929, the Guomindang government issued the "Declaration on the Revocation of Consular Jurisdiction". In January of the following year, the propaganda department of the Guomindang Peking Special City Party Steering Committee printed the book entitled *The Movement for the Abolition of Consular Jurisdiction* (*Chefei lingshi caipanquan yundong* 撤廢領事裁判權運動). In it, a special section explains the difference between consular jurisdiction and extraterritoriality, putting special emphasis on "we must make strict differences [between both] so as not give the imperial powers who enjoy consular jurisdiction any pretext".[101] Around 1930, the Guomindang government and some Western countries signed consular exchanges on how to deal with this foreign privilege; in the Chinese version, the term "consular jurisdiction" was used in most cases.[102] This shows the official cognition of this issue and the clear atti-

---

99 Liu Yan (1928), *Bei qinhai zhi Zhongguo*, pp. 1–2.

100 "Waijiao taolun weiyuanhui bianzheng falü yongyu" 外交討論委員會辯正法律用語 (The Committee for Discussing Foreign Policy Identifies and Corrects Legal Language), *Xinwen bao*, 22 November 1928, p. 13.

101 Zhongguo guomindang Beiping tebie shi weiyuanhui xuanchuanbu (1930), *Chefei lingshi caipanquan yundong*, p. 7.

102 For example, as signed with Mexico on 30 October 1929, "Guanyu Moguo fangqi lingshi caipanquan huanwen" 關於墨國放棄領事裁判權換文 (Exchange of Notes with Mexico on

tude of the Guomindang government. It is also one of the reasons why the term "consular jurisdiction" was favoured by the Chinese people and more widespread than "extraterritoriality" before 1938.

After the full outbreak of the War of Resistance in 1937, however, a new phenomenon soon became notable, namely, a shift in the daily usage of the term "extraterritoriality" in Chinese newspapers. It was applied more often than "consular jurisdiction" to a surprising extent. Seen from the databases of the *Shenbao* and the different editions of the *Dagongbao* between 1938 and 1949, the usage of "extraterritoriality" every year was more frequent than that of "consular jurisdiction", at times by a large margin. Although the usage in the *Dongfang zazhi* varied to some degree, on the whole "extraterritoriality" was used more often.

It is my contention that this phenomenon is related to Japan's full-scale aggression against China and to the outbreak of the War of Resistance against Japan in earnest. After the Marco Polo Bridge Incident and Japan's massive invasion of China, the Chinese people faced imminent danger: both for the whole country and for the nation. Concern with the abolition of extraterritoriality was no longer a matter of the highest urgency. It was not important whether the designation was "extraterritoriality" or "consular jurisdiction". Instead, it was the Western countries, such as America, England, France, *etc.*, which, with a view to confronting Japan and maintaining their own positions and interests in China, almost immediately became engaged in negotiations with Japan. In December 1937, for example, Japan's military leaders announced in Shanghai that citizens of third countries in China were required to obey Japanese military law. The American ambassador in Japan immediately sent a diplomatic note to the Japanese government demanding that it guarantee America's "extraterritorial status".[103] On 11 October 1938, the *Shenbao* published an article translated from the *North China Herald* on a jointly formulated letter by US citizens in China against the Japanese invasion and occupation of China; it also specifically demanded that Japan "recognised and guaranteed the extraterritorial status which Americans, according to the treaty, enjoy in China".[104] On 26 November, the *Shenbao* reported on a declaration of the foreigners of all nations, resident in China, who, in a telegraphic message, asked all governments to "restrain Japan strictly". The telegraphic message also specifically pointed out that, "according to the current treaties, Japan should recognise and respect the

---

Renouncing Consular Jurisdiction) and with Norway on 23 April 1931, "Guanyu zai Hua lingshi caipanquan zhi huanwen" 關於在華領事裁判權之換文 (Exchange of Notes on Consular Jurisdiction in China).

103 "The American Ambassador in Japan (Grew) to the Japanese Minister for Foreign Affairs (Ugaki)", *FRUS, Japan, 1931–1941*, vol. 1, p. 615.

104 "Meiqiao lianhe hui weida mudi" 美僑聯合會偉大目的 (The Great Goal of the Federation of US-citizens living in China), *Shenbao*, 11 October 1938.

extraterritorial status of the peoples of all countries [residing in China]".[105] This was by no means an isolated instance. At the end of the year 1938, the Japanese government published the "Third Konoe Declaration" in order to deceive the public and induce traitors to capitulate. It declared itself to be actively willing to contemplate "the revocation of extraterritoriality and the return of the concessions", *etc.* This was in line with the treaty signed between China and Manzhouguo two years earlier, "On the Revocation of Extraterritoriality in Manzhouguo and the Transfer of Administrative Rights to the South Manchurian Railway" in November 1937. The *Shenbao* published this as well as Chinese and foreign reactions to it. Chiang Kai-shek, for example, attacked the Japanese conspiracy. Britain, America and France also immediately notified the Japanese government expressing that they were willing to negotiate the question of the abolition of exterritoriality with an "independent and self-governed China", and that they would not accept Japanese involvement.[106] This went so far that the Chinese-British and the Chinese-American treaties of 11 January 1943, which revoked extraterritoriality, were a direct reaction to the conclusion of a treaty between Japan and the Wang Jingwei-government signed two days earlier, the "Agreement on the Return of the Concessions and Revocation and Abolition of Extraterritoriality" ("Guanyu jiaohuan zujie ji chexiao he feichu zhiwai faquan xieding" 關於交還租界及撤銷和廢除治外法權之協定). This kind of juggling with the extraterritoriality question between the British, American, French and Japanese did, in fact, serve to influence the symbolic use and transmission of the concept. From 1902, when the governments of Britain, the United States and France and Japan issued communications to the Chinese, which dealt with legal privileges in China, the words "extraterritoriality" or "extraterritorial rights" were normally employed in English, as it had already become a formality to translate this into Chinese as *zhiwai faquan*. After the outbreak of the comprehensive war of resistance, Britain, the US and other countries, to some extent, became the "active ones" using the concept of "extraterritoriality" and the Chinese character lexical symbol. The Chinese media, such as the *Shenbao*, often directly reported about the contents of this "war of words" between

---

105 "Waiqaio gongtong xuanyan fabiao, dian qing ge gai zhengfu yanli zhiciai Riben, neirong ji gong jiu xiang" 外侨共同宣言发表，电请各该政府严厉制裁日本，内容计共九项 (Publication of a Common Declaration of Foreigners from all Nation, Asking by Telegram all Governments Strictly to Restrain Japan, Nine Points in All), *Shenbao*, 26 Novermber 1938.

106 "Jiang weiyuanzhang tongsu Jinwei miao lun" 蔣委員長痛斥近衛謬論 (The Head of the [Military Affairs] Committee Jiang [Jieshi] Accuses Konoe's of Absurd Statements), *Shenbao*, 29 December 1938, "Meiguo zhi Ri zhaohui quanwen" 美國致日照會全文 (Complete Text of Diplomatic Communication of the US to Japan), *Shenbao*, 4 January 1939, "Yingguo zhi Ri zhaohui shengming, yuan yu duli zizhu Zhongguo tanpan" 英國致日照會聲明，願與獨立自主中國談判 (Announcement of Diplomatic Note of England to Japan, that it is Willing to Enter Negations with an Independent and Self-governed China), *Shenbao*, 17 January 1939.

Japan and the West. The term "extraterritoriality" was quite often used in order to attain the goal of jointly restricting and opposing Japan's invasion of China. Thus, it is not particularly surprising that the term circulated frequently. In addition, as Western countries such as Britain and the United States gradually became China's allies in World War II, they became more active in negotiations with the Chinese government on the abolition of extraterritoriality. Since the goal of abolishing the privilege was similar and the object was the same, the day when it would become a reality did not seem to be very far away. For this reason, both during the period of World War II and afterwards, China had actually already entered the "period of the abolition of extraterritoriality". Whether it was in negotiations with Britain, the United States or other countries, or when reporting on relevant issues in the media, it seemed no longer necessary to use "consular jurisdiction" instead of "extraterritoriality" in order to protect rights; instead, it had become possible to relax on the issue in order to avoid new problems cropping up unexpectedly. In the end, when China and the United States, Britain, France and more than ten other countries officially signed treaties to revoke this privilege, most of the Chinese texts used the term *zhiwai faquan* (like the Sino-American Treaty for the Relinquishment of Extraterritorial Rights in China ["Zhong Mei guanyu quxiao Meiguo zai Hua zhiwai faquan ji chuli youguan wenti zhi tiaoyu yu huanwen" 中美關於取消美國在華治外法權及處理有關問題之條約與換文], and the Sino-British Treaty for the Relinquishment of Extra-Territorial Rights in China ["Zhong Ying guaxu quxiao Yingguo zai Hua zhiwais faquan jiqi youguan tequan tiaoyue" 中英關於取消英國在華治外法權及其有關特權條約] *etc.*). Only the treaties with Portugal and Switzerland, which had been signed with China beforehand, retained the term "consular jurisdiction".[107]

Apart from the reasons explained above, the increased popularity of the term *zhiwai faquan* over *lingshi caipanquan* was also related to the limits of the scope of the connotation of the latter, which could not completely cover some other persisting factors of "jurisdiction beyond one's own boundaries". The judicial privilege of foreign powers in China and its related content were quite

---

107 The Chinese title of the Chinese-Swiss Treaty is: "Guanyu Ruishi fangqi zai Hua lingshi caipanquan jiqi youguan tequan huanwen" 關於瑞士放棄在華領事裁判權及其有關特權換文 (Exchange of Diplomatic Notes on Switzerland's Renouncement of Consular Jurisdiction in China and Related Privileges, 1946), the treaty with Portugal was "Guanyu quxiao Putaoya zai Hua lingshi caipanquan ji chuli qita shixiang zhi huanwen" 關於取消葡萄牙在華領事裁判權及處理其他事項之換文 (Exchange of Diplomatic Notes on Portugal's Renouncement of 'Consular Jurisdiction' in China and the Regulation of Other Aspects, 1947). Already in June 1918 in an appendix to the Chinese-Swiss "Treaty on Friendly Relations", the term "consular jurisdiction" had been applied: "in respect to consular jurisdiction (i.e., 'extraterritoriality') … later on, when China successfully has reformed it legal system, Switzerland and other treaty powers will renounce their consular jurisdiction in China"; Wang Tieya (1959), *Zhongguo jiu yuezhang huibian*, vol. 2, p. 1374.

EXTRATERRITORIALITY IN MODERN CHINA

209

extensive, so that they were by no means covered by the expression "consular jurisdiction".

Wang Jianlang 王建朗 once divided the exercise of extraterritoriality into three types: the first is through the consular court, the second is through a "common court" established in the area of the concession, and the third is through special courts established in China by Britain, the US and other countries.[108] The latter two, obviously, were not completely included in the concept of "consular jurisdiction". As early as 1926, Wang Chonghui 王寵惠 (1881–1958), a diplomat who knew both law and English, pointed out that "If we consider the current practice of extraterritoriality; in China, its scope is wider than that of consular jurisdiction. In fact, that which is subject to extraterritorial jurisdiction is far outside the realm of consular jurisdiction".[109] In 1928, the diplomatic historian Liu Yan also stressed:

That which is called 'extraterritoriality' by foreigners cannot in its entirety be included in the concept of 'consular jurisdiction' and has a meaning which is mixed with other rights. For this reason in 1924 in the Chinese-Russian agreement … Soviet-Russia promised to abolish extraterritoriality and consular jurisdiction. If China determines that the foreigner's 'extraterritorial jurisdiction' in China refers to the 'consular jurisdiction' in China, why then, in the Sino-Russian agreement, should extraterritoriality and consular jurisdiction be listed together? This is the most recent awareness of the Chinese diplomatic authorities.'[110]

During the late Qing dynasty and the Republic of China, the term and the concept of "consular jurisdiction" became popular, and, although it was used by some people and even by the national government to replace "exterritoriality" in the end, it nonetheless failed to do so.

In fact, if one untangles the puzzle of "legitimacy" caused by "diplomatic immunity", it is not difficult to discover that the term "extraterritoriality" not only had an advantage in expressing the contents of the privilege of the powers, it was also often used by the Chinese to sum up and reflect the ubiquity of the privileged position of the foreign powers in China. Moreover, in terms of the outer appearance of the Chinese characters, "extraterritoriality", in directly expressing the "non-normal" privileged position of the said foreign powers, and the linguistic effect of the extraordinary humiliation which the Chinese people suffered from, is slightly superior to "consular jurisdiction". This becomes

---

108 Wang Jianlang (2000), *Zhongguo feichu bu pingdeng tiaoyue de licheng*, p. 3.

109 "Zhongguo weiyuan duiyu zai Zhongguo zhiwai faquan shixing zhuangkuang zhi yijiansju" 中國委員對於在中國治外法權現在實行狀況之意見書 (Written Opinion of the Chinese Committee Members of the Practice of Extraterritoriality in China), in: *Diaochao zhiwai faquan weiyuanhui baogao shu(Ying-Han duizhao)* (1926), p. 298.

110 Liu Yan (1928), *Bei qinhai zhi Zhongguo*, p. 2. For the content of the 1924 Chinese-Russian Treaty, Cf. Wang Tieya (1959), *Zhongguo jiuzhang huibian*, vol. 3, p. 425.

especially visible when one has read a large amount of historical documents on the critique of imperialism in the post May Fourth period.

Although, during the period of the comprehensive anti-Japanese war, the term "extraterritoriality" spread widely, and, even in terms of the numbers of its being mentioned exceeded that of the term "consulate jurisdiction", and although there were some differences between the two, in the actual use in newspapers, both terms reflect the judicial privileges enjoyed by the foreign powers which invaded China and the political inequality embodied by them. But, on the other hand, both terms are often more or less equal, and they are quite often used indiscriminately.

If one concentrates on checking the dictionaries of the humanities and the social sciences of the period for definitions and explanations of the connotations of "extraterritoriality", one can still observe a number of contradictions, which add to a sense of cognitive confusion.

Some years ago, with the help of Zhu Xingxing, I examined 22 dictionaries of the humanities and the social sciences, which contained the lemma "extraterritoriality" and were published after 1919. Reading the relevant definitions was still cause for some confusion. The explanations of "extraterritoriality" in these dictionaries, basically have two different forms. One is to interpret "extraterritoriality" exclusively as diplomatic immunity, and clearly distinguish it from "consular jurisdiction" (marked by A in the table below), while the other sees "extraterritoriality" as having two meanings, which can refer to both "diplomatic immunity" and to "consular jurisdiction" and related privileges (marked by B in the table below).

Table I: "Extraterritoriality" in post 1919 dictionaries

Title	Year	Place of publication and publisher	Compiler	Form
Sifa faling cidian 司法法令辭典 (Dictionary of Judicature and Law)	1924	Shanghai: Shijie shuju	Tang Shenfang 唐慎坊	A
Zhong-Ying-Fa waijiao cidian 中英法外交辭典 (Chinese-English-French Diplomatic Dictionary)	1925	Nanjing: Waijiaobu	Treaty Department of the Ministry for Foreign Affairs.	B
Falü cidian 法律辭典 (Law Dictionary)	1927	Beijing: Chaoyang daxue	Li Zuyin 李祖蔭	A
Shehui wenti cidian 社會問題辭典 (Dictionary of Social Problems)	1929	Shanghai: Minzhi shuju	Chen Shousun 陳綬蓀	B

EXTRATERRITORIALITY IN MODERN CHINA

Title	Year	Place of publication and publisher	Compiler	Form
Xin shuyu cidian 新術語辭典 (Dictionary of New Technical Terms)	1929	Shanghai: Nanqian shuju	Wu Nianci 吳念慈 and others	A
Zhonghua baike cidian 中華百科辭典 (Encyclopedic Dictionary of China)	1930	Shanghai: Zhonghua shuju	Shu Xincheng 舒新城	A
Shehui yundong cidian 社會運動辭典 (Dictionary of Social Movements)	1930	Shanghai: Mingri shudian	Wang Weimo 王偉模	B
Zhongguo falü da cidian 中國法律大辭典 (Great Dictionary of Chinese Legal Terms)	1931	Shanghai: Shijie shuju	Zhu Caizhen 朱採真	B
Xin mingci cidian 新名詞辭典 (Dictionary of New Terms)	1932	Shanghai: Kaihua shuju	Hong Chao 洪超	A
Falü zhengzhi jingji da cidian 法律政治經濟大辭典 (Great Dictionary of Legal, Political and Economic Terms)	1932	Shanghai: Changcheng shuju	Yu Zheng-dong 余正東	A
Falü da cidian 法律大辭典 (Great Dictionary of Legal Terms)	1934	Shanghai: Dadong shuju	Wang Hanchang 汪翰章 and others	A
Zhengzhi falü da cidian 政治法律大辞典 (Great Dictionary of Legal and Political Terms)	1934	Shanghai: Shijie shuju	Gao Xisheng 高希聖 and others	B
Xin mingci cidian 新名詞辭典 (Dictionary of New Terms)	1934	Shanghai: Xin shengming shuju	Xing Moqing 邢墨卿	A
Xin zhishi cidian 新知識辭典 (Dictionary of New Knowledge)	1935	Shanghai: Tongnian shuju	Society for Compiling and Translating New Dictionaries 新辞书编译社	A
Falü di cishu 法律大辭書 (Dictionary of Legal Terms)	1936	Shanghai: Shangwu yinshuguan	Zheng Jingyi 鄭競毅 and others	A

Title	Year	Place of publication and publisher	Compiler	Form
Hua Ying shuangjie fazheng cidian 華英雙解法政辭典 (Chinese-English Dictionary of Law and Politics with Explanations in Both Languages)	1936	Tianjin, Baicheng shuju	Zhang Chongen 张崇恩	A
Cihai 辭海 (Sea of Words)	1937	Shanghai: Zhonghu shuju	Shu Xincheng 舒新城	A
Wang Yuwu da cidian 王雲五大辭典 (Wang Yunwu's Great Dictionary)	1937	Shanghai: Shangwu yinshuguan	Wang Yunwu 王雲五	B
Waijiao da cidian 外交大辭典 (Great Diplomatic Dictionary)	1937	Shanghai: Zhonghua shuju	Society for Diplomatic Studies	A
Ciyuan 辭源 (The Origins of Words)	1939	Shanghai: Shangwu yinshuguan	Fang Yi 方毅	A
Xin zhishi cidian 新知识辞典 (Dictionary of New Knowledge)	1948	Shanghai: Beixin shuju	Gu Zhijian 顧志堅	A
Zhishi xin cidian 知識新辭典 (New Dictionary of Knowledge)	1949	Beijing: Lizhi shuju	Hu Lizhi 胡立知	A

It needs to be stressed that the table above is certainly not complete. The treatment of the glosses for "diplomatic immunity" and "consular jurisdiction" in the "B" dictionaries are by no means in all cases in the language dictionary style, which offers direct correspondences. It certainly has biases, which I will not deal with further here. Nonetheless, our table is still quite useful for understanding some related questions. Among the 22 dictionaries in the table, 16 define "extraterritoriality" merely as "diplomatic immunity", which is 73 per cent. The "B" dictionaries, for which "extraterritoriality" is defined as not only covering "diplomatic immunity" but also "consular jurisdiction" and related privileges, are a group of only 6 dictionaries and merely constitute 27 per cent of the total sample. These findings are not consistent with the observation that, in newspapers and journals, the intermingling of the two terms, "diplomatic immunity" and "consular jurisdiction" clearly constitutes the mainstream. How can this contradiction be explained? I think it is possible to understand it by taking into account the following three aspects: at first, in respect of the definitions found in these dictionaries, the compilers did not start from the actual use of the vocabulary in order to arrive at generalisations and abstract concepts; instead, most of them use the definitions found in different loan-word dictionaries with small adaptations, and there was no lack of copying, repeating and adopting from each other. As already mentioned, dictionaries of law and politics which define "diplomatic immunity" as "extraterritoriality" show up as early as during the late Qing period. Secondly, the editing of these dictionaries was mostly aimed at spreading "new knowledge". Their word-definition often took a kind of pioneer attitude in order to spread what they acknowledged to be new knowledge, and they were by no means satisfied with the understanding and usage of parts of the normal circulating knowledge. Such an attitude was anything but rare at the time. Thirdly, except for two or three of these dictionaries, the vast majority of them were compiled between 1919 and 1937. This was precisely the period in which the people and officials were instigated by nationalism and which emphasised the difference between consular jurisdiction and extraterritoriality, in order to advocate anti-imperialist propaganda, and, in the process of negotiations with the foreign powers, it was a time, in which the former was consciously adapted in order to replace the latter. The emergence of such a situation is no more than the concentrated and amplified reflection of this cognitive tendency. In any case, in modern China, to understand extraterritoriality merely as diplomatic immunity, and to propagate an understanding that it does not have anything to do with consular jurisdiction for such a long time and in such a scope, was still beyond what I had expected. But this fact shows a certain "ahistoricism" or at least an inability to express historical complexity among those writings on intellectual history concepts which completely ignore or under-estimate the fact that the "extraterritoriality" concept in modern China is not the same as the knowledge on consular jurisdiction. In this regard, the clinging of the *Cihai* to a rather similar definition of extraterritoriality is, in fact, merely a certain continuation of the history of the Republic of China. At the same time, modern Chinese tried to replace extraterritoriality with the concept of "consular jurisdiction". Their, ultimately, unsuccessful attempt to strive actively for discursive power in the arena of International law is also worthy of special attention and deep-reaching reflection.

Conclusion: The Restraining of Concepts by the Strong and the Discursive Weapons of the Weak

The understanding and the application of the concept of "extraterritoriality" by modern Chinese people is rooted in the West. Its obtaining of a final form, its diffusion and its application at the same time were all closely related to the Western colonial aggression in Asian countries such as Japan and China. In

Britain and the United States, the word-form of the concept is "exterritoriality" and "extraterritoriality" and its literal meaning was always "legal power outside the scope of local rule" or "the privilege not to be subject to the laws of other countries". Since the mid-nineteenth century, however, through the dealings with Asian countries, the actual connotation of the concept gradually underwent a structural evolution, that is to say, from merely referring to diplomatic immunity, the item "consular jurisdiction" and "related judicial privileges" was added. In the end, this resulted in the formation of a contradictory conceptual structure, which could point at both diplomatic immunity based upon an understanding of equality, and unequal consular jurisdiction, as granted by a treaty. What was ambiguously transmitted to the Chinese through the Tongwenguan's early translation of Wheaton's *Principles of International Law* was a wide understanding of "extraterritoriality" with this kind of contradictory structure. This, however, only happened in respect of the academic connotation of the specialised terminology of Western International Law.

At the same time, in the daily use of the English mass-media and newspapers, especially in writings on Eastern countries such as China and Japan, "exterritoriality" and "extraterritoriality" often do not have the meaning of diplomatic immunity, but were directly used to refer to consular jurisdiction and the related privileges granted by the unequal treaties. This was because, from the perspective of England, the US and other strong countries, the scope of those enjoying consular jurisdiction was extended to all their subjects and, in fact, also included those who originally enjoyed diplomatic immunity. For those countries which were already strong and enjoying the unilateral judicial privilege of extraterritoriality, diplomatic immunity became meaningless, and, naturally, there was no need to worry about the contradictions and conflicts between the two. It was precisely because of this that, when British, American and other powers used it in their daily written practices, both the word and the symbolic connotation of extraterritoriality—often intentionally, or even unintentionally— were limited to the integrated conceptual level of "consular jurisdiction" and related judicial privileges. It thus obtained a certain language dominance which completely obscured the originally existing connotation of "diplomatic immunity". In the past, when studying the concept of "extraterritoriality", Chinese scholars have largely ignored this point. However, when perusing the English newspapers, written by foreigners who had come to China, it was precisely this point which left a lasting impression on me.

In fact, be it in modern China or in Japan, the contradictory understanding and the choice of application which emerged around the terms "extraterritoriality", "consular jurisdiction" and "diplomatic immunity" can all be traced back to the root of the difference between the original legal meaning of the concept of "exterritoriality" and "extraterritoriality" and its use in daily life.

What troubled China's intellectual élites, or, more exactly, what constituted the cognitive dilemma for Chinese intellectual élites, was, in fact, not just the contradictory meaning structure of the Western concept of "extraterritoriality" itself, but also the linguistic dominance in the sense of "consular jurisdiction" that accompanied it, and the Western discourse hegemony embodied by it.

When the concept of "extraterritoriality" was introduced to China during the late Qing period, Japan, serving as a "middleman", had an important impact. Beginning in the 1880s, the Chinese characters *zhiwai faquan*, coined by the Japanese in order to translate the term "extraterritoriality", sporadically entered China. The content of this concept at the outset pointed to a legal privilege which was related to the guiding idea of "consular jurisdiction". Despite the fact that, because of the different Chinese and Japanese habits of word formation, it was, to a certain extent, responsible for mis-readings or mis-interpretations when it first came to China, it still—either because of the concept of the word itself or because of the mainstream connotation of the word, which was to express a "legal privilege" dominated by consular jurisdiction—remained in circulation without change.

Beginning with the reform movement of 1898 and then from the beginning of the twentieth century, when the country was completely awakened to the concept of national sovereignty, the diffusion and use of words and concepts such as "extraterritoriality", "consular jurisdiction", *etc.*, gradually increased. Influenced by Japanese and Western works on International Law, the concept of "diplomatic immunity", which had originally been part of the content of "exterritoriality" and "extraterritoriality" was also introduced into China in a clearer way. Stimulated by a kind of nationalist sensitivity, some people tried to separate the two conceptual layers of exterritoriality and extraterritoriality and their inherent contradictions from each other, and even bring them into opposition, emphasising that extraterritoriality had originally been limited to the meaning of "diplomatic immunity". The goal was to prevent Westerners from using the designation "extraterritoriality" in the sense of equal "diplomatic immunity" in order to practice extraterritoriality in the sense of consular jurisdiction and other intruding privileges. Thus, there were a number of Chinese who preferred to adopt the term "consular jurisdiction" in order to express the totality of the legal privileges of the powers in China, and intentionally avoided the term "extraterritoriality". As a result, in terms of the instances of usage in the media, beginning in the late Qing period, the former gradually surpassed "extraterritoriality". During the late Beiyang period and especially under the Guomindang government, since this tendency of understanding was publicly endorsed by the government and strategically practiced, its influence was further strengthened.

However, after Japan launched its full-scale war of aggression against China, and because countries such as Britain, the US, France and others became

China's allies in World War II, and were used to referring to their complete legal privileges in China as "extraterritoriality", the Chinese, aware that these privileges were in the process of being abolished, did not want to create further obstacles. In addition, the term "consular jurisdiction" does not accurately cover the entire content of the legal privileges. For this reason, the circulation situation during this period in respect of employing "extraterritoriality" in order to denote the whole content experienced a certain reversal. In the end, although extraterritoriality, as a symbol of foreign aggression in China, was abolished, some Chinese tried to use the concept of "consular jurisdiction" to replace "extraterritoriality" completely, but, as it was an ambiguous concept which was riddled by the above-cited contradictory meaning structure, their hope was not fulfilled. Moreover, the content of extraterritoriality, as understood by the masses, differed from its scholarly definition of "diplomatic immunity", which was included into a number of dictionaries and has continued to this very day.

It is worth noting that, due to the impact of Chinese, Western and Japanese interaction, and the need for self-improvement of the principles of International Law at later stages in the use of "extraterritoriality", some adaptive adjustments did occur. Early on, at the end of the nineteenth century, there were already people who thought that "exterritoriality" was *zhiwai faquan*, in the sense of "diplomatic immunity", and "extraterritoriality" was *zhiwai faquan*, in the sense of "consular jurisdiction",[111] and they tried to separate the two and use them differentially in order to avoid contradictions. After the 1920s, this differentiated use increased. The fact that, in the English media, the term "extraterritoriality" was used much more than "exterritoriality" was also related to this. This is the reason why, in the *Encyclopedia of American Foreign Policy*,[112] we can still see both the terms clearly differentiated from each other.[113]

The above is an introduction to the dissemination of the concept of "extraterritoriality". However, the dissemination and the use of concepts cannot, in fact, be easily separated. Looking at the overall situation of the application of the concepts of "extraterritoriality" and "consular jurisdiction" in modern China enables us to distinguish between two periods, with considerable change. During the late Qing period and the early Republic, members of the élite, with Huang Zunxian and others as typical representatives, used the concept in order to point out to the foreign powers the dangers for Chinese sovereignty. They expressed the weight of the burden of humiliation, and, in a form of flexible

---

111 Cf. Piggot (1892), *Extraterritoriality*, p. 3.

112 Davids, Nielson (2002), "Extraterritoriality", p. 82.

113 In 1926, the missionary Evan Morgan published a bilingual dictionary of neologisms in Shanghai. In it, "extraterritoriality" was translated as *lingshi caipanquan* ("consular jurisdiction"). In explaining the concept of *zhiwai faquan* in the sense of "diplomatic immunity", he stressed that this was different from "consular jurisdiction"; See Morgan (1926), *Chinese New Terms*, p. 57, 229.

protest, the hope that it could be abolished as soon as possible. Towards the inner-Chinese public, it was used in order to reveal the status of the humiliation of the country, and stimulate the awareness of the national crisis and the enthusiasm for reform. They especially used the Japanese experience of abolishing extraterritoriality as an incentive model, and called on China to emulate the West and Japan and carry out political reforms. First, however, came legal reforms, and, for these, it played a very direct role in mobilisation and became an important topic of public discussions during the Reform and new-policy era.

After the May Fourth Movement, because of the changes in China's internal and external positions, the Chinese no longer considered extraterritoriality as the unavoidable price which China had to pay for its backwardness and a price which had to be endured. Instead, they blamed it for its "illegitimacy" as a scholarly principle, and time and time again embarked on anti-imperialist movements which aimed at abolishing this kind of privilege. Consistent with this, the concept of "extraterritoriality" no longer primarily served as a component of a discourse which aimed at reforms after the example of the West, but was regarded as one of the distinctive signs and symbols of Imperialist aggression against China. Thus, for the Chinese, it became a discourse weapon for protesting against Imperialist intrusion. It even became a conceptual tool which served to construct the legitimacy of revolution, especially of the anti-imperialist national revolution. The description and analysis of the harm brought about by extraterritoriality has become a core part of the historiography of the Imperialist aggression against China and has also become an important component of the emerging modern revolutionary history. This also shows its symbolic function for revolutionary political mobilisation.

Today, the extraterritoriality of the foreign powers in China has already become a relic of history. I am convinced, however, that a conceptual history of "extraterritoriality" is of help to allow us to understand the complex interaction between China, Japan and the West in modern times. It also helps us to understand the historical destiny of the modern Chinese nation-state. This, in turn, teaches us to cherish the political ideal of the equal co-existence of countries and the friendly intercourse of nations.

(Translated by Iwo Amelung)

Bibliography

Aoki Hiroyu 青木治世 (2008), "Wan Qing guanyu zengshe zhu Nanyang lingshi de zhenglun – jian lun jindai guoji, lingshi caipanquan, bu pingdeng tiaoyue de tizhi" 晚清關於增設駐南洋領事的爭論 - 兼論近代國際法、領事裁判權、不平等條約體制 (The Late Qing Controversy about Increasing the Number of Consuls in the

Southern Ports—at the same Time Providing a Discussion of the System of International law, Consular Jurisdiction and Unequal Treaties) , in: Wang Jianliang, Luan Jinghe (eds.), *Jindai Zhongguo, Dongya yu shijie*, Beijing: Shehui kexue wenxian chubanshe, pp. 600–618.

Aoyama Harutoshi 青山治世, Zhu Lin 朱琳 (tr.) (2013), "Jindai Zhongguo he Riben de 'jiaocuo' yu 'fenqi—raowei lingshi caipanquan wenti" 近代中國和日本的交錯與分歧——圍繞領事裁判權問題 (Interlacing and Disagreement between Modern China and Japan – the Issue of 'Consular Jurisdiction'), *Shehui kexue yanjiu*, 2013: 6, pp. 160–170.

Bulitun baikequanshu, guoji zhongwenban (xiudingban) 不列顛百科全書, 國際中文版 (修訂版) (Encyclopedia Britannica, International Chinese Edition, revised), Beiing: Zhongguo da baikequanshu chubanshe 2007.

Chen Lihu 陳立虎 (ed.) (2015), *Dong Wu faxue xianxian wenlu – Guoji faxue juan* 東吳法學先賢文錄 國際法學卷 (Records of Former Legal Scholars of Suzhou – International Law), Beijing: Zhongguo zhengfa daxue chubanshe.

Cheng Guangming 程光銘 (1919), *Lingshi caipan quan chehui zhi yanjiu* 領事裁判权撤回之研究 (Research on the Withdrawal of Consular Jurisdiction), n.p.

Dai Dongyang 戴東陽 (2004), "Riben xiugai tiaoyue jiaoshe yu He Ruzhang de tiaoyue renshi" 日本修改條約交涉與何如璋的條約認識 (Japan's Treaty Revision Diplomacy and He Ruzhang's Understanding of Treaties), *Jindaishi yanjiu*, 2004: 6, pp. 161–197.

– (2007), "Shilun Huang Zunxian dui bu pingdeng tiaoyue de renshi" 試論黃遵憲對不平等條約的認識 (On Huang Zunxian's Knowledge of Unequal Treaties), in: Wang Xiaoqiu (ed.), *Huang Zunxian yu jindai Zhong Ri wenhua jiaoliu,*: Shenyang: Liaoning shifan daxue chubanshe, pp. 206–226.

DeConde, Alexander, Richard Dean Buns and Fredrik Logevall (eds.) (2002), *Encyclopedia of American Foreign Policy*, New York: Charles Scribner's Sons 2nd edition.

Diao Minqian 刁敏謙 (1919), *Zhongguo guoji tiaoyue yiwu lun* 中國國際條約義務論 (On the Obligations Deriving from China's International Treaties), Shanghai: Shangwu yinshuguan (English original 1917).

Diaochao zhiwai faquan weiyuanhui baogao shu (Ying-Han duizhao) 調查治外法權委員會報告書(英漢對照) (Report of The Commission on Extra-territoriality in China [Anglo-Chinese edition]) (1926), Shanghai: Shangwu yinshuguan.

Ding Weiliang (W.A.P. Martin) 丁韙良 (tr.)(2002), *Wanguo gongfa* 萬國公法 (Elements of International Law [Originally written by Wheaton]), Shanghai: Shanghai shudian chubanshe.

Dongfang zazhi 東方雜誌 (The Eastern Miscellany), Shanghai, Changsha, Chongqing, Hong Kong 1904–1948.

Dongya bao 東亞報, Kobe 1898.

Encyclopedia Americana, International Edition (1985), New York: Grolier Incorporated.

Fuller, Joseph V. (1943), *Papers Relating to the Foreign Relations of the United States, Japan, 1931–1941*, Washington DC: United States Government Printing Office. (abbreviated as FRUS).

Gao Hancheng 高漢成 (2017), "Zhiwai faquan, lingshi caipanquan ji qita—ji yu yuyixue shijiao de lishi fenxi" 治外法權、領事裁判權及其他 - 基於語義學視角的歷史分析 (Extraterritoriality, Consular Jurisdiction and Others—a Study Based on Historical Semantics), *Zhengfa luntan*, 5, pp. 105–116.

- (2018), "Zhongguo jindai 'zhiwai faquan gainian de cihuishi" 中國近代「治外法權」概念的詞彙史 (A Lexical History of the Concept of 'Extraterritoriality' in Modern China), *Xiamen daxue xuebao (Zhexue shehui kexue ban)*, 2018: 5, pp. 112–122.
Gilbert, Rodney (1926), *What's Wrong with China?*, London: John Murray.
- (1929), *The Unequal Treaties: China and the Foreigner*, London: John Murray.
Gu Tinglong 顧廷龍 (ed.) (1992), *Qingdai zhujuan jicheng* 清代硃卷集成 (Collection of Vermillion Essays during the Qing-dynasty), Shanghai: Chengwen chubanshe.
Gu Weijun 顧維鈞 (1925), *Waiguo zai Hua zhi diwei* 外國在華之地位 (The Foreign Position in China), Beiping: Waijiaobu tushuchu (translated from the author's Ph.D. thesis, Columbia University 1911).
Guo Yuanlin 郭院林 (2012), *Fanghuang yu mitu: Liu Shipei sixiang yu xueshu yanjiu*, 彷徨与迷途：刘师培思想与学术研究 (Indecision and Losing One's Path: Researches on Liu Shipei's Thought and Learning), Nanjing: Fenghuang chubanshe.
Hao Liyu 郝立輿 (1925), *Lingshi caipanquan wenti* 領事裁判權問題 (The Problem of Consular Jurisdiction) Shanghai: shangwu yinshuguan.
Hart, Robert (1903), *These from the Land of Sinim—Essays on China Question*, London: Chapman & Hall.
He Ruzhang 何如璋 (1966), "Yu Liu Xianzhuang zhifu lun Riben yi gai tiaoyue shu" 與劉峴莊制府論日本議改條約書 (Letter to Governor-General Liu Kunyi on Japan's Efforts of Treaty Revision), in: Wen Tingjing (comp.), *Chayang sanjia wenchao: He Ruzhang, Lin Daquan, Qiu Jinxin*, Taibei: Wenhai chubanshe, j. 3, pp. 9–10.
He Xiangming 何襄明 (1943), "Feizhi tiaoyue zhiwai faquan ying xun de tujing" 廢止約定治外法權應循的途徑 (The Road which the Abolition of Extraterritoriality Follows), *Xin Zhonghua*, 1943: 2.
Hu Yilu 胡以魯 (1923), "Lun yi ming" 論譯名 (On Translating Words), in: Hu Yilu, *Guoyuxue caochuang*, Shanghai: Shangwu yinshuguan 1923, pp. 134–135.
Huang Xingtao 黃興濤 (2012), "Gainian shi fangfa yu Zhongguo jindaishi yanjiu" 概念史方法與中國近代史研究 (The Method of Conceptual History and Research on Modern Chinese History), *Shixue yuekan*, 2012: 9, pp. 11–14.
Huang Zunxian 黃遵憲 (2001), *Riben guozhi* 日本國志 (Treatise on Japan), Shanghai: Shanghai juji chubanshe.
Inoue Tetsujiro 井上哲次郎 (1881), *Tetsugaku ji* 哲學字彙 (Philosophical Dictionary), Tokyo: Toyokan.
Jiang Gongsheng 蔣恭晟 (1932), *Guochi shi* 國恥史 (History of National Humiliation), Shanghai: Zhonghua shuju.
Jiang Jianren 蔣堅忍 (1930), *Riben diguozhuyi qinlüe Zhongguo shi* 日本帝國主義侵略中國史 (A History of China's Invasion by Japanese Imperialism), Shanghai: Lianhe shudian.
Jiang Yihua, Zhang Ronghua 姜義華, 張榮華 (eds.) (2018), *Kang Youwei quanji* 康有為全集 (Complete Works of Kang Youwei), Bejing: Zhonghua renmin daxue chubanshe.
Kang Dashou 康大壽 (2000), "Jindai wairen zai Hua 'zhiwai faquan' shiyi" 近代外人在華「治外法權」釋義 (An Explanation of 'Extraterritoriality' Enjoyed by Modern Foreigners in China), *Shehui kexue yanjiu*, 2000: 2, pp. 108–112.
Kang Youwei 康有為 (2018), "Riben bianzheng kao" 日本變政考 (Research into the Reforms of Japan), in: Jiang Yihua, Zhang Ronghua (eds.), Kang Youwei quanji, Beijing: Zhonghua renmin daxue chubanshe, vol. 4, pp. 103–294.
Ku Hung-Ming (1901), *Papers from a Viceroy's Yamen*, Shanghai: Shanghai Mercury.

Li Guilian 李貴連 (1990), "Qingji falü gaige lingshi caipanquan" 清季法律改革與領事裁判權 (Legal Reform during the Qing and Consular Jurisdiction), *Zhongwai faxue*, 1990: 4, pp. 46–50.

Li Qicheng 李啓成 (2003), "Lingshi caipanquan zhidu yu wan Qing sifa gaige zhi zhaoduan" 領事裁判權制度與晚清司法改革之肇端 (The System of Consular Jurisdiction and the Beginning of Judical Reform during the Late Qing), *Bijiaofa yanjiu*, 2003: 4, pp. 16–28.

Li Xinrong 李欣榮 (2018), *Zichuang liangfa: Qingji xin xinglü de bianxiu yu fenzheng* 自創良法：清季新刑律的編修與紛爭 (A Good Method to Invent Something Oneself. The Compilation of a New Penal Code during the late Qing and Controversies around it), Beijing: Shehui kexue wenxian chubanshe.

Li Yang 李洋 (2015), "Cong ciyi dao yujing: 'Zhiwai faquan' wudu, wuyong, ji wuhui" 從詞義到語境：「治外法權」誤讀、誤用及誤會 (From Lexical Meaning to Context: "Extraterritoriality": Misreadings, Misuse and Misunderstanding), *Shehui kexue*, 2015: 2, pp. 152–163.

— (2013), "Zhiwai faquan, haishi lingshi caipanquan? Cong minguo yilai xuezhe lunzheng de jiaodian qieru" 治外法權，還是領事裁判權？- 從民國以來學者論爭的焦點切入 (Extraterritoriality or Consular Jurisdiction—Approaching the Problem on the Basis of Academic Discussions since the Republican Era), *Lishi xiaoxue wenti*, 2013: 6, pp. 113–117.

Li Yumin 李育民 (2009), "Wan Qing gaijin, shouhui lingshi caibanquan de mouhua ji nuli" 晚清改進、收回領事裁判權的謀劃及努力 (Plans and Efforts to Recover Consular Jurisdiction during the Late Qing Period), *Jindaishi yanjiu*, 2009: 1, pp. 35-53.

Liang Mindui 梁敬錞 (1930), *Zai Hua lingshi caipanqun lun* 在華領事裁判權論 (On Consular Jurisdiction in China), Shanghai: Shangwu yinshuguan.

Liu Yan 劉彥 (1928), Bei qinhai zhi Zhongguo (ji Zhongguo zui di xiandu yingquxiao bu pindeng tiaoyue) 被侵害之中國 (即中國最低限度應取消不平等條約) (Invaded China [i.e., China at Least should Cancel the Unequal Treaties]), Shanghai: Taipingyang shudian.

Ma Sidun 馬斯頓 (Karl von Martens), Liang Fang, Qing Chang 聯芳、慶常 (tr.), W.A.P. Martin (coll.) (2006), *Xingyao zhizhang* 星軺指掌 (*Guide diplomatique*), Beijing: Zhongguo zhengfa daxue chubanshe.

Morgan, Evan (1926), *Chinese New Terms*, Shanghai: Kelly & Walsh.

Nanyang zhoukan 南洋週刊, Singapore, 1938 -

Qian Xun, Dong Hongyi 錢恂、董鴻禕 (comp.) (1907), *Riben fagui jiezi* 日本法規解字 (Dictionary of Japanese Law), Shanghai: Shangwu yinshuguan (4th edition 1908).

Ransome, Arthurs (1927), *The Chinese Puzzle*, London: G. Allen & Unwin.

Piggott, Francis Taylor (1892), *Exterritoriality: The Law Relating to Consular Jurisdiction and to Residence in Oriental Countries*, London: William Clowes and Sons.

Qingyi bao 清議報 (The China Discussion), *Nagasaki 1898-1901*, (Reprint, Bejing: Zhonghua shuju 1991).

Renyin ke bianfa zhisheng weiyi 王寅科变法直省闱艺 (1903) (Examination Hall Essays of the Provincial Examinations of the 1902 Examinations), Shanghai : Shanghai shuju.

Sato Tooru 佐藤亨 (2007), *Gendai ni ikiru Bakumatsu Meiji shoki kango jten* 現代に生きる幕末 明治初期漢語辞典 (Dictionary of Modern Chinese Words during the Closing Days of Tokugawa and the Early Meiji Period), Tokyo: Meiji shoin.

Song Fangqing 宋方青 (2009),"Keju gefei yu Qingmo fazheng jiaoyu" 科舉革廢與清末法政教育 (The Reform and Abolition of the Traditional Examination System and Legal-political Education during the Late Qing), *Xiamen daxue xuebao (zhexue shehui kexue ban)*, 2009: 5, pp. 38–44.

Sun Baoxun 孫寶瑄 (2015), *Sun Baoxuan riji* 孫寶瑄日記 (The Diary of Sun Baoxuan), Beijing: Zhonghua shuju.

Sun Xiaolou, Zhao Yinian 孫曉樓、趙逸年 (eds.)(1937), *Lingshi caipanquan wenti* 領事裁判權問題 (On the Question of Consular Jurisdiction), Shanghai: Shangwu yinshuguan.

Tanabe Keiya 田邊慶彌, Wang Wozang 王我臧 (tr.) (1911), *Hanyi Riben falü jingji cidian* 漢譯日本法律經濟辭典 (Japanese Dictionary of Law and Economics Translated into Chinese), Shanghai: Shanwu yinshuguan 8th edition (first edition 1908).

Tang Bao'e 唐寶鍔 (1905), "Lun zhiwai faquan yu lingshi caipanquan zhi yitong" 論治外法權與領事裁判權之異同 (On the Similiarities and Differences between Extraterritoriality and Consular Jurisdiction), *Sichuan guanbao*, no 30, 1905, pp. 36–37.

Waijiao xuehui 外交學會 (comp.) (1937), *Waijiao da cidian* 外交大辭典 (Great Diplomatic Dictionary), Shanghai: Zhonghua shuju.

Wang, Dong (2005), *China's Unequal Treaties: Narrating National History*, Lanham MD: Lexington.

Wang Jianlang 王建朗 (2000), *Zhongguo feichu bu pingdeng tiaoyue de licheng* 中國廢除不平等條約的歷程 (The Process of Abolishing China's Unequal Treaties), Nanchang: Jiangxi renmin chubanshe.

Wang Jingwei 汪精衛 (1925), *Guoji wenti jueyi an bing liyou shu* 國際問題決議案並理由書 (A Letter on Resolving the International Problems and the Arguments for it), Guangzhou: Guomin geming jun zongzilingbu zhengzhibu.

Wang Rongbao , Ye Lan 汪榮寶, 葉瀾 (comp.)(1903), *Xin Erya* 新爾雅 (The New Erya), Shanghai: Mingquanshe.

Wang Tao 王韜 (1987), *Manyou suilu – Fusang youji* 漫遊隨錄 扶桑遊記 (Memories of my Peregrinations, Notes on Travels in Japan), Changsha: Hunan renmin chubanshe.

— (1959), *Taoyuan wenlu waibian* 弢園文錄外編 (Essays of Wang Tao, pt. 2), Beijing: Zhonghua shuju.

Wang Tieya 王鐵崖 (ed.) (1959), *Zhongguo jiu yuezhang huibian* 中外舊約章匯編 (Collection of China's Old Diplomatic Treaties), Beijing: Sanlian shudian.

— (ed.) (1996), *Zhonghua faxue da cidian - guoji faxue juan* 中華法學大辭典 - 國際法學卷 (Great Dictionary of Chinese Legal Science- International law), Beijing: Zhongguo jiancha chubanshe.

Wen Ching (1901), *The Chinese Crisis from Within*, London: Grand Richards.

Wheaton, Henry (1836), *Elements of International Law with a Sketch of the History of the Science*, Philadelphia PA: Carey, Lea and Blanchard.

Woodhead, H.G.W., *The Truth about the Chinese Republic*, London: Hurst & Blackett.

Wu Jintang 吳金堂 (1934), *Diguozhuyi qin Hua shi* 帝國主義侵華史 (A History of Imperialism's Invasion of China), Nanjing: Zhongyan lujun junguan xuexiao zhengzhi xunlian chu.

Wu Junru 吳君如 (1929), *Diguozhuyi dui Hua de sanda qinlüe* 帝國主義對華的三大侵略 (The Three Great Imperialist Invasions of China), Shanghai: Minzhi shuju.

Wu Songgao 吳頌皋 (1929), *Zhiwi faquan* 治外法权 (Extraterritoriality), Shanghai: Shangwu yinshuguan.

Wu Yixiong 吴义雄 (2006), "Yapian zhanzheng yiqian Yingguo zai Hua zhiwai faquan zhi yunxiang yu changshi" 鴉片戰爭前英國在華治外法權之醞釀與嘗試 (The Fermentation and Experimentation of British Extraterritoriality in China prior to the Opium War), *Lishi yanjiu*, 2006: 4, pp. 70–89.

Xia Zhengnong 夏徵農 (ed) (1989), *Cihai* 辭海 (Sea of Words), Shanghai: Shanghai cishu chubanshe.

Xinwen bao 新聞報, Shanghai 1893–1949.

Xue Fucheng 薛福成 (1987), "Chou yang quyi—yuezhang" 籌洋芻議·約章 (My Humble Opinion on Managing Foreign Relations—Concluding Treaties), in: Ding Fenglin, Wang Xinzhi (eds.), *Xue Fucheng xuanji*, Shanghai: Shanghai renmin chubanshe, pp. 527–529.

Yan Fu 嚴復 (2004), "Lun guojia yu wei lixian yiqian you keyi xing bi yi xing zhi yaozheng" 論國家於未立憲以前有可以行必宜行之要政 (On Important Politics which the Country Prior to the Establishment of a Constitution could Follow and on those which it should Follow), in: Song Yingxiang, Pi Houfeng (eds.), *Yan Fu ji, bupian*, Fuzhou: Fujian renmin chubanshe, pp. 49–51.

Yang Tianhong 楊天宏 (2005), "Beiyang waijiao yu 'zhiwai faqun' de chefei 北洋外交与"治外法权"的撤废 (The Diplomacy of the Beiyang Government and the Abolition of Extraterritoriality", *Jindaishi yanjiu*, 2005: 3, pp. 83–116.

Yang Chao 楊焯 (2015), *Ding yi Wanguo gongfa yanjiu* 丁譯《萬國公法》研究 (Researches on Wanguo gongfa translated by W.A.P. Martin), Beijing: Falü chubanshe.

Zhang Shiming 張世明 (2013), "Zailun Qing mo bianfa xiulü gaige zhaoduan yu feichu lingshi caipan" 再論清末變法修律改革肇端於廢除領事裁判權 (Further Discussion on the Abolition of Consular Jurisdiction as begin for law reform during the late Qing), *Zhongguo renmin daxue xuebao*, 2013:3, pp. 128–137.

Zhao Xiaogeng 趙曉耕 (2005), "Shixi zhiwai faquan yu lingshi caipan" 試析治外法權與領事裁判權 (Analysing Extraterritoriality and Consular Jurisdiction), *Zhengzhou daxue xuebao*, 2005: 5, pp. 70–74.

Zhongguo guomindang Beiping tebie shi weiyuanhui xuanchuanbu 中國國民黨北平特別市黨務指導委員會宣傳部 (1930), *Chefei lingshi caipanquan yundong* 撤廢領事裁判權運動 (The Movement for the Abolition of Consular Jurisdiction).

Zhongguo jindai jingjishi ziliao congkan bianji weiyuanhui, Zhonghua renmin gongheguo haiguan zongshu yanjiushi 中國近代經濟史資料叢刊編輯委員會,中華人民共和國海關總署研究室 (tr. and eds.) (1994), *Xinchou tiaoyue liding hou de shangyue tanpan* 辛醜條約訂立以後的商約談判 (Negotiations on Commercial Treaties after the Signing of the Boxer Protocol in 1901), Beijing: Zhonghua shuju.

"Zhong Ri tongshang tiaoyue" 中日通商條約 (Japan-China Treaty on Commerce and Navigation), *Shiwubao*, no 1, Qiangxuebao, Shiwubao Beijing: Zhonghua shuju 1991, vol. 1, p. 51.

Zhongwai ribao 中外日報, Shanghai 1898–1911.

Discourses on "National Humiliation" and "National Ruin" as Reflected in Late Qing and Early Republican Era History Textbooks

Li Fan

With the establishment of a new school system and new institutions of learning during the final years of the Qing dynasty, textbooks of various kinds came to play an increasingly important role in the field of education, particularly in elementary education. And history textbooks were no exception. [1] Especially during the first few years of the Republican era, the new government had a myriad of issues to deal with that it had inherited from the Qing dynasty and it took over a number of endeavours that had been commenced in the last decade of imperial China. Thus, when it came to issuing new textbooks, many were simply adapted from Qing editions. Therefore, albeit *prima facie* compiled under different historical circumstances, late Qing and early Republican history textbooks may actually be treated as a coherent corpus of sources and will be treated as such in the present study. Compared with the long tradition of historiographical writing in China, history textbooks arguably constitute an entirely new genre of historical narrative and they perform a function not previously fulfilled by traditional historiography, namely, the teaching of history as a means of properly socialising the future citizens of a nation-state. For this reason, the specific make-up and contents of history textbooks are particularly symptomatic for the mentality of their times. And this holds especially true for the discursive tools that they employ. An examination of late Qing and early Republican era history textbooks reveals that the discourses surrounding "national humiliation" (*guochi* 國恥) and "national ruin" (*wangguo* 亡國) are among the predominant modes of discourse encountered in these sources. Far from being a particularity of history textbooks, "national humiliation" and "national ruin" are nothing less than paragons—"textbook examples", if you will—for the "discourses of weakness" during the historical period in question, thus reflecting a much broader discursive practice. An inquiry into Discourses of Weakness via history textbooks will not only deepen our understanding of the history of modern

---

1 During the late Qing, textbooks were primarily used in primary schools, secondary schools and normal schools, which had recently been established. "History textbooks" in this article therefore refer to those used by these schools as well as those used in the field of social education.

224 LI FAN

Chinese textbooks, but also benefit research into conceptual history as well as the history of discourses.

I. "Histories of National Ruin and Humiliation" and the "History of National Ruin and Humiliation" in History Textbooks

During the waning years of the Qing dynasty, China faced an unprecedented crisis. The defeat during the First Sino-Japanese War (1894–95) and the signing of the Treaty of Shimonoseki, along with the subsequent series of events, ushered in a period of deeply felt disgrace and repeated setbacks, which elevated the slogan of the "national ruin and extinction of the race " (*wangguo miezhong* 亡國滅種), to one of the major themes of discussion of the period. The following few examples may suffice to illustrate this point: the Qing government (represented by Li Hongzhang 李鴻章 (1823–1901) and Li Jingfang 李經方 (ca. 1855–1934)) signed the Treaty of Shimonoseki in 1895. In the wake of this event, the public debate concerning "national humiliation" and "national ruin" drew ever more widespread popular attention, which may be illustrated by two particularly representative works of this kind, Liang Qichao's 梁啟超 (1873–1929) short essay entitled "Records of the Demise of Poland" (*Bolan miewang ji* 波蘭滅亡記) of 1896 and the *Record of the Partition and Destruction of Poland* (*Bolan fenmie ji* 波蘭分滅記) by Kang Youwei 康有為 (1858–1927), which Kang submitted to the throne on 24 July 1898. Kang and Liang implored the Guangxu 光緒 emperor (r. 1875–1908) to let the fall of Poland serve him and China as a warning from history and to make haste to introduce reforms in order to achieve the self-strengthening of the country.

The discussion regarding "national humiliation" and "national ruin" gained even more prominence in both monographs and in the popular press after the Boxer Protocol had been signed in 1901. In 1903, Chen Qi 陳崎 (fl. 1903) published the *Collectanea on National Humiliation* (*Guochi Congyan* 國恥叢言), for which he acted as compiler and translator, and he dedicated the first part of the work to "A History of Foreign Aggression" (*Waihuanshi* 外患史)". Shen Wenjun's 沈文濬 (fl. 1909) *A Brief History of National Humiliation* (*Guochi xiaoshi* 國恥小史) appeared in 1909 and narrates the series of incursions by the Western powers into China in their chronological order, from the First Opium War (1839–42) onwards. Works of this kind became models for subsequent accounts of China's history of national humiliation,[2] and it was in these works that the two characters *guo* 國 and *chi* 恥 came specifically to connote the shame

---

2 See Yu Danchu (1996), *Aiguozhuyi yu Zhongguo jindai shixue*, pp. 155–160.

suffered by China because of foreign encroachment, and "national humiliation" henceforth became a standard expression with a fixed meaning. During the same time period, works on "national ruin" (rather than "humiliation") were compiled and translated in even greater numbers. According to one scholar's statistic, 30 individual volumes of this kind appeared between 1901 and 1910 alone. Of these, seven deal with the fall of Korea, four deal with India and Egypt respectively, and three narrate the fall of Poland.[3]

The founding of the Republic of China in 1912 did not fundamentally change either the fact or the scale of China's internal conflicts against the backdrop of foreign aggression. On 9 May 1915, President Yuan Shikai 袁世凱 (1859–1916) proclaimed that he had accepted all but the fifth set of Japan's infamous Twenty-One Demands, which were widely perceived to be specifically tailored to bring about the destruction of China.[4] The ninth of May was thus designated as "National Humiliation Commemoration Day" in some areas of China (although it was not officially adopted by the Nationalist government until 1928) and the incident initiated yet another tidal wave of publications on the history of China's national humiliation, such as Lü Simian's 呂思勉 (1884-1957) *A Brief History of National Humiliation* (*Guochi xiaoshi* 國恥小史; the same title as Shen Wenjun's work of eight years earlier). Thereafter, the number of official National Humiliation Days steadily increased and national humiliation histories kept being churned out non–stop.

As the principal material of history education in public schools, history textbooks not only had to convey basic historical knowledge, but also assumed the task of guiding the future citizens by promoting orthodox conceptions of history as well as instilling in the students an officially sanctioned value system. For this reason, history textbooks and the manner of their compilation reflect scholarly standpoints as well as (and perhaps even to a greater degree than the former) the attitude of the contemporary political regime towards a given historical fact or event. The norms for education in general and history education in particular were detailed in official documents such as "regulations" (*zhangcheng* 章程) and "standards" (*biaozhun* 標准). Influenced by the prevailing atmosphere, school regulations concerning history courses stated in no uncertain terms that:

All those who teach history ought to place special emphasis on the elucidation of the relations between (historical) facts, identifying the origins of culture and imbuing [in

---

3 Zou Zhenhuan (1996), "Qing mo wangguoshi 'bianyi re'", pp. 327–328.

4 The last group demanded, among other things, that China hire Japanese advisors to take control over China's police force as well as the country's finances.

their charges] the capacity to discern the causes for [a nation's] strength and weakness, and rise and fall so as to rouse (*zhenfa* 振發) the aspirations of the citizens (*guomin* 國民).[5]

Exhortations of this kind evidently have to be understood in the light of the perceived severity of China's prevailing crisis which was often succinctly paraphrased with the above-mentioned formula predicting imminent "national ruin and extinction of the race". This dire state of affairs, however, was not conceptionalised as a historical inevitability, but rather as a challenge to be faced by the Chinese people. Against this backdrop, the people charged with the compilation of history textbooks—and, in so doing, being responsible for the history education of the nation's next generation of citizens—naturally had to contrive arguments and narratives that corresponded to both the prevailing popular visions and the officially promulgated school regulations.

These narratives were often structured around the double threat of "national ruin and extinction of the race" as a historical phenomenon. In other words, historical developments of this kind were made particularly prominent so as to awaken and amplify the (young) people's sense of crisis and their consciousness for the need for self-strengthening with the final goal of—as the school regulation cited above puts it—"imbuing in them the capacity to discern the causes for a nation's strength and weakness, and rise and fall so as to rouse the aspirations of these (future) citizens". In this way, the two motifs "national humiliation" and "national ruin" became pivotal elements in the discursive structure of late Qing history textbooks. And, as China's fundamental crisis did not abate with the fall of the dynasty, the existing discourses in history textbooks did not change in any significant way in the first few years following the foundation of the Republic.

Table 1: History textbooks of the late Qing and early Republican period

Title	Editor/Author	Year
Mengxue Zhongguo lishi jiaokeshu 蒙學中國歷史教科書	Ding Baoshu 丁保書	1903
Zhongguo lishi jiaokeshu 中國歷史教科書	Xia Zengyou 夏曾佑	1904–1906
Zuixin zhongxue jiaokeshu: Xiyang lishi 最新中學教科書·西洋歷史	unknown	1906

5 Kecheng jiaocai yanjiusuo (ed.) (2001), *20 shiji Zhongguo zhong-xiaoxue kecheng biaozhun, jiaoxue dagang huibian*, p. 42.

Title	Editor/Author	Year
Zhongguo lishi jiaokeshu 中國歷史教科書	Chen Qingnian 陳慶年	1909
Zhongguo lishi jiaokeshu 中國歷史教科書	Wang Rongbao 汪榮寶	1909
Xiyang lishi jiaokeshu (Zhongxuexiao yong) 西洋歷史教科書（中學校用）	Fu Yuefen 傅岳棻	1911
Gongheguo jiaokeshu Dongya ge guo shi (Zhongxuexiao yong) 共和國教科書東亞各國史（中學校用）	Fu Yunsen 傅運森	1913
Zhongxue Zhonghua lishi jiaokeshu 中學中華歷史教科書	Zhang Qin 章嶔	1913
Zhongdeng lishi jiaokeshu: Dong-Xiyang zhi bu 中等歷史教科書·東西洋之部	Zhao Yinian 趙懿年	1913
Xinzhi Dongyageguoshijiaoben (Zhongxuexiaoshiyong) 新制東亞各國史教本（中學校適用）	Li Bingjun 李秉鈞	1914
Shifan xuexiao xin jiaokeshu: Waiguoshi 師範學校新教科書·外國史	Fu Yunsen 傅運森, Xia Tingzhang 夏廷璋	1914
Xinzhi benguoshi jiaoben (Zhongxuexiao shiyong) 新制本國史教本（中學校適用）	Zhong Yulong 鐘毓龍	1914
Xinzhi benguoshi jiaoben (Shifan xuexiao shiyong) 新制本國史教本（師範學校適用）	Zhong Yulong 鐘毓龍	1915

There is an essential distinction to be made between the respective discourses on "national humiliation" and "national ruin" as they appear in history textbooks. The "national humiliation" trope primarily appears in textbooks on domestic history (*benguoshi* 本國史), whereas the notion of "national ruin" is mainly to be encountered in foreign history (*waiguoshi* 外國史) textbooks. But what was actually meant by "domestic" and "foreign" history respectively? During the late Qing period, this distinction very much depended on one's political standpoint, and thus opinions diverged accordingly. Reformers, proponents of a constitutional monarchy and the general reading-public naturally identified their "own nation" with the people and territory under the rule of the Qing dynasty. However, for certain people in the revolutionary camp who forcefully advocated to "remove the Manchu and restore the Han" (*pai Man xing Han* 排滿興漢), the Manchu were considered an alien race. In their eyes, and guided by the Western concept of a sovereign nation-state, China had indeed ceased to exist once the country had fallen under alien (that is, Manchu) rule. Phrases such as "China has already been ruined" (*Zhongguo yi wang* 中國已亡), seemingly counterfactual at first, thus imply that the Qing dynasty was not part of "our nation". Consequently, some histories of national ruin penned by members of the revolutionary camp (or their sympathisers) are actually histories on the fall of the Ming dynasty, *i.e.*, the last ethnically Han-Chinese dynasty.

Be that as it may, contemporary history textbooks, by their very nature, represented official sentiments to a substantial degree and took recognition of the Qing dynasty as something of a given. That is, the editors generally did not call the legitimacy of the ruling dynasty into question, although there was, indeed, a small minority of revolutionary-minded people who acted as schoolbook editors. The potentially divisive issue of national identity was thus largely sidestepped in the officially sponsored textbooks, which means that the line dividing the "history of our nation" and "foreign history" is drawn quite clearly here. The issue ceased to be relevant after the founding of the Republic.

In the case of domestic history textbooks, writing about "national humiliation" in order to achieve the goals of history education (as articulated in the quotation above), was quite often a conscious effort on the part of the compilers. Accordingly, it is pointed out by Ding Baoshu 丁保書 (fl. 1903), editor and author of the *Primary School Textbook of Chinese History* (*Mengxue Zhongguo lishi jiaokeshu* 蒙學中國歷史教科書), that:

The alternation of (ruling) clans and dynastic change, annexations and losses of territory, [that is] the change and development of [a nation's] territory over time, is [always] a vital factor in history. But how much more so is this the case in the modern era, as the nations of the European West secretly conspire to seize [Chinese territory], occupy strategic locations, and calling this concessions [*i.e.*, territories that are nominally leased only for a time] [but really means] that all our [key] ports and [trading] places have been lost?

I therefore compiled [the relevant historical events] from the Spring and Autumn and Warring States Period (770–256 BCE) until the recent past. In each case, these are accompanied by maps and detailed notes so that (the students) may know the causes that led to [territorial]annexations from time immemorial and [through that knowledge] will come to feel the pain of our present loss. For it is our task not only to impart knowledge but also to eradicate our national humiliation.[6]

In a similar vein, Wang Rongbao 汪榮寶 (1878–1933) stated in the *Textbook of Chinese History* (*Zhongguo lishi jiaokeshu* 中國歷史教科書), for which he acted as editor:

The strength of the European presence in the east is ever expanding. Since the First Opium War, we have crossed swords with the foreigners on many occasions and inevitably lost every war, and every defeat inevitably meant that we had to forfeit a certain

---

6 Ding Baoshu (1903), *Mengxue Zhongguo lishi jiaokeshu*, pp. 2–3.

portion of our sovereignty. As for the so-called "treaties" to [let foreigners] lease harbours, exploit mines, and lay railway tracks, these have been forced on us and the Eastern expansion of Western strength has thus turned into a scourge akin to a flood or an attack by wild beasts—once it has commenced, there is no stopping it. The *Book of Changes* states: "When [societal] changes arise, [...] are there [not] anxieties and calamities?" (*Yi zhi xing ye,* [...] *qi you youhuan hu* 易之興也 [⋯] 其有憂患乎).[7] The "Zuo-Commentary" says: "A state may be restored [when it is faced with] a multitude of adversities" (*Duo nan suoyi xing bang* 多難所以興邦).[8] The meaning (of these words) is that calamity quite possibly harbours the opportunity for a future restoration (*zhongxing* 中興).[9]

And Zhong Yulong 鐘毓龍 (1880–1970), editor and author of the *Textbook of Domestic History for the New School System* (*Xinzhi benguoshi jiaoben* 新制本國史教本), also emphasised (in the edition for use in normal schools, *i.e.,* teacher-training schools) that:

It is the purpose of this book to elaborate on the distinguishing characteristics of the people of our country and furthermore to examine the causes behind its poverty and weakness. I have paid particular attention to [Chinese] society, traditions, institutions, and learning, as well as the diplomatic failures of modern times, so as to awaken [in the reader] patriotic feelings and a desire to eradicate [our national] humiliation.[10]

And in the middle school edition, he wrote:

In modern times, [our] diplomatic failures became more severe from one day to the next. One can hardly keep track of all the indemnities that we had to pay, territories we had to cede, troops we lost, and insults our country had to suffer. At that time, we had to endure insults, but today we should attempt to stand up and take action. This book focuses specifically on the point of national humiliation in the hope that the students

---

7 Translator's note: This quotation contains a rather large ellipsis. The original passage translates into something like: "The origin of Yi [= the *Book of Changes*] was in middle antiquity. Those who composed Yi knew suffering and sorrow." (Rutt (2002), *The Book of Changes,* p. 42.) As is so often the case with citations from traditional Chinese literature in late Qing sources, the intended meaning deviates quite significantly from common interpretations. In any case, Wang Rongbao evidently reads "change" rather than "*Book of Changes*" and correlates the emergence of socio-historical ruptures with widespread feelings of uncertainty and dismay.

8 Translator's note: In modern colloquial language, this saying is often abbreviated as *duonanxingbang* ("much distress regenerates a country"). It alludes to the "Zuo-Commentary" (*Zuozhuan* 左傳; an exegetical work on the terse *Spring and Autumn Annals* that takes the form of a narrative history) for the "Fourth Year of Duke Zhao's Reign" (*Zhao Gong si nian* 昭公四年) which reads: "What [kind of result] the troubles of a neighboring state will bring, cannot be predicted. Perhaps their troubles are (indeed) numerous, but only result in (the people) [resolving to] strengthen their country and to enlarge their territory. Perhaps their troubles are nonexistent, but they will (nevertheless) forfeit their country and lose the realm which they had guarded." (Cf. Legge (1872), *The Ch'un Ts'ew with The Tso Chuen,* p. 596.) The obvious lesson is that the existence of difficulties need not be indicative for a state's future prospects.

9 Wang Rongbao (1909), *Zhongguo lishi jiaokeshu,* p. 2.

10 Zhong Yulong (1915), *Xinzhi benguoshi (Shifan xuexiao shiyong),* shang, p. 2.

who read it, learn to be wakeful and vigilant, and that their patriotism and their desire to cleanse (our national) humiliation may grow stronger.[11]

These statements clearly demonstrate the editors' intentions: they make use of the historical realities of "national humiliation" to construct a discourse of weakness in order to guide the students towards independence and self-strengthening, and to encourage them to join together and do their utmost to realise the country's goals of "cleansing humiliation" and "restoring the country".

Regarding actual textbook practice and the treatment of specific historical facts and events, the editors generally elaborated in detail on the repeated encroachments of the Western powers from the First Opium War, the curtailing of China's sovereignty, the unequal treaties the country had to sign following these conflicts, as well as China's unceasing loss of vassal states. For example, in its account of China's entire history from antiquity to the present (*i.e.*, the time in which the author lived), the *Primary School Textbook of Chinese History*, which consists of only 140 pages in total, usually limits itself to brief narratives. By contrast, the history of national humiliation during the late Qing period was detailed in great length and occupies 18 pages of the work. The *Middle School Textbook of Chinese History* (*Zhongxue Zhonghua lishi jiaokeshu* 中學中華歷史教科書, compiled by Zhang Qin 章嶔 (1879–1931), recounts the series of events in the late Qing period that forced China to surrender parts of its sovereign rights and suffer insults to its national dignity in 28 consecutive entries under the larger heading "Foreign Relations during the Qing" (*Qing zhi waijiao* 清之外交).[12] This list makes up the largest individual part of the entire book and, although the editors only provide historical information without commenting on it, it is enough to read through this lengthy enumeration of events to become shocked and horrified. The *Textbook of Domestic History for the New School System (For Use in Middle Schools)* (*Zhongxuexiao shiyong* 中學校適用) contains a chapter entitled "Foreign Aggression during the Qing" (*Qing zhi waihuan* 清之外患), which is further subdivided into the following sections: "The Opium War" (*Yapian zhi zhanzheng* 鴉片之戰爭), "The Anglo-French Alliance" (*Ying-Fa zhi lianjun* 英法之聯軍), "The Forfeiture of the Northeastern Territories" (*Dongbei zhi cudi* 東北之蹙地), "The Loss of the Ryukyu Islands" (*Liuqiu zhi sangshi* 琉球之喪失), "The Forfeiture of the Northwestern Territories" (*Xibei zhi cudi* 西北之蹙地), "The Loss of Vietnam" (*Annan zhi sangshi* 安南之喪失), "The Lost Naval Battle of Fuzhou" (*Majiang zhi sangshi* 馬江之喪師), "The Loss of Myanmar" (*Miandian zhi sangshi* 緬甸之喪失), "The Loss of Sikkim and Bhutan" (*Zhemengxiong Budan zhi sangshi* 哲孟雄布丹之喪失), "The Loss of

---

11 Zhong Yulong (1914a), *Xinzhi benguoshi (Zhongxuexiao shiyong) yi*, pp. 2–3.

12 Zhang Qin (1913), *Zhongxue Zhonghua lishi jiaokeshu: Xia ce*, pp. 36–52.

Siam" (暹羅之喪失), "The Loss of Korea" (*Chaoxian zhi sangshi* 朝鮮之喪失), "The First Sino-Japanese War" (*Zhong-Dong zhi zhanzheng* 中東之戰爭), "The Leasing of Military Ports" (*Jungang zhi zujie* 軍港之租借), and "The Stripping of Rights and Sovereignty" (*Liquan zhi qinduo* 利權之侵奪). Here, it is described how China suffered more and more aggression and humiliation over the course of the nineteenth century. The narratives were accompanied by maps illustrating, according to their names, "Foreign Aggressions against the Qing" (*Qing waihuan tu* 清外患圖), "Negotiations between China and Russia" (*Zhong-E jiaoshe tu* 中俄交涉圖), and "Qing Negotiations with Britain and France" (*Qing yu Ying Fa jiaoshe tu* 清與英法交涉圖) and were concluded by stating:

The powers were in [constant] competition with each other, so it seemed unavoidable that their squabbling would eventually turn into conflict. Thus, the concept of "spheres of influence" was created [which basically means that China] was clandestinely and intangibly carved up. [China] has been hit with onslaughts of foreign aggression like a clockwork, and this all began with the war of 1894.[13]

Similar statements can also be found in other history textbooks. And even though works of this kind might do little more than present objective facts while refraining from adding subjective comments, this already suffices to achieve the goals behind the discourse on "national humiliation" which they helped to construct and promote.

Turning to textbooks on foreign history, in these too, the editors often made a conscious effort specifically to emphasise stories of "national ruin" in order to keep the Chinese people on the alert. In their *New Textbook for Normal Schools: Foreign History* (*Shifan xuexiao xin jiaokeshu: Waiguoshi* 師範學校新教科書·外國史), Fu Yunsen 傅運森 (fl. 1914) and his collaborators wrote:

In compiling this book, we hope to have drawn clear demarcation lines and provided a balanced structure. As for the era following the intrusion of Western power into the east, we have given a particularly detailed account of it and a whole chapter is devoted to the partition and annexation of the pacific islands in order to inspire [the reader] to be alert and fearful.[14]

And Li Bingjun 李秉鈞 stated in the *Textbook of the History of the Countries of East Asia for the New School System (For Use in Middle Schools)* (*Xinzhi Dongya geguoshi jiaoben (Zhongxuexiao shiyong)* 新制東亞各國史教本（中學校適用）):

In the fourth chapter, this book discusses the national situation of Japan before and after the Meiji Restoration and carefully details the country's annexation of Ryukyu, Taiwan, and Korea. When covering this chapter, the teacher should enumerate the various incidents [in modern history] when our motherland lost sovereign rights and

---

13 Zhong Yulong (1914b), *Xinzhi benguoshi (Zhongxuexiao shiyong) san*, pp. 101–112.
14 Fu Yunsen (1914), *Shifan xuexiao xin jiaokeshu: Waiguoshi*, p. 2.

territories. In so doing, he or she will bring forth spontaneous expressions of patriotism in the ordinary student.[15]

And Zhao Yinian 趙懿年 (fl. 1913) remarked in the *Intermediate Level History Textbook: East and West* (*Zhongdeng lishi jiaokeshu: Dong-Xiyang zhi bu* 中等歷史教科書·東西洋之部):

After the Russo-Japanese War, [China's] situation grew worse and worse from one day to the next, and the reasons to be apprehensive multiplied. [If we] remind ourselves of the decline and fall of various countries and draw lessons from the rise of Japan, how can we, the people of our civilised oriental motherland, not understand that we must take action?[16]

These statements make the position of the compilers fully evident. They had the explicit intention of warning the Chinese people by writing histories of the fall of other nations.

As for the ways in which they present historical facts, foreign history textbooks are also divided into chapters, sections, and sub-sections, and use maps as additional visual aids to present a vivid picture of the historical processes that lead to a given country's demise. For example, *The Republic's Textbook of the History of the Countries of East Asia (For Middle Schools)* (*Gongheguo jiaokeshu Dongya geguoshi (Zhongxuexiao yong)* 共和國教科書東亞各國史（中學校用）) dedicates 70 pages in order to summarise the history of East Asia, from antiquity to modern times, in rather tersely worded textual segments, of which more than one-seventh are devoted to the fall of East Asian countries in the modern era, including sections such as "The Fall of Vietnam" (*Annan zhi wang* 安南之亡), "The Fall of Myanmar" (*Miandian zhi wang* 緬甸之亡), "The Fall of Ryukyu" (*Liuqiu zhi wang* 琉球之亡) and "The Destruction of Korea" (*Chaoxian miewang* 朝鮮滅亡). These ten pages or so offer far more detailed content than is provided in the other parts of the book. Furthermore, the "agony" of the individual countries' national ruin is additionally highlighted by an illustrative map entitled "The Powers' Influence in East Asia" (*Lieqiang zai Dongya shili tu* 列強在東亞勢力圖).[17] And, to give another example, one part of the *Textbook of Western History (For Middle Schools)* (*Xiyang lishi jiaokeshu (Zhongxuexiao yong)* 西洋歷史教科書（中學校用）) entitled the "Record of the Modern World" (*Xianshi ji* 現世記), contains chapters on topics such as "The Powers' Partition of Africa" (*Lieguo fenge Feizhou* 列國分割非洲), "The Powers Invade Asia" (*Lieguo qinlüe Yazhou* 列國侵略亞洲), and "The Powers Seize the Islands of Oceania" (*Lieguo*

---

15 Li Bingjun (1914), *Xinzhi Dongya geguoshi jiaoben (Zhongxuexiao shiyong)*, p. 2.

16 Zhao Yinian (1913), *Zhongdeng lishi jiaokeshu: Dong-Xiyang zhi bu*, p. 3.

17 Fu Yunsen (1913), *Gongheguo jiaokeshu Dongya geguoshi (Zhongxuexiao yong)*, pp. 59–70.

rangqu Dayangzhou zhu dao 列國攘取大洋洲諸島). This work recounts the histories of ruin from several continents, but focuses on Asia in particular.[18]

Similar to the textbooks on domestic history, these works also attempt to give an emotionally neutral account of historical facts and events. However, as the relevant events were nevertheless depicted in great detail, the historical process that led to the demise of the nations in question is actually able to speak for itself, and these narratives thus still serve to further the agenda of the "national ruin" discourse.

It needs to be clarified that substantial content relating to the histories of national ruin—specifically, the demise of Asian countries—are found in textbooks on domestic history as well as works on foreign history. However, in the former, this is labelled "national humiliation", rather than "national ruin", as it is the negative impact of the demise of China's neighbours *on China itself* that is really the focus of the narrative. The different labels thus stem from different perspectives on the same historical events. Nevertheless, this shows that the two discourses are certainly interconnected and that, in some respects, they overlap.

If we take a general survey of the discourses of "national humiliation" and "national ruin", as seen in late Qing and early republican history textbooks, we can see that the textbooks are, first and foremost, concerned with conveying historical facts and offering objective accounts of events. (An exception here are, of course, the "Editor's Intentions" (*Bianji dayi* 編輯大意) and similar texts that betray the personal views and motivations of the editors.) However, in so doing, certain historical facts are certainly given more prominence than others, and the inherent "selectivity" of historical content (*i.e.*, the fact that textbook editors and historians in general need to make an informed choice as to which facts, events, and ideas to include and exclude) plays a crucial role here.

Be that as it may, compared with other works dedicated to the history of national humiliation or the histories of national ruin in which the writers expressed their opinions explicitly, history textbooks were rather more subtle and opted for more implicit ways to convey "subjective" views. This difference may be largely explained by the general nature of textbooks. After all, textbooks are essential resources for teachers and students alike, and they form the basis of historical knowledge, and how it is conveyed, in schools. They are thus primarily concerned with the objective presentation of historical facts. In addition, school textbooks represent the official point-of-view and cannot employ highly emotionalised language in quite the same unscrupulous way in which popular histories of national humiliation and national ruin are able to do.

---

18 Fu Yuefen (1909), *Xiyang lishi jiaokeshu (Zhongxuexiao yong)*, pp. 10–23.

II. History Textbooks and the "Renewal of Historiography"

The wide adoption of new-style history textbooks as media for historical narratives in late Qing and early Republican China coincided with the rise and growth of the "Renewal of Historiography Movement" (*Xin shixue yundong* 新史學運動, hereafter simply called "New History"). In the context of this "renewal", the evolutionary view of history became the leading mode to conceptualise historical development. Historiographical works of all types developed their arguments in abidance with the evolutionary view of history, and history textbooks were no exception. Compilers of history textbooks, be they conservatives, reformists or revolutionaries, were heavily influenced by ideas of progress and evolution, and incorporated them into their products during the compilation process. This point has already been widely recognised in scholarly works on the topic.

Essentially, the evolutionary view, which predicates a gradual development from barbarism to civilisation and from backwardness to progress following a (mostly) straight trajectory, is the most typical example of a linear view of history. This is because linear views of history regard historical development as moving towards a set goal; that is, history, as well as civilisation, are thought to develop—in a straight line—from lower to higher conditions until they reach an ideal state. As history progresses, different countries and nationalities, due to a variety of multiple factors, are, at any given moment, located at different rungs of the evolutionary ladder. For late Qing and early Republican intellectuals, China's evidently disadvantaged position in the world's evolutionary process ranked among the greatest of their anxieties, and one core question for them was how China might be led out of this predicament and how its status in the process of evolution might be raised. Upon this basis, we can surmise that the way history textbooks shaped and constructed the discourses on "national humiliation" and "national ruin", in their essence, reflected this anxiety and, furthermore, explained what practical demands had to be met in order for China to escape from this difficult situation. Some textbooks voiced their intentions in this regard very clearly. For example, in a summary of modern Chinese history, it says in the *Textbook of Domestic History for the New School System* (middle school edition):

The [time period] from the Yuan and Ming dynasties until the end of the Qing marks the modern era (*jinshi* 近世). [...] Since the middle period of the Ming dynasty, China had had encounters with various civilised Western countries which esteem martiality (*shangwu* 尚武) and value practical [learning] (*chongshi* 崇實). China was consequently thoroughly and unavoidably defeated in every respect and on all fronts, being neither able to compete with them in military strength, nor being able to match them in the fields of academic learning (*xueshu* 學術) or technology (*gongyi* 工藝). Even when it came to the people's sense of patriotism and its ability to govern itself, [China] paled in comparison, as these attributes hardly existed at all [among the people]. Consequently, China's national strength declined every day, new territories were lost every day, the financial situation worsened every day, the people were more and more hard pressed to make a living every day, and the threat of partition (*guafen* 瓜分) came to loom over the country's head.[19]

This narrative clearly reveals the aforementioned common perception that China had manoeuvred itself in an unfavourable situation in the global evolutionary struggle, and reflects the widespread anxiety in the face of the countries contemporary crisis. The discourses on "national humiliation" and "national ruin" are thereby drawn upon to stir up patriotic feelings and to heighten the aspirations of the Chinese people. For this reason, narratives informed by nationalist sentiments are most prevalent in history textbooks and a large number of them can be said to actually flaunt their nationalist agendas. The *Primary School Textbook of Chinese History*, for instance, says as much in its "Editor's Intentions":

Exchange and traffic keep expanding, and boundaries keep growing. Today, competition between the yellow race and the white race resembles the competition between the Han nationality (*Hanzu* 漢族) and the non-Han nationalities (*fei-Hanzu* 非漢族) in the past. I therefore compiled this book to defend our race and boost our national prestige. If there is someone who deems himself a defender of our race and an opponent of foreign humiliation, he must exclaim: We must not be feeble! Thereby we can strengthen our youthful spirit.[20]

Zeng Saihua 曾鯤化 (fl. 1904; writing as "Mr. Hengyang yitian" 橫陽翼天氏) argues in a similar spirit and explains the reasons behind compiling his *History of China* (*Zhongguo lishi* 中國歷史) in the following way:

Today, if we want to animate the national spirit, we first have to destroy the myriad kinds of corruption and decay which have been festering since the dawn of history, and, in their stead, plant the flag of a glorious, brilliant, heroic, and magnificent new history. In this way, we will serve as the vanguard of our country's nationalism.[21]

As is well-known, nationalism is the product of the establishment of modern nation-states. But its concrete form is specific to the particular nation-state in question. When people in China's modern period discuss the history of "national humiliation" or the history of "national ruin", their arguments are inevitably developed under this overarching premise. And the discourses of "national humiliation" and "national ruin" as they find expression in history textbooks are equally based upon this assumption. Therefore, when history textbooks relate the "painful and bitter" history of "national humiliation" and

---

19 Zhong Yulong (1914b), *Xinzhi benguoshi (Zhongxuexiao shiyong) san*, p. 1.
20 Ding Baoshu (1903), *Mengxue Zhongguo lishi jiaokeshu*, p. 3.
21 Zeng (as Mr. Hengyang yitian) (1904), *Zhongguo lishi*, p. 2.

"national ruin", they emphasize time and again the importance of "moulding" the citizenry and stress the duties and responsibilities that a proper citizen is supposed to assume. Xia Zengyou's 夏曾佑 (1863–1924) *Textbook of Chinese History* (*Zhongguo lishi jiaokeshu* 中國歷史教科書; later changed to: *Zhongguo gudaishi* 中國古代史 (History of Ancient China)), for instance, places particular emphasis on the process of the evolution of the "people's intelligence" (*minzhi* 民智) in its narrative, and gives prominence to the role of the "citizens" (*guomin* 國民) in shaping China's history.[22] In this way, it contributes to the process of shaping the image of the Chinese citizen. Similarly, Zhao Yinian, in his summary of the modern history of Japan in his *Intermediate Level History Textbook: East and the West*, points out:

With the advent of the modern era, the white people began to rampage across Asia. Britain seized India and Myanmar, France seized Vietnam, and Russia seized the countries of Central Asia. Japan, apprehensive of these [developments], launched political reforms and took self-strengthening measures. High-born and low-born people all exerted themselves and thus made a hegemon (*ba* 霸) out of Japan. It is evident that, during the early modern period, the countries of Asia had not only been suffering from political stagnation, but had also experienced a gradual cultural decline. And it was precisely at this juncture that the [fruits of the] civilisation of the Europeans were first imported [into Asia] and have continued to do so ever since. This really was a time of global exchange (*shijie jiaotong* 世界交通). In the past, trade and [cultural] exchanges within Asia had been dominated by China; but now, China had become one of the beneficiaries of global exchange. Breathing new life into the civilisation of the motherland, adopting new cultural items from other continents, restoring [China's] qualification as the master [of Asia] which she had held in former days, and inspiring [China to become] the mainspring of global exchange—[achieving] these [aims] depends on the efforts of our citizens! It depends on the efforts of our citizens![23]

Statements such as these are fairly typical examples of the expectations demanded of the Chinese citizens as they are formulated in the context of the "national ruin" discourse and they strove to imbue the citizens with a sense of responsibility concerning their own destiny. In his *Textbook of Western History (For Middle Schools)*, Fu Yuefen 傅岳棻 (1878–1951), when summarising the history of the modern world, says:

In the latter half of the nineteenth century, internal competition between the European countries had reached its apogee. They employed policies of diplomacy to form alliances, to assist those they were in league with, and to maintain international peace. They built up their strength, equipped armies and enhanced their military power, adopted modern technology, and established standing national armies. As soon as their national power had grown formidable enough, they went forth and made a beeline for the east. The partition of Africa, the dividing of the islands of Oceania (*Dayangzhou* 大洋洲; *i.e.*,

---

22 Xia Zengyou (2000 [1904–1906]), *Zhongguo gudaishi*.
23 Zhao Yinian (1913), *Zhongdeng lishi jiaokeshu: Dong-Xiyang zhi bu*, p. 46.

the South West Pacific), and the gobbling up and nibbling away (*jingtuncanshi* 鯨吞蠶食) of Central Asia, as well as the areas to the south and north of it, were all the inevitable outcomes of these developments. Japan, however, [even] as a tiny island-country, braved the tidal wave of Western might as it gradually moved east, stood unmoving like a mountain and was not to be shaken. [The Japanese] were finally able to surmount the unrelenting [power of the West] and to rouse themselves to action. They mustered the entire strength of the whole country and frustrated Russia's plans to expand to the south and east. What a magnificent feat! The *Book of Master Guan* says: "Concerning the reasons why a ruler might be inferior or superior and a state secure or in danger, nothing is more important than troops" (*Jun zhi suoyi bei-zun, guo zhi suoyi an-wei, mo yao yu bing* 君之所以卑尊國之所以安危莫要於兵). It also says: "When internal politics are not in order, outside actions are ill-advised" (*Neizheng buxiu, waiju bu ji* 內政不修外舉不濟). That being the case, it is imperative, in this coliseum in which the weak are the meat and the strong devour (them), to put our domestic affairs in order and implement the maxim that "all citizens are soldiers" (*guomin jie bing* 國民皆兵) so as to be able to look as a bird of prey from above down on the new world of the twentieth century.[24]

Summaries of the contemporary political situation like the ones cited above are not just supposed to stimulate a "civic consciousness" and patriotic feelings in the Chinese people. At the same time, they also put forward positive ways to cope with this situation. In the example above, the text, inspired by the precedent of Japan, admonishes the reader that "it is of the utmost importance to put the domestic affairs in order and implement the maxim that 'all citizens are soldiers'". Only in this manner would it be possible for China to stand steady as a rock in the new world of the twentieth century. Calls of this kind clearly reflect the contemporary sense of urgency and the popular desire to see China returned to the status of a rich and powerful country. The discourses on "national humiliation" and "national ruin", as articulated in these textbooks, in many respects echo the prevalent anxiety regarding China's place in an evolutionary order ruled by the "law of the jungle" and the powerful conviction that it requires a strong form of nationalism to mould and mobilise the citizens and to commence and complete the construction of a modern nation-state in order to cast off the spectre of backwardness.

It should also be pointed out that the prevalence of historiographies of "national humiliation" and "national ruin" as well as the existence of broader public discourses on these topics, were, on the one hand, very much contingent upon a specific historical context. However, on the other hand, they must be regarded in equal measure as an intellectual continuation of traditional ways to write history. The traditional view of historiography has, in the Chinese context, continuously been dominated by the idea "of using history as a mirror" (*yi shi wei jian* 以史為鑒), that is, of drawing lessons for the present from historical precedents. Furthermore, this idea was by no means restricted to the field of

---

24 Fu Yuefen (1909), *Xiyang lishi jiaokeshu (Zhongxuexiao yong)*, pp. 23–24.

historiography proper, but possessed an important political dimension which was embraced—at least ostensibly—by the highest political powerholders in each and every dynasty.

One might even say that, considering how politicised historiography had been in imperial and pre-imperial China, "using history as a mirror" had almost been the sole pursuit of historians in the pre-modern era. The grim prospect of "national ruin and racial extinction" during the late Qing and early Republican era gave new impetus to the traditional credo "of using history as a mirror" and China's new historians adopted this idea more passionately than ever. Writing about historical cases of national ruin and narrating processes of decline thus became a common practice at the time.[25]

The discourses on "national humiliation" and "national ruin", as manifested in contemporary history textbooks actually inherited much from the long-held view that history could provide lessons for the present and became an integral part of this new historiographical trend. For example, in compiling his *Textbook of Chinese History*, Xia Zengyou emphasised that,

there is no greater wisdom than knowing what will come (in the future). In order to be able to know what will come, one cannot but draw inferences from past events.[26]

That is, the goal of studying history (and history education) has to be to "gain knowledge of the future based upon past events" (*ju wangshi er zhi weilai* 據往事而知未來). Xia thought that, particular in times when "the world is about to change" (*renshi jiang bian* 人事將變), the study of history was of vital importance for understanding the dangers and difficulties on the way ahead.[27] Such attitudes concerning historiography are strongly informed and shaped by the aforementioned traditional idea of "using history as a mirror". This can also be seen in the preface to Chen Qingnian's 陳慶年 (fl. 1909) *Textbook of Chinese History* (*Zhongguo lishi jiaokeshu* 中國歷史教科書). Here, it is pointed out that:

Education by means of the written word is nothing other than education by means of history. To use history to instruct the world is to teach the world foresight and careful thinking. We are not to blame for those who presently choose not to study history and, as a result, drag out an ignoble existence and are limited to a shallow understanding. If one studies history, one may comprehend [the events of] a thousand years and examine a hundred generations and thus advise a single place or manage all four corners of the earth. All the information one possesses is inferred from history. [...] The country is only

---

25 There already has been some research on "historical lessons of national ruin" and "historical lessons of decline and fall" in modern China, such as Yu Danchu (1996), *Aiguozhuyi yu Zhongguo jindai shixue*, pp. 242–259; Liu Yajun (2010), "'Shuaiwang shijian' yu wan Qing shehui biange", pp. 51–58.

26 Xia Zengyou (2000 [1904–1906]), *Zhongguo gudaishi*, p. 3.

27 Ibid.

complete if its knowledge is complete. And its knowledge is only complete if its history is complete. A complete history is the instrument to create complete knowledge.[28]

In statements like these, "history" (*shi* 史 or *lishi* 歷史) (and the study of history) is elevated to the highest possible rank of human activities, and "historical lessons" (*shijian* 史鑒) are envisioned as indispensable tools in leading the world and the nation. In this framework, history textbooks and history education are naturally endowed with a particularly significant function.

Some textbooks express the importance of historical precedents of national humiliation and national ruin in a markedly straightforward fashion:

In recent times, the world has been changing more and more drastically. Of those countries that shape the course of world events, almost none are located in Asia, but rather in Europe. And our Asia has suffered greatly under their unrestrained cruelty. People of talent who understood the current situation not only widely adopted those of their methods that could be put to good use, but furthermore explored the origins and [historical] developments [of these methods] and traced how they were handed down in history so as to enlighten the people of our country and broaden their view.[29]

Or, to offer another example:

China's situation today is characterised by extreme poverty and extreme weakness. That it has come to this, was not because of [events of] a single day and night, but was rather the result of (a multitude of) historical developments over the course of thousands of years. Two main factors have created China's present [place in] history: One, esteeming civility (*shang wen* 尚文); and two, valuing that which has no substance (*chongxu* 崇虛), whereby the latter is really a consequence of the former. Because [the Chinese] have [historically] esteemed civility, they did not pay attention to military preparedness and as for [practical endeavours such as] industry and commerce (*shiye* 實業), these they have regarded with nothing but contempt. [...] Poverty begets internal strife; weakness begets external aggression. For about a few thousand years, there has hardly been a dynastic period when the threats of [internal] strife and [external] aggression did not exist. The Han were the first to encounter them and those Manchu, Mongols, Hui, and Tibetans who were assimilated into the Han continued to experience [events of this kind] in later times. As this has been going on until the present, we are now in a truly desperate situation. The blessings of the Qing dynasty have come to an end and external aggression becomes fiercer every day. We [therefore] hope that the people of the whole country will be of one mind and make it their ambition to maintain stability within and resist foreign aggression without. Then, all national affairs would run smoothly. [...] [In this book], we thus relate past events in detail relating to (questions of) division and unity, war [and peace], rise and fall, and strength and weakness, (in an effort) to show that China's current situation has not been brought about by mere accident. There is a poem that reads: "When brother fights brother in their own walls, they may yet resist an attack from without." [Even so,] restrain from raising your weapon against someone from your

---

28 Chen Qingnian (1909), *Zhongguo lishi jiaokeshu*, p. 2.

29 *Zuixin zhongxue jiaokeshu: Xiyang lishi* (1906), pp. 1–2.

own home, lest the fisherman reap the benefits.[30] [These are words of caution] that all the people of our country ought to heed carefully and conscientiously![31]

All of these texts argue that it is their purpose to furnish contemporary Chinese society with "guideposts" in the form of historical precedents (and the lessons to be drawn from them), thus highlighting the practical value of historical narratives. In addition, due to the unique nature of textbooks as vehicles of education together with the wide circulation that they received, "historical lessons" framed in terms of the discourses on "national humiliation" and "national ruin" were able to exert influence far beyond the realms of academia and politics: they were able to spread and become—if you will—part and parcel of the common people's *Zizhi Tongjian* 資治通鑒 (Comprehensive Mirror in Aid of Governance).

During the late Qing and early Republican era, the "New History" school became a major player in the field of historiography. Having openly declared that opposition to China's "old history" would be at the forefront of its agenda, one would not expect that "historical lessons" would be valued very highly in the context of "New History", yet, this did not mean that there was absolutely no room left for it, either. In fact, the evolutionary view of history advocated by the "New History" school certainly left room where "historical lessons" of a more traditional variety could fit. Because historiography guided by the theory of evolution tends to take the form of linear narratives, this means that causal relationships in the process of historical evolution need to be specially emphasised. "Using history as a mirror" essentially entails summarising historical experiences and lessons, and letting them serve as points of reference for the present, which equally implies a conviction that history is guided by generalisable causalities. As a consequence, we can observe that there was indeed a large space for the two to blend together. As one textbook editor who adhered to the ideas of the "New History" school put it:

History [deals] exclusively [with] the traces of the past. Nonetheless, by investigating the traces of the past, one can draw inferences and gain knowledge about [the factors that] created the present situation. This is why the discipline of historical research is to be valued.[32]

In statements like this, the traditional view "of using history as a mirror" is fittingly blended together with ideas of causality, as espoused by the "New History" school. Moreover, the notion that history might serve as a mirror for the

---

30 The "fisherman" alludes to a famous parable about a snipe and a clam (representing two warring states) that, being locked in a fight, are both caught by a passing fisherman (a third, more powerful rival state).

31 Zhong Yulong (1914a), *Xinzhi benguoshi (Zhongxuexiao shiyong) yi*, pp. 1–2.

32 Ibid., p. 1.

present was hardly unique to the Chinese context, but can also be found in Western historical thought.[33] One can, however, make the argument that it was more prominent in China. "Historical lessons" were therefore not categorically excluded from history textbooks even if they originated with the "New History" school and were strongly informed by Western historiography. The discourses on "national humiliation" and "national ruin" can thus be regarded as modern-day formulations of "historical lessons", with the twist that the beneficiaries of these lessons were no longer merely monarchs and other rulers but also included the general public.

The idea that history may serve as a mirror (as either a historiographical or political concept) has actually been called into question by a number of scholars in recent years.[34] Some have even pointed out that, in the wake of the momentous socio-political transformations during the late Qing period, the evocation of historical precedents had proven itself to be no longer able to address practical problems effectively. Proposals such as "drawing on other peoples' experiences and putting them to use" (*jie taren zhi yueli er yong zhi* 借他人之閱歷而用之) or "making use of the other countries' historical records from the past century" (*yi geguo jin bainian lai shisheng wei yong* 以各國近百年來史乘為用), it is argued, constitute little more than continuations of the traditional idea of "using history as a mirror" (*i.e.*, of conveying criticisms and admonitions based upon particular cases) and their practical effect is therefore quite questionable. Regarding the development of history as an academic field, it is remarked by these same voices that,

[Finding themselves] in the midst of momentous changes, the majority of Western historians has already abandoned the belief that individual historical precedents can be imitated or serve as models [and are instead convinced that] individual historical events can no longer provide an immediate basis for action.[35]

Seen in this light, the idea of "using history as a mirror" as expressed in the discourses of "national humiliation" and "national ruin" in late Qing and early Republican history textbooks, appears as little more than an attempt to put old wine into new bottles, which would mean that the scope of its effect was probably rather limited. There is, therefore, a lot of room left for further inquiry into the various and, at times, truly elaborate ways in which history both is and has been narrated and conceptualised in historical, as well as contemporary, history textbooks.

(Translated by Mei Chen and Sebastian Riebold)

---

33 As is evident in the famous phrase *historia magistra vitae est* ("history is life's school master") inspired by a passage in Cicero's *De Oratore*.

34 See Liu Jiahe (2010), "Guanyu 'yishiweijian' de duihua", pp. 95–104; Sun (2001), "Cong lishi guiji kan 'yi shi wei jian' de deshi, pp. 26–31; Deng (2014), "Yi shi wei jian ruhe keneng – Jiyu zhishi shengchan de shijiao", pp. 52–56.

35 Liu Yajun (2010), "'Shuaiwang shijian' yu wan Qing shehui biange", pp. 57–58.

Bibliography

Chen Qingnian 陳慶年 (1909), *Zhongguo lishi jiaokeshu* 中國歷史教科書 (Textbook of Chinese History), Shanghai: Shangwu yinshuguan.

Deng Xize 鄧曦澤 (2014), Yi shi wei jian ruhe keneng—Jiyu zhishi shengchan de shijiao 以史為鑒如何可能——基於知識生產的視角 (How can "Using History as a Mirror" be Possible—An Inquiry from the Perspective of Knowledge Production), *Tianjin shehuikexue*, 2, pp. 52–56.

Ding Baoshu 丁保書 (1903), *Mengxue Zhongguo lishi jiaokeshu* 蒙學中國歷史教科書 (Primary School Textbook of Chinese History), Shanghai: Wenming shuju.

Fu Yuefen 傅嶽棻 (1909), *Xiyang lishi jiaokeshu (Zhongxuexiao yong)* 西洋歷史教科書 （中學校用）(Textbook of Western History (For middle schools)), Shanghai: Shangwu yinshuguan.

Fu Yunsen 傅運森 (1913), *Gongheguo jiaokeshu Dongya geguo shi (Zhongxuexiao yong)* 共和國教科書東亞各國史 （中學校用） (The Republic's Textbook of the History of the Countries of East Asia (For Middle Schools)), Shanghai: Shangwu yinshuguan.

Fu Yunsen 傅運森 and Xia Tingzhang 夏廷璋 (1914), *Shifan xuexiao xin jiaokeshu: Waiguoshi* 師範學校新教科書·外國史 (New Textbook for Normal Schools: Foreign history), Shanghai: Shangwu yinshuguan.

Kecheng jiaocai yanjiusuo 課程教材研究所 (ed.) (2001), *20 shiji Zhongguo zhong-xiaoxue kecheng biaozhun, jiaoxue dagang huibian: Kecheng (jiaoxue) jihuajuan* 20 世紀中國中小學課程標準·教學大綱彙編：課程（教學）計劃卷 (Compilation of Twentieth Century Curricula Standards and Syllabi for Middle and Primary Schools: Course (teaching) plans), Beijing: Renmin jiaoyu chubanshe, 2001.

Legge, James (1872), *The Chinese Classics, Volume V: The Ch'un Ts'ew with The Tso Chuen*, Hongkong: Lane, Crawford & Co., Part II.

Li Bingjun 李秉鈞 (1914), *Xinzhi Dongya geguo shi jiaoben (Zhongxuexiao shiyong)* 新制東亞各國史教本 （中學校適用） (Textbook of the History of the Countries of East Asia for the New School System (For use in middle schools)), Shanghai: Zhonghua shuju.

Liu Jiahe 劉家和 (2010), "Guanyu 'yi shi wei jian' de duihua" 關於 "以史為鑒" 的對話 (On the "Using History of as a Mirror" Dialogue), *Beijing shifan daxue xuebao* 1, pp. 95–104.

Liu Yajun 劉雅軍 (2010), "'Shuaiwang shijian' yu wan Qing shehui biange" "衰亡史鑒" 與晚清社會變革 ("Historical Lessons of Decline and Fall" and the Transformation of Late Qing Society), *Shixue lilun yanjiu*, 4, pp. 51–58.

Rutt, Richard (2002), *The Book of Changes (Zhouyi). A Bronze Age Document. Translated with Introduction and Notes*, London: Curzon.

Sun Jiazhou 孫家洲 (2001), "Cong lishi guiji kan 'yi shi wei jian' de deshi" 從歷史軌跡看 "以史為鑒" 的得失 (The merits and flaws of 'Using history as a mirror' seen from trajectory of history), *Shixue yuekan* 1, pp. 26–31.

Wang Rongbao 汪榮寶 (1909), *Zhongguo lishi jiaokeshu* 中國歷史教科書 (Textbook of Chinese history) (Formerly: *Benchaoshi jiangyi* 本朝史講義 (Lecture Notes for the History of the Present Dynasty)), Shanghai: Shangwu yinshuguan.

Xia Zengyou 夏曾佑 (2000 [1904–1906]), *Zhongguo gudaishi* 中國古代史 (History of Ancient China), Shijiazhuang: Hebei jiaoyu chubanshe.

Yu Danchu 俞旦初 (1996), *Aiguozhuyi yu Zhongguo jindai shixue* 愛國主義與中國近代史學 (Patriotism and Modern Chinese Historiography), Beijing: Zhongguo shehui kexue chubanshe.

Zeng Saihua 曾鰓化 (as Mr. Hengyang yitian 橫陽翼天氏) (1904), *Zhongguo lishi* 中國歷史 (History of China), Tokyo: Dongxinshe.

Zhang Qin 章嶔 (1913). *Zhongxue Zhonghua lishi jiaokeshu: Xia ce* 中學中華歷史教科書：下冊 (Middle School Textbook of Chinese History: last volume), Shanghai: Wenming shuju.

Zhao Yinian 趙懿年 (1913), *Zhongdeng lishi jiaokeshu: Dong-Xiyang zhi bu* 中等歷史教科書·東西洋之部 (Intermediate Level History Textbook: East and West), Shanghai: Kexue huibian yibu.

Zhong Yulong 鐘毓龍 (1914a), *Xinzhi benguoshi (Zhongxuexiao shiyong) yi* 新制本國史（師範學校適用）（中學校適用）一 (Textbook of Domestic History for the New School System (For Use in Middle Schools), Vol. 1), Shanghai: Zhonghua shuju.

— (1914b), *Xinzhi benguoshi (Zhongxuexiao shiyong) san* 新制本國史（師範學校適用）（中學校適用）三 (Textbook of Domestic History for the New School System (For Use in Middle Schools), Vol. 3), Shanghai: Zhonghua shuju.

— (1915), *Xinzhi benguoshi (Shifan xuexiao shiyong) shang* 新制本國史（師範學校適用）上 (Textbook of Domestic History for the New School System (For use in normal schools), first part), Shanghai: Zhonghua shuju.

Zou Zhenhuan 鄒振環 (1996), "Qing mo wangguoshi 'bianyi re' yu Liang Qichao de Chaoxian wangguoshi yanjiu" 清末亡國史 "編譯熱" 與梁啟超的朝鮮亡國史研究 (Research into the Histories of National Ruin "Compilation Craze" at the End of the Qing and Liang Qichao's History of the Fall of Korea), *Hanguo yanjiu luncong*, 2, pp. 327–328.

Zuixin zhongxue jiaokeshu: Xiyang lishi 最新中學教科書·西洋歷史 (Latest Textbooks for Middle Schools: Western History) (1906), Shanghai: Shangwu yinshuguan.

The Discourse on "National Humiliation" during the Early Period of the Chinese Communist Party—The Case of *The Guide Weekly* (1922–1927)

Li Lifeng

The rise of nationalism and the construction of the nation-state are, without a doubt, two of the most fundamental developments in modern China. In Benedict Anderson's view, the nation-state, as an "imagined community", is the outcome of the technologies of production and the relations of production of modern capitalism. In particular, the nation-state relies on the national imaginary created and informed by print capitalism.[1] The formation of such an imagined community is inextricably intertwined with creating an "invented tradition" as well as differentiating, in the here and now, between the self and the other.[2] By means of the former move, the existence of the community is projected into the remote past, and the latter strategy aids the development of a "reflective self".[3]

The Chinese experience was unique in the respect that the country was forced onto the road to modern nationhood by the gunboat diplomacy of the Western powers. Consequently, at the very time when China was constructing a historical memory of its own, it also had to face the collective trauma and crisis of identity brought about by the aggression of the Western powers. In a certain way, the construction of the modern Chinese nation-state is thus closely and intimately interwoven with a sense of "national humiliation" (*guochi* 國恥). This mentality is, on the one hand, a catalyst for the ideology of nationalism, but it also an important representation thereof.

Previous scholarship has already explored from multiple angles the ways in which modern Chinese intellectuals have supplied a solid "historical basis" for the Chinese nation-building project through their use of historical imaginaries and the re-construction of memories. Shen Songqiao (Shen Sung-chiao) 沈松僑, in his analysis of the myth of the Yellow Emperor as it was widely circulated in late-Qing intellectual circles, observed that ruptures exist between this version of the myth and the traditional legends of the Yellow Emperor.[4] Upon this

---

1 Anderson (1991), *Imagined* Communities.
2 Hobsbawm (1983), "Introduction: Inventing Traditions", pp. 1–14.
3 Giddens (1991), *Modernity and Self-Identity*.
4 Shen Songqiao (1997), "Wo yi wo xue jian Xuanyuan".

basis, he investigated the nation-building process in modern China and its inherent contradictions and conflicts. In a similar study, he also discussed the relationship between historiography and the national imaginary in the genealogies of national heroes constructed by late-Qing intellectuals.[5] Yang Ruisong (Jui-sung Yang) 楊瑞松 investigated how the expression "four hundred million people" (*si wanwan ren* 四萬萬人), which started out as a mere population figure, came to symbolise a community of "compatriots" in modern China who share blood and kinship ties, thus moulding a national identity which carries the connotation of a high degree of homogeneity.[6]

In contrast to the aforementioned scholars, who directly studied the construction of nationalism, John Fitzgerald approaches the issue from the perspective of the history of political culture. He traced the origins of what he calls "politics of awakening" (and the "awakening" metaphor) to imperial China and the ideas of the European Enlightenment, and delineates its further development in the process of state- and nation-building in modern China.[7] Rudolf G. Wagner delved into the same topic even more deeply. He minutely described how the "body" metaphor, as it appears in both word and image in the popular media of modern China, helped to promote a sense of crisis and national identity in the Chinese populace.[8]

These studies, to differing degrees, all touch upon the relationship between foreign aggression, the sense of national humiliation, and the construction of the modern Chinese nation-state. However, due to limitations in both the focus and the angle of inquiry of the research, there is—as of yet—no in-depth analysis of the ways in which the Chinese Communist Party (CCP) both narrated and remembered national humiliation in order to advance revolutionary propaganda and mobilization. In the present paper, I shall explore these topics by focusing on *The Guide Weekly* (*Xiangdao zhoubao* 向導週報), the first official newspaper of the CCP.

The Guide was founded in Shanghai in September 1922. Cai Hesen 蔡和森 (1895–1931) served as its first editor-in-chief, followed by Peng Shuzhi 彭述之 (1895–1983), who was, in turn, succeeded by Qu Qiubai 瞿秋白 (1899–1935). Chen Duxiu 陳獨秀 (1879–1942), at the time General Secretary of the Central Committee of the CCP, supported the publication ever since its founding and frequently contributed articles. Because the CCP was suppressed by the Kuomintang (KMT) authorities, the newspaper office, together with the CCP central leadership, was relocated first to Beijing, then to Guangzhou, and, at the end of 1926, established itself in Wuhan, the revolutionary centre in those years.

---

5 Shen Songqiao (2000), "Zhen Dahan zhi tiansheng".

6 Yang Ruisong (2012), "Jindai Zhongguo de 'Si wanwan'".

7 Fitzgerald (1998), *Awakening China*.

8 Wagner (2011), "China 'Asleep' and 'Awakening'".

In 1927, following the Shanghai Massacre (also called April 12 Incident) and the 715 Incident, *The Guide* was forced to cease publication on 18 July.

During its five year run, the paper published 201 issues. When the weekly was first launched, less than 3,000 copies of each issue were printed. At the beginning of 1925, by the time of the Fourth National Congress of the CCP, this number had more than doubled to over 7,000 copies, and had even reached 50,000 copies when the Fifth National Congress convened in 1927. *The Guide* had become one of the most well received newspapers at that time.[9]

By analysing the relevant narratives of *The Guide*, we may gain an understanding of the manner in which the CCP, which had just made its debut on the Chinese political stage, drew on the logic of remembering, analysing, and cleansing of the perceived national humiliation, successfully merged the idea of class struggle with the narrative framework of national liberation and subsequently realised its goal of mobilising the people for the Communist revolution.

I. Commemorating National Humiliation: From the Boxer Protocol to the May Thirtieth Movement

The violation of China's territorial sovereignty in modern times had already begun in 1840 with the outbreak of the First Opium War. However, it was not until 1895, when the Middle Realm was defeated by the "flyspeck country" of Japan in the First Sino-Japanese War and forced to sign the Treaty of Shimonoseki, that a true sense of "national humiliation" began to spread widely in both the officialdom and in the general public.

In 1897, the reform-minded Manchu Uksun Šeofu (Zongshi Shoufu 宗室壽富, 1865–1900) along with Kang Youwei 康有為 (1858–1927), among others, initiated the "Sense-of-Shame Study Association" (Zhichi xuehui 知恥學會) in Beijing. In his "Preface to the [Mission Statement] of the Sense-of-Shame Study Association" (*Zhichi xuehui xu* 知恥學會敍), published in the reform journal *The Chinese Progress* (*Shiwubao* 時務報), Liang Qichao 梁啟超 (1873–1929) stated that, as the foreign threat had become ever more pressing, value must be placed in having a sense of shame. Compared to Japan, he wrote, China as yet possessed few people of quality and therefore

[Uksun Šeofu] wishing to instil a lasting sense of shame in them, drew up a proposal and encouraged the foundation of a (study) society so as to call on the support of the entire realm.[10]

---

9 Ma Fulong (2012), "Xiangdao".

10 Liang Qichao (1897), "Zhichi xuehui xu".

The corresponding "Postface", written by Šeofu, enumerates all the occasions between the Opium Wars and the First Sino-Japanese War when the Western powers had seized the opportunity to pounce and gobble up parts of Qing China's sphere of influence. The repeated defeats in battle and the losses of territory that the country had suffered were, according to the author, a matter of great shame and humiliation, and he professed to his fellow countrymen that one could not but have a sense of shame. To instil a sense of shame,

> there is no better way than to engage in study. Study leads to wisdom, wisdom leads to strength, strength leads to the great countries seeing us as one of their own, and the small countries holding us in awe. To refrain from study leads to ignorance, ignorance leads to weakness, weakness leads to the great countries despising us, and the small countries offending us.[11]

At the same time, discussions concerning "national humiliation" became quite popular and started to appear in various publications. In 1898, the *Journal of Sichuan Learning* (*Shuxuebao* 蜀學報) printed an article entitled "Highlighting National Humiliation to Foment Public Indignation" (*Ming guochi yi ji gongfen yi* 明國恥以激公憤議). At the very beginning of the article, we find a string of alarming assertions that betray a profound anxiety concerning the perilous nature of the national situation:

> Alas! The horror of war. The threat of partition. They censure us for our flaws, break open our cracks, bait us when we are famished, kick us when we are limping. All that to get us in a stranglehold, tie us in bonds, cut us into slices. And finally, they will turn us into another Poland, another India.[12]

The famous political caricature *Shiju quantu* 時局全圖 (Complete Illustration of the Contemporary Situation), which was successively published first in Hong Kong, then Shanghai and elsewhere, brought the very real danger that China was faced with—to be divided up like a melon or split like a bean—before the eyes of the Chinese people in a most concise and impressing fashion, further contributing to the development and diffusion of a sense of national humiliation.[13]

The Revolution of 1911 brought an end to the monarchy and created the first republic in Asia. However, under the rule of the government in Beijing, the state of China's sovereignty did not in any way take a turn for the better; on the contrary, it degraded even further. Time and time again, the Chinese people were plagued by diplomatic setbacks and even violence and bloodshed. On 7 May 1915, the Japanese government issued its infamous Twenty-One Demands,

---

11 Shoufu (1897), "Zhichi xuehui houxu".

12 Deng Rong (1898),"Ming guochi", p. 1a.

13 For the different versions of the *Shiju quantu* and its evolving meaning, see Wagner (2011), "China 'Asleep' and 'Awakening'".

THE GUIDE WEEKLY (1922–1927)

249

which seriously infringed upon China's sovereignty. Two days later, President Yuan Shikai 袁世凱 (1859–1916) felt compelled to comply with them. When the news became public, the acceptance of the Twenty-One Demands was immediately regarded as a grave insult to the Chinese people and the two dates "7 May" and "9 May" were declared "National Humiliation Days" and remembered as such henceforth. The young Mao Zedong 毛澤東 (1893–1976) was reportedly genuinely distraught and, that summer, he expressed his feelings in the following words: "On 7 May, our republic was deeply humiliated. How are we to get our revenge? It's up to my pupils!"[14] Not long after the incident had occurred, several pamphlets and booklets on the topic of national humiliation began to appear. The two volumes of *National Humiliation*, published under the umbrella "The Sense of Shame Press" (*Zhichi she* 知恥社), for instance, gave an introduction to the origins of national humiliation, discussed how the various parts of the country had reacted following the news of 9 May, and explained the stance of the central government as well as the attitudes of the provincial governments. It also offered the Japanese arguments regarding the incident and summarised the international discourse.[15] Furthermore, we have the *Mirror of National Humiliation* (*Guochi jian* 國恥鑒) written by Sun Xinyuan 孫鑫源 (fl. 1915) which provides discussions of various modes of disgrace: the ceding of territory, the violation of national borders, consular jurisdiction (*i.e.*, extraterritorial rights), the loss of economic rights, the concessions and leased territories, the delineation of spheres of influence, and the principle of equal profit-sharing.[16] Hereafter, a multitude of written works, maps, and other publications dedicated to the subject matter of national humiliation began to mushroom.[17] It also became a common practice to declare all these dates to be "National Humiliation Days" on which a humiliating event had occurred or China's sovereignty had been further violated. Whenever this happened, people and groups from all walks of society commemorated the occurrence via cables, articles, rallies, and demonstrations. According to a 1928 survey by the Ministry of the Interior of the national government in Nanjing, there were already 26 "National Humiliation Commemoration Days" annually.[18]

As the official organ of the Central Committee of the CCP, it was *The Guide*'s principal task to promote the guiding principles and policies of the party. Furthermore, it had the task of "critiquing and spreading the news of current domestic and international events", which meant that its political propaganda

---

14 Mao Zedong (1915). "Ming chi pian tizhi", p. 11.

15 Zhichi she (ed.) (1915), *Guochi*.

16 Sun Xinyuan (1915), *Guochi jian*.

17 Gongmin jiuguo tuan (ed.) (1919), *Guochi tongshi*; Henan sheng zhengfu (ed.) (1922), *Zhonghua guochi ditu*; Shen Wenjun (1925), *Zengding guochi xiaochi*.

18 See *Shehui kexue cidian* (1929), pp. 497–498.

consisted in a blend of news reports and social commentaries. In addition to lengthy commentaries and articles, *The Guide* successively introduced columns entitled "Commentary on Current Events" (*shishi duanping* 時事短評), "This Week in China" (*Zhongguo yi zhou* 中國一周), "This Week in the World" (*shijie yi zhou* 世界一周), "Correspondence from Everywhere" (*gedi tongxin* 各地通信), and "Pricking Awl" (*cuntie* 寸鐵; i.e. short critical comments on miscellaneous topics—often contributed by Chen Duxiu—which were often sharply worded, hence the name of the column). In these, significant national and international events were treated as the occasion demanded. Looking at the topics discussed in the news reports, commentaries, and propaganda materials of *The Guide* and the points of view expressed therein, it is evident that they nearly all, to a greater or lesser extent, carried undertones of the prevalent sense of national humiliation.

The publication provides rather detailed and thorough discussions of the series of military defeats and diplomatic setbacks from the Opium Wars onwards. Here, special attention is placed on the altercation with the Eight Nation Alliance (*Baguo Lianjun* 八國聯軍) in 1900 and the signing of the Boxer Protocol the following year, the Twenty-One Demands of 1915, and the May Thirtieth Movement of 1925. The corresponding "National Humiliation Days" (7 September, 7 or 9 May, and 30 May respectively) also became key moments in the context of the revolutionary propaganda of the CCP during this period.

The Boxer Uprising was an anti-foreign movement that caught the attention of both observers in China and abroad alike and resulted in an allied force of eight countries, namely, the British Empire, the United States, France, Germany, Russia, Japan, Austria-Hungary, and Italy, encroaching on Chinese soil. On 7 September 1901 (*xinchou* 辛丑), the losing side, China, was obliged to sign the Boxer Protocol (or Xinchou Treaty). This marked the apex of the string of humiliating events and violations of sovereignty that had occurred in modern Chinese history. Before long, the date of the signing of the treaty was regarded as a major symbol for national humiliation and entered the collective memory as such.

In 1924, on the eve of the 23rd anniversary of the signing of the Boxer Protocol, *The Guide Weekly* published a "7 September" special issue which featured commemorative articles by Chen Duxiu and his collaborators. These pieces spoke very highly of the Boxer Movement, calling it a dramatic prelude to the "history of the national revolution" or "history of the national movement". In the article, Chen Duxiu vehemently denounced any and all judgements to the effect that the Boxers had been an exclusively anti-foreign movement. The critics of the Boxers, he argued, solely focused on their "savage anti-foreignism" with total disregard for the causes of their anti-foreign sentiments. These were brought about by "the gore and resentment caused by the ruthlessness of foreign troops, diplomats, and missionaries that the whole of China had had to endure ever since the Opium Wars".[19] Peng Shuzhi offered a re-appraisal of the origin and failure of the Boxer Movement and pointed out that the emergence of the Boxers was the necessary outcome of imperialist aggression towards China. The Boxers failed because they lacked knowledge about revolutionary organisation and strategy, and had been co-opted by reactionary forces.[20] Cai Hesen extolled the Boxer's "anti-foreign spirit" which he regarded as the "legacy of tragedy, tears, and suffering in the history of the Chinese national revolution". According to him, their movement had been doomed to failure from the very start because it did not modernise properly. The 1911 Revolution, in turn, came to nought, as it constituted but a "pathetic attempt to imitate modern *bourgeois*-ification (*zichan jiejihua* 資產階級化)". The national revolution could only hope to succeed by combining an anti-imperialist political programme with the Boxer's anti-foreign spirit.[21] In September 1925, *The Guide* once again published a "7 September" special issue. In his substantial article "The Significance of the Boxer Movement and the Prospects of the May Thirtieth Movement" (*Yihetuan Yundong zhi yiyi yu Wu-Sa Yundong zhi qiantu* 義和團運動之意義與五卅運動之前途), Qu Qiubai provides a re-assessment of the shortcomings and meaning of the Boxer Movement based upon the Marxist theory of social classes. In his view, the May Thirtieth Movement is to be seen as a continuation of the Boxer's struggle to resist foreign aggression. However, with regard to the key questions of the guiding role of the proletariat, class struggle and class consciousness, and prospect of becoming a world revolution, the former surpasses the latter by far.[22]

The Twenty-One Demands of 1915 were very probably the root cause behind the wide dissemination of the sense of national humiliation in China. Each year on 7 or 9 May, periodicals such as the *Shanghai News* (*Shenbao* 申報) or *Social Welfare* (*Yishibao* 益世報) carried large-format political advertisements and published an account of the course of events of that year along with the content of the Twenty-One Demands. They would report on the various activities in which people from all walks of life engaged in memory of May 1915 so as to enable the people to recall the national disgrace elicited by this incident.[23] However, in 1924, the Beiyang government imposed a strict prohibition on people attending gatherings in commemoration of national humiliation on 7 or

---

19 Chen Duxiu (1924b), "Women duiyu Yihetuan liang ge cuowu de guannian".
20 Peng Shuzhi (1924), "Diguozhuyi yu Yihetuan yundong".
21 Cai Hesen (1924), "Yihetuan yu guomin geming".
22 Qu Qiubai (1925b), "Yihetuan yundong zhi yiyi".
23 See Peng Nansheng (2010), "Quru de jiyi".

9 May. *The Guide* launched an immediate attack and proclaimed: "This is yet more proof that the warlords are the tools of the imperialists."[24]

On 7 May, the weekly printed an article entitled "An Urgent Call to All Compatriots on Occasion of National Humiliation Day" (*Guochi jinianri xigao quanguo tongbao* 國恥紀念日檄告全國同胞). It enumerated all the occasions in recent years when foreign countries such as Japan or England had exploited China economically or killed Chinese nationals and declared: "Let us raise our heads high, or we will surely die!"[25] On the anniversary of the Twenty-One Demands in 1925, *The Guide* explained the nature and origin of the national humiliation associated with 7 May. The relevant piece described how Japanese imperialism, from the First Sino-Japanese War, to the Russo-Japanese War, to World War I, had encroached ever deeper on China's sovereignty and called on the masses to overthrow Japanese imperialism and the pro-Japanese Beiyang government.[26]

On 7 May, thousands of students in Beijing had been barred from observing the 7 May national humiliation day. Enraged, they besieged and assaulted the residence of minister of education, Zhang Shizhao 章士釗 (1881–1973). Soon after, *The Guide* published an article and reported on what had occurred. It called this angry upheaval, born out of the yearning to commemorate the disgrace of 7 May, an "awakening to anti-imperialism" and a "mass movement to attack the Anfu Club traitors" and appealed to the masses to unite, rise, and make a stand against the Beiyang government.[27] The horrific events on 30 May of that year caused both the commemoration of national humiliation as well as anti-imperialist propaganda to reach their highest point during the entirety of modern Chinese history up to that point.

On 15 May, when Chinese worker Gu Zhenghong 顧正紅 (1905–1925) was shot and killed by a Japanese guard, workers in Shanghai went on strike in angry protest. The Central Committee of the CCP responded promptly and made an urgent public announcement the following day to the effect that organisations belonging to the party throughout the country ought to appeal to trade unions, peasant and student associations, and other social organisations to support—by all possible means—the Shanghai strikers in their fight.[28] On 17 May, *The Guide* reported on the shooting and called upon the people to "rise up and overthrow

---

24 Chen Duxiu (1924a), "Junfa shi diguozhuyizhe de gongju".

25 *Xiangdao*, 64 (7 May 1924), pp. 509–510.

26 Shuanglin (1925), "Wu-Qi guochi yu Riben diguozhuyi".

27 Cai Hesen (1925), "Wu-Qi jinian Beijing xuesheng fendou"; Zhao Shiyan (as Luojing) (1925), "Beijing Wu-Qi nuchao", pp. 1071–1072.The Anfu Club was the political wing of the so-called Anhui Clique, one of several mutually hostile factions during the Warlord Era (1916–1928).

28 "Zhongyang tonggao di sanshi'er hao" (1989 [1925]), pp. 415–416.

Japanese imperialism, overthrow the traitorous, pro-Japanese government".[29] On 19 May, the CCP Central Committee issued a public notice calling for an "anti-Japanese mass movement".[30] On 28 May, the Central Committee convened an emergency meeting and decided to establish a federation of trade unions in Shanghai. In addition, it mobilised a great number of people to hold a demonstration protesting against the imperialism in the foreign concession at Shanghai. During the march on 30 May, which was accompanied by rallies and public speeches, a clash occurred between students and the Shanghai Municipal Police. The British policemen opened fire and shot more than ten people dead. Dozens were wounded. Such were the events underlying what came to be known as the May Thirtieth Movement which shook both China and the world.

The Beiyang Era (1912–1928) saw repeated occurrences of acts of violence perpetrated by the Western powers against Chinese people. However, in terms of political fallout and historical significance, other, similar incidents pale utterly in comparison with the massacre on 30 May 1925. Following the incident, the Central Committee issued a letter entitled "Announcement to the Chinese Masses" via *The Guide*. The introductory paragraph puts the message in no uncertain terms: "Shanghai, where blood and guts are splattered everywhere, has now become the slaughterhouse of foreign imperialism!"[31]

Immediately after this, the announcement pointed out that the massacre bore witness to the efforts of Japanese and British imperialism to "repress by iron and by blood (*tie xue zhenya* 鐵血鎮壓)" China's working class and the national movement, and calls on "the people of all oppressed classes nationwide to resist the savage slaughter of imperialist brutality".[32] At the same time, the periodical published an article by Zheng Chaolin 鄭超麟 (1901–1998) with a detailed introduction to the course of events, that is to say, the massacre in Shanghai and the ensuing popular protests, between 30 May and 4 June.[33] In the following months, every weekly issue contained follow-up reports and detailed discussions on the topic. The main points included: 1) The May Thirtieth Massacre was the necessary outcome of the oppression of small countries by the imperialist nations and the continuation of the enslavement and slaughter of the Chinese people by the powers carried out since the Opium Wars and the Boxer Uprising; 2) The May Thirtieth Movement was the necessary outcome of the continuous escalation of the Chinese people's resistance against imperialism between the time of the Taiping Heavenly Kingdom and the Boxer Movement;

---

29 Zheng Chaolin (1925b), "Shanghai Riben zibenjia qiangsha Zhongguo gongren", p. 1060.

30 "Zhongyang tonggao di sanshi'san hao" (1989 [1925]), pp. 417–418.

31 "Zhongguo Gongchandang wei fankang diguozhuyi yeman canbao de datusha gao quanguo minzhong shu" (1925), p. 1075.

32 Ibid.

33 Zheng Chaolin (1925a), "Diguozhuyi tusha Shanghai shimin".

3) The incident on 30 May was a political, not a legal, affair. The struggle of the Chinese people could not be appeased by punishing the murderers or granting compensation for the victims. The movement aimed to repeal the Unequal Treaties and rescind the privileges of imperialism in China.[34]

In fact, since that time and until the periodical was shut down two years later, nearly every issue of *The Guide* carried pieces that directly or indirectly touched upon the incident on 30 May. "30 May" (stylised as *wu-sa* 五卅, 5-30, in Chinese) had by then become a symbolic number for implementing a national revolution. On both occasions, the one year anniversary of the May Thirtieth Movement in 1926, and again the two year anniversary in 1927, *The Guide* published special commemorative issues to review the series of events which led up to the incident, but also (and more importantly) engaged the people in the fight to topple foreign imperialism and abolish domestic warlordism.[35]

The May Thirtieth Massacre had occurred against the backdrop of the commemoration of another national humiliation, namely, 7 May, that is to say, Japan's Twenty-One Demands of 1915. These two grave incidents of national humiliation thus became compounded and reinforced each other to the degree that they roused an unprecedented anti-imperialist fervour. The CCP took advantage of the national righteous indignation stirred up by the incident on 30 May and launched a mass movement against imperialism on a previously unheard-of scale. Furthermore, under the slogan of "Down with Imperialism!", the party successfully created an image for itself as the standard-bearer of nationalism. It is therefore not hard to imagine that the CCP leadership spoke of the May Thirtieth Movement only in the highest terms in the belief that this event had spurred the rapid expansion of the native anti-imperialist movement, caused the firm consolidation of a united front on the part of all social classes against imperialism, and created "an unprecedented national liberation movement that not only pervades the entire country but is also carried out in a conscious and organised manner".[36] This marked the dawn of a new period in Chinese history—the period of national revolution (*guomin geming* 國民革命).[37]

Beyond the commemoration of 7 September, 7 or 9 May, and 30 May, *The Guide Weekly* also carried an irregularly scheduled special column called "Daily Record of Foreign Aggression" (*waihuan rizhi* 外患日志) which thematised

---

34 See, for example, Chen Duxiu (1925g), "Women ruhe yingfu cici yundong de xin jumian".

35 See, for example, "Wu-Sa zhounian jinian gao quanguo minzhong" (1926); Qiu Qubai (1927), "Wu-Sa er zhou jinian".

36 Xincheng (1925), "Minzu jiefang yundong".

37 Qu Qiubai (1925a), "Wu-Sa hou fan-diguozhuyi lianhe zhanxian de qiantu", pp. 1146–1147. Translator's note: Both *guomin geming* and *minzu geming* 民族革命 are translated as "national revolution" in this article. For the latter, the more accurate albeit rather cumbersome alternative "ethno-national revolution" is used in the instances where the two are systematically distinguished. (See, for example, the quote by Wang Jingwei below.)

recent occasions when the powers had browbeaten or insulted China.[38] Every time one of the Western powers was responsible for the killing of Chinese people, the weekly would publish a report at the first opportunity and without fail make sure to call it a matter of "national humiliation" so as to excite the outrage and fighting-spirit of the populace. On 5 September 1926, three British warships (HMS *Cockchafer*, HMS *Widgeon*, and the armed steamer *Kiawo*) clashed with a force of Chinese defence troops on a riverbank in Wan County, Sichuan province. During the altercation, the British naval vessels even shelled a densely populated area of the county seat, an act which resulted in thousands of military and civilian casualties on the Chinese side. The event is known as the "Wan-hsien Incident" (*Wan xian can'an* 萬縣慘案; lit. Wan County Massacre) and provoked strong reactions in China and elsewhere in the world.[39] Following the tragedy, the CCP promptly joined together with members of the left wing of the KMT and established the "Wan County September-Fifth-Massacre Reinforcement Association" (*Wanxian jiu-wu can'an houyuan hui* 萬縣九五慘案後援會) which organised large-scale demonstrations in protest against Britain's actions. At the same time, the CCP published a "Letter Informing the Masses" in *The Guide* and sternly condemned the repeated violent provocations by British troops since the beginning of the Northern Expedition in July 1926. The letter called on the people to mobilise and "form a second, even more expansive, anti-British May Thirtieth Movement". Only in this way, it was argued, "can we hope to prevent the British imperialist brigands from committing a second or third atrocity of this nature".[40]

In 1926, Qu Qiubai wrote an article looking back on the past ten years of the history of the Chinese revolutionary movement. He discovered that the month of May was particularly dense in days remembering events that were deemed significant to national humiliation or revolution, and thus called it "Revolution-May" (*Geming de Wuyue* 革命的五月): The First of May is a memorial day to "mount, on an international scale, a show of force [against] the world *bourgeoisie* by jointly going on strike to take stock of the military prowess of the world proletariat". The fourth of May is "a day of remembrance because it marks the anniversary of the Chinese revolutionary student's movement". The 5th of May commemorates the birthday of Karl Marx. The 7th and 9th of May are National Humiliation Days in memory of Japan's imposition of the Twenty-One Demands on China. And 30 May marks the day on which the foreign powers, through their savagery, inadvertently facilitated the formation of an

---

38 Issues 64, 68, 72, and 79, for instance, do not contain this column.

39 Jizhe (1926), "Canwurendao zhi Yingguo diguozhuyi".

40 "Zhongguo Gongchandang wei Yingguo diguozhuyi tusha Wan xian gao minzhong shu" (1926).

"anti-imperialist united front under the leadership of the proletariat".[41] Looking at the commemoration of national humiliation thus reveals one aspect of how the national humiliation discourse was of major significance for revolutionary mobilisation.

II. The Roots of National Humiliation: Genealogies of "Foes" and "Friends"

As stated above, the aftermath of the First Sino-Japanese War and, arguably even more so, of the Twenty-One Demands, had witnessed a gradual upsurge of a sense of national humiliation and nationalist mentalities within all strata of Chinese society and in both official and civic circles. However, during the founding period of the CCP, the party had not yet put forward political demands associated with a nationalist agenda. The political programme promulgated by the First National Congress of the CCP professed "it is the fundamental political goal of the party to realise a socialist revolution", to "overturn the regime of the capitalist class" through class struggle, and ultimately to "abolish all differences between the social classes". No mention was made of recovery of sovereignty or national independence.[42] Be that as it may, before long, the CCP also came to realise that nationalism bore a special significance for mass mobilisation.

In June 1922, the CCP issued a statement concerning the current political situation. It maintained that the "feudal power of the warlords" was still the chief target of attack but the starting-point of the argument had shifted to the oppression of the Chinese people by "international imperialism".[43] Not long afterwards, a declaration of the plenary session of the Second National Congress of the CCP unequivocally characterised "overthrowing the warlords" to create peace domestically, as well as "eliminating the oppression of international imperialism" to realise national independence as the two key objectives of political struggle.[44] A year later, when the Third National Congress was convened, the catchphrases "anti-imperialism" and "anti-warlordism" were re-iterated a second time.[45] From then on, imperialism and warlordism were ever more firmly established as the arch-enemies of the Chinese revolution.

---

[41] Qu Qiubai (1926), "Zhongguo zhi geming de Wuyue yu Makesizhuyi", pp. 1426–1428.
[42] "Zhongguo Gongchandang di yi ge gangling" (1989 [1921]), p. 3.
[43] "Zhongguo Gongchandang guanyu shiju de zhuzhang" (1989 [1922]), pp. 33–46.
[44] "Zhongguo Gongchandang di er ci quanguo daibiao dahui xuanyan" (1989 [1922]), p. 115.
[45] "Chen Duxiu zai Zhongguo Gongchandang di san ci quanguo daibiao dahui shang de baogao" (1989 [1923]), p. 169.

THE GUIDE WEEKLY (1922–1927)

Moreover, in communist rhetoric, anti-imperialism not only came to match, but gradually even overtook, resistance against the warlords in importance as evidenced by the "Resolution on the Plan of Advancing the National Movement" (*Guomin yundong jinxing jihua jueyi'an* 國民運動進行計劃決議案) passed in November 1923. The text, arguing upon the basis of "nationalism as understood in the Three Principles of the People (*Sanmin Zhuyi* 三民主義)", stated:

The anti-imperialist movement is of more vital importance to the Chinese national movement than the movement against the warlords. When there is a conflict between warlords and imperialists, we have to aid the warlords in resisting the foreigners. We must absolutely never rely on an external force to overpower the warlords.[46]

Less than two months of time passed between the start of the publication of the *The Guide* in September 1922 and the summoning of the Second National Congress of the CCP. In its "Manifesto" (*Benbao xuanyuan* 本報宣言), printed in the first issue of the journal, *The Guide* had stated its purpose clearly from the outset and maintained that "unity and peace" were what the vast majority of the Chinese people presently desired. However, due to the warlords within, who had carved out pieces of territory and were now engaged in fighting amongst themselves, and the imperialist oppression from without, "the people of China are unable to develop self-determinately". Only by "overthrowing warlordism" and "eliminating international imperialism" could the people hope to achieve unity and peace.[47]

Every week, in its surveys of the general trend of global events and the discussions of important news in current politics, *The Guide* outlined veritable genealogies of what it deemed to be the friends and foes of the Chinese revolution in order to reveal the true roots of national humiliation and point the way towards eliminating the national disgrace. All events of national humiliation up to that point, from "7 September", via "7 May", to "30 May", had stemmed from invasions, interference, and slaughter caused by "international imperialism". The respective perpetrating countries were, in the eyes of *The Guide*, without question obstructions to the Chinese national liberation and were enemies of the national revolution. A country's rank in this detailed account of enemy states was, on the one hand, directly related to the degree to which it had violated Chinese sovereignty. On the other hand, the evaluation to a significant extent also depended on how it figured in the CCP's imagination of the international order within the framework of the Marxist theory of social classes.

Analysing anti-imperialist propaganda from the period of national revolution reveals that Britain, Japan, the US, and France were usually regarded as the principal external enemies of the Chinese revolution. In particular, Britain and

---

46 "Guomin yundong jinxing jihua jueyi'an" (1989 [1923]), p. 200.
47 "Benbao xuanyan" (1922).

Japan stood out as "first-order enemies" (*touhao diren* 頭號敵人) since these two countries violated China's sovereignty particularly gravely and irritated the Chinese people most deeply. According to the *Lexicon of the Social Sciences* (*Shehui kexue cidian* 社會科學辭典) published in 1929, of the 26 National Humiliation Days observed by the Chinese people, 15 concerned Britain and 7 Japan.[48] These two countries also bore sole responsibility for causing the two most significant and emblematic incidents in the formation and dissemination of a sense of national humiliation in China, that is, the imposition of the Twenty-One Demands and the May Thirtieth Massacre respectively. The United States and France were also deemed "imperialist countries" which ruled tyrannically over small nations. France was additionally labelled a "counter-revolutionary country", as it oppressed its own workers and strikers.[49] However, the US and France had seldom been directly responsible for creating violent incidents, and the Chinese people did not treat them with the same degree of outrage and indignation. Thus, they were considered to be enemy states of minor importance.

China's Japanese neighbour showed greater aggression and posed a more serious threat for China than any other country. It had also been the originator of the infamous Twenty-One Demands. An article in *The Guide* pointed out that, as a rising capitalist nation in Asia, Japanese capitalism "was fierce and brutal in nature and had received the backing of warlordism" from the very outset. Because the island nation had just become embroiled in competition with the economic strength of the Euro-American powers, but possessed only a confined territory and almost no natural resources to speak of, it could not but opt for outward expansion, which was first of all directed against China.[50] The Middle Realm was "the only market for Japan to sell its goods, a land rich in coal and iron deposits, and a route of escape and a granary for the troops in wartime". To call off the invasion of China would be tantamount to "pronouncing a death sentence over Japanese capitalism" and therefore it would "have no choice but to continue its invasion".[51]

Great Britain was the oldest imperialist country on record and was, arguably, the unspoken leader of the Western powers. Its encroachments on China had had a longer history than any other country and it had been the ringleader behind the massacre on 30 May 1925, which is why Chen Duxiu called England an "implacable enemy who had incessantly oppressed China".[52]

---

48 *Shehui kexue cidian* (1929), pp. 497–498.
49 "Faguo di zhengzhi jingji zhuangkuang" (1924), p. 523.
50 Shuanglin (1925), "Wu-Qi guochi yu Riben diguozhuyi", p. 1051.
51 Zhang Guotao (1923), "Zhongguo yi tuoli le guoji qinlüe de weixian me?", p. 48.
52 Chen Duxiu (1925d), "Shanghai datusha", p. 1077.

The United States had attained virtual hegemony over the world economy in the wake of World War I and was seeking markets for its commodities as well as new places in which to invest capital. But almost all the viable colonies had already been distributed between countries such as England, Japan, and France, leaving only China as "a possible domain to feed American free development and free competition". The US thus "had no choice but to exert all its strength towards seizing the Chinese market".[53]

France had, in the past, repeatedly collaborated with Britain in attacks against China. In the twentieth century, the country had damaged China's sovereign rights in the Gold-franc Case (*Jinfulang an* 金佛朗案) (when it had demanded that China redeems France's share of the Boxer Indemnity in gold), when it had refused to return Guangzhou Bay on time, when it had refused to convene a conference on customs and raise tariffs, and when it had interfered in negotiations between China and Russia.[54]

All of these countries had, time and time again, interfered in China's internal affairs and violated its sovereignty, and were therefore the immediate causes of China's national humiliation. They also counted among the external enemies that had to be crushed in the advancement of national liberation.

On the ninth anniversary of the imposition of the Twenty-One Demands on 7 May 1924, *The Guide* published a letter to its compatriots nationwide. Its object of attack was, first and foremost, Japan, followed by Britain, the US, and France. The text argued that, ever since the Washington Naval Conference (November 1921–February 1922), a shift had occurred in international relations from Japan "oppressing us on its own" to "a new situation in which [the abovementioned four countries] oppress us in co-operation".[55] After the incident on 30 May, Chen Duxiu labelled Britain "the king of imperialism" and said that Japan, which had followed Britain's lead, "had obtained interests in China that in no way came into conflict with those of Britain". British and Japanese imperialism was thus the "enemy before the eyes" of the Chinese national movement. The US, while not fully endorsing Britain's policy, "would, in the end, undertake concerted action with the other powers" in order to help to preserve the overall interests of imperialism in China and to implement its own Open Door Policy.[56] By contrast, nations such as Germany, Austria, and Russia, although they had also been imperialist countries in the past, and, for instance, taken part in the incursions of the Eight-Nation Alliance during the events of 1900 and were thus directly responsible for the national humiliation associated with 7 September, had been transformed into "anti-imperialists" after their

---

53 Zhang Guotao (1923), "Zhongguo yi tuoli le guoji qinlüe de weixian me?", p. 47.
54 Liu Renjing (1924), "Faguo zhi xin zhengju", pp. 550–551.
55 "Guochi jinianri xigao quanguo tongbao" (1924), p. 509.
56 Chen Duxiu (1925b), "Cici yundong zhong zhi diguozhuyi yu junfa", pp. 1135–1136.

defeat at the hands of the Entente countries in World War I. Their approach towards China had also become one of "peaceful trade" which stood in diametrical opposition to Britain, the US, France, and Japan, countries which continued to "exploit and trample on" (*boxue jianta* 剝削踐踏) the Chinese. China, therefore, no longer needed to regard them as its enemies.[57]

Not long after *The Guide* had been established, Cai Hesen put forth his personal views on the place of China in the contemporary international order. He was of the opinion that China, along with all other oppressed peoples, had for a long time been "caught in the relentless embrace of imperialism, faced on all sides with the threat of exploitation and territorial dismemberment". The Great War that had erupted in 1914 and had engulfed the whole world, however, had left a "great transformation" (*jueda bianhua* 絕大變化) of the international situation in its wake:

Imperialist Russia has been transformed into a republic of workers and peasants in which all systems of exploitation have been eradicated root and branch. And imperialist Germany has been transformed into a country subjugated by the Entente powers.

The community of oppressed peoples now had "the opportunity to escape from the snares of imperialism, unite with the great anti-imperialist nations, and pursue independence and self-determination". With regard to China, Cai argued, one ought to "support unreservedly the policy of creating a Chinese-German-Russian alliance and shed the fetters of Britain, the US, France, and Japan".[58] In this context, the enemies of former days, Germany and Russia, now had to be included in the "non-imperialist" (*fei-diguozhuyi* 非帝國主義) camp, if not the "anti-imperialist" (*fan-diguozhuyi* 反帝國主義) camp, and had become the possible friends of the Chinese revolution. Commentaries in *The Guide* discussing current international developments more often than not revealed a sympathetic attitude toward the defeated nations of World War I and gave expression to the belief that they, just like China, had suffered the ravages of war at the hands of countries such as Britain, the US, and France.[59] These voices even denounced an alleged "French imperialist scheme to carry out the partition of Germany".[60]

Following the October Revolution of 1917, Russia had become the first "proletarian nation" in world history. For the Chinese communists, Soviet Russia represented the successful pioneering effort to implement in practical terms the theories of historical materialism and class struggle which provided tangible material, as well as crucial intellectual backing, for their own agenda. Not long

---

57 Chen Duxiu (1925d), "Shanghai datusha", p. 1078.
58 Cai Hesen (1923d), "Zhong-De-E san guo lianmeng", pp. 25–26.
59 Cai Hesen (1923c), "Peichang wenti", pp. 144–145.
60 Cai Hesen (1923a), "Deguo de fenli yundong", p. 340.

after the October Revolution had erupted, the Soviet government declared its intention to renounce any and all privileges that the Tsarist Russian regime had secured for itself within Chinese borders. Following a string of secret consultations, it officially signed the "Sino-Russian Framework Agreement to Resolve Outstanding Issues" (*Zhong-E jiejue xuan'an dagang* 中俄解決懸案大綱) along with other related diplomatic papers on 31 May 1924. The Soviet government declared that it renounced all the extraterritorial rights of old Russia in China and took the initiative to repeal the Unequal Treaties between the two countries. This was an absolutely unprecedented development in the history of China's relations with the outside world, and stood in stark contrast to the stance of the Western powers which insisted on clinging obstinately to their system of Unequal Treaties with China.[61] It is not hard to imagine that this move had a strong impact on the world view of the Chinese people and on their national sentiment.

Ever since the founding of the CCP, Soviet Russia had been regarded as the truest and most powerful friend of the Chinese revolution. At the Second National Congress of the CCP, convened in 1922, it was declared that Soviet Russia

is the world's first country of workers and peasants. It is the motherland of the proletariat and the motherland of the toiling masses. And it represents a bulwark of resistance for workers and peasants from all over the globe against the world's imperialist countries.[62]

Furthermore, the Congress argued, one ought to launch an appeal to the workers and oppressed masses of China and urge them to "join the united front of the world's working class", safeguard "the motherland of the proletariat" and protect the "vanguard [in the struggle to] liberate all oppressed peoples".[63]

Essays commenting on Sino-Russo relations that were published in *The Guide* were always careful to distinguish clearly between the Soviet Russia of the present and the "old Russia" that had, on previous occasions, displayed aggression towards China. They emphasised their sympathy and support of Soviet Russia for the liberation movements of small nations and underscored its commitment in the struggle against Western imperialism.[64] In this vein, Chen Duxiu wrote:

Lenin's October Revolution truly and firmly based itself upon an internal proletarian revolution to topple the militarist and imperialist regimes of the Russian Tsar and Alexander Kerensky (1881–1970). And it helped Finland, Poland, and other ethnic minorities

---

61 Wang Qisheng (2006), *Guo-Gong hezuo*, p. 141.
62 "Guanyu 'Shijie dashi yu Zhongguo Gongchandang' de yijue'an" (1989 [1922]), pp. 59–60.
63 Ibid.
64 Zhang Tailei (1924), "Liening yu Yihetuan", 654–655.

within the country to accomplish national self-determination, that is to say, independence and autonomy.[65]

In his view, the Russian Revolution provided a perfect example of how a class revolution within China could be productively combined with the various global efforts of national liberation, and was the historical precedent upon which the Chinese revolution should strive to model itself.

As for other "small eastern nations" such as Turkey, India, and Korea, which had suffered imperialist aggression and oppression like the Chinese had, China should share in their hatred of a common enemy and join with them in a collective struggle to achieve national independence. An article in *The Guide* analysed the state of the world revolution and provided a list of "colonies and oppressed nations" that "had already witnessed ferocious revolutionary independence movements" which included Ireland, Turkey, India, Persia, Egypt, the Philippines, Korea, and Vietnam.[66]

One country on this list merits particular attention, as the CCP leadership did not tire of continually citing it as a case in point. This was the Republic of Turkey, which had been established following a successful revolution after the collapse of the Ottoman Empire in the aftermath of World War I. Turkey had defeated the British and Greek army in 1922 and reclaimed its territorial integrity and national sovereignty. At the same time, it had abolished the sultanate, which had lasted for hundreds of years, and put a republic in its place. *The Guide* offered high praise for Turkey's success, calling it "not a victory of Islam over Christianity, nor a victory of the yellow race over the white race, and, least of all, a victory of Asians over Europeans", but, instead, "a victory won by the oppressed Turkish nation in revolt against European imperialist exploitation".[67] In analyses of China's domestic politics, the journal also frequently mentioned Turkey as a model to consult and follow. The hope was that the Chinese Nationalist Party would be able to strive to represent truly the interests of the people, just like the Republican People's Party (CHP) had done, and that the Chinese revolutionaries would lead their compatriots and ensure revolutionary victory, just like Mustafa Kemal Atatürk (1881–1938) had done.[68] In appeals to the people to resist foreign aggression or to overthrow the Northern Warlords, Turkey, again, served as an example:

---

65 Chen Duxiu (1925e), "Shiyue Geming yu dongfang", p. 1849.
66 Cai Hesen (1922), "Zhongguo guoji diwei", pp. 17–18.
67 Gao Junyu (1922), "Tu'erqi guominjun", pp. 22–23.
68 Zhang Tailei (as Chunmu) (1923), "Xiu jian guomin de Zhongguo Guomindang", p. 213.

THE GUIDE WEEKLY (1922–1927)

If Turkey's Republican People's Party had not first stopped the invasion by England and France, how would it have been able to topple the government in Constantinople (which is the same as China's Beijing government) and govern Turkey?[69]

Turkey's central role notwithstanding, *The Guide* paid close and constant attention to the national liberation movements in India, Mongolia, and Korea as well, provided information in the form of commentaries or translations, and discussed how the lessons to be drawn from their experiences might help to inspire the Chinese revolution.[70]

Friend-foe relationships at international level corresponded one-to-one to a given country's internal political situation and its class structure. The reason why the so-called "imperialist countries" of Britain, Japan, the US, and France had been able to carry-out their wanton acts of aggression, plunder, and murder was that China's Northern Warlords had shown complete and utter submission and timidity in their dealings with them. Chen Duxiu thus differentiated national humiliation into "external humiliation" and "internal humiliation". "When Europeans, Americans, or Japanese kill and injure the Chinese, or shame and insult the Chinese" that, of course, was a matter of national humiliation. But the "cowardly dim-wittedness" (*nuoruo hunkui* 懦弱昏聵) of the Beiyang government was, in his view, an even worse instance of "great shame and humiliation for the Chinese nation". According to his view, "to fawn shamelessly and ignominiously on foreign powers" constitutes "a more flagrant form of national humiliation than any other".[71] The Northern Warlords were not only the "wicked remnants of autocracy" but also formed a "super-government" (*chaoji zhengfu* 超級政府) above the Chinese civil government and acted as "lackeys" (*nupu* 奴僕) and "accomplices" (*bangxiong* 幫兇) for foreign imperialism.[72] Putting the "powers" (*lieqiang* 列強) on an equal level with the "warlords" (*junfa* 軍閥) as the two principal enemies of the Chinese revolution thus became a central theme in mass mobilisation campaigns in the national revolution.

In June 1924, *The Guide* issued a proclamation to commemorate the 3 June strike of 1919 and especially used a large-size font to set-off the slogan "Struggle for National Sovereignty Without, Remove Traitors Within".[73] If one were to seek to obtain the success of the revolution and the liberation of the nation, it argued, one would need to wage war simultaneously against outside foes and internal enemies. To "topple imperialism" and to "overthrow the warlords"

---

69 Cai Hesen (1923b), "Guomindang ying haozhao guomin fandui guomin de qinlüe", p. 293.

70 Such as Yongzhao (1923), "Yi jiu er er Yindu guomin yundong de fenxi", pp. 153–156; Dengdebu (1922), "Menggu jiqi jiefang yundong", pp. 43–44. The author is probably a Mongolian named "Dendev".

71 Chen Duxiu (1923b), "Hua-Yangren xuerou jiazhi de guijian", p. 182.

72 Chen Duxiu (1923c), "Zenme dadao junfa", p. 152.

73 "'Liu-San' jinian" (1924), p. 541.

were, in other words, two sides of the same coin. With such formidable internal and external enemies, one would have to unite all the possible forces that could be united. Only then could the revolution hope to stand any chance of success. This was precisely what provided the rationale behind the idea of a revolutionary "united front".

According to the CCP's analysis based upon the theory of social classes, it was the proletariat that suffered the greatest oppression. The working class "owned nothing but the shackles that tied them", but also undeniably possessed organising force and intellectual leadership. It was the vanguard in the fight against imperialist oppression.

In the wake of the May Thirtieth Incident, a multitude of peasants, students, businessmen, and soldiers became part of the "revolutionary masses" and joined the ranks of the anti-imperialist movement as they came to experience the violation of their interests and a growing sense of national humiliation caused by the encroachments of the Western powers.[74] The power of the *bourgeoisie* had been curtailed by the twin forces of imperialism and warlordism, just like that of the workers and peasants, but, by virtue of their class, so the argument went, the former was feeble by nature and prone to wavering. Chen Duxiu divided the Chinese capitalist class into three parts: first, came the revolutionary *bourgeoisie*. They endorsed the revolution because the warlords and imperialists had hindered the development of industry and commerce. Second, the anti-revolutionary *bourgeoisie*, had been relying on the Western powers' and the warlords' good favour and had accumulated a "tainted" form of commercial capital. It naturally supported them and opposed the revolution. Third came the non-revolutionary *bourgeoisie*. The businesses and enterprises run by its members were small-scale operations; the non-revolutionary *bourgeoisie* had no particular political demands, and adopted a passive and non-committed stance towards a democratic revolution.[75] Similarly, Mao Zedong, in his text "Analysis of the Classes in Chinese Society" (*Zhongguo shehui ge jieji de fenxi* 中國社會各階級的分析), written in 1926, provided his classic assessment of the individual social classes' respective relationships to the revolution:

To sum up, it can be seen that our enemies are all those in league with imperialism: the warlords, the bureaucrats, the comprador class, the big landlord class and the reactionary section of the intelligentsia attached to them. The leading force in our revolution is the industrial proletariat. Our closest friends are the entire semi-proletariat and petty *bourgeoisie*. As for the vacillating middle *bourgeoisie*, their right-wing may become our enemy and their left-wing may become our friend but we must be constantly on our guard and not let them create confusion within our ranks.[76]

---

74 Qu Qiubai (1925a), "Wu-Sa hou fan-diguozhuyi lianhe zhanxian de qiantu", pp. 1145–1148.
75 Chen Duxiu (1923d), "Zichan jieji de geming yu geming de zichan jieji", pp. 162–164.
76 Mao Tse-tung (1965 [1926]), "Analysis of the Classes in Chinese Society", p. 20.

In this manner, the Chinese Communist Party integrated class-analysis with their observations of the current international developments. On both layers of analysis—the international and domestic stage, respectively—it firmly established a genealogy of friends and foes along clear categories. Concerning the issue of the origins of national humiliation, this approach offered (on the surface, at least) a fair and reasonable interpretation. Furthermore, the second related issue of how China's national disgrace might be wiped out was also addressed by delineating a course of action completely in line with the above-mentioned analysis. We will turn to this issue in the following section.

III. Eliminating National Humiliation: National Revolution and Class Revolution

The *Record of Rites* (*Liji* 禮記) states:

If there is cause for shame due to [a certain] matter, this (only) suffices to stimulate them [i.e., the people]. If there is cause for shame due to [a matter concerning] the country, this suffices to rouse them.[77]

The rise and spread of a sense of national humiliation and the discourse of national humiliation are often the harbingers of modern nationalism. And when the shame of the nation and its sense of honour are sublimated into the determination to cleanse the disgrace, this becomes a powerful tool for mass mobilisation.

In the early years of the twentieth century, nationalist ideas such as cleansing humiliation and revitalising China began to take shape in the hearts and minds of the Chinese people. In 1902, the *Xinmin Congbao* 新民叢報 (New People's Gazette) edited by Liang Qichao once expressed it in this way:

Since ancient times, the saying goes: 'If there is cause for shame due to [a certain] matter, this (only) suffices to stimulate them. If there is cause for shame due to [a matter concerning] the country, this suffices to rouse them.' If [shame] can cause our countrymen to be, from now on, unified in their convictions, be they of high or low standing, and to make a determined effort to become strong, would [the incurrence of shame] not turn out to be like the case of the old frontiersman who lost his horse, that is, to turn out to be a blessing after all?[78]

---

77 *Liji*, 27.8: *Liji Zhengyi* (1936), p. 102. The passage in question (attributed to Confucius) actually discusses marriage ceremonies but has been translated here so as to reflect the early twentieth century re-interpretation of the paragraph. For a more traditional reading refer to Legge (1885), *Li Ki*, p. 266.

78 *Xinmin congbao* 1 (8 February 1902), p. 106.

In 1905, the *Eastern Miscellany* (*Dongfang zazhi* 東方雜誌) wrote:

After (the war of) 1894, wanting to wash away the humiliation of cessions and indemnities, everyone talked about self-strengthening. After [the Boxer Uprising in] 1900, wanting to relieve the pain of reparations and loss of sovereignty, everyone talked about independence.[79]

Going further into the twentieth century, following the founding of the CCP, the re-organisation of the KMT along the lines of the Communist Party of the Soviet Union, and the formation of the national revolution, the revolutionary elite gradually came to realise where the roots of national disgrace were located. Accordingly, they purported that launching a national revolution was the only practicable way to topple foreign imperialism and domestic warlordism and turn China into an independent, united, and strong modern nation. The logical chain from raising awareness about national humiliation, to commemorating national humiliation, and finally to eradicating said humiliation is commonly found in arguments used in both propaganda pieces as well as in commentaries in *The Guide Weekly*. Just as apparent is the publication's commitment to see these steps realised. In May 1924, an article written in commemoration of the "9th of May National Humiliation" pointed out that remembrance entails more than reminding people not to forget a certain disgrace, it means to "eventually think of [ways to] eliminate the humiliation". The specific date of 9 May

already goes beyond remembering the national humiliation of the fourth year of the Republican Era [*i.e.*, 1915] and constitutes a periodical call of rebuke by the Chinese national independence movement against the powers. At the same time, it marks a day on which to exhort our fellow countrymen to march onwards and upwards.[80]

The special issue on occasion of 7 September (*i.e.*, the date of the signing of the Boxer Protocol) the same year emphasised that "days of national humiliation" are "when the tide of anti-imperialist sentiments is the highest in the entire country". Our compatriots should "rise with force and vigour to wash away this great shame and humiliation".[81] Out of the small community of people that had used terms such as "sense of shame" to refer to themselves, a fully-fledged "society to cleanse humiliation" had emerged.

The Guide Weekly had previously made mention of groups and organisations such as "The eradication of the humiliation of the murder of our compatriots by the Japanese society" (*Riren cansha tongbao xuechi hui* 日人殘殺同胞雪恥會), "The eradication of the humiliation of the atrocities in Qingdao and Shanghai society of Hunan" (*Qing-Hu can'an Hunan xuechi hui* 青滬慘案湖南雪恥會), or "The eradication of the humiliation of the savage slaughter of our compatriots

---

79 "Zicun pian", p. 100.
80 Zhengchang (1923), "Women di chulu", p. 519.
81 Wei (1924), "Ruguo yangmin zhi xinchou heyue", p. 656.

by British warships in Wan County society" (*Wan xian Ying lun canbi tongbao xuechi hui* 萬縣英輪慘斃同胞雪恥會).[82]

Reportedly, "organisations such as support groups and societies for the eradication of humiliation sprang up in places all over China" after the May Thirtieth Incident had occurred.[83] Following the Wan County tragedy of 1926, *The Guide* published an open telegram to all regions with the expressed objective of "restraining their brutal ferocity, expanding our national sovereignty and the eradication of this matter of great shame and humiliation even at the cost of one's life".[84] Chen Duxiu, in a short piece on occasion of the anniversary of the May Thirtieth Incident, discussed the relationship between commemoration and mobilisation, and between national humiliation and the cleansing of humiliation very thoroughly and to the point:

We not only want to remember the butchery wrought by our enemies, we also want to remember our resistance. We not only want to remember our resistance, we also want to carry on our resistance. We not only want that there be remembrance for the 30th of May, we demand a May Thirtieth remembrance movement. If there is only remembrance but no movement—and let it be a remembrance of ten years, or a hundred years, or even a thousand years—our remembrance will always just be remembrance, and their slaughter, aggression, and coercion will remain slaughter, aggression, and coercion. This kind of farcical travesty of remembrance would do nothing more than to aggravate the anguish of those members of the May Thirtieth Movement who died that day and the disgrace of those who did not.[85]

This means, in conclusion, that one ought, through the efforts and struggle of one's fellow countrymen, turn national humiliation days into "memorial days in honour of the independence and liberty of the Chinese nation".[86] And this is, in fact, how it turned out. Every act of remembering national humiliation went beyond the commemoration of national humiliation itself and inevitably took the shape of a campaign to incite the masses to rise up and make a stand. Words and concepts such as "tragedy/massacre" (*can'an* 慘案) and "national humiliation" were always connected to activities such as "resistance" (*fankang* 反抗), "revolution" (*geming* 革命), "overthrow" (*dadao* 打倒), or "topple" (*tuifan* 推翻) and directed towards the final goals of cleansing humiliation and winning the independence of the nation.

The struggle to eradicate national humiliation may be regarded as the fundamental logic underlying the entire national revolution movement. Indeed, regarding this point, the interests and commitments of KMT and CCP appear

---

82 *The Guide* issues 116, p. 1068; 122, p. 1124; 173/174, p. 1776.

83 Chen Duxiu (1925f), "Women ruhe jixu fan-diguozhuyi de zhengdou", p. 1153.

84 "Ge fatuan dian" (1926), p. 1787.

85 Chen Duxiu (1926a), "Duiyu Shanghai Wu-Sa jinian yundong zhi ganxiang", p. 1504.

86 Longchi (1926), "Fei yue yundong yu Jiu-Qi jinian", p. 1726.

congruent. However, substantial differences nonetheless existed between the two parties as to how the success of the revolution could be guaranteed and the independence of the nation achieved. The KMT followed Sun Yat-sens ideas as expressed in his Three Principles of the People, namely, his interpretation of nation (*minzu* 民族), people's rights (*minquan* 民權), and people's livelihood (*minsheng* 民生). The word "people" in the context of the Three Principles refers to the whole body of citizens. With the sole exception of the Northern Warlords, who had to be crushed by the national revolution, people of every description belonged to the ranks of the citizenry. The Northern Warlords were counted among the enemies of the revolution mainly because they purportedly represented the interests of foreign imperialism in China.

By contrast, the national humiliation narrative of the CCP was unique in the sense that the communists had clearly stamped it with the brand of class analysis. The complementary pairs of "external enemies and internal enemies", "the humiliation of the nation and the humiliation of the class", "the overthrow of imperialism and the overthrow of the warlords" were integrated into a two-fold discursive framework constructed around the concepts of "nation" and "class". The Northern Warlords featured as internal enemies of the revolution not only because they were seen as accomplices of imperialism, but also because they represented the interests of the reactionary classes within China. The national revolution was therefore neither a national revolution solely dedicated to overthrowing imperialism, nor a national revolution solely dedicated to bringing down the warlords, but a class revolution of the lowest rung of workers and peasants against the landlord class and the *haut bourgeoisie*.

When *The Guide* celebrated its third anniversary, Chen Duxiu wrote an article looking back on the history of the young CCP, in which he observed that the watchword for many of the party's activities had changed from "democratic revolution" (*minzhu geming* 民主革命) to "national revolution" (*guomin geming*). He reasoned that the CCP had initially adopted the motto "democratic revolution" in continuation of the intellectual tradition of the 1911 Revolution and emphasised the need for a democratic revolution to topple the autocratic regime of the Northern Warlords. However, this motto was "inevitably and purely geared towards capitalism. The socio-economic conditions of a colony or a semi-colony make a revolution akin to the *bourgeois* revolution in eighteenth century Europe impossible". The text "On Nation-building" (*Zaoguo lun* 造國論) that had appeared in the second issue of *The Guide* had, accordingly, substituted it with the phrase "national revolution". Afterwards, this expression was, in turn, adapted by the KMT and thus "became a widespread pan-Chinese slogan".[87]

---

87 Chen Duxiu (1925a), "Benbao san nian lai geming zhengce zhi gaiguan", p. 1173.

THE GUIDE WEEKLY (1922–1927)

Be that as it may, the concept of a national revolution was most certainly not a CCP invention. By the beginning of the twentieth century, if not earlier, it had already begun to appear in the Chinese press. The *Compilation of the Citizen's Daily* (*Guomin riribao huibian* 國民日日報彙編) published in 1903, for instance, mentioned that "Russia's autocratic system is enough to provide the motive force behind its national revolution (*guomin geming*)".[88] And Wang Jingwei's 汪精衛 (1883–1944) inaugural statement to *The People's Virtue* (*Mindebao* 民德報), founded in Paris in 1913, reads:

> Therefore, those who speak of an ethno-national revolution (*minzu geming*) desire to make the [levels of] happiness of the [individual] ethnicities equal, as they are not equal. And those who speak of a national revolution (*guomin geming*) desire to make the [levels of] happiness of the [individual] social- and economic groups equal, as they are not equal.[89]

By 1916, at the latest, we find the idea of revolution further differentiated into "armed" (*wuli* 武力) and "peaceful" (*pinghe* 平和) revolution, revolution against outside forces as opposed to revolution against internal forces, as well as "dynastic revolution" (*chaodai geming* 朝代革命) in contrast to "national revolution".[90]

However, when the term "national revolution" had been used on these earlier occasions, it had always referred to the struggle of the people of a given country for economic rights and political equality, and had, in a sense, always been designated an "internal revolution". To combine the notion of national revolution with the efforts of small nations to win independence and liberation for themselves was, indeed, a conceptual novelty employed by both the KMT and the CCP. But the CCP subsequently developed it even further into a single comprehensive concept that encompassed ethno-national, democratic, and class revolution.

The introduction of the discourse of class into the narratives of national humiliation and nationalism by the CCP was clearly reflected at both international and domestic level. First, conflicts between different ethnic groups and different countries could now be regarded as manifestations of class struggle at international level. The origins of China's national humiliation in modern times were naturally to be found in the encroachments and oppression of the imperialist powers, but relations between the powers and small nations were by no means purely a matter of international relations. Rather, class relationships manifested themselves in the realm of international relations. In this global perspective, the powers appeared as capitalist countries, while the Soviet Russia and

---

88 *Guomin riribao huibian* 1 (7 August 1903), p. 3.

89 Wang Jingwei (1913), "Mindebao fakanci", p. 16.

90 Zhang Jiasen (1916), "Ying-Fa-Mei geming", p. 14.

China were proletarian countries. The humiliation of the nation was therefore equally a matter of the humiliation of the class and anti-imperialist struggle was at the same time class struggle. Because of this, the Chinese revolution was not only a revolution for the benefit of the liberation of the Chinese nation alone, but was of significance for a prospective world revolution. In the words of Trotskyist revolutionary Zheng Chaolin: "The Chinese proletariat will stand at the forefront of the world proletariat and will play a major part in digging the grave of imperialism."[91]

Second, within the domestic revolutionary movement, ethno-national struggle and class struggle were tightly and inseparably interwoven. Class struggle went beyond the struggle between the different social classes within a given country, and resistance against outside enemies had to be included as one of its issues. Warlord rule undoubtedly remained the immediate target of the national revolution, but its ultimate goal was to shake great-power oppression and attain national liberation. As Chen Duxiu points out:

National revolution (*guomin geming*) and national liberation (*minzu jiefang* 民族解放) are words nearly identical in meaning. To resist foreign imperialist oppression is, therefore, the central task of the national revolutionary movement.[92]

In the context of national revolution, "the anti-imperialist movement is our foremost measure and also our most fundamental one, everything else can merely help to alleviate symptoms".[93] However, at the same time, one must not neglect the enemy within in favour of ousting foreign influences. Qu Qiubai accordingly differentiated between "internal" and "external" forms of class struggle. The former meant the struggle of the commoner class in opposition of the Manchu nobility; the latter meant the struggle of the Chinese nation against imperialism. The reason why the Boxer Movement had failed was because its followers had been "deceived by a narrow sense of nationalism and statism (*guojiazhuyi* 國家主義)", had lacked a clear class-consciousness and thus had fallen prey to the Chinese noble class, who had co-opted them for its own aims.[94]

Under the CCP's theory of class analysis, different classes played different roles in the context of the anti-imperialist national revolution. Accordingly, proletariat, semi-proletariat, petty *bourgeoisie*, *bourgeoisie*, big landowners and *haute bourgeoisie* along with their deputies, the Northern Warlords were respectively assigned tags such as "leading anti-imperialist force" (*fankang diguozhuyi de lingdao liliang* 反抗帝國主義的領導力量), "traitors to the interests of the nation"

---

91 Zheng Chaolin (1925c), "Zhongguo fan-diguozhuyi yundong", p. 1180.
92 "Jia gemingdang yu fan-gemingdang", p. 594.
93 Wengong (1924), "Guomin geming yu fan-diguozhuyi yundong", p. 641.
94 Qu Qiubai (1925b), "Yihetuan yundong zhi yiyi", p. 1168.

(*minzu liyi de pantu* 民族利益的叛徒), or "faithful flunkies of imperialism" (*diguozhuyi de zhongshi zougou* 帝國主義的忠實走狗). Consequently, if one desired to realise the goals of national revolution and national liberation, one would also need to pursue the course of class revolution.

When *The Guide* was first published in September of 1922, co-operation and accommodation between the two parties was still progressing smoothly, clearly reflected in the fact that the CCP's evaluation of the KMT was exceedingly positive. An article entitled "What is the KMT?" (*Guomindang shi shenme* 國民黨 是什麼) thus confidently asserted:

The Chinese Nationalist Party is a revolutionary party which represents the national revolution [as a whole] and not a political party which represents any particular class because, in its party programme, it pursues the general interests of the nation and not the special interests of a particular class.[95]

The KMT membership was primarily made up of intellectuals (representing the *bourgeoisie*) and workers (*i.e.*, the proletariat), both of which were deemed to be supporting the forces of the national revolution. The author furthermore frankly stated:

The industry within China has, as of yet, not developed to a degree for the opposition between the classes to create a clear-cut, unbridgeable divide between them. For this reason, political parties representing only one class have naturally had no chance to develop.[96]

Chen Duxiu emphasised that the continued existence of warlord politics was only possible because "the power of the democratic revolution was still unfocussed", and appealed to all revolutionaries to "gather in the democratic-revolutionary Chinese Nationalist Party so that it might become a strong and powerful revolutionary party".[97] The "momentary social interests" of the individual classes had to be "subordinated to the more long-term interests of the nation".[98] Conversely, he issued a plea to the KMT to "lead the revolutionary *bourgeoisie*, rally the revolutionary proletariat, and bring about a *bourgeois* democratic revolution".[99]

Even though *The Guide* was occasionally critical towards the KMT, this was limited to remarks such as "[the KMT] is not close to the citizens", or that "[the KMT] has not in any way met its responsibility to muster the people's spirit in the slightest".[100] In June 1924, it still praised the KMT for its "struggle for the

---

95 Zhiyan (1922), "Guomindang shi shenme", p. 16.
96 Ibid.
97 Chen Duxiu (1923c), "Zenme dadao junfa", p. 152.
98 Chen Duxiu (1923a), "Guomindang yu Anfu jiaotong", p. 182.
99 Chen Duxiu (1923d), "Zichan jieji de geming yu geming de zichan jieji", p. 164.
100 Zhang Tailei (as Chunmu) (1923), p. 213.

nation, and the rights and livelihood of the people", and called it "the only enemy" of the imperialist powers and the Northern Warlords that they "will absolutely be unable to appease".[101]

However, beginning in early 1925, and especially after Sun Yat-sen's death in March of that year, the relationship between KMT and CCP became more and more strained. The CCP leadership started to discuss publicly the inevitability of class struggle in the course of the national revolution. The hitherto rather positive image of the KMT in *The Guide* was likewise increasingly reversed, and, in the end, the party was included in the ranks of "the enemies of the revolution".

In the summer and autumn of 1925, a public verbal altercation erupted between senior KMT statesman Dai Jitao 戴季陶 (1891–1949) and CCP leader Chen Duxiu. In a booklet entitled *The National Revolution and the Chinese Nationalist Party* (*Guomin geming yu Zhongguo guomindang* 中國革命與中國國民黨), Dai Jitao, in discussing the issues of the leadership and direction of the national revolution, launched a fierce assault against Chen Duxiu's notion of class struggle. In response, Chen Duxiu published an open letter in *The Guide* that was phrased no less harshly. In this letter, Chen claimed that the fundamental error of Dai and his "faction to eliminate communism" (*paichu gongchan pai* 排除共產派) was that they "only see the demands of the national struggle and do not see the demands of the class struggle". This mistaken idea, he argued, not only obliterated the interests of the classes, but also caused the national struggle to suffer immense losses. In his rebuttal, Chen used the Canton Merchants' Corps Uprising (1924), the May Thirtieth Movement, and the Shakee Massacre (1925) as examples to demonstrate that the mass of peasants and workers was a supporting force of the national revolution, whereas big businessmen and big landowners had to be seen as destructive. "These facts already clearly tell us: There is, indeed, a need for class struggle within the national struggle." This need was, following Chen, due to the fact that it was foreign capitalist imperialism that maintained control of the economic lifeline of colonies and semi-colonies. Given such conditions, there is objectively little chance for a national capitalist class to develop, and there is even less likelihood that European-American type *bourgeois* revolution would occur. The national revolution therefore had to rely on the strength of the peasant and proletarian masses, and the strength of the peasant and proletarian masses, in turn, had to grow out of their immediate interests and by their engagement in class organisation and class struggle. Consequently, to advocate the suspension of class struggle in colonial or semi-colonial conditions constituted a sure way both to undermine and to destroy the national struggle.[102] The letter provides a clear and thorough discussion of the

---

101 "'Liu-San' jinian" (1924), p. 541.
102 Chen Duxiu (1925c), "Gei Dai Jitao de yi feng xin".

relationship between (as Mao Zedong calls them) antagonistic (*neibu maodun* 內部矛盾) and non-antagonistic contradictions (*waibu maodun* 外部矛盾), and national struggle and class struggle respectively. It marked, to a large extent, a turning-point for the CCP in the sense that the focus of the work of the party shifted from national revolution to class revolution.

The year 1926 witnessed the gradual deterioration in the relationship between the two major parties. The Canton *Coup*, or *Zhongshan* Incident (*Zhongshan jian shijian* 中山艦事件), was soon followed by a KMT resolution that severely restricted communist activity in its ranks. The KMT's right wing grew increasingly suspicious of the CCP and re-doubled its efforts to push the rival aside. On the one hand, *The Guide* spoke in defence of the ideas of the CCP, while, on the other, it condemned the KMT for ousting its communist members. The article entitled, "Conference of the KMT-Rightists" (*Guomindang youpai dahui* 國民黨右派大會), written by Chen Duxiu, for instance, not only denounced the anti-communists moves of the KMT in the wake of the *Zhongshan* Incident, but also criticised the Kuomintang at an ideological level, arguing that the party's right wing had deviated from the original intentions of Sun Yatsen regarding his key concepts of Nationalism, People's Rights, and the People's Livelihood.[103] With the April 12 Incident (also known as the Shanghai Massacre) in 1927, collaboration between KMT and CCP broke down completely and the image of the KMT in the party organ underwent a total reversal.

The KMT's right wing—representative of feudal warlordism and the feudal *bourgeoisie*—proved itself utterly unable to permanently cooperate with the revolutionary proletariat and its political party (the Communist Party).[104]

The "revolutionary party that had represented the national movement" of former days had thus officially degenerated into yet another stooge of imperialism and feudal warlordism, an enemy of the proletariat and the toiling masses, and was, therefore, a target that the Chinese revolution would need to destroy.

IV. Conclusion: National Humiliation and Awakening

The defeat against Japan in 1895 marked a major turning-point in the course of modern Chinese political and intellectual history. The continual, violent provocations in the shape of military defeats and unequal treaties remoulded, to a significant degree, the historical consciousness and world view of China's intellectuals, and pushed the country towards an era of political and intellectual

---

103 Chen Duxiu(1926b), "Guomindang youpai dahui".
104 Chen Duxiu (1927), "Zhongguo Guomindang de weixian jiqi chulu", p. 2198.

transformation.[105] It was precisely during this period of rapid change and upheaval that the continuous imaginative and constructive efforts of various modern Chinese intellectuals gradually helped to give form to the "imagined community" that is the Chinese nation-state.

On the one hand, relying on metaphors and images of "body" and "treatment of disease" and contrasting narratives such as "strength and weakness" or "asleep and awakened", modern intellectuals, in their efforts to instil a sense of crisis in the Chinese people, constructed the image of a "sickly China" (*bingti Zhongguo* 病體中國) that was embroiled in a strenuous struggle in a cruel and ruthless environment ruled by the "Law of the Jungle" (*ruorou qiangshi* 弱肉強食).[106] On the other hand, these same intellectuals conducted a thorough revision of the traditional works on Chinese history and established a nationalised "New Historiography" centred around origin myths (such as the Yellow Emperor) and genealogies of heroes (such as the heroic Song dynasty general Yue Fei 岳飛) in order to arouse feelings of national identity in their compatriots.[107] This drastic contrast created by the juxtaposition of a brilliant, glorious past and a present ostensibly characterised by the sickness and frailty of the Chinese nation forms the basis of the narrative of "national humiliation" in modern China.

The thirty years between the Treaty of Shimonoseki and the Boxer Protocol, and the Twenty-One Demands and the May 30th Massacre, respectively, saw multiple occurrences which were subsequently interpreted as having contributed to China's national humiliation. At the same time, the sense of national humiliation of the Chinese people grew in depth as well as the extent to which it provided an inexhaustible motive force for the efforts of mass mobilisation of the intellectual elite and the revolutionary political parties. In the 1920s, the newly-founded CCP and the re-organised KMT became the two main actors on the Chinese political stage. In a sense, the elites of both parties can be seen as nationalists endowed with a pronounced sense of "national humiliation" and who were motivated by incidents of national humiliation, which drew on the narrative of national humiliation as a rhetorical tool, and pronounced the cleansing of national humiliation to be a goal that merited diligent attention.

To link the narrative of national humiliation to the national revolutionary movement is a political strategy reminiscent of Lenin and features the watchwords "representation" and "awakening". KMT and CCP were, of course, long-term political opponents, but, in a certain respect, they may also be seen as "two melons growing on the same vine" (*yi gen teng shang jie de liang ge gua* 一根籐上的兩個瓜). They were both the product of modern Chinese society and showed a

---

105 See Chang (1971), *Liang Ch'i-ch'ao*.
106 See Yan Jianfu (2013), "'Bingti Zhongguo'".
107 Shen Songqiao (2000), "Zhen Dahan zhi tiansheng".

THE GUIDE WEEKLY (1922–1927)

high degree of similarity in styles of organization.[108] Both parties revered Leninist principles of party-building and were both ideologically guided by a specific "-ism". In addition, and no less importantly, whether we consider Sun Yat-sen's three-fold differentiation of the Chinese populace into "those who are quicker to realise" (*xianzhixianjue* 先知先覺), "those who are slower to realise" (*houzhi houjue* 後知後覺), and "those who remain ignorant" (*buzhi bu jue* 不知不覺)[109], or the discourse of the CCP on the relationship between the vanguard and the masses,[110] it is evident that both parties embody comparable political ideas, namely, that the elite should represent and awaken the masses. Due to the unceasing and persevering "awakening" and "mobilisation" endeavours of the revolutionary elite, the sense of national humiliation and the commemoration of national humiliation, step by little step, turned into a national revolution with the explicit purpose of cleansing national humiliation.

But this is only one part of the story. Both KMT and CCP set themselves the task of representing and awakening the masses. However, they strongly differed regarding the political ideologies underlying these aims. The KMT insisted that it would be able to represent the entire nation. The "people" in the Three Principles of the People—Nationalism, People's Rights, and the People's Livelihood—always referred to the whole body of citizens, and not merely a particular class thereof. In this sense, one is certainly justified in calling this party a "Nationalist Party" (*minzudang* 民族黨).

The "representative politics" (*daibiao zhengzhi* 代表政治) of the CCP, in contrast, were based upon the Marxist theory of class analysis. It claimed to be the one true representative of the interests of the proletarian class and furthermore argued to have obtained the right to "awaken" the other underprivileged classes by merit of having been part of the "united front". Within the CCP's framework of social classes, the KMT had forfeited all rights to calling itself a representative of the whole nation and was instead defined as the fickle and compliant representative of the *bourgeoisie*. When conditions were right, it would degenerate into an enemy of the people and an enemy of the revolution along with the class which it represented. In this way, the CCP introduced the theory of class struggle into the nationalist ideology with the result that the two had merged into one in the context of the national revolution of the 1920s.

Social anthropologist and philosopher Ernest Gellner (1925–1995) once derisively summarised the Marxist theory of nationalism in the following way: "The awakening message was intended for classes, but by some terrible postal error was delivered to nations."[111] John Fitzgerald, in a similar vein, pointed out

---

108 Zhang Kaiyuan, "Xu", p. 3.
109 Sun Zhongshan (1981 [1924]), "Jianguo fanglüe", p. 161.
110 See Li Lifeng (2013), "'Qunzhong' de miankong".
111 Gellner (1983), *Nations and Nationalism*, pp. 124, 129.

that, in the Chinese case, the mailman must have delivered the awakening message for the classes and the awakening message for the nation to the same address.[112] In so doing, the CCP undoubtedly contributed a new chapter to the tidal wave of nationalism that had swept the globe ever since the nineteenth century.

(Translated by Sebastian Riebold)

Bibliography

Anderson, Benedict (1991), *Imagined Communities: Reflections on the Origin and Spread of Nationalism*, London: Verso Books.

"Benbao xuanyan" 本報宣言 (This Publication's Manifesto) (1922), *Xiangdao* 1.

Cai Hesen 蔡和森 (1922), "Zhongguo guoji diwei yu chengren suwei'an Eluosi" 中國國際地位與承認蘇維埃俄羅斯 (China's International Status and the Recognition of Soviet Russia), *Xiangdao*, 3, pp. 17–18.

— (1923a), "Deguo de fenli yundong" 德國的分立運動 (Germany's Partition Movement), *Xiangdao*, 44, p. 339–340.

— (1923b), "Guomindang ying haozhao guomin fandui guomin de qinlüe" 國民黨應號召國民反對國民的侵略 (The KMT should Appeal to the People to Oppose Aggression by the People), *Xiangdao*, 39, p. 293.

— (1923c), "Peichang wenti yu diguozhuyi" 賠償問題與帝國主義 (The Question of Reparations and Imperialism), *Xiangdao*, 18, pp. 144–145.

— (1923d), "Zhong-De-E san guo lianmeng yu guoji diguozhuyi ji Chen Jiongming zhi fandong" 中德俄三國聯盟與國際帝國主義及陳炯明之反動 (The Three-nation Alliance between China, Germany, and Russia, International Imperialism, and Chen Jiongming's Counter-movement), *Xiangdao*, 4, pp. 25–26.

— (1924), "Yihetuan yu guomin geming" 義和團與國民革命 (The Boxers and the National Revolution), *Xiangdao*, 81, 652–654.

— (1925), "Wu-Qi jinian Beijing xuesheng fendou de yiyi" 五七紀念北京學生奮鬥的意義 (The Meaning of the Struggle of Beijing's Students during the Commemoration of 7 May), *Xiangdao*, 115, pp. 1059–1160.

Chang, Hao (1971), *Liang Ch'i-ch'ao and Intellectual Transition in China, 1890–1907*, Cambridge: Harvard University Press.

Chen Duxiu 陳獨秀 (1923a), "Guomindang yu Anfu jiaotong" 國民黨與安福交通 (The KMT's Connections to the Anfu Club), *Xiangdao*, 25, p. 182.

— (1923b), "Hua-Yangren xueroujiazhi de guijian" 華洋人血肉價值的貴賤 (The Relative Worth of Chinese and Foreign Lives), *Xiangdao*, 25, p. 182.

— (1923c), "Zenme dadao junfa" 怎麼打倒軍閥 (How to Overthrow the Warlords), *Xiangdao*, 21, p. 152.

---

112 Fitzgerald (1996), *Awakening China*, pp. 315–348.

- (1923d), "Zichan jieji de geming yu geming de zichan jieji" 資產階級的革命與革命的資產階級 (The Revolution of the Bourgoisie and the Revolutionary Bourgeoisie), *Xiangdao*, 22, pp. 162–164.
- (1924a), "Junfa shi diguozhuyizhe de gongju you yi zhengju" 軍閥是帝國主義者的工具又一證據 (Another Piece of Evidence that the Warlords are Imperialist Tools), *Xiangdao*, 67, p. 538.
- (1924b), "Women duiyu Yihetuan liang ge cuowu de guannian" 我們對於義和團兩個錯誤的觀念 (Our Two Misconceptions Concerning the Boxers), *Xiangdao*, 81, pp. 645–646.
- (1925a), "Benbao san nian lai geming zhengce zhi gaiguan" 本報三年來革命政策之概觀 (This Publication's Survey on the Revolutionary Measures of the Last Three Years), *Xiangdao*, 128, p. 1173.
- (1925b), "Cici yundong zhong zhi diguozhuyi yu junfa" 此次運動中之帝國主義與軍閥 (Imperialism and Warlords in this Movement), *Xiangdao*, 124, pp. 1135–1136.
- (1925c), "Gei Dai Jitao de yi feng xin" 給戴季陶的一封信 (A Letter to Dai Jitao), *Xiangdao*, 129, pp. 1186–1190.
- (1925d), "Shanghai datusha yu Zhongguo minzu ziyou yundong" 上海大屠殺與中國民族自由運動 (The Shanghai Massacre and the Chinese National Liberty Movement), *Xiangdao*, 117, p. 1077.
- (1925e), "Shiyue Geming yu dongfang" 十月革命與東方 (The October Revolution and the East), *Xiangdao*, 178, p. 1849.
- (1925e), "Women ruhe jixu fan-diguozhuyi de zhengdou" 我們如何繼續反帝國主義的爭鬥 (How do we Continue the Anti-imperialist Struggle?), *Xiangdao*, 126, p. 1153.
- (1925f), "Women ruhe yingfu cici yundong de xin jumian" 我們如何應付此次運動的新局面 (How do we Deal with the New Dimension of this Movement?), *Xiangdao*, 120, pp. 1104–1105.
- (1926a), "Duiyu Shanghai Wu-Sa jinian yundong zhi ganxiang" 對於上海五卅紀念運動之感想 (Thoughts on the May Thirtieth Commemoration Movement in Shanghai), *Xiangdao*, 156, p. 1504.
- (1926b), "Guomindang youpai dahui" 國民黨右派大會 (Conference of the KMT's Rightists), *Xiangdao*, 150, pp. 5–8.
- (1927), "Zhongguo Guomindang de weixian jiqi chulu" 中國國民黨的危險及其出路 (The Danger of the KMT and how to Escape it), *Xiangdao*, 200, p. 2198.

"Chen Duxiu zai Zhongguo Gongchandang di san ci quanguo daibiao dahui shang de baogao" 陳獨秀在中國共產黨第三次全國代表大會上的報告 (Chen Duxiu's Report at the Third National Congress of the CCP) (1989 [1923]), in: Zhongyang dang'anguan 中央檔案館 (ed.), *Zhong-Gong Zhongyang wenjian xuanji* 中共中央文件選集 (Selected Documents of the Central Committee of the CCP), Beijing: Zhong-Gong Zhongyang dangxiao chubanshe, vol. 1, p. 169.

Deng Rong 鄧榕 (1898), "Ming guochi yi ji gongfen yi" 明國恥以激公憤議 (Highlighting National Humiliation to Foment Public Indignation), *Shuxuebao*, 12, pp. 1a–3b.

Dengdebu 登德布 (1922), "Menggu jiqi jiefang yundong" 蒙古及其解放運動 (Mongolia and its Liberation Movement), *Xiangdao*, 5, pp. 43–44.

"Faguo di zhengzhi jingji zhuangkuang" 法國底政治經濟狀況 (The Political and Economic Condition of France) (1924), *Xiangdao*, 65, pp. 523–524.

Fitzgerald, John (1998), *Awakening China: Politics, Culture, and Class in the Nationalist Revolution*, Stanford CA: Stanford University Press.

Gao Junyu 高君宇 (1922), "Tu'erqi guominjun shengli de guoji jiazhi" 土耳其國民軍勝利的國際價值 (The International Value of the Victory of the Turkish Militia), *Xiangdao*, 3, pp. 22–23.

"Ge fatuan dian" 各法團電 (Telegram to all Corporations) (1926), *Xiangdao*, 173/174, p. 1787.

Gellner, Ernest (1983), *Nations and Nationalism*, Ithaca NY: Cornell University Press.

Giddens, Anthony (1991), *Modernity and Self-Identity: Self and Society in the Late Modern Age*, Stanford CA: Stanford University Press.

Gongmin jiuguo tuan 公民救國團 (ed.) (1919), *Guochi tongshi* 國恥痛史 (The Painful History of National Humiliation), Shanghai: Gongmin jiuguo tuan.

"Guanyu 'Shijie dashi yu Zhongguo Gongchandang' de yijue'an" 關於 "世界大勢與中國共產黨" 的議決案 (Concerning the Resolution on "The Global Situation and the CCP") (1989 [1922]), in: Zhongyang dang'anguan 中央檔案館 (ed.), *Zhong-Gong Zhongyang wenjian xuanji* 中共中央文件選集 (Selected Documents of the Central Committee of the CCP), Beijing: Zhong-Gong Zhongyang dangxiao chubanshe, vol. 1, pp. 59–60.

"Guochi jinianri xigao quanguo tongbao" 國恥紀念日檄告全國同胞 (An Urgent Call to All Compatriots on Occasion of National Humiliation Day) (1924), *Xiangdao* 64, p. 509–510.

Guomin riribao huibian 國民日日報彙編 (Compilation of the Citizen's Daily), 1 (7 August 1903), p. 3.

"Guomin yundong jinxing jihua jueyi'an" 國民運動進行計劃決議案 (Resolution on the Plan of Advancing the National Movement) (1989 [1923]), in: Zhongyang dang'anguan中央檔案館 (ed.), *Zhong-Gong Zhongyang wenjian xuanji*中共中央文件選集 (Selected Documents of the Central Committee of the CCP), Beijing: Zhong-Gong Zhongyang dangxiao chubanshe, vol. 1, p. 200.

Henan sheng zhengfu (ed.) 河南省政府 (ed.) (1922), *Zhonghua guochi ditu* 中華國恥地圖 (Atlas of China's National Humiliation).

Hobsbawm, Eric (1983), "Introduction: Inventing Traditions", in: Eric Hobsbawm, Terence Ranger (eds.), *The Invention of Tradition*, Cambridge: Cambridge University Press, pp. 1–14.

"Jia gemingdang yu fan-gemingdang" 假革命黨與反革命黨 (Fake Revolutionary Parties and Anti-revolutionary Parties) (1924), *Xiangdao*, 74, p. 594–595

Jizhe 記者 (1926), "Canwurendao zhi Yingguo diguozhuyi tusha Wan xian"慘無人道之英國帝國主義屠殺萬縣 (The Abominable Slaughter Committed by the British Imperialists in Wan County), *Xiangdao*, 173/174, p. 1774.

Legge, James (1885), *The Li Ki, XI–VLVI* (Sacred Books of the East, volume 28), Oxford: Clarendon Press.

Liji zhengyi 禮記正義 (The Correct Meaning of the Record of Rites) (1936), Shanghai: Zhonghua shuju, vol. 17.

Li Lifeng 李里峰 (2013), "'Qunzhong' de miankong—jiyu jindai Zhongguo qingjing de gainianshi kaocha" "群眾" 的面孔 - 基於近代中國情境的概念史考察 (The Face of the "Masses"—A Conceptual and Historical Investigation of Modern China), in: Wang Qisheng 王奇生 (ed.), *Ershi shiji Zhongguo geming de zai chanshi* 二十世紀中國革

命的再闡釋 (A New Interpretation of the Twentieth Century Chinese Revolutions), Beijing: Zhonghua shuju, pp. 31–57.

Liang Qichao 梁啟超 (1897), "Zhichi xuehui xu" 知恥學會敍 (Preface to the [Mission Statement] of the Sense-of-Shame Study Association), *Shiwubao*, 40, pp. 3–4.

Liu Renjing 劉仁靜 (1924), "Faguo zhi xin zhengju yu dui Hua waijiao" 法國之新政局與對華外交 (The New Political Situation in France and its China Policy), *Xiangdao*, 69, pp. 550–551.

"'Liu-San' jinian yu zuijin junfa lieqiang zhi lianhe jingong" "六三" 紀念與最近軍閥列強之聯合進攻 (The Commemoration of 3 June and the Recent Joint Attack of the Warlords and the Powers) (1924), *Xiangdao*, 68, p. 541.

Longchi 龍池 (1926), "Fei yue yundong yu Jiu-Qi jinian" 廢約運動與九七紀念 (The Movement to Break the Treaty [of 1901] and the Commemoration of 7 September), *Xiangdao*, 170, p. 1726.

Ma Fulong 馬福龍 (2012), "Xiangdao: Hei'an de Zhongguo shehui de yi zhan mingdeng" 《向導》: 黑暗的中國社會的一盞明燈 (*The Guide* - A Beacon in a Dark Age of Chinese society), *Shanghai dangshi yu dangjian*, pp. 36–37.

Mao Zedong 毛澤東 (1915), "Ming chi pian tizhi" 《明恥篇》題志 (On understanding shame), in: Idem, *Mao Zedong zaoqi wengao* 毛澤東早期文稿 (Early Writings of Mao Zedong), Changsha: Hunan renmin chubanshe (1990), p. 11.

– (1926), "Zhongguo shehui ge jieji de fenxi" 中國社會各階級的分析 (Analysis of the Classes in Chinese Society), *Zhongguo nongmin*, 2, pp. 12–13.

– (1965 [1926]), "Analysis of the Classes in Chinese Society", in: Idem, *Selected Works of Mao Tse-tung*, Oxford: Pergamon Press (1965), vol. 1, pp. 13–21.

Peng Nansheng 彭南生 (2010), "Quru de jiyi: Yi 'Nian Yi Tiao' guochi jinian wei taolun zhongxin" 屈辱的記憶：以 "廿一條" 國恥紀念為討論中心 (Remembering Humiliation: An Inquiry centred on the 21 Demands), *Jiangsu shehui kexue*, 5, pp. 208–215.

Peng Shuzhi 彭述之 (1924), "Diguozhuyi yu Yihetuan yundong" 帝國主義與義和團運動 (Imperialism and the Boxer Movement), *Xiangdao*, 81, pp. 646–652.

Qu Qiubai 瞿秋白 (1925a), "Wu-Sa hou fan-diguozhuyi lianhe zhanxian de qiantu" 五卅後反帝國主義聯合戰綫的前途 (The Prospects of the Anti-imperialist United Front in the Wake of 30 May), *Xiangdao*, 125, pp. 1146–1147.

Qu Qiubai 瞿秋白 (1925b), "Yihetuan yundong zhi yiyi yu Wu-Sa yundong zhi qiantu" 義和團運動之意義與五卅運動之前途 (The significance of the Boxer Movement and the Prospects of the May Thirtieth Movement), *Xiangdao*, 128, pp. 1167–1172.

– (1926), "Zhongguo zhi geming de Wuyue yu Makesizhuyi" 中國之革命的五月與馬克思主義 (The Month of May in the Chinese Revolution and Marxism), *Xiangdao*, 151, pp. 1426–1428.

– (1927), "Wu-Sa er zhou jinian yu guomin geming lianhe zhanxian" 五卅二周紀念與國民革命聯合戰綫 (The Two-year Anniversary of the May Thirtieth Incident and the Nation Revolution's United Front), *Xiangdao*, 196, pp. 2135–2139.

Shehui kexue cidian 社會科學辭典 (Lexicon of the Social Sciences) (1929), Shijie chuban shuju.

Shen Songqiao 沈松僑 (Sung-chiao Shen) (1997), "Wo yi wo xue jian Xuanyuan—Huangdi shenhua yu wan Qing de guozu jiangou" 我以我血薦軒轅 - 黃帝神話與晚清的國族建構 (I Present my Blood to Xuanyuan—The Myth of the Yellow Emperor and the Construction of Chinese Nationhood in the Late Qing), *Taiwan shehui yanjiu jikan*, 28, pp. 1–77.

— (2000), "Zhen Dahan zhi tiansheng—Minzu yingxiong puxi yu wan Qing de guozu xiangxiang" 振大漢之天聲 - 民族英雄譜系與晚清的國族想象 (A Cry to Awaken the Great Han—Genealogies of National Heroes in the National Imagination of the Late Qing), *Zhongyang yanjiuyuan jindaishi yanjiusuo jikan*, 33, pp. 77–158.

Shen Wenjun 沈文濬 (1925), *Zengding guochi xiaoshi* 增訂國恥小史 (A Short History of National Humiliation - Expanded and Revised), Shanghai: Zhongguo tushu gongsi.

Shoufu 壽富 (1897), "Zhichi xuehui houxu" 知恥學會後敘 (Postface to the [Mission Statement] of the Sense-of-Shame Study Association), *Shiwubao*, 40, 3–4.

Shuanglin 雙林 (1925), "Wu-Qi guochi yu Riben diguozhuyi" 五七國恥與日本帝國主義 (The National Humiliation of 7 May and Japanese Imperialism), *Xiangdao*, 114, pp. 1051–52.

Sun Xinyuan 孫鑫源 (1915), *Guochi jian* 國恥鑒 (Mirror of National Humiliation), Shanghai: Wenming shuju.

Sun Zhongshan 孫中山 (Sun Yat-sen) (1981 [1924]), "Jianguo fanglüe" 建國方略 (The Fundamentals of National Reconstruction), in: Idem, *Sun Zhongshan xuanji* 孫中山選集 (Selected Works of Sun Yat-sen), Beijing: Renmin chubanshe, p. 161.

Wagner, Rudolf G. (2011), "China 'Asleep' and 'Awakening.' A Study in Conceptualizing Asymmetry and Coping with it", *Transcultural Studies*, 2011:1, pp. 4–139.

Wang Jingwei 汪精衛 (1913), "Mindebao fakanci" 民德報發刊詞 (Inaugural Statement of The People's Virtue), *Dongfang zazhi*, 9: 11, p. 16.

Wang Qisheng 王奇生 (2006), *Guo-Gong hezuo yu guomin geming (1924–1927)* 國共合作與國民革命 （1924－1927） (Nationalist-Communist Co-operation and the National Revolution (1924-1927)), Jiangsu: Jiangsu renmin chubanshe.

Wei 慰 (1924), "Ruguo yangmin zhi xinchou heyue" 辱國殃民之辛丑和約 (The Disgraceful and Disastrous 1901 Peace Treaty), *Xiangdao*, 81, p. 656.

Wengong 文恭 (1924), "Guomin geming yu fan-diguozhuyi yundong" 國民革命與反帝國主義運動 (The National Revolution and the Anti-imperialist Struggle), *Xiangdao*, 80, p. 641.

"Wu-Sa zhounian jinian gao quanguo minzhong" 五卅周年紀念告全國民眾 (Informing the Nation's Masses of the Anniversary of 30 May) (1926), *Xiangdao*, 155, pp. 1488-1489.

Xincheng 心誠 (1925), "Minzu jiefang yundong de xin shiqi" 民族解放運動的新時期 (A New Period in the National Liberation Movement), *Xiangdao*, 127, p. 1172.

Xinmin congbao 新民叢報 1 (8 February 1902), p. 106.

Yan Jianfu 顏健富 (Guan Kean-fung) (2013), "'Bingti Zhongguo' de shiju yinyu yu zhiliao cuilian"—lun wan Qing xiaoshuo de shenti/guoti xiangxiang "病體中國" 的時局隱喻與治療淬煉——論晚清小說的身體/國體想像 ("Sickly China" as Metaphor and Remedy—Images of the Body and the National Body in Late Qing Fiction), *Tai Da wen-shi-zhexue bao*, 79, 83–118.

Yang Ruisong 楊瑞松 (Jui-sung Yang) (2012), "Jindai Zhongguo de 'Si wanwan' guozu lunshu xiangxiang" 近代中國的 "四萬萬" 國族論述想象 (The "Four Hundred Million" in the Discourse on the Nation in Modern China), *Dongya guannianshi jikan*, 2 (2012), pp. 283–336.

Yongzhao 永釗 (1923), "Yi jiu er er Yindu guomin yundong de fenxi" 一九二二印度國民運動的分析 (An Analysis of the 1922 National Movement in India), *Xiangdao*, 19, pp. 153–156.

Zhang Guotao 張國燾 (1923), "Zhongguo yi tuoli le guoji qinlüe de weixian me?" 中國已脫離了國際侵略的危險麼？(Has China Already Escaped the Dangers of International Aggression?), *Xiangdao*, 6, p. 48.

Zhang Jiasen 張嘉森 (1916), "Ying-Fa-Mei geming hou jianguo shiye zhi bijiao" 英法美革命後建國事業之比較 (A Comparison of Nation-building Efforts after the English, French, and American Revolutions Respectively), *Dongfang zazhi*, 13:11, p. 14.

Zhang Kaiyuan 章開沅 (2003), "Xu" 序 (Preface), in: Wang Qisheng 王奇生, *Dangyuan, dangquan yu dangzheng—1929–1949 nian Zhongguo guomindang de zuzhi xingtai* 黨員、黨權與黨爭 - 1924~1949 年中國國民黨的組織形態 (Party Members, Party Power, and Party Struggle—The Organisational Make-up of the KMT 1924-1949), Shanghai: Shanghai shudian chubanshe, p. 3.

Zhang Tailei 張太雷 (as Chunmu 春木) (1923), "Xiu jian guomin de Zhongguo Guomindang" 羞見國民的中國國民黨 (The KMT is Embarrassed to see the People), *Xiangdao* 29, p. 213.

Zhang Tailei 張太雷 (1924), "Liening yu Yihetuan" 列寧與義和團 (Lenin and the Boxers), *Xiangdao*, 81, pp. 654–655.

Zhao Shiyan 趙世炎 (as Luojing 羅敬) (1925), "Beijing Wu–Qi nuchao de jingguo" 北京五七怒潮的經過 (The Tide of Outrage in Beijing on 7 May), *Xiangdao*, 116, pp. 1071–1072.

Zheng Chaolin 鄭超麟 (1925a), "Diguozhuyi tusha Shanghai shimin zhi jingguo" 帝國主義屠殺上海市民之經過 (Imperialists Slaughter Shanghai Citizens), *Xiangdao*, 117, pp. 1082–1084.

– (1925b), "Shanghai Riben zibenjia qiangsha Zhongguo gongren" 上海日本資本家槍殺中國工人 (Chinese Worker Shot Dead by Japanese Capitalists in Shanghai), *Xiangdao*, 115, p. 1060.

– (1925c), "Zhongguo fan-diguozhuyi yundong zai shijie geming shang de yiyi" 中國反帝國主義運動在世界革命上的意義 (The Significance of the Chinese Anti-imperialist Movement in the World Revolution), *Xiangdao*, 128, p. 1180.

Zhengchang 正厰 (1923), "Women di chulu" 我們底出路 (Our Way Out), *Xiangdao*, 65, p. 519.

Zhichi she 知恥社 (ed.) (1915), *Guochi* 國恥 (National Humiliation), Shanghai: Zhichi she.

Zhiyan 隻眼 (1922), "Guomindang shi shenme" 國民黨是什麼 (What is the KMT?), *Xiangdao*, 2, p. 16.

"Zhongguo Gongchandang di er ci quanguo daibiao dahui xuanyan" 中國共產黨第二次全國代表大會宣言 (Declaration of the First National Congress of the CCP) (1989 [1922]), in: Zhongyang dang'anguan 中央檔案館 (ed.), *Zhong-Gong Zhongyang wenjian xuanji* 中共中央文件選集 (Selected Documents of the Central Committee of the CCP), Beijing: Zhong-Gong Zhongyang dangxiao chubanshe, vol. 1, p. 115.

"Zhongguo Gongchandang di yi ge gangling" 中國共產黨第一個綱領 (The First Programme of the CCP) (1989 [1921]), in: Zhongyang dang'anguan 中央檔案館 (ed.), *Zhong-Gong Zhongyang wenjian xuanji* 中共中央文件選集 (Selected Documents of the

Central Committee of the CCP), Beijing: Zhong-Gong Zhongyang dangxiao chubanshe, vol. 1, p. 3.

"Zhongguo Gongchandang guanyu shiju de zhuzhang" 中國共產黨關於時局的主張 (Positions of the CCP Regarding the Current Political Situation) (1989 [1922]), in: Zhongyang dang'anguan中央檔案館 (ed.), *Zhong-Gong Zhongyang wenjian xuanji* 中共中央文件選集 (Selected Documents of the Central Committee of the CCP), Beijing: Zhong-Gong Zhongyang dangxiao chubanshe, vol. 1, pp. 33–46.

"Zhongguo Gongchandang wei fankang diguozhuyi yeman canbao de datusha gao quanguo minzhong shu" 中國共產黨為反抗帝國主義野蠻殘暴的大屠殺告全國民眾書 (A Letter of the CCP Instructing the Nation's Masses to Oppose the Brutal Slaughter of the Imperialists) (1925), *Xiangdao*, 117, p. 1075.

"Zhongguo Gongchandang wei Yingguo diguozhuyi tusha Wan xian gao minzhong shu" 中國共產黨為英國帝國主義屠殺萬縣告民眾書 (A Letter of the CCP Informing the Nation's Masses of the Slaughter Committed by the British Imperialists in Wan County) (1926), *Xiangdao*,173/174, p. 1771.

"Zhongyang tonggao di sanshi'er hao" 中央通告第三十二號 (32nd Announcement of the Central Committee) (1989 [1925]), in: Zhongyang dang'anguan 中央檔案館 (ed.), *Zhong-Gong Zhongyang wenjian xuanji* 中共中央文件選集 (Selected Documents of the Central Committee of the CCP), Beijing: Zhong-Gong Zhongyang dangxiao chubanshe, vol. 1, pp. 415–416.

"Zhongyang tonggao di sanshi'san hao" 中央通告第三十三號 (33nd Announcement of the Central Committee) (1989 [1925]), in: Zhongyang dang'anguan 中央檔案館 (ed.), *Zhong-Gong Zhongyang wenjian xuanji* 中共中央文件選集 (Selected Documents of the Central Committee of the CCP), Beijing: Zhong-Gong Zhongyang dangxiao chubanshe, vol. 1, pp. 417–418.

"Zicun pian" 自存篇 (On Self-preservation) (1905), *Dongfang zazhi*, 2:5, p. 100.

The Boundaries of the Chinese Nation: Racism and Militarism in the 1911 Revolution

Clemens Büttner

Within weeks of the 10 October 1911 uprising in Wuchang 武昌 and the spread of the anti-Qing 清 revolt to numerous provinces, the leaders of China's revolutionary movement could rest assured that both their mobilisation strategy and the courtship of their desired instrument of action, had led to the coveted results: a growing emphasis on ethnically justified—and largely racist—anti-Manchu rhetoric since the early 1900s had expedited the unification and growth of the previously loose and discordant revolutionary movement, and an increasing endorsement of military values and virtues—with strong *militaristic* connotations—had contributed to bringing many units of the New Armies (*Xinjun* 新軍) on to their side. It was these troops, stirred up by years of revolutionary agitation, that possessed the will and the means to challenge the authority of the Manchu Court effectively.

The ethnic[1] and militaristic ideas that the revolutionaries promoted complemented each other well. The former aimed at constructing a "we/Han 漢" *versus* "them/Manchus" dichotomy, thereby drawing the image of a clearly discernible enemy that served a mobilising purpose for the revolutionary cause. The latter, by installing the professional soldier as a role model to all, promoted the values and virtues that the future Chinese republican citizen ought to possess: patriotism, discipline, a martial spirit combined with the willingness to make sacrifices, loyalty, and a sense of duty towards the nation-state. Both discourses rested on the assumption that the world abided by Social Darwinist

---

1 I use the term "ethnic", as it provides a quite fitting description of the actual contents of the Chinese discourse on (Han) ethnicity. Anthony D. Smith asserts that an "ethnic community" is characterised by the following features: "1. a collective proper name; 2. a myth of common ancestry; 3. shared historical memories; 4. one or more differentiating elements of common culture; 5. an association with a specific 'homeland;' 6. a sense of solidarity for significant sectors of the population. (…) Such a community must be sharply differentiated from a *race* [Smith's emphasis] in the sense of a social group that is held to possess unique hereditary biological traits that allegedly determine the mental attributes of the group." Smith (1991), *National Identity*, p. 21. While matters of race in the above-mentioned sense were also discussed by Chinese advocates of an ethnic nation, their focus lay on questions associated with ethnicity in the above-mentioned sense. For an overview of the corresponding Chinese thinking, see, for example, Gasster (1969), *Chinese Intellectuals and the Revolution of 1911*, Chap. 3.

principles, that a national community could only survive if it was fit enough to fight for its continued existence.

However, within weeks of the Uprising, the revolutionaries became acutely aware of the consequences of their racist mobilisation strategy—and they were dismayed at the outcome of having their ideas translated into action. Before long, countless Manchus and banner-people had been killed by troops in revolt, and the revolutionary authorities in the various provinces hurried to urge publicly a halt to racist violence, stressing the *political*—not racial—character of their revolution. Nevertheless, it was not the human victims that gave the revolutionaries pause. What they feared for was the actualisation of the one goal to which they *truly* aspired: a strong and united Chinese state. Violence was not only a danger to those who had—for supposedly ethnic reasons—profited from the Qing political system, it was also, above all, a danger to the territorial integrity of the fading polity.

Moreover, anti-Manchu violence, its primarily political rationale notwithstanding, made other non-Han ethnicities in the Empire feel just as unsafe as the Manchus. This, together with years of calls for national self-rule of the Han majority and the acknowledgment by some that other ethnicities in China were also justified to demand their national autonomy, quickly brought the—as James Leibold has termed it—geo-body of the Qing Empire on the verge of breaking apart.[2] Declarations of independence from various territories in early 1912 contradicted the revolutionaries' vision of a Chinese state with the same borders as the collapsing Empire. Consequently, measures to preserve China's territorial integrity and popular cohesion were taken. In ideological respect, this meant that the nation that was to invigorate the nascent Chinese nation-state encountered its boundaries even *before* the Republic of China was officially established: any notion of a Chinese nation that posed a challenge to the vision of a new state with the borders of the Qing Empire was out of the question.

It is these boundaries of Chinese nationalist thinking in the revolutionary period that I wish to address in this chapter. While doing so, my focus will rest on the development of the early twentieth century ethnic and militaristic discourses on the Chinese nation, and my analysis will be guided by the following conceptual assumptions: (1) The hypothesis that any notion of a Chinese nation was to be subordinated to geopolitical requirements suggests that the understanding of China as a —in the words of John Fitzgerald—"nationless state" whose nation "… has been created and recreated in the struggle for the state"[3] holds true. However, when one takes a closer look at the ethnic and militaristic discourses on the nation, then the picture of a Chinese nation emerges which was certainly confined by certain concepts of the state, but which was still

---

2 Leibold (2007), *Reconfiguring Chinese Nationalism*, Chap. 1.

3 Fitzgerald (1995), "The Nationless State", pp. 76, 75–78.

clearly distinguishable from the state. Initially, the Chinese national community that came to be envisioned was characterised by shared ethnic/cultural/historical markers. I argue, however, that it was eventually superseded by the idea of a nation that was defined by a *specific set of behavioural patterns, value concepts, and virtues* that was deemed desirable from a political state-centred point of view. These patterns, concepts, and virtues were militaristic in the sense of Alfred Vagts' definition, who, in his seminal 1937 study *A History of Militarism*, specified that the term "militarism" connotes, among other things, "… an emphasis on military considerations, spirit, ideals, and scales of value, in the life of states".[4] In this respect, the Chinese nation's main point of reference turned out to be the military, not the state.

(2) With regard to its role in the process of conceiving a Chinese national identity, militaristic ideas would, from late-1911 onwards, gradually surpass their ethnic counterpart in importance. Initially, however, the ethnicity-based approach to national identity formation was at an advantage. After all, in the years leading up to the Revolution, it was not sufficient to stress the alleged maliciousness of the Manchus in their dealings with a victimised Han people. It also had to be asserted in *positive* terms what it was that characterised the Han Chinese. Zhang Binglin 章炳麟 (1869–1936) and others did just that by postulating the existence of a shared Han ancestry and history, a unique language and culture.[5] Nonetheless, China's revolutionaries were neither willing (nor able) to divorce this discourse from anti-Manchuism, nor could they remedy the one *main* deficiency that characterises such attempts to create a specific identity in general. Rogers Brubaker goes to the heart of the matter by asserting that "race, ethnicity, nationhood are not precise analytical concepts; they are vague vernacular terms whose meaning varies considerably over place and time".[6] Because of this inherent vagueness, the *pre*-Revolutionary discourse on ethnicity crystallised around the emphasis of anti-Qing sentiment as its most "concrete" element. *After* the Revolution, the most tangible element of the ethnic discourse turned out to be the state, whose now-envisioned multi-ethnic character had to be justified.[7]

It was because of its pronounced anti-Manchuism that the ideas of ethnic discourse immediately began to pose a considerable danger to the revolution-

---

4 Vagts (1959), *A History of Militarism*, p. 14. According to Vagts, the other traits of militarism are "a domination of the military man over the civilian, [and] an undue preponderance of military demands" (ibid.).

5 Cf. e.g. Zhang Binglin (1907a), "Zhonghua Minguo jie"; Brubaker (2009), "Ethnicity, Race, and Nationalism", pp. 26–28, provides a good overview of different means of constructing—and asserting—membership in a given ethnic group.

6 Brubaker (2009), "Ethnicity, Race, and Nationalism", p. 27.

7 With regard to the construction of ethnic identity, Cf. e.g. Horowitz (1985), *Ethnic Groups in Conflict*, Chap. 2.

aries' vision of a wealthy and powerful Chinese nation-state when fighting broke out in October 1911. The originally identity-creating resource of ethnic nationalism had to be fundamentally reshuffled in order not to turn it into an obstacle to the revolutionary state-building project. At the same time, and because of the negative effects of racist thought and actions on the said state-building project, the discourse on militarism also underwent a transformation: as it had, from its very beginning, been perceived as a means of awakening the Chinese people to their duties to the (future) nation-*state*, it was suddenly at an advantage when the revolutionaries had, in 1912, to assume actual responsibility *for* the state: as soon as the revolutionaries turned from challengers into the wielders of political power, their nationalist objectives also shifted and the notion of a national community united by a spirit of duty to the state became incomparably more attractive.

(3) The apparent ease with which the conceptual foundations of the Chinese nation could be exchanged suggests a high degree of mutability of the image of the Chinese nation—a finding that is consistent with Frederik Barth's argument in *Ethnic Groups and Boundaries* that the question of national identity—of belonging to a specific group, and not others—is, in fact, not a matter of defining "objectively" discernible differences between certain groups. It should instead, writes Barth, be perceived as a matter of *setting up boundaries* between one's own group and others. If national identity formation is therefore understood as a *process of demarcation*, and not the stipulation of immutable markers of belonging, the continuous existence of one group can be assumed even if its defining parameters are constantly and fundamentally re-imagined. As long as individuals feel themselves to be part of a certain group and pledge allegiance to it, the group exists.[8] In the Chinese case, the defining parameters that would have to be accommodated were the physical borders of the Qing Empire, and the means with which to accommodate them was the envisioning of a community upon basis of certain behavioural patterns, value concepts, and virtues—not ethnic or other markers.

However, while the specific defining contents of the who and the what of the Chinese nation were not as important as the demarcation processes which they entailed, (4) the substitution of ethnic with militaristic notions of the nation would not have gone that easily if two related factors had not been met. The first one was their common Social Darwinist starting-point: both messages, those of ethnicity or of militarism, fit very well within the then dominant view that envisioned the world as a place of struggling nation-states. The second factor was that the intellectual leadership of both discourses largely comprised

---

8 Bart (1969), "Introduction", pp. 14–16. Also, cf. Brubaker, *Ethnic Groups in Conflict*, p. 29.

the *same personnel*, cutting right through the—admittedly blurry[9]—dividing line between the revolutionary and reform factions.

Taken together, these four points underscore the assumption that the early twentieth century discourse on the Chinese nation was characterised by two seemingly contradictory features: a high degree of *mutability* in terms of content, strictly *limited*, however, by the actual borders of the Chinese geo-body. To China's revolutionaries, to determine clearly the identity of the Chinese nation was never as important—or, at least, as tangible—as its embodiment: the territory of the state that they envisioned. And yet, even though the discourse boundaries were preset by the state- and border-fixation of Chinese nationalist thinking, it was not the image of a nation defined by its state that emerged—it was one defined by its militaristic conceptions.

In order to substantiate these claims, I will, in a first step, briefly outline the Social Darwinist starting-point that informed both the ethnic and the militaristic discourses on the nation. In a second step, I will provide an introduction to the militaristic strand of Chinese nationalist ideology. While its ethnic counterpart is very well researched, Chinese militaristic thinking is an understudied topic. To substantiate the claimed complementary nature of both discourses, I will then highlight the high degree of overlapping content and exchange as well as interaction between their participants.[10] In a third step, I will deal with the gradual supplementation of ethnic with militaristic notions of the nation in the wake of the Revolution, when the danger to the territorial integrity of the Qing geo-body had to be reacted to.

Social Darwinism - The Common Starting-point

In 1895, after China's painful defeat at the hands of its supposedly inferior neighbour Japan, Chinese reform-oriented individuals reinforced their efforts to find an explanation for—and remedy to—the persistent weakness of their homeland. In the course of their search for answers, two subjects of discussion emerged in the late nineteenth century. These subjects were the development and evolution of human races, and the formation and safeguarding of strong and sovereign nation-states. Both discourses stemmed from the same intellec-

---

9 Cf. Gasster (1969), *Chinese Intellectuals and the Revolution of 1911*, Chaps. 3–4, whose accounts of Anti-Manchuism and the efforts to establish a republic provide ample proof of the near-impossibility of distinguishing between reformers and revolutionaries on ideological grounds.

10 In order to highlight inter-discourse exchanges and not to distort the discourse chronology, I will (wherever possible) refer to primary sources in their original publication format, usually articles or article series in the periodical press.

tual starting-point, and they co-existed in the parallel and often overlapping ethnic and militaristic discourses on the Chinese nation.

The above-mentioned starting-point was provided in March 1895, roughly two weeks before the Sino-Japanese peace talks began at Shimonoseki 下関市. In that month, Yan Fu's 嚴復 (1853–1921) highly influential series of articles entitled "The Sources of Strength" (Yuan qiang 原強) was published in the Tianjin 天津 newspaper *Zhibao* 直報.[11] In this series, Yan introduced China's intellectuals to the basic Social Darwinist ideas that were to inform both the ethnic and the militaristic discourse on national rejuvenation in the decade preceding the 1911 Revolution and beyond.

In face of looming humiliation at the negotiating table, Yan Fu sternly demanded that China's long-standing weakness now comprehensively—and relentlessly—be analysed and overcome. After all, the vast Qing Empire had been easily brought to its knees by "a navy of but a few vessels [and] a people of just some ten-thousand men".[12] However, Yan's interest did not lie with evaluating the condition of China's armed forces, its educational system, or its political institutions. For him, to work on their improvement was but to attend to the *symptoms* of a sickness. If China was to survive, the *roots* of its current ailment had to be addressed: the shortcomings of the wisdom of its people (*minzhi* 民智), the virtuousness of its people (*minde* 民德), and the (physical) strength of its people (*minli* 民力).[13]

Yan based this argument upon the realisation that the root of Western superiority did not lie with weaponry or institutions. Instead, "[t]he Westerner's secret was in their attitude, their philosophy",[14] as James Pusey has put it. They held an outlook on world that rested on the wholehearted acceptance of Charles Darwin's (1809–1882)—and Herbert Spencer's (1820–1903)—theories. By establishing that all life had evolved from a single source, Yan maintained, Darwin's *On the Origin of Species* (first published in 1859) had fundamentally

---

11 Yan Fu (1895), "Yuan qiang" had such an impact on the Chinese reading public that Liang Qichao approached Yan Fu in October 1896 and requested permission to reprint the text in his journal *Shiwubao* 時務報. Yan, however, asked for some time to rework the manuscript, as he deemed it unsatisfactory at the time. Even though Yan eventually submitted a fundamentally reworked version of his article later that year, it was not published in *Shiwubao* (Wang Shi (1986), *Yan Fu ji*, vol. 1, p. 5n*). The revised manuscript was only published in 1901 in the *Block-printed Series of [Works by] Mr. Yan [Fu] from Houguan* (Houguan Yan shi congke 侯官嚴氏叢刻, (Yan Fu (1982 [1901]), "Yuan qiang", 1a–29b). Both Schwartz (1964), *In Search of Wealth and Power*, Chap. III) and Pusey (1983), *China and Charles Darwin*, Chap. 2, have based their respective analyses of the text upon the revised manuscript published in 1901. I, by contrast, refer to the 1895 original version of "The Sources of Strength", as it was *precisely* this text that triggered Chinese interest in Social Darwinism.

12 Yan Fu (1895), "Yuan qiang", no. 33, p. 1.

13 Ibid., no. 37, p. 1.

14 Pusey (1983), *China and Charles Darwin*, p. 55.

altered Western science, politics, and religion. What made the Westerners superior to the Chinese was that the former had already internalised the two key messages of Darwin's research: that all species had to fight for their existence (*zheng zicun* 爭自存), and that a species' continued existence was dependent on the constant opportunity to pass on favorable [genetic] endowments (*yi yizhong* 遺宜種).[15]

Yan Fu summarised Darwin's message as follows:

That which is called "fighting for one's existence", means that [in the beginning] men [and] living things are randomly born into the world, equally enjoying the benefits of heaven, earth, [and] nature. [But when they] meet each other, [then] conflict arises, [and] man [and] man [as well as] living thing [and] living thing fight each other for their existence. In the beginning, race and race fight each other, and [upon] forming groups [and] forming states, groups fight groups, and states fight states. Thus, the weak become the prey of the strong, [and] the stupid become the peons (*yi* 役) of the wise. [Only] when one persists [in fighting] can [one] pass on favorable [genetic] endowments [to one's descendants]. Certainly, [species so refined] are tenacious [and] enduring (*qiangren* 強忍), imposing [and] exceptional (*kuijie* 魁桀), nimble [and] agile (*qiaojie* 趫捷), ingenious [and] intelligent (*qiaohui* 巧慧). [They] are the [species] most suited to the climate, geography, [and] all [other] circumstances of [their] times.[16]

With these lines, Yan Fu announced the two main pillars of Social Darwinist thinking to his readers—and determined that a close connection between the phenomena of fighting for one's existence and of passing on favorable genetic endowments existed: only *after* successfully having fought for its continued existence could an intra-species process of genetic refinement begin. Such a process had to continue in perpetuity, as all species constantly had to adapt to changing living conditions. Accordingly, the Chinese people—in order to remedy their three afore-mentioned shortcomings—had to be made aware of the implications of Darwin's findings for their own condition.[17] The Chinese had to internalise this realisation, adapt their moral proclivities accordingly, and make themselves physically fit to stand the tests of evolution.

Yan Fu stressed that humankind was subjected to the same evolutionary forces as all the other species. In one regard, however, it stood apart: humans, in order to enhance their individual chances for survival, were able to form

---

15 Yan Fu (1895), "Yuan qiang", no. 32, p. 1. Yan referred to the third and the fourth chapter of Darwin's book: "Struggle for Existence", and "Natural Selection" (Darwin 1859, Chaps. 3, 4). The revised version of "The Sources of Strength" featured different terms for these two concepts: "*wujing*" 物競 (struggle for existence), and "*tianze*" 天澤 (natural selection), respectively (cf. Yan Fu (1982 [1901]), "Yuan qiang", p. 1b).

16 Yan Fu (1895) "Yuan qiang", no. 32, p. 1.

17 Ibid., no. 32, p. 1; no. 33, p. 2.

groups (*qun* 群) and work together.[18] Grouping allowed for an effective division of tasks and labour and the comprehensive implementation of rules of conduct that structured and safeguarded the functioning of social life. It was in this respect that Herbert Spencer had expanded on Darwin's theory, wrote Yan. By pointing out that the processes of group formation and preservation were part of evolution, Spencer had been able to account for the rise and fall, the strength and weakness of any country in the world. A thorough understanding of sociology (*qunxue* 群學, lit. "science of group formation"), Spencer's field of study, thus held the key to enhancing China's own chances of survival, argued Yan.[19]

Thus, by 9 March 1895, when the final part of "The Sources of Strength" was published in *Zhibao*, Yan Fu had provided *the* seminal compilation of the intellectual strands that were to characterise the following debate on China's weakness: a seemingly scientific explanation for—and remedy to—the Chinese ailment, an evolutionary framework of world history into which China could be fitted, as well as core concepts of nationalist thinking: that the Chinese were a specific group (distinct from others) with a legitimate claim on the territory of their homeland. It was upon this basis that others would come to ponder about China as a community of individuals and the means to fortify it. While Yan Fu had, as indicated, been clear in emphasising the *interdependency* between fighting for one's survival and the strengthening of the race (or other groups), his reform- or revolutionary-oriented successors would usually favour one of these points over the other.

During the autumn and winter of 1897–98—and merely five years after a first Chinese-language article on human races had been circulated in China[20]—the most influential early anthropological text written by a Chinese author was published: the series of articles enitled"A Study of the [Human] Races in the Various Countries" (Geguo zhongleikao 各國種類考), authored by Tang Caichang 唐才常 (1867–1900).[21] In his series, Tang informed his readers on peoples from the different continents, lecturing on their respective origins and purported qualities. Yet, the main purpose of his text lay beyond providing an introduction to the anthropological knowledge of his times: his overarching aim was historiographical, to make the—momentarily discouraging—Chinese case an integral part of global developments. This desire, noted Tang, was borne by

---

18 Cf. e.g. ibid., no. 34, pp. 1–2, where Yan sketched the main characteristics of the four human races.

19 Ibid., no. 32, pp. 1–2, cf. also Dikötter (1992), *The Discourse of Race*, pp. 102–103.

20 In the autumn of 1892, the article entitled "The Theory of Dividing Mankind in Five Types" (Ren fen wulei shuo 人分五類說), written by an (unnamed) western author (cf. Dikötter (1992), *The Discourse of Race*, p. 56), was published in the seventh issue of the journal *Gezhi huibian* 格致匯編; "Ren fen wulei shuo" (1892).

21 Tang Caichang (1897), "Shixue di'wu: Geguo zhongleikao". Regarding the composition of this text, cf. Ishikawa (2003), "Anti-Manchu Racism".

his worries about the continuing existence of the Chinese race which had arisen after he had read "The Sources of Strength" in 1895.[22]

Besides Yan, who had dedicated little space to the subject in his series of articles,[23] Tang Caichang expounded in detail that humankind was—upon basis of skin colour—divided into the four main races (*dazhong* 大種) of "yellow", "white", "red", and "black" men. According to him, the yellow and the white races were inherently superior to the red and the black ones. However, at least for the time-being, there was also no denying that the yellow race was inferior to its white counterpart. And yet, noted Tang Caichang, the origins of humankind could be traced back to the Asian continent—and to China, specifically. It had been from China, declared Tang with some pride, that humankind had set out to settle in all parts of the world.[24]

To restore a sense of pride in his compatriots was not the main goal that Tang Caichang pursued, however: in an appendix that he later added to his "A Study of the [Human] Races in the Various Countries",[25] entitled "The Joining of [Human] Races" (Tongzhong shuo 通種說), he argued that crossbreeding with members of superior races was a way to improve the race (*jinzhong* 進種; namely, the races of yellow, black, and red skin). By this means, the inherent qualities (regarding intelligence, mindset, *etc.*) of inferior races could be improved.[26]

Seen from this vantage point, anthropology seemed to be a scientific tool with which the Chinese—by means of genetic improvement—could be delivered from their hardships.[27] Roughly two months earlier,[28] but to less public

---

22 Tang Caichang (1897), "Shixue di'wu: Geguo zhongleikao", no. 15, p. 3a. "A Study of the [Human] Races in the Various Countries" was only the final portion of a greater series of articles by Tang Caichang, entitled "Historiography" (Shixue 史學) and published uninterruptedly in the first 27 issues of *Xiangxue xinbao* 湘學新報 (from issue 21 onwards called *Xiangxuebao* 湘學報). The parts published in Issues 10 and 11 were written by an associate of Tang, Cai Zhonghao 蔡鐘浩 (1877–1900).

23 Yan Fu (1895), "Yuan qiang", no. 34, p. 1.

24 Tang Caichang (1897), "Shixue di'wu: Geguo zhongleikao", no. 15, pp. 3b, 5a–b.

25 Shortly after the conclusion of the article series in *Xiangxuebao*, Tang added the appendix "The Theory of Joining [Human] Races" (Tongzhong shuo 通種說) to a reprint of the text in *Private Words from the Studio of Sensing the Falling Darkness* (Juedian Mingzhai neiyan 覺顛冥齋內言, 1898), a collection of many of his *Xiangxue (xin)bao* articles, Tang Caishang (2002 [1898]), *Juedian Mingzhai neiyan*, j. 3, pp. 49b–54b.

26 Tang Caishang (2002 [1898]), *Juedian Mingzhai neiyan*, j. 3, pp. 49b, 51a–53b. For Tang, a disciple of Kang Youwei, the world would enter into the Age of Great Peace (*Taiping zhi shi* 太平之世) after all human races had converged, sharing the same blood (*xue* 血), vital energy (*qi* 氣), character traits (*xing* 性), and sentiments (*qing* 情). Tang Caishang (2002 [1898]), *Juedian Mingzhai neiyan*, j. 3, p. 51b.

27 See Ishikawa (2003), "Anti-Manchu Racism and the Rise of Anthropology in Early 20th Century China", p. 13.

28 The first part of Tang's article series was published on 7 September 1897, in *Xiangxue xinbao*, while Liang's article was published in the June 30, 1897 issue of *Shiwubao*.

resonance, Tang's friend and teacher Liang Qichao 梁啟超 (1873–1929) had published a short article that argued in likewise fashion, albeit without adopting Tang's standpoint that the yellow race should be crossbred with the white race. Instead, in his article entitled "On China's Future Strength" (Lun Zhongguo zhi jiangqiang 論中國之將強), Liang argued that a conscious effort by the "Chinese race" (*Huazhong* 華種) to acquire western knowledge and to combine it with its own superior (Confucian) teachings would herald China's return to the top. This argument—the first part lifted from Yan Fu, the second part taken from Kang Youwei's 康有為 (1858–1927) New Text Confucianism (*Jinwen jingxue* 今文經學)[29]—was then buttressed with anthropological ideas. According to Liang, the yellow race was superior to peoples of black, red, or brown skin,[30] as the latter races were physically incapable of achieving the intellectual accomplishments of white and yellow men:

All men of black, red, [or] brown colour are, [because of] microorganisms (*weishengwu* 微生物) in their blood vessels, and [because of] the angular dimensions (*jiaodu* 角度) of their brains, completely different from white men. Only the yellow [man's micro-organisms and dimensions of his brain] are very close to [those of] the white [man]. Therefore, among all things that the white man can achieve, there is not one that the yellow man cannot achieve [as well].[31]

Upon the basis of this assessment, Liang then came to the conclusion that the yellow race, unlike the brown and the black races, was not *per se* predestined for enslavement, servitude, and subservience. The Chinese, as part of the yellow race, possessed the mental faculties to decide over their fate themselves—they only had to be roused.[32]

In the years following the failure of the Hundred Days' Reform of 1898, Liang gradually removed himself from the intellectual orbit of Kang Youwei. In 1902, when Liang Qichao published his series of articles entitled "A New Historiography" (Xin shixue 新史學), he had already perceptibly distanced himself from Kang's utopian vision of a future Great Unity. Instead, Liang now expanded on Tang Caichang's idea of relating anthropological theories to the course of history of humankind, commencing the fourth part of his series of articles entitled "The Relationship between History and Human Races" (Lishi yu renzhong zhi guanxi 歷史與人種之關係), with the following line:

---

29 Liang Qichao (1897), "Lun Zhongguo zhi jiangqiang", pp. 2a–2b. Correspondingly, the bright future Liang envisioned for China was that of Kang's Great Unity (*Datong* 大同) (ibid., p. 4b).

30 Unlike Tang, Liang counted five human races on basis of skin colour: white, yellow, black, red, and brown (ibid., pp. 3b–4a).

31 Ibid., p. 2a.

32 Ibid., pp. 2b, 3b–4a, 4b. The red race, Liang predicted, would soon be extinct (ibid., p. 3b).

History—what is it? The account of the development of human races and their struggles [with each other]—and that's it.[33]

By invoking ideas originally brought forward by Yan Fu, Liang then ranked the five human races upon the basis of their ability to group together and to distinguish themselves actively from others. It was by lengthy processes of demarcation, he stated, that clear divisions between the various human races (*zhongjie* 種界) had been established. The white and the yellow races were at the vanguard, since they, as "historical human races" (*lishi de renzhong* 歷史的人種), had been able to join together (*zijie* 自結) by themselves. By contrast, the black, the red, and the brown races, as "non-historical human races" (*fei lishi de renzhong* 非歷史的人種), had been joined together by external forces.[34] The white race was still superior to its yellow counterpart, however, as it was the only human race of universal historical (*shijieshi* 世界史) significance. Such a race—and, at that moment, it was the white sub-race of the Teutons, specifically—could capitalise on a culture and military force (*wenhua wuli* 文化武力) whose influence transcended its original living area. It was because of its culture and military prowess that a race of universal historical significance did not only shape its own developmental path, but also that of others, asserted Liang.[35]

For Liang Qichao, as for Yan, then, the ability of individuals to group together was a key factor in determining the fate of a race or country, and it was also present in Tang Caichang's series of articles.[36] Yet, these men were not only interested in the act of group formation and demarcation, they also concerned themselves with the questions of *how* a group could be founded and *what* function it ought to assume. Given the precarious situation of the Chinese and the desire to improve their condition, these (and other) *literati* asked these questions with specific regard to the group that was to populate their homeland. Of course, their answers were predetermined by the ubiquitous new image of a merciless Social Darwinist world in which only the fittest survived.[37] Various contemplations of the Chinese "(ethnic) nation" (*minzu* 民族) (see below) and the related matter of nationalism as *the* means of fostering unity among a group were written. An important early source of inspiration had been provided in 1895, when Timothy Richard's translation of Robert Mackenzie's 1880 populist

---

33 Liang Qichao (1902), "Xin shixue", no. 14, p. 10.

34 Ibid., no. 14, pp. 19–20.

35 Ibid., no. 14, pp. 23, 30.

36 Tang Caichang (1897), "Shixue di'wu: Geguo zhongleikao", no. 15, pp. 3a–3b.

37 In 1898, Yan Fu's translation of Thomas Huxley's *Evolution and Ethics* (Huxley (1893), *Evolution and Ethics*) was published (see Hexuli 2002 [1898], *Tianyan lun*), a text which popularised Darwin's (and Spencer's) evolutionary thinking among Chinese *literati*; cf. Chow (2001), "Narrating Nation, Race, and National Culture", p. 53.

treatise entitled *The 19th Century* had been published in Shanghai.[38] It was (amongst others) this book that acquainted China's reform-oriented intellectuals with the —in the words of Kai-wing Chow—

... [the] fundamental principles that constituted a nation-state. Chinese intellectuals looked to language, custom, history, and religion for the common bond of the nation. They found none. (...) A political regime could no longer be justified in terms of virtuous leadership but only in the sovereignty of the people—the Chinese nation.[39]

Yet, even though it proved hard to reach an agreement on the questions of who and what the Chinese nation were, the unifying effects of nationalism were commonly acknowledged—as was the following equation: the stronger the group, the stronger the state. Liang Qichao was one of the first to elaborate on the idea of grouping that had first been brought forward by Yan Fu. The latter had asserted that evolutionary advantages could be gained from assembling into a group, but, in "The Sources of Strength", Yan had not commented on the mechanisms that underlay group formation and the functions that the group ought to assume. These questions were tackled by Liang, who—between April and September 1899—published a lengthy translation of the 1874 monograph *Deutsche Statslehre* (sic) *für Gebildete* [German Political Science for Educated People] by the Swiss jurist Johann Caspar Bluntschli (1808–1881) in his journal *Qingyibao* 清議報. This translation—entitled "On the Nation-state" (Guojia lun 國家論) and essentially a plagiarism of a Japanese translation by Azuma Heiji 吾妻兵治 (dates unknown)—gave Chinese intellectuals a first impression of bluntschlian political thinking.[40] Yet, it only was in October 1903 that the Swiss' ideas would make a deeper impact, when Liang presented them not in the form of a translation but as a summary appraisal in his journal *Xinmin congbao* 新民叢報. In his article entitled "The Theories of Bluntschli, Master of Political Science" (Zhengzhixue dajia Bolunzhili zhi xueshuo 政治學大家伯倫知理之學說), Liang explained that Bluntschli had come to the conclusion that national sovereignty was directly related to social unity.[41] This line of reasoning rested on two assumptions: that (1), it was the duty of the state to create and maintain

---

38 Makenxi (2002 [1895]), *Taixi xinshi lanyao*; for the 1880 original, cf. Mackenzie (1880), *The 19th Century*. For the decidedly ethnic connotation of the term *minzu*, cf. Matten (2012), "China is the China of the Chinese", p. 75n72, and, especially, Chow (2001), "Narrating Nation, Race, and National Culture".

39 Ibid., p. 51.

40 Bolunzhili (1899), "Guojia lun". The Japanese translation Liang had plagiarised was the 1899 text *Science of the State* (*Kokkagaku* 國家學; Buruntīri (1899), *Kokkagaku*) as Marianne Bastid-Bruguiere (2004), "The Japanese-Induced German Connection of Modern Chinese Ideas of the State", has shown.

41 Liang Qichao (1903b), "Zhengzhixue dajia Bolunzhili zhi xueshuo". A considerably shorter earlier draft of this article had already been published in late May 1903 in *Xinmin congbao*; cf. Liang Qichao (1903a), "Zhengzhixue dajia Bolunzhili zhi xueshuo".

The Boundaries of the Chinese Nation

inner unity and social cohesion, and to protect its citizens from foreign menace; and (2)—and more importantly—that a people had to be *willing* to assemble into a state. In this respect, statehood became the result of the *voluntary* decision of a hitherto only loosely linked group: an "(ethnic) nation" (*minzu*), merely related with each other on natural or habitual grounds. After having acted upon this decision, an "(ethnic) nation" would evolve into a "state-people" (*guomin* 國民) that were willing to exert themselves for the greater good of the nation-state (*guojia* 國家).[42]

The relationship between a united people's willingness to apply themselves for their homeland and its chances of survival in the universal struggle of evolution had already been established by Liang Qichao a couple of months earlier, in one part of his series of articles entitled "Renewing the People" (Xinmin shuo 新民說). In the issue of 26 February 1903 of *Xinmin congbao*, he had addressed the existing relationship between one's duties to the state and the rights that could be gained from performing them:

Duties (*yiwu* 義務) and rights (*quanli* 權利) are interdependent. (...) Where do rights emerge from? [They] emerge from victories (*sheng* 勝) [in the struggle for survival] and [the resulting natural] selection [opportunities] (*bei ze* 被擇). Wherefrom does victory arise? From struggling and attaining excellence (*huo you* 獲優). What is excellence? To fulfil [one's] duties to an extent that exceeds [the extent to which] ordinary men (*changren* 常人) [fulfil their duties].[43]

It was thus clear to Liang that all rights had to be earned through diligent performance of one's duties to the state. However, the struggle that accompanied the earning of these rights was not just an internal matter: each nation-state was part of a highly competitive international system in which fighting was the *only*

---

42 Liang Qichao (1903b), "Zhengzhixue dajia Bolunzhili zhi xueshuo", pp. 26–27. For the differences between *guomin* and *minzu*, cf. also ibid., pp. 26–34. I translate the term *guomin* as "state-people" since this translation conveys both components of the Chinese term and highlights Liang's indebtedness to Bluntschli's original term "Staatsvolk". In Bluntschli's words: "Das Verhältnisz des Volkes zum Staate ist ein so natürliches und enges, dasz die Sprache geneigt ist, die Gesammtbevölkerung eines Staates auch dann Volk zu nennen, wenn dieselbe aus mehreren Völkern oder nur aus einem Theile eines Volkes besteht. Wir sind demnach genöthigt, das Volk im natürlichen Sinne, Naturvolk (Nation) von dem Volke im staatlichen Sinne, dem *Staatsvolk* (Bluntschli's emphasis; C.B.) zu unterscheiden. Das letztere ist dann jeder Zeit das lebendige Gesammtwesen, welches den Staat erfüllt und in demselben lebt, wie das Individuum in dem Körper, den es bewohnt"; Bluntschli (1857), *Allgemeines Staatsrecht*, p. 70. The English translation of "state-people" for "Staatsvolk" comes from Hobsbawm (1992), *Nations and nationalism since 1780*, p. 73. Bluntschli himself voiced his discontent with the fact that the ideas he associated with the term "Volk" were usually associated with the term "nation" in English publications; cf. Bluntschli (1874), *Deutsche Statslehre für Gebildete*, p. 36.

43 Liang Qichao (1902–06), "Xinmin shuo", no. 26 (1903), p. 1.

296 CLEMENS BÜTTNER

means to assert one's position.[44] For Liang (and others), this fact informed their observations in the then unfolding discourse on the Chinese nation-state.

A Fortified People and its Nation-state: The Discourse on a "Militaristic State-People" and the "Esteem of Martial Qualities"

By 1903, when Liang Qichao introduced his readers to the bluntschlian idea that national unity derived from allegiance to a specific state (not ethnic markers), he was already a staunch opponent of the revolutionaries' anti-Manchu ideology. Nonetheless, in late December 1898, early January 1899, it had been he himself who—by justifying it in Social Darwinist terms—had been instrumental in putting the then growing anti-Manchuism into "scientific" terms.[45] In the short two-part article "Political Reform has to Begin with Levelling the Divisions between Manchus and Han" (Lun bianfa bi zi ping Man-Han zhi jie shi 論變法必自平滿漢之界始), Liang had declared the Manchu rulers to be members of an inferior race (liezhong 劣種) in comparison with their Han subjects. While both Manchus and Han were sub-races of the main yellow race, the fate of the Manchus at large—and the Empire under their control—rested on their ability to overcome their divisions with the Han, to improve racially and to unite—and then to fight the real enemy of China: the white race.[46] By arguing in this fashion, he inadvertently re-focused the Chinese debate on human races: the hitherto predicted future clash of the white and yellow races became relegated to a secondary position, and the anticipated conflict between Han and Manchus came into focus.

---

44 In this respect, cf. e.g. the sixth part of "Renewing the People" (published 22 April 1902 in *Xinmin congbao*), where Liang—when referring to the German jurist Rudolf von Ihering's 1872 lecture *Der Kampf um's Recht*—based himself on the altered fifth edition of the text; cf. von Ihering (1879), *The Struggle for Law*, Liang Qichao, "Xinmin shuo" (1902–06), no. 6 (1902), p. 2.

45 Cf. Zarrow (2012), *After Empire*, pp. 150–3; Rhoads (2000), *Manchus & Han*, pp. 3–5. In order to fuel feelings of enmity towards the Qing Court, various recollections of atrocities committed by the invading Manchus during the Ming-Qing transition in the seventeenth century resurfaced in the late nineteenth century and were reprinted in great number. The gist of their intended message was that, if China was to survive, the Qing rulers had either to reform or be disposed. Prominent examples of texts that vividly described Manchu brutality during the conquest of the Ming Empire (1368–1644) included the *Record of Ten Days in Yangzhou* (Wang Xiuchu (1982), *Yangzhou shi ri ji*) and the *Brief Account of the Massacre of the Inhabitants of the Captured City of Jiading* (Zhu Zisu (1982), *Jiading tucheng jilüe*).

46 Liang Qichao (1898/99), "Lun bianfa bi zi ping Man-Han zhi jie shi", no. 1, pp. 1a, 2a, no. 2, pp. 1a–2b.

However, while Liang Qichao believed in the existence of qualitative differences between the various races and sub-races, he remained convinced of the basic mutability of their qualities.[47] Many of his ideological opponents, by contrast, were prone to essentialising these differences. For instance, the article of August 1901 entitled "The Destruction of the Country" (Wangguo pian 亡國篇) in the final issue of the Tōkyō-published *Guominbao* 國民報 argued that the survival of the Han race was actually dependent on the destruction of the Qing Empire and its replacement with a truly *Chinese* state. Any suggestion of a Han-Manchu rapprochement was dismissed as detrimental to the desired survival of the Han race.[48] In this respect, the anonymously written article was an exemplary expression of one of the key features of revolutionary anti-Manchu and racial thinking: its *political* motivation. Dissatisfaction with the Qing rulers was—to a certain extent—based upon their purported ethnic otherness, but it was mainly their alleged political incompetence, their unwillingness to reform, and their mistreatment of the Han that fueled hostile sentiments.[49]

Thus, on the surface, the issue was whether a rejuvenation of China could be achieved together *with* the Manchus or not. Below the surface, however, lay the interlinked questions of who the Chinese state-people ought to be comprised of—and why. To answer these questions, the revolutionaries, on the one hand, invoked common ancestry, history, culture, *etc.* Liang Qichao and his followers, on the other, emphasised the importance of two characteristics: individual willingness to assemble into a nation-state and individual readiness to serve it selflessly in the pursuit of the greater good. This readiness found exemplary expression in the eager payment of taxes and, especially, in the unhesitant performance of military service.[50]

In April 1903, when Liang put the following assessment of his times in writing, he had been aware of the direct link between a state's international status and its military capabilities for years:

The world of today is indeed [one] that is called a world of "armed peace" (*wuzhuang heping* 武裝和平). At the congresses of the great powers, [there is] daily talk of ending war, but [while they] agree to conclude treaties to make peace [and to establish] friendly relations, [they simultaneously] write motions to build up their armaments. In [this] age of "might is right" (*qiangquan zhi shi* 強權之世), only those who are ready to fight can [live] peacefully.[51]

---

47 Cf. Zarrow (2012), *After Empire*, p. 151.

48 "Wangguo pian" (1901), pp. 1–2.

49 Rhoads (2000), *Manchus & Han*, pp. 11, 13–18; Gasster (1969), *Chinese Intellectuals and the Revolution of 1911*, pp. 65–70.

50 Cf. e.g. Liang Qichao (1902–06), "Xinmin shuo", no. 26 (1903), pp. 4–5.

51 Ibid., no. 29 (1903), p. 8.

By 1903, however, Liang's quite commonplace insight had gained a new dimension of meaning. Ever since the *débâcle* of the Hundred Days' Reform, he had been living in the Meiji Empire, a state that prided itself for its martial "bushidō spirit" (*bushidō no seishin* 武士道の精神).[52] The Japanese endorsement of all things military impressed Liang Qichao deeply: in the short article entitled "Praying for Death in Battle" (Qi zhansi 祈戰死), published in late December 1899 in *Qingyibao*, he came to the conclusion that the main difference between the Japanese and Chinese rested with the latter's disdain of war.[53] Nonetheless, it had been the appreciation of bushidō by the Japanese people that had led to their rise, and China must develop a corresponding mindset—a "soldierly soul" (*binghun* 兵魂), as Liang called it in the article entitled "Where is China's Soul?" (Zhongguohun an zai hu 中國魂安在乎).[54]

Apart from equating the "soldierly soul" with an "esteem of martial qualities" (*shangwu* 尚武), as he did in the said article,[55] Liang Qichao would remain silent on the matter for the foreseeable future.[56] But, in the meantime, two specialists in military affairs would step forward to close this gap: in the course of the year 1902, both Cai E 蔡鍔 (1882–1916) and Jiang Baili 蔣百里 (1882–1938)—military students in Japan at the time—took up the notion of a state-people and expanded on it by developing the concept of a "militaristic state-people" (*junguomin* 軍國民),[57] a national people characterised by the possession of the mindset and practical skillset of the military man and distinguished on the grounds of their willingness to give their lives for the greater national good. By establishing a link between bluntschlian notions of nation-statehood and milita-

---

52 Cf. e.g. Inoue Tetsujirō (1901), *Bushidō*, pp. 3–4.

53 Liang Qichao (1899a), "Qi zhansi", p. 2b. "Praying for death in battle" was part of Liang Qichao's "Freely Written Memorandum [from the] Ice-Drinker's Chamber" (Yinbingshi ziyoushu 飲冰室自由書).

54 Liang Qichao (1899b), "Zhongguohun anzai hu", p. 3a.

55 Ibid., p. 2b. The idea that an "esteem of martial qualities" would strengthen China stemmed from Zhang Zhidong 張之洞 (1837–1909) (Zhang Zhidong (1973 [1898]), *Quanxuepian: waipian*; Cf. also, *Guangxu chao Donghualu* (1984), vol. 5, pp. 4113–4114).

56 In late March-early April 1903, Liang published the two-part article "On the Esteem of Martial Qualities" (Lun shangwu 論尚武) in *Xinmin congbao*, as part of the series "Renewing the People" Liang Qichao (1902–06), "Xinmin shuo", 28 (1903) and 29 (1903).

57 My decision to translate *junguomin* as "militaristic state-people" is based upon the following considerations: since the term was coined in Japan and its principles are grounded in Japanese precedent (cf. Xie Benshu (1989), "Lun 'junguomin zhuyi'", pp. 56–58, *'junguo'/'gunkoku'* will be translated as "militaristic". This decision is substantiated by the fact that Liang Qichao himself used the Japanese term for "militarism" (*gunkoku shugi* 軍国主義) in a corresponding manner; cf. Liang Qichao 1904, *Zhongguo zhi wushidao*, "zixu", p. 3. Furthermore, the goals pursued with the "education of a militaristic state-people" were equivalent to that which is described as militarism: a preponderance of military considerations, virtues, and values in the civilian sphere; cf. Vagts (1959), *A History of Militarism*, p. 14. In addition, in order not to obscure the influence of Bluntschli's thinking, *guomin* will be translated as "state-people".

ristic ideas, they argued that only a fortified people were fit to persist in the Social Darwinist world of the time. As military students, these two young men were directly subjected to Japanese military teaching methods and content. By the time of writing their respective texts—Cai penned the series of articles entitled "A Militaristic State-people" (Junguomin pian 軍國民篇), while Jiang wrote "The Education of a Militaristic State-people" (Junguomin zhi jiaoyu 軍國民之教育)—both men were enrolled at Japanese military educational facilities.[58]

While Cai E's article provided some information on the key characteristics of a "militaristic state-people", his main objectives were to analyse why the Chinese people had failed to develop the kind of martial spirit (*shangwu jingshen* 尚武精神) that distinguished the Japanese,[59] and to incite the Chinese to remedy this shortcoming. The "doctrine of a militaristic state-people" (*junguomin zhuyi* 軍國民主義), Cai declared, was a commonly accepted concept in the western world and in Japan. In these countries, its principles were part of general education, and it was valued highly by their peoples. Its effects became visible in the appreciation of the military profession as well as the soldiers' spirit and skillset. Quoting a saying he attributed to the Japanese, Cai stated:

[To provide for] an army is the obligation of the state-people. The knowledge of the military man (*junren* 軍人), [his] spirit, [and his practical] skillset, are not reserved to those who join the army—the state-people of the whole country ought to possess them.[60]

It was for this reason that the Japanese people were of an unyielding and bellicose mindset. The Han nation (*Hanzu* 漢族), by contrast, was too submissive and subservient, and clearly not yet ready to evolve into a state-people.[61] This deplorable mindset had solidified into a common disdain of the military profession, lamented Cai, a disdain that was founded on a wrong understanding of the military man and his great service to the country. The soldierly profession was not one reserved to good-for-nothings—to enlist was actually a noble deed:

---

58 Cai E (1902), "Junguomin pian", Jiang Baili (1902), "Junguomin zhi jiaoyu". In late 1901, both men entered the preparatory Seijō Army Academy (Rikugun Seijō Gakkō 陸軍成城学校). In December 1903, they enrolled at the Army Officers Academy (Rikugun Shikan Gakkō 陸軍士官学校) from which they graduated in late 1904 (Deng Jiangqi (2006), *Cai E sixiang yanjiu*, p. 329; Tao Juyin (1985), *Jiang Baili zhuan*, p. 8). In later years, both men were held in high regard for their military professionalism, cf. e.g. Hou Anghao (2011), "Jindai junshixue qikan de chuangban jiqi xueshu gongneng", pp. 91, Green (2003), "The Spirit of the Military (Junren Hun)", pp. 123–4.

59 Cai E faulted China's educational system, teachings, literature, customs, the physical weakness of its people, its lack of adequate arms, and history; cf. Cai E (1902), "Junguomin pian", no 1, pp. 83–88, no 3, pp. 65–72, no. 7, pp. 67–69.

60 Ibid., no. 1, p. 80.

61 Ibid., no. 1, pp. 81, 84.

300 CLEMENS BÜTTNER

[The soldier willingly] relinquishes [his right to decide about his own] life and death, he renounces [all] desires, he abandons all that which man enjoys and [embraces] all that which causes man suffering. [He] gives up the selfishness of one man and puts [himself] into the service of the public [good] (*gong* 公) of one country—what could be of greater magnanimity?[62]

The Japanese people (and others) appreciated the great sacrifices of the military man to the country, but as long as the Chinese themselves will not come to appreciate their own soldiers, all future confrontations with other countries will end in dismal defeat.[63]

Cai E's text was written in righteous anger by a man who had—for the good of China—deliberately decided to become that which his compatriots despised: a soldier. The same applied to his close friend Jiang Baili, although his article was less of a fiery appeal to a national awakening and more of a guideline of how actually to educate a militaristic state-people. "The education of a militaristic state-people" largely comprised translations of Japanese source materials on the matter, to which Jiang had added his own comments. Like Cai, Jiang emphasised the close relationship that ought to exist between the military man and the nation-state:

Military service is the responsibility of the state-people, the defence of the country is [their] duty. The wars of today are wars of the whole body of the state-people (*guomin quanti* 國民全體). (...) Apart from the state-people, [there] is no entity [that would suffice] to shoulder the responsibility of the life and death, the misfortune and fortune [of the whole nation-state].[64]

Any people that was to survive in these Social Darwinist times had to be prepared for the performance of its obligations towards the nation-state. To this end, all aspects of life had to be militarised:

All organisations in society should be regulated according to military laws. All organs of national defence should be built according to military considerations. The spirit of society (*shehui zhi jingshen* 社會之精神), [its] customs and habits, all ought to be related to the military man's spirit in a meaningful [way].[65]

In the course of activating such a militaristic spirit, the following pre-requisites had to be met, and the following steps had to be taken: (1) a feeling of "love of one's country" (*aiguo* 愛國) had to be developed, a sentiment that arose from personally being responsible for the military security of the state. However, love of one's country had to arise in a people *before* the nation-state could be founded. Furthermore, the individual's willingness to sacrifice his or her life for the greater good could only develop if the people assembled into the all-

---

62 Ibid., no. 1, p. 87.
63 Ibid., no. 1, p. 88.
64 Jiang Baili (1902), "Junguomin zhi jiaoyu", p. 33.
65 Ibid., pp. 34–5.

encompassing social unit of the nation-state.[66] (2) A notion of public virtues (*gongde* 公德)—of the willingness to subordinate oneself to greater concerns than one's own—had to be mediated, and the most effective way to do so was through the communal experience of military life:

[If a soldier] dies, [he dies] together [with his brothers in arms]. If [he] lives, [he] lives together [with his brothers in arms]. It is the military man's highest virtue (*meide* 美德) to sacrifice [his] life for the [greater good] of the whole body. Thus, for the troops, public virtues are the core element of [their] organisation, and with respect to [mediating] public virtues, the troops are the best instrument for educating [the people].[67]

(3) A "sentiment of honour" (*mingyuxin* 名譽心) had to be fostered, a sentiment that could only be gained through fastidious performance of one's duties to the nation-state. (4) The individual's body and will had to be hardened by means of accustoming it to a frugal lifestyle (*zhisu* 質素) and training its perseverance (*rennaili* 忍耐力). Only thus prepared for hardships could one serve the nation-state adequately.[68]

All these behavioural standards were perfectly epitomised by the professional soldier, and still—deplored Jiang—the Chinese scorned him. They also displayed an arrogant aversion to hardships in general, an aversion they justified on the grounds of their alleged cultural superiority. In—what was for Jiang—a rare moment of righteous anger, he therefore lambasted his countrymen:

China truly is a rotten country; its stupid and frail [men] are incapable of assuming [any] responsibility [for the greater good of the nation-state]. (...) Those who say: "I wish for civilisation"—they have not yet understood that sufferings [accompany] the pursuit of civilisation. [They] wish to enjoy the pleasures of civilisation before [having had to fight and suffer for their attainment].[69]

In the face of the perpetual natural struggle for survival, the most viable way to ensure China's thriving was to impart the spiritual and practical skillset of the soldier on everyone, implored Jiang: "State-people! State-people! The stage of contest has been set, and nothing is more urgent than to disseminate military knowledge!"[70]

In the spring of 1903, then, Liang Qichao would summarise and refine the core messages of his two friends' articles. In the seventeenth part of the series of articles entitled "Renewing the People"—"On the Esteem of Martial Qualities" (Lun shangwu 論尚武)—he turned his attention to the esteem of martial qualities by emphasising their importance for the creation of nation-statehood:

---

66 Ibid., p. 36.
67 Ibid., p. 37.
68 Ibid., pp. 39–40.
69 Ibid., p. 41.
70 Ibid., p. 45.

[The esteem of martial qualities] is that which the nation-state depends on for [its] establishment, and [it] is that which civilisation relies on for its preservation. In the words of Bismarck: "That which the Ecumene (*Tianxia* 天下) can rely on, [is] not international law (*gongfa* 公法)! [It] is nothing but black iron, nothing but red blood!"[71]

It had been the prevalence of such a martial spirit among its people that had paved the way for Germany's swift international rise. Now, there was "not one [person] who did not receive the education of the military man [or] does not possess the [professional] qualifications (*zige* 資格) of the military man"[72] in the German Empire. Germany had attained its dominant international status within a very short time, and therefore its (perceived) emphasis on all things military seemed to be the most viable option for the Chinese people to assemble into a nation-state and rise.[73] With his article, Liang thus essentially stipulated all the key messages of the then ensuing debate on a militaristic state-people.[74]

Liang Qichao argued for the education of a militaristic state-people in the same way in which Cai and Jiang had, but, with regard to its nationalist value, he strengthened their line of argument: Liang was very articulate at underscoring that the emergence of a martial spirit did, in fact, *precede* all feelings of love of one's country. In Germany, for instance, the emergence of nationalism had been informed by Bismarck's seemingly bellicose iron-and-blood politics.[75] By establishing this order—more precisely, by asserting that the individual's esteem of martial qualities *predated* all feelings of nationalism or patriotism and the will to assemble into a nation-state—the discourse on a militaristic state-people was shielded from the otherwise conceivable accusation that it drew the picture of a nation whose only *defining* characteristic was its political manifestation—the nation-state. If that were the case, the whole pre-revolutionary discourse on the Chinese nation—whose explicit goal it had been to construe a nation *independent* from the state (currently being under the control of the Manchus, as it was)—would have been reduced to absurdity. But by asserting the primacy of martiality, Cai E, Jiang Baili, and Liang Qichao did, in fact, envision a *militaristic* nation, a nation characterised by spiritual qualities and practical abilities explicitly attributed to the professional soldier. The advantage of such an imagined community was twofold: since the question of national belonging was thus reduced to compliance with a specific mind- and skillset, the otherwise necessary—and

---

71 Liang Qichao (1902–06), "Xinmin shuo", no. 28 (1903), p. 1.

72 Ibid., no. 28 (1903), p. 1.

73 Ibid., no. 29 (1903), p. 8.

74 Later articles that concerned themselves with the notion of a militaristic state-people would take up these ideas and alter or refine them only to a small degree, e.g. by putting a stronger emphasis on the necessity of physical training, cf. Bingwu (1911), "Junguomin jiaoyu zhi cao'an" or delving into the reasons for China's lack in martiality; cf. Guanghan (1904), "Junguomin de jiaoyu".

75 Liang Qichao (1902–06), "Xinmin shuo", no. 28 (1903), pp. 1–2.

THE BOUNDARIES OF THE CHINESE NATION

highly dividing—task of determining whatever exclusionary (Han)-*Chinese* identifying markers could be circumvented, *and* membership in the Chinese national community—irrespective of ethnicity—became open to all who, upon acquiring said militaristic mind- and skillset, developed feelings of responsibility towards their homeland.

In one respect, however, the concept of a militaristic nation was still assailable: while the creators of the notion of a militaristic state-people had circumnavigated the risk of reducing the nation to its political manifestation, they had basically sacrificed the "Chineseness" of the Chinese nation. After all, the gist of Cai's and his fellow campaigners message was that belonging to the nation was open to all who acquired the mind- and skillset of the military man. The resulting lack of "Chineseness" was further aggravated by the fact that the notion of a militaristic state-people had—essentially *in toto*—been lifted from the Japanese precedent. For this reason, Liang Qichao would soon take it upon himself to assert that the esteem of martial qualities was actually a genuinely *Chinese* character trait: in late December 1904, Liang's (self-proclaimed and somewhat counter-intuitively titled) textbook *China's bushidō* (*Zhongguo zhi wushidao* 中國之武士道) was published in Shanghai.[76] In the "Author's Preface" (zixu 自序), Liang claimed:

[I], the New Historian (*Xin shishi* 新史氏; *i.e.*, Liang Qichao; C.B.) ... says: "Martiality (*wu* 武) was the earliest natural instinct (*tianxing* 天性) of the Chinese [ethnic] nation (*Zhongguo minzu* 中國民族). [That] the Chinese nation is [now] without martiality, [this] is [only its later developed] second natural instinct."[77]

Accordingly, in the times of the Warring States (*Zhanguo* 戰國, 475–221 B.C.), the various Chinese states had still had to be militaristic (*junguo zhuyi* 軍國主義) and possessed by a martial spirit in order to survive. Only with the political unification and the establishment of imperial rule had China lost its own "bushidō spirit", and its people had become effeminate.[78] Now, this original spirit of the Chinese had to be restored. To this effect, Liang Qichao compiled a list of qualities that the true warrior (*wushi* 武士)—as the archetypical embodiment of a state-people—ought to possess. The main gist of this list was that the individual *always* had to attach the utmost importance to the benefit of the nation-state, irrespective of his or her personal well-being. The individual's *unreserved* loyalty had to belong to the nation-state alone.[79]

---

76 In the book's "instructions for use" (fanli 凡例), Liang defended his decision to use the—admittedly Japanese term—"bushidō" on the grounds of its "elegance and [comprehensive] meaning"; Liang Qichao (1904), *Zhongguo shi wushidao*, "fanli", p. 1.

77 Ibid., "zixu", p. 1.

78 Ibid., "zixu", pp. 3, 11–12.

79 Ibid., "zixu", pp. 5–7.

304 CLEMENS BÜTTNER

However, Liang Qichao could not, of course, convincingly declare martiality to be a specifically *Chinese* character trait. His attempts at establishing a national identity upon the basis of an indigenised "bushidō spirit" could only be deemed successful if it was related to another—more tangible—element. A "martial spirit" might indeed be conceived as a characteristic of the Chinese people, but the same could also be said of other peoples. As a result, the actual "Chineseness" of the nation that Liang envisioned had to be derived from its members' connection to a specific—namely, Chinese—*state*.

This state-orientation of militaristic nationalism made it highly attractive to the Qing rulers who, by then, were fighting for their political survival: not only did it hold the prospect of a thoroughly militarised—and thus strong, disciplined, and obedient—people, it also, from their perspective, was pleasingly silent on the matter of ethnicity, *the* main weak point of the Manchu Court's claim to legitimate power. In its early days, moreover, the idea of educating a militaristic state-people was not yet firmly directed *against* the Qing: in the spring of 1903, for instance, a meeting of over one thousand *literati* in Shanghai concluded with the demand that the throne take measures to instil the "spirit of a militaristic state-people" (*junguomin zhi jingshen* 軍國民之精神) into the Chinese people.[80] In early 1906, the Court itself decreed that all educational facilities in the Empire ought to incorporate the "doctrine of a militaristic state-people" in their curricula, as a means to prepare their students physically and mentally for military service.[81] Official advocacy of the concept of educating a militaristic state-people was to continue right until the end of the Empire.[82]

The Interplay between Militaristic and Ethnic Notions of the Nation

The Qing Court's enthusiastic embrace of the concept of a militaristic state-people did not mean that its creators were loyal supporters of the Manchu Court. By 1903, Liang Qichao's support of a constitutional monarchy was wavering at best, and both Cai E and Jiang Baili were clearly inclined towards revolution.[83] Nonetheless, many of the early supporters of the concept of a militaristic state-people were not (yet) clearly opposed to the prospect of continued rule of the Manchu Court. However, their—already timid—faith in the

---

80 Cf. Lü Yujun, Chen Changhe (2007), "Qingmo Minchu de junguomin jiaoyu sichao de xingqi jiqi shuailuo", pp. 93–97.
81 "Jiaoyu zongzhi" (1906), p. 7.
82 Cf. e.g. *Qingchao xu wenxian tongkao* (1935 [1921]), vol. 2, j. 111, "xuexiaokao shiba", p. 8698.
83 See Boorman (1967-71), *Biographical Dictionary*, vol. 1, p. 313; vol. 3, p. 288.

ability of the Qing to reform themselves and strengthen China was irredeemably destroyed in the first half of 1903, the year in which the Court threw away its last chance of taking the lead in a patriotic movement of Chinese students both on the mainland and in Japan who had rallied together to resist Russian encroachment in Northeast China: in the course of the Boxer Uprising, Tsarist Russia had occupied Manchuria and stationed 200,000 troops in the region. They remained even after the signing of the Boxer Protocol on 7 September 1901. In order to settle the question of Russia's withdrawal from Manchuria, an additional agreement between the Qing and the Russian Empire was signed on 4 April 1902. It stipulated that the region be evacuated in three stages over the course of eighteen months. But while the first evacuation wave took place as planned in October 1902, the Russian government did not comply with the agreement to withdraw the second portion of its troops in April 1903. Furthermore, the previously returned cities of Mukden (*i.e.*, Shenyang 沈陽) and Niuzhuang 牛莊 were re-occupied by Russian forces.[84]

It was because of Russia's blatant disregard of the 1902 agreement that Chinese students came together throughout the whole Empire, as well as in Tōkyō, in the spring of 1903 to voice their criticism of the Tsarist regime.[85] In order to underscore their willingness to resist Russia in Manchuria actively, many students formed volunteer corps (*yiyongdui* 義勇隊) and began to train for combat. These corps, they offered, would fight side by side with the Qing's armed forces in Manchuria. But the Manchu Court reacted negatively: in China, student activities were suppressed, and the Japanese authorities were asked to disband the local student volunteer corps that had already been organised into the so-called Student Army (*Xueshengjun* 學生軍).[86] To China's patriotic youth, the Throne had now shown its true colours. Its interest was not China's well-being, only the retention of its power, even if that meant bowing to the illegal pressures of the Russians (or others).

On 11 May 1903, the Student Army was re-organised into the Association for the Education of a Militaristic State-People (*Junguomin Jiaoyuhui* 軍國民教育會).[87] Its establishment was justified by the need to instil a fighting spirit (*douzhi* 鬥志) in the people. Otherwise, they argued, there would soon be no one left in China to advocate war against Russia. Fighting, however, was inevitable if the Chinese were not to become slaves of the Slavs.[88] To this effect, a convention was drawn up in which the Association's members pledged to cultivate a martial spirit (*yangcheng shangwu jingshen* 養成尚武精神) among themselves, and to

---

84 Hsü (1980), "Late Ch'ing foreign relations", pp. 127–129.
85 Weston (2004), *Power of Position*, p. 61; Zhang Yufa (1982), *Qingji de geming tuanti*, p. 256.
86 Ibid., 259–60; Zarrow (2012), *After Empire*, p. 155; Young (1959), "Ch'en T'ien-hua", p. 115.
87 Yang Tianshi, Wang Xuezhuang (1979), *Ju E yundong: 1901–1905*, p. 106.
88 "Junguomin Jiaoyuhui zhi chengli" (1903), p. 144.

invest their patriotism (*aiguo zhuyi* 愛國主義) in the service of China. The members of the Association were also to take it upon themselves to protect China's territorial integrity and—invoking Yan Fu—to increase the physical strength of the Chinese people (by means of physical training, *etc.*).[89]

In the early days of the Association, its activities were not explicitly directed against the Manchu Court. Even though the Association for the Education of a Militaristic State-People was the direct outcome of the Qing's refusal to co-operate with China's patriotic youth both in China and abroad,[90] it was made clear in the announcement of its establishment that the Chinese students in Japan would not become active either on the political stage or on the battlefield without the prior consent of the Court.[91] By 5 July 1903, however, such restraint had clearly been abandoned. From that day on, the members of the Association for the Education of a Militaristic State-People began to wear badges with a portrait of the Yellow Emperor (Huangdi 黃帝)[92]—a gesture of great significance, as it symbolised the final renunciation of the Qing Court's claim to legitimate authority over China: from middle of 1903 onwards, numerous articles in the revolutionary periodical press began to position the Yellow Emperor as the first legitimate ruler of China and the progenitor of the Han race—but not of the Manchus.[93]

For this reason, it seemed as if the ethnic turn of the Association for the Education of a Militaristic State-People signified the—albeit temporary—triumph of ethnic nationalism over its militaristic counterpart in the political discourse. This impression was supported by other developments at the time, above all the so-called "*Subao* case" (*Subao* an 蘇報案) in Shanghai: in May 1903, the newspaper *Subao* published long passages of Zou Rong's 鄒容 (1885–1905) overtly racist anti-Manchu pamphlet *The Revolutionary Army* (*Gemingjun* 革命軍). The newspaper's decision resulted in a severe official backlash: Zhang Binglin, who had written an approving introduction to the text, as well as Zou Rong, were both arrested and sentenced to perennial prison terms. Of equal importance was the fact that the revolutionary faction in Japan had gained further momentum through the inauguration of two radical Chinese journals in Tōkyō: *Zhejiangchao* 浙江潮 was published for the first time in February 1903,

---

89 "Junguomin Jiaoyuhui gongyue" (1903), pp. 2, 5.

90 It has to be noted, however, that the Court's leeway to accept the students' offer was limited by the fact that students were by law prohibited from engaging in political affairs; cf. Weston (2004), *Power of Position*, p. 63.

91 "Junguomin Jiaoyuhui zhi chengli" (1903), p. 145.

92 Chow (2001), "Narrating Nation, Race, and National Culture", p. 59.

93 Cf. Dikötter (1992), *The Discourse of Race*, pp. 116–118. The growing willingness to differentiate between sub-races of the yellow race, perceptible since around 1900, also signified the gradual departure of the anticipation of a "great race war" between the yellow and the white races; cf. Chow (2001), "Narrating Nation, Race, and National Culture", p. 54.

Jiangsu 江蘇 in April. These two periodicals proved to be powerful challengers to Liang Qichao's journalistic predominance, as had hitherto been ensured by the influence of *Xinmin congbao*.[94] However, the—in hindsight—most conclusive indication of the (momentary) victory of ethnic nationalism in the Chinese nationalist discourse was Sun Yat-sen's 孫逸仙 (1866–1925) embrace of racist anti-Manchu ideas to mobilise support for his movement.[95]

And yet all these developments convey only an incomplete picture of the dynamics of the discourse on the Chinese nation at the time. After all, the ethnic and the militaristic discourses on the nation were anything but mutually exclusive. To advocate national ideas of a community of values was not tantamount to the rejection of an ethnically-defined nation, and an emphasis of ethnicity-based markers of identity did not preclude the possibility of an appreciation of the goals of the advocates of militaristic nationalism. The participants of both sides in the nationalist discourse could easily find common ground by focusing on the starting-point of their deliberations—Social Darwinism.

Seen from this point of view, it is hardly surprising that the two names that are strongly associated with anti-Manchu racist ideas can be found on the list of members of the Association for the Education of a Militaristic State-People: Chen Tianhua 陳天華 (1875–1905) and Zou Rong. The former called for the merciless killing of everyone who did harm to the Han (as descendants of the Yellow Emperor), while also maintaining that the Manchus, because of their racial inferiority, were no real threat to the Han.[96] The latter was infamous for depicting the Manchus as an inferior animal-like race that ought to be completely annihilated if the Han were to cleanse themselves of the "great shame" (*da chiru* 大恥辱) of 260 years of foreign domination.[97]

And yet, at the same time, these men were also very much at home with the discourse that their acquaintances Cai E and Jiang Baili had initiated: until his death at his own hands on 8 December 1905, Chen remained undecided in his opinion of the Manchu Court. For instance, even in an inflammatory text such as his "Alarm Bell" (Jingshizhong 警世鐘), distributed in the autumn of 1903 after the Qing had declined the Chinese students' offer to resist Russia with them, he stated that he would accept a Manchu government as long as it would honestly strive for reform, put an end to the racial discrimination of the Han, and fight foreign encroachment with determination.[98] In ideological accordance

---

94 Chow (1997), "Imagining Boundaries of Blood", pp. 43–45; Pusey (1983), *China and Charles Darwin*, p. 179.

95 Leibold (2004), "Positioning Minzu", p. 172.

96 Chen Tianhua (1957 [1903]), "Jingshizhong", p. 121. Cf. also Young (1959), "Ch'en T'ienhua", p. 123.

97 Zou Rong (1968 [1903]), *Gemingjun*, p. 1. John Lust's translation was consulted; cf. Tsou Jung (1968), *The Revolutionary Army*, p. 58. Cf. also Zarrow (2012), *After Empire*, p. 156.

98 Chen Tianhua (1957 [1903]), "Jingshizhong", pp. 125–126.

with militaristic nationalists, he also underscored that the Chinese had to embrace the military profession and its mindset if they wanted to stand a chance in the struggle for survival.[99] This kind of ideological duality stayed with him until his death, as became evident in his "Suicide Note" (Juemingshu 絕命書), written on the day before his demise (and published in *Minbao* 民報 on 2 August 1906). In the note, he eloquently emphasised the *dual* racial-political character of the Chinese revolutionary movement and defended his own viewpoint:

The current discussions of revolution have become detached and self-contended. I, [Chen Tianhua], was also a man engaged [in these discussions]. Among the revolutionaries, there are those who put emphasis on (ethnic) nationalism, [and] those who put emphasis on political questions. Usually, that which I stood for attached importance to political [matters] and made light of (ethnic) nationalist [matters], as is self-evident in the books which I have written. Formerly, [there were still those who] longed for Manchu political reforms, for the softening of racial divisions, so that [we] could ward off the foreign aggression [together]. Recently, however, the advocacy of (ethnic) nationalism [has become dominant, the notion] that—in the end—Manchus and Han cannot coexist. We attack them with words, they attack us [physically]. Our attacks on them only started in recent years, their attacks on us have been going on for 200 years. When we retreated, they pushed forward—how could [one thus] hope that they would dispel [our] suspicions [of them] and become willing to work together with us? [And yet, if one] desires that China will not be destroyed, [then one must] make a clean break [with the past], take over the reins of government from the Manchus and make them [aware of their new position]. If they realise [the end of their] Heavenly Mandate (*Tianming* 天命) [for the rule of China], then it will be possible to treat them [generously], like the Tokugawa 德川 are [treated by the Meiji Emperor in Japan]. The Manchu (ethnic) nation would be attributed equal status as [part of] the state-people, [since], in this era of civilisation, [we] have to break with the [habit] of killing from hatred. The reason why I attacked the Manchus was not because of that what the advocates of [racial] revenge say, but only because of political problems. According to political convention (*zhengzhi gongli* 政治公例), it is the rule that the majority [and] superior race rules over the minority [and] inferior race. That the minority [and] inferior race rules over the majority [and] superior race contradicts [this principle]. This was [always] my [standpoint] on revolution.[100]

Zou Rong, who died in prison on 3 April 1905, was not as ambivalent in his hatred of the Manchus as Chen Tianhua was. Nonetheless, his ideas were also permeated with key concepts of the discourse on a militaristic nation. Above all, Zou fully embraced the notion of a state-people that willingly assumed responsibility for its national well-being and won its sovereign and independent rights by means of fighting. According to him, it was the duty of the Han race— incomparably superior to the Manchus—to rise in revolution against the

---

99 Ibid., pp. 131, 133–134, 136.
100 Chen Tianhua (1906), "Chen Xingtai xiansheng juemingshu", pp. 3–4.

Qing.[101] Integrating these ideas into the Social Darwinist understandings of his time, Zou understood revolution to be a *universal* principle of evolution, and he, therefore, could refer to the example of other revolutionary movements as a source of inspiration for the Han race. Having studied the American Revolution, Zou stated, he compiled a list of proposals that the Chinese ought to observe in their own revolutionary endeavour: accordingly, Zou Rong called for the expulsion (or killing) of the Manchus and the establishment of a Chinese central government—and he reminded his compatriots of the duties that were associated with national sovereignty: the duty to pay taxes, the duty of loyalty to the nation-state—and, in first place—the duty of all men to transform themselves into a militaristic state-people.[102]

The incorporation of these ideas into Zou Rong's pamphlet was not coincidental. Both Cai E and Jiang Baili were close acquaintances of Zou during his stay in Japan, and they had been directly involved in the process of drafting *The Revolutionary Army*.[103] Cai and Jiang, for their part, had been brought close to the anti-Manchu revolutionary movement by the untimely death of Tang Caichang—one of the crucial disseminators of Social Darwinist-tinged racial ideas in Chinese thinking. On 22 August 1900, Tang (and others) had been executed by Qing authorities after their plan to instigate an uprising in Hankou 漢口 had been exposed.[104] Cai E's growing doubts in the ability of the Manchu Court to reform itself, and his flirtation with racist ideas found a first expression in a short poem he published in *Qingyibao* on 23 October 1900. In his "Random Thoughts in Ten [Verses]" (Zagan shi shou 雜感十首), written with the deaths of Tang and Tan Sitong 譚嗣同 (1865–1898) still fresh in mind, he expressed his disappointment in the Han race's inability to throw off the yoke of its Manchu overlords.[105]

After that, Cai E began to support the case of an anti-Manchu revolution actively. He associated himself with Chen Tianhua, Huang Xing 黃興 (1874-1916), Song Jiaoren 宋教仁 (1882-1913), and others and became involved in various revolutionary activities in Tōkyō. Nonetheless, Cai E also remained convinced of the veracity of the assumption that China could only be saved by military means, a conviction that not only found expression in his series of articles on a militaristic state-people, but also in the role that he played in the 1911 Revolution in Yunnan, the National Protection War (*Huguo zhanzheng* 護

---

101 Zou Rong (1968 [1903]), *Gemingjun*, pp. 25–26, 35–36, 41–42. John Lust's translation was consulted; cf. Tsou Jung (1968), *The Revolutionary Army*, pp. 99, 113, 122.

102 Zou Rong (1968 [1903]), *Gemingjun*, pp. 42–43. John Lust's translation was consulted; cf. Tsou Jung (1968), *The Revolutionary Army*, p. 123.

103 Liu Yusheng (1960), *Shizaitang zayi*, p. 149, Deng Jiangqi (2006), *Cai E sixiang yanjiu*, p. 48.

104 Wu Yangxiang (2009), "Jiang Baili zaonian de sixiang shijie", p. 32; Deng Jiangqi (2006), *Cai E sixiang yanjiu*, pp. 43–44, 46.

105 Cai E (1900), "Zagan shi shou", p. 1.

國戰爭) of 1915–16, and the professional military career he was to pursue until his early death in 1916.[106]

Jiang Baili's political biography was quite similar to that of Cai. After his arrival in Japan in the wake of Tang Caichang's failed uprising, he befriended Cai E and soon found entry into revolutionary circles in the Japanese capital. Unlike Cai, however, Jiang embraced the racial and racist ideas of his compatriots more comprehensively. He became very involved with the radical journal *Zhejiangchao* and published numerous articles that disseminated ethnic—and racist—ideas. For instance, for the first two issues of *Zhejiangchao*, Jiang provided an article on "The Nature of the Russian People" (Eren zhi xingzhi 俄人之性質) in which he maintained that they were unable to assemble into a strong group because of their heterogeneous—part Asian, part European—racial background.[107] In his two-part article entitled "A Discussion of Two Important Recent Theories" (Jinshi er da xueshuo zhi pinglun 近時二大學說之評論), Jiang addressed Chinese circumstances: directly referring to Liang's dictum that the people must be renewed, he argued that China could only be saved if the Qing government was done away with. As long as a foreign race was ruling over China, no national rejuvenation would be possible.[108]

"A discussion of two important recent theories", published in October and November 1903 in *Zhejiangchao*, had been written with the events of the spring and summer still fresh in mind. The Manchu Court's reaction to the Volunteer Corps had disappointed Jiang Baili to such an extent that he called on his Chinese fellow students to concentrate on the expulsion of the Manchus.[109] However, and just as Cai E had, Jiang also chose to complete his studies at the Japanese Imperial Army Officers Academy. He partook in the 1911 Revolution and dedicated the rest of his life to the military strengthening of China.[110]

Naturally, Chen Tianhua, Zou Rong, Cai E, and Jiang Baili were far from being alone with their open-minded opinions of the Chinese nation. Ultimately, for them, as for many other political thinkers and activists, the main interest rested with the actual strengthening of the Chinese polity. To a certain extent, therefore, most participants in the pre-revolutionary nationalist discourse incor-

---

106 Tian Fulong (ed.) (1997), *Yi Cai E*, p. 141; Deng Jiangqi (2006), *Cai E sixiang yanjiu*, pp. 49–55.
107 Jiang Baili (1903a), "Eren zhi xingzhi", no. 1, pp. 81–83; no. 2, pp. 77–9. Also cf. Dikötter (1992), *The Discourse of Race*, p. 110.
108 Jiang Baili (Feisheng) (1903b), "Jinshi er da xueshuo zhi pinglun", no. 8, pp. 1–2; no. 7, p. 8; no. 9, pp. 11–15. Cf. also Jiang Baili (Feisheng) (1903b), no. 8, pp. 1–2, 7–8; no. 9, pp. 11–5. Cf. also Wu Yangxiang (2009), "Jiang Baili zaonian de sixiang shijie", p. 33.
109 Yang Tianshi, Wang Xuezhuang (1979). *Ju E yundong: 1901–1905*, pp. 289–290.
110 See Setzekorn (2015), "Jiang Baili".

porated ideas of both the ethnic and the militaristic discourse into their own articles.[111]

Only for a short time after 1904 did the development of a schism between the advocates of ethnic and militaristic notions of the nation seem imminent. In that year, Yan Fu, the doyen of Chinese Social Darwinist thinking, came to find himself compelled to remind his compatriots of the fact that successful group formation was but one side of the struggle for survival: in his translation of Edward Jenks' (1861–1939) *A History of Politics*, Yan Fu promoted the Englishman's view that the ascent of modern statehood had been caused by the effects of warfare, that the modern state's structural origins lay in military organisation, and that it was military matters that—mainly through the common bond of military service—created social cohesion at national level.[112] This, *per se*, did not arouse the anger of the revolutionaries. After all, Yan, like them, dreamt of a strong and wealthy China. However, Yan Fu had become convinced that the prospective Chinese nation-state primarily ought to be defined by its military function. By implication, then, all activities that jeopardised social cohesion, as the basis of military strength, must be avoided. In a commentary on Jenks' assessment that all legislation ought to be based upon state considerations,[113] he wrote:

The Manchus won the country some 300 years ago, and yet, clear racial divisions between the Manchus and the Han still exist. (...) [Correspondingly], while the present [political] groups disagree on [the degree to which] the new and the old [ought to be embraced], they all hold the same [positive] view of [ethnic] nationalism (*minzu zhuyi* 民族主義). Today, [they] talk of joining together in groups (*hequn* 合群), tomorrow, [they] talk of driving the foreigners away, [they] even talk of driving the Manchus away. As for talking of militarism (*junguo zhuyi* 軍國主義), of hoping that everyone embraces [this doctrine]—there is virtually no one [who holds this view]! (...) But will [ethnic] nation-

---

111 Wang Jingwei 汪精衞 (1883–1944), for instance, analysed the organizational peculiarities of the Qing military sphere. It was there, argued Wang, that Manchu's unequal treatment of the Han became especially apparent and had safeguarded their continued rule; see Wang Jingwei (1905/06), "Minzu de guomin", no. 2, pp. 9–13. Elsewhere, Wang appropriated the bluntschlian distinction between (ethnic) nations and state-peoples and tried to bridge the gap between racial notions of the nation and a state's constitutive state-people (ibid., no. 1, p. 3). Hu Hanmin 胡漢民 (1879–1936) invoked the process of evolution—and not history—to justify opposition to the Manchu. Cf. Hu Hanmin (1906), "Shu Houguan Yan shi zuijin zhengjian", p. 13. Wang's and Hu's thought, as well as that of others, such as Zhu Zhixin 朱執信 (1885–1920), Yang Du 楊度 (1875–1931), Chen Tianhua, Zou Rong, Liang Qichao, and Zhang Binglin have been studied at length by Gasster, (1969), *Chinese Intellectuals and the Revolution of 1911*, Chaps. 3, 6, and Pusey (1983), *China and Charles Darwin*, Chaps. 6, 7.

112 Zhenkesi (2002 [1903]), *Shehui tongquan*, "juan shang", p. 5a; "juan xia", pp. 4a, 26a. Cf. also Jenks (1900), *A History of Politics*, pp. 2, 73, 140. Yan Fu circumscribed Jenks' term "military organization" (Jenks (1900), *A History of Politics*, p. 140), as "militaristic society" (*junguo shehui* 軍國社會), cf. Zhenkesi (2002 [1903]), *Shehui tongquan*, "juan xia", p. 26a.

113 See Jenks (1900), *A History of Politics*, pp. 124–125.

alism be [an adequate means] to strengthen our race? I [Yan Fu] have concluded that it certainly cannot [serve this purpose]![114]

It was especially these lines that triggered a forceful reaction from the revolutionary camp. In addition, the revolutionaries also had to deal with the challenge of Liang Qichao who had begun to query the conclusiveness of their anti-Manchu thought. In the course of the ensuing heated debate, Hu Hanmin rejected the notion that ethnic nationalism and militarism were mutually exclusive, and that common feelings of racial identity were necessary for the creation of a sense of common belonging. Wang Jingwei maintained that ethnic nationalism was necessary to rid China of the monarchical system, and Zhang Binglin, like Hu, argued that racism and national cohesion complemented each other. Furthermore, he asserted that all militarily strong modern states were ethnically homogenous.[115] However, none of Yan's critics called into question that a nation-state had to be militarily potent. They only took umbrage with the assertion that ethnic nationalism was counter-productive to the goal they all pursued: strong statehood.

Revolutionising the Army and Winning the War

Due to the interplay of various factors, the concept of a militaristic nation was to gain in influence again in the second half of the 1900s. The years 1907–08 were a time of setbacks for the revolutionaries: Sun Yat-sen's [Revolutionary] Alliance (Tongmenghui 同盟會) instigated various unsuccessful revolts, infighting weakened the revolutionary camp, and China's secret societies could not be convinced of joining the revolutionaries as their fighting force. For these reasons, a new strategy had to be sought out—and the revolutionaries' focus began to shift to the New Armies. As they were the most modern and professional part of the Qing military establishment, their usefulness relied on a steady and sufficient supply of well-trained professional military men. This demand was increasingly met by Chinese military students who returned from Japan. While they were there, however, they were heavily targeted by propaganda efforts undertaken by the Revolutionary Alliance, and upon their return to the

---

114 Zhenkesi (2002 [1903]), *Shehui tongquan*, "juan xia", p. 20a.

115 Hu Hanmin (1906), "Shu Houguan Yan shi zuijin zhengjian", pp. 5–7, Wang Jingwei (1905/06), "Minzu de guomin", no. 2, p. 18, Zhang Binglin (1907b), "Shehui tongquan shangdui", pp. 16–17, 20–21. For more details regarding this issue, cf. Pusey (1983), *China and Charles Darwin*, pp. 326–330.

troops in China, they often began to disseminate revolutionary ideas in the military themselves.[116]

These developments were encouraging for the revolutionaries, but it would still take until 1909 for Sun Yat-sen to be convinced that the Chinese armed forces were no less reliable than secret societies. And yet, China's armed forces truly came into the focus of the revolutionaries only after Yuan Shikai 袁世凱 (1859–1916) had temporarily been forced into retirement.[117] The most effective means to stir the troops' revolutionary spirit was to disseminate anti-Manchu tracts by Chen Tianhua, Zou Rong, and the like. These texts were written in easily comprehensible vernacular and stressed the racial superiority of the Han in comparison with the inferior Manchus, they depicted the Qing rulers as corrupt and evil, and called for their annihilation.[118]

However, anti-Manchu agitation was only one of the mobilising forces at work in the New Armies. From the beginning, the calls for the education of a militaristic state-people had also been accompanied by an increasing glorification of the military man and his professional sphere. Like the concept of a militaristic state-people itself, the notion of the venerability of the soldier on the grounds of his profession was a reiteration of Japanese ideas. As shown above, Cai E had compared the Japanese favourably to the Chinese with regard to their appreciation of the military man and the great service that he did for his country,[119] and Jiang Baili had invoked a similar image in "The Education of a Militaristic State-People", when he had written admiringly about the honour of the Japanese soldier:

Which [Japanese man] does not wish to be endowed with the glorious honour [of the military man], stepping over bones on battlefields in enemy territory, shedding blood on [his own] country's territory for the just [national] cause? (...) The military man's sentiment of honour [and] the might of the country—they are but one![120]

Jiang's suggestion that the common man should model himself on the military man found even clearer expression in articles by others. For instance, in "On the Doctrine of Esteeming Martial Qualities" (Lun shangwu zhuyi 論尚武主義), published on 27 June 27 1905 in *Dongfang zazhi* 東方雜誌, its anonymous author demanded:

Value the honour of the military man, heighten the [social] position of the military man, promote the education of a militaristic state-people, spread the awe-inspiring [spirit] of

---

116 See Gasster (1980), "The republican revolutionary movement", pp. 505–506, 508–509, Wong (1989), *Search for Modern Nationalism*, pp. 67–83.

117 Tao Juyin (1957), *Beiyang junfa tongzhi shiqi shihua*, vol. 1, pp. 22–23.

118 Fung (1975a), "Military Subversion in the Chinese Revolution of 1911", pp. 113–115, 118–119.

119 Cai E (Fenhesheng) (1902), "Junguomin pian", no. 1, p. 80.

120 Jiang Baili (1902),"Junguomin zhi jiaoyu", p. 39.

[China's] bushidō, so [that] to die in battle may become the highest joy, [that] to defy death may become the highest [expression] of virtuousness, [and that] to submit to military service may become the due responsibility of the state-people.[121]

Of course, civilian notions of the national and moral superiority of the military man were very much welcomed by the Chinese military establishment. After all, it still had to ward off the long prevailing view that the military profession was reserved only for good-for-nothings. Now, however, the military man was frequently depicted as *the* archetypal member of a developed state-people: he was willing to give his all—even his life—selflessly for the greater good of the nation-state, he shunned spoils and riches, and he had, in the lengthy processes of education and training, been furnished with the spiritual qualities and practical skillset that were deemed indispensable for persisting in the universal struggle for survival. The more the military man was imagined as an exemplary *national* individual,[122] the more was he inclined to believe in such statements. Claims of his particular qualification to participate in national matters must also seem quite convincing, since they were rooted in the fact that he had undergone lengthy professional socialisation processes to acquire it. If this line of reasoning was brought to its logical conclusion, then the military man must indeed be better suited to assume responsibility for the well-being of the nation-state than others: since he had been specifically trained for it, he simply *must* be better prepared to do his job than civilians.

Accordingly, the units of the New Armies that revolted in Wuchang in October 1911 were by no means will-less instruments of the revolutionary faction, merely incited by anti-Manchu propaganda to rise up in arms against the Qing. Racist mobilisation strategies had obviously played an important role in stirring up the New Armies—the quickly rising death toll among the Manchus was ample proof of that[123]—but it was also the *military* revolutionary authorities in various provinces that first called for an end of the killings: to halt the continuing violence against Manchus in Wuchang, the Hubei 湖北 Military Government (*Junzhengfu* 軍政府) decreed a ban on retributive activities against banner-people on 23 October 1911. On the same day (and again two days later), military authorities in Shaanxi 陝西 took comparable measures. On 13 November 1911, Cai E, then military governor of Yunnan 雲南, cabled reassurances to the prefectural magistrate of Chuxiong 楚雄 county, emphasising that "this is a

---

121 "Lun shangwu zhuyi" (1905), p. 99.

122 Cf. e.g. Zhuangyou (1903), "Guomin xin linghun", pp. 5–6; Yang Du (1907), "*Zhongguo xinbao xu*", p. 1.

123 Rhoads (2000), *Manchus & Han*, pp. 187–205, refrains from estimating the overall number of victims of anti-Manchu violence during the revolution, but it must have been in the ten-thousands. Cf. also, Esherick (1976), *Reform and Revolution in China*, p. 182.

THE BOUNDARIES OF THE CHINESE NATION

political revolution (*zhengzhi geming* 政治革命), and not a racial revolution (*zhongzu geming* 種族革命)".[124]

While such measures to restore order might also be explicable without reference to the ideological convictions of Chinese military men, the incident that came to be known as the Luanzhou Armed Remonstrance (*Luanzhou bingjian* 灤州兵諫) was not: on 29 October 1911, 5,000 troops of the 20th Division stationed at the strategically important traffic hub of Luanzhou (roughly 150 km east of Beijing) refused to board trains that were supposed to transport them south to face the revolutionary enemy. Their commander Zhang Shaozeng 張紹曾 (1879–1928), as well as Lan Tianwei 藍天蔚 (1878–1922), commander of the 2nd Mixed Brigade, and others memorialised the Throne to give their opinion of the political developments of the last weeks and to make twelve demands.[125] The two men—both graduates of the Japanese Imperial Army Officers Academy, with Lan Tianwei also having been active in the Resist Russia Movement—criticised the Qing, saying that the Court had, until now, only taken military measures against the insurgents. However, in order to resolve this conflict truly, the Court also ought to take political action. In their following demands, Zhang and Lan then outlined a roadmap that was to lead to the establishment of a constitutional monarchy and the restoration of peace: the inauguration of a parliament, the drafting of a constitution, an amnesty for all political offenders, *etc.* Their entitlement—as military men—to participate actively in political affairs was underscored with their final demand:

[Regarding] the constitution [and] the organic law of the parliament [that] are now to be drafted, as well as all [other] important issues of the nation-state—should circumstances demand a settlement [of any dispute], then military men have the right to participate (*canyu* 參預) [in the process of their resolution].[126]

After some hesitation, the Court finally gave in. On 3 November 1911, it announced the promulgation of the *Great Precepts in Nineteen Articles* (*Zhongda xintiao shijiu tiao* 重大信條十九條), a framework for a future constitution that was to curtail the powers of the Emperor and the nobility considerably. Many of their provisions were almost verbatim copies of Zhang's and Lan's demands, but the desired codification of a military prerogative to "participate" in political

---

124 See Yang Tingyuan (1982), "Ji E junzhengfu de chuqi waijiao huodong", p. 47 (dated 23 October 1911) for Hubei, Guo Xiren (1957), "Congrong jilüe", p. 69 (dated 23 October 1911) and Guo Xiaocheng (1957), "Shanxi guangfuji", pp. 41-42 (dated 25 October 1911) for Shaanxi, Cai E (1984a [1911]), "Zhi Chuxiongxian yishihui quanxuesuo dian", p. 78 (dated 13 November 1911) for Yunnan. Cf. also, Rhoads (2000), *Manchus & Han*, pp. 189–192.

125 For accounts of the Armed Remonstrance, cf. Rhoads (2000), *Manchus & Han*, pp. 180–185, Fung (1980), *The military dimension of the Chinese revolution*, pp. 218–219.

126 *Zhonghua Minguo shishi jiyao (chugao): 1911* (1973), pp. 754, 753–4.

decisions did not feature on the list.[127] Nonetheless, two days later the Luanzhou Armed Remonstrance came to its conclusion.

By then, the end of the Qing Dynasty was only a matter of time. On 18 December 1911, after revolutionary authorities in both Wuchang and Shanghai had pledged to guarantee the Court's security and livelihood, negotiations between the revolutionaries and the Throne were officially begun, and on 1 January 1912—before the specific terms for the Manchu abdication had been laid down—the Republic of China under the provisional presidency of Sun Yatsen was proclaimed. Notwithstanding this, little actual progress was made in the next weeks, and military men intervened once again: on 26 January 1912, a group of more than 40 Qing military officers under the leadership of Duan Qirui 段祺瑞 (1865–1936) cabled Beijing to express their disapproval of the Manchu Court's delaying tactics ever since it had issued the *Great Precepts*. In addition, the officers urged the Qing finally to abdicate from the throne, which the Xuantong 宣統 Emperor (r. 1908–1912) did on 12 February.[128]

While military political activity on the imperial side usually stemmed from soldierly initiative without prior invitation by the Court, the revolutionaries explicitly welcomed active military participation in politics. As early as late 1906, Sun Yat-sen's [Revolutionary] Alliance had prepared an "[Inaugural] Manifesto of the Military Government" (Junzhengfu xuanyan 軍政府宣言) that was to be distributed on the day of the outbreak of the Revolution. In this well-known document, the prospective timetable of the establishment of republican rule was presented, and it began with the following lines:

Today, the army of the state-people (*guominjun* 國民軍) has risen [and] established the Military Government [in order] to wash away the 260 years of mutton stink [that the Manchus exude], to recover [our] 4,000 year old fatherland, [and] to work for the welfare of 400 million men—this is not only the unrefusable duty of the Military Government, our whole state-people ought to regard [this] as their personal duty![129]

Thus, it was clearly the military (assumed to be controlled by the revolutionaries, of course) that were to lead the way to China's national rejuvenation. During the second phase of the revolutionary project, the period of rule by a provisional constitution, the military government was to relinquish its rights at

---

127 "Zhongda xintiao shijiu tiao" (1911), pp. 5–8; Rhoads (2000), *Manchus & Han*, p. 184 has pointed out the similarity between Zhang's Twelve Demands and the Nineteen Articles.

128 Zhang Guogan (1958), *Xinhai Geming shiliao*, pp. 304–306. Military pressure was only one factor in the actual abdication. Rhoads (2000), *Manchus & Han*, p. 222, argues that Manchu resistance against giving up the Throne only ended after Liangbi 良弼 (1877–1912), a member of the imperial lineage, fell victim to an assassination attempt on 26 January.

129 Sun Zhongshan (1981 [1906]), "Zhongguo Tongmenghui geming fanglüe", p. 296.

THE BOUNDARIES OF THE CHINESE NATION

local level. Only in the final, third phase was military rule to come to its definitive end.[130]

Even though the document was written roughly five years before the revolution actually broke out, it would still hold sway in the autumn of 1911: most of the Chinese provinces that tergiversated from the Empire followed the lead of Hubei and established military governments under the leadership of military governors (*dudu* 都督) who were professional soldiers. The precedent had been set in Wuchang during the revolutionaries' search for an eminent personality to head the military government. Before Li Yuanhong 黎元洪 (1864–1926), commander of the 21st Mixed Brigade, had conceded (or had been coerced to concede) to assume the military governorship of Hubei on 11 October 1911, the civilian president of the provincial assembly, Tang Hualong 湯化龍 (1874–1918) had also been approached with the offer to head the province's revolutionary authorities. However, Tang had declined, invoking the needs of these times:

At this moment, [we live] in military times. I [Tang Hualong], am not a military man, I do not know how to employ military force. With regard to [the upcoming] military issues, [I therefore] ask you gentlemen to [alter your] plans [accordingly], for I would be incapable of providing the best [service].[131]

It was also because of this kind of reasoning that Li Yuanhong—a professional soldier of high rank and good reputation—was chosen to head the Hubei Military Government. But even though Tang justified his refusal to become Military Governor on the grounds of the military needs of his time, it was still a *political* position that he thus handed over to a military man.[132] In this respect, the notion of a special aptitude of the soldier to deal with political affairs—on the grounds of his professional socialisation—became reinforced once again.

---

130 Ibid., 296–8. After the Revolution broke out, adherence to the 1906 timetable was still reiterated. Cf. e.g. Cai E's official "Announcement to the Compatriots in the Whole Province" (Bugao quansheng tongbaowen 布告全省同胞文) from November 1911, Cai E (1984b [1911]), "Bugao quansheng tongbaowen", p. 98.

131 Cao Yabo (1982), *Wuchang Geming zhenshi*, vol. 2, p. 36; Cf. also, Fung (1975b), "Li Yüan-hung and the Revolution of 1911.", pp. 155–156; McCord (1993), *The Power of the Gun*, pp. 70–81, 83, 83n10.

132 Cf. e.g. the profile of requirements posed at a military governor in the document entitled "The Relations between the Military Government and the Local State-People's Armies" (Junzhengfu yu gechu guominjun zhi guanxi 軍政府與各處國民軍之關係), which – like the "[Inaugural] Manifesto of the Military Government" was part of "The General Revolutionary Plan of the Chinese [Revolutionary] Alliance" (Zhongguo Tongmenghui geming fanglüe 中國同盟會革命方略; Sun Zhongshan (1981 [1906]), "Zhongguo Tongmenghui geming fanglüe", p. 298–299.

The Qing geo-body, the Nation, and the Militarisation of the State

The increasing participation—and intervention—of the military in Chinese politics was only one result of the revolutionary events of October 1911. In part, the increasing assumption of political control by professional soldiers was due to the necessity of having to *fight* for control of the country. However, years of efforts to enhance the social reputation of the soldierly profession had also considerably contributed to these developments. By depicting the military man as *the* role model of a people that was to be politically conscious and only motivated by considerations of the greater good of the nation-state, it was unsurprising that he began to assert his national *political* role. In this respect, the 1911 Revolution brought militaristic nationalist ideology and political realities in conformity with each other, and the era of military-political entanglement that essentially was to characterise the whole Republican era began.

But it was not only militaristic ideology that encountered political realities. The same could also be said of the ethnic nationalist discourse whose principles also became translated into action. Beginning with the Wuchang Uprising, Manchus, as well as other non-Han ethnicities, became the target of Han-inflicted racist violence. However, now facing the prospect of *actually* having to assume political responsibility, the revolutionaries swiftly abandoned their racist rhetoric. But it was not primarily the lives of countless (potential) victims of Han racism that concerned them. What was at stake for them was the chance of realising their vision of a Chinese Republican state with the same territorial expansion as the (multi-ethnic) Qing Empire.

When faced with this dilemma, it was not difficult for Sun Yat-sen—whose embrace of racist anti-Manchu ideology had always been more purposeful and less fueled by conviction—to renounce the notion of an ethnic Han nation. Even years before he assumed the provisional presidency, he had been reluctant to advocate anti-Manchu ideas wholeheartedly. For instance, in a speech which he had given on occasion of the first anniversary of the revolutionary journal *Minbao* in late November 1906, he emphasised that the hate of the revolutionaries ought to be focused only on those Manchus who did harm to the Han, not on all Manchus.[133]

The primarily political rationale that underlay Sun's rejection of the Manchus could be traced back even further. In late 1894, when he had founded the Society to Revive China (*Xing Zhonghui* 興中會), he had pledged to expel the Qing rulers on the grounds of their perceived inability to deal with foreign aggression.[134] However, Sun Yat-sen's criticism of the Manchu Court did not

---

133 Sun Zhongshan (1906), "Ji shi'er yue er ri benbao jiyuan jieqingzhu dahui shi ji yanshuoci", p. 85.

134 Gasster (1980), "The republican revolutionary movement", pp. 466–467.

THE BOUNDARIES OF THE CHINESE NATION

extend to the territorial expression of their rule—the Qing Empire. In Japan, in 1899, he made a detailed "Current Map of China" (Shina gensei chizu 支那現勢地図) in which he drew up plans for a future railway system that was to connect all the territories of the state. In this plan, Manchu, Mongol, Uyghur, and Tibetan territories were also declared to be parts of China. James Leibold has put the objective of Sun's thinking in apt words: "[T]he emperor had to go, but the empire, or at least its territory, was to remain."[135]

Soon after the start of the Revolution, the safeguarding of the territorial integrity of the (former) Qing geo-body suddenly became more urgent: on 1 January, Outer Mongolia and Tibet declared their independence from China, Inner Mongolia began to make likewise preparations, and Xinjiang was by then already *de facto* ruled autonomously by its governor Yang Zengxin 楊增新 (1864–1928).[136] Sun, however, was not willing to let go of his vision of the Republic's territorial expansion, as he reiterated in his inaugural "Declaration of the Provisional President" (Linshi Da Zongtong xuanyanshu 臨時大總統宣言書), given in Nanjing on 1 January 1912. In his speech, Sun Yat-sen emphasised:

> The nation-state's foundation rests on [the ability] of the people to unite the Han, Manchu, Mongol, Hui, [and] Tibetan territories into one single state (*yiguo* 一國) and to unite the Han, Manchu, Mongol, Hui, [and] Tibetan [ethnic] nations into one single people (*yiren* 一人). This is called the unification of the (ethnic) nations (*minzu zhi tongyi* 民族之統一).[137]

Prior to the establishment of the Republic, other revolutionaries had not put the same stress on preserving the territorial integrity of the Empire after its future demise. In July 1907, for instance, Zhang Binglin had stated in his article "Explaining [the concept of a] Chinese Republic" (Zhonghua minguo jie 中華民國解) that the future state, on grounds of the ethnicity of their inhabitants, also ought to comprise Vietnamese and Korean territories. Tibetans, Hui, and Mongols, however, should be allowed to decide for themselves if they wanted

---

135 Leibold (2007), *Reconfiguring Chinese Nationalism*, p. 34. For the map, see Sun Zhongshan (1899), "Shina gensei chizu".

136 Leibold (2007), *Reconfiguring Chinese Nationalism*, p. 39; Leibold (2004), "Positioning 'Minzu'", p. 178.

137 Sun Zhongshan (1912), "Linshi Da Zongtong xuanyanshu", pp. 1–2. Sun's call to inter-ethnic unity of 1 January 1912 had, in a way, already been anticipated by Cai E in November 1911. At that time, the military governor of the ethnically highly heterogeneous province of Yunnan had informed his provincial compatriots of the key changes that would go along with the establishment of the Republic. He told them about the new polity's name (calling it *Zhonghuaguo* 中華國, however), its political system (democratic [*minzhu guoti* 民主國體]), its flag (red with the character "*Zhong*" 中 for China written in white at its centre), and that the Han, Hui, Mongolian, Manchurian, Tibetan, Yi, and Miao ethnicities should all be regarded as integral parts of the body politic as well; see Cai E (1984b [1911]), "Bugao quansheng tongbaowen", pp. 97–98.

to remain a part of China or become independent (that the Manchus had to be excluded from the Republic was clear to Zhang). Thus, Zhang—as one of the few participants in the discourse on ethnicity—would, at least in principle, concede that other ethnic groups possessed the same right to self-determination as the Han did.[138] And yet, in the days following the start of the Revolution, even Zhang Binglin would join in with those who had begun to call for a multi-ethnic "Republic of the Five [Ethnic] Nations" (*Wuzu Gonghe* 五族共和)[139] with the Empire's borders.

The resulting renunciation of racist rhetoric and the de-emphasising of ethnic nationalism also found abundant expression in early Republican legislation. The most prominent example of this could be found in the third and fifth articles of the *Provisional Constitution of the Republic of China* (*Zhonghua Minguo linshi yuefa* 中華民國臨時約法, promulgated on 11 March 1912). The third article stipulated that "[t]he territory of the Republic of China comprises 22 provinces, Inner [and] Outer Mongolia, Tibet, [and] Qinghai". Article 5 stated: "The people (*renmin* 人民) of the Republic of China are without exception equal; there is no discrimination on grounds of race, class, or religion."[140] Yet, it was also in more specific legislation that the new multi-national spirit of the Republic was invoked. In an order dated from 22 April, in which President Yuan Shikai decreed that the administration over Mongolia, Tibet, and Xinjiang was to remain with the Ministry of Internal Affairs (*Neiwubu* 內務部), he re-iterated the Republic's new nationalist parlance:

[We] now have a Republic of the Five [Ethnic] Nations. The Mongol, Tibetan, Hui, and [Uyghur] territories are also part of the sovereign territory (*lingtu* 領土) of the Republic of China, and [correspondingly], the Mongol, Tibetan, Hui, [and Uyghur ethnic] nations are [integral] parts of the Republican state-people. [Thus, we] must not, as in the times of imperial rule, [degrade them] again by giving [them] the [outdated] name of "dependent territories" (*fanshu* 藩屬).[141]

---

138 Zhang Binglin (1907a), "Zhonghua Minguo jie", p. 8. Furthermore, in his rebuttal of Yan Fu's rejection of ethnic nationalism, Zhang re-iterated again that, in principle, other ethnicities in China had the same right to national sovereignty as the Han; cf. Zhang Binglin (1907b), "Shehui tongquan shangdui", pp. 19–20. Wang Jingwei, by contrast, supported the notion that bigger races ought to assimilate smaller ones; cf. Pusey (1983), *China and Charles Darwin*, pp. 331–332.

139 Leibold (2004), "Positioning 'Minzu'", p. 179. For other advocates of a multi-ethnic republic after the outbreak of the Revolution, cf. Matten, (2012), "'China is the China of the Chinese'", pp. 86–88.

140 "Zhonghua Minguo linshi yuefa" (1912), Articles 3, 5. The three Manchurian provinces of Fengtian 奉天, Jilin 吉林, and Heilongjiang 黑龍江 were counted among the 22 provinces; see Lee (1970), *The Manchurian Frontier*, pp. 152–167.

141 "Linshi Da Zongtong ling" (1912), p. 3.

THE BOUNDARIES OF THE CHINESE NATION

With regard to the Manchus specifically, Yuan decreed on 24 May a ban on the sale of any kind of literature that was anti-Manchu in content or slandered the Qing Dynasty. He emphasised that any vilification of the Manchus (or other non-Han ethnicities) went against the "aims of the Republic" (*Minguo zongzhi* 民國宗旨).[142]

This new inclusiveness eventually became connected to global matters. After Sun Yat-sen had relinquished the provisional presidency in March, he even went so far as to declare that the very principles of Social Darwinism were obsolete. In a speech delivered on 30 August 1912 in Beijing, he stated that Western academia had already abandoned the notions of struggling for survival and the survival of the fittest, and that, correspondingly, the future wealth and power of the Chinese Republic did not lie with the precepts of Social Darwinism, but with co-operation and the willing performance of one's duties.[143]

Such a positive assessment of global developments was not shared by many, however. Most still regarded China's international position to be highly precarious: hostile imperialistic powers were lurking at the Chinese borders, and only a united people of the "Five [ethnic] nations" would be able to ensure China's survival.[144] Unfortunately, the people were not yet fit for this challenge, a fundamental weakness that was, especially for the Chinese military sphere, a matter of great concern and a reason for thorough discussion in the military periodical press. As early as 1904, the military educator Liao Yuchun 廖宇春 (1870–1923) had lamented in an article about "China's Military Preparedness" (Lun Zhongguo wubei 論中國武備) that China—because of its prevalent lack of interest in martial qualities—"... simply does not wish to become a powerful country".[145] This flaw had to be remedied, of course, and therefore, the Chinese people had to be taught to esteem martial qualities—by means of publicly exalting the military man and by having to undergo compulsory military service.[146]

Upon basis of this reasoning, the army was then often depicted as the school of the nation as, for instance, one Zhenfei 震飛 (dates unknown) maintained in his article entitled "Training the Soul" (Lian hun pian 練魂篇), published in September 1906 in *Nanyang bingshi zazhi* 南洋兵事雜誌: "Although the troops are [only] one part of the people, they may be regarded as the manufacturing place of the whole militaristic state-people."[147] Since it was mainly his purported spiritual qualities that were used to justify calls for the social elevation of the professional soldier, the envisioned military training of the people *en*

---

142 *Zhonghua Minguo shishi jiyao (chugao): 1912* (1971), pp. 534–535.

143 Sun Zhongshan (1982 [1912]), "Zai Beijing Hu-Guang Huiguan xuejie huanyinghui de yanshuo", p. 423.

144 Leibold (2007), *Reconfiguring Chinese Nationalism*, p. 38.

145 Liao Yuchun (1904), "Lun Zhongguo wubei", p. 2b.

146 He Zhongliang (1906), "Shangwu jiaoyulun", p. 2b–3a.

147 Zhenfei (1906), "Lian hun pian", pp. 13–14.

masse was to concentrate on cultivating the appreciation of soldierly virtues and values. More specifically, discipline and obedience as the most tangible expressions of such a mindset were especially emphasised. It was argued that it would be beneficial to the country if discipline were to be as strictly enforced in society as it was in the army. As one Zhuang'e 莊諤 (dates unknown) said in his comparison piece entitled "Education of the Troops and Education of the State-People" (Jundui jiaoyu yu guomin jiaoyu 軍隊教育與國民教育), published in mid-December 1906:

Everybody knows that the rules [of conduct] of the troops are strict. The rules [of conduct] of our state-people cannot be any [less] strict than [those] of the troops. In the nation-state, the rules of the nation-state apply. In society, the rules of society apply. (…) To be able to comply firmly with rules in [one's] professional work (*yewu* 業務) [and] one's personal conduct - how could [this] not be an indispensable quality of a civilised state-people (*wenming guomin* 文明國民)?[148]

From the viewpoint of a professional soldier like Zhuang'e, "careless state-peoples" (*qingbo zhi guomin* 輕薄之國民) had to be subjected to strict rules in order to make them become aware of their duties to the nation-state.[149] If, therefore, discipline was enforced among the people, their spirits would be rectified and the nation-state would prosper. If each member of the people could be brought to subordinate to the rules willingly, then the proper functioning of society—simply put, a network of overlapping hierarchical relationships—could be ensured. Correspondingly, the viewpoint that the armed forces ought to be regarded as *the* role model to the state-people was re-iterated.[150] This belief in the magnificence of the military man had already been put into apt words by a brother-in-arms of Zhuang'e who had confidently asserted in 1906: "The military man stands above the myriad people, [he] is the [true] representative of the state-people, [he] is the shield and rampart of the nation-state."[151]

This growing tendency of military men—on the grounds of their professional qualities—to glorify themselves must, of course, seem worrisome to the civilian state. Accordingly, from early on—and even though it had been the troops which had brought revolutionary victories—attempts were made to rein in the military and assert civilian control of the state.[152] At the same time, however, the allure of a thoroughly militarised nation-state, of a well-organised,

---

148 Zhuang'e (1906), "Jundui jiaoyu yu guomin jiaoyu", p. 3.

149 Ibid.

150 Ibid., p. 4.

151 Jianfei (1906), "Lun junren zhi jingshen", p. 3. Others were at least equally praiseful of the military man; cf. e.g. "Jingshen jianghua" (1907), p. 1.

152 Cf. "Gaojie junren xunling" (1913), "Lujun xingshi tiaoli" (1915), "Lujun shenpan tiaoli" (1915).

disciplined, obedient, and fortified people at the regime's disposal continued to hold considerable sway. Thus, on 2 September, 1912, the Ministry of Education (*Jiaoyubu* 教育部) made the Republic's "Educational aims" (Jiaoyu zongzhi 教育宗旨) known to the public, counting the education of a militaristic state-people as one of them.[153] Roughly three years later, in October 1915, President Yuan Shikai himself felt compelled to re-iterate that the esteem of martial qualities was a key component of the Republic's educational aims. He declared that a country's strength was intimately linked to the strength of the people, who, in turn, had to apply "the ways of esteeming martial qualities" (*shangwu zhi dao* 尚武之道) to strengthen themselves. These ways comprised the training and toughening of the body and—more importantly—awareness of personal responsibility of the individual to the state. This awareness had, of course, to be translated into actual services rendered to the country—to be exact: military service.[154]

The increasing association of the notions of esteeming martial qualities and militarism with educational aims and the matter of (compulsory) military service (which, nonetheless, would only be implemented in 1936[155]) might suggest that the function of military virtues and values as the nation-*defining* tool that Liang Qichao had envisioned them to be in 1903 was coming to its end. Yet, even though the Republic and many of its representatives were busy advocating the new notion of a multi-ethnic Chinese nation,[156] some continued to refer to martial qualities as the cause of the formation of China. In May 1915, for instance, the Beiyang 北洋 general and later one-time president of the Republic Feng Guozhang 馮國璋 (1859–1919) argued upon the basis of the single components of the character "*guo*" 國 (namely, "*wei*" 囗 for "encompass", "*ge*" 戈 for "weapon", "*kou*" 口 for "population", and "*yi*" 一 for the "individual") that the true meaning of "country" hailed from antiquity, when the people from a common area all had the duty to pick up their weapons and defend their home if need be. It was from there that China's political unification and national sovereignty had arisen. This line of argument brought Feng to the following conclusion: "[To say that] the doctrine of a militaristic state-people really was the cause of the birth of our national [community]—[that] is not calumny."[157] Gradually, however, the Chinese educational system had lost sight of this fact,

---

153 "Jiaoyubu gongbu jiaoyu zongzhi" (1912), p. 28.

154 "Da Zongtong banding jiaoyu yaozhi: shangwu" (1915).

155 Wang Xiaowei (1997), *Zhongguo junshi zhidushi: Bingyi zhidujuan*, pp. 381–382. The duty of the Chinese people to render military service compulsory had originally been codified in the provisional constitution of 11 March 1912 ("Zhonghua Minguo linshi yuefa" (1912), Article 14) but no steps to its actual implementation had been taken.

156 Cf. e.g. Matten (2012), "'China is the China of the Chinese'", pp. 85–96.

157 Feng Guozhang (1915), "Junguomin jiaoyu yanjiu chuyi", no. 84, p. 8.

and it led to the reprehensible rise of individualism (*geren zhuyi* 個人主義) and egotism.[158]

This line of argument notwithstanding, Feng's main interest did not lie with defining the Chinese nation, it rested with furnishing the state-people with those attributes that made them useful to the *state*: namely, that they be disciplined, fortified, and obedient. Not even the increasingly horrible news from the European battlefields of World War I and the—albeit only temporary—realisation that the ways of "might is right" could not be pursued indefinitely,[159] was capable of leading to an abandonment of militaristic ideas. In the early 1930s—only a few years after the conclusion of the Northern Expedition to unite (at least nominally) China under the *aegis* of the Guomindang 國民黨 (GMD)—its core principles were re-activated, albeit under the banner of "fascism" (*faxisidi zhuyi* 法西斯蒂主義). At that time, the Chinese modernisation project was not going well—administrative inefficiency and corruption abounded, the GMD was divided into various hostile factions, internal unrest was prevalent—and Chiang Kai-shek 蔣介石 (1887–1975) and numerous party ideologues were looking for ways to unite the Party and the people, increase effectiveness, and overcome the political standstill. In late 1931, the young Party member Liu Jianqun 劉健群 (1903–1972) proposed a revitalisation of the GMD by building up a new organisation within the Party structure that was to serve as its ideological engine. Chiang took up Liu's ideas and ordered a group of young and loyal military officers to make the necessary preparations, and, in late January 1932, the organisation that came to be known as the Blue Shirt Society (*Lanyishe* 藍衣社) was established.[160]

The goals of the society were—in their own words—"fascist". Lloyd E. Eastman has put it as follows: "The appeal of fascism to the Blue Shirts was that it seemed to provide a proven and unambiguous method of the goal of national salvation."[161] However, the demands that the Blue Shirts made on the individual and on society were not new. Chiang Kai-shek was inebriated by the prospects of the national wealth and power that the—seemingly new—approach of fascism held, but, in fact, its ideas were, in principle, exact replications of those that had been developed within the discourse on a militaristic state-people some 30 years earlier. The proximity of the fascist and militaristic ideas that were promoted becomes especially obvious in the article entitled "Facism and China" (Faxisidi zhuyi yu Zhongguo 法西斯蒂主義與中國), published in the journal *Qiantu* 前途 on 1 February 1934 by the GMD ideologue Chen Qiuyun 陳秋雲 (dates unknown). In his article, he expounded the

---

158 Ibid.

159 Cf. e.g. Yingning (1919), "Junguo zhuyi yu guomin jiaoyu zhi qiantu", pp. 6–7, 10–11.

160 Eastman (1972), "Fascism in Kuomintang China", pp. 2–3.

161 Ibid., p. 4.

THE BOUNDARIES OF THE CHINESE NATION

benefits of fascism for the Chinese Republic: the implementation of fascism would lead to the establishment of a perfect nation-state (*jianquan zhi guojia* 健全之國家) and a strong government, and it would lead to a fortification of the Republic. Fascism would foster a healthy sense of obedience towards the national leader (who was characterised by his intelligence and knowledge in military and political affairs), and it would impart an individual sense of responsibility for the well-being of the country. The individual would only be motivated by his or her duties to the state—and never by his or her rights. Furthermore, fascism would promote the individual willingness to join together and to develop the willingness to make sacrifices for the greater good. Fascism would encourage the people to face hardships and to fight; it would facilitate the establishment of social order and enable the people to face foreign threats.[162]

Unfortunately, all this had still to be realised in the Republic. As Chen wrote: "The great worry of China today is that the nation-state proves unable to unite the people, [and] that the people do not know how to love [and] protect the nation-state."[163] What China therefore needed now was political centralisation, a capable leader at the top, and the unquestioning execution of commands. Not that GMD ideology was to blame for lack of socio-political developmental successes. What was to blame was the inadequate conduct of the individual: if the Revolution was to succeed, then the individual had to develop a spirit of obedience towards the leader, a spirit of willingness to relinquish his or her rights, and a spirit to endure hardships and to fight.[164]

Yet, the "new" ideology of the Blue Shirts was not only with regard to its content a reiteration of the ideas of the militaristic discourse of the first decade of the twentieth century. It also suffered from the same problem that Liang Qichao had only been able to solve inadequately at that time: How to establish the specific "Chineseness" of these ideas? Liang had attempted to show that Japanese bushidō concepts were actually Chinese, and in the course of the ill-fated New Life Movement (*xin shenghuo yundong* 新生活運動) of the 1930s, whose purpose was a wholesale militarisation of society, the GMD tried to indigenise their behavioral demands by relating them to revived Confucian ideas of morality and an increasing rejection of certain Western ideas.[165] Yet, just as Liang had, the GMD ideologues also failed to establish an indisputable link between their behavioural demands and the Chinese *nation*. All they—like Liang—could achieve was to connect their demands on the people to the *state* that supposedly represented the nation. For the discourse participants, this was probably not deemed problematical. After all, they had—at least to some

---

162 Chen Qiuyun (1934), "Faxisidi zhuyi yu Zhongguo", pp. 1–3.
163 Ibid., p. 5.
164 Ibid., p. 5.
165 For the GMD efforts, see Eastman (1972), "Fascism in Kuomintang China", pp. 18–22.

degree—succeeded in establishing the notion of a nation that was independent from the state: what was to define the Chinese nation was not the state, but its *militaristic* conduct, its value concepts, and the virtues that guided the behaviour of the citizens *towards* the state.

Bibliography

Barth, Fredrik (1969), "Introduction", in: Fredrik Barth (ed.), *Ethnic Groups and Boundaries: The Social Organization of Culture Difference*, Bergen: Universitetsforlaget, pp. 9–37.

Bastid-Bruguiere, Marianne (2004), "The Japanese-Induced German Connection of Modern Chinese Ideas of the State: Liang Qichao and the *Guojia lun* of J.K. Bluntschli", in: Joshua A. Fogel (ed.), *The Role of Japan in Liang Qichao's Introduction of Modern Western Civilization to China*, Berkeley, CA: Institute of East Asian Studies, University of California & Center for Chinese Studies, pp. 105–124.

Bingwu 病武 (1911), "Junguomin jiaoyu zhi cao'an" 軍國民教育之草案 (Draft for the Education of a Militaristic State-People), *Nanfengbao*, 2, pp. 14a–18b.

Bluntschli, [J.C.] (1857), *Allgemeines Staatsrecht: Erster Band*, 2nd ed. Munich: Literarisch-artistische Anstalt der J.G. Cotta'schen Buchhandlung.

— (1874), *Deutsche Statslehre für Gebildete*, Nördlingen: C.H. Beck'sche Buchhandlung.

Bolunzhili 伯倫知理 (= J.C. Bluntschli) (1899), "Guojia lun" 國家論 (On the Nation-State), translated by Liang Qichao 梁啟超, *Qingyibao*, no. 11, pp. 1a–3b; no. 15, pp. 4a–6b; no. 16, pp. 7a–9b; no. 17, pp. 10a–12b; no. 18, pp., 7a–9b; no. 19, pp. 16a–18b; no. 23, pp.1a–2b; no. 25, pp. 3a–4b; no. 26, pp. 5a–7b; no. 27, pp 8a–10b; no. 28, pp. 1a–2b; no. 29, pp. 3a–4b; no. 30, pp. 5a–6b; no. 31, pp. 7a–8b.

Boorman, Howard L. (ed.) (1967–71), *Biographical Dictionary of Republican China*, 4 vols., New York and London: Columbia University Press.

Brubaker, Rogers (2009), "Ethnicity, Race, and Nationalism", *Annual Review of Sociology* 35, pp. 21–42.

Buruntīri 伯崙知理 (= J. C. Bluntschli) (1899), *Kokkagaku* 国家学 (Science of the State), translated by Azuma Heiji 吾妻兵治, Tōkyō: Zenrin yakushokan.

Cai E 蔡鍔 (Fenhesheng 奮翮生) (1900), "Zagan shi shou" 雜感十首 (Random Thoughts in Ten [Verses], *Qingyibao*, 61, shiwen cisuilu, [p. 1].

— (Fenhesheng 奮翮生) (1902), "Junguomin pian" 軍國民篇 (The Militaristic State-People), *Xinmin congbao*, no. 1, pp. 79–88; no. 3, pp. 65–72; no. 7, pp. 67–72; no. 11, pp. 45–51.

— (1984a [1911]), "Zhi Chuxiong xian yishihui quanxuesuo dian" 致楚雄縣議事會勸學所電 (Telegram to the Institute for the Exhortation of Learning of the Assembly for the Discussion of Official Business of Chuxiong County), in: Zeng Yeying (ed.), *Cai Songpo ji*, Shanghai: Shanghai renmin chubanshe, p. 78.

— (1984b [1911]), "Bugao quansheng tongbaowen" 布告全省同胞文 (Announcement to the Compatriots in the Whole Province), in: Zeng Yeying (ed.), *Cai Songpo ji*, Shanghai: Shanghai renmin chubanshe, pp. 97–98.

Cao Yabo 曹亞伯 (1982). *Wuchang Geming zhenshi* 武昌革命真史 (True History of the Wuchang Revolt), 3 vols., Shanghai: Shanghai shudian.

Chen Qiuyun 陳秋雲 (1934), "Faxisidi zhuyi yu Zhongguo" 法西斯蒂與中國 (Facism and China), *Qiantu*, 2 (2), pp. 1–5.

Chen Tianhua 陳天華 (1906), "Chen Xingtai xiansheng juemingshu: fu ba" 陳星台先生絕命書：附跋 (Suicide Note of Mr. Chen Xingtai (= Chen Tianhua): with attached postscript), *Minbao*, 2, pp. 1–10.

– (1957 [1903]), "Jingshizhong" 警世鐘 (Alarm Bell), in: Chai Degeng *et al.* (eds.), *Xinhai Geming*, Shanghai: Shanghai renmin chubanshe, vol. 2, pp. 112–143.

Chow, Kai-wing (1997), "Imagining Boundaries of Blood: Zhang Binglin and the Invention of the Han 'Race' in Modern China", in: Frank Dikötter (ed.), *The Construction of Racial Identities in China and Japan: Historical and Contemporary Perspectives*, Honolulu, HI: University of Hawai'i Press, pp. 34–52.

– (2001), "Narrating Nation, Race, and National Culture: Imagining the Hanzu Identity in Modern China", in: Kai-wing Chow, Kevin M. Doak, and Poshek Fu (eds.), *Constructing Nationhood in Modern East Asia*, Ann Arbor MI: University of Michigan Press, pp. 47–83.

"Da Zongtong banding jiaoyu yaozhi: shangwu" 大總統頒定教育要旨：尚武 (The President Promulgates the Main Aims of Education: The Esteem of Martial Qualities) (1915), *Jiaoyu yuebao* 10, pp. 82b–83b.

Darwin, Charles (1859), *On the Origin of Species by Means of Natural Selection, or the Preservation of Favoured Races in the Struggle for Life*, London: John Murray.

Deng Jiangqi 鄧江祁 (2006), *Cai E sixiang yanjiu* 蔡鍔思想研究 (A Study of Cai E's Thought), Changsha: Hunan Shifan Daxue chubanshe.

Dikötter, Frank (1992), *The Discourse of Race in Modern China*, Hong Kong: Hong Kong University Press.

Eastman, Lloyd E. (1972), "Fascism in Kuomintang China: The Blue Shirts", *The China Quarterly*, 49, pp. 1–31.

Esherick, Joseph W. (1976), *Reform and Revolution in China: The 1911 Revolution in Hunan and Hubei*, Berkeley, CA, *et al.*: University of California Press.

Feng Guozhang 馮國璋 (1915), "Junguomin jiaoyu yanjiu chuyi" 軍國民教育研究芻議 (My Humble Opinion on the Research of the Education of a Militaristic State-People), *Jiaoyu zhoubao* (Hangzhou) no. 84, pp. 3–8; no. 85, pp. 5–12.

Fitzgerald, John (1995), "The Nationless State: The Search for a Nation in Modern Chinese Nationalism", *The Australian Journal of Chinese Affairs*, 33, pp. 75–104.

Fung, Edmund S.K. (1975a), "Military Subversion in the Chinese Revolution of 1911", *Modern Asian Studies*, 9 (1), pp. 103–123.

– (1975b), "Li Yüan-hung and the Revolution of 1911", *Monumenta Serica*, 31, pp. 151–171.

– (1980), *The military dimension of the Chinese revolution: The New Army and its role in the Revolution of 1911*, Vancouver and London: University of British Columbia Press.

"Gaojie junren xunling" 誥誡軍人訓令 (Admonitory Instructions to Military Men) (1913), *Zhengfu gongbao* 239 (5 January), pp. 7–9.

Gasster, Michael (1969), *Chinese Intellectuals and the Revolution of 1911: The Birth of Modern Chinese Radicalism*, Seattle, WA, and London: University of Washington Press.

– (1980), "The republican revolutionary movement", in: John K. Fairbank, Liu Kwang-Ching (eds.), *The Cambridge History of China*, vol. 11: *Late Ch'ing, 1800–1911*, pt. 2, Cambridge *et al.*: Cambridge University Press, pp. 463–534.

Green, Colin Robert (2003), "The Spirit of the Military (Junren Hun): The Tradition and Its Revival in the Republican Period", Ph.D. diss., University of British Columbia.

Guanghan 逛漢 (1904), "Junguomin de jiaoyu" 軍國民的教育 (The Education of a Militaristic State-People), *Zhongguo baihuabao*, 10, pp. 29–34.

Guangxu chao Donghualu 光緒朝東華錄 (Records of the Guangxu Reign from the Eastern Gate), 5 vols., 2nd ed., 1984. Edited by Zhu Shouming 朱壽明, Beijing: Zhonghua shuju.

Guo Xiaocheng 郭孝成 (1957), "Shanxi guangfuji" 陝西光復記 (Record of the Recovery of Shaanxi), in: Chai Degeng *et al.* (eds.), *Xinhai Geming*, Shanghai: Shanghai renmin chubanshe, vol. 6, pp. 38–51.

Guo Xiren 郭希仁 (1957), "Congrong jilüe" 從戎紀略 (A Brief Record of [My Time] of Enlistment), in: Chai Degeng *et al.* (eds.), *Xinhai Geming*, Shanghai: Shanghai renmin chubanshe, vol. 6, pp. 60–103.

He Zhongliang 賀忠良 (= Taga Muneyuki 多賀宗之) (1906), "Shangwu jiaoyulun" 尚武教育論 (On the Education of Esteeming Martial Qualities), *Wubei zazhi*, 20, pp. 1a–3b.

Hexuli 赫胥黎 (= Thomas H. Huxley) (2002 [1898]), *Tianyanlun* 天演論 (The Theory of Evolution), translated by Yan Fu 嚴復, in: *Xuxiu siku quanshu*, vol. 1297: *zibu, Xixue yizhu lei*, Shanghai: Shanghai guji chubanshe.

Hobsbawm, E.J. (1992), *Nations and nationalism since 1780: Programme, myth, reality.* 2nd ed., Cambridge *et al.*: Cambridge University Press.

Horowitz, Donald L. (1985), *Ethnic Groups in Conflict*, Berkeley, CA, Los Angeles, CA, London: University of California Press.

Hou Anghao 侯昂好 (2011), "Jindai junshixue qikan de chuangban jiqi xueshu gongneng—yi '(Zhejiang) Bingshi zazhi' weili" 近代軍事學期刊的創辦及其學術功能——以 "（浙江）兵事雜誌" 為例 (The Founding of Modern Periodicals on Military Science and their Academic Function—exemplified by '(Zhejiang) Bingshi zazhi'), *Junshi lishi yanjiu*, 2, pp. 89–95.

Hsü, Immanuel C.Y. (1980), "Late Ch'ing foreign relations", in: John K. Fairbank, Liu Kwang-Ching (eds.), *The Cambridge History of China*, vol. 11: *Late Ch'ing, 1800–1911*, pt. 2, Cambridge: Cambridge University Press, pp. 70–141.

Hu Hanmin 胡漢民 (1906), "Shu Houguan Yan shi zuijin zhengjian" 述候官嚴氏最近政見 (A Description of the Newest Political Views of Mr. Yan [Fu] from Houguan [in Fujian]), *Minbao*, 2, pp. 1–17.

Huxley, Thomas H. (1893), *Evolution and Ethics*, London and New York: Macmillan and Co.

Inoue Tetsujirō 井上哲次郎 (1901), *Bushidō* 武士道(Bushidō), Tōkyō: Heiji zasshisha.

Ishikawa, Yoshihiro 石川禎浩 (2003), "Anti-Manchu Racism and the Rise of Anthropology in Early 20th Century China", *Sino-Japanese Studies* 15, pp. 7–26.

Jenks, Edward (1900). *A History of Politics*, New York: The Macmillan Company.

Jianfei 劍飛 (1906). "Lun junren zhi jingshen" 論軍人之精神 (On the Spirit of the Military Man), *Nanyang bingshi zazhi*, 1, pp. 3–9.

(Jiang) Baili 蔣百里 (1902), "Junguomin zhi jiaoyu" 軍國民之教育 (The Education of a Militaristic State-People), *Xinmin congbao*, 22, pp. 33–52.

Jiang Baili 蔣百里 (Feisheng 飛生) (1903a), "Eren zhi xingzhi" 俄人之性質 (The Nature of the Russian People), *Zhejiangchao* (Tōkyō) , no. 1, pp. 79–85; no. 2, pp. 77–85.

Jiang Baili 蔣百里 (Feisheng 飛生) (1903b), "Jinshi er da xueshuo zhi pinglun" 近時二大學說之評論 (A Discussion of Two Important Recent Theories), *Zhejiangchao* (Tōkyō), no. 8, pp. 1–8; no. 9, pp. 9–16.

"Jiaoyubu gongbu jiaoyu zongzhi" 教育部公布教育宗旨 (The Ministry of Education Publishes Educational Aims) (1912), *Dongfang zazhi*, 9: 4, p. 28.

"Jiaoyu zongzhi" 教育宗旨 (Educational Aims) (1906), *Xuebu guanbao*, 1, pp. 3b–9a.

"Jingshen jianghua" 精神講話 (Introduction to the Spirit [of the Military Man]) (1907), *Nanyang bingshi zazhi*, 6, pp. 1–3.

"Junguomin Jiaoyuhui gongyue" 軍國民教育會公約 (Pact of the Association for the Education of a Militaristic State-People) (1903), *Jiangsu*, 2, pp. 152–157.

"Junguomin Jiaoyuhui zhi chengli" 軍國民教育會之成立 (Establishment of the Association for the Education of a Militaristic State-People) (1903), *Jiangsu*, 2, pp. 144–146.

Lee, Robert H.G. (1970), *The Manchurian Frontier in Ch'ing History*, Cambridge, MA: Harvard University Press.

Leibold, James (2004), "Positioning 'Minzu' within Sun Yat-sen's Discourse of Minzuzhuyi", *Journal of Asian History*, 38 (2), pp. 163–213.

— (2007). *Reconfiguring Chinese Nationalism: How the Qing Frontier and its Indigenes Became Chinese*, New York: Palgrave Macmillan.

Liang Qichao 梁啟超 (1897), "Lun Zhongguo zhi jiangqiang" 論中國之將強 (On China's Future Strength), *Shiwubao*, 31, pp. 1a–4b.

— (Rengong 任公) (1898/99), "Lun bianfa bi zi ping Man-Han zhi jie shi" 論變法必自平滿漢之界始 (Political Reform has to Begin with Levelling the Divisions between Manchus and Han), *Qingyibao*, no. 1 pp. 1a–3b; no. 2, pp. 1a–3b.

— (Rengong 任公) (1899a), "Qi zhansi" 祈戰死 (Praying for Death in Battle), *Qingyibao*, 33, pp. 2a–2b.

— (Rengong 任公) (1899b), "Zhongguohun anzai hu" 中國魂安在乎 (Where is China's Soul?), *Qingyiba,o* 33: 2b–3a.

— (Zhongguo zhi xinmin 中國之新民) (1902), "Xin shixue" 新史學 (A New Historiography), *Xinmin congbao*, no. 1, pp. 39–48; no. 3, pp. 57–63; no. 11, pp. 35–44; no. 14, pp. 19–30; no. 16, pp. 31–36; no. 20, pp. 29–33.

— (Zhongguo zhi xinmin 中國之新民) (1902–06), "Xinmin shuo" 新民說 (Renewing the People), *Xinmin congbao*, no. 1, pp. 1–10; no. 2, pp. 1–7; no. 3, pp. 1–7; no. 4, pp. 1–12; no. 5, pp. 1–11; no. 6, pp. 1–15; no. 7, pp. 1–8; no. 8, pp. 1–8; no. 9, pp. 1–7; no. 10, pp. 1–8; no. 11, pp. 1–13; no. 12, pp. 1–7; no. 13, pp. 1–7; no. 16, pp. 1–7; no. 19, pp.1–7; no. 20, pp. 1–18; no. 24, pp. 1–13; no. 26, pp. 1–7; no. 28, pp. 1–8; no. 29, pp. 1–9; no. 38–39, pp. 1–18, no. 40–41, pp. 1–11; no. 46–48, pp. 1–12; no. 3 (1), pp. 1–12; no. 3 (24), pp. 1–10.

— (Liren 力人) (1903a), "Zhengzhixue dajia Bolunzhili zhi xueshuo" 政治學大家伯倫知理之學說 (The Theories of Bluntschli, Master of Political Science), *Xinmin congbao* 32, pp. 9–16.

— (Zhongguo zhi xinmin 中國之新民) (1903b), "Zhengzhixue dajia Bolunzhili zhi xueshuo" 政治學大家伯倫知理之學說 (The Theories of Bluntschli, Master of Political Science), *Xinmin congbao*, 38/39, pp. 19–53.

— (Yinbingshi zhuren 飲冰室主人) (1904), *Zhongguo zhi wushidao* 中國之武士道 (China's bushidō), Shanghai: Guangzhi shuju.

Liao Yuchun 廖宇春 (1904). "Lun Zhongguo wubei" 論中國武備 (On China's Military Preparedness), *Wubei zazhi*, 4, lunshuo, pp. 2a–4a.

"Linshi Da Zongtong ling" 臨時大總統令 (Order of the Provisional President) (1912), *Xibei zazhi* (Beijing) , 1 (1) (22 April), mingling, p. 3.

Liu Yusheng 劉禺生 (= Liu Chengyu 劉成禺) (1960), *Shizaitang zayi* 世載堂雜憶 (Miscellaneous Recollections from Shizai Hall), Beijing: Zhonghua shuju.

Lü Yujun, Chen Changhe 呂玉軍，陳長河 (2007), "Qingmo minchu de junguomin jiaoyu sichao de xingqi jiqi shuailuo" 清末民初的軍國民教育思潮的興起及其衰落 (The Rise and Decline of the Trend of Educating a Militaristic State-People in the Late Qing and Early Republican Era), *Junshi lishi yanjiu*, 3, pp. 91–99.

"Lujun shenpan tiaoli" 陸軍審判條例 (Army Court Ordinance) (1915), *Zhengfu gongbao*, 1034 (26 March), mingling, pp. 3–13.

"Lujun xingshi tiaoli" 陸軍刑事條例 (Army Criminal Ordinance) (1915), *Zhengfu gongbao*, 1027 (19 March), mingling, pp. 4–21.

"Lun shangwu zhuyi" 論尚武主義 (On the Doctrine of Esteeming Martial Qualities) (1905), *Dongfang zazhi*, 2:5, pp. 98–100.

Mackenzie, Robert (1880), *The 19th Century: A History*, London: T. Nelson and Sons.

Makenxi 馬懇西 (= Robert Mackenzie) (2002 [1895]), *Taixi xinshi lanyao* 泰西新史攬要 (The Essentials of Recent Western History), translated by Li Timotai 李提摩太 (= Timothy Richard), in: *Xuxiu siku quanshu*, vol. 1297: *zibu, Xixue yizhu lei*, Shanghai: Shanghai guji chubanshe.

Matten, Marc A. (2012), "'China is the China of the Chinese': The Concept of Nation and Its Impact on Political Thinking in Modern China", *Oriens Extremus*, 51, pp. 63–106.

McCord, Edward A. (1993), *The Power of the Gun: The Emergence of Modern Chinese Warlordism*, Berkeley, CA, Los Angeles, CA, Oxford: University of California Press.

Pusey, James Reeve. (1983), *China and Charles Darwin*, Cambridge, MA, and London: Council on East Asian Studies, Harvard University.

Qingchao xu wenxian tongkao 清朝續文獻通考 (Continued General History of Institutions of and Critical Examination of Documents of the Qing Dynasty) (1935 [1921]), edited by Liu Jinzao, 4 vols., Beijing: Shangwu yinshuguan.

"Ren fen wulei shuo" 人分五類說 (The Theory of Dividing Mankind in Five Types) (1892), *Gezhi huibian*, 7, pp. 9a–10b.

Rhoads, Edward J.M. (2000), *Manchus & Han: Ethnic Relations and Political Power in Late Qing and Early Republican China, 1861–1928*, Seattle, WA, and London: University of Washington Press.

Schwartz, Benjamin (1964), *In Search of Wealth and Power: Yen Fu and the West*, Cambridge, MA: Harvard University Press.

Setzekorn, Eric (2015), "Jiang Baili: Frustrated Military Intellectual in Republican China", *Journal of Chinese Military History* 4 (2), pp. 142–161.

Smith, Anthony D. (1991), *National Identity*, London: Penguin.

Sun Zhongshan 孫中山 (Sun Wen 孫文) (1899). "Shina gensei chizu" 支那現勢地図 (Current Map of China), Tōkyō: Tōhō Kyōkai.

— (Minyi 民意) (1906), "Ji shi'er yue er ri benbao jiyuan jieqingzhu dahui shi ji yanshuoci" 紀十二月二日本報紀元節慶祝大會事及演說辭 (Record of the Events and Speeches of the Celebration Meeting [on Occasion of] the First Anniversary of this Journal's [Foundation] on 2 December), *Minbao*, 10, pp. 81–114.

— (1912), "Linshi Da Zongtong xuanyanshu" 臨時大總統宣言書 (Declaration of the Provisional President), *Linshi zhengfu gongbao* 1, lingshi, pp. 1–3.

- (1981 [1906]), "Zhongguo Tongmenghui geming fanglüe" 中國同盟會革命方略 (The General Revolutionary Plan of the Chinese Revolutionary Alliance), in: Guangdongsheng Shehui Kexueyuan Lishi Yanjiushi *et al.* (eds.), *Sun Zhongshan quanji, di'yi juan: 1890–1911*, Beijing: Zhonghua shuju, pp. 296–318.
- (1982 [1912]), "Zai Beijing Hu-Guang Huiguan xuejie huanyinghui de yanshuo" 在北京湖光會館學界歡迎會的演說 (Speech Delivered in Beijing at the Welcoming Party for the Academic Circle of the Provincial Guild of Hu-Guang), in: Guangdongsheng Shehui Kexueyuan Lishi Yanjiushi *et al.* (eds.), *Sun Zhongshan quanji, di'er juan: 1912*, Beijing: Zhonghua shuju, pp. 422–424.

Tang Caichang 唐才常 (1897), "Shixue di'wu: Geguo zhongleikao" 史學第五：各國種類考 (Historiography, pt. 5: A Study of the [Human] Races in the Various Countries), *Xiangxue xinbao*, no. 15, pp. 3a–6b; no. 16, pp. 4a–7b; no. 17, pp. 3a–6b; no. 18, pp. 4a–7b; no. 19, pp. 6a–9b; no. 20, pp. 4a–7b; no. 21, pp. 4a–7a; no. 22, pp. 3a–6b; no. 23, pp. 4a–7b; no. 24, pp. 4a–7b; no. 25, pp. 7a–10b; no. 26, pp. 8a–11b; no. 27, pp. 4a–6a.

- (2002 [1898]), *Juedian mingzhai neiyan* 覺顛冥齋內言 (Private Words from the Studio of Sensing the Falling Darkness), in: *Xuxiu siku quanshu*, vol. 1568: *jibu, bieji lei*, Shanghai: Shanghai guji chubanshe.

Tao Juyin 陶菊隱 (1957), *Beiyang junfa tongzhi shiqi shihua, di'yi ce: Xinhai Geming qianhou he Di'yi-ci Nan-Bei Zhanzheng shiqi (1895 nian zhi 1913 nian)* 北洋軍閥統治時期史話，第一冊：辛亥革命前後和第一次南北戰爭時期（一百九五年至一九一三年）(Narrative History of the Period of the Rule of the Northern Warlords, vol. 1: Period of the Xinhai Revolutionary era and the First South-North War (1895–1913)), Beijing: Sanlian shudian.
- (1985), *Jiang Baili zhuan* 蔣百里傳 (Biography of Jiang Baili), Beijing: Zhonghua shuju.

Tian Fulong 田伏隆 (ed.) (1997), *Yi Cai E* 憶蔡鍔 (Remembering Cai E), Changsha: Yuelu shushe.

Tsou Jung (1968). *The Revolutionary Army: A Chinese Nationalist Tract of 1903*, translated by John Lust, The Hague: Mouton.

Vagts, Alfred (1959), *A History of Militarism: Civilian and Military*, revised ed., New York: The Free Press.

von Ihering, Rudolf (1872), *Der Kampf um's Recht*, Vienna: Verlag der G. J. Manz'schen Buchhandlung.

von Ihering, Rudolph (1879), *The Struggle for Law*, translated by John J. Lalor, Chicago, IL: Callaghan and Company.

Wang Jingwei 汪精衛 (1905/06), "Minzu de guomin" 民族的國民 (An [Ethnically] National State-People), *Minbao*, no. 1, pp. 1–31; no. 2, pp. 1–23.

Wang Shi 王栻 (ed.) (1986), *Yan Fu ji* 嚴復集 (Collected Writings of Yan Fu), 5 vols., Beijing: Zhonghua shuju.

Wang Xiaowei 王曉衛 (1997), *Zhongguo junshi zhidushi: Bingyi zhidujuan* 中國軍事制度史：兵役制度卷 (History of the Chinese Military System, vol. [5]: Military Service System), edited by Chen Gaohua and Qian Haihao, Zhengzhou: Daxiang chubanshe.

Wang Xiuchu 王秀楚 (1982), *Yangzhou shi ri ji* 揚州十日記 (A Record of Ten Days in Yangzhou), in: Zhongguo Lishi Yanjiushe (ed.), *Yangzhou shi ri ji*, Shanghai: Shanghai shudian, pp. 229–246.

"Wangguo pian" 亡國篇 (The Destruction of the Country) (1901), *Guominbao*, 1 (4), pp. 1–7.

Weston, Timothy B. (2004), *The Power of Position: Beijing University, Intellectuals, and Chinese Political Culture, 1898–1929*, Berkeley, CA, Los Angeles, CA, London: University of California Press.

Wong, Young-tsu (1989), *Search for Modern Nationalism: Zhang Binglin and Revolutionary China, 1869–1936*, Hong Kong: Oxford University Press.

Wu Yangxiang 吳仰湘 (2009), "Jiang Baili zaonian de sixiang shijie" 蔣百里早年的思想世界 (The Thought World of Jiang Baili during [His] Early Years), *Hunan Daxue xuebao (shehui kexueban)* 23 (5), pp. 31–35.

Xie Benshu 謝本書 (1989), "Lun 'junguomin zhuyi'" 論 '軍國民主義' (On the 'Doctrine of a Militaristic State-People'), *Guizhou shehui kexue*, 10, pp. 56–61.

Yan Fu 嚴復. 1895, "Yuan qiang" 原強 (The Sources of Strength), *Zhibao*, no. 32, pp. 1–2; no. 33, pp. 1–2; no. 34, pp. 1–2; no. 35, pp. 1–2; no. 36, pp. 1–2; no. 37, p. 1.

– (1982 [1901]), *Houguan Yan shi congke* 侯官嚴氏叢刻 (Block-printed Series of [Works by] Mr. Yan [Fu] from Houguan) (Jindai Zhongguo shiliao congkan xubian, di'shiba ji, 116), Taibei: Wenhai chubanshe.

Yang Du 楊度 (1907), "*Zhongguo xinbao* xu" 中國新報敘 (Preface to the *Zhongguo xinbao*), *Zhongguo xinbao* 1, pp. 1–8.

Yang Tianshi, Wang Xuezhuang 楊天石, 王學莊 (eds.) (1979), *Ju E yundong: 1901–1905* 拒俄運動 ： 1901-1905 (The Resist Russia Movement: 1901–1905), Beijing: Zhongguo shehui kexue chubanshe.

Yang Tingyuan 楊霆垣 (1982), "Ji E junzhengfu de chuqi waijiao huodong" 記鄂軍政府的初期外交活動 (Records of Early Diplomatic Activities of the Hubei Military Government), in: Zhongguo Renmin Zhengzhi Xieshang Huiyi Quanguo Weiyuanhui Wenshi Ziliao Yanjiu Weiyuanhui (ed.), *Xinhai Geming huiyilu*, Beijing: Wenshi ziliao chubanshe, vol. 7, pp. 42–55.

Yingning 嬰寧 (1919), "Junguo zhuyi yu guomin jiaoyu zhi qiantu" 軍國主義與國民教育之前途 (The Future of Militarism and the Education of a State-People), *Jiaoyu zhoubao* (Hangzhou) 231, pp. 1–11.

Young, Ernest P. (1959), "Ch'en T'ien-hua (1875–1905): A Chinese Nationalist", *Papers on China (Harvard University)*, 13, pp. 113–162.

Zarrow, Peter (2012), *After Empire: The Conceptual Transformation of the Chinese State, 1885–1924*, Stanford, CA: Stanford University Press.

Zhang Binglin 章炳麟 (Zhang Taiyan 章太炎) (1907a), "Zhonghua Minguo jie" 中華民國解 (Explaining [the Concept of] a Chinese Republic), *Minbao*, 15, pp. 1–17.

Zhang Binglin 章炳麟 (Zhang Taiyan 章太炎) (1907b), "Shehui tongquan shangdui" 社會通詮商兌 (A Discussion of [and] Deliberations [on Yan Fu's Translation of Jenks'] 'A History of Politics'), *Minbao* ,12, pp. 1–24.

Zhang Guogan 張國淦 (ed.) (1958), *Xinhai Geming shiliao* 辛亥革命史料 (Historical Materials on the Xinhai Revolution), Shanghai: Longmen lianhe shuju.

Zhang Yufa 張玉法 (1982), *Qingji de geming tuanti* 清季的革命團體 (Revolutionary Organisations in the Last Years of the Qing [Era]), Taibei: Zhongyang Yanjiuyuan Jindaishi Yanjiusuo.

Zhang Zhidong 張之洞 (1973 [1898]), *Quanxuepian: waipian* 勸學篇：外篇 (Exhortation to Learn: Outer chapters) (Jindai Zhongguo shiliao congkan, dijiu ji, 84), Taibei: Wenhai chubanshe.

Zhenfei 震飛 (1906), "Lian hun pian" 練魂篇 (Training the Soul), *Nanyang bingshi zazhi*, 1: 9–16.

Zhenkesi 甄克思 (= Edward Jenks) (2002 [1903]), *Shehui tongquan* 社會通詮 (A Comprehensive Explanation [of the Concept] of Society), in: *Xuxiu siku quanshu*, vol. 1300: *zibu, Xixue yizhu lei*, Shanghai: Shanghai guji chubanshe.

"Zhongda xintiao shijiu tiao" 重大信條十九條 (Great Precepts in Nineteen Articles) (1911), *Beiyang guanbao* 2959, pp. 5–8.

"Zhonghua Minguo linshi yuefa" 中華民國臨時約法 (Provisional Constitution of the Republic of China] (1912), *Linshi zhengfu gongbao*, 35 (11 March), pp. 1–9.

Zhonghua Minguo shishi jiyao (chugao): Minguo jiyuan qian 1 nian (1911) 1 zhi 11 yuefen 中華民國史事紀要（初稿）：民國紀元前一年（一九一一）一至十一月份 (Abstracts of the Main Historical Events of the Republic of China (First Draft): First to Eleventh Month of Year 1 (1911) Before the Republic) (1973), edited by Zhonghua Minguo shishi jiyao bianji weiyuanhui, Taibei: Zhonghua Minguo Shiliao Yanjiu Zhongxin.

Zhonghua Minguo shishi jiyao (chugao): Minguo yuannian (1912) 1 zhi 6 yuefen 中華民國史事紀要（初稿）：民國元年（一九一二）一至六月份 (Abstracts of the Main Historical Events of the Republic of China (First Draft): January to June of Year 1 (1912) of the Republic] (1971), edited by Zhonghua Minguo shishi jiyao bianji weiyuanhui, Taibei: Zhonghua Minguo Shiliao Yanjiu Zhongxin.

Zhu Zisu 朱子素 (1982), *Jiading tucheng jilüe* 嘉定屠城紀略 (Brief Account of the Massacre of the Inhabitants of the Captured City of Jiading), in: Zhongguo Lishi Yanjiushe (ed.), *Yangzhou shi ri ji*, Shanghai: Shanghai shudian, pp. 249–269.

Zhuang'e 莊諤 (1906), "Jundui jiaoyu yu guomin jiaoyu" 軍隊教育與國民教育 (Education of Troops and Education of the State-People), *Nanyang bingshi zazhi* 4, tonglun, pp. 1–5.

Zhuangyou 壯游 (1903), "Guomin xin linghun" 國民新靈魂 (The New Soul of the State-People), *Jiangsu* (Tōkyō) , 5, sheshu, pp. 1–9.

Zou Rong 鄒容 (1968 [1903]), *Gemingjun* 革命軍 (The Revolutionary Army), in: *The Revolutionary Army: A Chinese Nationalist Tract of 1903*, edited by John Lust, The Hague: Mouton.

The Idea of "Intellectual Warfare" and the Dispersion of Social Darwinism in Late Qing China (1897–1906)

Sebastian Riebold

> The problem of the reputation and fame of Kemet [the Ancient Egyptian name for Egypt] as one of the cradles of civilization, if not *the cradle* of human wisdom, posed a great embarrassment to [the] advocates of Negro inferiority. [...] Napoleon's 1798 invasion of Kemet paved the way for the solution. *When Napoleon entered Kemet he took an intellectual army along with his soldiers.* These intellectuals, charged with the responsibility of investigating and reporting on the remains of the amazing ancient Nile Valley civilization, placed the surviving works of the African ancestors into captivity, carting much off to Europe and holding the remainder in bondage in the land of its origin.[1]

> The refined man worries about our weakness, and [does] not [worry] about the enemy's strength. He worries about our stupidity, and does not worry about the enemy's intelligence. When a country is assaulted by an enemy and is unable to overcome them, this is not the result of the enemy's strength. The fault lies with our weakness. *When (a country) is ensnared by an enemy and unable to realize this, this is not the result of the enemy's intelligence. The fault lies with our stupidity.*[2]

I. Introduction

Around the turn of the century, old China saw itself attacked on all fronts: from revolutionaries and rebels within, and from foreign powers without; and literally (by Western "gunboat diplomacy") as well as figuratively: almost all traditional institutions and values believed to have been foundational to the Chinese world order were increasingly called into question. The ubiquity of war and "struggle"—the latter notion having been informed by newly introduced Darwinian ideas—led to the conceptual reframing of various non-military fields of social activity in terms of warfare. In the case of trade and commerce, this process of reframing has already been amply documented.[3] Less well known to date, at least in sinological scholarship outside of Greater China, is the idea of "Intellectual Warfare" (*xuezhan* 學戰), sometimes (albeit seldom) also referred to as

---

1 Carruthers (1999), *Intellectual Warfare*, p. 7. The second emphasis is my own.

2 Lü Zuqian (12th century), *Zuo shi boyi*, juan 12.

3 The idea of "commercial warfare" (see below) is most prominently associated with the merchant reformer Zheng Guanying 鄭觀應 (1842–1922). See: Wu (2010), *Zheng Guanying*, pp. 130–134; 187–193; Wang Ermin (1995), *Zhongguo jindai sixiangshi lun*, pp. 233–382; Ma Min (2006), "Zhongguo jindaihua sichao de yi ge cemian—shangzhan."

"Knowledge Struggle" (*zhizheng* 智爭).[4] Although arguably something of a "fringe" idea, and not being connected to any of the eminent thinkers of the late Qing, the notion enjoyed remarkable popularity for a time and can be traced well into the twentieth century. However, the intellectual warfare idea experienced real prominence only in the very last years of the Qing dynasty and the first years of the Republican Era.[5]

The introduction and subsequent reception and acculturation of Darwinian evolution and social Darwinism in turn-of-the-century China has already received considerable scholarly attention and serves mostly as a backdrop to the following inquiry.[6] The key observation regarding social Darwinism's early history in the Chinese cultural sphere as it pertains to the idea of intellectual warfare is that, while social Darwinism established the "survival of the fittest" as a key category of human history, in and of itself it had little to say about the specific mechanisms of the "struggle for existence" and "natural selection". In other words: Why is something (and particular a race or nation) "weak" or "unfit"? "Fitness" is necessarily a very general category and to equate "fitness" with physical or military strength, while seemingly standing to reason, is not at all a conceptual inevitability—and it certainly was not in late nineteenth and early twentieth century China. As I will hope to demonstrate, traditional, established and (from the perspective of Chinese literati) more readily workable concepts such as "wealth and strength" (*fuqiang* 富強) or war were, to some degree, conflated with "new" categories such as "fit", "inferior/superior", and "struggle".

---

4 "Intellectual Warfare" has been the subject of a number of studies, but, to the best of my knowledge, never been thoroughly investigated. Cf. Chen Zhongchun (2004), "Lun Nanxue hui de jiangxue huodong ji weixin sixiang"; Zhou Wu (1988),"Lun 'xuezhan' sichao"; Xiong Zhiyong (1998),"Bingzhan, shangzhan, xuezhan yu wan Qing junshi jindaihua de xiandao diwei"; Fang Ping (1994), "Lüe lun wan Qing 'xuezhan' sichao". Wang Dongjie seems to be the only scholar who has explicitly linked the notion to social Darwinism (Wang Dongjie (2007), "'Fanqiuzhuji'—Wan Qing jinhuaguan yu Zhongguo chuantong sixiang quxiang"). Huang Xingtao and Hu Wensheng have discussed "Intellectual Warfare" in the context of modern China's "intellectual transformation" around the time of the Hundred Days' Reform (Huang Xingtao and Hu Wensheng (2005), "Lun Wuxu Weixin shiqi Zhongguo xueshu xiandai zhuanxing de zhengti mengfa") and Wang Ermin has traced the historical development of the idea from similar notions (Wang Ermin (1995), *Zhongguo jindai sixiangshi lun*, esp. pp. 244–248).

5 Some of the more substantial pieces the discussion of which lies outside the scope of the present study include: Xia Shixing (1920), "Xuezhan lun"; Jiang Hongtao (1929), "Xuezhan shuo"; Bai Chongxi (1939), "Bingzhan yu xuezhan"; Tu Daotan (1943), "Lun Zhongzu xuezhan".

6 The most comprehensive work remains Pusey (1983), *China and Charles Darwin*. For more recent scholarship see Yang Haiyan (2013), "Knowledge Across Borders"; Ke Zunke and Li Bin (2016), "Spencer and Science Education in China"; Shen (2016), "Translation and Interpretation".

Of such conceptual interactions, I would argue, the most significant concerns the amalgamation of the Darwinian "struggle for survival" with the idea and experience of war. For, in the case of war, we are venturing not merely in the realm of abstract concepts but rather deal with metaphors that are anchored in real-world experiences.[7] Furthermore, the vocabulary of war provided a convenient tool to put the alien, abstract framework of social Darwinism into a more concrete "conceptual guise", that is, to link it to a more familiar semantic field. The struggle for survival might be (as leading intellectuals alleged) a "universal law" of history and nature, but war had been a constant reality for China for decades.

As "fitness" is, as argued above, conceptually open, it proved not to be too much of a challenge for turn-of-the-century Chinese thinkers to apply it to those social fields that they deemed most crucial for a strong and modern nation. To be sure, they generally did not do so under the exclusion of everything else, but they differed significantly in their priorities. For the purpose of the following analysis, I would thus suggest the metaphor of a ray of white light that passes through a prism as a means of illustrating the reception of Darwinian thought in late Qing China: as these ideas interacted with the existing "intellectual lattice" (*i.e.*, the material of the prism), Darwinian thought "dispersed" into different "colours".[8] In turn-of-the-century Chinese sources we thus find expressions such as "military warfare" (*bingzhan* 兵戰), "commercial warfare" (*shangzhan* 商戰), "mental warfare" (*xinzhan* 心戰), "industrial warfare" (*gongzhan* 工戰), "agricultural warfare" (*nongzhan* 農戰), and "religious warfare" (*jiaozhan* 教戰).[9] In what follows, I will trace only one of these "dispersed light rays" and focus on the idea of "intellectual warfare". Previous scholarship has so far done little to illuminate the inherent ambiguity of the idea: Is it "war" between or within academic disciplines? Or between academic traditions (as Jonathan Swift's famous satire "Battle of the Books" depicts it)? Does it denote warfare that heavily relies on knowledge? Or rather warfare within the sphere of knowledge?

---

7 Lakoff and Johnson (2003 [1980]), *Metaphors We Live By*, pp. 19–22 and especially chapter 22 (The Creation of Similarity), pp. 147–155. The metaphor "argument is war" is discussed on pp. 4–7 and in chapter 15 (The Coherent Structuring of Experience), pp. 77–86.

8 Wang Dongjie has made a similar distinction between "competing in strength" (*jing yu li* 競於力) and "competing in principles" (*jing yu li* 競於理). Wang Dongjie (2007), "'Fanqiuzhuji'— Wan Qing jinhuaguan yu Zhongguo chuantong sixiang quxiang", pp. 325–326.

9 Some of these, most notably "commercial warfare", significantly pre-date any mention of Darwin in China. However, the basic metaphor proposed here still holds, as it is precisely my contention that the new item of knowledge ("the light") interacts with the body of knowledge that was already present. For "mental warfare", see Wang Ermin (1995), *Zhongguo jindai sixiangshi lun*, pp. 244–247.

This metaphor, however, can only contribute to the explanation of the *diversification* of the social Darwinist discourse during the period in question. The second, related issue concerns its reception and dissemination. I argue that, prior to its initial introduction into the Chinese intellectual sphere, the war metaphor had already helped to prepare the ground for the rapid diffusion of social Darwinism in China (although it probably did little to further its actual comprehension). While James Pusey is certainly justified when he observes that the Darwinian "praise for struggle" went against mainstream Chinese thought, we should not underestimates the degree to which Chinese thinkers were and have always been willing to reinterpret and re-evaluate traditional ideas in light of contemporary challenges. [10] Darwinism provided a new vocabulary to articulate an already firmly rooted sense of "national crisis" that was increasingly communicated not via a select number of thinkers but in a nationwide Discourse of Weakness characterised by vivid, even graphic language. In this context, I would argue, the war metaphor is particularly potent, as has been acknowledged since Lakoff and Johnson's seminal work on the cognitive power of metaphorical language. As Austrian sociologist Heinz Steinert puts it:

(the starting of a) war is the supreme 'populist moment', the perfect situation to enlist the greatest possible number, preferably the whole nation, to work for a shared goal, thereby causing us to forget small discrepancies and even opposing interests.[11]

"War"—as all cognitive metaphors—derives its plausibility and conceptual power from its underlying experiential basis (*i.e.*, there are actually observable war-like phenomena and conflicts present). [12] In this way, metaphor and experience reinforce each other: the former focusses attention on the latter while the latter provides evidential ground for the former. Metaphors thus play a key role in the "social amplification" of war.[13]

How far the war metaphor was taken at times in turn-of-the-century China, can be exemplified by the following paragraph from Wang Kangnian's 汪康年 (1860–1911) "A Discussion of Commercial Warfare" ("Shangzhan lun" 商戰論) published in *Shiwubao* 時務報 (The Chinese Progress) on 15 December 1896. Here, mercantile competition is clearly associated with warfare:

If you tie the hands and feet of brave warriors and then bring them to fight with others, will that work? If you place shackles on brave generals and place strong soldiers in

---

10 Pusey (1983), *China and Charles Darwin*, pp. 60–67; cf. ibid., pp. 6–7.

11 Steinert (2003), "The Indispensable Metaphor of War", p. 266.

12 Ibid., pp. 275–281, especially p. 281: "Not only is the war experience entrenched (!) in everyday practices, the type of enthusiasm that can mainly be mobilized for defending against a national catastrophe is routinely invoked by populist entertainment and populist politics. They both rely on situations of threat and emergency and demand universal participation and a concerted effort by all. No one is allowed to stand aside; all are included against the enemy."

13 Kasperson, R. E. et al. (2005), "The Social Amplification of Risk".

bonds and then bring them to war with others, will that work? Yet, today, we confine our merchants to a place where [their movements] are impeded and [their freedom] is curbed, place them in a despondent situation, and still expect them to be able to successfully compete with the merchants of all the other countries. This is like travelling south with the shaft pointing north.[14]

I shall present the sources that I base my analysis upon in fairly strict chronological order so as to account for the sudden and momentous changes that constantly re-arranged the world of thought of modern China even in the rather short time-span under discussion here. In this manner, I have identified three major turning-points, each of which is associated with a commensurate "spike" in writings on intellectual warfare: the post-war reform era, the New Policies and the reform of the Civil Service Examinations in the wake of the Boxer Uprising, and the time following the promulgation of the Qing dynasty's Educational Aims of 1906. As will be shown, the term "intellectual warfare" first appears in a series of articles in the journal *Xiangbao* 湘報 (Hunan News) in 1897/98. However, the trope did not fully merge with the newly introduced Darwinian ideas until about five years later. By 1906, the concept of intellectual warfare had been developed in a number of directions, not all of which are easily reconcilable.

In the first section, I will first give a brief overview of what I believe to be the key characteristics of the "prism" that is the late Qing Chinese intellectual sphere. Naturally, I will only focus on a few ideas that are, in my opinion, key for the emergence of the idea of intellectual warfare in late nineteenth century China.

II. Ideas on Intelligence, Ignorance, and National Peril before 1898

The importance of "learning" (*xue* 學) in Chinese culture (past and present) has been well established, almost to the point of having become a stereotype. Time and time again, Chinese men and women of letters throughout history have re-affirmed their conviction that "learning" (e.g., emulating the sages of antiquity, learning from other cultures) constitutes the basis not only for personal growth and self-cultivation (*xiushen* 修身) but also for successful rule and societal stability and prosperity. What "learning" actually entailed, changed—dramatically at times—according to historical context, and was naturally contested and subject to constant reinterpretation. But the fundamental tenet, that is, the primacy of "learning", remained largely unchallenged. "Learning" and its patronage on

---

14 Heck (2000), *Wang Kangnian*, p. 193; Wang Kangnian (1896), "Shangzhan lun".

340   Sebastian Riebold

the side of government and society at large has, throughout Chinese intellectual history, been regarded as the very hallmark of civilisation.

The lines quoted in the second epithet above, for instance, stem from a twelfth century commentary on the following entry in the "Zuo-Commentary" to the *Spring and Autumn Annals* (year 20 of Duke Xi's 僖 reign):

> The refined man may say that (the state of) Sui 隨 suffered this invasion, because it had not measured its [own] power. The errors of those who move only after they have measured their power are few. Do success and defeat come from one's self or from others?[15]

Notice that the original text does not mention either "intelligence" or "stupidity". However, the Song dynasty commentator Lü Zuqian 呂祖謙 (1137–1181) evidently deemed these to be factors of victory in defeat just as significant as (military) strength and weakness—or, alternatively, he saw intelligence as an integral part of a country's "force" (*li* 力).

We find a similar belief expressed in another text of ancient Chinese wisdom, the *Book of Documents* (*Shangshu* 尚書),[16] which is one of the Five Classics, the foundational canonical texts of the complex edifice of ideas conventionally called "Confucianism". The "Pledge of Zhonghui" (*Zhonghui zhi gao* 仲虺之誥) states:

> Annex the weak, and assault the ignorant; take [their state] from those who have allowed it to fall into disorder, and insult those [states] that are going to ruin. When you expedite the ruin [of what is of itself about to perish], and strengthen what is of itself able to persevere, how the states will all flourish![17]

Leaving aside questions of philology and interpretation for the moment (the translation above is based on the translation by James Legge which presumably reflects the conventional late-nineteenth century reading rather closely; the *Documents* employ—or at least mimic—rather archaic language and are notoriously ambiguous), it seems rather clear that the passage above condones military interventions in "uncivilised" territories and its wording is almost eerily reminiscent of what is known as the "White Man's Burden", i.e., the "obligation" of self-identified civilised nations to subjugate "inferior" peoples in order to "civilise" them, *i.e.*, it is *for their own good*.

There are good reasons to believe that it was precisely this reading that was intended by one of late-Qing most influential and vocal thinkers, Kang Youwei (1858–1927), one of the key people behind the reform movement of 1898 (and, as we will see, many of the proponents of the idea of intellectual-warfare shared

---

15 Legge (1872), *The Chinese Classics, Volume V*, Part I, p. 178.

16 The "Pledge of Zhonghui" is one of the "spurious" chapters of the *Documents* of uncertain provenance and is likely not as ancient as traditionally assumed.

17 Translation informed by Legge (1865), *The Chinese Classics, Volume III*, Part I, p. 181.

this conviction). Kang evidently found the passage quoted above to be particularly instructive and cited it on multiple occasions,[18] most notably perhaps in his fifth memorandum to the Guangxu emperor, submitted to the throne in January of 1898:

The "Pledge of Zhonghui" says: "Annex the weak, and assault the ignorant; take [their state] from those who have allowed it to fall into disorder, and insult those [states] that are going to ruin." We have committed ourselves into a state of weakness and ignorance. So how can we keep others from annexing and assaulting us? We are already moving with every passing day towards disorder and ruin. So how can we resent others for taking our territory and insulting us? Without discerning where the sickness is located, it is impossible to administer the proper treatment or drug; not understanding the symptoms of upheaval, yet keeping to the old methods, one will cause untold and long-lasting harm.[19]

There are a lot of points to be remarked in this dense paragraph, but I want to hone in on only one particular aspect; that is, the explicit (almost causal) link drawn between "level of intelligence" and the fate of a country. Other contemporary thinkers, most notably perhaps Yan Fu (1853–1921), equally expressed their conviction that education ("broadening the people's intelligence") was one, if not *the*, key component of national salvation. As I see it, however, Kang goes one step further and argues—drawing on the *Documents* to buttress his argument—that ignorance *invites* (*zhaogong* 召攻), even demands, aggression and humiliation from without.[20]

To what degree Kang was informed and influenced by social Darwinism in early 1898 is hard to ascertain,[21] and, as will become clear below, the link between intellectual warfare and the struggle for survival between nations was not explicitly drawn until later. What needs to be pointed out, however, is that when Kang speaks about "ignorance" (or "intelligence"), he is not talking about predetermined ("genetic"), unchanging traits. Intelligence is honed by learning, and ignorance is proof of a lack of learning, and not of any biological difference, let alone racial inferiority—it is a cultural difference. We have here a very deeply entrenched belief that predates social Darwinism in China or the "national shock" of 1894/95 by far. To give only one prominent example, at least a decade earlier, we find the following assessment by pioneering reformer Feng Guifen 馮桂芬 (1809–1874):

---

18 The first mention I could find is from November 1895. It is quoted in Pusey (1983), *China and Charles Darwin*, p. 57.

19 Kang Youwei (1981 [1898]), "Shang Qing Di di wu shu", p. 203.

20 Ibid.

21 Pusey (1983), *China and Charles Darwin*, pp. 83–94. For Kang's "pre-Darwinian" evolutionary thought, see ibid., pp. 15–47.

The intelligence and ingenuity of (the people of) China, is surely above that of the various barbarian tribes [including the Westerners]. They have simply not made much use of them in the past. [...] At first, we will take them as our teachers and emulate them. When we have established [a foundation], we will match them and make (what they have given us) greater. In the end, we will deliberate (on it) and overtake them. Herein truly lies the way of self-strengthening.[22]

Notice how Feng relates "self-strengthening" to intelligence and learning.

In contrast to both Kang and Feng, when Yan Fu summarises the mechanism of natural selection in the opening paragraph of his famous essay "On the Origin of Strength" (*Yuanqiang* 原強), he is very much talking about biological traits.

All people and all animals vie for survival. [...] The weak are liable to become the meat of the strong, and *the ignorant are liable to become the servants of the intelligent*. If there is [a species] that was able to survive [...], this means that it [has proven itself to be] the fittest regarding [characteristics such as] strength, endurance, eminence, and ruthlessness or vigour, agility, *cunning, and wisdom* [...].[23]

This is not to say that Yan entirely agreed with the proposed mechanisms of natural selection[24] and thought characteristics such as strength and intelligence to be unchanging. Indeed, it is arguably the key characteristic of the reception of Darwinism in China that Chinese thinkers refused to replace the belief in a "pre-ordained fate" (*ming* 命) with a new, "scientifically based" biological (i.e., racial) determinism. The conviction that only the strong were "fated" to survive was tied to the equally firm conviction that societies could progress, that is, grow *stronger*.[25] In any case, most agreed that the "yellow race" was not in any way inferior to the "white race" (see Section V). The apparent differences between the two in terms of "strength" and "brains", glaring, as they may be, could and would eventually be overcome. The eminent Hunan reformer (and later revolutionary) Tang Caichang 唐才常 (1867–1900) made this distinction very clear:

---

22 "Zhi yangqi yi" 製洋器議 (Proposal concerning the Production of Foreign Instruments): Feng Guifen (1885), *Jiaobinlu kangyi*, vol. 2, p. 42b. Feng's text has a complex textual history and the chapter may have been included in alternative versions prior to 1885.

23 Yan Fu (1986 [1895]), "Yuan qiang", p. 5; cf. Houang (1977), *Les Manifestes de Yen Fou*, pp. 50–51.

24 In particular, Yan believed "human selection" to be potentially disastrous: "[W]e must realise that the art of human selection may be applied to flora and fauna, but it must under no circumstances find employ within human society. [...] Therefore I say, if one seeks strength by means of human selection, it will result only in weakness." Yan Fu and Feng Junhao (1998), *Tianyan lun*, p. 194.

25 Pusey (1983), *China and Charles Darwin*, pp. 51–58.

[Nations perish] not because their races are infertile, or their intelligence weak, or their weapons un-sharp. They perish in the end because they have not the government, philosophy, and learning to preserve themselves.

In other words, the rise and fall of nations is a matter "not of Heaven [or nature] but of human endeavour".[26]

We can say with some confidence that few Chinese thinkers around 1900 would have contradicted Tang's last statement. However, there was considerable disagreement concerning the right course of action, the degree and pace of reform, and the priorities that one ought to dedicate to China's various "construction sites"; *i.e.*, should defence be prioritised, or rather industry, or agriculture, or science?[27] These were often explicitly weighed against each other in the discourse on intellectual warfare. Now, to the best of my knowledge, Kang Youwei never made the conceptual leap to posit the existence of intellectual warfare. He did, however, concur that military warfare was not the most fearful peril. In the same 1895 memorandum cited above, he writes:

In an era of unity, the country is necessarily sustained by agriculture and the hearts of the people may thus be appeased. In an era of contention, the country is necessarily sustained by commerce and thus [one's profits] may equal one's opponent's profits. To change this would be disastrous. [...] Moreover, in the past, countries were vanquished by weapons, everyone knows this. Today, countries are vanquished by commerce but everyone overlooks this. When one uses weapons to destroy another, the country will be ruined but the people will still. exist. When one uses commerce to destroy another, the people will be ruined and the country will follow. China will probably find her demise in this way.[28]

Initially, Kang probably only reached the emperor and his inner court with these words. However, a year later, another reformer, the above mentioned Wang Kangnian, used the newly established popular reform journal *Shiwubao* to convey a similar idea in his treatise "A Discussion of Commercial Warfare". He begins his essay with the following words:

All the countries in the world, without exception, ensure their survival through war. If they wage war, they remain vigilant and there is nothing that does not flourish. If they do not wage war, they become self-complacent and there is nothing that does not go to ruin. There are three tools of war: religion to seize [the other country's] people, weapons to seize its territory, and commerce to seize its wealth.[29]

---

26 Pusey (1983), *China and Charles Darwin*, p. 135.

27 The case of science is discussed in detail in Iwo Amelung's contribution to this volume.

28 Kang Youwei (1981 [1895]), "Shang Qing Di di er shu", p. 127. This is a quotation from Kang's famous second memorial to the Guangxu emperor. The text is otherwise known as the "Public Vehicle Petition" (*Gongche shangshu* 公車上書) and was composed in protest by Kang and others following the signing of the Treaty of Shimonoseki.

29 Wang Kangnian (1896), "Shangzhan lun", p. 1.

By 1896, the notion that modern wars were fought by more than just weapons, and on more than just one battlefield, and that some of these modes were more devastating than others, had thus become widespread among China's growing reformist movement. These notions now only had to be combined with established ideas about learning, ignorance, and national ruin, as I have outlined them above, under the proper institutional conditions, in a suitable intellectual atmosphere. This "intellectual cauldron" turned out to be pre-revolutionary Hunan.[30]

III. Origins: "Struggle for Intellectual Survival"

The first expression of the intellectual warfare idea seems to have been a short notice announcing the foundation of the Practical Application Study Society (*Zhiyong xuehui* 致用學會), located in Longnan 龍南 (Hunan Province), which was presumably published in *Xiangbao* in July or late June of that year:[31]

Today's people of talent, being agitated, say: "[The people today] do not realise that when the Occident (*Taixi* 泰西) makes use of economic warfare, they are really using intellectual warfare." When merchants are without learning, how can they engage in warfare? When learning is without [study] societies, how can merchants be educated? Present-day China therefore must make it its number one priority to open study societies. For, the reason why the hearts of the people are not stirred [to action] is that they are not sufficiently conversant with the current political situation; and the reason why they are not sufficiently conversant with the current political situation is that they do not read newspapers. [...] Study societies must therefore purchase a broad variety of useful Chinese and foreign newspapers and make them available for all comrades for their perusal.[32]

From the *en passant* mentioning of the term alone, it is already quite clear that, as early as mid-1897, the notion of intellectual warfare must not have been very alien to a reader of reform newspapers. In any case, whoever penned the

---

30 For the end of the reform movement in Hunan and Tang Caichang's brief career as a revolutionary, see Hürter (2002), *Tang Caichang*, pp. 233–283; Esherick (1976), *Reform and Revolution in China*, pp. 11–33.

31 The founders were Huang Zun 黄尊 of Nanzhou 南洲, Yi Shunyu 易順豫 of Longyang 龍陽, as well as Chen Changtan 陳昌曇, Hu Rong 胡榮, and Mei An 梅安. The earliest version of the text that I had access to dates from 1898 and was published in Macao. It gives "the sixth month of the 23rd year of the reign period Guangxu" as the founding date of the study society and I believe it to be likely that the original announcement would have been published shortly thereafter in a regional journal.

32 Huang Zun et al. (1898), "Zhiyong xuehui zhangcheng xu", p. 9b.

THE IDEA OF "INTELLECTUAL WARFARE" 345

announcement did not deem it necessary to explain the concept in any way, which bespeaks of an earlier origin and wider use.

Be that as it may, the concept of intellectual warfare, as far as I can see, came to the focus of scholarly attention only with an 1898 initiative in Hunan's capital of Changsha to establish a study society exclusively dedicated to illuminating the relationship between learning and the conduct of war. The Intellectual Warfare Society (*Xuezhan hui* 學戰會), as it was called, issued a list of its rules and basic tenents in *Xiangbao* in May of 1898 and had 13 founding members, including Huang E 黃崿 (fl. 1898; born in Shanhua 善化 County), and a certain He Tingzao 何廷藻. For the present inquiry, the Statutes of the Intellectual Warfare Society (*Xuezhan hui zhangcheng* 學戰會章程) are not very informative, but the society did articulate its fundamental creed at this point that "military warfare is inferior to commercial warfare, commercial warfare is inferior to intellectual warfare" (*bingzhan buru shangzhan, shangzhan buru xuezhan* 兵戰不如商戰商戰不如學戰).[33]

The previous issue of *Xiangbao* had already carried a more essayistic piece entitled "Inaugural Statement of the Intellectual Warfare Society" (*Xuezhan hui qi* 學戰會啟),[34] in which founding member Huang E outlined the group's purpose in more detail and elaborated on its commitment to "promote and expound the teachings of our race, and join and solidify the hearts of our people, thereby creating a country of true luminaries" (*chang ming wu zhongjiao gujie wu minxin er cheng zhen haojie zhi guo* 昌明吾種教固結吾民心而成真豪傑之國). These "modern heroes", however,

will not be provided with spears and lances, and will not be given armour and helmets; they will not devote themselves to the deeds of warriors (*zhuangshi* 壯士), and will not bother with the performing arts [lit.: "the exercises of dancers"].[35]

The last remark is evidently meant to counter any and all suspicions that the students of the Intellectual Warfare Society would only learn to become just as "effeminate" (*wenruo* 文弱) as their traditional, "old China" counterparts. The "champions" of the new China envisioned by Huang are distinct from both, uneducated, brutish warriors as well as from delicate, unworldly men of letters.[36]

---

33 Huang E et al. (1898), "Xuezhan hui zhangcheng", 234a.

34 The text is almost incomprehensible in places and appears in large parts to be a pastiche of a sixth century text entitled "Letter to Wang Sengbian" (*Yu Wang Sengbian shu* 與王僧辯書) which was written by the famous compiler Xu Ling 徐陵 (507–583).

35 Huang E (1898), "Xuezhan hui qi", p. 230b.

36 On physical education in the late Qing and Republican era see Schillinger (2016), *The Body and Military Masculinity*; Morris (2004), *Marrow of the Nation*. The image of China as the "Sick Man of East Asia" is discussed by Jui-sung Yang in his contribution to this volume.

In its convictions, the Intellectual Warfare Society is directly opposed to people from the (in the words of historian Luo Zhitian) "materialist group" such as the eminent statesman Zhang Zhidong 張之洞 (1837–1909), who argued that learning "is spread through power" and "power means the military".[37] Huang reverses this hierarchy:

What this [society] hopes to accomplish is for those who are well-versed in Western learning to again and again demonstrate that conventional warfare (*bingzhan*) and commercial warfare (*shangzhan*) are inferior to intellectual warfare; and we will work diligently and conscientiously to assure that the teachings of our race (*wo zhong jiao* 我種教) will persevere whenever a group (*qun* 群) fights against another group, man fights against nature (*tian* 天), public and private [interests] wage war, or man and things wage war.[38]

"Intellectual wars" are thus fought on a variety of "battlefields": First (and foremost), it is one of the modes in which groups (nations, races) may be pitted against each other. However, for Huang, "fighting" nature (*i.e.*, studying, comprehending, and exploiting natural phenomena and resources) and "fighting" inanimate things (such as natural disasters) and animals equally fall into the purview of intellectual warfare.

Huang goes on to illustrate the idea of intellectual warfare with a series of examples from world history. It is, however, recent events in East Asia that are his immediate concern:

Let us consider the truly egregious misery [inflicted on] Taiwan and Jiaozhou Bay. Germany studies and respects Confucianism [*i.e.*, to understand better their Chinese subjects] and encourages the people of Jiaozhou [to study].[39] Japan institutionalised Chinese as a school subject and educates Taiwanese scholars. But can it really be the case that [Germany and Japan] do this in order to benefit the students and not because they really wish to keep the common people ignorant? The Germans say [with regard to this]: We use [these measures] to subdue the "savages" (*yeman* 野蠻). And the Japanese say: We are thus able to exert complete control over [this part of] China. How can there be anyone who admires [Germany and Japan's] [supposed efforts to] enlighten [the Chinese people in their territories]? How can there be any who admire their [supposed efforts] to remove our weakness?[40]

---

37 Luo Zhitian (2015), *Inheritance Within Rupture*, pp. 243–244.

38 Huang E (1898), "Xuezhan hui qi", p. 230b. The dichotomy between "public" and "private" was frequently invoked in late Qing political discourse, but not usually framed as a war. See Zarrow (2012), *After Empire*, Chapter 2, esp. pp. 63–69.

39 On the "ambiguities of colonial governance in Qingdao" see Mühlhahn (2012), "Negotiating the Nation", esp. pp. 38–43. Colonial Jiaozhou had in fact a very high school density and commensurately high per capita student enrolment. Schultz-Naumann (1985), *Unter Kaisers Flagge*, p. 183.

40 Huang E (1898), "Xuezhan hui qi", p. 230a.

The last sentence is, admittedly, rather obscure.[41] However, what Huang seems to be attempting to do here is to debunk the myth of the "White Man's Burden", *i.e.*, the notion that Western colonialism really does more good than harm. The actions of the German Empire and of Japan in Jiaozhou and on Taiwan respectively, are seen in a similar light as Napoleon's invasion of Egypt (Kemet) by Africana scholar Jacob H. Carruthers in his 1999 book entitled *Intellectual Warfare* and whose evaluation is quoted in the first epithet to this article. "Learning" may become a tool of subjugation and colonialism, and accomplish a level of destruction that is more devastating than any military action, and may have repercussions long after the guns have gone silent.

The "Inaugural Statement" goes on to offer yet more pieces of historical evidence to support the claim that it is really learning which—again and again— proves to be the decisive factor in warfare: the British chieftain Caratacus (r. 43–50 CE), who led an (initially) successful guerrilla campaign against the Roman occupiers; the American Revolution; the events of the *Vormärz* that led to the Frankfurt Parliament (1848–49);[42] and the series of reforms in Japan following Commodore Perry's forceful opening of the country that led to the abolition of the *han* 藩 (fief) system and culminated in the establishment of a centralised government during the Meiji Restoration.

In all of these cases, [the abovementioned countries] had learning, [study] societies, and were able to form a group (*qun*). As for the present, there are a few more examples worth considering: Why did [Yaqub Beg's regime in the] Tarim Basin (*Huibu* 回部) vanish? Why did Poland perish? Why did India go into decline? And why did the Chinese vassal states of Korea, Vietnam, Burma and Ryukyu fall into oblivion, one after the other? [Implied answer: They did not have learning and societies.] We can thus conclude that, if one lacks a strategy, how can one possibly fight for oneself? If one lacks [the ability to] fight, how can one possibly persevere? If one lacks [the ability to] persevere, how can one form a group?[43]

"Learning" thus stands at the top of a cascade of societal effects that start with successful conduct of war and end in creating "social cohesion"—arguably, the "most thought after good" in turn-of-the-century China and the central concern of virtually every "nationalist" reformer. According to some modern assessments, study societies did, indeed, play a key role in reform era Hunan and

---

41 The original text reads: 豈有慕於明之亡我之弱已焉哉.

42 The text mentions a "set-back suffered by Prussia at the hands of France" (*Pu jue yu Fa* 普蹶於 法). This may refer to the "Rhine crisis" of 1840 or the February Revolution when workers and students in France deposed the Citizen King Louis-Philippe; their actions resulted in the declaration of the Second Republic. Both events impacted the revolution of 1848 in the German states.

43 Huang E (1898), "Xuezhan hui qi", p. 230a.

elsewhere.[44] The link that Huang sees between learning, study societies, and social cohesion is thus more than mere grandstanding.

We know precious little about the inner workings of the Intellectual Warfare Society aside from the rules put forward in the society's statutes. However, two additional articles published some months after the group was officially established, further elucidate the discourse on intellectual warfare in late-nineteenth century Hunan and offer at least an indirect glimpse into the activities of the society. That being said, neither article admits to having been indebted to the work of the group in any way, and their authors clearly developed the idea of intellectual warfare in two quite different directions. Indeed, as we will see later on, there is a certain "fuzziness" associated with the idea that characterises the discourse as a whole. Nonetheless, they represent the closest thing that we have to a "work product" of the Intellectual Warfare Society.

The first essay to be discussed, entitled "Treaties on the Dictum that Military Warfare is Inferior to Commercial Warfare which is Inferior to Intellectual Warfare" (*Bingzhan buru shangzhan shangzhan buru xuezhan shuo* 兵戰不如商戰商戰不如學戰說) is one of the only pieces of writing on the subject that was written by an identifiable historical figure (and a rather well-known one at that), Cao Dianqiu 曹典球 (1877–1960). About 20 years of age at the time, Cao was an acquaintance of Yan Fu's (by 1901 at the latest), and went on to become superintendent (*jiandu* 監督) of the Advanced School of Industry and Commerce Hunan (*Hunan Gaodeng Shiye Xuetang* 湖南高等實業學堂), the forerunner of Central South University (*Zhongnan Daxue* 中南大学), from 1908–1912. He served as President of Hunan University (then called Hunan Provincial University) from March 1931 to October 1932, and served in various functions in the People's Republic of China after 1949.[45]

In his "Treatise on Intellectual Warfare", Cao argues that China is currently engaged in a war with the Western world that is not fought on a traditional battlefield but in the realm of learning.

For decades now, we have been sending students [abroad], set up schools, and established translation bureaus. Those [entrusted with] drafting [political measures] to work towards self-strengthening and to resist the foreigners say: Weapons! Commerce! And yet, why has our country not made an inch of progress and not achieved the slightest result? To cover it in a few words: it is because of a lack of learning.[46]

While not exactly denying that the West poses a very real and dangerous military threat and that China needed to "plug the leaking vessel" (塞漏巵), i.e., to

---

44 Chen (2010), "Civilization and Competition".

45 Liu Liyan, *Red Genesis*, pp. 29–42; Zhu Youzhi and Guo Qin (2011), *Hunan jin-xiandai shiye renwu zhuanlüe*, pp. 284–287.

46 Cao Dianqiu (1898), "Bingzhan buru shangzhan shangzhan buru xuezhan shuo", p. 657a.

THE IDEA OF "INTELLECTUAL WARFARE" 349

stop the draining of funds and profits from the country,[47] he stresses that it is not weapons, and trade and commerce, as such, that are important for warfare, it is *knowledge about weapons and commerce* that matters. China's gravest mistake, according to Cao, had been to hire foreign experts to take charge of these fields. Not so much because they had acted against the interests of China (Sir Robert Hart famously considered himself to be an agent of the Qing Empire, as did Charles G. Gordon, "Chinese Gordon"),[48] but because, in so doing, China had indefinitely "shelved" addressing the deeper underlying issue, that is, the lack of expertise among its own subjects. Therefore, China continued to "rely on the support of foreigners for everything" (*shishi jie yangji wairen* 事事皆仰給外人). In Cao's view, this problem had only recently started to dawn on people:

> Those who presently concern themselves with current affairs gradually come to the realisation that Western instructors must not be hired. The day when the leaders of our government [as well] come to understand the clever schemes and jealous hearts of the other nations (*bizu* 彼族) and implement orderly measures to open the people's intelligence and to offer incentives to people of ability will mark the beginning of a major turning-point in the intellectual war between China and the West.[49]

Furthermore, Cao continues, as a matter of fact, "a [possible] restoration of China is a bewildering and dreadful [prospect] for Europe" (*Zhongguo zhi weixin, Ouzhou zhi qi ju ye* 中國之維新歐洲之奇懼也) proven by the fact that European "intelligence gatherers" pay close attention to the developments in the Middle Realm:

> Of all the instances in which [in the past] China has hired instructors, established schools, or set up study societies, an untold number of them were reported on in Western newspapers. Those who do not know [what this really signifies] believe that [this shows that] (the West) admires China, praises China. Those who *do* know it believe that they survey China, envy China, and that they monitor whether (China's) learning is (more) accomplished or not, so as to find ways to match it [provided that it is necessary].[50]

The exact same thing had allegedly happened with regard to Japan during the Meiji Restoration. Cao rounds up his argument by quoting Wang Kangnian (see quotation at the end of Section I) and reiterating his initial observation:

> In the words of Mr. Wang Rangqing 汪穰卿 (= Kangnian): "All the countries in the world, without exception, ensure their survival through war." Thus, since the West-

---

47 Ibid.

48 For a study that attempts to reconcile both Chinese and foreign perspectives during Chinas "semi-colonial" period see Bickers (2011), *The Scramble for China.*

49 Cao Dianqiu (1898), "Bingzhan buru shangzhan shangzhan buru xuezhan shuo", p. 657a.

50 Ibid.

erners [demonstrably] go so far as to survey us and envy us, [the present situation) constitutes a state of fierce warfare between China and the West.[51]

All things considered, Cao is remarkably optimistic with regard to China's outlook in the currently raging intellectual war with the European powers. Indeed, he confidently declares that European thought lags behind China in important fields of inquiry, namely, "ritual studies" (*lixue* 禮學) and possess nothing akin to the "various schools of (Zhou-period) thought" (*zhuzixue* 諸子學).

Finally and quite characteristically for a discourse of weakness, he provides a short list of the necessary reform steps that ought to be taken in order to ameliorate China's ability to engage successfully in intellectual warfare. Not without a good measure of pomposity, he concludes thus:

If one were to implement [these measures] for three years—considering China's vastness and the brilliant intelligence of the yellow race—could we possibly fail to subdue Europe, dominate the East, overtake North and South America, and hold sway [over the entire world]? That is utterly implausible! That is utterly implausible![52]

We will encounter similarly bellicose words time and again. In the discourse on intellectual warfare, the "battle lines" are clearly and quite exclusively drawn between China and the West, with the rest of the world being literally only of historical interest. It should also be noticed how Cao almost "romanticises" intellectual warfare. There is no indication that he views it in any way as a horrific means of exercising control over other nations, as was done in the "Inaugural Statement of the Intellectual Warfare Society". If anything, he views it as a commendable tool for Chinese world dominance.

The anonymous writer behind the second article entitled "Discussion of the Dictum that Military Warfare is Inferior to Commercial Warfare Which is Inferior to Intellectual Warfare" (*Bingzhan buru shangzhan shangzhan buru xuezhan lun* 兵戰不如商戰商戰不如學戰論), shares the latter's basic observation, but does not view it so lightly. Indeed, there are a few indications that the author of "Discussion on Intellectual Warfare" is much less enthusiastic about intellectual warfare and the outlook that it offers than Cao. It begins by suggesting a cosmological necessity of war:

The world cannot be without war. In an age of savagery, [conflicts are fought] by means of military warfare. In an age of civilisation, [they are fought] by means of commercial warfare or by means of intellectual warfare. I have reflected on this long and intensely and [have come to the conclusion] that the junctures when the world has transformed and advances were [always] the result of the world fighting wars. Therefore, the world

---

51 Ibid.
52 Ibid., p. 657b

THE IDEA OF "INTELLECTUAL WARFARE"   351

only exists as long as there is war and if there was no war, the world would [simply] grind to a halt.[53]

It is noteworthy that intellectual warfare and commercial warfare are actually similarly placed on the "ladder" of historical evolution (with a slight edge given to the former). Moreover, if humanity were to cease waging wars (or had categorically refrained from doing so in the past), our world would become "a world in which birds and beasts vie for supremacy and where the human race has become extinct" (*wei qinshou zhengduo zhi shi er wei renzhong juemie zhi shi* 為禽獸爭奪之世而為人種絕滅之世).

While the authors of the article "Discussion on Intellectual Warfare" ground their arguments more firmly in a philosophical basis, the actual concern lies once again with China's actual present situation, not abstract philosophy:

Ever since the Occident has engaged [with us] in mutual trade, it has beheld the race (*zhonglei* 種類) of this most civilised country and seen how much its strength is lacking. And thus, the Westerners have been sneering at us, ridiculing us, calling us "Aboriginals" (*tufan* 土番) and a country only half-civilised (*banjiao zhi guo* 半教之國). This (attitude) stands in outrageous and flagrant defiance of the principle of equality (*pingdeng zhi yi* 平等之義). I have pondered [their behaviour] with ardent disapproval and concluded: the reason why the Westerners today [dare to] mock our China (*Zhina* 支那) and humiliate our China (*Caina* 采拿)[54] is that our race is unable to engage in warfare.[55]

The necessity of warfare seen both from the standpoint of cosmology as well as *realpolitik* notwithstanding, the text expresses strongly doubts that further military built-ups will improve China's ability to wage war. The shape of modern warfare has changed to such a degree that "if China wishes to fight, it must do so by means of commercial or intellectual warfare (*yu zhan bi yi shangzhan yi xuezhan* 欲戰必以商戰以學戰)". Europe, they go on to argue, has long realised this. Since any modern (conventionally fought) war will inevitably turn into a total war that would "imperil commerce and ruin the country" (*hai shang wangguo* 害商亡國), the European countries have ostensibly managed to channel their primeval inclination as human beings towards combat into a less destructive, more "sublime" pursuit and now primarily "use learning to determine who is strong and who is weak (以學爭強弱)".[56]

The text anticipates the natural objection that this portrayal of present-day Europe is warped and rather naïve and weaves the following counter-argument into its own line of reasoning to forestall such voices:

---

53 "Bingzhan buru shangzhan shangzhan buru xuezhan lun" (1898), p. 577a.
54 A rare phonetic transliteration of the English "China".
55 "Bingzhan buru shangzhan buru xuezhan lun" (1898), p. 577a.
56 Ibid.

"You say that the Westerners employ intellectual warfare. Why, then, did they resort to brute force and inhumane barbarism during the events of Jiaozhou Bay and Dalian Bay,[57] and [why did they] make excessive demands of us and coerce us into compliance?" [To this] I answer: "They dared to act in this manner because China is lacking in learning."[58]

The entire argument of "Discussion on Intellectual Warfare" may thus be summarised as follows: 1) China is too weak militarily to confront the West on this particular "front". In addition, giving pride of place to the military when it comes to national priorities is historically obsolete. Therefore, since war is (for the time being, at least) a "necessary evil", if not the driving factor of human development, the country needs to engage in alternative modes of warfare. 2) Shifting towards intellectual warfare would at the same time demonstrate to the other countries (and the European powers in particular) that China deserves to be treated equally on the international stage. (After all, small countries such as Belgium and Switzerland are not being bullied even though they are much weaker in terms of territory, manpower, and resources than China is.) Presumably, at least the author implies as much, this would eventually compel the other nations to cease their military aggression against China.

All things considered, the second text is somewhat less confident concerning China's prospects, but nonetheless closes with the assurance that "the race can be protected" (*zhong keyi bao* 種可以保) and that "there is yet hope that the 400 million [members of the] yellow race will not become [*i.e.*, suffer the same fate as] black slaves or redskins [*sic!*]" (*siwanwan zhi huangzhong bu wei heinu hongren you jiji ye* 四萬萬之黃種不為黑奴紅人猶幾及也).[59]

To summarise, the textual evidence clearly points to post-1895 Hunan as the "cradle" of the intellectual warfare idea. However, as J.R. Pusey has amply demonstrated, Darwinian thought was by no means readily, let alone uncritically, adopted in Hunan. Tang Caichang, for instance (by 1898, not yet fully committed to revolution and armed resistance), was enough of a "realist" to acknowledge that the Darwinian vision adequately described the present world, but was equally convinced that humanity as a whole (and perhaps Hunan in particular) was on a gradual, preordained path towards the utopian state of the "Great Unity" (*datong* 大同).[60] It thus seems feasible that the evolutionary development from "military warfare" to "intellectual warfare", as suggested by the members and spiritual successors of the members of the Intellectual War-

---

57 On Jiaozhou see note 39 above. For the events that led to the cession of Dalian (historically known as Port Arthur) on the Liaodong peninsula see Otte (2007), *The China Question*, pp. 74–132.

58 "Bingzhan buru shangzhan buru xuezhan lun" (1898), pp. 577a–577b.

59 Ibid., p. 577b.

60 Kang's magnus opum (begun in the late 1880s) and parts were published intermittently. However, it was not fully available in print until 1935.

fare Society, in some way reflects this hopeful trajectory. As a matter of fact, the last sentence of "Discussion on Intellectual Warfare" cautions that intellectual warfare is in fact not the penultimate step of socio-cultural development, because "if the Universal Principle remains unclarified, learning is not sufficient to avoid disaster and calamity" (*gongli bu ming ze xue buzu yi mian huohuan* 公理不明則學不足以免禍患). The ultimate goal of learning thus has to be the explication of the "Universal Principle" (*gongli* 公理) and to move humanity towards the Great Unity.[61] Learning pertaining to areas of study that do not seek to do so, but, instead, aim solely at gaining an advantage in intellectual warfare, is thus relegated to a less lofty status.

Be that as it may, the Great-Unity ideal all but disappeared from the intellectual warfare discourse after 1900 (the year in which Tang was executed for sedition) and made way for the alternative conviction that a world without conflict had to be born out of bloody conflict.[62] Fuelled by yet more acts of "national humiliation" (the Boxer Protocol of 1900 and later the Russo-Japanese War) as well as domestic political developments, namely, the New Policies after 1901, the intellectual warfare discourse developed a life independent of its Hunanese origins with the dawn of the new century. In particular, the war metaphor perpetuated by the discourse on intellectual warfare grew inextricably linked to the jargon of social Darwinism and to visions of "national ruin" (*wangguo* 亡國).

IV. Let it all Come Together: The "Intellectual Struggle for Survival"

On 16 July 1901, the prolific intellectual and reformer Liang Qichao published part one of his essay entitled "New Methods to Vanquish Nations" (*Mieguo xinfa lun* 滅國新法論). Much like his teacher Kang Youwei (Section II), he, too, acknowledged that a country's destruction or preservation was not only a matter of military strength but also a matter of "intangible" (*wuxing* 無形) factors. However, in contrast to Kang, Liang did not illustrate insights from ancient sages with examples from recent history, but attempted to identify specifically

---

61 On *gongli* see Hürter (2002), *Tang Caichang*, pp. 112–114, 132–137. This is a key idea in the thought of Tang Caichang: "What is the universal principle? [It is] the way towards the Great Unity." Ibid., p. 114.

62 Cao's article and "Discussion on Intellectual Warfare" were reprinted in *Xiangbao wenbian* 湘報文編 (1902), however.

"modern" (*i.e.*, "new") modes of destruction.[63] Basically, Darwin had replaced the mythological adviser Zhonghui as an authority on "national ruin".

Liang begins his essay with the observation that, in former times, states vanquished other states "by overwhelming them and attacking them" (*yi ta zhi fa zhi* 以撻之伐之); today, this is done "by coaxing them and persuading them" (*yi ao zhi xiu zhi* 以噢之咻之). Formerly, the act of vanquishing another state had been "abrupt" (*zhou* 驟) and "obvious" (*xian* 顯); today it is "gradual" (*jian* 漸) and "subtle" (*wei* 微). He goes on:

> Formerly, those who vanquished countries were like tigers and wolfs; today, they are like foxes and racoon dogs. In some cases, countries are vanquished by international trade; in others, they are vanquished by controlling their debt. In some cases, countries are vanquished by training their troops for them; in others, by installing advisors; and in still others by building roads. In some cases, countries are vanquished by fanning or inflaming factional struggles; in others, by pacifying civil strife; and, in still others, by supporting revolutions. Provided that the essence [of the country to be destroyed] is already exhausted, the [aggressor's] opportunity is ripe and they may, in one fell swoop, change the country's name and change the colouring of its maps. If the essence is not yet exhausted and the opportunity is not yet ripe, it can happen that the name will be kept and the colouring will remain the same for another a hundred and some years.[64]

In Liang's view, China's "race had not yet run", as its "essence" was carried by its people of which there were still millions upon millions. China's greatest danger lay, instead, "within", specifically with its own government:

> Let me now direct a few words of honest admonition to [China's] 400 million people: Do not worry that others will topple [our country] and establish a [new] state [in its stead]; do not worry that others will overthrow [the government] and establish a [new] dynasty. Whoever has a mind to plot against another, will surely take advantage of their stupidity and will not use their intelligence [against them]. They will surely take advantage of their weakness and will not use their strength [against them]. They will surely take advantage of their [state of] disorder and will not use their good governance [against them]. In present-day China, the one who is most stupid and most weak, to the point of causing chaos, is none other than the current government.[65]

Liang's essay contained almost all of the pieces of the fully mature intellectual warfare discourse: the nod to Darwin, the conviction that the nature of international conflict had profoundly changed in the modern period, and the belief that education could provide the saving remedy.[66] However, "learning" is conspic-

---

63 Cf. Kang Youwei (1981 [1898]), "Shang Qing Di di di wu shu", p. 205. Kang expounded Zhonghui's words drawing on a plethora of examples from recent (world) history, ending each section with the same formulaic phrase to emphasize that these events had played out according to the principles laid down by the classical text.

64 Liang Qichao (1999 [1901]), "Mieguo xinfa lun", p. 467.

65 Ibid., p. 473.

66 Ibid., p. 474.

uously missing from his list of "new methods". Nor did he link the new, abstract, foreign concept of "struggle" to the more general and familiar notion of "warfare".

Although there seems to be a noticeable gap in the relevant sources for the years between the Hundred Days' Reform and the commencement of the New Policies, it is evident that the evocation of "intellectual warfare" had become something of a rhetorical commonplace by the time Liang had published his "New Methods", and by 1902/03 at the latest.[67] In 1902, for example, the *Hangzhou Vernacular Newspaper* (*Hangzhou baihuabao* 杭州白話報) featured an article that proclaimed the present to be a "world of education" 教育的世界 and an "era of knowledge struggle and intellectual warfare" (*zhizheng xuezhan de shidai* 智爭學戰的時代).[68] The same year, the *Shanghai News* (*Shenbao* 申報) of 17 October ran a piece written by a certain Liu Kun 劉焜 (1867–1931) in which he discusses the intellectual development of the Western world and begins with a familiar-sounding statement:

Whoever uses weapons to make war weakens his people. Whoever uses commerce to make war weakens his [missing character; = country?]. Whoever uses learning to make war weakens the race. The great powers of the entire globe vie for honour and contend for glory. Only our yellow race studies the old and follows established [ways]. This is to be feared! This is to be feared![69]

Interestingly, Liu seems to caution the reader *not to* engage in intellectual warfare and remains sceptical that "learning" should take priority over military affairs, arguing for a more comprehensive form of education that echoes Yan Fu's tripartite construct of "people's power" (*minli* 民力), "people's intelligence" (*minzhi* 民智), and "people's virtue" (*minde* 民德) which the author sees to have been realised in ancient Sparta. Namely, while Sparta elevated "the esteeming of martiality" (*shangwu* 尚武) to be the principle aim of their system of education, it actually consisted of three tiers: physical education (*tiyu* 體育), mental education (*zhiyu* 智育), and moral education (*deyu* 德育). Athens, on the other hand, solely "esteemed civility" (*shangwen* 尚文) and thus provided a less well-rounded education for its citizens.

Regarding the Orient, Japan and Russia are close to the Spartan [model] and China resembles Athens. And since the judgement regarding who is strong and who is weak is

---

67 Apart from the articles discussed below, see, for example: "Yu tongzhi shu" (1960 [1903]) (*Youxue yibian* 7, May); "Guang shangxue yi kai shang zhi shuo shang" (1904) (*Shenbao*, 11330, 31 October 1904). I cannot hope to discuss them all within the confines of this article.

68 Huanghai Fenglang (1902), "Lun jinri zui yao de liang zhong jiaoyu", p. 2a. Quoted in: Wang Rongguo (1987), "Jiaoyu jiuguo", p. 136.

69 Liu Kun (1902), "Xiguo xueshu daoyuan Xila".

evident, it is equally [easy] to understand which [main (educational)] purpose [*i.e.*, *shangwu* or *shangwen*] is superior and which is insufficient.[70]

For Liu, Sparta had thus evidently won its intellectual war with Athens. However, there was no agreement on this in the discourse on intellectual warfare around 1903, as the corresponding source in Section V shows.

When tracing the further development of the intellectual-warfare trope and its journey to Shanghai, we can, however, go a step further and offer more compelling evidence, as the following source testifies. An article in *Shenbao* entitled "I Taught you with Assiduous Repetition" (*Hui er zhunzhun* 誨爾諄諄)[71] from 23 August 1903 explicitly states that the author had received a letter from a friend in Changsha who introduced the idea to him. The article actually consists of a transcript (or at least, a retelling) of a recent speech held by Provincial Governor 巡撫 of Hunan, Zhao Erxun 趙爾巽 (1844–1927), who had assumed office in January of 1903, in front of the student body of a polytechnic academy:

When [people] shoot at each other with small-calibre Gruson guns, this is tangible warfare (*youxing zhi zhanzheng* 有形之戰爭). Its damage is obvious and superficial. As for intangible warfare (*wuxing zhi zhanzheng* 無形之戰爭), it can topple another state or annihilate another race without the enemy being aware of it. Its damage is concealed and furious. When the people of the entire country dedicate themselves wholeheartedly to learning, new principles will be revealed daily and the people's intelligence will be greatly enlarged. This is called intellectual warfare. Whoever is victorious, will become hegemon (*ba* 霸).[72]

Similarly, the victors in commercial warfare will prove themselves to be "strong" (*qiang* 强) and the victor of industrial warfare will become "wealthy" (*fu* 富). The "great men and eminent scholars" (*weiren shuoshi* 偉人碩士) of both East and West, Zhao continues, are in agreement that these three areas deserve unlimited access to financial resources and public support. Yet, "learning" still reigns supreme:

This being the case, if [people working] in the field of industry and technology (*gongyi* 工藝) only did their utmost and [conducted further] research and sought to improve upon that which is already excellent (*jing yi qiu jing* 精益求精), then they could, on the large scale, [contribute to] enrich the country and to retrieve economic rights that have flown abroad. And on the small scale, they could bring prosperity to their families so that they may enjoy endless profits. [Considering this,] could you students, having aspirations in

---

70 Ibid.

71 The title is taken from a verse in the *Book of Odes* (*Shijing* 詩經): "I taught you with assiduous repetition, And you listened to me with contempt." Legge (1871), *The Chinese Classics, Volume IV*, Part II, p. 517.

72 "Hui er zhunzhun" (1903).

THE IDEA OF "INTELLECTUAL WARFARE" 357

this field of study as well as the benefit of instruction by brilliant teachers possibly do less then fully exert yourselves?[73]

We thus see that the intellectual warfare trope appears quite frequently in the early twentieth century Chinese language press. Examples can be found in more highbrow publications (*Jingshi wenchao*, see below), vernacular periodicals (*Hunan baihuabao*), commercial (foreign run) newspapers (*Shenbao*), and radical, Japan-based journals (*Jiangsu*, see below). Indeed, the years between 1902 and 1905 seem to mark the "heyday" of the intellectual warfare discourse in both scope and depth. Be that as it may, systematical, comprehensive reflections on the topic are nonetheless few and far between; or, to put it differently, the trope is often *employed* but seldom *expounded*. And indeed, after the Intellectual Warfare Society had been, as far as can be ascertained, dissolved in the wake of the shattering of the Hunanese reform movement, another substantial treatise on the idea was not published until 1903.[74] We will turn to this particular source presently.

The article in question appeared in the first issue of the journal *Jingshi wenchao* 經世文潮 (Tidings Concerning Statecraft; henceforth abbreviated as *JSWC*) and headed the journal's section on education. In fact, it was the very first article to appear in *JSWC*, directly following the journals inaugural introduction. I take this to mean that the editors ascribed some importance to the issue. The article is densely argued, but roughly divides into two parts: the first part discusses the historical evolution of intellectual warfare; the second part deals with the apparent contradiction that, given that intellectual warfare ostensibly "evolved" from military warfare, how come military warfare still exists and is, in fact, rampant in East Asia?

Much like the text entitled "Discussion on Intellectual Warfare" discussed in Section III, the *JSWC* text unequivocally identified intellectual warfare as a modern phenomenon. War "has existed since there was a world" (*zi zhao you shijie zhi ri shi* 自肇有世界之日始), but intellectual warfare "actually only began in modern civilisations" (*shi wanjin zhi wenming kai zhi* 實晚近之文明開之). As humanity evolved, it developed agriculture and technology, and

although, at that time, their [new-found] commitment to encourage learning was not yet equal to their customary veneration of martiality, it nonetheless further developed over time and gradually progressed and became more and more inclined to esteem mental [rather than physical] capabilities (*chongshang naoli* 崇尚腦力).[75]

The emergence of "fully-fledged" intellectual wars in the recent past, however, was a kind of "adaptive response" of humankind to new environmental (or

---

73 Ibid.

74 And it would take until 1915 for the next lengthy treatise to appear. See conclusion.

75 "Xuezhan" (1903), p. 9b.

rather, historical) pressures: specifically, Malthusian pressures, as the text will go on to argue.[76] The shape of intellectual warfare is already outlined at the very beginning of the article:

I have delved into facts and deeds from time immemorial and investigated the recent events on the five continents. And when I contemplate [the reasons] that have led to [a country's] rise or fall and inquire into [the conditions] of success or failure, I cannot but bemoan the havoc wreaked by intellectual warfare. Compared to the menace of conventional war (*gange* 干戈; lit. shield and halberd), the effects caused by it are many times, if not a hundred times [more serious], and the final victory is many times, if not a hundred times [more decisive]—and that is a very conservative estimate.[77]

This is far removed from the "romantic" rendition that depicts intellectual warfare as a more civilised, less destructive kind of warfare that bespeaks humankind's road to a utopian global society. In fact, it is the exact opposite: learning (not only the "hard sciences") has made the destructive potential of wars much greater. Add to this the Darwinian vision of "national ruin and racial extinction" and intellectual warfare becomes a dreadful prospect, indeed. As a matter of fact, the influence of Liang Qichao's (1873–1929) "New Methods" on "Intellectual Warfare" is blatantly obvious.[78] Military warfare is characterised as "sudden" (*dun* 頓) and "obvious", whereas intellectual warfare is "gradual" and "subtle"—these, aside from the first one, are Liang's exact same words! The text continues: When a race is extinguished by military warfare,

this may be likened to a tiger that breaks limbs and tears at the body or a sudden wind and abrupt rainfall. People would still have the opportunity to rescue and lend aid to the victims. [...] When a race is annihilated by intellectual warfare, this may be likened to a fox that saps the essence and sucks the marrow. Every day [the victims] wane further and further and every month they are more and more exploited. [In this way] their vitality (*yuanqi* 元氣) is greatly harmed and death and doom soon follow. In this case, not even (a genius like) [the legendary physician] Bian Que 扁鵲, would be able to avert the consequences that must ensue.[79]

Such drastic visions had been relatively absent from the intellectual warfare discourse before 1903. To be sure, the Hunanese intellectuals had been aware of, influenced by, and reacted to Darwinian thought, but the texts on intellectual warfare of the "first wave" show comparatively little of this influence. Spe-

---

76 Ibid., p. 9a. T. R. Malthus (1766–1834), in his famous *An Essay on the Principle of Population* of 1798 had argued that, while food production follows an arithmetic progression, population growth follows a geometric series: "If we do not find a method to prevent this [from continuing the way it has], the affliction of overpopulation (*renman* 人滿) will be [mathematically] unavoidable and wars and suicide will run amok without hope of bringing them under control." Ibid.

77 Ibid., p. 8a.

78 Ibid., p. 10a.

79 Ibid., p. 10a–10b.

cifically, the tell-tale Darwinian phrases and names (such as Darwin, Malthus, survival of the fittest, natural selection) that feature on virtually every page of "Intellectual Warfare" played no major role in 1898. Conversely, one of the *Shenbao* articles discussed above does use the key formula "survival of the fittest" (*yousheng liebai* 優勝劣敗) in connection to the idea of intellectual warfare.[80] But as things stand, the author of "Intellectual Warfare" goes much further and all but *equivocates* intellectual warfare with social evolution:

Today, there are two acknowledged principles of evolution: elimination by nature (*ziran zhi taotai* 天然之淘汰) and elimination by human forces (*renli zhi taotai* 人力之淘汰). [...] At present, elimination by nature has become diminished and insufficient and elimination by human forces thus arose. What is "elimination by human forces"? It is intellectual warfare.[81]

In other words: the mechanisms of evolution themselves evolve and are subject to change.

The distinction between "natural" and "manmade" selection had already been made by Yan Fu in his translation of "Evolution and Ethics". However, in his commentary, Yan had made it perfectly clear that he saw "human selection" as the greatest imaginable threat to societal well-being and social cohesion.[82] To be sure, the author of "Intellectual Warfare" discusses the *international*, rather than the *intranational*, level, but they clearly foresee a similarly devastating effect on the world if "elimination by human forces" is allowed to have a free hand.

"All well and good," one might say, "but if the West is indeed so culturally advanced and has, as you, the author, alleges, "shifted its mind away from building up their military might in order to plan towards encouraging learning and cultivating talent" (*yi qi zhengjunjingwu zhi xin yi tu quanxue yucai zhi shi* 移其整軍經武之心以圖勸學育才之事), then why do they have weapons at all? Should they not have "dissolved all military bodies and dismantled all military equipment" (*san zuwu chi wubei* 散卒伍弛武備) long ago?" This challenge (although not in these exact words) is posed by an imagined interlocutor at the beginning of the second part of "Intellectual Warfare". "Discussion on Intellectual Warfare" had responded to a similar question by arguing that the West deals peacefully (in the domain of learning) exclusively with equals, but defaults to force, violence, and even outright slaughter when confronting so-called "inferiors". "Intellectual Warfare" argues slightly differently: within and among the "enlightened" (*kaiming* 開明) advanced societies of the present, peace is the norm and war an aberration,

---

80 "Hui er zhunzhun" (1903).
81 "Xuezhan" (1903), p. 8b–9a.
82 See note 24.

Everything that is ostensibly used to raise armies, in actuality, serves to protect the people. [...] For, promoting prosperity is the means by which the body and the intellect (of the nation) are made stronger. It ensures that the intelligence [of the people] may grow ever higher and that intellectual warfare will be engaged in ever more ferociously.[83]

Proponents of intellectual warfare of the "second generation"—no longer convinced that Kang Youwei's utopian vision was feasible (certainly not in the near future)—sought to reshape Chinese society's "hierarchy of values", rather than suggest that there was no place at all for the military in the modern world. The last section of the essay echoes the sino-chauvinism of Cao Dianqiu:

All of the characteristics [of intellectual warfare described above] may be found by anyone who dips but a little bit into Western history. It is only the particularly dim-witted who have not made a study of it. When Columbus first arrived in America, there was an abundance of native tribes (lit.: "red barbarians"; *hongyi* 紅夷). Today, though, they are [usually] only found in museum displays. (Interlinear commentary: A certain American newspaper argued that one ought to pass a law to protect the [remaining] Native Americans, lest their race become extinct. [In this way,] they could be used in [ethnographic] studies.) Furthermore, I once heard the following from someone who had just returned from Honolulu (*Tanxiangshan* 檀香山): When the Englishman [James Cook?][84] first arrived on this island, he conducted a census and counted 200,000 people. By 1900, there were only 20,000 people were left. That said, does this really indicate that the Europeans went ahead and slaughtered all these barbarians?

I would rather argue that [the "barbarians"] had been ignorant and unenlightened, and that their chance for survival had been slim. And thus they were annexed (*bingtun* 幷吞) thanks to the intellect of the Europeans and were not even aware of it. But alas! Is this only [true for] the indigenous peoples of America and of Hawaii? How will those who call themselves the 400 million Han perceive these [historical cases]? "The cart in front has already overturned, and yet, whoever follows behind in the same rut still draws closer." Whenever I ponder this , I inevitably become so terrified that my hair stands on end and I will surely burst into tears.[85]

We have seen that there is an inherent ambiguity to the intellectual-warfare idea: Is it more of a danger and a curse? Or is it an opportunity? By comparing and contrasting "Intellectual Warfare" with the texts from Section III, we can draw the following tentative conclusion: it depends on the "level of advancement" of a given nation. Nations that recognise one another as being on the same evolutionary level, engage in the "civil" kind of intellectual warfare as envisioned, for example, by Cao Dianqiu. Nations that have (allegedly) completely fallen behind in the struggle for existence (like the Hawaiians, the Native Americans, and the

---

83 "Xuezhan" (1903), p. 10b.

84 The text has *Xidunguo* 吸頓郭 as the name of the Englishman. It is unclear who this refers to but Cook was the first European to visit Hawaii and The Butterworth Squadron under Captain William Brown was the first European mission to visit what is now Honolulu harbour.

85 "Xuezhan" (1903), p. 10b–11a.

peoples of Africa) cannot expect to be afforded the same "courtesy". For them, intellectual warfare is a truly perilous option in which they stand to lose virtually everything—and can only hope that their opponents are "kind enough" to let some of their people live. China, of course awkwardly "sits on the fence", so to speak. It has the potential to join the West as an equal, but has about just as much chance to go the same way as Poland and India.[86]

The author's dubious interpretation of the historical events described above notwithstanding, it is clear what kind of message they wish to convey: the truly dreadful thing is the danger that an ignorant Chinese populace would be unable to "read the signs" and draw the appropriate lessons from examples such as these.[87] The toppling of the front cart *may potentially* serve as a warning, but who is to say if it is actually heeded? In fact, this is exactly what the ancient thinker Xunzi feared, when he made use of the same aphorism:

When sagely wisdom is not used, the stupid will lay schemes. The chariots in the van have already overturned, but the rearguard still knows no need to alter the course - when will they be awakened?[88]

Xunzi describes here a historical setting that is not wholly unlike turmoil-ridden late Qing China, and expresses his concern that, even at a time of evident crisis, those who know better (like himself, naturally) will not be heard.[89] As it turns out, proponents of the intellectual warfare idea judged the prospects of the "yellow race" in the intellectual war between China and the West to be excellent, provided that their naturally endowed intelligence was fostered by proper education. But this raises an interesting point: within the framework of intellectual warfare, the Xunzian dilemma is only of concern if the intellectual war is conceptualised as being fought between the "educated masses" of the contending nations, rather than a handful of "intellectual champions" representing each side. It is argued in "Intellectual Warfare", for instance, that:

The disaster of military warfare is a struggle on the stage of politics. The disaster of intellectual warfare is a struggle on the stage of skills and crafts (*shu yi* 術藝). Political struggle means that collectives fight each other. Only states can engage in it. A struggle of skills and crafts means that people fight on their own. Even individuals can take charge of it.[90]

---

86 Alternatively, the interpretation depends on one's own outlook on the world. Tang Caichang, for instance, divided Western thought into two camps, the "evolutionists" who essentially believe that "might makes right"; and the "physiologists" who equally believe in the existence of "fit and unfit", and "good and bad", but hold that these need to be treated with medicine and benevolence. Hürter (2002), *Tang Caichang*, pp. 132ff.

87 Cf. Li Fan's contribution on history education in this volume.

88 *Xunzi* 25.35: Knoblock (1994), *Xunzi*, p. 182.

89 Ibid., pp. 169 (quotation), 170–171.

90 "Xuezhan" (1903), p. 10a.

Again, who are these people? Or rather, what does it take to become a viable "intellectual warrior"? To quote yet another text by Liang Qichao, "On the World-Changing Power of Scholarship" (*Lun xueshu zhi shili zuoyou shijie* 論學術之勢力左右世界) (1902):

I wish to respectfully inform the scholars of our country: all of you have the power to influence the world. Why do you not use it? Even if I grant you that you will not be able to become [the likes of] Bacon, Decartes or Darwin, can you not manage to become like Voltaire, Fukuzawa Yukichi or Tolstoi? And even if you will not be able to influence the world, can you not manage to influence one country? And if you can influence our country, this will be the means by which our country will be enabled to influence the world.[91]

This adds yet another dimension to the intellectual warfare discourse and links this rather eccentric idea to a discussion that became paramount in the era of educational reform during the last years of the Qing dynasty and beyond: namely, should "specialised training" (*zhuanmen* 專門) be given priority, or rather "popular education" (*putong jiaoyu* 普通教育, or *puji jiaoyu* 普及教育).

V. Educational Reform: The "Intellectuals' Struggle for Survival"

It is hardly surprising that the intellectual warfare trope was a staple rhetorical device for educational reformers, particularly after the turn of the century when the focus of the debate shifted from high level education (*i.e.*, the Civil Service Examination) to the education of the "masses". For many, it was now an "army" of citizens that had received at least an elementary form of education that provided the "soldiers" needed for intellectual warfare, rather than the "luminaries" of the Intellectual Warfare Society or the prospective candidates of the (reformed) Civil Service Examination that publications like *JSWC* attempted to reach. Secondly, intellectual warfare was increasingly conceptualised as the final stage of a "race war" between the "yellows" and "whites" in which the other races ("black", "brown", and "red") had already been eliminated, as will be seen presently.

Much as the article "Intellectual Warfare" had spearheaded the *JSWC*, the intellectual warfare trope stands prominently at the beginning of a text published on 3 June the same year (1903) in *Jiangsu* 江蘇. It is entitled "A Comprehensive Discussion of Education" (*Jiaoyu tonglun* 教育通論) and was written by one Yunwo 云窝 (probably a pseudonym). The author shares the assessment of his peers concerning the remaining "battle lines":

---

91 Liang Qichao (1999 [1902]), "Lun xueshu zhi shili zuoyou shijie", p. 560.

The Idea of "Intellectual Warfare" 363

The world of today has become the era of the struggle between the yellow race and the white race. The other three races [brown, red, and black] will surely return to nothingness (*wuheyou zhi xiang* 無何有之鄉) within the next few hundred years. This is absolutely certain.[92]

As things stand, the "whites" have a considerable head start as "most of the world has fallen into the hands of the Caucasians" (*shijie dashi ji quyu baizhongren zhi shou* 世界大勢既趨於白種人之手). However, as formidable as they might appear, they but stand "at the initial stage of progress and not at its apex" (*jinhua zhi chujie er fei Jinhua zhi jidian* 進化之初階而非進化之極點) which means that "even an extremely poor and weak country" (*zhi pinruo zhi guo* 至貧弱之國) may catch up with them in due time.[93] This refers to China specifically; there is no indication that Yunwo has any hope for or is indeed interested in other "poor and weak" nations.

"Comprehensive Discussion" opens with the now familiar statement that, in the context of the struggle for survival, "nothing is more devastating than intellectual warfare" (*lihai zhi lie mo shen yu xuezhan* 利害之烈莫甚於學戰)".[94] Whoever loses will disappear in the "vortex of natural elimination" (*ziran taotai zhi xuanwo* 自然淘汰之旋渦) and their race will become completely wiped out.

On the surface, all [I] seem to say is that military warfare, commercial warfare, agricultural warfare, and industrial warfare are enough to rejuvenate another country or to destroy another country. [But] if we look on the inside, then the question of why someone wins or loses a military, commercial, agricultural, or industrial war, is inevitably decided by means of intellectual warfare. If the intellectual domain does not make progress, then even a person like Qin Shihuang, Genghis Khan, or Napoleon could not make a single move.[95]

Like Liu Kun (see Section IV), Yunwo cites the examples of ancient Athens and Sparta and reiterates the usual judgement that Athens had "esteemed civility" whereas Sparta had "esteemed martiality". However, they then take a completely different turn: instead of highlighting Sparta's prowess during its own time, it is pointed out that only Athens' legacy (Athens' "offspring", to put it in biological terms) survives to this day: Rome "had [all of] Greece as its mother and gave birth to Europe", but it was Athens' Socrates, Plato and Aristotle, who were the progenitors of all the intellectual lineages of Western learning.[96]

---

92 Yunwo (1960 [1903]), "Jiaoyu tonglun", p. 552.

93 Ibid., p. 553.

94 Ibid., p. 551.

95 Ibid.

96 It is unclear whether Yunwo means that Rome inherited its *culture* from Athens and its *military might* from Sparta, but the main point they wish to get across remains: There is no trace left of Sparta in the Western intellectual tradition. Yunwo (1960 [1903]), "Jiaoyu tonglun", p. 553.

However, while the author shows great respect towards history's "great men", Section 2 of "Comprehensive Discussion"—which is tellingly headed "Everyone should Receive an Education" (*Renren dang shou jiaoyu* 人人當受教育)—makes it clear that the text argues in favour of popular education:

Not all people need to become heroes and luminaries but they must absolutely not fail to become people of impeccable character. [...] The essential factor for a nation equally does not lie with obtaining a lot of heroes and luminaries. It instead centres it's hope on the strong, the young, the men and the women of the entire country becoming people of impeccable character (*wanquan renge zhi ren* 完全人格之人).[97]

In other words, intellectual warfare relies on intellectual "foot soldiers" rather than "heroes". Interestingly, the war metaphor is not taken any further at this point. For example, there is no explicit distinction made between regular soldiers (the educated masses) and other ranks (the "heroes and luminaries" serving as "generals", for instance).

An argument that is even more elaborate was made in the 1903 February issue of the periodical *Student Body of Hubei* (*Hubei xueshengjie* 湖北學生界). The strongly worded polemic "The Students' Struggle" (*Xuesheng zhi jingzheng* 學生之競爭) unequivocally states that the fate of China in this "cut-throat" world rests with its students:

Twentieth century China is the students' China. Her restoration can only be brought about by students. Her ruin can only be brought about by students.[98]

The author calls China's students to battle on all fronts: foreign relations (*waijiao* 外交), army and navy (*luhaijun* 陸海軍), agriculture (*nongye* 農業), technology (*gongyi* 工藝), and commerce (*shangwu* 商務).[99] As it turned out, popular education did become a reality in the wake of the early twentieth century political reforms initiated by the Qing government in 1902. The government's official Educational Aims (*Jiaoyu zongzhi* 教育宗旨) of 1906 stressed the importance of both general education and specialisation, but it was precisely this formulation on which a new debate could ignite itself: Which of the two was to be prioritised?

From the early period of educational reform, there survive three particularly intriguing sources that testify to the ways in which the intellectual-warfare trope was received "at the grass roots level", *i.e.*, not only by those who discussed educational reform, but by those upon whom it had its most direct impact: students. In 1907, the *Zhili Education Miscellany* (*Zhili Jiaoyu zazhi* 直隸教育雜誌) published three student essays all entitled "Discussion on Intellectual Warfare" (*Xuezhan lun* 學戰論). The student's names and their schools appear in the

---

97 Ibid., p. 556.

98 Li Shucheng (1960 [1903]), "Xuesheng zhi jingzheng", p. 454.

99 Ibid., pp. 454–455.

respective bylines (consequently, I will refer to the authors' names to tell them apart). Two were published in the same issue of the journal, another a few weeks earlier. The contributions were written by one Shi Zuolan 石作蘭 (fl. 1906) from *Tianjin guangye zhongxuetang* 天津廣業中學堂 (issue 7), and Wu Weijun 吳為均 (fl. 1906) and Liu Zhongjun 劉鍾俊 (fl. 1906) both from *Zhuozhou guanli gaodeng xiaoxuetang* 涿州官立高等小學堂 (issue 12). Tianjin and Zhuozhou are both located in today's Hebei Province, *i.e.*, in northern China, near Beijing. We can thus not only deduce that the intellectual warfare trope had by 1907 permeated virtually every strata of (literate) society, but also that it had travelled further north within the same timeframe. We may further estimate that Wu and Liu were between the ages of 13 and 16, and that Shi was their senior by at least 4 years but not older than 20.[100]

In these essays, the amalgamation of Darwinian ideas and the war metaphor in the context of the discourse on intellectual warfare, which, as we have seen, had been established by 1903, is clearly reflected: "The survival of the fittest is an (iron) law of evolution" (*yousheng liebai zhe tianyan zhi li ye* 優勝劣敗者天演之理也); "The struggle for survival is an (absolute) constant of the human condition" (*shengcun jingzheng zhe renqing zhi chang ye* 生存競爭者人情之常也;[101] and humans are portrayed as having an inborn "mind for struggle" (*jingxin* 兢心).[102]

Particular striking is the use of the war metaphor: Learning is likened to "a formless (instrument of) black iron or an intangible bared blade" (*wuxing zhi heitie bairen* 無形之黑鐵白刃) by Shi Zuolan, who then continues:

[A country] that does not [stress the continual improvement of learning] but instead lets its learning slowly and increasingly grow lax, is like [an army] that, being besieged on all sides (*simian Chuge* 四面楚歌) decides to abandon all its armour and to cast away all its weapons. How thoroughly will it be defeated and overthrown? What a frightful [prospect]![103]

And Wu Weijun writes using similarly vivid language:

When learning pushes energetically forward, it is quicker than cannons or rifles; when learning deeply penetrates, it is sharper than any edged or pointed weapon. When [in the pursuit of] learning one conducts a thorough investigation, this is no less than devising a campaign strategy from inside an army tent; when [in the pursuit of] learning one strives

---

100 According to the 1906 school regulations, students entered school at age 7. Lower primary schools covered grades 1–5, higher primary schools grades 6–9 and middle/vocational/normal schools grades 10–13. Zarrow (2015), *Educating China*, p. 22. Naturally, the three students in question could not have entered the education system under the 1906 rules (!) and the ages must thus be regarded as educated guesses.

101 Liu Zhongjun (1907), "Xuezhan lun", p. 114.

102 Shi Zuolan (1907), "Xuezhan lun", p. 111.

103 Ibid., p. 112.

to comprehend something [completely], this is no less than planning for a victory a thousand miles ahead.[104]

As for the contemporary debate on the respective merits of elementary and specialised education, Liu and Wu both seem to come down on the side of "more education is better":

How can those who regard learning as an arduous undertaking and willing accept [spending their lives] drifting through the world dull-wittedly hope to remain standing in this mighty and violent vortex of wars that is the twentieth century without being swept away by the racing currents and becoming eliminated?[105]

Indeed, as Peter Zarrow points out, lower primary school (the level that Liu and Wu had just graduated from) was as high as most students in late Qing China went![106] This would mean, from the perspective of intellectual warfare, that the majority of the "army" of educated young people had received only five years of elementary education (mostly in the Classics and arithmetic) and had, for example, not yet begun to learn any foreign language.[107] By comparison: the Prussian *Volksschule* had consisted of eight years of primary education while the Empire of Japan extended compulsory education to six years in 1907. Wu seems to have been less concerned with such statistics, but rather with the state of higher learning in China:

When I look on our scholars today, I find myself completely taken aback. They do not seek to [understand] the foundation but only stick to the skin and hair (*i.e.*, superficial knowledge). They have not been able to pass [new insights] on to their students and are only proficient in [spreading] gossip. [...] In this manner, it is already impossible to establish learning firmly, let alone to be able to study war![108]

This, of course, makes sense, when the pool of possible future scholars is rather limited to begin with.

Of the three essays, Shi's is, arguably, the most insightful, perhaps owing to his being older and, presumably, being more mature. He makes an effort to derive China's intellectual potential from antiquity,[109] specifically from the "various traditions" of the Warring States Period (see Cao Dianqiu in Section III), and lists what he views as ancient Chinese exponents of engineering, military science, agronomy, economics, jurisprudence, and logic (lit.: "the study of names", *mingxue* 名學). These are characterised by him (not without an over-

---

104 Wu Weijun (1907), "Xuezhan lun", p. 116.

105 Liu Zhongjun (1907), "Xuezhan lun", p. 115.

106 Zarrow (2015), *Educating China*, p. 1.

107 Ibid., pp. 1, 23 (table).

108 Wu Weijun (1907), "Xuezhan lun", pp. 115–116

109 Much like the contemporary National Essence Movement attempted to do. Hon (2003), "National Essence, National Learning, and Culture".

tone of hero worship) as "original creations by sublime and unusual talents who [dared to] break new ground" (*kuiwei qite zhi cai dupishengmian* 魁偉奇特之才獨闢生面).[110] He continues:

> Later generations elaborated on [the ancient knowledge] carried it forward. Having expert knowledge in only one of these is enough to subdue all nations and to be a match for the entire globe. For what reason was [China] defeated in military warfare as soon as she encountered the other nations? In commerce, she was again defeated; and yet again in industry and agriculture. If [China], having fought a hundred wars and having suffered a hundred defeats, wishes to relieve her pain and resist her strong enemies, she cannot but return to the domain of learning and seek a great turn for the better. [...] China's warships are not robust, her cannons are not effective, her finances are not plentiful, and her soldiers are not élite. Why, then, can one still say that [China] has the ability to surpass the entire globe? It is because the Chinese people (*Huaren* 華人) are [by nature] sensible, intelligent, talented, and perceptive (*cong hui ying da* 聰慧穎達), and thus they can be encouraged to learn.[111]

With this assessment, we have almost come full circle: intellectual warfare is, once more, optimistically depicted as taking place on an alternative, "virtual" battlefield without bloodshed and casualties: it is a mode of struggle that has been completely relegated to the realm of thought and ideas. Furthermore, it is a form of struggle that can be engaged in *even after the military conflict has already been decided* to the detriment of China. However, I hope to have also demonstrated that this vision, which, in certain respects, inherits the utopian ideals of thinkers such as Kang Youwei and Tang Caichang, comes with a critical caveat: This variant of intellectual warfare is contingent upon the recognition of the county as a "civilised" nation by the other so-called "civilised nations".[112]

We have seen that the intellectual warfare trope persisted through multiple historical watersheds during the period under consideration: the *coup d'état* of 1898 (shortly after its initial conception), the New Policies and the reform and abolition of the civil service examination, and the introduction of popular primary education. The historical survey could be considerably extended, as I pointed out in the introduction, but this is beyond the purview of the present article. In the conclusion, I will—as a way to summarize the empirical findings of sections III–V, briefly explore the fate of the trope in the Republican Era.

---

110 Wu Weijun (1907), "Xuezhan lun", pp. 111–112. The similar "*dukaishengmian* 獨開生面" is a standing expression.

111 Shi Zuolan (1907), "Xuezhan lun", p. 112.

112 Compare this to the distinction between "positive" and "negative competition" made by Wang Jingwei around 1920 in his "Human-Co-Existentialism" which is discussed by Yang Zhiyi in her contribution to this volume.

VI. Conclusion: The Limits of the War Metaphor

The Revolution of 1911 prompted yet another surge in writings on intellectual warfare. First, the original texts of the Intellectual Warfare Society (the "Statutes" and the "Inaugural Statement") were reprinted in the compilation *Xiangbao leizuan* 湘報類纂 (Assorted Selections from the Hunan News) of 1911. A wave of new original articles appeared shortly thereafter.[113] Of these, a 1915 article in three parts offers the most comprehensive overview of the state of the intellectual-warfare discourse in early Republican China. Naturally, like any original piece of writing, all three sections offer ideas, variations, and twists not previously encountered, but these, I must, regretfully, disregard for the time being, and will instead focus on elements that were presented in the discussion above.

The "Intellectual Warfare Trilogy" (for lack of a better name) is very tidily argued, as each part is dedicated to precisely one topic. And as the authors themselves point out, Part One explores the issue of "using learning to make war" (*yi xue wei zhan* 以學而為戰), whereas Part Two discusses the topic of "using warfare to preserve one's learning" (*yi zhan er cun qi xue* 以戰而存其學).[114] In the terms of the analysis above, Part One corresponds to the "realist" vision of intellectual warfare that regards learning primarily as providing an intellectual basis for strategy, tactics, and instruments of war, thus making warfare more destructive. However, the author employs rather toned down, less drastic diction when compared, for instance, to "Intellectual Warfare" of 1915. What we see instead is a re-interpretation and narrowing of the meaning of "learning" to denote "practical learning" (*shixue* 實學) or even "science" (*kexue* 科學) specifically.

Part Two accordingly corresponds to the "utopian" conceptualisation of intellectual warfare. The author appeals to his peers (*i.e.*, China's students!) to make Chinese learning known to the world. By this, they evidently mean "classical" Chinese learning. There is nothing to indicate that a country could choose to "fight" not with its own, but with the enemy's "weapons". In the twenty-first century, by contrast, there is certainly competition between "national systems of thought", but nations also compete for, for example, Nobel Prizes—and these are awarded for achievements in fields of inquiry believed to be universal, not nation specific.

Part Three, finally, addresses the question of primacy between elementary and specialised education, which, it would seem, remains of relevance even a decade after the Qing government's Educational Aims had been promulgated.

---

113 Zhu Gancheng (1916), "Shijie si dazhan"; He Yiming (1915), "Xuezhan shuo"; Ou Ting (1913),"Xuezhan pian".

114 Fei (1915), "Xuezhan zhong", p. 1.

The author, while vehemently denying that there exists a clear-cut dichotomy, argues for specialised education, and laments that:

In today's community of students, there is truly no lack of people who finish elementary education and are [already] satisfied. How tragic![115]

From a Chinese perspective, the year 1915 witnessed at least two major developments: World War I (which had proven to continue for far longer than was initially estimated) and, more importantly, Japan's infamous Twenty-One Demands and the beginning of the New Culture Movement. The trilogy of essays discussed above does not betray much impact of these events (aside from the rise of "Mr. Science", perhaps), even though the first article in the series was published on 24 November, months after the ratification of Japan's demands by the Chinese government on 25 May. It would certainly be worthwhile to continue on the trajectory delineated by the present study and trace the development of the intellectual warfare trope through this tumultuous period of modern Chinese history, but I shall end my inquiry here and instead close with a brief outlook.

The present investigation started out from the observation that social Darwinism (or Darwinian thought, as I prefer to call it) was not simply "broadcast" (in the literal, agricultural sense of the word) throughout late Qing China by print culture, and intellectual and personal networks, but also "dispersed" into various, but distinguishable, facets. This article has subsequently focused on one of these facets, namely "Intellectual Warfare" and traced the development of this notion from reform era Hunan, to a variety of journals and newspapers published around 1903, and continued until approximately 1906. As I hope to have plausibly shown, the discourse on intellectual warfare was, at every step of the way, intimately linked with the current discussions on learning, educational reform and, more generally, the situation of China in global politics and its prospects in a world ostensibly governed by the "Law of the Jungle". As such, the intellectual warfare trope is located at the intersection of at least two major Discourses of Weakness in early twentieth-century China: the discourse on "national ruin", and the discourse on "national salvation through education" (*jiaoyu jiuguo* 教育救國).[116] Being less cumbersome to handle than either of these, the discourse on intellectual warfare struck me as a suitable case-study to capture a representative cross-section of late Qing Discourses of Weakness.

---

115 Fei (1915), "Xuezhan xia", p. 3.

116 I have tentatively explored the discourse on national ruin in Eikeschulte et al (2018), "Visions of Decline", pp. 100–112. See also Karl (2002), *Staging the World*, pp. 12–17, 33–49. There is a plethora of scholarship dedicated to the second topic: Schulte (2013), "Joining Forces to Save the Nation"; Wang Rongguo (1987), "1900–1910 nian Zhongguo zichan jieji de 'jiaoyu jiuguo' sixiang". For a review of relevant Chinese language articles see Xu Zhenglin and Qu Fengrui (2013), "Jin sanshi nian lai jiaoyu jiuguo yanjiu shuping".

Thus far, the question of to what degree and in which sense a limit can be placed on a Discourse of Weakness' ability to "indicate and mobilize" has rarely been posed. Daniel Hausmann and Klaus Seidl have both pointed to the inner dynamics of Discourses of Weakness.[117] Furthermore, Benjamin Steiner goes even further and has argued that historical developments in general may have "unintended consequences".[118] This begs the question of how "intention", as an analytical category, has to be incorporated into analyses of Discourses of Weakness. Here, I want to make but one additional, related point that serves more as an outlook than a fully-fledged argument and offers the opportunity to hark back to this article's initial theoretical reflections on the ubiquity of the war metaphor.

Throughout the entire history of the idea, as far as I have been able and willing to cover it in the present article, the discourse on intellectual warfare had an additional dimension that I saw myself unable to adequately address in the main body of this study. Educational reform in early twentieth century China was always "haunted" by the conviction of some actors that all the things education ostensibly wished to accomplish (as outlined, for instance, in the Educational Aims of 1906), namely, patriotism, public-mindedness, discipline, physical fitness, *etc.*, could be better, more thoroughly, achieved by popular militarisation.[119] Indeed, this conviction *did* leave its mark on popular education in late Qing and early Republican China.[120]

I do not presume to be able, at this point, to demonstrate convincingly the precise pathway by which the intellectual-warfare trope (and similar manifestations of the war metaphor) actually facilitated China's increasing militarisation in the Republican period and earlier, but it seems clear that framing education and learning in terms of war most certainly did little to work against such tendencies in Chinese society.[121] I am thus left wondering whether China's (civilian) educational reformers did, in the end, fatally undermine their own agenda by invoking the war metaphor in non-military discourse, thereby playing into the hands of their ideological and political rivals. Or to put it differently: We ought to ask, following moral philosopher James Childress, whether the war

---

117 See Daniel Hausmann's contribution to this volume where he characterises late Qing Chinese Discourses of Weakness to a "basso continuo" that are, at least in part, markedly "undetermined" and "flexible". Seidl distinguishes between (intended) "results" and (unintended) "effects" of Discourse of Weakness. Seidl (2018), "Representations of Weakness", pp. 50–52.

118 Steiner (2015), *Nebenfolgen in der Geschichte*, pp. 18–20 and passim.

119 Schillinger (2016), *The Body and Military Masculinity*, pp. 255–267.

120 Ibid., pp. 290–303.

121 Following Hans van den Ven, "militarism" is here simply understood as a general "appreciation of qualities normally associated with the military" and does not refer to the domination of politics by military actors (Hans van den Ven, "The Military in the Republic", p. 353n4). See also Clemens Büttner's article in this volume.

metaphor in early twentieth century China was truly "generative", i.e. a metaphor that enabled new insights, or whether it, on the contrary, obscured the issues at hand and limited contemporary visions about the proper course of action.[122]

Bibliography

Bai Chongxi 白崇禧 (1939). "Bingzhan yu xuezhan" 兵戰與學戰 (Military Warfare and Intellectual Warfare), *Juesheng*, 24, pp. 8–9.

Bickers, Robert (2011). *The Scramble for China. Foreign Devils in the Qing Empire, 1832–1914*, London: Allen Lane.

"Bingzhan buru shangzhan buru xuezhan lun" 兵戰不如商戰商戰不如學戰論 (Discussion of the Dictum that Military Warfare is Inferior to Commercial Warfare which is Inferior to Intellectual Warfare) (1898). *Xiangbao*, 145, pp. 577–578.

Cao Dianqiu 曹典球 (1898). "Bingzhan buru shangzhan shangzhan buru xuezhan shuo" 兵戰不如商戰商戰不如學戰說 (Treaties on the Dictum that Military Warfare is Inferior to Commercial Warfare which is Inferior to Intellectual Warfare), *Xiangbao*, 165, pp. 657a–657b.

Carruthers, Jacob (1999). *Intellectual Warfare*, Chicago: Third World Press.

Chen Hon-Fai (2010). "Civilization and Competition: Study Societies and State Formation in Late Qing China", *Social and Cultural Research*, Occasional Paper No. 10, pp. 1–42.

Chen Zhongchun 陳忠純 (2004). "Lun Nanxue hui de jiangxue huodong ji weixin sixiang" 論南學會的講學活動及維新思想 (On the Educational Activities and Reformist Thought of the Southern Study Society), *Xuzhou Shifan Daxue xuebao (Zhexue shehui kexue ban)* , 30.4, pp. 99–103.

Childress, James F. (2001). "The War Metaphor in Public Policy: Some Moral Reflections". In J. Carl Ficarrotta (ed.), *The Leader's Imperative: Ethics, Integrity, and Responsibility*, West Lafayette: Purdue University Press, pp. 181–197.

Eikelschulte, Nadine et al (2018). "Visions of Decline in Transhistorical Perspective—Narratives, Images, Effects". In Iwo Amelung, Hartmut Leppin, and Christian A. Müller (eds.), *Discourses of Weakness and Resource Regimes. Trajectories of a New Research Program*, Frankfurt am Main: Campus, pp. 67–139.

Esherick, Joseph Q. (1976). *Reform and Revolution in China. The 1911 Revolution in Hunan and Hubei*, Ann Arbor: Center for Chinese Studies, University of Michigan.

Fang Ping 方平 (1994). "Lüe lun wan Qing 'xuezhan' sichao" 略論晚清 "學戰" 思潮 (A Brief Discussion of the Trend of Intellectual Warfare in the Late Qing), *Shilin*, 1, pp. 41–46.

Fei 飛 (1915). "Xuezhan (shang, zhong, xia)" 學戰（上、中、下） (Intellectual Warfare (I, II, III)), *Qinghua zhoukan*, 56 , pp. 1–3; 57, pp. 1–3; 59, pp. 1–3.

---

122 Childress (2001), "The War Metaphor in Public Policy", pp. 194–195. On generative metaphors see Schön (1993 [1979]), "Generative metaphor", pp. 138–139, 150–161.

Feng Guifen 馮桂芬 (1885). *Jiaobinlu kangyi* 校邠廬抗議 (Protests from the Jiaobin Studio), vol. 2.

"Guang shangxue yi kai shang zhi shuo shang" 廣商學以開商智說上 (Expanding Education in Commerce to Broaden the Knowledge of Merchants, Part One) (1904). *Shenbao* 11330, 31 October.

Heck, Ewald (2000). *Wang Kangnian (1860–1911) und die* Shiwubao, Sankt Augustin: Institut Monumenta Serica.

He Yiming 何一鳴 (1915). "Xuezhan shuo" 學戰說 (Treaties on Intellectual Warfare), *Xuesheng*, 2:2, pp. 15–16.

Hon, Tze-ki (2003). "National Essence, National Learning, and Culture: Historical Writings in Guocui xuebao, Xueheng, and Guoxue jikan", *Historiography East & West*, 1.2, pp. 242–286.

Houang, François (1977). *Les Manifestes de Yen Fou*, Paris: Fayard.

Huang E 黃崿 (1898). "Xuezhan hui qi" 學戰會啟 (Inaugural Statement of the Intellectual Warfare Society), *Xiangbao*, 58, 230a–231a.

Huang E 黃崿 et al (1898). "Xuezhan hui zhangcheng" 學戰會章程 (Statutes of the Intellectual Warfare Society, *Xiangbao*, 59, 234a–234b.

Huang Xingtao 黃興濤 and Hu Wensheng 胡文生 (2005). "Lun Wuxu Weixin shiqi Zhongguo xueshu xiandai zhuanxing de zhengti mengfa—jian tan Qing mo Min chu xueshu zhuanxing de neihan he dongle wenti" 論戊戌維新時期中國學術現代轉型的整體萌發——兼談清末民初學術轉型的內涵和動力問題 (On the Origins of the Fundamental Transformation of Chinese Scholarship and its Connotations and Impetus during the Late Qing and Early Republican Era), *Qing shi yanjiu*, 4, pp. 36–50.

Huang Zun 黃尊 et al (1898). "Hunan Longnan Zhiyong xuehui zhangcheng xu" 湖南龍南致用學會章程序 (Preface to the Statutes of the Practical Application Study Society of Longnan, Hunan), *Zhixinbao*, 43, 9a–10b.

Huanghai Fenglang 黃海鋒郎 (1902). "Lun jinri zui yao de liang zhong jiaoyu" 論今日最要的兩種教育 (On the Two Most Important Kinds of Education Today), *Hangzhou baihuabao*, 2.9, pp. 1a–3b.

"Hui er zhunzhun" 誨爾諄諄 (I Taught You with Assiduous Repetition) (1903). *Shenbao*, 10899, 23 August.

Hürter, Jens (2002). *Tang Caichang (1867–1900). Reformer, Denker und Rebell in China an der Schwelle zur Moderne*, Münster: LIT.

Jiang Hongtao 江鴻濤 (1929). "Xuezhan shuo" 學戰說 (Treatise on Intellectual Warfare), *Xuesheng wenyi congkan*, 5.9, pp. 75–77.

Kang Youwei (1981 [1895]). "Shang Qing Di di er shu" 上清帝第二書 (Second Memorial to the Qing Emperor). In Tang Zhijun 湯志鈞 (ed.), *Kang Youwei zhenglun ji* 康有為政論集 (Collection of the Political Writings of Kang Youwei), Beijing: Zhonghua shuju, vol. 1, pp. 114–136.

— (1981 [1898]). "Shang Qing Di di wu shu" 上清帝第五書 (Fifth Memorial to the Qing Emperor) In Tang Zhijun 湯志鈞 (ed.), *Kang Youwei zhenglun ji* 康有為政論集 (Collection of the Political Writings of Kang Youwei), Beijing: Zhonghua shuju, vol. 1, pp. 201–210.

Karl, Rebecca (2002). *Staging the World. Chinese Nationalism at the Turn of the Twentieth Century*, Durham: Duke University Press.

Kasperson, R. E. et al. (2005). "The Social Amplification of Risk: A Conceptual Framework". In J. X. Kasperson and R. E. Kasperson (eds.), *The Social Contours of Risk: Volume 1: Publics, Risk Communication and the Social Amplification of Risk*. London: Earthscan, pp. 99–114.

Ke Zunke and Li Bin (2016). "Spencer and Science Education in China". In Bernhard Lightman (ed.), *Global Spencerism. The Communication and Appropriation of a British Evolutionist*, Leiden: Brill, pp. 78–102.

Knoblock, John (1994). *Xunzi. A Translation and Study of the Complete Works, Volume III, Books 17–32*, Stanford: Stanford University Press.

Lakoff, George and Mark Johnson (2003 [1980]). *Metaphors We Live By*, Chicago: Chicago University Press.

Legge, James (1865). *The Chinese Classics, Volume III: The Shoo King, or the Book of Historical Documents*, London: Trübner & Co., Part I.

— (1871). *The Chinese Classics, Volume IV: The She King, or the Book of Poetry*, Hongkong: Lane, Crawford & Co., Part II.

— (1872). *The Chinese Classics, Volume V: The Ch'un Ts'ew with The Tso Chuen*, Hongkong: Lane, Crawford & Co., Part I.

Li Shucheng 李書城 (1960 [1903]). "Xuesheng zhi jingzheng" 學生之競爭 (The Students' Struggle). In Zhang Nan 張枏 and Wang Renzhi 王忍之 (eds.), *Xinhai geming qian shi nian jian shilun xuanji* 辛亥革命前十年間時論選集 (Anthology of Opinion Pieces from the Decade Prior to the 1911 Revolution), Hong Kong: Sanlian shudian, vol. 1, Part 1, pp. 452–459.

Liang Qichao 梁啟超 (1999 [1901]). "Mieguo xinfa lun" 滅國新法論 (New Methods to Vanquish Nations). In Zhang Pinxing 張品興, Yang Gang 楊鋼, and Wang Xiangyi 王相宜 (eds.), *Liang Qichao quanji* 梁啟超全集 (Complete Works of Liang Qichao), Beijing: Beijing chubanshe, vol. 2, pp. 467–474.

— (1999 [1902]). "Lun xueshu zhi shili zuoyou shijie" 論學術之勢力左右世界 (On the World-Changing Power of Scholarship). In Zhang Pinxing 張品興, Yang Gang 楊鋼, Wang Xiangyi 王相宜 (eds.), *Liang Qichao quanji* 梁啟超全集 (Complete Works of Liang Qichao), Beijing: Beijing chubanshe, vol. 3, pp. 557–560.

Liu Kun 劉焜 (1902). "Xiguo xueshu daoyuan Xila" 西國學術導源希臘 (Western Scholarship Has its Source in Greece), *Shenbao* 10596, 17 October.

Liu Liyan (2012). *Red Genesis. The Hunan First Normal School and the Creation of Chinese Communism, 1903–1921*, Albany: State University of New York Press.

Liu Zhongjun 劉鍾俊 (1907). "Xuezhan lun" 學戰論 (Discussion of Intellectual Warfare), *Zhili Jiaoyu zazhi*, 12, pp. 114–115.

Luo Zhitian (2015). *Inheritance Within Rupture. Culture and Scholarship in Early Twentieth Century China*, translated by Harris, Lane J. and Mei Chun, Leiden: Brill.

Lü Zuqian 呂祖謙 (12th century). *Zuo shi boyi* 左氏博議 (Erudite Discussion of Mr. Zuo's Commentary), Qinding Siku Quanshu edition.

Ma Min 馬敏 (2006). "Zhongguo jindaihua sichao de yi ge cemian—shangzhan" 中國近代化思潮的一個側面——商戰 (One Aspect of China's Modernisation—Commercial Warfare), available at: http://www.xinfajia.net/2091.html (3 August 2018).

Morris, Andrew D. (2004). *Marrow of the Nation. A History of Sport and Physical Culture in Republican China*, Berkeley: University of California Press.

Mühlhahn, Klaus (2012). "Negotiating the Nation. German Colonialism and Chinese Nationalism in Qingdao, 1897–1914". In Bryna Goodman and David S. G. Goodman (eds.), *Twentieth-century Colonialism and China. Localities, the Everyday, and the World*. London: Routledge, pp. 37–56.

Otte, Thomas G. (2007). *The China Question. Great Power Rivalry and British Isolation, 1894–1905*, Oxford: Oxford University Press.

Ou Ting 偶亭 (1913). "Xuezhan pian" 學戰篇 (Essay on Intellectual Warfare), 2 parts, *Zhenxiang huabao*, 1.14, pp. 11–13; 1.15, pp. 20–22.

Pusey, James R. (1983). *China and Charles Darwin*, Cambridge (Massachusetts): Harvard University Press.

Schillinger, Nicolas (2016). *The Body and Military Masculinity in Late Qing and Early Republican China. The Art of Governing Soldiers*, Lenham: Lexington Books.

Schultz-Naumann, Joachim (1985). *Unter Kaisers Flagge: Deutschlands Schutzgebiete im Pazifik und in China Einst und Heute*, München: Universitas.

Schön, Donald A. (1993 [1979]). "Generative Metaphor: A Perspective on Problem-Setting in Social Policy". In Andrew Ortony (ed.), *Metaphor and Thought*, Cambridge: Cambridge University Press, pp. 137–163.

Schulte, Barbara (2013). "Joining Forces to Save the Nation: Corporate Educational Governance in Republican China". In Jennifer Y. J. Hsu and Reza Hasmath (eds.), *The Chinese Corporatist State: Adaption, Survival and Resistance*, London: Routledge, pp. 10–28.

Seidl, Klaus (2018). "Representations of Weakness: Functions, Images, Effects". In Iwo Amelung, Hartmut Leppin, and Christian A. Müller (eds.), *Discourses of Weakness and Resource Regimes. Trajectories of a New Research Program*, Frankfurt am Main: Campus, pp. 45–66.

Shen, Vincent (Shen Qingsong 沈清松) (2016). "Translation and Interpretation: the Case of Introducing Darwinian Evolutionism into China", *Zhexue yu wenhua* 43.1; pp. 3–25.

Shi Zuolan 石作蘭 (1907). "Xuezhan lun" 學戰論 (Discussion on Intellectual Warfare), *Zhili jiaoyu zazhi* 7, pp. 111–112.

Steiner, Benjamin (2015). *Nebenfolgen in der Geschichte. Eine Historische Soziologie Reflexiver Modernisierung*, Berlin: De Gruyter Oldenbourg.

Steinert, Heinz (2003). "The Indispensable Metaphor of War: On Populist Politics and the Contradictions of the State's Monopoly of Force", *Theoretical Criminology* 7.3, pp. 265–291.

Tu Daotan 塗道坦 (1943). "Lun Zhongzu xuezhan" 論"種族學戰" (Intellectual Race War), *Minzu zhengqi* 1.5/6, pp. 14–19.

Ven, Hans van de (1997). "The Military in the Republic", *The China Quarterly*, 150 (Special Issue: Reappraising Republican China), pp. 352–374.

Wang Dongjie 王東杰 (2007). "'Fanqiuzhuji'—Wan Qing jinhuaguan yu Zhongguo chuantong sixiang quxiang (1895–1905)" 「反求諸己」——晚清進化觀與中國傳統思想取向（1895–1905）("Seek the Cause in Oneself'—Late Qing Evolutionism and the Trajectory of Traditional Chinese Thought). In Wang Fansen 王汎森 et al, *Zhongguo jindai sixiangshi de zhuanxing shidai* 中國近代思想史的轉型時代 (The Transformative Period of Modern Chinese Intellectual History), Taibei: Lianjing chuban gongsi, pp. 315–351.

Wang Ermin 王爾敏 (1995). *Zhongguo jindai sixiangshi lun* 中國近代思想史論 (Discussions of Modern Chinese Intellectual History), Taibei: Taiwan shangwu yinshuguan.

Wang Kangnian 汪康年 (1896), "Shangzhan lun" 商戰論 (A Discussion of Commercial Warfare), *Shiwubao*, 14, pp. 1–3.

Wang Rongguo 王榮國 (1987). "1900–1910 nian Zhongguo zichan jieji de 'jiaoyu jiuguo' sixiang 1900–1910年中國資產階級的 "教育救國" 思想 (The Idea of "National Salvation through Education" of the Chinese Capitalist Class, 1900–1910), *Xiamen daxue xuebao (Zhexue ban)* , 3, pp. 136-143.

Wu Guo (2010). *Zheng Guanying* 鄭觀應. *Merchant Reformer in Late Qing China and his Influence on Economics, Politics, and Society*, Amherst: Cambria Press.

Wu Weijun 吳為均 (1907). "Xuezhan lun" 學戰論 (Discussion on Intellectual Warfare), *Zhili jiaoyu zazhi*, 12, pp. 115-116.

Xia Shixing 夏時行 (1920). "Xuezhan lun" 學戰論 (Discussion on Intellectual Warfare), *Fengxian xianli di yi gaodeng xiaoxue youhui zazhi*, 3, pp. 88-89.

Xiong Zhiyong 熊志勇 (1998). "Bingzhan, shangzhan, xuezhan yu wan Qing junshi jindaihua de xiandao diwei" 兵戰、商戰、學戰與晚清軍事近代化的先導地位 (Military Warfare, Commercial Warfare, Intellectual Warfare and the Guiding Role of Military Modernisation during the Late Qing), *Jingzhou zhiye jishu xueyuan xuebao (Shehui kexue ban)* , 3, pp. 25-28, 72.

Xu Zhenglin 徐正林 and Qu Fengrui 屈鳳銳 (2013). "Jin sanshi nian lai jiaoyu jiuguo yanjiu shuping—jiyu CNKI de shuju fenxi" 近三十年來教育救國研究述評———基於 CNKI的數據分析 (A Review of Research on National Salvation through Education of the last 30 years—Based on the Analysis of Data from the China National Knowledge Infrastructure), *Dangdai jiaoyu luntan*, 253, pp. 64–69.

"Xuezhan" 學戰 (Intellectual Warfare) (1903), *Jingshi wenchao*, 1, 8a–11a.

Yan Fu 嚴復 (1986 [1895]). "Yuan qiang" 原強 (On the Origin of Strength). In Wang Shi 王栻 (ed.), *Yan Fu ji* 嚴復集, Beijing: Zhonghua shuju, vol 1, pp. 5–14.

Yan Fu 嚴復 (author/trans.) and Feng Junhao 馮君豪 (ed.) (1998). *Tianyan lun* 天演論 (On Evolution), Zhengzhou: Zhongzhou guji chubanshe.

Yang Haiyan (2013). "Knowledge Across Borders: The Early Communication of Evolution in China". In Bernhard Lightman et al (eds.), *The Circulation of Knowledge Between Britain, India and China: The Early-Modern World to the Twentieth Century*, Leiden: Brill, pp. 181–208.

"Yu tongzhi shu" 與同志書 (A Letter to My Comrades) (1960 [1903]). In Zhang Nan 張枏 and Wang 王忍之 (eds.), *Xinhai geming qian shi nian jian shilun xuanji* 辛亥革命前十年間時論選集 (Anthology of Opinion Pieces from the Decade Prior to the 1911 Revolution), Hong Kong: Sanlian shudian, vol. 1, Part 2, pp. 393–400.

Yunwo 云窩 (1960 [1903]). "Jiaoyu tonglun (jielu)" 教育通論（節錄）(A Comprehensive Discussion of Education (Excerpt)). In Zhang Nan 張枏 and Wang Renzhi 王忍之 (eds.), *Xinhai geming qian shi nian jian shilun xuanji* 辛亥革命前十年間時論選集 (Anthology of Opinion Pieces from the Decade Prior to the 1911 Revolution), Hong Kong: Sanlian shudian, vol. 1, Part 2, pp. 551–559.

Zarrow, Peter (2012). *After Empire. The Conceptual Transformation of the Chinese State, 1885–1924*. Stanford: Stanford University Press.

– (2015). *Educating China: Knowledge, Society, and Textbooks in a Modernizing World, 1902–1937*. Cambridge: Cambridge University Press.

Zhou Wu 周武 (1988). "Lun 'xuezhan' sichao" 論 "學戰" 思潮 (On the Trend of Intellectual Warfare), *Shehui kexue*, 2, pp. 49–53.

Zhu Gancheng 祝幹丞 (1916). "Shijie si dazhan: Bingzhan buru shangzhan, shangzhan buru xuezhan, xuezhan buru jiaozhan" 世界四大戰：兵戰不如商戰，商戰不如學戰，學戰不如教戰 (The World's Four Great Wars: Military warfare is inferior to commercial warfare, commercial warfare is inferior to intellectual warfare, intellectual warfare is inferior to religious warfare), *Xinminbao*, 3.10, pp. 4–7.

Zhu Youzhi 朱有志 and Guo Qin 郭欽 (2011). *Hunan jin-xiandai shiye renwu zhuanlüe*湖南近現代實業人物傳略 (Biographical Sketches of Hunanese People of Industry and Commerce of the Modern and Present Era), Changsha: Zhongnan Daxue chubanshe.

The Revolutionary Army: A Chinese Nationalist Tract of 1903, edited by John Lust, The Hague: Mouton.

Part III:
Prognosis for the Sick Man—Ruin,
Resistance and Restauration

Evolution of the Late Qing Historical Writing on the Decline of Poland

Zou Zhenhuan

Chinese academia's attention on Chinese historical writing on the extinction of Poland first emerged in the context of the research on the late Qing historiography of national ruin (*wangguo* 亡國). Among the earliest works was Yu Danchu's 俞旦初 article "Histories of National Ruin in Modern China's patriotism" ("Zhongguo jindai aiguozhuyi de 'wangguo shijian'" 中國近代愛國主義的"亡國史鑒").[1] Yu's article is the first that notices the three translated versions of *Pŏrando suibŏ* senshi by Shibue Tamotsu 涉江保. It also discusses "The Story of Poland's National Ruin" (*Bolan wangguo de gushi* 波蘭亡國的故事), which was published in the *Hangzhou Vernacular Newspaper* 杭州白話報 in 1901, "The Whole Story of Poland's National Ruin" (*Bolan miewang shimo ji* 波蘭滅亡始末記), published in the *Jingji congbian* 經濟叢編 in 1901, "Reasons for the National Ruin of Poland" (*Bolan wangguo zhi you* 波蘭亡國之由), which was published in the *Waijiaobao* 外交報 (*Journal of Diplomacy*) in 1903 and so forth. The author, however, did not read much of this material.

The article "Research on the Late-Qing 'Compilation and Translation Fever' of Histories of National Decline and Liang Qichao's 梁啟超 (1873–1929) History of the Ruin of Korea" (*Qingmo wangguoshi bianyi re yu Liang Qichao de Chaoxian wangguo shi yanjiu* 清末亡國史"編譯熱"與梁啟超的朝鮮亡國史研究, written by Zou Zhenhuan 鄒振環, focuses mainly on late Qing histories of the national ruin of Korea but also takes note of Kang Youwei's 康有為 (1858–1927) "Record of the partitions and extinction of Poland" (*Bolan fenmie ji* 波蘭分滅記) and Liang Qichao's historiography of national decline.

Using the history of the national decline of Poland as an example, the article points out that the writing on the decline of foreign countries by Late Qing scholars was used in order to warn their compatriots of the danger and the misery which "national ruin and the extinction of the race" (*wangguo miezhong* 亡國滅種) could cause. The late Qing fever for compiling and translating histories of decline was an important part of the patriotic historiography of that time.[2]

---

1 Yu Danchu (1984), "Zhongguo jindai aiguozhuyi de 'wanggguo shijian' chu kao".

2 Cf. Zou Zhenhuan (1996), "Qingmo wangguoshi bianyi re yu Liang Qichao de chaoxian wangguoshi yanjiu". Other articles introducing the historiography on the national decline of

With the increase of academic research on Chinese nationalism, more works which look into the problem from such a perspective have appeared, such as Rebecca Karl's *Staging the World: Chinese Nationalism at the Turn of the Twentieth Century*.[3] Karl's book gives an account of the twentieth-century Chinese interpretations regarding histories of national ruin – including the question of how they present the reasons for the ruin of Poland and the Polish people's fight against foreign invasion, and how these histories enabled Chinese readers to understand the historical connections between such terms as *tongzhong* (同種, same race), *wangguo* (亡國, national ruin) and *renmin* (人民, the people). The book extensively discusses the Peking opera *Guazhong lanyin* (瓜種蘭因, *Seeds of the Melon, Cause of the Orchid*) adapted by Wang Xiaonong 汪笑儂 (1858–1918) from the *History of Poland's Fall and Ruin* (*Bolan shuaiwang shi* 波蘭衰亡史). The opera depicts how Poland failed in wars, pleaded for peace, ceded territories and paid reparations. The ostensibly accounted foreign historical events did, in fact, point to the acts of the Qing government. Writing about this opera libretto, Karl's book reveals how China had to find its place in the global world as well as the importance of constructing a "national citizen" (*guomin* 國民)-consciousness. Feng Kexue's 馮克學 master thesis entitled "The History of the Ruin of Poland and Late Qing Nationalist Writing" (*Bolan wangguo shi yu wan Qing minzuzhuyi shuxie* 波蘭亡國史與晚清民族主義書寫) suggests that the history of the decline of Poland in connection with concepts related to nationalism promoted the growth of nationalism during the late Qing dynasty. In his thesis, Feng discusses how the history of the national decline of Poland was introduced to China as common historical knowledge. The author conducts a textual analysis of the Late Qing works on the history of the national ruin of Poland and shows that, as China's national crisis deepened, in addition to interpretations by scholars, the word "Poland" became something akin to a symbol for "national ruin". It introduces interpretations of the history of the national decline of Poland by reformers as well as by revolutionaries in order to show how late Qing narratives of the history of the Polish national ruin were related to perceptions of the national state, emphasis on military affairs and racial identity, as well as the Chinese understanding of these concepts at that time.[4]

While there is a considerable amount of research dealing with the compilation and translation of histories of Polish national ruin during the late Qing

---

Poland include: Yan Yunliang (1982), "Wei kanxing de Kang Youwei liang bu zhuzuo", Kong Xiangji (1982), "Cong 'Bolan fenmie ji' kan Kang Youwei wuxu bianfe shiqi de zhengzhi zhuzhang" and Liu Yajun (2010), "Shuaiwang shiji yu wan Qing shehui bianqe". They all discuss the historiography of the national decline of Poland from the perspective of political and social transformation.

3 Karl's book has been translated and was published in Chinese in 2008, cf. Karl (2008), *Shijie da wutai—shjiu, ershi shijizhi jiao Zhongguo de minzuzhuyi*.

4 Feng, Kexue (2012), "Bolan wangguo shi yu wan Qing minzuzhuyi shuxie".

dynasty, a detailed examination of the question of how the historiography of Polish national decline evolved is still missing. None of the works mentioned above gives a clear account of the compilation and translation of Shibue Tamotsu's *Pōrando suibō senshi* in the Chinese world. The focus of this article lies in the evolution of the historiography of Polish national decline in late Qing China. It begins with an examination of the literature on Polish history starting with the *Haiguo tuzhi* (Treatise on the Maritime Countries) and its treatment of Polish history as written by Western scholars. It goes on to discuss the earliest works regarding Poland in compilations and translations of histories of national decline during the late Qing period. It then analyses the writings of reformers who focused on the history of the ruin of Poland, especially during the Hundred Days' Reform of 1898 in China as well as how, within the framework of the pre-1911 wave of "histories of national ruin", Chinese intellectuals translated the Japanese scholar Sibue Tamotsu's *Pōrando suibō senshi* in a way that made Poland a symbol of national decline and demise, and how they later used it as a nationalist ideological resource in order to spur group consciousness among the people and overthrow the corrupt Qing rule.

1. Poland in Geographic Works Written by Westerners in the Chinese Language, as Quoted in the *Haiguo tuzhi*

Wei Yuan's 魏源 (1794–1857) fifty-volume *Haiguo tuzhi* (海國圖志, Treatise on the Maritime Countries) was published in 1844. Its 1847 edition was expanded to sixty volumes and the 1852 edition to 100 volumes. Volume 46 of the 100-volume edition includes a part entitled "The Historical Evolution of Poland" (*Polanguo yange* 波蘭國沿革), whose major sources were the "Records of Foreign Lands" (*Zhifang waiji* 職方外紀), "Complete Collection of World Geography" (*Wanguo dili quantu ji* 萬國地理全圖集) and "Geography of Foreign Nations" *Waiguo dili beikao* 外國地理備考).[5] As far as I know, the earliest Chinese work introducing Poland is the *Zhifang waiji*, written by the Italian missionary Giulio Aleni 艾儒略 (1582–1649) in 1623. The book was the first geographic work written in the Chinese language, after Matteo Ricci's 利瑪竇 (1552–1610) world map, that gives a systematic introduction to the cultural geography of the world.[6] The second part of the book entitled "Europe" (Ouluoba 歐邏巴) deals with *Boluoniya* (波羅尼亞, Polonia).

---

5 See Chen Hua (1998), *Hai guo tu zhi*, vol. 2., pp. 1320–1322.
6 See Zou Zhenhuan (2011), *Wan Ming hanwen xixue jingdian*, pp. 255–288.

Northeast of *Yalemaniya* (亞勒馬尼亞, Alemaña, *i.e.*, Germany) is *Boluoniya*. [It is a country] extremely rich. The landscape is largely plain with widespread forests of fruits. There are so many of them that the people there cannot exhaust the [fruit], and often leave it on the trees. Salt and furs are also local products. Salt there is as transparent as crystals, whose taste is very strong. The people there are nice-looking, gentle, harmonious and unpretentious. They are very hospitable to guests. Burglars and robbers are non-existent. Their people do not even know of burglars or robbers in their life. The king does not pass the position to his son, instead, he lets the ministers choose a sage new monarch. Generations of their kings abide by national laws which are not changed even slightly. On some occasions, the son of the old king is selected, but the selection must be done while the old kings is still holding the position; otherwise, it could not happen. It is the same with selecting ministers or kings of other countries. The country is divided into four regions. [The king] resides in a region for three months, within one year he has visited all the borders. The climate is quite cold. The sea freezes during the winter months. Travellers often spend several days and nights on the ice, travelling while being guided by the stars. [The country] has a tributary called *Boduoliya* ["Podolia" transliterated], whose land is also very fertile. If one plants grain in one year enough for three years will be harvested. Grasses and vegetables can grow five to six *chi* 尺 within three days.[7]

According to the explanation by Xie Fang 謝方, *Boluoniya* is the transliteration of "Polonia". The Polish Commonwealth existed between 1569 and 1795 and this is the reason why Aleni wrote "The king does not pass the position to his son, instead, he lets the ministers choose a sage new monarch". In addition, *Zhifang waiji* twice mentions "amber" as a Polish product,

amber is found near the seashore. It is grease that leaks out from rock gaps at the bottom of the sea. It resembles oil at first. When the weather is warm, it comes up to the surface of the sea and solidifies upon meeting the wind. When the weather is cold, it solidifies the moment it leaks out from the gap. It is often washed up by gales to the seashore.[8]

The part entitled "Marine Products" ("Haichan" 海產) in Volume 5 "A General Account of the Four Oceans" ("Sihai zongshuo" 四海總說) mentions amber again: "Amber is a local product of Europe's *Boluoniya*. It can be found at a distance of 3000 *li* along the sea. The pieces have been washed ashore by the winds and tides and amass there. Local people use them to make implements."[9] Amber is fossilised tree resin which has lost volatile components and reached a stable status through a long period of being buried underground. "Amber is found near the seashore" refers to the coast of the Baltic Sea, which is famous for its abundance in amber. A large amount of orange, brown or red amber in the shapes of irregular lumps, icicles or drops are contained in the glauconite

---

7 Aleni, Giuilio, Xie Fang (2000), *Zhifang waiji jiaoshi* p. 95.

8 Ibid., p. 95.

9 Ibid., p. 154.

HISTORICAL WRITING ON THE DECLINE OF POLAND

sand-layer which formed 40–60 million years ago. The Chinese people love amber, Aleni's extensive introduction of it was clearly aimed at meeting their taste.

Another Western geographic work in the Chinese language which mentions Poland and is quoted by the *Haiguo tuzhi* is the *Reference Book of Foreign Geography* (*Waiguo dili beikao* 外國地理備考) written by Portuguese author José Martinho Marques 瑪吉士 (1810–1867) during the Late Qing. dynasty[10] The author of this book selected material from a large number of foreign-language sources and wrote in very fluent classic Chinese. Much importance was attached to the book by Chinese scholars even at that time. It was proofread by the famous scholar Chen Li 陳澧 (1810–1882), and, in 1847, Pan Shicheng 潘仕成 (1804–1873) included it into his *Collecteana of the Immortals of the Seas and Mountains* (*Hai shan xianguan congshu* 海山仙館叢書). Marques' book also was entitled *New Explanations to the Reference Book of Geography* (*Xinshi dili beikao* 新釋地理備考). It is not clear whether the book had been published as a monograph before it was included into the *Hai shan xianguan congshu*. Later, parts of the book were included and published in the first volume of Wang Xiqi's 王錫祺 *Collected Works on Geography from the Xiaofanghu Studio* (*Xiaofanghuzhai yudi congchao* 小方壺齋輿地叢鈔). Marques' book consists of ten volumes. The first and second volume deal with natural geography. The first volume consists of twenty sections including records on geography (*dili zhi* 地理志), on the Earth (*diqiu lun* 地球論), on the rotation of the Earth (*diqiu xunhuan lun* 地球循環論), the order of the Earth and the five planets (*diqiu wuxing xuzhi* 地球五星序秩), on solar and lunar eclipses (*riyue shi lun* 日月蝕論), on the spherical Earth 地圓論, on the frigid, temperate and torrid zones 寒溫熱道論, on longitudes and latitudes 經緯二度論, on the time zones of the Earth 地球時刻道論, and on the four seasons 辨四季寒暑論. The second volume consists of 22 sections which discuss natural phenomena such as air, clouds, the wind, thunder and lightning, earthquakes, volcanoes and so on. It is accompanied by sixteen illustrations on, for example, the geographical zones, the longitudes and latitudes, *etc.*

The third volume is entitled "General Discussion on the Origins of the Laws and Morals of the Different Countries and the Fundaments of Politics and Trade" (*Bangguo fadu yuanyou zhengzhi maoyi genben zonglun* 邦國法度原由政治貿易根本總論). The fourth to the tenth volumes are "A General Account of the Earth" (*Diqiu zonglun* 地球總論), "A Complete Account of Europe"

---

10 José Martinho Marques, also known under the designation 大西洋瑪吉士 (Marques from the Western Ocean), was a member of the Marques family and had dwelled in Macao for a long time, see *Macao Daily* (*Aomen ribao* 澳門日報 July 13th 1987, p. 8–9) and Tan Zhiqiang (1994), "Aomen yu Zhongguo jindai guoji guanxi zhishi zhi yinjin", p. 190. Marques was born on March 2, 1810 in São Lourenço, Macau and died in the same parish on July 4, 1867. He studied at the St. Joseph's Seminary since young and was student of Joaquim Alfonso Goncalves 江沙維. Marques was fluent in both Cantonese and Mandarin.

(Ouluoba quanzhi 嘔囉吧全志), "A Complete Account of Asia" (*Yaxiya quan-zhi* 啞細啞洲全志), "A Complete Account of America" (*Yamilijiazhou quanzhi* 啞美哩咖洲全志) and "A Complete Account of Oceania" (*Asaiyanizhou quanzhi* 啊噻啞呢洲全志).[11] "A Complete Account of Europe" mentions Poland.

In the year of 1814, there was a country named Polonia, which was completely ruled by this country [Russia]. The country lies between the 50th and the 55th parallels north, and between the 15th and the 22nd meridian east. It borders Russia in the east, Prussia in the northwest, and the country of Galicia to the south. The size of the country is about 1250 *li* in length and about 800 *li* in width, covering an area of about 63,700 square *li*. It has a population of 3,925,000 persons. The landscape is flat, with plenty of lakes and rivers in between. Fields are fertile, grains and fruit grow in abundance, woods and forests are dense, and birds and beasts multiply. Local products include silver, bronze, iron, tin, coal, white jade, patterned gems, sulphur, porcelain and so forth. The climate is temperate. The horizon stretches far without being obstructed by mountains. In the north, the wind blows so strongly that people hardly remain on their feet. The [major] religion is Roman Catholicism. Other religions are followed by some of the people, there is no ban on them. Craftsmanship there is rather mediocre. Artisan work-shops are rare. The nation is divided into eight provinces: Mazovia, whose capital is Warsaw and is managed by a viceroy sent each year by the Russian emperor, Kraków whose capital is Miechów, Sandomierz whose capital is Radom, Kalisz whose capital is also named Kalisz, Lublin whose capital is also named Lublin, Plock whose capital is also named Plock, Podlasie whose capital is Siedlce, and Augustów whose capital is Suwałki. Prosperous commercial cities of the nation are Warsaw, Lublin, Kraków, Kalisz and so on.[12]

From the translated names, it becomes clear that the author of the *Waiguo dili beikao* made use of the *Zhifang waiji* when writing the book, only that he added a "mouth"-radical to every character when translating names or place-names. When quoting from the *Dili beikao*, Wei Yuan made changes and made omis-sions—in contrast to what he did with the *Zhifang waiji*. For example, he changed the characters for Russia from 呃囉嘶 to 峨羅斯 or 厄羅斯, and Prussia from 吥嚕哂啞國 to 布魯西亞國; he also deleted the mouth radical from almost all people's and place names.[13]

Bolan 波蘭 as the designation for Poland probably made its earliest appear-ance in the *Complete Illustrated Collection of World Geography* (*Wanguo dili quantu ji* 萬國地理全圖集, which was compiled by Karl Friedrich August Gützlaff (郭實臘) in 1843 and 1844. After quoting from Gutzlaff's work, Wei Yuan continued to write:

---

11 Marques (1849), "Xinshi dili beikao", vol. 1.
12 Ibid., vol. 6, pp.45–46.
13 Chen Hua (1998), *Hai guo tu zhi*, vol. 2, p. 1321.

HISTORICAL WRITING ON THE DECLINE OF POLAND — 385 omitted

The nation of Poland used to rule its people independently. Because the members of the nobility were constantly fighting each other, Russia, Austria and Prussia partitioned most of its territory. In the twelfth year of the Daoguang 道光 reign (1832), there was a deadly insurrection, but the rebels failed after more than ten battles. The country was returned to Russia to be ruled by it. The country produces grains, honey and timber. Most of the people are serfs of the nobility. The capital is called Warsaw and there are 150 thousand residents, among whom 30 thousand are Jewish. They like to seize things.[14]

Western authors' introduction to the Polish situation were thus mostly rather objective descriptions of geography, customs and local products. The author of the *Waiguo dili beikao* writes, however, "[Poland] is managed by a viceroy sent each year by the Russian emperor", and Wei Yuan also adds, "The country is ruled by Russia". Both are thus pointing out Poland's demise, but the *Haiguo tuzhi* does not include any remark referring to historical lessons to be learned from national decline nor does it address any nationalist sentiments.

2. The Misery of Poland's National Ruin in the Works of Chinese Reformers.

During the reform movement of the late Qing dynasty, Chinese reformers attached a great deal of attention to history books as a means for saving the nation and securing its existence. By August 1897 Liang Qichao 梁啟超 (1873–1929), had already published an article entitled "Records of the Extinction of Poland" ("Bolan miewang ji" 波蘭滅亡記) in the third issue of the newspaper *Shiwu bao* (時務報 *Chinese Progress*). The article focuses on describing the misery of Poland after its people had become what Liang calls Russia's "slaves from a ruined country" (*wangguo nu* 亡國奴):

I have heard that Poland has been defeated by Russia again. The Russians spared no effort to track down the rebels. Whoever appeared to be even slightly involved in the plot was sent to Siberia and the Caucasus Mountains and ordered to serve in the army. Thirty thousand Polish people were sent to the Caucasus to cultivate wasteland and were not allowed to bring their families with them. These people all used to be powerful nobles, gentry, rich or scholar-officials, [but now] they were put into prisoner's carts on the roads, being chased like sheep or dogs. Their lands and properties were confiscated by the alien nation, their wives and children becoming slaves and beggars of the alien people. In March 1835, the Russian emperor mandated that all Poles older than seven years of age who were poor or parentless were to be sent to the borders areas. At first, they snatched young children during the night, later they abducted them in the daytime. On the 17 May of this year, there was a long line of carts with numerous children inside

---

14 Ibid., vol. 2, pp. 1320–1321.

who were to be sent to Siberia. When the carts were about to move, the parents of the children wailed and shouted and climbed onto the carts and wanted to travel along. They were beaten up by angry soldiers and fell to the ground. Some of them went under the carts, willing to be crushed to death by the hooves and wheels. Their blood and flesh lay on the streets and tracks. *En route*, the children were only fed with coarse food. Those who became ill were immediately thrown off from the cart and left to die on the roadside, their bread still lying beside them. It went so far that officials and people were not allowed to speak Polish any longer and were forced to speak Russian, instead. In all schools and colleges, everything was taught in Russian. Once, there were scholars and young people who gathered in Vilnius, conversing in Polish. They were arrested by police patrols and charged with felony. Alas! When a country is not able to compete and is shackled and yoked by others, the misery is beyond description![15]

Between 1600 and 1700, Poland used to be a powerful nation of Europe. Then, the politics of the country deteriorated. The lords and the people alike became accustomed to sluggishness. Ministers in position were corrupt, lazy and negligent of their duty. Riots took place frequently, and the country was not able to extricate itself from these problems. Because of this, both the public and the private people became poor. The situation worsened daily. In the year 1763, Russia sent Hermann Karl von Keyserling as envoy to Poland. He used a large sum of money to bribe the people in Poland. Because of this, the officials of the Polish court had the intention of relying on Russia politically. Even among the commoners, more than half wanted to become Russians. In October of that year, the Polish king died, and Russia used military force to appoint who it preferred to be the new king, and concluded a secret pact with Prussia, which contained a provision that the Polish king's title should not be hereditary. "When the old king dies, a new king should be elected by the people. If a new king is appointed arbitrarily, he should be dethroned by our two nations together." In 1765, riots broke out in Poland, and Poland begged for military aid from Russia to contain the bandits. Russian troops used the opportunity to commit much arson and robbery. At the time, Poland was already extremely weak. All the ministers of the court were under Russia's thumb. Realising that the Polish people were still quite united, the Russians secretly bribed their powerful representatives and envoys, so that they would all harbour treacherous feelings against each other. The Polish court suppressed the armed uprising. It banned all public meetings and discussions of politics. The Polish people's morale became weaker and weaker. In 1772, Russia, Austria and Prussia concluded a public pact about the partition of the Polish territory. Russia gained 19,800 square *li*, Austria obtained 13,500 square *li* and Prussia received 6,300 square *li*. They forced the Polish king to submit a written statement giving up the territories and pleading for peace. Poland's remaining territory was now only 42,000 square *li*. Turkey proposed a righteous army to oppose the three powers and aid the weak, but this was immediately foiled by Russia. The European nations were all afraid of Russia's power. Being anxious and seeking to protect themselves, they did not get involved into the Polish issue again. In 1789, Russia secretly discussed with Prussia about swallowing up Poland completely, lest its people made more trouble. In 1793, 80,000 troops pressed on to the Polish borders. The Polish military man Tadeusz Kościuszko led an uprising to resist Russia but failed. He subse-

---

15 Liang, Qichao (1897), "Bolan miewang ji."

quently fled to Italy. In 1795, Russia, Austria and Prussia partitioned Poland once again. They forced the Polish king to resign, promising him an annuity of 200,000 silver coins to live on and to pay the governmental debts for him. In this way, Poland was destroyed. When Alexander I became the Russian tsar, he tried to comfort the Polish people by granting favours, valuing them even more than the Russians. In March 1818, he went to Poland himself to open its parliament. He issued an edict to the public stating: "Your country used to have a parliament. The reason why I have re-established the parliament is that your people are wise and are able to understand the overall situation. It is not the case that I am unwilling to grant the same thing to the Russian people, but they are so coarse, ignorant and stubborn that I do no dare to hasten it." The Polish were pleased by his words, and deeply believed in his affection At the time, Russia appointed Józef Zajączek as the viceroy of Poland in order to manage the affairs of the country. The tsar's younger brother, Duke Constantine Pavlovich, was appointed as commander-in-chief. The viceroy had to obey his commands and was deceived by the duke, and, before he was even able to realise [the privileges accorded to the Polish], they were abolished. Poland's newspaper publishing houses were banned from printing, and Polish soldiers were sent home. The whole of Poland became the territories of the three nations [Russia, Austria and Prussia]. When Napoleon had come to power in France earlier, he had granted independence to the Poles and had created the Duchy of Warsaw. Following Napoleon's defeat, the various nations met for the Congress of Vienna [1814–15], and there they agreed that Poland would become a kingdom, with the king's title concurrently held by the Russian tsar. After that, the Polish people made several attempts to recover their country. Between 1830 and 1835, and between 1863 and 1865, they twice engaged in bloody battles. Year after year, they were crushed by powerful Russia, either because of miscalculations on the part of their commanders, or because they were outnumbered. The viceroyalty was abolished and [Poland] came under direct control of St. Petersburg. Poland was lost again.[16]

The last part of the article was entitled "Commentary", and here Liang wrote:

When Russia devoured other countries in order to expand [its own territory]; although it used its military might in order to restrain [its adversaries], it also used tricks and schemes. It used religion in order to lure them [the other countries] to its side, or it obtained control with the help of marriages, or it coerced [its adversaries] with the help of its nobles. It employed this way to destroy other countries and to obliterate a ruling house. Poland's internal politics were corrupt, and the accumulated weakness grew steadily. It was as if there were foxes and mice in your home, but you rely on tigers and wolves for your own protection. It is only when they start to choose to eat the meat [in the house] that you begin to look at each other in dismay. This is a useless plan and can only can be conferred the title of the greatest stupidity and should not have been adopted. In Europe, the situation of stationing troops has become more serious. Compassionate scholars promote the learning of international law, hoping that, by employing the principles of righteousness, violence can be restrained and the weak can be relieved. When I look at the amoral treaty between Russia, Prussia and Austria, these three countries, without any justification, sent out their armies and, in one moment of time, they

16 Ibid.

took a territory of 240.000 *li* and portioned partitioned it. The other states remained indifferent and did not raise a hand. How then can one speak approvingly of international law?

Not trying to protect oneself and being willing to be protected by other countries, using others to protect oneself, alas—this only means quickening one's own demise and that is all. The countries which are Russia's neighbours today, such as Sweden and Denmark, don't have more territory or people than Poland, but they still firmly exist today. Does this not also show that Poland was itself responsible for its fall, and that it wasn't destroyed by Russia?[17]

"Records of the Extinction of Poland" is not a long article, but it was the earliest work of the late Qing period which dealt with the history of the national demise of Poland. In 1901, Liang Qichao wrote an article entitled "On a New Method of Destroying Countries", which was serialised in volumes 85 to 89 of the *Qingyi bao* ("Mieguo xinfa lun" 滅國新法論) between July and August of that year. In this work, Liang regards the history of Poland's national demise as a typical example of "inflaming fights between parties in order to extinguish [a country]," which he counted among the "new methods for destroying a country".[18]

In 1898, Kang Youwei wrote his "Account of the Partition and Destruction of Poland" (*Bolan fenmie ji* 波蘭分滅記). This was an important work which aimed to encourage the Guangxu-Emperor "to carry on with determination" during the later stage of the Hundred Days' Reform. Works such as the *Catalogue of the Tenthousand Trees Thatched Cottage* (*Wanmu caotang congshu mulu* 萬木草堂叢書目錄) by Zhang Bozhen 張伯楨 (1877–1946) claimed that Kang's book had been "confiscated" in the *coup* that put an end the reform. The library of the Palace Museum holds the original copy which was presented to the emperor during the reform, in two cases. Except for the Preface, the work consists of seven volumes in three books. The book has white pages without lines and the text is written in ink in neat handwriting. At the bottom-right hand corner of each page is the signature of the author "Secretary of the Board of Works, Kang Youwei".[19] Each volume of the book deals with several issues, which are arranged chronologically. The single parts are entitled the following way: 1. The Origins of Poland's Partition and Fall; 2. The Old Country of Poland; 3. Russian Tsarina Catherine's Autocracy in Poland; 4. Russia Arrests Polish Patriots at Will; 5. Polish Patriots Plan the Recovery of their Country and Fight Russia; 6. Russia Usurps Power and the Dethronement and Enthronement of the Polish King; 7. Russia Fights the Patriotic Party, which has been Formed by Polish Righteous Persons; 8. The Reasons for the Partition of

---

17 Ibid, p. 141.

18 See Zou Zhenhuan (1996),"Qingmo wangguoshi 'bianyi reȝ yu Liang Qichao de Chaoxian wangguoshi yanjiu."

19 Kong Xiangji (2008), *Kang Youwei bianfa zouzhang jikao*, pp. 432–433.

HISTORICAL WRITING ON THE DECLINE OF POLAND

Poland by Prussia, Austria and Russia; 9. Russia Forces Poland to Give up Reform and Conducts the Second Partition; and 10. Poland's Third Partition and its Demise. Kang's book mainly deals with the three partitions of Poland in 1772, 1793 and 1795 by Russia, Prussia and Austria, during the period when Józef Poniatowski, the minister favoured by Catherine II, was in power. In the latter half of the eighteenth century, mid- and lower-level Polish nobles and the newly emerged *bourgeoisie*, launched, under the influence of the Western European enlightenment movement, a patriotic reform movement which was crushed by a military intervention of Catherine II.

Poland was partitioned for the first time by Russia, Prussia and Austria in 1772. Through his account of how Poland, which had once been a major European nation was partitioned and destroyed by foreign powers because of political corruption, Kang Youwei intended to warn the Guangxu Emperor and to mobilise scholar officials to join the reform. According to Kang's analysis, the fall of Poland had the following reasons: first, there was the stubbornness of the nobles and ministers in power, who spared no effort in obstructing reform and in suppressing patriots.

Those who spoke of new studies were accused of heresy. Those who mentioned techniques were scolded for performing wicked crafts. Those who were in favour of opening mines were obstructed by the claim that the Earth's *qi* would be flushed out. Those who spoke about travelling were accused of colluding with the enemy. Those who advocated nourishing the people were chided for advocating the "right of the people". Those who spoke out for the opening of the parliament, were prevented from doing so and accused of treason. Whoever spoke of new laws, new studies and new policies was slandered and attacked by the conservatives, who even fabricated rumours and confused right with wrong, so that those who spoke of reform were kept silent out of fear. Everywhere, they set up mechanisms with the intention of framing and maligning these people.[20]

For this reason, Poland continued to follow old ways and was gradually trapped in a situation of weakness. Second was the Polish king's fear and dependence on the very intrusive tsarist Russia. He not only refused to use talented people, but also helped arrest and kill Polish patriots. Nobles and ministers were bribed by Russia, while common people trusted Russia blindly. "The Russian ambassador was worried about a rebellion of the national party. He ordered the Polish king to arrest righteous members of the party. The Polish king was afraid that disobedience on his part would enrage Russia and thus complied as best he could. At that time, the court ministers had already been bribed and were all obedient." Several times, Kang mentions that "the Polish king was weak and cowardly. He was controlled by the Russian viceroy, who often coerced him to give orders to the Polish people".[21] Influenced by the French Revolution, the

---

20 Kang Youwei (2007) "Bolan fenmie ji", p. 406.
21 Ibid., p. 419–420.

Polish Congress passed a constitution on 3 May 1791, which resulted in another military intervention by Catherine II. In 1793, Russia and Prussia partitioned Poland for the second time. In 1794, the Polish people revolted under the leadership of the national hero Kościuszko, but the revolt was immediately suppressed by Russia. In 1795, Russia, Prussia and Austria partitioned Poland for a third time. In his book, Kang Youwei revealed such agonising historical facts as how the tsarist Russia sent troops, bribed nobles and ministers, and eventually partitioned Poland overtly. Kang pointed out that "Russia is a nation of tigers and wolfs, whose major concern is engulfing another country's territory. This is known to the whole world". He continued, "the Polish king and his mother were repeatedly insulted by Russian officials. His queen and concubines were all captured by the Russians and assaulted." The mother of the Polish king poisoned herself after being assaulted. The king also died of depression.[22] Kang specifically emphasised the reasons for Poland's demise, namely, the delay in reform, which resulted in the country being partitioned twice by Russia and Prussia. As a result, the king and the talented ministers started to consider reform but were prevented from doing so by conservative nobles and ministers. After the third partition, the whole nation from top to bottom wanted reform, but Russia intervened and sent troops to surround the congress, forcing Poland to abolish new policies and to return to the old rules. Poland fell within only a few years thereafter. Kang earnestly exhorted the Guangxu-Emperor "to keep in mind the lessons from Poland's decline and fall by day and night, and to have determination in strengthening [the nation]". "One looks at Poland's partition and fall and knows that a nation has no choice but has to strive to be independent." Kang also made a reference to the Chinese reality and wrote:

In order to get Liaodong back, we did, in fact, rely on the power of Russia, and we granted them railways. This year, we gave Russia Lüshun and Dalian. It is unlikely for us to not become like Poland! Our nobles and ministers today are unwilling to establish an 'institutional office' (*zhiduju* 制度局) to carry out reform. If we start reforming now, there will still be some hope; if we wait several years, the Russian railways in Manchuria will be finished and they will come all the way to the south. For this reason, we still intend to draft a constitution, but I fear that there will still be conservatives who will not allow it. Are we not making ourselves their Poland? And are the conservatives not helping Russia to partition ourselves?[23]

While *Bolan fenmie ji* mainly focuses on describing the facts of Poland's history, each volume, however, was followed by the comments by Kang Youwei, comments of various length.[24] In his comments to the preface and to each volume, Kang Youwei adopted a writing style full of emotions. Bearing a clear goal in

---

22 Ibid., p. 422.
23 Ibid., preface. p. 397.
24 See Yang Yuliang (1982), "Wei kanxing de Kang Youwei liang bu zhuzuo."

HISTORICAL WRITING ON THE DECLINE OF POLAND

mind, he extensively pointed out how the Polish king's conservativeness, his isolation from the people and his lack of courage in promoting pro-reform talent eventually led to the "ravage and encroachment" by other countries including Russia. Kang vividly depicted an appalling scene of partition and fall in which "the population did not have any clothes, and even the noblemen began to suffer. Spilled brain mass and ripped out intestines littered the land, streams of blood formed a river".[25] In his comment, Kang pointed out that the reason for Poland's failure to reform was the king's lack of resolution: "Had the Polish king decided to carry out reform, with his wisdom, he could have been called a sage king. But he was hindered by ministers domestically and threatened by powerful neighbours from the outside. For this reason he was notable to follow his earlier plans. In the end, he lost his nation and left himself to be insulted. He was unable to protect his wife and children. His suffering is rare in history."[26]

Kang Youwei's *Bolan fenmie ji* is not a just an article, but rather a piece with the format and the system of a historical work that deals with agonising lessons from Poland's decline and fall. *Bolan fenmie ji* was presented to the Emperor during the later stage of the Hundred Days' Reform (in mid-August, 1898). The goal of writing was not only to discuss why Polish history should be studied and how to learn from the reforms of other countries, but earnestly to urge Emperor Guangxu to establish the "Office of Institutional Reform" as soon as possible, as "there are many new policies to be adopted and everything needs to start anew", otherwise "we really would become [another] Poland".[27] The book also presents a number of implicit comparisons to current issues which could not be put forward directly. For example, by describing the Polish conservative ministers' obstruction of reform, Kang unmasked similar practices of the Chinese conservatives, hoping that the Guangxu Emperor could sweep away those obstructions and carry the reform through to its end. By making use of the *Bolan fenmie ji*, Kang Youwei presented to Emperor Guangxu an agonising lesson in which the deferment and irresolution surrounding a reform resulted in sabotage by the conservatives and foreign intervention, going so far as to say that, if reforms ended in failure, the nation could be partitioned. This was the lesson that could be drawn from Poland's mistakes.[28] After the book had been presented to the emperor, the Guangxu emperor was deeply affected by it. Kang Youwei said:

After the birthday of the Empress dowager, I presented the 'Records of the Partition and the Demise of Poland' to the throne, which describes the tragic experience of

---

25 Kang Youwei (2007) "Bolan fenmie ji", preface. p. 397.

26 Ibid., pp. 422–423.

27 Ibid., p. 406.

28 Wang, Xiaoqiu (2003), *Jindai Zhongguo yu shijie*, pp. 85–90.

Poland, when partitioned and destroyed by Russia and Austria. It points out how the scholars and the population suffered from the cruelty of persecution, the disaster brought about by the Russian control of the country's king and his extreme suppression by the conservative party. Later, when the king angrily engaged in reform, the Russians sent private soldiers in order to suppress it and did not allow the reform; soon [Poland] was destroyed by partition. I described this with utter pain. The Emperor read it and was so moved that he sobbed. He awarded me 2000 *liang* silver as a reward for having compiled the book.[29]

During the Hundred Days' Reform, Liang Qichao's "Bolan miewang ji" and Kang Youwei's "Account of the Partition and Destruction of Poland" focused on the reasons for Poland's demise so as to warn the Chinese that, if no reform took place, China would not escape the fate of eventually being partitioned in the same way as Poland. At the later stage of the Reform, Kang Youwei presented *Bolan fenmie ji* to Emperor Guangxu. Using Poland's partition as an example, Kang hoped that the Guangxu emperor would call up all his courage to promote further the reform of China's political system. The two reform thinkers both tried to use the history of the demise of Poland as an important intellectual resource for realising their goal of political mobilisation and political action.

3. Shibue Tamotsu and His *Porando suibo senshi* which entered China in the wave of "*Wangguo* Historical Lessons"

The signing of the Boxer Protocol in 1901 rendered early twentieth-century China into a lamb in the slaughterhouse. Britain controlled the Yangtze River area, France controlled Guangdong, Guangxi and Yunnan, Germany controlled Shandong, Japan controlled Fujian, Russia considered the three northeastern provinces as its ready meat, and the United States was waiting to devour the most delicious parts. Enlightened Chinese people felt a "spirit-destructing and heartbreaking" pain. They constantly asked themselves: "Why are our people so numb and indifferent as if they were dead ash and withered trees. Being slaves seems to be irrelevant to them. In the Confucian analects it is written: 'Despair is the greatest sorrow.' It would already be intolerable if one person's heart were dead. When a whole country's heart is dead, its demise is imminent."[30] Therefore, this period saw another wave of compilations and translations of the history of the demise of Poland. As far as I know at least three Chinese versions of the book *A History of the Wars of the Decline and Demise of Poland (Porando suibo*

---

29 Kang Youwei (2000), "Kang Nanhai zibian nianpu", p. 155.
30 Zou Zhenhuan (1990), "Wan Qing liu Ri xuesheng yu riwen xishu de hanyi huodong".

senshi 波蘭衰亡戰史) written by Japanese scholar Shibue Tamotsu 澀江保 (1857–1930) were published: the first is a single-volume version translated by the "Society for the Translation of Books" (*Yishui huibianshe* 譯書彙編社) in 1901, the second being a version titled "History of Forgotten Facts about Poland" (*Bolan yishi* 波蘭遺史), translated by Chen Danran 陳澹然 (1859–1930) and published by the Jiangxi official gazette publishing house in 1902, the third being the one translated by Xue Gongxia 薛公俠, published by *Jingjin shuju* 鏡今書局 in Shanghai in 1904.

Shibue Tamotsu (1857–1930) was originally named Shigeyoshi 成善. Members of the Shibue family had been the domain's medical practitioners 藩醫 of the Hirosaki Domain 弘前藩 (today's city of Hirosaki in the Aomori Prefecture) for generations. Tamotsu loved reading from when he was a child. At the age of four, he had already started studying Confucian works guided by a teacher, while also studying Chinese medicine. In March 1871, the fifteen-year-old Shibue Tamotsu went alone to Tokyo and started studying English at a school established by Seki Shinpachi 尺振八. In 1875, Shibue graduated from a normal college at the age of nineteen. He then taught at different schools and colleges. In the meantime, he translated a *Brief History of America*. In October 1879, he resigned from his job to pursue further studies at Keio Public School 慶應義塾. In September 1881, in order to support his family, he became headmaster of Aichi Middle School 愛知中學. Shibue published as many as about 150 pieces of written or translated works with publishers such as Hakubunkan 博文館.

Shibue's *Pōrando suibō senshi* was originally published by one of the most famous publishing agencies in Japan's modern history, Hakubunkan. Hakubunkan had been established by Ōkashi Sahei 大橋佐平 (1835–1901) in his hometown of Tokyo in 1887 and stopped doing business in 1947. In its more than 60 years' history, due to the tremendous influence of the many books and magazines which it published, Hakubunkan created a "Hakubunkan" era in Japan's modern publishing industry. As Li Dongmu 李冬木 has pointed out, "The rapid development of Hakubunkan's publishing enterprise in the Meiji era was possible because it met the demand for enlightenment of the times".[31] Hakubunkan's publications were already drawing the attention of the Chinese publishing industry during the late Qing period. Guangzhi publishing house in Shanghai, for example, in 1903, translated Hakubunkan's *History of 30 Years of Meiji Restoration* (*Riben weixin sanshi nian shi* 日本維新三十年史) and, in 1906, published *A Complete Account of the Russo-Japanese War* (*Riben zhanshi benmo* 日俄戰紀本末, translated by Zhao Shen 趙伸. According to the statistics made by Li Dongmu, during the eight years between January 1890 and January 1898, Hakubunkan published more than 50 works written or translated by Shibue

---

31 See Li Dongmu (1998), "Shibu Tamotsu yi 'Zhina ren qizhi'".

Tamotsu with their contents ranging from history to geography, from anthropology to electrical technology, from literature to hypnotherapy, as well as geometry, arithmetic, gymnastics, the studies of supernatural monsters, and handicrafts. Among these works, the proportion dealing with Western thought, history and literature is considerable. For example, in the 100-volume *Tsūzoku kyōiku sōsho* (通俗教育叢書, *General Education Series*) published in January 1890, 22 of the volumes are works of Shibue. The best known, however, are the 24 volumes which were published as part of his *Collecteana of the History of Wars of the Nations of the World* 萬國戰史叢書 in September 1894 and which were praised as a "masterpiece" of the literature on military history in Japan at that time.[32]

Shibue Tamotsu finished the original version of *Pōrando suibō senshi* in 1895. The work consists of two volumes. In 1901, the *Publishing House for Translated Books* 譯書出版社, which was run by Chinese students who had studied in Japan, published a single-volume translation. The book, entitled *Bolan shuaiwang zhanshi*, contains three sections and twelve chapters. At the beginning of the Preface 緒言, three major reasons for Poland's fall are given: first, the "malady of the public election of kings", which was responsible for the "emergence of factions and cliques in the nation". "The factions stood against each other and jostled with each other. The people could not be united. Foreign countries took advantage of the cleavage and fed those involved with bribes. Interventions gradually took place, followed by pervasive threats and cruel oppression. The nation was finally swallowed up." Second was the "disaster of foreign intervention", which, in particular, pointed to the invasion schemes of Tsarist Russia: "When the disaster has not developed, it is rather easy to prevent it; once the disaster has happened, it is very hard to find a remedy." The third was the "exclusion of the public from politics". "Although a public election system was carried out in Poland", everything was, in fact, manipulated by "dominant nobles", whereas "the people (*renmin* 人民) were excluded". The people were not allowed to be concerned about politics nor to participate in it. As a result, "the people considered their country as a stranger and saw national affairs as though they were observing fire from a safe distance". According to the author, "People are the root of the country". "A national disaster is something, which affects the country; if something affects the country, this is not something which is outside of the people. There is nothing else [than the people] which forms what is called a country/nation (*guo*). This means that what they are exposed to is the same and this it is. When the people do not know about the affairs of the country, this is the root of discord [within the country] and those who desire [to take it over] act as an evil and brutal enemy." To the author, all

---

32 See ibid. A considerable number of Hakubunkan's publications also spread to Korea..

this was absolutely impermissible. In his review of this book, Gu Xieguang 顧
燮光 pointed out that,

Poland was a major nation of the West. Its size was smaller only than Russia; its military power was prominent at the time. But it was not long before Poland was partitioned by Russia, Prussia and Austria; its nobles and commoners were extinguished in the same way. Oh, how sad this is! This book is divided into three sections with a total of 12 chapters. It suggests three reasons for the demise of Poland: 1. The malady of the public election of kings; 2. The disaster of the foreign intervention; and 3. The exclusion of the people from politics. These are elaborated in abundant detail and can serve as a warning from history. If we try to find out how the disaster could become so severe, then it is because the followers of the religions mistreat each other. Russia took advantage of this cleavage and coerced them unscrupulously. How can we not fear the potential of religion in causing a nation to fall?[33]

On 19 December 1901, the *Zhong wai ribao* 中外日報, *Chinese and Foreign Daily* published an advertisement regarding the recent publication of *Bolan shuaiwang zhanshi*, which says "the book deals with the three partitions of Poland in detail. Its account of the Russian viceroy's political machinations and Polish patriots' sacrifice of their lives for the nation are particularly alarming. Now Russian power is shifting to the East. Having occupied Lüshun, they are again thinking about occupying Manchuria.[...] Hopefully, when people read this book, they will know that the Russians have a blueprint already."

Chen Danran, a holder of a *juren*-degree, which he had been awarded in 1893, translated Shibue Tamotsu 's *Pōrando suibo̅ senshi* as *Bolan Yishi*. The book was published by the Jiangxi official gazetteer publishing house in 1902. However, Chen did not completely follow the structure of Shibue's original book in his translation; instead, he

as much as possible emulated the 'chronicle of events' style structure [...] in the original version personal names and place names are badly mixed up and not uniform because the author took it from different translated Western books, which employed different transliterations. It was extremely difficult to correct this, because it is very hard to agree on what is wrong or correct.

The translated version includes two sections. The first section is entitled "A General Account of Poland." Its first chapter is entitled "The Establishment of the Polish Nation", the second chapter, "The Nation Ruled by a Foreign King", and the third, "Russia's and Sweden's Designs on Poland.". The second section is entitled "Reasons for the Fall of Poland", which is divided into four chapters, the first being "The Cruelty of the Russian King", the second, "Righteous Persons Trying to Recover the Nation", the third, "The Bar Confederation", and the fourth, "Poland's Partition by Three Nations". The original book's practice

---

33 Gu, Xieguang (2007), *Yishu jingyan lu*, vol. 1, p. 251.

of using both Western and Chinese calendars was adopted by Chen. In his translation, Chen also referred to other works by Shibue. For example, when discussing Copernicus in the first chapter of "The Establishment of the Polish Nation", he writes,

Copernicus was born in Toruń, Poland. He was born in the year 1473 of the Western calendar (the ninth year of the Chenghua reign of the Ming dynasty, a year of *guisi*) and died in the year 1543 of the Western calendar (the 22nd year of the Jiajing reign, a year of *guimao*). He explored the two theories regarding whether the Earth orbits round the Sun or the reverse, and wrote *De revolutionibus orbium coelestium*. According to Copernicus, standing on the Earth and looking at the Sun, it seems as though the Sun were orbiting round the Earth, which is not true. The Earth spins in two ways, one called rotation and the other revolution. Rotation means that the Earth spins on its axis one time per day; Revolution means that the Earth spins on the orbit round sun one time each year. This argument was much criticised at his time. Catholics, for example, considered the theory to be against the Bible, but what is truth could not be worn away, and Copernicus was revered by generations and generations.

The book also includes a number of quotations from Shibue's other works as well as notes from Chen's own research under the signature of "Obscure monk" (Huizeng 晦僧). At the end of the second chapter of the second section, Chen, for example, remarks:

The contradictions originally existing in this book almost cannot be counted. The names of persons and the place names of all the countries are completely messed up, so that, for those translating, it almost is impossible to check them [....]; at times, the facts are not clear. The book, for example, says that, in 1769, father and son Pulaski were already dead and, later on it says that Pulaski was again appointed as Polish commander in chief. All these contradictions are really severe.

The *Yishu jingyan lu* writes: "The book has been revised by Chen Danran. The translation is similar to the original translation of Shibue. Chen Danran, however, is able to handle the words of classical scholars; for this reason, he was able to wash away all complicated words."[34]

The National Library in Beijing holds a copy of the book's reprinted version of 1916, whose publisher is unknown. Chen Danran writes:

In the year 1902, I sojourned in Jiangxi, when Japan and Russia were making trouble. I was afraid that our compatriots would get near to these two countries and, in this way, repeat Poland's way to ruin, so I got this book and made amendments to it. I waited to have it published by the "Official Gazette" in order to make it known in the Empire. Now more than a decade has passed. Domestic troubles are frequent. Scholar-officials are eager to follow the example of Poland.

---

34 Ibid., vol. 1, p. 234.

Thus, the book was reprinted to warn the people "not to become slaves". In his introduction to the reprinted version, Chen writes,

The fall of Poland started from the collusion of the various factions with foreign countries. The foreigners seized the opportunity and destroyed the country. It is the same with today's China. Poland was a big country on the Baltic coast. Its demise happened only one hundred years ago. The plot of annexation started from the Russian tsarina Catherine II. The Prussian king Frederick, being Poland's neighbour, was also envious, so he persuaded Russia and Austria to combine the military forces of the three countries to partition the Polish territory. For three times, troops were despatched.

After Poland's demise, people sighed upon seeing how the Russian viceroys tyrannically abused their power and how the nobles Tadeusz Kosciuszko and General Wodzicki sacrificed their lives for the country. This sad example is not very far away in history; how can we not be frightened? In the wake of the Sino-Japanese war, our ministers were indignant about Japan's annexation of the Southern Liaoning Province and started to think about getting close to Russia so as to avenge the disgrace. Zhang Zhidong 張之洞 first proposed that Xinjiang be ceded to Russia so as to [use Russia in order to] avenge the humiliation. Li Hongzhang 李鴻章 was deeply hurt by the Treaty of Shimonoseki and when later the railways of the three northeastern provinces were taken by Russia. Then, the Russo-Japanese war broke out and the right to the Southern Manchurian railway was taken by Japan. Japan started to bring more calamity than Russia. In the year 1914 after the battle of Qingdao [between Germany and Japan], Eastern Mongolia and Shandong fell into the hands of the strong neighbour and nothing could be done about it. Japan's conspiracy against our country started from Tomizu Hirondo's proposal to annex China. His main idea was to help the South gain independence in order to cut the Northern armies from their financial sources. Then the Japanese could enter Manchuria and Mongolia, seize the capital, sweep across the North-China plain and attempt to go south. Today, Yunnan, Guizhou, Guangxi and Guangdong are confronting the Northern regime and, the difference between the south and the north becomes so great that they do not see each other as neighbours any longer. This is all based upon the tricky strategy of Tomizu. The people of our country are already facing such a calamity. It will not stop until we have become another Poland. Alas! Isn't this divine will?

The year 1904 saw yet another translation of *Pōrando suibō senshi* by Xue Gongxia 薛功俠 (1876–1944), which was printed by the Jingjin shuju in Shanghai.

Xue Gongxia earned his *xiucai* degree in 1898. Influenced by Kang Youwei's and Liang Qichao's reform, Xue determinedly abandoned a traditional career *via* imperial examinations and instead devoted himself to the dissemination of new ideas and new knowledge. He had studied in Japan and assisted Jin Songcen 金松岑 in translating Miyazaki Tōten's 宮崎滔天 (1871–1922) *My Thirty-three Year Dream (Sanshisan nian luohua meng* 三十年落花夢*)*.

Xue's *History of the demise of Poland (Bolan shuaiwang shi* 波蘭衰亡史*)* consists of six chapters. The first chapter, entitled "Outset" 發端 is further divided into four sections, namely, "Introduction" 緒言, "The Original Ruling Dynasty of Poland"," A Biography of Jan Sobieski", and "Sweden and Russia Meddle into the Polish Affairs". The second chapter, entitled "Immediate Causes of Poland's Partition, Part I", is divided into three sections, namely, "The Russian Tsarina's Moves on Poland", "The Arrest of Patriots and the Disbandment of the Congress", and "The Patriots' Resistance against Russia". The third chapter, entitled "Immediate Causes of Poland's Partition", is divided into four sections, namely, "Russia's Attack on Turkey", "The Bar Confederation", "The Plan of the Bar Confederation does not Work out", and "The Dissolution of the Bar Confederation". The fourth chapter, entitled "The First Partition of Poland", is divided into four sections, namely, "The Collaboration between Prussia, Austria and Russia", "Policies of the Three Countries and their Alliance", "The Discussions about the Partition", and "The Initial Partition of Poland". The fifth chapter, entitled "The Second Partition of Poland", is divided into four sections, namely, "The Plan to Revise the Constitution", "Poland's Alliance with Prussia and the Issue of the New Constitution", "Russia's and Prussia's Armies' Entry into Poland", and "Another Partition of Poland". The sixth chapter, entitled "The Third Partition of Poland", is divided into four sections, namely, "The Plan of the Patriotic Faction to Raise Troops", "Brief Biography of Tadeusz Kościuszko", "The Battle between the Patriotic Army and the Armies of Russia and Prussia", and "Poland's Partition and Fall". The appendix, entitled "Poland's Situation after its Fall", has ten sections, namely, "Founding the Duchy of Warsaw", "Russia-annexed Poland, Prussia-annexed Poland and Austria-annexed Poland", "The Tyrannical Rule of Duke Constantine Pavlovich", "Righteous Revolt by the Polish People", "A Brief Biography of Adam Mickiewicz", "The Defeat of the Polish Army and the Russian's Troops Entering Warsaw", "Alas, Poland Fell", and "The Recent Moves of Poland". The book focuses on how Polish people, during the process of Poland's fall, struggled for national emancipation and launched multiple large-scale revolts, and the appearance of a number of national heroes and patriotic military men such as Tadeusz Kościuszko, Jan Kiliński, Jan Dąbrowski, Edward Dembowski, Józef Bem and Walery Wróblewski. The book includes an introduction by Liu Yazi 柳亞子 under the pseudonym "Zhongguo shaonian zhi shaonian Liu Renquan" (中國少年之少年柳人權, Youth of the Chinese Youths Liu Human Rights). The then 18-year-old young revolutionary Liu Yazi was much inspired after having read the translated *Bolan shuaiwang shi*. His passion against Qing rule grew stronger. In the introduction, Liu wrote:

There is nothing which is more painful than losing one's heart. There is nothing to be grieved more than a lost nation. Although there are differences in losing one's nation, the surviving people are not aware of the tragedy of the destruction of the ancestral temple and being cut off from one's clan. The humiliation of being a slave, like an ox or a horse! With a blushing face, they try to calm down; indifferently, they forget about it. Gradually, they will arrive at a stage of deliberate misrepresentation, treating the thief as a son. They will consider somebody else's country as their own country and somebody else's ruler as their own ruler...

Since Taiwan and the Penghu-Island have been lost, our country has been occupied. The northern barbarians have ravaged it for more two-hundred years. During this endless night, the kingly atmosphere of the central plain has vanished completely; it is like a gathering of women with cackling voices. Where is the strong wind of a great king? My poor compatriots, they are on the verge of a merger between the Chinese and the barbarian races and being drowned in the disastrous floods of the Heilongjiang river. Should one not ask about the cause of driving out [the barbarians] and recovering the territory?

Liu was of the opinion that late Qing China was already facing the predicament of being just like Poland, but that the Chinese people's resolution to exert themselves and save the nation was even weaker than that of the Polish patriots.

By now the whole world is connected. The wind from Europe makes great waves. Those scholars who are semi-enlightened, are intimidated by the prospect of being carved up like a melon. They are mobilising for their cause in order to turn around the public opinion of one generation, but China's becoming Poland has by no means been started today. From the point of view of spirit, China will never become Poland; up to now, we have not seen men like those generations of men of moral integrity who resist Russia and follow each other. They follow each other and, even in front of a rain of projectiles and a forest of rifles, they are without fear. Even if one throws them out into the icy weather or into a snowy cellar, they do not regret.

During the Russo-Japanese War, when the "Polish army of volunteers' war proclamation was sung in all five continents", "who would have expected that the veterans of the Xiang and of the Huai army as well as the members of the reform party, would still be proud of having served the illegitimate dynasty as running dogs?" In order to resist the invasion of the imperialists, Liu encouraged the Chinese readership to learn from the example of "the unity of the patriotic party and the Kościuszko-uprising", and their war spirit and their daring "to raise the flags and beat the war-drums and to denounce St. Petersburg". The Chinese were also expected to learn from the heroic spirit of those Polish people who joined the Russian Nihilist party in order to resist tsarist rule. Liu Yazi pointed out that, as long as the Chinese people "could have, as the Polish have, the spirit of not forgetting the motherland, those other races who call themselves king would not, for a long time, be able to trample on our land and devour our profit, let alone those who have just established their zone of influence!" He also wrote: "My friend the hibernating dragon [i.e., Xue Gongxia] has translated the *History of the Demise of Poland* in order to express, time and time again, his intention of preserving the race and hating the enemy. After ten years of bloody war and nine generations of hatred, Poland's success cannot be far."

His ultimate hope was that, through reading Shibue's *History of the Demise of Poland*, "our nation could suddenly wake up; our nation could learn from the example; our nation could desist from being discouraged". Thus, it could stand up with courage and strive for national freedom and independence.[35]

Shibue's *Porando suibo senshi* focuses on praising the Polish patriots' heroic deeds of resisting invasion during the process of decline and fall. By depicting the Polish revolutionary patriots' struggle against foreign invasion and domestic tyranny as well as their endeavour to recover national independence in the wake of the fall of the nation, Liu Yazi hoped to inspire the Chinese people to learn from the Polish patriots' martial spirit of fighting in bloody battles in order to resist invasion and to seek national independence, so that the people would actively devote themselves to the cause of the anti-Qing national revolution.

The *Guomin bao* 國民報, *Journal of the Nationals*, for example, a newspaper which began its formal publication in Tokyo on 10 May 1901, was founded by the revolutionaries-in-exile Qin Lishan 秦力山 (1877–1906) and Shen Xiang-yun 沈翔雲 (1888–1914). In its issues 2–4 of 1901, *Guomin bao* published a serialised article entitled "On China's decline and fall" ("*Zhongguo miewang lun*" 中國滅亡論), which also took up the Polish patriots' deeds of refusing to resign themselves to the fate of decline and fall and instead rising up in resistance, so as to inspire the Chinese people: "Poland fell, but it fell after fighting to the death. It was a fall of martyrdom."[36] A major reason for radical intellectuals to translate *Porando suibo senshi* was that they not only wanted to explore how Poland experienced its decline and fall, but that they wanted to make it clear to the Chinese public how the Poles resisted foreign enslavement and struggled for national independence. They wanted to point out how Poland had transformed itself from a fallen nation to one in which patriots were still sparing no effort in seeking national recovery. This was called "The country has fallen but the people does not perish", "Although the nation Poland has fallen, the spirit of its people remains. How could we say that it would not be revived!"[37] Another line ran: "Though the Polish motherland has fallen in form, the Polish national spirit has not demised."[38] As long as the national spirit still existed, there was still hope of regaining independence.

III. The Polish *Wangguo* History as a Nationalist Symbol

As a symbol for nationalism, *Porando suibo senshi* drew the attention of many readers at the time. Zhou Zuoren's 周作人 (1885–1967) diary between January

---

35 See Shibue Tamotsu (1904), *Bolan shuaiwang shi*, preface by Liu Renquan.
36 "Zhongguo miewang lun" (1901).
37 "Minzu jingshen lun" (1960), p. 838.
38 Ibid.

HISTORICAL WRITING ON THE DECLINE OF POLAND

1902 and April 1903 contains a number of entries regarding two of Hakubunkan's publications entitled *Japan in Danger* (*Leiluan dongyang* 累卵東洋 by Ohashi Otowa 大橋乙羽 published in 1898 (translated into Chinese by Youyazi 憂亞子) and Shibue Tamotsu's *Porando suibo*, which had been published 1895. The two books were left to Zhou Zuoren by Lu Xun 魯迅 (1881–1936) when Lu visited his family in Shaoxing 紹興 before heading to study in Japan. Zhou Zuoren read the books many times. In his diary entry for the fourth day of the first month of the 28th year of Guangxu (9 March 1902), Zhou wrote that *Porando suibo senshi* was bound in Western style. "It was a cause for the utmost happiness."[39] "Cause for happiness" here refers to Zhou's feeling upon receiving the book as though it were a heaven-sent treasure. On the seventh day of the second month, Zhou finished reading the book. When re-reading it on the nineteenth day of the third month (26 April), he wrote "When I had finished reading, I unconsciously started to sigh again and again".[40] His sighing was undoubtedly caused by Poland's misery and the Polish patriots' courage to recover their nation. And in the seventh month of the year, Zhou noted that he had read *Porando suibo senshi* again.[41]

The reformer and businessman Zheng Guanying 鄭觀應 (1842–1922), wrote a long poem after reading *Porando suibo senshi*:

If, for a moment, one investigates the other countries on the Earth, one can measure the principles of growth and decline and surviving and perishing.

The surrounding groups of stars form the firmament, the convergence of land and sea form the area [of the globe].

Humans let spirit and blood converge to connect the whole of the body, and, because of this, they are able to employ their senses through the ears and the eyes.

If a small group suddenly emerges, it can successively form a large group, the wise men will not let lie waste the power of the group.

A leader ruling a large number of people can be called emperor. Only by respecting the virtuous will he be able to pacify and control the masses through the ages.

The people are the basis of the state; who could doubt this? Ruler and subject are bound together and assist each other, like the two wings of a bird.

When it comes to the later days of an Empire, the autocratic government becomes stricter. Despicable officials neglect the suffering of the people but the officials still behave as though peace and prosperity reigned.

Paralysed by fear, they look askance [at the common people]; this terrible situation can be easily observed.

But the Imperial court still goes so far to protect them [the officials] against the people, like protecting against a flood of the river. Clamping down on them, binding them and bitterly suppressing them.

---

39 Lu Xun bowuguan (1996), *Lu Xun bowuguan zang Zhou Zuoren riji*,, p. 317.
40 Ibid., p. 329.
41 Ibid., p. 345.

It is unaware of the fact that the wisdom of the people is the basis of wealth and power and is only concerned with the question of whether the people behave correctly.

When the flood can no longer be contained everything will get out of hand. The popular morale will slacken and the destiny of the nation will necessarily become unclear and obstructed.

Where can one go, in order to look for upright and powerful men? Only some honorific power is retained, but one is, in fact, utterly isolated.

When I read the "History of the Polish war", every time, I close the book, I have to sigh for a long time. As to peace and disorder, joy and sorrow, there is nothing which is not taken up by the book. The way two great powers (meaning the separatist regimes of Russia and Prussia) overstepped their limits provides us with a grievous lesson.

If, on an early day, one can unite with the masses, open them with sincerity and impartiality, such hatred and grudge could be avoided.

If ruler and the people are of one heart and are united with each other, how could the country be annexed and swallowed up by somebody else?

The good way of reform has not been adopted and this is a disaster brought about by the selfish interest of the vulgar high officials. (In this way, one can see that autocracy does not work if the monarch is not enlightened).

Lazy and idle, slipping almost imperceptibly for more than one hundred years (Today it is more than a hundred years since the destruction and fall of Poland), it is as if the cart behind does not see the handrail of the cart ahead.

This makes me wringing my hands in even greater despair. Strong powers are waiting on all sides so that my heart becomes full of sorrow. The strong powers use the protection of China's interest as an excuse to interfere in the internal politics of the country.

The foreign powers pretend to protect China's interest, but, in fact, they interfere in China's internal affairs, not only in the case of officials who are promoted or demoted, (the promotion and demotion of officials as well as the determination of the taxes and tariffs was originally a part of China's internal affairs, but already we can no longer make our own decisions).

Many foreign concessions have been left to self-government; this is the same as providing the wood for the handle of an axe (using the power of officials in order to extort profit and letting the traders and the people suffer; foreigners are buying land at official prices, they build railways and do not pay taxes, they even occupy land and they recruit the local population for their militia).

The Boxer Protocol, which was the result of the Boxer Rebellion, went even further, mandating the destruction of the Taku forts and the city wall of Tianjin, demanded land in order to establish a foreign concession, and allowed the erection of battery and a fort in order to station foreign troops for defence. The beautiful motherland was transformed into a gloomy scenery without people.

Now it is already necessary to inure our compatriots for future trials; they need to become determined and resolute heroes who do not hesitate to shatter the hardest rocks.

The hearts of those who are not the sons and daughters of China must be different; if we rely on foreign support, we need to be careful and to be wary of treacherous persons.

Historical Writing on the Decline of Poland

Russia, be it in the North, South, East, and West, it always tries to make those on the outside to adopt Russian citizenship.

I feel glad, however, that the Emperor determinedly announces a new era, so that the people can directly express their feelings.

If the Emperor is able to arrogate all the powers to himself and to control the great plans of the nation, then the current Emperor will not be inferior to the Meiji-Emperor of Peter the Great.

If one wants to compete with them in respect to their aspiration to attain supremacy, it is necessary to master all sorts of techniques and to train all kinds of talent.

Work out a constitution and establish awareness of civic obligations, allow the businessmen and craftsmen to obtain benefits in order to encourage trade and commerce.

Let knowledge and information circulate widely; let the upper and lower layers of society communicate with each other. To enlighten the people is the most important policy.

Open a parliament, so that the wishes of the higher authorities will become known to the lower strata and the higher strata of society know about the status of the lower. The established practices of Europe and America are certainly worth adopting.

Adopt even more consciously the Mencius well-established truism: Consider the people as important, the state as less important and the rulers as unimportant.

Those who have misgivings and do not dare to speak up should be touched by the awe-inspiring righteousness of the songs of the Polish people.

Send the message to our compatriots to spare no effort in strengthening themselves, let them rub their eyes and awake united to a new destiny.[42]

However, Zheng Guanying did not clarify which version of the translation he had read.

The revolutionary journal *China in the Twentieth Century* (*Ershi shiji zhi Zhina* 二十世紀之支那) which was aimed at Late-Qing Chinese students studying in Japan was founded by Song Jiaoren 宋教仁(1882–1913) and Huang Xing 黃興 (1874–1916) in Tokyo in 1905. In the journal's first issue of June 1905, there is an article entitled "First Remarks on China in the Twentieth Century" (*Ershi shiji zhi Zhina chu yan* 二十世紀之支那初言) in which the author, Wei Zhong 衛種 (literally: "Guarding the race"), also used Poland's fall as an example in order to inspire patriotic passion among the Chinese people:

Even though the disaster of the partition [of the nation] is visible directly, we need to be aware that partitioning our country will not necessarily happen in one step. Russia, Prussia and Poland partitioned Poland for the first time in 1772. In 1792, the second partition occurred. It took until 1795 for this partition to be completed. It is certainly not true to say that there had been no opportunity for national recovery. In the end, Poland perished because patriotism was not universal enough among the Polish people, with the result that they could not unite. For this reason, all the uprisings they attempted failed. I do not fear the partition by the strong powers but I only hope that the people of our country will be vitalized. And it is not only like this, even if the whole country

---

42 Zheng Guanying (1988). "Du 'Bolan shuaiwang zhanshi' shugan" vol. 2, pp. 1350–1351.

belongs to other people, if the patriotic feeling of our people becomes more developed, so that we can wait for it to be sufficient enough to become independent. America in the year 1779 actually constitutes a historical precedence. And, in the last year, there was the independence of 'Majianai'[43]. These are all our teachers; I can no longer bear the suffering from the fall of China and I am only looking forward to the people of our country becoming patriotic.[44]

Yang Dusheng 楊篤生 in 1903 published a book entitled *New Hunan* (*Xin Hunan* 新湖南), which he had written under the pseudonym *Hunan zhi Hunan ren* (湖南之湖南人, A Hunan Person from Hunan). The work includes six parts: "Introduction" 緒言, "The Nature of the Hunan People and their Responsibilities", "The Deadly Peril of the Current Situation", "The Mutual Criticism of the Old and New Parties in Hunan must Result in [Taking] one Road", "Destruction and Independence", and so on. The work also includes a comprehensive map of the Hunan Province. The first edition of *Xin Hunan* was published in Japan. It was re-printed twice between 1910–1913 and had a considerable influence on the intelligentsia at that time. In its third part, "The Deadly Peril of the Current Situation", the author mentioned Poland's decline and fall many times:

After Poland was partitioned by Russia and Germany, the Polish language was banned from being spoken and written. Polish landlords who owned property were expropriated by Russia and Germany. They were forced to give up all their property and savings. If things like that happen, when people are from the same continent and of the same race, how then could they possibly feel pity for our race?

What the Russians did, in respect of Poland, was to use Polish people in order to kill Polish people. The disaster which the Poles were suffering from became ever more serious and the power to resist the Russian people became weaker from day to day. Once they had encroached on Poland's sovereignty, they butchered and maimed several hundred determined people. They also removed several 10,000 persons to Siberia. Innocent children and weak women slipped under the wheels of the carriages and the horses' hooves. Later on they [the Russians] together with the Prussians divided Poland's land and appropriated it. How great must be the anger of the Polish people who are weeping blood! Up to today, they have not managed to have the name of their country returned. Because the Polish people are trembling with fear and are scared to bits of the Russians. The Russian efficiency lies in using the Polish in order to attack the Polish, and there is nothing else![45]

---

43 Note by the translators: The original text is: 而客歲又有馬加奈獨立之事. No state became independent in 1904, the only state to become independent in 1903 (if the article was written in 1904 already, but published in 1905 only) was Panama, which however according to the pronounciation most likely is not meant. It thus was impossible to determine what the author might have meant.

44 Wei Zhong (1905), "Ershi shiji zhi Zhina chuyan".

45 "Hunan zhi Hunnan ren" (1906), *Xin Hunan*, pp. 624,627–628.

Although the book criticised the royalist remarks made by reformers such as Kang Youwei and Liang Qichao and called for the people to rise up and overthrow the despotic rule of the Qing, many passages regarding the situation in Poland were quite close to Liang Qichao's writing.

In the early twentieth-century, among the cries that warned the people to be aware of Russia's greediness for Chinese territory and the foreign powers' intention of "partitioning China as if it were a melon, and cutting it as if it were a bean (*guafen dou pou* 瓜分豆剖*)* so that China could be spared from following the same old road of India and Poland to ruin,[46] "Poland" also appeared many times in the examination questions of various schools. For example, Shanghai's Qiuzhi College's 求志書院 examination topic in spring 1901 was "Examine the complete course of events of Russia's Annexation of Poland" (*Lun E bing bolan shimo kao* 論俄併波蘭始末考).[47]

The Imperial University (*Jingshi daxuetang* 京師大學堂) opened a crash-course class in 1902 in order to recruit students for its school for training officials (*shixueguan* 仕學館), and at its Normal College (*shi fan guan* 師範館),"Poland" was also used as part of its examination questions. A question in the first examination of September runs as follows: "The corruption of Poland's internal policy was not necessarily worse than that of Turkey. Poland, however, was partitioned while Turkey maintained its integrity. What are the reasons for this?"[48] According to *Shenbao*'s 申報 correspondent to Ningbo, in an examination called "Policy essays in the canonic scriptures, history and current affairs for *Shengyuan* of Ningbo prefecture", which was conducted by the Provincial Educational Officer Zhang Xiejun 張燮鈞 in November 1902, there was a question that went:

The hatred between Poland and Russia is stronger than the hatred between Yan and Qi; the crimes of the Turks, however, exceed those of the most heinous tyrants. For this reason, Russia, when it wanted to partition Poland, took a war of revenge against Turkey as their excuse. Their intention was to annex and their words of revenge were just an excuse. Now, in regard to this meaning, is there anything else you would relate to it? Please try to discuss this with a calm heart![49]

Examinations often play an important guiding role for youth, and therefore, "the miserable situation after the demise of Poland" and the impassioned

---

46 "Lü E pian" 慮俄篇 (Worrying about Russia), *Shenbao*, August 22, 1903, p. 1.

47 "Shanghai qiuzhi shuyun xinchou chuji keti" 上海求志書院辛丑春季課題 (Examination Questions of the Shanghai Qiuzhi College in Spring 1901), *Shenbao*, April 17, 1901, p. 1.

48 "Daxue shiti"大學試題 (University Examination Questions),*Shenbao*, November 7, 1902, p. 2.

49 "Yongshi san zhi" 甬試三志 [Three Records of Examinations in Ningbo], *Shenbao*, December 2, 1902, p. 2.

speech by "the revolutionary patriot Kościuszko" often appeared in all kinds of compositions written by students.

A Brief Conclusion

History writing on Poland first appeared in the *Zhifang waiji*, written by the Italian missionary Giulio Aleni in 1623. The Portuguese author, José Martinho Marques' book, *Waiguo dili beikao*, written in the mid-nineteenth century, also contained information about Poland's decline and fall, but these works, written by Westerners using the Chinese language and cited in Wei Yuan's book *Haiguo tuzhi*, did not betray any nationalist sentiment. The article "Bolan miewang ji" written by Liang Qichao and published in *Shiwu bao* on 29 August 1896, was the first among the Late-Qing history writings that took a perspective of depicting Poland as a "ruined country" and thus providing a historical lesson. Kang Youwei also wrote *Bolan fenmie ji* thereafter. The two reformist thinkers were the first that used the "the history of Poland's ruin" as an important ideological resource for the Reformists during the political mobilisation of the Hundred Days' Reform. Following the turmoil of the year 1900 and the signing of the Boxer Protocol, the perception that China would became a ruined country became even more grave. In the wave of "historical lessons from ruined countries", the Japanese scholar Shibue Tamotsu's book *Pōrando suibō senshi* entered China, with three translated versions, which appeared during 1901–1904. Inspired by a strong nationalist spirit, "Poland" once again became a political symbol of the nation's fall. This symbol was further used as a nationalist ideological resource in order to awaken group consciousness among the people to combat foreign imperialist invasions and to overthrow the corrupt Qing rule.

(Translated by Mei Chen and Iwo Amelung)

Bibliography

Aleni, Giulio (Ai Rulüe) 艾儒略, Xie Fang 謝方 (annot.)(2000), *Zhifang waiji jiaoshi* 職方外紀校釋 (Annotated *Records of the the Foreign Lands*), Beijing: Zhonghua shuju.
Chen Hua 陳華 et al. (annot.)(1998), *Hai guo tu zhi* 海國圖志, Changsha: Yuelu shushe.

HISTORICAL WRITING ON THE DECLINE OF POLAND 407

Feng Kexue 馮克學 (2012), "Bolan wangguo shi yu wan Qing minzuzhuyi shuxie" 波蘭亡國史與晚清民族主義書寫 (The History of the Decline of Poland and the Late Qing Nationalist Writing). MA thesis, Nanjing University, 2012.

Gu Xieguang 顧燮光 (2007), *Yishu jingyan lu* 譯書經眼錄 (Bibliography of Translated Books), vol. 1 in: Xiong Yuezhi (ed.), *Wan Qing xinxue shumu tiyao*, Shanghai: Shanghai shudian chubanshe.

Hunan zhi Hunnan ren 湖南之湖南人 (1960), *Xin Hunan* 新湖南 (New Hunan), in: Zhang Dan, Wang Renzhi (eds), *Xinhai geming shinian jian shijian xuanji*, Beijing: Sanlian, pp. 612–648.

Kang, Youwei 康有為 (2000), "Kang Nanhai zibian nianpu" 康南海自編年譜 (Self-compiled Chronical Autobiography of Kang Youwei), in: *Zhongguo shixue hui* (ed.), *Wuxu bianfa*, Shanghai: Shanghai renmin chubanshe, vol. 4, pp. 155–165.

— (2007), "Bolan fenmie ji" 波蘭分滅記 (Account of the Partition and Destruction of Poland), in: Jiang, Yihua and Zhang, Ronghua (eds.), *Kang Youwei quanji*, Beijing: Zhongguo renmin daxue chubanshe, vol. 4, pp. 395–423.

Karl, Rebecca (2002), *Staging the Word: Chinese Nationalism at the Turn of the Twentieth Century*, Durham NC: Duke University Press.

— (2008), *Shijie da wutai – shjiu, ershi shiji zhi jiao Zhongguo de minzuzhuyi* 世界大舞臺——十九、二十世紀之交中國的民族主義 (Staging the Word. Chinese Nationalism at the Turn of the Twentieth Century), Beijing: Sanlian shudian.

Kong Xiangji 孔祥吉 (1982), "Cong 'Bolan fenmie ji' kan Kang Youwei wuxu bianfa shiqi de zhengzhi zhuzhang" 從〈波蘭分滅記〉看康有為戊戌變法時期的政治主張 (Looking at Kang Youwei's Political Proposals during the Time of the 1898 Reform from the Perspective of the 'Records of the Division and Extinction of Poland'), *Renwen zazhi*, 5, pp. 80–84.

— (ed.) (2008), *Kang Youwei bianfa zouzhang ji kao* 康有為變法奏章輯考 (An Editorial Examination of the Reform Memorials of Kang Youwei), Beijing. Beiing tushuguan chubanshe.

Li Changsen 李長森 (2011), "Dui huayu xuexiao chuanjian you yoingxing de renwu ji jianjiao chuqi de iaozhang—Aomen ligong xueyuan yuyan ji fanyi gaodeng xuexiao bainianshi yanjiu zhi ba" 對華語學校創建有影響的人物及建校初期的校長——澳門理工學院語言暨翻譯高等學校百年史研究之八 (Persons who were Influential on the Founding of the Chinese School and School Presidents of the Founding Period of the School—Research into the One Hundred Years of History of the School of Languages and Translation of the Macao Polytechnic Institute) , *Journal of Macao Polytechnic Institute*, 14: 1, pp. 128–142

Li Dongmu 李冬木 (1998), "Shibue Tamotsu yi 'Zhina ren qizhi' yu Lu Xun – Lu Xun yu riben shu zhi yi" 澀江保譯〈支那人氣質〉與魯迅——魯迅與日本書之一 (Shibue Tamotsu's Translation of Chinese Characteristics and Lu Xun – Lu Xun and Japanese books No. 1), *Kansai gaidai daikaku yanjiu lunwenji*, 67, pp. 269–286.

Liang Qichao 梁啟超 (1897), "Bolan miewang ji" 波蘭滅亡記 (Records of the Extinction of Poland), *Shiwu bao*, No. 3, 29 August 1897.

Liu Yajun 劉雅軍 (2010), "Shuaiwang shiji yu wan Qing shehui biange" 衰亡史鑒'與晚晴社會變革 (Histories of Decline and Extinction and the Social Reforms during the Late Qing, *Shixue lilun yanjiu*, 4, pp. 59–68.

Lu Xun bowuguan 鲁迅博物馆 (comp.) (1996), *Lu Xun bowuguan zang Zhou Zuoren riji* 鲁迅博物館藏周作人日記 (Zhou Zuoren's Diary Stored at the Lu Xun Museum), Zhengzhou, Daxiang chubanshe.

Marques, José Martinho (Ma Jishi) 瑪吉士 (1849), "Xin shi dili beikao" 新釋地理備考 (New Explanations to the Reference Book of Geography), in: Pan Shicheng (comp.) *Hai shan xianguan congshu*, vol. 1.

"Minzu jingshen lun" (1960), 民族精神論 (On the National Spirit), in: Zhang Dan, Wang Renzhi (eds), *Xinhai geming shinian jian shijian xuanji*, Beijing: Sanlian, pp. 837–849 (originally *Jiangsu*, 7–8 [1904]).

Shenbao 申報, Shanghai 1872 ff.

Shibue Tamotsu 澀江保, Xue Gongxia 薛公俠 (trsl.) (1904), *Bolan shuaiwang shi* 波蘭衰亡史 (History of the Demise of Poland), Shanghai: Jingjin shuju.

Tan Zhiqiang 譚志強 (1994), "Aomen yu Zhongguo jindai guoji guanxi zhi zhi yinjin" 澳門與中國近代國際關係知識之引進 (Macau and the Introduction of Modern International Relations Knowledge to China), in: Wu, Zhiliang (ed.), *Dong Xifang wenhua jiaoliu*, Macao: Macao Foundation, 1994, p. 189–191.

Wang Xiaoqiu 王曉秋 (2003), *Jindai Zhongguo yu shijei – hudong yu bijiao* 近代中國與世界——互動與比較 (Modern China and the World: Interaction and Comparison), Bejing: Zijincheng chubanshe.

Wei Zhong 衛種 (1905), "Ershi shiji zhi Zhina chuyan" 二十世紀之支那初言 (Introductionary Remarks on [the Publication of] Twentieth Century China", *Ershi shiji zhi Zhina*, p. 1.

Yang Yuliang 楊玉良 (1982), "Wei kanxing de Kang Youwei liang bu zhuzuo—'Bolan fenmie mi', 'Lieguo zhengyo bijiao biao' jian jie" 未刊行的康有為兩部著作-〈波蘭分滅記〉、〈列國政要比較表〉簡介, (Two Works of Kang Youwei, which were not published—brief introduction to "Records of the Division and Extinction of Poland' and 'Comparative Table of the Important Politics of the Different Countries'"), *Gugong bowuyuan yuankan* , 1982: 4, pp. 62–67.

Yu Danchu 俞旦初 (1984), "Zhongguo jindai aiguozhuyi de 'wangguo shijian' chu kao" 中國近代愛國主義的"亡國史鑒 (Histories of National Ruin in Modern China's Patriotism), *Shijie lishi*, 1, pp. 23–31.

"Zhongguo miewang lun" (1901), 中國滅亡論 (On China's Demise), *Guomin bao* 2–4.

Zheng Guanying 鄭觀應 (1988), "Du 'Bolan shuaiwang zhanshi' shugan" 讀《波蘭衰亡戰史》書感 (Feelings when Reading *A History of the Wars of the Decline and Demise of Poland*), in: Xia Dongyuan (ed.), *Zheng Guanying ji*, Shanghai: Shanghai renmin chubanshe, vol. 2, pp. 1350–1351.

Zou Zhenhuan 鄒振環 (1990), "Wan Qing liu Ri xuesheng yu riwen xishu de hanyi huodong" 晚清留日學生與日文西書的漢譯活動 (Chinese Students Studying in Japan during the Late Qing and the Translation of Japanese Western books into Chinese), in: *Zhongguo jindai xiandai chubanshi xueshu taolunhui wenji*, Beijing: Zhongguo shuji chubanshe, pp. 93–105.

— (1996), "Qingmo wangguoshi bianyi re yu Liang Qichao de Chaoxian wangguoshi yanjiu" 清末亡國史編譯熱與梁啟超的朝獻亡國史研究 (Research on the Late-Qing 'Compilation and Translation Fever' of Histories of National Decline and Liang Qichao's History of the Decline of Korea), *Hanguo yanjiu luncong*, 2, pp. 325–355.

- (2011), *Wan Ming hanwen xixue jingidan: Bianyi, quanshi, liuchuan yu yingxiang* 晚明漢文西學經典：編譯、詮釋、流傳與影響 (The Chinese Western-learning Canon during the Late Ming: Translation and Editing, Annotations, Circulation and Influence), Shanghai: Fudan daxue chubanshe.

Selfish Faint Hearts, Ardent Fighters, and Gallant Heroines?—Characters in Plays about the Taiwan Republic

Mirjam Tröster

Spear in hand, determined, and proud—this is how a woman on horseback leads a troop of female warriors and male indigenous volunteers into battle against the Japanese army in Taiwan in 1895. Not only do they withstand heavy shelling by the Japanese, but they also appear to be immune to the enemy's attack. And, it seems, the only people wounded or killed happen to be Japanese soldiers.

This description refers to a colour woodblock print, which dates from around 1896.[1] Flags and inscriptions on this print reveal whom we are supposed to deal with: among the ornaments on one of the flags, we see a tiger, while an inscription identifies the woman on horseback as "Miss Liu Yuegu" (Liu Yuegu *xiaojie* 劉月姑小姐), signifying an alleged daughter of Liu Yongfu 劉永福 (1837–1917), commander of the anti-Japanese resistance forces in Southern Taiwan in 1895.[2] A further inscription states:

There was news this month that Miss Liu led a troop of women, killing innumerable Japanese. Soldiers of the raw savages [*shengfan* 生番; *i.e.*, members of the indigenous population of Taiwan] supported them. The Japanese army thereupon suffered a crushing defeat.

The print is but one of several illustrations that depict women fighting Japanese soldiers in the Taiwan War of 1895 (Yiwei Zhanzheng 乙未戰爭), *i.e.*, during the military resistance against the Japanese occupation of Taiwan in the wake of the First Sino-Japanese War (Jiawu Zhanzheng 甲午戰爭, 1894–1895).[3] The

---

1 "Liu xiaojie yu wonu duizhen tu" 劉小姐與倭奴對陣圖 (Miss Liu Confronts the Dwarf-Slaves [*i.e.*, the Japanese] in Battle), original in the *Dubosc collection*, British Museum, http://www.britishmuseum.org/research/collection_online/collection_object_details/collecti on_image_gallery.aspx?assetId=248338001&objectId=234195&partId=1 (last accessed 8 October 2018); see, also, the reprint in Lust (1996), *Chinese Popular Prints*, illustration no. 19.

2 Cf. also, Lust (1996), *Chinese Popular Prints*, p. 230.

3 Cf. for instance, Davidson (1903), *The Island of Formosa Past and Present*, p. 349 and insert between pp. 348 and 349. For an overview, see Wei Chi (2011), "Yiwei Taiwan kang-Ri". As Yin Hwang shows, the print belongs to the genre of "victory pictures" (*desheng tu* 得勝圖) of the nineteenth century, which show (imagined) Qing 清 victories in war; Hwang (2014), *Victory Pictures*; for a short discussion of the print, see ibid., p. 176. For conceiving of the armed

above-mentioned print's fanciful re-imagination of history resonates with a range of topics that this chapter examines: it tells a *story of the resistance efforts* against Japan (comprising the *Taiwan Republic* —symbolised by the tiger on the flag—and a *possibly victorious outcome of the war*). What is more, it visualises (partly fictitious) *protagonists* of this particular historical situation, who *struggle to "save the country"* (*jiuguo* 救國).

Moving from print culture to the theatre stage and from the late nineteenth into the first half of the twentieth century, this chapter focuses on two plays of Republican China (Zhonghua Minguo 中華民國) that deal with the Taiwan Republic (Taiwan Minzhuguo 臺灣民主國) including the military resistance efforts against the Japanese occupation of Taiwan in 1895. It compares *Qiu Shuyuan Destroys his Family to Save the Nation*, aka *The Regret of Taiwan* (*Qiu Shuyuan huijia jiuguo, youming Santai yihen* 邱菽園毀家救國，又名三臺遺恨， 1910s, author unknown; *Qiu Shuyuan* below)[4] to the war drama *Taiwan* 臺灣 (Taiwan, 1942) by Xu Jiarui 徐嘉瑞 (1895–1977) in order to extricate the different models to save the country that the two plays propose. With the performance history of the first play unclear and only scarce extant traces relating to the performance of the latter, I will base my analysis upon the written texts, with a brief but important detour to the performance of *Taiwan* in the latter part of the chapter.

I. Setting the Scene

In 1895, both civilian and military efforts were made to prevent the loss of Taiwan to Japan. For those interested in the exploration of different ways to deal with the weakness of a country, the Taiwan Republic (including the Taiwan War) thus constitutes a temporally circumscribed "object" of investigation that encompasses multiple aspects. Like a burning-glass, it brings the strategies to counter the weakness of the country, the actors involved in these efforts, and the possible challenges to focus. What is more, divergent narratives about the Taiwan Republic and the main agents involved in anti-Japanese resistance abound, so that the brief period lends itself even more easily to imaginative retellings. Accordingly, within the framework of broader discourses of weakness

---

resistance against the occupation of Taiwan in the wake of the Treaty of Shimonoseki (Maguan Tiaoyue 馬關條約, 1895) as a separate war, see Lamley (1970), "The 1895 Taiwan War of Resistance" and Alsford (2018), *Transitions to Modernity in Taiwan*, pp. 2–3.

4 This translation of the scenario's title is largely based on the translation proposed by Siyuan Liu in Liu (2013), *Performing Hybridity*, p. 105. *Santai* 三臺 also vaguely alludes to the imperial administration; cf. Hucker (1985), *A Dictionary of Official Titles*, p. 403.

in late Qing 清 and Republican China, narratives about the loss of Taiwan emerged. From the mid-nineteenth century—and reinforced after the loss of the First Sino-Japanese War—apprehensions about the possibility of the country perishing pervaded the discourses of the élite in China. Various causes for the country's weakness were identified and suggestions for possible remedies flourished as this book amply illustrates. Some of these suggestions focussed more on technological and military aspects (as in the case of the self-strengthening movement (*yangwu yundong* 洋務運動) of the second half of the nineteenth century), while others called for a transformation of the political system by means of either reform or revolution. Still others called for an even more fundamental change in the mind-set of the people. Ideas about the best way to educate the people thus played a prominent role. In his well-known essay "On Theatre" (*Lun xiqu* 論戲曲) published in 1904, Chen Duxiu 陳獨秀 (1879–1942) emphasised the power of theatre as a tool of enlightenment at a time in which the country was in severe crisis. In contrast to the establishment of schools and newspapers and to the writing of fiction, the staging of theatre plays could, according to Chen, reach everyone in society:

I think we only [have to] reform theatre, perform more new plays which hint at current affairs and enlighten the habits [in society]. People of all ranks of society can be moved when they watch [a theatre performance]. Even the deaf can see it, [even] the blind can hear it. Is this not the most convenient way to enlighten the habits [in society]?[5]

Theatre as an art form appeals to all senses and is apt to arouse emotions. Granted, if one chooses the appropriate subject matter such as current affairs, it becomes an ideal medium to educate and enlighten the people.

According to many writings of the late nineteenth century onwards, one group that was in particular need of education was that of Chinese women. In many essays or fictional works of the late Qing and Republican China (especially by male writers), women epitomised the weak (*ruozhe* 弱者)[6]—symbolising the "'oppressed'",[7] the most unenlightened, or both.[8] The weakness of women, in this reasoning, was symptomatic of the weakness of the country.[9] Having said this, an analysis of drama that deals with attempts to save

---

5 San'ai (1904), "Lun xiqu", p. 6. For a translation of the text, see, also, Chen Duxiu (2002), "On Theatre".

6 For a study on how women writers engaged with this trope and on its empowering function, see Yan (2006), *Chinese Women Writers*. See, also, Dooling (2005), *Women's Literary Feminism* for related tropes and alternative voices in the women's literature of the first half of the twentieth century.

7 Dooling (2005), *Women's Literary Feminism*, p. 25.

8 Cf. Yan (2006), *Chinese Women Writers*, p. 15.

9 Hershatter (2007), *Women in China's Long Twentieth Century*, pp. 79–80; He (2008), "Women and the Search for Modernity", p. 47; Croissant et al. (2008), "Introduction", p. 1.

the country from perishing can, therefore, not overlook the role that these plays accord to women.

The two plays discussed below insert female characters into a broader narrative of 'saving the country'. More generally, *Qiu Shuyuan* and *Taiwan* propose two different models to do so. In this chapter, I will show that, although both plays share a *basic narrative of active resistance* to counter the imminent loss of the country caused by both external and internal enemies, they not only highlight different *ways to achieve this goal*, but also pin their hope on different *individuals or groups of people* to whom they assign the *capability of saving the country*. In other words, the two plays provide different answers to the question concerning who can (best) save the country and by which means. Both the actors and the approaches to overcoming weakness are thus intimately interconnected in these plays. The solutions that they offer boil down to the following: while *Qiu Shuyuan* ultimately celebrates a double tracked approach that is based upon the cooperation and joint action of different actors, *Taiwan* essentially narrows these options for resistance down to military action led by a resolute individual hero. Similarly, we can observe a transformation from a comparatively jaunty narrative ending on a note of optimism in the play of the 1910s to a 1940s version that oozes with a sense of urgency. Not surprisingly for theatre plays, and mirroring a strong focus on historical agents in histories of 1895, dramatic characters epitomise the different approaches of the two texts discussed in this chapter. For this reason, the analysis of the two plays lays particular emphasis on their use of dramatic characters and the degree of agency that the plays allot to specific characters, specifically their ability to contribute to saving the country.

Based upon Jens Eder's conceptualisation of literary characters, I understand these as complex constructs made up of four interconnected aspects. They are "fictional beings" populating a fictional world, "artefacts" constituted by representational devices, "symbols" referring to *topoi* and themes beyond the literal, and "symptoms" for processes and decisions that link production and reception.[10] In the analysis below, I combine this conceptualisation of characters with an understanding of agency as the "capability of the individual to 'make a difference' to a pre-existing state of affairs or course of events",[11] to use Anthony Giddens' words. Conceiving of characters as fictional beings, we treat them as "quasi-human" inhabitants of a fictional world, who manifest

---

10 Eder (2010), "Understanding Characters". As for the aspect of characters as symptoms, one might, for instance, ask why a specific character might have been inserted into the play and what this tells us about society at the time of production/reception.

11 Giddens (1984), *The Constitution of Society*, p. 14. Anthony Giddens conceives of agency and structure as being interdependent; see, also, Emirbayer and Mische (1998), "What is Agency?", for a conceptualisation that stresses the temporal dimension of agency.

different degrees of the capability of acting in that world. We might thus ask the following questions, among others: Does a character make a change to the state of affairs in the fictional world? Are there any barriers that he or she encounters? Do other characters bar him or her from speaking or moving about freely, or ridicule him or her, for example? If we turn to characters as artefacts, we look into how the (degree of) agency of a character is created in the play—in other words, into its stylistic or dramaturgical function. We might, for instance, focus on the impact of a character's actions for the development of the plot, which is often (but not necessarily) dependent on the space allotted to a character in the text. We might also be interested in the degree to which genre conventions, intertextual relations, or the use of comic devices pre-determine and hence steer or control a character's capability of acting. Concerning the third aspect of characters as symbols, we can conceive of the fictional world that evolves from a play as a model for society—in our case, for a society that is faced with the possible loss of the country. A character's capability of acting in the fictional world then symbolises the agency of a person or social group in the extra-fictional world in this specific model of society. If the model of the world that evolves when a reader or spectator reads or watches the play calls into question prevalent ideas of agency or agents in society, it may even open space for enlarging the reader's or the audience's capability of acting in society.

Zooming in on characters as symbols and symptoms also profits from looking into character constellations[12] because dissecting character constellations is

closely connected to questions of ideology, politics, and understanding texts as indicators of collective dispositions, problems, wishes and fears in a certain time and culture.[13]

In short, a closer look into the characters of the two plays helps us to uncover the anxieties, priorities, and hopes concerning the feasibility of saving the country that circulated in the 1910s and the early 1940s, respectively.

Before turning to the plays and their interrelation with society, however, the following section provides an overview of the historical events in Taiwan in 1895. It specifically highlights the role of two historical figures which the two plays transform into fictional characters, namely Tang Jingsong 唐景崧 (1841–1903) and Liu Yongfu. Having summarised the historical events, I will then turn to an analysis of characters in the two plays. By delving deeper into the two

---

12 Character constellation is an "abstraction" that "puts all the characters of a fictional world in relation to each other"; Eder et al. (2010), "Characters in Fictional Worlds: An Introduction", p. 26.

13 Ibid., p. 27.

II. The Taiwan Republic and the Taiwan War of 1895

In a nutshell, one of the (albeit short-lived) attempts to prevent Japanese occupation of Taiwan was the establishment of the Taiwan Republic. When Qing China lost the First Sino-Japanese War, the cession of Taiwan and the Penghu Islands (Penghu Qundao 澎湖群島) to Japan formed part of the stipulations laid down in the Treaty of Shimonoseki (Maguan Tiaoyue 馬關條約, signed on 17 April 1895). As this treaty states, the Qing had to transfer the province of Taiwan to Japan within two months.[14] With no support to be expected from the Qing court, the gentry in Taiwan counted on the Western powers:[15] planning to establish a self-ruled (*zizhu* 自主) republic (*minzhu zhi guo* 民主之國),[16] they hoped to attract international assistance upon the basis of international law, because, as self-ruled entity, so the reasoning went, the Taiwan Republic could not be ceded by another country—in this case, Qing China—against its will.[17] The gentry finally succeeded in convincing the originally hesitant governor Tang Jingsong, who at first had "refused their request to serve as president",[18] to "throw in his lot with [their] plan".[19] Tang ignored the order of the court to return to the mainland and finally consented to serve as president of the Taiwan Republic, which was inaugurated on 25 May 1895.[20] The gentry quickly set up a parliament and presented state symbols—such as the famous yellow tiger flag (*huanghu qi* 黃虎旗) upon which the representation of the flag in the print mentioned in the introduction is based.[21] The Taiwan Republic also used a reign

---

14 Morris (2002), "The Taiwan Republic", p. 9. Cf. Lamley (1968), "The 1895 Taiwan Republic", for an overview of the events.

15 Cf. e.g., Wang (2013), "Modernity", pp. 166–169. For the role that the diplomat Chen Jitong 陳季同 (1851–1907) played see Lamley (1968), "The 1895 Taiwan Republic".

16 For the use of *minzhu*, *minzhuguo*, and *zizhu* in the context of the Taiwan Republic, cf. Lamley (1968), "The 1895 Taiwan Republic", pp. 750–751; Wang, "Modernity", p. 168, n26.

17 Cf. Lamley (1968), "The 1895 Taiwan Republic", pp. 741, 743, 744; Morris (2002), "The Taiwan Republic", pp. 4, 13; Gordon (2007), *Confrontation over Taiwan*, p. 190; Wang (2013), "Modernity", pp. 166–168, 174.

18 Morris (2002), "The Taiwan Republic", p. 13.

19 Ibid., p. 11. Divergent evaluations of Tang Jingsong's role coexist; cf. e.g., Kerr (1974), *Formosa*, p. 14; Morris (2002), "The Taiwan Republic", p. 11; Gordon (2007), *Confrontation over Taiwan*, p. 189–194.

20 Morris (2002), "The Taiwan Republic", p. 14.

21 Lamley (1968), "The 1895 Taiwan Republic", p. 754; Morris (2002), "The Taiwan Republic", p. 15.

SELFISH FAINT HEARTS, ARDENT FIGHTERS, AND GALLANT HEROINES? 417

name, though, which was "Eternal Qing" (Yongqing 永清), thus demonstrating allegiance to the Qing dynasty. This reign name, as well as some of Tang Jing-song's correspondence with the court, bespoke a certain ambivalence on the part of at least some of the protagonists involved in the Taiwan Republic.[22] Hence, "the 1895 Republic referenced both the modern nation-state and the Qing empire, indicating that both ideas had a measure of legitimacy for the Republic's founders".[23]

However, apart from the élite, most residents of Taipei 臺北 (Taibei) were hardly enthusiastic about the republic.[24] Part of the reasons for their lack of support was the feeling that they had been betrayed by Qing officials: a great number of them had left Taiwan, and rumours about their embezzling money had started to spread early on.[25] Moreover, skirmishes among different Qing troops sent to Taiwan had broken out. On several occasions, this led to violence and the killing of residents, which Tang did not have the power to prevent.[26] When the Japanese army landed in North-Eastern Taiwan and made a quick advance on Taipei,[27] the situation in the city got increasingly out of hand.[28] In this situation, on 5 June 1895, the president secretly escaped to the mainland.[29] The Northern period of the Taiwan Republic thus ended,[30] and the gentry soon decided to open the city gates to the Japanese army. The local population welcomed both the army and, soon after, Kabayama Sukenori 樺山資紀 (1837–1922), the first Japanese governor-general of Taiwan.[31]

Outside Taipei, however, military resistance against Japanese occupation continued.[32] In central Taiwan, volunteer forces fought the Japanese army in a guerrilla war. One of their prominent leaders was Qiu Fengjia 丘逢甲 (1864–

---

22 Lamley (1968), "The 1895 Taiwan Republic", pp. 752–753; Morris (2002), "The Taiwan Republic", p. 16; Wang (2013), "Modernity", pp. 168–169.

23 Harrison (2016), *Legitimacy, Meaning and Knowledge*, p. 73. For a concise discussion of this ambivalence and the evaluation on the part of contemporaries as well as historians that this position yielded, see Wang (2013), "Modernity", pp. 169–179.

24 Cf. the eye-witness account of James W. Davidson (1872–1933); Davidson (1903), *The Island of Formosa Past and Present*, pp. 281–282.

25 Morris (2002), "The Taiwan Republic", pp. 9–11, 15; Gordon (2007), *Confrontation over Taiwan*, pp. 190–191.

26 Morris (2002), "The Taiwan Republic", pp. 9, 12.

27 Gordon (2007), *Confrontation over Taiwan*, p. 201.

28 See Morris (2002), "The Taiwan Republic", pp. 16–17.

29 Ibid., p. 17.

30 Cf. Alsford (2018), *Transitions to Modernity*, who uses the terms "Northern" and "Southern period" to subdivide the Taiwan Republic into the period in which Tang Jingsong was president and the time of continued resistance until the fall of Tainan.

31 Morris (2002), "The Taiwan Republic", pp. 17–18.

32 Cf. Lamley (1970), "The 1895 War of Taiwan Resistance" for the period of military resistance. Lamley highlights the rivalry between the three most prominent resistance leaders, Tang Jingsong, Qiu Fengjia, and Liu Yongfu; cf. also, Lamley (1968), "The 1895 Taiwan Republic".

1912), a Hakka (*kejia* 客家) member of the local gentry involved in the founding of the Taiwan Republic, who left for the mainland in late July.[33] Liu Yongfu, the leader of the Black Flag Army (Heiqi jun 黑旗軍), who was famous for his success in battles of the Sino-French War (Zhong-Fa zhanzheng 中法戰爭, 1884–1885), was based in Southern Taiwan, where he "promised to make a stand".[34] Nominal commander-in-chief of the Taiwan Republic,[35] Liu now organised the Southern period of the republic in Tainan,[36] although he did not accept the seals of presidency.[37] As Harry J. Lamley argues, this "republic" was much more based upon loyalty to Liu than on democratic principles.[38] When the Japanese army was about to take the upper hand in early October 1895, "Black Flag General Liu deserted his 'republic' and his troops, disguised himself as an old woman, and sailed off to Amoy across the Strait, taking the treasury with him as his own reward".[39] Tainan fell on 21 October 1895 with Kabayama declaring Taiwan pacified. The Taiwan War had thus ended, although guerrilla fighting continued into the early twentieth century.[40]

Stories about the Taiwan Republic—including the war—circulated in China early on. In his *Gleanings of Chit-chat* (*Huizhu shiyi* 揮麈拾遺), published in 1901, the Singaporian journalist, poet, and reformer Qiu Shuyuan 邱菽園 (Khoo Seok Wan, *i.e.*, Qiu Weixuan 丘煒萲, 1874–1941) [41] addresses his *literati* friend Qiu Fengjia. He is curious about the anti-Japanese resistance in Taiwan:

You once said that I [should] take all records of the anti-Japanese resistance in Taiwan that [have been published] in new books printed by all those lead-type presses in Shanghai as [pure] hearsay [written by] outsiders; what is worse, matters relating to the two commanders Tang [Jingsong] and [Liu] Yongfu are arbitrarily [depicted in such a way that they are] detested and loved, flattered and vilified, only confusing what was seen and heard.[42]

---

33 Alsford (2018), *Transitions to Modernity*, p. 191. For biographical information on Qiu see Momose (1943): "Ch'iu Fêng-chia". For Qiu and his poetry engaging with the "loss" of Taiwan see Tsai (2017): *A Passage to China*, pp. 54–112.

34 Kerr (1974), *Formosa*, p. 15.

35 Lamley (1968), "The 1895 Taiwan Republic", p. 752.

36 Kerr (1974), *Formosa*, p. 15; Alsford (2018), *Transitions to Modernity*.

37 Lamley (1968), "The 1895 Taiwan Republic", p. 755.

38 Ibid., pp. 755–756. According to Leonard H.D. Gordon, Liu established a parliament (*yiyuan* 議院); Gordon (2007), *Confrontation over Taiwan*, p. 202.

39 Kerr (1974), *Formosa*, p. 15. According to Niki J.P. Alsford, Liu disguised as a labourer, while Tang Jingsong escaped in the disguise of a woman; Alsford (2018), *Transitions to Modernity*, p. 182.

40 Lamley (1970), "The 1895 Taiwan War of Resistance", p. 55; Gordon (2007), *Confrontation over Taiwan*, p. 203.

41 For a short biography, see Lee (2012), "Khoo Seok Wan".

42 Qiu Shuyuan (1958), "Huizhu shiyi", pp. 547–548.

Qiu Fengjia's assessment does not, of course, bar Qiu Shuyuan from adding a further narrative about the events, concentrating on his friend's experiences in Taiwan. Several authors were likewise quick to take up the subject matter. Even a short glimpse into an anthology of literary works about the First Sino-Japanese War published in 1958 by the writer A Ying 阿英 (1900–1977) indicates a vivid interest in what had happened in Taiwan on the part of writers in the late Qing period.[43] Most of the writings collected in the anthology are poems. Fiction writing about the Taiwan War began when the war was still being fought.[44] These texts, in general, perceive of resistance against Japan as part and parcel of the First Sino-Japanese War. Moreover, Liu Yongfu takes centre-stage in many of the writings. To mention but one example: the last 12 of the 33 chapters of Hong Xingquan's 洪興全 (dates unknown) *Tale of the Dwarfs* [*i.e.*, Japanese] (*Shuo wo zhuan* 說倭傳, 1900), also known as *The Romance of China's Big War in the East* (*Zhongdong dazhan yanyi* 中東大戰演義) deal with Liu's battles in Taiwan and his return to China.[45] An early, albeit slightly veiled, response to the cession of Taiwan on the theatre stage was Wang Xiaonong's 汪笑儂 (1858–1918) *Weeping at the Ancestral Shrine* (*Ku zumiao* 哭祖廟, 1895). Adapting a passage from *The Romance of the Three Kingdoms* (*Sanguo yanyi* 三國演義, fourteenth century), a character in this Beijing opera (*jingju* 京劇) laments the fact that land (*jiangshan* 江山) had been presented to others without getting anything in return (*bai song* 白送).[46]

In the 1910s and early 1940s, respectively, two theatre plays also turned to the events, adding yet more versions to the rumours mentioned by Qiu Shuyuan above. These are *Qiu Shuyuan* (1910s) and *Taiwan* (1940s). Both plays were created in times fraught with tension between China and Japan, in other words, in times in which the need felt to strengthen China was linked to resisting Japan, albeit to a different extent. Arguably, this is one of the reasons why both plays refrain from staging the final defeat of the military forces on Taiwan.[47] Since

---

43 In his introduction, A Ying emphasises that only three people active in the war were "praised exuberantly" by the poets of the time. Among these, two had fought in the Taiwan War, namely Jian Dashi 簡大狮 (1870–1999) and, especially, Liu Yongfu; the third was Zuo Baogui 左寶貴 (1837–1894); A Ying (ed.) (1958), *Jiawu Zhong-Ri Zhanzheng wenxue ji*, p. 12.

44 See, for instance, the novels Tales of Heroines in Taiwan (*Taiwan jinguo yingxiong zhuan* 臺灣巾幗英雄傳, 1895) and *True Account of the War in Taiwan* (*Taizhan shiji* 臺戰實記, 1895). The first novel tells the story of a woman who, after her husband's death, organises an army and co-operates with a daughter of "Liu Yongfu" to fight the Japanese army in Taiwan; Qian Zhonglian et al. (eds.) (2000), *Zhongguo wenxue da cidian*, p. 1584; cf. also, Hanan (2005), *Chinese Fiction of the Nineteenth and Early Twentieth Centuries*, Chapter 1, note 23.

45 Hong Xingquan (2012), *Shuo wo zhuan*.

46 Wang Xiaonong (1957), p. 140. See, also, Goldstein (2007), *Drama Kings*, p. 95.

47 This is not without precedence: As Davidson vividly describes, "improbable" (p. 349) accounts and pictorial representations of defeating or at least the putting to rout of the Japa-

both plays re-imagine the history of resistance in Taiwan, the narrated time of the two plays overlaps, although they give different importance to the two periods of the Taiwan Republic. Furthermore, both plays introduce fictional characters that are not related to the historical events, some of whom are women. If we remember the intimate connection between women and the state of the country that many texts written in the first half of the twentieth century create, this does not come as a surprise. What makes a comparison even more rewarding is that the narratives of resistance that the two plays weave, as well as the devices upon which they draw, differ in many respects. I will begin the discussion of the plays in chronological order.

III. *Qiu Shuyuan Destroys his Family to Save the Nation*

The first of the two plays to be discussed is *Qiu Shuyuan Destroys his Family to Save the Nation*. We know of *Qiu Shuyuan* because a scenario (*mubiao* 幕表) still exists, that is to say an outline presenting the place, the characters, the entrances and exits, and the plot, as well as the main elements of the dialogue.[48] Although the concrete year(s) of the play's performance could so far not be ascertained, theatre scholars concurrently date *Qiu Shuyuan* to some time around 1911 to 1917.[49] The scenario summarises nine acts, in the first three of which members of the Taiwan gentry (*shenshi* 紳士) in collaboration with "Liu Yongfu"[50] coax

---

nese army on Taiwan circulated during the war; Davidson (1903), *The Island of Formosa Past and Present*, p. 348–349. Another example can be found in the print described in the introduction.

48 In 1989, Wang Weimin published the scenario based upon a handwritten copy dating from 1953 and stored in the collection *Xinjiu jugao* 新舊劇稿 (Manuscripts of old and new plays) at the Department of Drama at the Central Academy of Drama in Beijing (Zhongyang Xiju Xueyuan Xiju Wenxue Xi 中央戲劇學院戲劇文學系); Wang Weimin (1989), *Zhongguo zaoqi huaju xuan*, pp. 697–700, see, also, ibid., p. 12. Unfortunately, this copy could not be located at the Central Academy of Drama in summer 2016. Note that according to Fu Xiaohang and Zhang Xiulian (1994), *Zhongguo jindai xiqu lunzhu zongmu*, pp. 693, 712, an undated collection of the same name published by Li Tianran 李天然 (dates unknown) exists. Li Tianran most likely refers to the theatre actor of the same name performing in new drama in the 1910s and early 1920s, and the manuscript might be based upon this collection.

49 Wang Weimin, for instance, only included scripts published or performed before 1918 into his anthology. He mentions the scenario in the contexts of plays performed "around [the time of] the Xinhai Revolution"; Wang Weimin, *Zhongguo zaoqi huaju xuan*, pp. 9, 10. Dong Jian (2003), *Zhongguo xiandai xiju zongmu tiyao*, users' guide and pp. 128–129 lists the play under 1918, the year under which he groups all the new dramas with unascertained performance/publication dates.

50 In the remainder of the chapter (except for direct quotations), I use inverted commas for names of dramatic characters to more easily differentiate between characters and historical figures.

"Tang Jingsong" into taking office as president of the independent republic. In the following five acts, the Taiwanese gentry and army fight to protect the island's independence. An agent planted by the Japanese army tries to convince "Tang" either to renounce independence or to leave Taiwan, which "Tang" finally does. When one of the characters, "Qiu Shuyuan", tries to stab the traitor, he is arrested by the Japanese and can only be rescued from captivity by cunning. Making use of ploys and military ambush tactics, the Taiwanese/Chinese finally obtain victory over the Japanese. When the play ends, all traitors have either been killed or arrested, and the Japanese commanders are on the run, while the sounds of "Long live Taiwan!" resound on stage.

The use of scenarios instead of scripts was quite common in performances of the so-called "new drama" (*xinju* 新劇). New drama evolved from "Western" speech-based theatre, Chinese *xiqu* 戲曲 (classical music theatre), and the Japanese "new school drama" (*shinpa* 新派) in the 1900s and 1910s.[51] Its centre being located in Shanghai, new drama flourished in the mid-1910s, but was still performed in the second half of the 1910s and later.[52] An additional name, "civilised theatre" (*wenmingxi* 文明戲),[53] was

heaped on xinju [in the late 1910s] largely to mock its commercialism and theatrical hybridity, which was typified by scripts mixed with scenarios and improvisation, speech mixed with singing, female impersonation mixed with performance by actresses, and so on.[54]

In the beginning, at least, the theatrical form was deeply enmeshed in an agenda of social and political change. Although the form was criticised for allegedly having substituted the political impulse of its early years with shallow entertainment and melodrama by the mid-1910s, Siyuan Liu convincingly deconstructs this dichotomy, stating new drama's "agitational power" and its

---

51 See Liu (2013), *Performing Hybridity*, p. 1. *Shinpa* directly influenced some of "new drama's" pioneers when they were studying in Japan in the early twentieth century.

52 For the continued life of *wenmingxi*, see Liu (2013), *Performing Hybridity*, pp. 95–96. Zhao Ji dates the end of *wenmingxi* in Shanghai to 1929; Zhao Ji (2011), *Huaju yu Shanghai shimin shehui*, pp. 27, 228.

53 See, e.g., Zhao Ji (2011), *Huaju yu Shanghai shimin shehui*, pp. 22, 23. I use the terms interchangeably. See Wang Fengxia (2008), "Zuowei 'gongming' de wenmingxi: wenmingxi de leixing he xingtai" for *wenmingxi* as an umbrella term.

54 Liu, *Performing Hybridity*, p. 8. Actor Xu Banmei 徐半梅 (= Xu Zhuodai, 1880–1958), with a twinkle in his eyes, alludes to the proliferation of the term *wenming* 文明 (civilised) at the time when he calls *wenmingxi* a "nickname" (*chuohao* 綽號) given to new drama mainly by illiterate prostitutes and concubines, who were not able to read performance advertisements and simply conjectured that since "a marriage without wind and percussion instruments is called civilised marriage, so theatre without wind and percussion instruments must be called civilised theatre"; Xu Banmei (1957), *Huaju chuangshiqi huiyilu*, p. 124; cf. also, Eberstein (1983), *Das Chinesische Theater im 20. Jahrhundert*, p. 28, note 17.

"search for commercial success" were interwoven.[55] In the mid-1910s, many *wenmingxi* companies responded to political events such as Japan's *21 Demands* (Ershiyi Tiao 二十一條, 1915) and Yuan Shikai's 袁世凱 (1859–1916) self-proclamation as emperor in late 1915.[56] *Wenmingxi* productions about "lost countries" (*wangguo* 亡國) occupy an important position among the patriotic plays that were produced in this context. As Liu describes,[57] "[m]any of these plays staged lost nations [*sic*] by focusing on internal corruption, foreign brutality, patriotic heroism, and the misery of the ordinary citizen under colonialization".[58] Judging from its subject matter, *Qiu Shuyuan* fits well into this "return" of patriotic plays,[59] which used drama to alert the audience to the problems that placed the country in danger.

This choice of subject matter resonates with a broad interest in so-called "lost countries" in late Qing and early Republican China. Rebecca Karl shows that the use of the topos of *wangguo* at that time connected China to the global history of imperialism.[60] Not only did the idea of the perishing of a country flourish in "histories about lost countries" (*wangguo shi* 亡國史), but music theatre (or, opera)—later followed by new drama—also joined in, with the major aim of using entertainment for enlightenment and mobilisation.[61] The "most celebrated and written about 'new-style' opera of the first decade of the twentieth century",[62] *Guazhong lanyin* 瓜種蘭因 (1904),[63] stages the fictitious partition of Poland by Turkey. While, as Karl suggests, the opera turns the stage into a microcosm of the world, it

helps indicate how China's late Qing crisis-ridden situation came to be linked to a geographically far-off yet conceptually proximate imaginary of others perceived to be engaged in a shared contemporary moment of historical crisis and change.[64]

If we take this opera as paradigmatic example, the following plot elements form part of a "*wangguo* play": invasion of a country by an external enemy, betrayal and internal disunity, and ineffectual politicians, most prominently the head of state.[65] Comparing this list with the plot synopsis of *Qiu Shuyuan* presented

---

55 Liu (2013), *Performing Hybridity*, 59.

56 Ibid., 83–94, esp. p. 83.

57 Ibid., p. 85.

58 Ibid.

59 Liu (2013), *Performing Hybridity*, p. 87.

60 Karl (2002), *Staging the World*.

61 Cf. ibid., p. 32.

62 Ibid., p. 46.

63 The title can be translated as "Planting the Melon Seed, Cause of the Orchid", translation based upon Karl (2002), *Staging the World*, p. 29; see ibid., pp. 29–30 for further explanation.

64 Ibid., p. 29.

65 Cf. ibid., p. 30.

SELFISH FAINT HEARTS, ARDENT FIGHTERS, AND GALLANT HEROINES?   423

above, there is reason to regard the play as a late example of this subgenre.[66] One main difference comes to mind, though: the story of the *wenmingxi* play is located in Taiwan and not in a "geographically far-off" place. As mentioned above, earlier Chinese fictional renderings of anti-Japanese resistance in Taiwan in 1895 in general imagined these events as part of the First Sino-Japanese War—that is, as part of a war whose outcome epitomised the weakness of *China*, not that of another country. In the analysis below, it will thus be illuminating to see whether this entails any significant modifications to the above-mentioned pattern.

To understand better the significance of *Qiu Shuyuan* in this context, I will, as a final step before delving into the play, add a few comments on how Taiwan as a "lost country" has fared in other texts about this subject matter. Three general answers to this question can be identified. First, Taiwan is occasionally mentioned in conjunction with other "lost countries" such as Poland, Korea, and Vietnam,[67] turning Taiwan into simply a further addition to the list and stripping it of its explicit links to China that exceed those of the other countries. Secondly, if anthologies collecting histories of "lost countries" add a specific chapter on Taiwan at all, they do not necessarily focus on the year 1895, but define the "loss" or "perishing" of Taiwan in different terms. This is, for instance, the case with Yang Nancun's 楊南邨 (dates unknown) *Shijie wangguo baishi* 世界亡國稗史 (*Unofficial History of the Lost Countries in the World*), published in 1917. An entry called "Santai yihen lu 三臺遺恨錄" (Record of the Regret of Taiwan) concludes the anthology.[68] It does not deal with 1895, however, but with the more recent anti-Japanese activities of Luo Fuxing 羅福星 (Ra Fukusei, 1886–1914) in Taiwan in 1913, in this way (re-) establishing relations between Taiwan and China upon a new basis, namely, revolution.[69]. Thirdly, the events of 1895 form part of the history of the perishing of Taiwan told by the text, but are put into broader perspective. Liu Yazi 柳亞子(= Yalu 亞盧, 1887–1958) published an article entitled "Three Hundred Years of the History of Taiwan" (*Taiwan sanbai nian shi* 臺灣三百年史) in *Jiangsu* 江蘇 in 1903/1904.[70] This article can be interpreted as a wake-up call for his country-

---

66 Cf. also, Liu (2013), *Staging Hybridity*, p. 105, where Siyuan Liu clearly connects the play to the "tradition of lost nation history and popular resistance".

67 Cf. e.g., an essay published in 1903 by Tang Tiaoding 湯調鼎 (Erhe 爾和, 1878–1940), cited in Karl (2002), *Staging the World*, p. 108.

68 Yang Naicun (1917), "Santai yihen lu". It remains to future research to bring to light whether the fact that the title of the entry is almost identical to the alternative title of *Qiu Shuyuan, The Regret of Taiwan* (*Santai yihen*), is pure coincidence.

69 For the Luo Fuxing uprising of 1913, see Kiang (1992), *The Hakka Odyssey*, p. 153; Lamley (2007), "Taiwan Under Japanese Rule", p. 218.

70 Yalu (1903), "Taiwan sanbai nian shi", and Yalu (1904), "Taiwan sanbai nian shi (xu qianqi)".

men. It perceives of the Japanese occupation of Taiwan as the culmination of a longer history of imperialism on the island:[71]

A sound of explosion awoke our Taiwanese compatriots [*tongbao* 同胞] from their nightmare that had lasted more than 300 hundred years.[72]

According to Liu Yazi, the crucial moment in the history of Taiwan can be dated to the Manchu 滿族 conquest of the island in 1683 when "the tragedy of the perishing of the country started to be performed on the stage of Taiwan".[73] When it comes to the events in 1895, his account is similarly tinged in anti-Manchu rhetoric:

Patriotic men with ideals united to establish an independent army; [they] declared internationally and domestically that they were not [willing to] accept Japanese fetters and would no longer submit themselves to the rule of the Manchus.[74]

Liu then goes on to describe the establishment of the republic and blames the failure of the struggles of resistance on "traitors to the Han" (*hanjian* 漢奸) collaborating with the Japanese, on Qing troops "not willing to go to war with Japan", and on Tang Jingsong and others, who were "slaves of the Manchu-Qing" (*Manqing nuli* 滿清奴隸).[75] As he puts it, the "the seed of self-rule [*zili zhongzi* 自立種子] had thus been eradicated".[76] As these excerpts show, the article imagines the Taiwanese and the people on the mainland to share a common desire to shed off the shackles of Manchu domination. In this logic, overthrowing the Manchu is the only possible way to save (Han) China, while self-rule (*zili* 自立) and independence (*duli* 獨立) represent an ideal that must be achieved (again). In this reasoning, then, for a short moment the Taiwan Republic foreshadowed the advent of a new era. Moving on to *Qiu Shuyuan*, the next section shows the efforts it takes to realise the ideal of independence—albeit on the stage.

---

71 That Taiwan was grouped together with what he calls "inferior nations" (*liedeng minzu* 劣等民族) such as Indians and Koreans at the Osaka World Exhibition in 1903 induced Liu to write the article; Yalu (1903), "Taiwan sanbai nian shi", p. 53.

72 Yalu (1904), "Taiwan sanbai nian shi (xu qianqi)", p. 53.

73 Yalu (1903), "Taiwan sanbai nian shi", p. 70.

74 Yalu (1904), "Taiwan sanbai nian shi (xu qianqi)", p. 53.

75 Ibid.

76 Ibid.

III.1. Characters in *Qiu Shuyuan Destroys his Family to Save the Nation*—Weakening the Country

The characters in *Qiu Shuyuan* are developed from a variety of sources. While some are based upon historical figures such as Tang Jingsong and Liu Yongfu, others vaguely link up with characters from other literary texts, while others again are freely invented. Some resemble the stock characters of *wangguo* plays, others fit in with well-established literary types that go beyond these or with the role categories of new drama. Literary types and role categories govern—albeit not unalterably—a character's repertoire of traits and actions, and hence directly influence its agency and raise expectations in the reader or spectator. This, in turn, impacts on whether a character is more likely to be perceived as being able to combat the weakness of a country or to do harm to it, instead.

Qiu Shuyuan pits characters whose actions work towards the demise of the country against those fighting for its survival, with a strong preponderance of the latter. Moreover, one character, "Tang Jingsong", establishes a link between both sides. I will start with an introduction to the opponents of the country, then focus on "Tang", and end the discussion with those co-operating to save Taiwan.

Two groups of antagonists can easily be distinguished in the play. In line with the pattern of a *wangguo* play introduced above, the readers or spectators encounter external and internal enemies to the country. It comes as no surprise that the external enemies are two conceited Japanese commanders called "Kabayama" 樺山 and "Japanese General Ōtori" 日將大鳥. In all likelihood, "Kabayama" refers to Kabayama Sukenori, the commander of the invasion force and first Japanese governor-general of Taiwan.[77] While the Japanese commanders should, in principle, have the highest degree of ability to change the situation in the country, their actions and plans are repeatedly thwarted.[78]

Several internal enemies collaborate with the Japanese commanders, among these the money-grubbing "Gong Zhaoyu" 龔照瑗, a namesake of the "Chief Commissioner of the Arsenal and Naval Yard" at Port Arthur (Lüshunkou 旅

---

[77] The scenario calls him a *dashuai* 大帥 (commander-in-chief). As a side-note: in the Qing dynasty, *dashuai*, fittingly, denoted a Provincial Governor; Hucker (1985), *A Dictionary of Official Titles*, p. 470. It is possible that the name of the second commander refers to Ōtori Keisuke 大鳥圭介 (1833–1911), who was not involved in the Taiwan War, but was instrumental in the events leading up to the First Sino-Japanese War; cf. Shan (2018), *Yuan Shikai*, pp. 51–52.

[78] They are manipulated by "Gong Zhaoyu" when they plan to kill "Qiu Shuyuan". Having spared the life of the latter, a group of servants led by a woman rescues "Qiu". What is more, at the end of the play, the commanders find themselves on the run.

順口), who is reported to have fled the port when the Japanese army arrived.[79] In the play, the scheming of "Gong" changes the fate of the main characters several times, thereby turning and twisting the plot. When "Kabayama" "orders [Gong] to persuade Tang to revoke independence" or to leave Taiwan, "Gong" obeys—turning himself into the embodiment of betrayal and of the disruptive forces damaging the country from within, which fits well into the pattern of a *wangguo* play.[80] "Gong" tries to achieve his goal by approaching "Tang's" henpecking wife, a character that I will introduce in some depth because it impacts strongly on the plot. Strong-willed, but selfish and, most importantly, unaffected by the promise of independence, which might secure the future of the country, she eagerly co-operates with "Gong" to convince "Tang" to escape Taiwan. This portrayal of "Tang's" wife not only echoes the early twentieth century trope of the unenlightened Chinese woman, it also draws heavily on the literary type of the shrewish wife so well-established in Chinese fiction.[81]

In Chinese, no single word exclusively denotes the shrew, but *pofu* 潑婦 is most commonly used.[82] Traits such as jealousy, selfishness, violence, and lustfulness are typical of the characters representing this literary type, but various combinations of these exist.[83] While, in many texts, the shrew, who is depicted as threat to the social order, is eventually punished, approaches to the theme of the shrewish—or henpecking—wife and her weak-willed husband range from satire to comedy.[84] The shrew was also one of the role categories in *wenmingxi*. Due to rapid changes in programming, which did not leave much time for rehearsal, and evidence of the continuing influence of *xiqu* on new drama, the use of role categories (*paibie* 派別) was very common in *wenmingxi* performances. Role categories—while also used in the performance of scripted plays—facilitated improvisation based upon scenarios.[85] The most often cited taxonomy of role categories in new drama was presented by Zhu Shuangyun 朱

---

79 This means that, as in the case of Ōtori, a tie to a historical figure in the First Sino-Japanese War that was not involved in the Taiwan War imposes itself on the reader. For the episode involving Gong Zhaoyu (1840–1901), see Harris (2018), *The Peking Gazette*, p. 274.

80 "Mubiao" (1989), p. 698.

81 This literary type was particularly prevalent in Chinese fiction of the seventeenth century; Wu (1988), "The Inversion of Marital Hierarchy", p. 363. See ibid., pp. 369–372 for a taxonomy. For a more detailed discussion see Wu (1995), *The Chinese Virago*.

82 Yang (2016), "Grafted Identities", p. 3.

83 Yang (2016), "Grafted Identities", pp. 2–3; see, also, Wu (1988), "The Inversion of Marital Hierarchy".

84 Cf. Wu (1995), *The Chinese Virago*.

85 Shi Yi (2010), "Wenmingxi dui Zhongguo chuantong xiqu de xucheng", pp. 73–74; Goldstein (2007), *Drama Kings*, pp. 100–101; Liu (2013), *Performing Hybridity*, pp. 70, 74–75, 104; Ma Junshan (2013), "Lun wenmingxi jiaose zhi"; for the difference between role categories in "new drama" and role types (*hangdan* 行當) in *xiqu*, see the latter, p. 198.

雙雲 (1889–1942) in 1914.[86] One of the categories that he lists is the shrew (*pola* 潑辣). Despite his *caveat* concerning the homogeneity of this role category, he characterises the majority of its representatives as "fierce and reckless".[87] This can easily be said of "Tang's" wife in *Qiu Shuyuan*, too. Selfish and jealous, her agency both as a fictional being and as an artefact is arguably the greatest among the antagonists because it is she who finally succeeds in forcing the president of the republic to leave, a scene to which I will come back below.

Her husband, "Tang Jingsong", contrasts with her strikingly. Not a bit as determined as his wife, he repeatedly switches positions and is driven to action by others. Apparently loyal to the Qing (and thus representing the weakness of the Qing and Qing China),[88] at the beginning of the play, he is determined to enforce the court's decision to cede Taiwan, shouting at "Qiu Shuyuan", who, as the spokesperson of the gentry, presents arguments in favour of resistance, and reviling "Liu Yongfu", who backs the gentry's arguments, as "not being loyal [to the court]".[89] When "Qiu" advocates independence (*duli* 獨立) and proposes that "Tang" be president, "Tang's" capability of acting crumbles. The members of the gentry now beg him on their knees to consent to the nomination. This already quite animated scene becomes even more physical when "Tang", now under great pressure, "hurriedly enters the inner [chambers]",[90] followed hot on his heels by "Liu" and the others. By replacing the parlour for the sanctum, a most improper place for dealing with the affairs of state, governor "Tang" disgraces the dignity of his office. Unable to argue his case successfully, he resorts to even more slapstick-like action, giving out the following order to his servant "Tang De" 唐德:

"Quickly, fetch a ladder!" [Tang] De exits, [then] enters with a ladder, which he leans against the bed. [Tang Jing]Song hides [in the canopy of the bed]. Liu [Yongfu] leads the crowd [into the room] to look for [Tang], he [then] pulls [Tang] down.[91]

"Tang" is thus forced to face the gentry and engage in a discussion about the rights and duties of a president. However, it needs the encouragement of his patriotic concubine "Guoying" 國英 for him to consent weepingly.

The scene takes a clear stance on "Tang's"—or Tang Jingsong's, for that matter—lack of agency: the president is not able to act. He is either urged to

---

86 Zhu distinguishes between male (*shenglei* 生類) and female (*danlei* 旦類) roles, which he further subdivides into eight male and six female role categories; Zhu Shuangyun (1914), *Xinju shi*, "paibie", pp. 1–3.

87 Zhu Shuangyun (1914), *Xinju shi*, "paibie", pp. 2–3.

88 Cf. Katherine Chou Hui-ling (2000), "Nü yanyuan", p. 25, note 4, stating that the play "ridicules the weakness of the Manchu Qing".

89 "Mubiao" (1989), p. 697.

90 Ibid.

91 Ibid., p. 698.

come to a decision by both the gentry and "Liu Yongfu" or he is persuaded to act by his concubine. The scene can be understood as symbolising the historical Tang Jingsong's comments about the gentry prevented him from leaving the island.[92] It can also be interpreted as a fictitious rendering of the so-called Li Wenkui Incident (Li Wenkui shijian 李文魁事件) of late April 1895, when Tang, apprehensive of the danger of an attack by a group of assailants, is said to have hid in the kitchen, only to be rescued by a cook and the military.[93]

To return to the play, "Tang" now symbolises the president. For a short moment, the image of "Tang" proving unsuitable to be head of state seems to change when he resists the efforts made by his wife and "Gong Zhaoyu" to cajole him into revoking independence. However, his egoistic wishes soon cause his fickle support of the republic to collapse: he is tempted to leave Taiwan on condition that he can take his concubine with him. His jealous and fierce wife—again taking the initiative— denies his wish and finally "forces" him off the stage.[94] Similar to earlier examples of this theme of the shrewish wife disrespecting traditional gender roles, this scene is

rich in allegorical meaning. As the family was regarded as the microcosm of the state, the anxiety produced by any reversal of domestic hierarchy bespeaks a fear of political chaos.[95]

Dragging her husband off the stage, the wife symbolically ends the first period of the republic and thus challenges the authority of the male members of the gentry and the military, who advocated the nomination of a head of state.

Concurrently, the scene provides an opportunity for a highly physical performance. "Tang's" use of slapstick-like actions adds a strong comic flavour to *Qiu Shuyuan*, identifying the role of "Tang" as belonging to the *huajipai* 滑稽派, the comic role category, which was particularly popular from 1914 onwards.[96] A short stage direction in Scene Two of the scenario substantiates this impression: upon the gentry's entry, "Tang" *zuo huaji* 做滑稽:[97] since Zhu Shuangyun describes linguistic adroitness as important characteristic of the role category, the president might have made a joke to deflect attention from the disputed

---

92 See, e.g., Gordon (2007), *Confrontation over Taiwan*, p. 193.

93 A group of people approached the governor's *yamen* 衙門 (official residence) because they were suspicious that Tang might escape from the island and take treasure with him. Several people who gathered outside the *yamen* were shot dead or injured; see Gordon (2007), *Confrontation over Taiwan*, p. 191, and Alsford (2018), *Transitions to Modernity*, pp. 44–45 for the incident.

94 "Mubiao" (1989), p. 698.

95 Wu (1995), *The Chinese Virago*, p. 12.

96 Ma Junshan (2013), "Lun wenmingxi jiaose zhi", p. 200.

97 "Mubiao" (1989), p. 697.

issue of declaring independence.[98] In addition, however, the stage direction foreshadows the highly physical action that ensues at the end of the scene. In fact, physical routines and slapstick-imbued improvisation were a distinguishing feature of the role category's performance style as comments of theatre practitioners such as Zhou Jianyun 周劍雲 (1893–1967) evidence. Zhou complains that actors of the comic role category "perform all sorts of movements in an excessive way".[99] As theatre scholar Ma Junshan states, exaggeration, including in the realm of bodily movement, was a defining characteristic of the comic role in *wenmingxi*.[100] As for *Qiu Shuyuan*, slapstick-like body movement that verges on farce is the main device to present the president as a laughing stock. The play in this way ridicules him as a person devoid of agency, as a person who is too weak to live up to the office of presidency.[101]

In popular literature, this connotation of Tang Jingsong's role as president lived on. In the expanded version of *Flowers in a Sea of Sins* (*Niehai hua* 孽海花, 1927–1930) by Zeng Pu 曾樸 (1871–1935), for example, a character comments on rumours about "Tang Jingsong":

Nowadays, if one talks about the seven days of Tang Jingsong's presidency, everybody laughs about his good start and poor finish, [saying that he] performed in a farce [*huajiju* 滑稽劇]. As a matter of fact, this was the sad history of a nation's perishing. Talking about this is really scary.[102]

---

98 Zhu Shuangyun (1914), *Xinju shi*, "paibie", p. 2. Cf. Liu (2013), *Performing Hybridity*, p. 105. For a short overview on the pervasiveness and changing connotation of the term *huaji* in early twentieth century, see Rea (2015), *The Age of Irreverence*, pp. 107–110.

99 Jianyun (1915), "Xinju pingyi", p. 255; see, also, Ma (2013), "Lun wenmingxi jiaose zhi", p. 200. Ouyang Yuqian 歐陽予倩 (1889–1962), in his reminiscences of the era of *wenmingxi*, shows much ambivalence in his evaluation of comic actors because "their acting was truly popular with the audience [and] augmented the audience's interest in new drama" and it could "serve to smash superstition and uncover the dark side of society", while "some did not hesitate to shatter the plot"; Ouyang Yuqian (1984), "Tan wenmingxi", pp. 221–222. The pejorative view of *huaji* actors was often justified by the unnaturalness of their performance, which contradicted the often conjured claim to "reasonable" (*heli* 合理) performance in *wenmingxi*; see Liu (2013), *Performing Hybridity*, pp. 146–149; since these objections were often uttered by actors who specialised in other roles categories, it is probable that rivalry was a driving force behind the respective statements; see ibid., pp. 148–149.

100 See Ma Junshan (2013), "Lun wenmingxi jiaose zhi", p. 200. *Wenmingxi*'s comical routines even impacted on the emergence of *huajixi* 滑稽戲, "a new genre of farce", which developed on the Shanghai stage in the 1910s, and which "combined repartee [...] with slapstic elements"; Rea (2015), *The Age of Irreverence*, p. 112. Cf. also, Ouyang Yuqian (1984), "Tan wenmingxi", p. 222; Liu (2013), *Performing Hybridity*, p. 149; and Ma (2013), "Lun wenmingxi jiaose zhi", p. 200.

101 Note that in *Qiu Shuyuan* the character performed in the *huaji* category is the one criticised, not the one who criticises others.

102 Dongya bingfu (1928), "Niehai hua", p. 15. For the different versions of the novel, see Zhang Bilai (1979), "Qianyan", pp. 2–3; Zimmer (2001), "Vorwort", pp. 12–14.

When watching *Qiu Shuyuan*, the audience might have felt a similar sense of unease evoked by the simultaneity of farce and laughter, on the one hand, and the demise of a country, on the other. This ambiguity serves a double function. Apart from entertaining the audience, comedy and farce can also have the additional effect of enlightening and of mobilising the audience. They can, in other words, have an empowering effect much needed in times of real or perceived weakness. Christopher Rea, in his study on the "age of irreverence", shows that, in the early twentieth century, authors made ample use of this device. As he puts it,

Chinese writers of the early twentieth century did not need a lover's encouragement to seek humorous ways to minister to the citizens of a dying empire (or, later, a sickly republic). Many threw themselves into cheering everyone up with gusto, conceiving of uses for laughter besides the palliative. Jokes could inspire reform; playfulness could lead to new discoveries; mockery could shame the powerful into better behaviour. Conversely, laughter could be a symptom of cultural illness.[103]

III.2. Characters in *Qiu Shuyuan Destroys his Family to Save the Nation*—Saving the Country

Qiu Shuyuan contrasts the hesitant and weak "Tang" with a group of idealists (*zhishi* 志士),[104] who oppose the cession of Taiwan and make up the plan to nominate a president. The group mainly consists of members of the gentry, including their spokesperson "Qiu Shuyuan", as well as "Provincial Military Commander" (*tidu* 提督)[105] "Liu Yongfu", who represents the military. The following section will introduce these two characters.

"Liu Yongfu" exerts agency in both the realms of the body and the mind. As his chase of "Tang Jingsong" proves, he does not shy away from physical action. Furthermore, devising a stratagem that secures victory over the Japanese army and their commanders at the end of the play, he proves capable of strategic thinking that results in a change in the country's future. His loyalty lies with the élite. In the last scene of the play, which twists history by ignoring the offer of conditional surrender that the historical Liu Yongfu made to the Japanese army,[106] "Liu" unveils more vehement traits when he cannot stop himself from killing a traitor who had urged "Kabayama" to sign a declaration of surrender. This fit of rage is suggestive of the "ardent role category" (*jiliepai* 激烈

---

103 Rea (2015), *The Age of Irreverence*, p. 4.
104 "Mubiao" (1989), p. 697.
105 "Mubiao" (1989), p. 697; for the title, cf. Hucker (1985), *A Dictionary of Official Titles*, p. 498.
106 Cf. Alsford (2018), *Transitions to Modernity in Taiwan*, pp. 181–182.

派) in new drama, which Zhu Shuangyun defines as: "chest full of anger, glares [at others], dashes ahead disregarding safety; hence fierce."[107] As this description suggests, the representatives of the ardent male category are likely to make changes to the fictional world or to the plot, respectively. The changes brought about by this anger and fierceness may not always lead to the desired results, as the example of "Liu Yongfu's" counterpart "Qiu Shuyuan", who equally falls into the role category of the ardent male, amply demonstrates.

At this point, a remark on the name of the title character is due. As mentioned in the introduction, the historical Qiu Shuyuan was a reform-minded journalist and poet in Singapore. He had close connections to Kang Youwei 康有為 (1858–1927) and other advocates of reform in China.[108] We saw above that Qiu also corresponded with Qiu Fengjia.[109] This connection becomes meaningful in order to explain the title of the play. It is quite possible that the name of the title character was meant to refer to Qiu Fengjia, one of the gentry who had led the resistance in 1895. A similar "mistake" is documented in articles printed in the *Shenbao* 申報 in late 1931 and early 1932, when Shanghai writer and critic Zheng Yimei 鄭逸梅 (1895–1992) returned once more to the history of the Taiwan Republic. Roughly three months after the Mukden Incident (Jiu Yiba Shibian 九一八事變, 1931), he published an article with the title of "Qiu Shuyuan at the Time of the Cession of Taiwan" (Gerang Taiwan shi zhi Qiu Shuyuan" 割讓臺灣時之邱菽園).[110] Regarding the cession as a "a major page in the history of national humiliation", he tells the story of a resistance leader called Qiu Shuyuan, who "invested the family property to assist the army, organised the Taiwan Republic, and recommended Tang Jingsong and Liu Yongfu as president and vice-president, respectively".[111] When the resistance had failed, so the article continues, he returned to his ancestors' home in Guangdong 廣東, and, from there, moved on to Singapore. It is obvious that Zheng Yimei mixes the biographical data of Qiu Shuyuan with those of Qiu Fengjia, a fact that an article published in the same paper was quick to complain about.[112] Like Zheng's article, the *wenmingxi* play may have exchanged the name of Qiu Fengjia for that of Qiu Shuyuan by accident. This would also explain why the title of the play suggests that "Qiu Shuyuan" destroys his family – something not taken up explicitly in the remainder of the scenario.

---

107 Zhu Shuangyun (1914), *Xinju shi*, 'paibie', p. 1.

108 Cf. Lee (2012), "Khoo Seok Wan".

109 Cf. Qiu Zhuchang (2004), *Qiu Fengjia jiaowang lu*, pp. 41–46.

110 Zheng Yimei (1931), "Gerang Taiwan shi zhi Qiu Shuyuan".

111 Ibid.

112 See Hua Shilin (1932), "Buzheng 'Gerang Taiwan shi zhi Qiu Shuyuan'"; for an earlier correction of the article focussing on the details of Qiu Shuyuan's life, see Wu □zai (1931), "Buji Qiu Shuyuan".

Taking the title more seriously, another explanation is also possible: Qiu Shuyuan is but one—albeit the most important—of several historical figures from whom the scenario borrows its name, but who were not directly related to the events in Taiwan in 1895.[113] Most of the persons to whom these names allude either played a role in the First Sino-Japanese War, or, as is the case with Qiu Shuyuan, were active contributors to debates in China and commented on the Taiwan Republic. This accumulation of historically inaccurate resemblances in terms of names corroborates the impression that the creators of *Qiu Shuyuan* were less interested in the history of Taiwan than in turning an imaginary Taiwan into a playing-field upon which to project their view of China. Furthermore, with the historical Qiu Shuyuan not being tinged by the history of an escape from Taiwan, his name becomes an apt choice for the title character of the play, which, in addition, includes overseas (Singaporean) Chinese into the play's vision for saving the country.

As mentioned above, the "Qiu Shuyuan" character in the play is prone to ardent behaviour. He acts on impulse and disregards his own safety to confront both the traitor "Gong Zhaoyu" and the Japanese commanders: a suicide note written by "Tang Jingsong's" concubine, "Guoying", which also informs him about the successful efforts that "Gong Zhaoyu" and "Tang's" wife have made for president "Tang" to escape from Taiwan (and which causes "Guoying" to commit suicide), strongly upsets him. The fact that, shortly afterwards, "Tang's" servant also cuts his throat finally causes him to dash to the Japanese headquarters, confront "Gong" and attempt to stab him. Arrested by Japanese soldiers, "Qiu" does not hesitate to insult the two Japanese commanders, which leads to his arrest. Put differently, his role category easily provokes action that propels the plot, while his ardent behaviour also temporarily results in him being completely impeded from further action.

However, "Qiu Shuyuan" does not just engage in physical action. He is much more successful in changing the course of the country's future as an orator. Like many characters of the ardent role category,[114] "Qiu Shuyuan" and, to a minor degree, "Liu Yongfu" concurrently belong to the category of orators (*yanlunpai* 言論派)—a category known for mainly improvised and often very long speeches on political affairs, which, in most cases, serve to propagate revolution (around 1911) or patriotism.[115] Although the prominence of these speeches had temporarily declined after the revolution, they regained

---

113 See, e.g., "Gong Zhaoyu" and "Japanese General Ōtori" above.

114 Cf. Ma Junshan (2013), "Lun wenmingxi jiaose zhi", p. 199.

115 Cf. e.g., ibid.; Zhao Ji (2011), *Huaju yu Shanghai shimin shehui*, p. 31; Ouyang Yuqian (1984), "Tan wenmingxi", p. 220. Scenarios in general only provide the name of the speaker and the main message of the speech; cf. also, Liu (2013), *Performing Hybridity*, 70.

SELFISH FAINT HEARTS, ARDENT FIGHTERS, AND GALLANT HEROINES? 433

importance during the boom of political plays in the mid-1910s.[116] Improvised speeches are a major device in *Qiu Shuyuan*, too. Starkly contrasting with "Tang's" comic routines, they dominate the first acts, thus providing ample space for the speakers to "make a change".[117] Although the speeches do not survive, we know from the plot outline that the orators – especially "'Qiu Shuyuan", who is seconded by "Liu Yongfu"—strongly oppose the cession of Taiwan and advocate independence and the nomination of a president as a way to save the country from perishing. With the views of the orators in unison, and "Tang's" concerns (*i.e.*, loyalty to the court) soon discredited by his *huaji* behaviour described above, the ideas that the orators disseminate emerge as the play's preferred solution to counter the country's decline: a (strong) republic with a president nominated by the élite and supported by the representatives of the army.

As this suggests, the orators' agency reaches beyond the level of the fictional world. In performance, the orator—addressee situation doubles, with the *yanlunpai* actors also addressing the audience, which, in general, was the urban population.[118] The play's orators spoke to the (future) citizens (*guomin* 國民) of the young and fragile republic.[119] In this environment, the orators met with the ground well-prepared for their speeches because, starting from the late Qing period, "public speaking" (*yanshuo* 演說) had increasingly gained in importance in moulding, persuading, and educating citizens.[120] In the *yanlunpai* actor, then, the roles of the actor and the orator converged. The theatre had now virtually turned into the classroom that Chen Duxiu had purported it to be in the early 1900s,[121] and laid claim to be able to induce change in favour of the strengthening of the country.

Moving back to the characters of the play, "Qiu's" power of persuasion causes the gentry to join him on his way to "Tang Jingsong's" residence and thus sets the events in motion. Similarly, at curtain fall, he re-establishes himself as the spokesperson of the gentry when he initiates their calls of "Long live Taiwan". And yet, "Qiu's" agency is not infinite, as his captivity proves. The protagonist has to rely on the support of others in order to re-establish his

---

116 Liu (2013), *Performing Hybridity*, p. 87.

117 In the scenario, the placeholders for speeches are marked by verbs such as *shenshuo* 申說 (state a reason), *quan* 勸 (advise), *zhuzhang* 主張 (advocate) among others; "Mubiao" (1989), pp. 697–698.

118 For an analysis of spoken drama including *wenmingxi* and Shanghai society see especially Zhao Ji (2011), *Huaju yu Shanghai shimin shehui*.

119 This holds true no matter whether *Qiu Shuyuan* was performed in the early 1910s or in the mid-1910s—which especially the subject matter and the scenario's combination of *huaji* elements with political speeches suggest. For a concise summary of competing concepts of the "citizen" in modern China see Goldman and Perry (2002), "Introduction", pp. 3–7.

120 Strand (2002), "Citizens in the Audience and at the Podium".

121 Cf. San'ai (1904), "Lun xiqu".

434 MIRJAM TRÖSTER

capability to act. At this crucial moment of the play, a young woman, "Liu Yanyu" 劉燕玉, "Liu Yongfu's" daughter, comes to his rescue. On hearing about the arrest, she

contrives a way and orders that [Liu] Yi [劉毅] and herself lead the female servants to disguise themselves as performing artists and seek an opportunity to rescue Qiu. [Liu Yong]fu and [Liu] Yi both give their consent.[122]

Act Eight stages their counterfeit performance, and the trick proves successful. This scene serves a double purpose: first, it allows for entertainment and slap-stick on stage. Secondly, it establishes "Liu Yanyu", the mastermind behind the ruse, as the female foil to the protagonist. "Unrestrained by convention and outstandingly brisk", she belongs to the role category of the gallant woman (*haoshuang* 豪爽).[123] Her wit and resolve free the protagonist from imprison-ment. On the symbolic level, she thus reverses the trope of the male rescuing the woman in danger, which was popular in the writings of (mainly) male authors of the first half of the twentieth century.[124] In *Qiu Shuyuan*, "Liu Yanyu" challenges the Japanese commanders just as the title character had himself done before. The means that she uses are different, though. While her male counter-part insults and tries to stab his opponents, "Liu Yanyu" exploits her oppo-nents' image of female performers as innocuous companions in entertainment and, possibly, objects of desire.

The scene plays on yet another, albeit related, trope that was widespread in the Chinese literature published in the first half of the twentieth century, name-ly, the "oppressed female body as an allegorical space on which to inscribe (his)stories of the nation",[125] in other words, the inscription of foreign encroachment on China on the body of women. When looking at the scene described above, this pattern first seems to be re-inscribed. Mirroring power relations, the leaders of the occupation troops gaze at the indigenous women's performance and do not hesitate to force them to drink alcohol, which repre-sents a clear manipulation of their bodies. Hence, for a short moment, it seems as if the occupation of the country was to be repeated on the level of gender relations. As planned beforehand, however, the women use this misconception on the part of their opponents, and turn the power relations upside down.

In the fictional world of the play more generally, female characters demon-strate a very high degree of agency. Like "Tang Jingsong's" wife and his concu-bine, "Liu Yanyu" causes changes to the plot at decisive moments. Nonetheless, *Qiu Shuyuan* does not allot the same space to female characters as to their male

---

122 "Mubiao" (1989), p. 699.
123 Zhu Shuangyun (1914), *Xinju shi*, 'paibie', p. 2.
124 Cf. Dooling (2005), *Women's Literary Feminism*, p. 3.
125 Dooling (2005), *Women's Literary Feminism*, p. 3.

SELFISH FAINT HEARTS, ARDENT FIGHTERS, AND GALLANT HEROINES? 435

counterparts. To give but one example: having fulfilled her dramaturgical function as a foil to the protagonist, "Liu Yanyu" does not re-appear in the play. Furthermore, as the quotation above shows, only upon the consent of her father and "Liu Yi", presumably her brother, she puts her plan to rescue "Qiu" into practice. Symptomatic of a time in which gender role models were under debate, "Liu Yanyu" thus emerges as an ambivalent and complex character in the play. This ambiguity mirrors the troubled relationship of woman and the *wenmingxi* stage, upon which most female roles were performed by female impersonators. Their often fierce rejection of actresses, which can—at least partly—be explained by fear of competition, starkly contrasts with the creation of strong and revolutionary female characters in a number of new dramas.[126]

"Liu Yanyu" shares this slightly ambiguous portrayal of a courageous woman with her namesake in *Destiny of Rebirth* (*Zaisheng yuan* 再生緣, late eighteenth century), a string ballad (*tanci* 彈詞) by the female writer Chen Duansheng 陳端生 (1751–*circa* 1796).[127] *Tanci* are a "popular form of prosimetric ballad that became irrevocably associated with women and their literary experience".[128] In this vein, *Destiny of Rebirth* is known for denouncing unequal gender relations in society.[129] Significantly, though, *Qiu Shuyuan* does not fully capitalise on this strand of the string ballad. The play establishes intertextual or, to borrow a term introduced by Wolfgang G. Müller, internymic relations to the *tanci*, by "shift[ing][…] the name of a fictional character […] to a figure in another text".[130] "Liu Yanyu" does not share her name with the cross-dressing protagonist of the *tanci*, however, but with a supporting character, which is "depicted as a devoted daughter and a chaste and kind-hearted wife".[131] Nevertheless, like the "Liu Yanyu" in the play, the "Liu Yanyu" in *Destiny of Rebirth* rescues one of the male characters—she saves the man that she loves from being murdered by her own brother.[132] An important difference in motivation can be made out,

---

126 See Chou (1997), "Striking Their Own Poses", pp. 141–150. See, also, Liu (2013), *Performing Hybridity*, pp. 153–173, esp. 165–173. While Chou illustrates the "very limited room for women" (p. 150) in new drama, Liu delineates the influence of female impersonation in *shinpa* on *wenmingxi*.

127 The *tanci* was completed by Liang Desheng 梁德繩 (1771–1847) and first published in 1822; Hieronymus (1999), *Frauenvorbilder*, p. 83. For an analysis of *Destiny of Rebirth* see, e.g., Guo (2015), *Women's Tanci Fiction*, pp. 38–59. String ballads were a common source of inspiration for *wenmingxi* companies in the second half of the 1910s; Ouyang Yuqian (1984), "Tan wenmingxi", p. 195; Zhao Ji (2011), *Huaju yu Shanghai shimin shehui*, p. 222.

128 Idema (2010), "Prosimetric and verse narrative", p. 331. The writing and distribution of *tanci* flourished in the Jiangnan 江南 region during the Qing. For a concise introduction to the form, including a discussion of *Destiny of Rebirth*, see Idema (2010), pp. 374–388.

129 See, also, CYP (1986), "Ch'en Tuan-sheng".

130 Müller (1991), "Interfigurality", pp. 102–103.

131 Guo (2015), *Women's Tanci Fiction*, p. 38.

132 Chen Duansheng (1822), *Zaisheng yuan quanzhuan*, scroll 1.

though: although the scenario may also insinuate a romantic subplot, the play does not elaborate on this aspect, but puts emphasis on the urgent task of rescuing the most outspoken proponent of independence, instead. Ultimately, the gallant action of the "Liu Yanyu" in the play contributes to save the country from perishing.

As in the cases of the henpecking wife (whose actions cause damage to the country) and of the patriotic concubine "Guoying", *Qiu Shuyuan* directly relates "Liu Yanyu's" exercise of agency to the ruin or strengthening of the country. This focus comes as no surprise if we understand the different groups of characters in the play (excluding the Japanese commanders) as representing groups of citizens in early twentieth century China. In her analysis of gender and citizenship in this period, Joan Judge describes how

> [f]emale political citizenship was [...] construed in terms of national duties rather than personal rights. The same was true for female social citizenship, which focused on the woman's obligation to make a contribution to society rather than on her rights to work or to consumption.[133]

As seen above, the theatre stage lent itself well to the education of (future) citizens. On these grounds, the insertion of female characters into the play becomes a necessity because women were not only among the audience at *wenmingxi* performances,[134] they were also citizens—albeit with fewer rights than their male counterparts. The female characters of the play presented female spectators with "negative" ("Tang's" wife) and "positive" ("Guoying", "Liu Yanyu") role models. Most forcefully, the models to emulate called on women's active commitment to the support of patriotic men in saving the country from perishing. Despite this focus, the female characters' strength, which cumulates in "Liu Yanyu's" gallantry and defiance of conventions, reverses the popular trope about women be equal to a weak China, and allows the reader or spectator to imagine alternative practices and gender norms.

III.3. *Qiu Shuyuan Destroys his Family to Save the Nation*—A Summary

To sum up, the naming of characters and the use of literary types and role categories can be distilled from *Qiu Shuyuan* as the main devices employed to steer the characters' agency and thus propose a model to counter the perishing of the country. The interweaving of references to historical figures with "quasi-

---

133 Judge (2002), "Citizens or Mothers of Citizens?", p. 36.

134 Male and female spectators were at times separated, though; see Katherine Chou Hui-ling (2000), "Nü yanyuan", p. 14.

historical" characters (the latter of which were not present in Taiwan in 1895) creates a twofold effect. On the one hand, it de-familiarises the Taiwan War so that "Taiwan", like other allegedly "lost countries", turns into a microcosm that serves as a reference-point for China. Since these historical and "quasi-historical" persons were either part of the events in Taiwan or of recent Chinese history and intellectual debates, however, the use of names contributes to turn the "Taiwan" of the play into "China" itself.

The following diagnosis of a perishing country and a model to overcome weakness stems from this chapter's examination of the inventory of characters in the scenario: at first glance, as befits a *wangguo* play, *foreigners who encroach on the country* are the most obvious danger for the country's survival. However, with the foreign commanders being successfully outwitted by a woman, their agents arrested or killed, and they themselves on the run at the end of the play, their capability to act turns out to be severely damaged. *Internal enemies* emerge as another risk which can harm the country. Quite clearly, these are *traitors* who directly co-operate with the foreign intruders out of *egoistic motives* such as avarice. In contrast to the fierce indictment of "traitors to the Han" in the history of Taiwan written by Liu Yazi, however, the issue of ethnicity is not broached in the scenario.

Unpatriotic and shrewish women—a well-established literary type represented by "Tang Jingsong's" wife—gladly join with the traitors. These different internal enemies are depicted as having a huge impact on the future course of the country. Yet, while the traitors are finally rendered innocuous in the play, the henpecking wife's actions have a detrimental effect and lead to a severe crisis for the republic, which loses its head of state.

The crisis is epitomised in the figure of the *president*, who selfish and faint-hearted, not only shows an extremely volatile commitment to the republic, he also proves incompetent to govern the country. Drawing on the *huaji* role category, the play presents the head of state not only as increasingly devoid of agency, but even as a laughing stock. This treatment is reminiscent of a dismissive attitude towards the Taiwan Republic that prevailed in many contemporary works on the events.[135] An early example of this can be found in Liang Qichao 梁啟超 (1873–1929), who, in his *Letters on Travelling Taiwan* (*You Taiwan shudu* 遊臺灣書牘, 1911), states that the suddenness of the republic's emergence makes it "resemble a joke" (*ru xi* 如戲).[136] *Qiu Shuyuan*, by contrast, does not ridicule the idea of establishing a republic. The problem instead lies with the person who holds office. The abundance of performance time which the scenario allots to characters of the role category of male orators that advocate independence and

---

135 Cf. e.g., Davidson's account in Davidson (1903), *The Island of Formosa*, pp. 275–313; see, also, Lamley (1968), "The 1895 Taiwan Republic", pp. 39–40.
136 Liang Qichao (1989), *Yinbingshi heji: zhuanji*, vol. 7, no. 22, p. 205.

438 MIRJAM TRÖSTER

the nomination of a president—as *pars pro toto* for the republic—proves this point.

The republic that the play envisions as a means to strengthen the country and to withstand internal and external assault is centred on the *élite*. The *civilian realm*, which is insinuated by the name of the title character, possibly also includes translocal networks, and does not act in isolation but cooperates with the *military*. This *co-operation* continues when the president turns out to be a failure and a second approach to save the country, namely, joint military action, moves into the foreground. Apart from the male protagonists, *courageous and patriotic women* contribute to save the country, even though they do not enter the battlefield. The most outstanding of these is the gallant "Liu Yanyu". The internymic relations of "Liu Yanyu" to a supporting character in *Destiny of Rebirth* foretells the rescuing of "Qiu Shuyuan" by the female character for those familiar with the *tanci*. Simultaneously, they also complicate the portrayal of "Liu Yanyu", creating an ambiguity that is symptomatic of changing gender relations both on the *wenmingxi* stage and beyond.

None of the characters—not even the title character—is an individual hero. Their agency only unfurls to the full as long as they co-operate. The representatives of the different groups mentioned above have to bundle their efforts and skills in order to gain victory in the end. The open ending of the play creates a celebratory mood concerning the defence of an independent republic. *Qiu Shuyuan* thus transforms the historical early demise of the Taiwan Republic into hope regarding its (*i.e.*, China's) future. In this, it links up with the new paradigm of action to counter victimisation, which Rebecca Karl describes for the early twentieth century.[137] Countries such as the Philippines that had actively struggled against the threat of colonisation were now presented as models for emulation even though their struggle had failed. In short, the "ability to struggle—to demonstrate civilization not only through textual claims but through contemporary action—"[138] was more relevant than the outcome of the struggle. In this vein, reminiscent of the point that Liu Yazi's had made in 1903/04, the fight for independence and for the establishment of the Taiwan Republic could be seen as model that foreshadowed the beginning of a new era in China itself.

Befitting the positive mood prevailing in the play and characteristic of the new drama in the mid-1910s, *Qiu Shuyuan* interweaves education, primarily in the form of ardent political speeches, with entertainment. To be able to laugh at the henpecked president and the drunk foreign commanders and to cheer the women on, who follow the dauntless daughter of the general into the abodes of the enemy, does not just amuse the audience. By offering an alternative to the urgency and gloom that pervades many texts on the perishing of the country,

---

137 Karl (2002), *Staging the World*.
138 Ibid., p. 115.

the play also popularises serious messages by ways of playfulness. Drawing on such a light-hearted approach was presumably out of the question to Xu Jiarui when he re-wrote the story of the Taiwan Republic once again, this time during the Second Sino-Japanese War (*Kang-Ri zhanzheng* 抗日戰爭, 1937–1945).

IV. Xu Jiarui: *Taiwan* (1942)

The five-act drama *Taiwan*, written by Communist teacher and scholar Xu Jiarui in 1942, starts with a kind of prologue that immediately locates the play within the framework of a country that is perishing: when students perform poorly at the morning exercise, their teachers understand this as an "omen for the impending ruin of Taiwan".[139] Right then, news about the cession of Taiwan and the proclamation of independence reach them, which evoke the students' patriotic feelings.

After the scene is set, the play divides into two parts that roughly symbolise the last moments of the Taiwan Republic's Northern period and the military conflict that followed in its wake, respectively. The first and rather short part (Act Two) dramatises the response of the Qing officials in Taiwan and their pleasure-seeking wives to the military victories of the Japanese army, including the imminent danger of the seizure of Taipei. Despite vacillating for a short while, the officials decide to take to their heels and cross the Taiwan Strait to the mainland—not without first embezzling money allocated to pay for arms and munitions to resist the Japanese occupation of Taiwan.

Acts Three to Five tell the story of the precarious Taiwan War. They focus on "Liu Yongfu", who co-ordinates the war efforts. In the midst of war, two female students, one of them his daughter-in-law, come to meet him on the battlefield, where they are shot by Japanese soldiers. Around the same time, "Liu Yongfu's" son dies in battle. "Liu" mourns the death of his family members before he ardently calls the soldiers to arms and the play ends.

In the preface to the script, Xu Jiarui, who felt emotionally attached to the historical events of 1895, the year of his birth,[140] claims that his play is loosely based upon Yao Xiguang's 姚錫光 (1857–1921) *Short Record of Military Affairs in the East* (*Dongfang bingshi jiliie* 東方兵事記略, 1897). The details and vividness of

---

139 Xu Jiarui (1943b), "Taiwan", p. 3. See Schillinger (2016), *The Art of Governing Soldiers*, pp. 290–303 for the introduction of physical drill into school curricula during the late Qing and early Republic. Xu personally is said to have laid great emphasis on physical exercise to counter the image of China as the "sick man of East Asia" (*Dongya bingfu* 東亞病夫); Xu Yan (2013), *Xu Jiarui lüezhuan*, p. 15.

140 Xu Yan (2013), *Xu Jiarui lüezhuan*, pp. 14–15.

this report on the First Sino-Japanese War, which, according to Xu, is itself "rich in dramatic flavour" and apt to "move" its readers, made a strong impact on the author of the drama.[141] Nonetheless, he decided to "insert many idealist elements and unhistorical characters"[142] because he either thought of them as conveying the truth or felt that they "increased the dramatic effect".[143] Indeed, as we will see below, these insertions—which speak more to the historical moment in which the play was produced—heighten the sense of urgency that permeates the play, and add to the characterisation of the protagonist as an outstanding man of action.

Rewriting history for the theatre stage was a widely adopted approach among writers during the later phase of the war.[144] During the Second Sino-Japanese War, theatre practitioners of varying backgrounds took part in an effort to popularise drama for the purposes of anti-Japanese resistance and wartime mobilisation. Before and during the first years of the war, theatre troupes in a huge and partly orchestrated move toured the country and staged sketches that were often—at least partly—improvised.[145] From about 1939, however, spoken drama productions based upon scripts re-gained prominence.[146] Since the audiences in the countryside preferred plays based upon historical events, many of these resistance dramas (*kangzhan huaju* 抗戰話劇) draw on historical subject matter in order to engage with contemporary events.[147] According to Chang-tai Hung, these historical plays (*lishiju* 歷史劇) pursued two main goals, namely,

cultivating political symbols in the fight against the Japanese invasion and spreading patriotic messages to a wider audience in the interior as well as in occupied cities like Shanghai. To realize these goals playwrights turned to heroes and heroines from the past.[148]

As this quotation shows, literary characters—heroes and, possibly, heroines—take centre-stage in these works. *Taiwan* is no exception. Thus, in the following,

---

141 Xu Jiarui (1943a), "Zixu", pp. 1–2.

142 Ibid., p. 3.

143 Ibid., p. 2. Xu's explanations, which are meant to justify his approach, have to be seen in the context of a debate about historical dramas at the time, which focused on whether or not historical accuracy was an adequate standard against which to measure fictional works; see Hung (1994), *War and Popular Culture*, pp. 79–80.

144 Ibid., pp. 64, 78–84; cf. also, *Eberstein (1983), Das Chinesische Theater im 20. Jahrhundert*, pp. 151–154, 162.

145 Hung (1994), *War and Popular Culture*, pp. 49–64; cf. also, *Eberstein (1983), Das Chinesische Theater im 20. Jahrhundert*, pp. 139–148.

146 Hung (1994), *War and Popular Culture*, pp. 63–64.

147 Ibid., p. 64. Especially from 1941/1942 onwards, when censorship tightened, historical plays served as disguise to utter dissent; ibid., p. 84. See, also, *Eberstein (1983), Das Chinesische Theater im 20. Jahrhundert*, pp. 151–154; Qian (2016), *Imperial-Time-Order*, pp. 122–123.

148 Ibid., p. 64.

I will first introduce some of the characters in *Taiwan* whose behaviour is depicted as weakening the country, and will then move on to a discussion of the protagonist, who dominates the play. This approach mirrors the structure of the play, which, in its first part, provides a study of those who hasten the perishing of the country, only to provide the ground for the emergence of the hero in its second part. Character constellation and structure thus collude as the main devices to visualise the agency of the characters and, above all, have "Liu Yong-fu" emerge as the only one who is possibly capable of saving the country.

IV.1. Characters in *Taiwan*—Treating the Future of the Country with Indifference

Of the different groups of people who harm the country in *Qiu Shuyuan* (foreign invaders, traitors, the shrewish wife, and the incompetent head of state), we meet the first three again in this play, albeit in a somewhat different form. Although Japanese soldiers only appear in Act Five of the drama, they emerge from the play as being more brutal, relentless, and capable of acting than the Japanese commanders in *Qiu Shuyuan*. We will look into one of the scenes that demonstrates their cruelty when discussing the death of two female students below. The group of traitors in *Taiwan* somewhat differs from those in the play of the 1910s. *Taiwan*, first of all, repeatedly names two culprits at court: these are "Li Hongzhang" 李鴻章 (1823–1901) and, most importantly, "Cixi" 慈禧 (1835–1908). Despite "Cixi" ranking among the main traitors, the play does not elaborate on her being Manchu, but stresses her egoistically-driven misuse of power, instead.[149] From the outset, the blame for the possible demise of the country is thus primarily put on those in power.

"Li Hongzhang" and "Cixi" are not the only ones depicted as betraying the country, though. Former Qing officials who are now in the service of the Taiwan Republic abandon Taiwan as soon as the Japanese army approaches. The collective escape of the officials symbolises the breakdown of the efficient administration of the republic. Only two of the characters are fleshed out more thoroughly, namely, a character called "Supervisor Feng" (Feng *duban* 豐督辦) and his wife. When "Feng" first hesitates before leaving Taiwan, it is his wife who convinces him to escape. Thus, similar to *Qiu Shuyuan*, *Taiwan* also puts part of the blame for the crisis of the country on the shrewish, henpecking wife. This said, "Mrs. Feng" in *Taiwan* still differs from "Tang Jingsong's" wife in *Qiu*

---

149 The characters mention that "Cixi" abandons Taiwan because she needs money to build the Summer Palace (Yiheyuan 頤和園); Xu Jiarui (1943b), "Taiwan", p. 4; for a reference to Li Hongzhang, see ibid., p. 41.

Shuyuan. In contrast to the latter, "Mrs. Feng" does not act out of jealousy. Money and the wish to lead a pleasurable life motivate her actions. She is part of a group of officials' wives who have had access to education when still on the mainland, but did not value this opportunity.[150] In Taiwan, they now kill time by playing mah-jong and wasting money. In stark contrast to their husbands, who—though gutless and corrupt—show some interest in state affairs, the women are neither interested in politics nor "do [they] understand the least about the important affairs of the country", as "Mr. Feng" puts it and they themselves happily confirm.[151] This does not mean, though, that "Mrs. Feng's" conduct does not make a difference to the country. In private, she manipulates the decision-making process of her husband. In contrast to "Tang Jingsong's" wife in *Qiu Shuyuan*, she does not do so by resorting to physical violence, but uses her "glib tongue",[152] instead. Having convinced her husband to leave, it does not take much to cajole him into embezzling money that the army urgently needs,[153] which has a detrimental impact on the war: according to "Liu Yongfu", the lack of money to equip and feed the soldiers appropriately is the main reason for the military setbacks that the army suffers.[154]

In a nutshell, the egotism of the husband and the wife collude. Spurred on by their wives, who are apathetic to the future of the country, the collective escape of the cowardly, greedy, and corrupt group of politicians, so the drama suggests, completely smashes the credibility of the republican endeavour. At plot level, this sets the scene for the second part of the play, which establishes (male) military resolve as a solution to save the country that outrivals the reliance on dysfunctional civilian institutions.

IV.2. Characters in *Taiwan*—Desperately Fighting the Death of the Country

The fictional rendering of Liu Yongfu—a historical figure who attracted increasing attention during the war—[155] clearly dominates the second part of the play, which casts him as one of the heroes taken from history that Chang-tai Hung mentions in the passage quoted above. Reminiscent of Chen Duxiu's

---

150 Ibid., p. 13.

151 Ibid., pp. 15–16.

152 Ibid., pp. 1, 20.

153 Ibid., p. 21.

154 E.g., ibid., p. 24. The capability of the historical Liu Yongfu to make a change on the battlefield was indeed impeded by a constant lack of money; see Lamley (1968), "The 1895 Taiwan Republic", p. 40.

155 See, for instance, the articles on Liu in the *1833–1949 Chinese Periodical Full-text Database.*

SELFISH FAINT HEARTS, ARDENT FIGHTERS, AND GALLANT HEROINES? **443**

praise of theatre for its ability to speak to the senses, heroes and heroines in resistance dramas have, according to Hung, the power to elicit a strong emotional response from the audience:

If the patriotic resistance struggle could somehow be reduced to human terms, if it could be individualized as a person—a flesh-and-blood human being endowed with authentic feelings and experiences—then powerful nationalistic reactions among the people might be evoked.[156]

In other words, resistance drama drew on the device of personification in order to mobilise more effectively the spectators of a performance to resist Japan. *Taiwan* likewise creates the image of a male hero who sticks out from the crowd not only in terms of courage but also in his spirit of absolute dedication to the cause of saving Taiwan/China. This characterisation summons the notion of the *yingxiong* 英雄, the "outstanding male" an idealised concept of masculinity, which Bret Hinsch succinctly describes:

More than just strong, the classic Chinese hero combines physical prowess with other ideal qualities, such as talent, wisdom, and devotion to honor, making him the personification of a range of manly traits.[157]

Indeed, in *Taiwan*, one of the female students addresses "Liu Yongfu" as a *yingxiong*. She makes recourse to an image of the historical Liu Yongfu that had emerged after his success in battle against the French in Vietnam when "Liu Yongfu was lionized as a commander of a type needed to save China".[158] The student says:

Regional Commander Liu, you were famous when we were children, a hero [*yingxiong*] who defended the country. One could say that your history [*sic*] in Northern Vietnam [Annam] was the most glorious page in the history of China.[159]

---

156 Hung (1994), *War and Popular Culture*, p. 76.

157 Hinsch (2013), *Masculinities in Chinese History*, "Ming Dynasty". Like femininity, masculinity is a complex notion that better be conceptualised in the plural. Concepts of masculinity are "idealized and normative models, discursive representations, and iconic figurations that, in fact, influence the far more complex reality of individual behavior and identity"; Schillinger (2016), *The Art of Governing Soldiers*, p. 18. These concepts not only change over time, but may also coexist; see ibid., pp. 18–19. For a concise discussion of the concept (also in the Chinese context) see Hinsch (2013), *Masculinities in Chinese History*, "Introduction". For a definition of *yingxiong*, see, also, Huang (2006), *Negotiating Masculinities*, pp. 89–91; see Louie (2002), *Theorizing Chinese Masculinity*, pp. 22–41 for a discussion of *yingxiong* in the framework of *wen* 文 (civil) and *wu* 武 (military).

158 Wagner (2007), "Joining the Global Imaginaire", p. 124. This image was forged by "combining information derived from newspapers, including Western newspapers, with rumors, wishful thinking, and propaganda"; see, also, ibid., p. 122.

159 Xu Jiarui (1943b), "Taiwan", p. 49.

By digging out "Liu Yongfu's" actions, convictions, and traits in the context of the play's character constellation, the following analysis will show how the resistance play adapts the notion of the *yingxiong* to the needs of wartime mobilisation.

The drama introduces "Liu Yongfu" as "50 years [of age], white-haired, composed, good at fighting",[160] thus highlighting both mental strength and physical prowess. Moreover, his age and white hair lend dignity and an air of wisdom to him, inducing the reader to put trust in his ability to save the country. The structure of the second part of *Taiwan* further re-inforces this impression when the line-up of visitors of "Liu Yongfu" is interrupted by a scene which shows him ruminating about the best strategy to save the country:

[Liu] Yongfu walks to and fro on stage; for the moment, there is no sound on stage; complete silence fills the space; [Liu] Yongfu walks to the wall and looks at the map; his finger draws the geographical features of the area around Taiwan; [he] repeatedly walks across the stage; sits at the desk; strokes his white hair, takes the mirror out of the desk and looks at himself, sighs; silence.[161]

"Liu's" movements and the sigh characterise him as a person who does not take responsibility lightly. What is more, by steering attention towards "Liu" as well as towards Taiwan, the scene establishes an intimate connection between the main character and the country's future.

The fact that the scene interrupts a flow of visitors that come to see "Liu Yongfu" makes it even more effective in enhancing the protagonist's position as a character who stands out from the others. The dialogues that ensue guarantee that most of the floor is provided to "Liu" and to the orders that he gives to others. "Liu Yongfu" imposes martial law, sends his female family members to the mainland, and entrusts his son, "Liu Chengliang" 劉成良, with the order to guard a crucial fortress, for instance. He also receives a leader of the volunteer forces, applauds their courage, and sends him to the frontline. Fighting against the external enemy in a spirit of unity thus emerges as a necessity in this play, too. Yet, reminiscent of Harry J. Lamley's depiction of the Taiwan Republic's Southern period, a clear hierarchy exists, in which co-operation is tantamount to subordination to the leadership of "Liu Yongfu", who exercises the highest degree of agency.[162]

The character's leading role and outstanding "guts"[163] are also recognised by another important visitor, the English consul, Mai Jialin 麥嘉林,[164] whose visit

---

160 Ibid., p. 1.
161 Ibid., p. 29.
162 Cf. Lamley (1968), "The 1895 Taiwan Republic", pp. 755–756.
163 Xu Jiarui (1943b), "Taiwan", p. 34.
164 The *Short Record of Military Affairs in the East* mentions a customs officer of this name who asked for the establishment of postal services in order for the Taiwan Republic to be able to

lends an air of international recognition to the resistance struggle led by "Liu Yongfu", and, in this way, enhances his agency in the play. The insertion of this scene is symptomatic of the moment of production of the drama and its reception. The play was written and performed in 1942 and published in the following year, at a time when the international recognition of China's war efforts was a topic within China and beyond.[165]

Moving back into the fictional world, "Mai" suggests that "Liu" issue stamps of the Taiwan Republic in order to feed his soldiers. Being concerned about the well-being of his soldiers, a (temporary) continuation of the republic appears necessary to "Liu Yongfu", who otherwise shows nothing but contempt for its institutions and its office holders. The most well-known of the latter is "Tang Jingsong". In fact, "Tang's" name is breached several times in a disparaging way by some of the characters.[166] But no character who refers to Tang Jingsong ever appears in the play. The position of the republic's president amounts to a blank, leaving its office-holder devoid of any opportunity to have an impact on the plot. "Liu Yongfu's" views of the republic and its representatives are made most explicit when, upon "Tang's" escape to the mainland, members of parliament beg "Liu" to accept the interim presidency, which, in their words, is the "will of the people (*renmin de gongyi* 人民的公意)".[167] "Liu" vehemently refuses to take office and rebuffs them ferociously. Furious about their daring to approach him with these matters in "such a critical moment",[168] he admonishes them severely: "There are many foreigners in Taiwan. Are you not afraid to make yourself the scorn of the whole world?"[169] Again, international recognition matters to him. The members of parliament, however, do not give up easily, which finally causes "Liu" to put himself in contradistinction to Tang Jingsong:

---

feed the soldiers; Yao Xiguang (2010), *Dongfang bingshi jilüe*, p. 140. The Takao Club based in Kaohsiung 高雄 (Gaoxiong) on its websites mention a British citizen named C.A. McCullum who worked for the Imperial Maritime Customs at that time, available at: http://www.takaoclub.com/personalities/IMCdata/index.htm (last accessed 25 August 2018). Ironically, he seems to have been among the three people persuading the soldiers at Anping 安平 to lay down arms when the Japanese navy was about to land there; Davidson (1903), *The Island of Formosa*, p. 363.

165 Although with the outbreak of the Pacific War, China's war efforts were finally recognized by the Allied powers, "this alliance would prove a very uneven one"; Mitter (2016), "The War Years", p. 163. In addition, China had to deal with the closure of the Burma Road (Yunnan – Burma Highway (Dian-Mian Gonglu 滇緬公路)) by Japan. See ibid., pp. 163–169 and Hsü (2000), *The Rise of Modern China*, pp. 601–603 for China's international relations at the time. It is also significant that the so-called "unequal treaties" were renounced in January 1943; Hsü (2000), *The Rise of Modern China*, p. 601.

166 E.g. Xu Jiarui (1943b), "Taiwan", pp. 17, 19–20.

167 Ibid., p. 30. The gentry (see. *Qiu Shuyuan*) is thus replaced by the "people" in this play.

168 Ibid., p. 31.

169 Ibid.

446   MIRJAM TRÖSTER

Let those who act as president, act as president, [but] let me be a human being. Let history write about Tang Jingsong that he was president of the Taiwan Republic, and write about me that I was a soldier who defended the country. [...] Tang Jingsong regards [the seal of the Republic] as an imperial seal that hands down the state power. I, however, regard it as a piece of stone. [...][170]

This scene is vaguely reminiscent of the scene in which the gentry-scholars come to nominate "Tang Jingsong" president in *Qiu Shuyuan*. The respective messages as well as the degree of agency of the two characters are in stark contrast, though. While "Tang Jingsong" emerges as laughing stock in the *wenmingxi* play precisely *because he rushes away from the cause of the republic*, "Liu Yongfu", in *Taiwan*, is not manipulated by the representatives of the republic. In contrast, he warns them of becoming the laughing stock of the world precisely *because they urge him to become president*, while he, in fact, is a man of (military) action, who is solely dedicated to saving the country on the battlefield.

Putting trust in neither the Taiwan Republic nor the court, there are no civilian authorities to which "Liu Yongfu" can pay allegiance any longer. Even though he is tired and disillusioned,[171] he does not give up in his desperate attempt to "defend the country", which turns out to be the only yardstick to him. But, in the long run, the country can only be strong if the current authorities are disempowered as soon as the war against the external enemies is won.

To understand this line of attack more easily, a word on the author of the play is due. [172] Xu Jiarui was an editor, a school and university teacher, and a very active member in a number of cultural associations located in wartime Kunming 昆明 such as the Yunnan 雲南 branch of the All-China Resistance Association of Writers and Artists (Zhonghua Quanguo Wenyijie Kangdi Xiehui 中華全國文藝界抗敵協會). Although more well-known for his poetry and his academic research on folk literature and local music theatre, he started to write anti-Japanese dramas after the Mukden Incident and—being a teacher—had them performed in local schools.[173] Simultaneously, Xu was a member of the Chinese Communist Party (Zhongguo Gongchandang 中國共產黨, CCP), although he had temporarily lost his connection to the party organisation in the late 1920s/early 1930s.[174] *Taiwan* was written, performed, and published

---

170 Ibid. One of the representatives calls him "obstinate" (*guzhi* 固執), insinuating that "Liu" was already convinced that the war will be lost; ibid., p. 32. This is one of the moments in the play that opens space for an additional reading, which is much more critical of the role of the protagonist; see, also, below.

171 Ibid., p. 25.

172 If not stated otherwise, the information on Xu's life is based on Xu Yan (2013), *Xu Jiarui lüezhuan*; Idem (2008), "Xu Jiarui nianpu".

173 Xu Yan (2013), *Xu Jiarui lüezhuan*, pp. 174–179; Idem (2008), "Xu Jiarui nianpu", pp. 47–52.

174 Xu Yan (2008), "Xu Jiarui nianpu", p. 646; Idem (1983), "Xu Jiarui xiaozhuan", pp. 311–313. See, also, Meng Shuhong (2016): "Xu Jiarui", p. 186; "Xu Jiarui" (1979), p. 439.

at a time when the co-operation between the CCP and the Nationalist Party (Guomindang 國民黨) had already started to break down.[175] Since China was still at war, however, notwithstanding all mutual distrust, the necessity to unite against the foreign enemy could not be denied. The biting denunciation of the civilian authorities paired with the plea to continue the fight against the Japanese army in Xu Jiarui's drama symbolises this tension.

Correspondingly, for "Liu Yongfu", giving up the fight for the country is out of the question. When two students beg him to "defend Taiwan to the death",[176] he angrily replies: "This is my duty, what [need is there to] send representatives?"[177] Patriotism and (soldierly) honour are the values that "Liu Yongfu" is determined to sacrifice his life for, while absolute resolve and a valiant fighting spirit are the ingredients that he needs to pursue his goal in order to save the country from demise. The last scene of the play pointedly summarises his priorities when he mourns the losses of his son, who—as one of the dramatist's "idealist" insertions to enhance the dramatic effect—has died in battle,[178] and of his daughter-in-law:

Within one day, I lost my son, I lost the wife of my son, and I lost my most important fortress. [...] Oh, my son! Although your mother is far away, your wife is sleeping by your side. She, too, has sacrificed her life for Taiwan. You should die content. [...][179]

Against the background of his relatives' death, the bravery of "Liu Yongfu" shines even more brightly. The scene thus further establishes him as a heroic character. As such, he does not have a choice but to transform quickly grief into determination. "Liu" orders: "Take the corpses away and advance!"[180] When his soldiers answer his call, the play ends.

Despite the fact that the failure of the Taiwan War was well-known, this partly open ending—another "idealist" insertion by Xu—can literally be interpreted as a call-to-arms in the Second Sino-Japanese War. I will give two slightly different explanations for this. First, the appeal to endurance establishes a link to Mao Zedong's 毛澤東 (1893–1976) "On Protracted War" (*Lun chijiu zhan* 論持久戰, 1938), which predicts a long but ultimately successful struggle against Japan.[181] As far as the resistance drama *Taiwan* is concerned, its partly open

---

175 Mitter (2016), "The War Years", p. 163; Hsü (2000), *The Rise of Modern China*, p. 590. Cf. Van Slyke (1986), "The Chinese Communist Movement During the Sino-Japanese War 1937–1945", pp. 665–671 for a more detailed account of the New Fourth Army Incident (South Anhui Incident, Wannan Shibian 皖南事變) of 1941.

176 Xu Jiarui (1943b), "Taiwan", p. 49.

177 Ibid.

178 According to Yao Xiguang (2010), *Dongfang bingshi jilüe*, p. 150, Liu's son did not die in battle.

179 Xu Jiarui (1943b), "Taiwan", pp. 56–57.

180 Ibid., p. 58.

181 Mao (1952), "Lun chijiu zhan"; Idem (1965), "On Protracted War". Cf. also, Xu Yan (2013), *Xu Jiarui lüezhuan*, p. 175. See Kun Qian for an analysis of historical dramas of the war period

ending creates continuity. It weaves a joint narrative of two wars—the First Sino-Japanese War (here represented by the Taiwan War) and the current struggle. As Xu writes in his preface to the drama:

The cession of Taiwan, the signing of the Treaty of Shimonoseki, and Liu Yongfu's defence of Taiwan to the death are an act in a tragedy, they are the greatest prelude to the Chinese nation's War of Resistance to Japan.[182]

The drama's ending suggests that the anti-Japanese resistance has not ended yet: The war has not been won, but nor has it been lost. Even though it might take time, victory is possible. The "Liu Yongfu" character in this context epitomises the necessary spirit of resolve. Secondly, the demise of a corrupt country might be necessary in order to build a new China. To use the words of a character in a drama of Xu Jiarui written in 1937: "While the old China perishes, the new China is born. Death means birth, no need for sorrow."[183]

IV.3. Characters in *Taiwan*—Women on the Battlefield

As the following analysis shows, a further aspect of the play directly relates to the exigencies of wartime mobilisation as they were defined by the CCP, namely, the role of women in war. We saw above that "Liu Yongfu" acknowledges that both his son and his daughter-in-law "sacrificed [their lives] for Taiwan". Yet, even a brief glimpse at the drama reveals that, according to the reasoning of the play, men and women are to contribute to the war in gender-specific ways. The characters of the two female students, another "idealist element" inserted by the author, illustrate this point. In Act Four of *Taiwan*, Chinese students in Tokyo decide to send a female student representative, "Yu Guoxiu" 余國秀, to Taiwan as a sign of the students' moral support.[184] As her name indicates, the "Splendour of the Country" is a patriotic young woman. Urged on by a male student, she enthusiastically embraces this opportunity to

---

against this background, e.g. dramas about the Southern Ming 南明 dynasty written by A Ying; Qian (2016), *Imperial-Time-Order*, pp. 115–147.

182 Xu Jiarui (1943a), "Zixu", p. 1. See, also, Xu Yan (2013), *Xu Jiarui lüezhuan*, p. 177.

183 Xu Jiarui (2008), "Paosheng xiang le", p. 261. See, also, Xu Yan (2013), *Xu Jiarui lüezhuan*, p. 175.

184 This scene suggests that in 1895 female Chinese students studied in Tokyo and together with the male students were involved in patriotic activities. The number of female students in Tokyo only substantially increased in the early 20th century, though; for periodization and an overview on changing gender views in this context see Judge (2005), "Between Nei and Wai". See, also, Chiang (2014), "Forces for Change", pp. 127–128.

act.[185] "Liu Yongfu's" daughter-in-law, "Hua Chuzhen" 華楚珍, accompanies "Yu Guoxiu" to Taiwan.

What follows are the only scenes in the two plays in which female characters are actually on the battlefield. As it turns out, however, their agency decreases in this environment. The male hero in *Taiwan* does not appreciate their presence: "You are really naughty children. You [should] study well! What do you race to the battlefield for?"[186] When he doubts that they have come to see him in this dangerous situation out of their own free will, even "Yu Guoxiu", the much more assertive of the two women, feels obliged to justify their behaviour. She not only calls "Liu" a *yingxiong*, but reveals that the students put their "last hope" on him, in this way sanctioning "Liu Yongfu's" position as paramount (male) authority in the play, and as the only one that they consider able to save the country.[187] When "Yu Guoxiu" then suggests that they collect donations to support the anti-Japanese resistance, the clear distinction of roles that the play assigns to men and women in wartime becomes even more apparent:

Yu   The great pains that the Regional Commander takes really move us to tears. Although I myself am a woman, [even I understand that] urging others to go to war empty-handed is an unreasonable matter. Alright, I want to do some work for you. I want to go to all of the coastal provinces for you, ask each provincial governor for help, and collect donations from the merchants of each province. I do not care whether this is successful or not, [but] want to set forth.

Yongfu   I am deeply grateful that you are so courageous, but I am afraid this will not lead to any [positive] outcome.[188]

"Liu Yongfu" still agrees to send "Hua Chuzhen" with her. When the latter asks him if she can go to meet her husband, who is guarding a strategically important fortress, "Liu" strongly rejects this wish and presents two reasons for doing so: first, the danger of going to the frontline, and, second, the possibly detrimental impact of women on soldiers on the battlefield:

Yongfu   That place is under shelling. How could you go [there]? This would not only mean [for you] to be in the utmost danger. I am afraid that [your presence would] shake the morale of the army. You accompany Miss Yu! [Quickly] leave! [You] cannot stay long[er] at this place.[189]

For "Liu", the place of women is not on the battlefield but far from the frontlines. They may contribute to the resistance by collecting money. It would be

---

185 Xu Jiarui (1943b), "Taiwan", p. 42.
186 Ibid., p. 48.
187 Ibid., p. 49.
188 Ibid., p. 50.
189 Ibid., p. 51.

450 MIRJAM TRÖSTER

even better—so "Liu's" comment upon the students' arrival suggests—for the women to stay away from the frontlines entirely and to study to prepare for the re-building of the country. Thus, the women's exertion of agency is spatially confined. In this way, the play not only distinguishes clearly between male and female tasks in times of war, it also goes a step further and equals the presence of women to peril on the battlefield, obliquely referring to the trope of the beauty who brings the country to collapse (*qingguo* 傾國). Consequently, women, or women's bodies, have to be "removed" from the battlefield as quickly as possible.

This is what literally happens in the play. When the students are on the retreat, they soon lose any capability to act. The "bleak and deserted battle-field"[190] frightens them terribly. Menace succeeds foreboding when the two students spot Japanese soldiers. Frightened, they go into hiding – only to come out of their hideout shortly afterwards, not suspecting that the soldiers have tricked them.[191] The Japanese soldiers then not only shoot at the naïve women, but turn them into objects of ridicule:

Japanese soldier A   Haha, Chinese! They come to ask for death.

All Japanese   Haha! Is it easy to kill Chinese?

Japanese soldier A   Chinese women, haha, are killed comfortably.

All Japanese soldiers   Chinese women, haha, are looking for death again.[192]

Despite their initial courage and although the women die performing their patriotic mission, the students thus symbolise weakness—the alleged weakness of China and, more specifically, of Chinese women. However, the play transforms the trope of the weak and unenlightened woman mentioned in the introduction: these two students neither lack education nor patriotism. They fall victim of both their own simple-heartedness and the cruelty of Japanese soldiers. What is more, however, their weakness results from their temporary transgression of the rules which the play posits as gender-appropriate behaviour during wartime: only when the borders of gender-specific spaces are not violated, can the weakness of the country possibly be overcome.

The scene described above and the respective message that it conveys contrast starkly with the "proliferation of female resistance symbols [in resistance drama] whose purpose was to mobilise the masses to stand up against Japanese

---

190 Ibid., p. 53.

191 Note the contrast to *Qiu Shuyuan*, in which a female character devises a ruse to rescue the title character.

192 Xu Jiarui (1943b), "Taiwan", p. 54.

SELFISH FAINT HEARTS, ARDENT FIGHTERS, AND GALLANT HEROINES? **451**

aggression".[193] The trope of the woman warrior—also common in pre-modern Chinese theatre—[194] is, of course, related more to fiction than fact.[195] Similarly, the military participation of women in the Communist revolution – including the war years – changed over time.[196] Nicola Spakowski observes that, when, in the late 1930s and early 1940s the CCP's views on mobilisation for war changed, their attitude towards female participation in the war changed, too. More than in the years before, it was now expected from women to do "women work", which meant to stay clear of the battlefront and engage in mobilisation for the war, instead.[197] As a result, the model of "women warriors" turned into a metaphor, an allegory for feeling and acting as a patriot.[198]

To understand fully the relevance of these changing norms for *Taiwan*, a brief note concerning the performance of the play is due. *Taiwan* was performed by the teachers and students of the Kunhua Girls' Middle School (Kunhua Nüzi Zhongxue 昆華女子中學) in Kunming in the school's auditorium in 1942.[199] This performance situation makes the frequent recourse to the subject matter of education in times of war even more plausible. In this way, the play is more directly connected to the experiences of the students. In addition, the fact that the drama was performed at the said middle school adds further meaning to the attitude towards the female role in wartime disseminated in the play. Kunhua Girls' Middle School is known both for its links to the underground party branch of the CCP—Xu Jiarui, too, had intermittently taught at the school— [200] and for its wartime mobilisation activities.[201] During the war, some of the school's students

abandoned their studies to enlist in "battlefield service battalions" that roved the anti-Japanese front lines in Hubei, Hunan, and Jiangxi provinces, encouraging the officers

---

193 Dooling (2005), *Women's Literary Feminism*, p. 24. For a discussion of female warriors and patriotic courtesans in wartime drama see Hung (1994), *War and Popular Culture*, pp. 64–78. A scene that contrasts strikingly with the scene described above can be found in the play *Qiusheng fu* 秋聲賦 (Rhapsody in the Sound of Autumn; 1941) by Tian Han 田漢 (1898–1968). In this scene, two Chinese women engage in a fierce battle with two Japanese soldiers and finally kill them. See Tian Han (1983), "Qiusheng fu", pp. 345, 364–365; for a discussion of the play (including a translation of the scene) see Luo (2014), *The Avant-Garde*, pp. 131–138.
194 Louise Edwards characterizes the gender transgression of fictional women warriors in pre-modern China as "'crisis femininity' in which exceptional events provide space for a temporary release from the norms of womanly behavior (passivity, gentleness and frailty) as they lead armies, wage war and defend cities"; Edwards (2016), *Women Warriors*, p. 10.
195 Hung (1994), *War and Popular Culture*, pp. 77–78. This does not mean that no women fought in battle at all; see, e.g., Spakowski (2009), *"Mit Mut an die Front"*, pp. 233–236.
196 Spakowski (2009), *"Mit Mut an die Front "*.
197 Cf. Spakowski (2009), *"Mit Mut an die Front"*, pp. 211–321 for a detailed analysis.
198 Ibid., pp. 214–215.
199 Xu Yan (2008), "Xu Jiarui nianpu", p. 651; Xu Yan (2013), *Xu Jiarui lüezhuan*, p. 179.
200 Yuan (2001), "Restore Schools for Girls", p. 9; Xu Yan (2008), "Xu Jiarui nianpu".
201 Yuan (2001), "Restore Schools for Girls", pp. 9–10.

452 MIRJAM TRÖSTER

and men who were fighting the Japanese, raising their spirits, and making contributions to the war against the enemy.[202]

Against this background, the play can be said to have prescribed an arguably new role model for the female students in Kunming, one that decreased their options for making a change in the war and hence their agency. This role model adapted the CCP's transformed view on the gender-specific tasks to be performed by men and women at war. The message of the urgency to resist Japan within the confines of appropriate gender roles was in concert with the CCP's main parameters for anti-Japanese resistance and mobilisation at the time. The visualisation of the negative consequences for women who transgress the related boundaries and pay with their life thus also constituted a warning to the women both in the audience and on the stage.

IV.4. Characters in *Taiwan*—A Summary

To conclude the analysis of *Taiwan*, the play's staging of the fight against the loss of the country singles out three main groups that harm the country. First, the *foreign enemies* exert more agency and act in a much more brutal and detrimental way than in the *wenmingxi* play discussed above. Secondly, the play also harks back to the trope of the henpecking wife that manipulates her husband and, in this way, contributes to the demise of the country. This re-cast incarnation of the *shrew* acts in a physically less violent way than "Tang's" wife in *Qiu Shuyuan*, but uses her sharp tongue, instead. Thirdly, in contrast to the *wenmingxi* play, the group of *traitors* is not composed of those who collaborate with the foreign enemies to work *against* the authorities, but of those that *represent* them, instead. The resistance drama paints a grim picture of civilian authorities (symbolising the Guomindang administration). Officials disclose their corrupt and selfish nature, and the "president" is erased from the play, while the parliamentarians turn out to be more concerned with formalities than with resisting the external enemy. The main device to exhibit the lack of trust in the civilian authorities, however, resides in the play's establishing of the (military) protagonist as an alternative to the republic and its representatives. He is moulded as the only character who resolutely fights to save the country until the end. Saving the country by military means thus evolves as the only valid option from the play.

The structure of the drama thus interacts with the character constellation by dividing the play into two clearly distinct parts that symbolise the two phases of

---

202 Ibid.

the republic, which represent the corruptness of the civilian authorities, on the one hand, and the resolve and capability of the male military hero, on the other. In addition, the line-up of characters meeting "Liu Yongfu", including the two female characters who glorify him and who differ from "Liu" so fundamentally in their lack of courage, add to the moulding of the protagonist into a character that stands out from the crowd. The orders he gives both make a change to the lives of individuals and keep the resistance-struggle alive. Moreover, switching to the character as an artefact, his decisions are the major driving forces of the plot in the second part of the play. "Liu's" sagacity and resolve, paired with his sense of honour, further characterise him as a *yingxiong*.

"Liu" differs from this ideal in two interrelated aspects, however: he feels tired and old, and we never see him prove his courage and physical strength in actual battle. However, he makes up for this by showing absolute stamina, zest for action, and an uncompromising fighting spirit—in short, mental strength. In this way, the resistance drama adapts the *yingxiong* model to a phase of the war in which hope for (quick) victory had dwindled. By ways of turning the spirit of the tired but unflinching hero into a model to emulate, the drama disseminates the clearly propagandistic message to continue fighting the Japanese army against all odds.[203] The re-definition of the *yingxiong* situates this play firmly within a specific time and place, that is, wartime China in the early 1940s, and also within a specific (Communist) political agenda.

The latter also surfaces in its popularisation of *gender roles at war*. The portrayal of women in *Taiwan* is disturbing. There are no strong female characters in the play. Among the pleasure-seeking wives, the shrew whose manipulation of her husband harms the country sticks out. Her capability to persuade, however, is conditioned by the fact that her wishes and plans have to converge with the egoistic wishes of her husband before they finally lead to the desired result.[204] Even more strikingly, the agency of the two patriotic female students is weak. Their actions have neither impact on the future course of the war or the country in the end, nor do they change the main plotline decisively, but only serve to spotlight the male hero more prominently.

---

203 If it were not for the time and place in which the play was written and performed, an alternative reading of the protagonist would suggest itself: The aged "Liu Yongfu" has suffered many setbacks, and his final call-to-arms is likely to lead directly to his death at the hands of the Japanese army. In other words, it is appealing to read the portrayal of this character against the grain, namely as an indictment of a military leader (*i.e.* Chiang Kai-shek 蔣介石 (Jiang Jieshi, 1887–1975)) who, devoid of agency, is unable to save the country.

204 The play thus refrains from turning the shrew into a representation of Soong May-ling 宋美齡 (Song Meiling, 1897–2003), who, in negative images of Chiang Kai-shek, was frequently depicted as domineering her husband; cf. Taylor (n.d.), "Enemy of the People".

V. Conclusion

The two theatre plays *Qiu Shuyuan Destroys His Family to Save the Nation* (1910s) and *Taiwan* (1942) both resort to the example of anti-Japanese resistance in Taiwan in 1895 in order to explore the weakness of the country and propose a model to save it from perishing. They hence share a basic narrative that tells the story of a country facing the threat to being "lost" to an "invader", while internal enemies, disunity, and incompetent political leadership hasten its demise. Although this narrative is evocative of similar plays about "lost countries" such as Korea, Poland, or Vietnam that were popular in late Qing and early Republican China, the example of Taiwan is taken from (Qing) China's own history. But "Taiwan" assumes a different meaning in the two plays. While *Qiu Shuyuan* establishes a relatively detached link to Taiwan, which it turns into a projection screen for China, with the events of 1895 foreshadowing the Chinese republic, the resistance drama written by Xu Jiarui weaves a direct thread from the anti-Japanese resistance on Taiwan in 1895 to the Second Sino-Japanese War, a difference that mirrors the "deafening silence [concerning explicit claims to sovereignty over Taiwan] between 1911 and [...] the Second World War".[205]

Based upon their different diagnoses of the most urgent weaknesses of the country, the two plays propose different treatments to save the country, that is to say, China, from perishing. *Qiu Shuyuan* suggests a two-layered approach. Even though it acknowledges the necessity of defending the country on the battlefield, it pins hope on the founding of an independent republic which will strengthen the country in the long run. In this vein, it not only warns of the potential harm done by egoistic individuals, but also alerts its readers and/or spectators to beware of politicians who are not capable of putting the agency that their office endows them with to good use. The strengthening of co-operation among a like-minded civilian and military élite—the main agents of the play—emerges as the preferred remedy to counter the country's weakness. Smart, courageous, and patriotic women complement the array of talents that the (future) republic needs. Accordingly, optimism and a strong belief in joint action pervade the play. The resistance drama rigidly narrows the legitimate approaches to remedying the weakness of the country down to the military. In the play of the early 1940s, the civilian authorities have completely lost their credibility. Confidence is instead put in the military (male) hero, who continues to pursue the seemingly hopeless resistance-struggle against all odds.

The two plays visualise their respective models to save the country at character level. Befitting *Qiu Shuyuan*'s emphasis on flexibility and the co-operation of different groups, the *wenmingxi* play uses a pot-pourri of different ways to

---

205 Hughes (1997), *Taiwan and Chinese Nationalism*, p. 5.

create its characters and define their potential agency. It makes ample use of role categories, which it combines with the use of literary types, historical and "quasi-historical" characters, as well as of internymic relations. The resistance drama, by contrast, mainly builds on an interweaving of its structure and character constellation to define its characters and visualise their different degrees of agency. In a nutshell, the play's complete structure is geared towards the protagonist.

Not surprisingly, with a view to their common point of departure, similar groups of characters appear in the two plays, although their concrete form and importance differs. Written and performed in times of war, external enemies that threaten the country gain in both importance and agency in the later drama. While a young woman still outwits the Japanese commanders in the *wenmingxi* play, for instance, the Japanese soldiers of the resistance drama set a trap and kill the patriotic female students. Similarly, regarding the group of internal enemies or traitors, there is an important change, too: *Qiu Shuyuan* identifies greedy individuals that co-operate with the external enemy to influence the political decision-makers as major threat to the country. In *Taiwan*, those who harm the country most are the representatives of state power. In both plays, henpecking wives collude with the traitors, most impressively so in the earlier play in which the shrew's actions contribute to sculpting the president into a most ridiculous character. Selfish and faint-hearted, the president only shows fickle support for independence, and is finally driven off stage (*i.e.*, across the Taiwan Strait) by his wife. In the resistance drama, the president even amounts to a mere blank, a nullity. Faint hearts—albeit not selfish ones—nonetheless also appear in *Taiwan*. They are now two female students who lose their initial courage on the battlefield.

Ardent male fighters struggle to save the country in both plays. In *Qiu Shuyuan*, these fighters combine the skills of an orator with that of a strategist in war, but are too hot-headed to achieve their goals on their own. It needs their joint action to rout the enemy. In *Taiwan*, the *yingxiong* supersedes the ardent fighters of the earlier play, and surpasses them in his capacity to act. Relating to the situation of China in the early 1940s, the body of this wartime hero may be tarnished, but his resoluteness and perseverance are unsurpassable. More than merely standing in for a person, he symbolises the spirit of mental strength and the resolve to resist the enemy against all odds.

Patriotic women are the last group of characters that appear in both plays. Whereas they greatly impact on the development of the plot of the *wenmingxi* play, the patriotic students' wish to contribute to the resistance efforts in the later drama comes to nothing, and they have hardly any capability to impact on the plot. As this indicates, the role of women in the two plays differs greatly. Even though, at first glance, the women in *Qiu Shuyuan* are not as dazzling as the female warrior that we encountered in the introduction to this chapter, their portrayal offers ample space for female agency. While the shrewish wife puts the republic in danger, her capability to act is even outshone by the gallant "heroine" who comes to the rescue of the title character. An undecidedness with regard to gender roles permeates the *wenmingxi* play, however. The shrewish wife, for instance, does not represent a so-called "new woman" (*xin nüxing* 新女性),[206] and the play stops short of turning the gallant female role into a protagonist of the play. Nonetheless, compared to the female characters in *Taiwan*, they are stronger and able to act more effectively in all respects—be that in their wickedness or in their gallantry. The playful and multi-layered approach to gender roles is absent from *Taiwan*, which presents us with a rather pale version of the shrew, and, what is more, has the female students shot on the battlefield. While women still have some power to harm the country, the main function of the female characters in the play is to make the hero stand out brightly. In short, if we include the female warriors on the battlefield in *Taiwan*, with which this chapter started, we can trace a clear line of development from these stunning women in the print to an ambivalent characterisation of women in *Qiu Shuyuan*, and subsequently to the depiction of rather sapless female characters in *Taiwan*. This describes a movement from strength to weakness, but also from the fantastic to the transitory moment of experimentation with new role models, and leads us on to a concrete model of action for female students in Kunming in 1942 both on the stage and beyond.

Qiu Shuyuan and *Taiwan* both draw on the example of the Taiwan Republic—including the Taiwan War—in order to educate the audience, at least in part. The devices that they choose are symptomatic of the different times at which the two plays were created. *Qiu Shuyuan* combines the speeches of orators with slapstick-like entertainment in order to popularise the ideas of resisting the enemy, and, more importantly, of strengthening the country by establishing an independent republic and nominating a president. It attempts to educate citizens by persuasion, as well as by making them complicit in laughter. The resistance drama, on the other hand, chooses the personification of a spirit of resolve and perseverance, as well as the visualisation of the consequences of transgressing desirable gender norms in times of war as principal educational devices used for wartime mobilisation. Propaganda and warning thus replace persuasion of (future) citizens. The story of Taiwan in 1895 is told according to the prevailing needs and visions of the time.

---

206 As Shu Yang argues, in the first half of the twentieth century, several purportedly negative characteristics of the shrew were transformed into components of the so-called "new woman"—the "modern" and progressive woman unconstrained by "traditional" role models; Yang (2016), "Grafted Identities".

This kind of imaginative re-writing of the Taiwan Republic, including the Taiwan War, has continued ever since, albeit to different degrees. The subject has, for instance, regained the attention of both writers and theatre directors on both sides of the Taiwan Strait in the last decade.[207] The second half of the 2000s witnessed several well-advertised films and performances on the topic. The most prominent of these, without doubt, is *Blue Brave: The Legend of Formosa in 1895* (*Yi ba jiu wu* 一八九五, 2008) by Hong Chih-yu 洪智育 (Hong Zhiyu, 1968–), which focuses on Hakka anti-Japanese resistance. Especially in works created in Taiwan and which link up with the imagination of a Taiwanese identity, the contribution of the population of Taiwan to the resistance struggle, and the issue of the degree of agency of the individual concerning Taiwan's future has moved to centre-stage. If we remain in the realms of theatre and education, Hsu Rey-fang's 許瑞芳 (Xu Ruifang, 1961–) *Open the City Gates in 1895* (*Yi ba jiu wu kai chengmen* 一八九五開城門) is an apt example.[208] In 2009, Hsu and her students of Tainan National University (Guoli Tainan Daxue 國立臺南大學) co-operated with the National Museum of Taiwan History (Guoli Taiwan Lishi Bowuguan 國立臺灣歷史博物館) to realise this project of theatre-in-education (*jiaoxi juchang* 教習劇場). *Open the City Gates in 1895* centres on the question of whether to resist the approaching Japanese army or, instead, open the gates of a city in central Taiwan to them. In the premises of the museum, the narrator and the actors and actresses collaborate with the pupils to re-enact history. The pupils not only watch recordings and scenes acted out by the actors and actresses, and listen to the narrator, but also invent rumours that might have been spread in 1895, develop arguments for both positions, and assume different roles themselves. Hence, in a totally different sense to the two plays discussed in this chapter, the performance explores the issue of agency both in history and today, and causes the students to relate to the past both intellectually and emotionally. Thus, yet another story of the events in Taiwan in 1895 is born. The worries, fears, and hopes of the local population now take precedence over the faint-heartedness of the president, the betrayal of the traitors, and the wickedness of the shrewish wife. They also supersede the victories of the stunning female warriors, the entertaining and courageous tricks of the gallant women, the fervent speeches of the ardent men, and the resolute call-to-arms of the wartime *yingxiong*.

---

207 For a comparison of two TV series on the topic produced in China and Taiwan, respectively, see Lee (2013), "All About 1895". Significantly, the Taiwan Republic is not broached in the mainland Chinese series; ibid., p. 507.

208 For the script and a DVD recording of one the play's performances at the National Museum of Taiwan History see Hsu Rey-fang (2009), *Yi ba jiu wu kai chengmen*.

Bibliography

A Ying 阿英 (ed.) (1958), *Jiawu Zhong-Ri zhanzheng wenxue ji* 甲午中日戰爭文學集 (Anthology of Literature on the First Sino-Japanese War), Beijing: Zhonghua shuju.

Alsford, Niki J.P. (2018), *Transitions to Modernity in Taiwan: The Spirit of 1895 and the Cession of Formosa to Japan*, London and New York: Routledge.

Chen Duansheng 陳端生 (2014), "Zaisheng yuan quanzhuan" 再生緣全傳 (Complete Tale of the Destiny of Rebirth), Baoningtang edition of 1822, in: *Xuxiu siku quanshu, Diaolong Full Text Database of Chinese and Japanese Ancient Books* (last accessed 9 November 2018).

Chen, Duxiu (2002), "On Theater", in: Faye Chunfang Fei (trans., ed.), *Chinese Theories of Theater and Performance from Confucius to the Present*, Ann Arbor MI: University of Michigan Press, pp. 117–120.

Chiang, Linda H. (2014), "Forces for Change: Overseas Education for Chinese Women at the Turn of the Republican Period in China", in: Ya-chen Chen (ed.), *New Modern Chinese Women and Gender Politics: The Centennial of the End of the Qing Dynasty*, London and New York: Routledge, pp. 123–131.

Chou, [Katherine] Hui-ling (1997), "Striking their own Poses: The History of Cross-Dressing on the Chinese Stage", *The Drama Review*, 41: 2, pp. 130–152.

Chou [Katherine] Hui-ling (Zhou Huiling 周慧玲) (2000), "Nü yanyuan, xieshizhuyi, 'xin nüxing' lunshu: wan Qing dao wusi shiqi Zhongguo xiandai juchang zhong de xingbie biaoyan" 女演員，寫實主義，'新女性' 論述—晚清到五四時期中國現代劇場中的性別表演 (Actresses, Realism, and the Discourse of the "New Woman": Gender Performance in Modern Chinese Theatre From the Late Qing to the May Fourth Period), *Xiju yishu*, no. 1 (93), pp. 4–26.

Croissant, Doris et al. (2008), "Introduction", in: Idem (eds.), *Performing "Nation": Gender Politics in Literature, Theater, and the Visual Arts of China and Japan, 1880–1940*, Leiden and Boston MA: Brill, pp. 1–15.

CYP [*sic*] (1986), "Ch'en Tuan-sheng", in: William H. Nienhauser, Jr. (ed.): *The Indiana Companion to Traditional Chinese Literature*, Bloomington IN: Indiana University Press, p. 236.

Davidson, James W. (1903), *The Island of Formosa Past and Present: History, People, Resources, and Commercial Prospects. Tea, Camphor, Sugar, Gold, Coal, Sulphur, Economical Plants, and Other Productions*. London and New York: Macmillan & Co.

Dong, Jian 董健 (ed.) (2003), *Zhongguo xiandai xiju zongmu tiyao* 中國現代戲劇總目提要 (Annotated Bibliography of Modern Chinese Theatre), Nanjing: Nanjing daxue chubanshe.

Dongya bingfu 東亞病夫 (= Zeng Pu 曾樸) (1928), "Niehai hua di-shiliu juan di-sanshier hui" 孽海花第十六卷第三十二回 (*Flowers in a Sea of Sins*, volume 16, Chapter 32), *Zhen mei shan*, 2:3, pp. 1–22.

Dooling, Amy D. (2005), *Women's Literary Feminism in Twentieth-Century China*, New York and Basingstroke: Palgrave Macmillan.

Eberstein, Bernd (1983), *Das Chinesische Theater im 20. Jahrhundert*, Wiesbaden: Harrassowitz.

Eder, Jens (2010), "Understanding Characters", *Projections*, 4:1, pp. 16–40.

Eder, Jens et al. (2010), "Characters in Fictional Worlds: An Introduction", in: Idem. (eds.), *Characters in Fictional Worlds: Understanding Imaginary Beings in Literature, Film, and Other Media*, Berlin and New York: Walter de Gruyter, pp. 3–64.

Edwards, Louise (2016), *Women Warriors and Wartime Spies of China*, Cambridge: Cambridge University Press.

Emirbayer, Mustafa and Ann Mische (1998), "What is Agency?", *American Journal of Sociology*, 203: 4, pp. 962–1023.

Fu Xiaohang 傅曉航 and Zhang Xiulian 張秀蓮 (eds.) (1994), *Zhongguo jindai xiqu lunzhu zongmu* 中國近代戲曲論著總目 (Index of Articles and Books on Modern Chinese Theatre), Beijing: Wenhua yishu chubanshe.

Giddens, Anthony (1984), *The Constitution of Society: Outline of the Theory of Structuration*, Cambridge: Polity Press.

Goldstein, Joshua (2007), D*rama Kings: Players and Publics in the Re-creation of Peking Opera, 1870–1937*, Berkeley CA et al.: University of California Press.

Goldman, Merle, and Elizabeth J. Perry (2002), "Introduction: Political Citizenship in Modern China", in: eadem (eds.), *Changing Meanings of Citizenship in Modern China*, Cambridge MA and London: Harvard University Press, pp. 1–19.

Gordon, Leonard H.D. (2007), *Confrontation over Taiwan: Nineteenth-Century China and the Powers*, Lanham MD: Lexington.

Guo, Li (2015), *Women's* Tanci *Fiction in Late Imperial and Early Twentieth-Century China*, West Lafayette IN, Perdue University Press.

Hanan, Patrick (2005), *Chinese Fiction of the Nineteenth and Early Twentieth Centuries: Essays by Patrick Hanan*. New York: Columbia University Press, E-Book (last accessed 12 January 2018).

Harris, Lane J. (2018), *The Peking Gazette: A Reader in Nineteenth-Century Chinese History*, Leiden and Boston MA: Brill.

Harrison, Mark (2016), *Legitimacy, Meaning and Knowledge in the Making of Taiwanese Identity*, New York: Palgrave Macmillan.

He, Chengzhou (2008), "Women and the Search for Modernity: Rethinking Modern Chinese Drama", *Modern Language Quarterly*, 69: 1, pp. 45–60.

Hershatter, Gail (2007), *Women in China's Long Twentieth Century*, Berkeley CA et al.: Global, Area, and International Archive, University of California Press.

Hieronymus, Sabine (1999), "Frauenvorbilder: Über fiktive und reale Heldinnen in der späten chinesischen Kaiserzeit am Beispiel von Meng Lijun und Qiu Jin", Ph.D. Thesis, Kiel University, Ann Arbor: UMI.

Hinsch, Bret (2013), *Masculinities in Chinese History*, Lanham MD: Rowman & Littlefield, E-Book (last accessed 23 August 2018).

Hong Xingquan 洪興全 (2012), *Shuo wo zhuan* 說倭傳 (Tale of the Dwarfs), arranged by Chen Shuliang 陳書良, Beijing: Zhongguo guoji guangbo chubanshe.

Hsu Rey-fang (Xu Ruifang) 許瑞芳 (2009), *Yi ba jiu wu kai chengmen* 一八九五開城門 (Open the City Gates in 1895), Tainan: Tainan Shiboguan.

Hsü, Immanuel C.Y. (2000), *The Rise of Modern China*, 6th edition, New York and Oxford: Oxford University Press.

Hua Shilin 劃士林 (1932), "Buzheng 'Gerang Taiwan shi zhi Qiu Shuyuan'" 補正割讓臺灣時之邱菽園 (Supplement to and Correction of "Qiu Shuyuan at the time of the cession of Taiwan"), *Shenbao*, 9 January 1932.

Huang, Martin W. (2006), *Negotiating Masculinities in Late Imperial China*, Honolulu HI: University of Hawai'i Press.

Hucker, Charles O. (1985), *A Dictionary of Official Titles in Imperial China*, Stanford CA: Stanford University Press.

Hughes (1997), *Taiwan and Chinese Nationalism: National Identity and Status in International Society*, London and New York: Routledge.

Hung, Chang-tai (1994), *War and Popular Culture: Resistance in Modern China, 1937–1945*, Berkeley CA et al.: University of California Press, http://ark.cdlib.org/ark:/13030/ft829008m5 (last accessed 9 October 2018).

Hwang, Yin (2014), "Victory Pictures in a Time of Defeat: Depicting War in the Print and Visual Culture of Late Qing China 1884–1901", Ph.D. Thesis, SOAS, University of London, http://eprints.soas.ac.uk/18449 (last accessed 29 August 2018).

Idema, Wilt L. (2010), "Prosimetric and Verse Narrative", in: Chang Kang-i Sun and Stephen Owen (eds.), *The Cambridge History of Chinese Literature, vol. 2, From 1375*, Cambridge MA et al.: Cambridge University Press, pp. 243–412.

Jianyun 劍雲 (1915), "Xinju pingyi" 新劇平議 (Discussion of New Drama), *Fanhua zazhi*, 5, pp. 251–257.

Judge, Joan (2002), "Citizens or Mothers of Citizens?: Gender and the Meaning of Modern Chinese Citizenship", in: Merle Goldman and Elizabeth J. Perry (eds.), *Changing Meanings of Citizenship in Modern China*, Cambridge MA and London: Harvard University Press, pp. 23–43.

— (2005), "Between Nei and Wai: Chinese Women Students in Japan in the Early Twentieth Century", in: Bryna Goodman and Wendy Larson (eds.): *Gender in Motion: Divisions of Labor and Cultural Change in Late Imperial and Modern China*, Lanham MD: Rowman & Littlefield, E-Book (last accessed 20 August 2018).

Karl, Rebecca (2002), *Staging the World: Chinese Nationalism at the Turn of the Twentieth Century*, Durham and London: Duke University Press.

Kerr, George H. (1974), *Formosa: Licensed Revolution and the Home Rule Movement, 1895–1945*, Honolulu HI: University of Hawai'i Press.

Kiang, Clyde (1992), *The Hakka Odyssey & Their Taiwan Homeland*, Elgin PA: Allegheny.

Lamley, Harry J. (1968), "The 1895 Taiwan Republic: A Significant Episode in Modern Chinese History", *The Journal of Asian Studies*, 27:4 , pp. 739–762.

— (1970), "The 1895 Taiwan War of Resistance: Local Chinese Efforts against a Foreign Power", in: Leonard H.D. Gordon (ed.), *Taiwan: Studies in Chinese Local History*, New York and London: Columbia University Press, pp. 23–77.

— (2007), "Taiwan Under Japanese Rule, 1895–1945: The Vicissitudes of Colonialism", in: Murray A. Rubinstein (ed.), *Taiwan: A New History*, Expanded Edition, Armonk NY and London: M.E. Sharpe, pp. 201–260.

Lee, Guan Kin (2012), "Khoo Seok Wan", in: Leo Suryadinata (ed.), *Southeast Asian Personalities of Chinese Descent: A Biographical Dictionary*, vol. 1, Singapore: Chinese Heritage Centre, Institute of Southeast Asian Studies, pp. 417–419.

Lee, Pei-Ling (2013), "All About 1895: An Ideological Analysis of TV Serials from the Two Sides of the Taiwan Strait", *Oriental Archive*, 81:3 , pp. 495–514.

Liang Qichao 梁啟超 (1989), *Yinbingshi heji: zhuanji* 飲冰室合集：專集 (Collected Works from the Ice-Drinker's Studio: Special Collection), vol. 7, no. 22–29, Beijing: Zhonghua shuju.

Liu, Siyuan (2013), *Performing Hybridity in Colonial-Modern China*, New York: Palgrave Macmillan.

Louie, Kam (2002), *Theorising Chinese Masculinity: Society and Gender in China*, Cambridge et al.: Cambridge University Press.

Luo, Liang (2014), *The Avant-Garde and the Popular in Modern China: Tian Han and the Intersection of Performance and Politics*, Ann Arbor MI: The University of Michigan Press.

Lust, John (1996), *Chinese Popular Prints*, Leiden et al.: Brill.

Ma Junshan 馬俊山 (2013), "Lun wenmingxi jiaose zhi de xingcheng yu yanbian" 論文明戲角色制的形成與演變 (The Formation and Development of the Role Category System in Civilised Theatre), *Jianghai xuekan*, no. 1, pp. 196–201.

Mao Zedong 毛澤東 (1952), "Lun chijiu zhan" 論持久戰 (On Protracted War), in: Idem, *Mao Zedong xuanji*, vol. 2, Beijing: Renmin chubanshe, pp. 429–506.

– (1965), "On Protracted War", in: Idem, *Selected Works of Mao Tse-tung*, vol. 2, Beijing: Foreign Languages Press, pp. 113–194.

Meng Shuhong 蒙樹宏 (2016), "Xu Jiarui" 徐嘉瑞 (Xu Jiarui), in: Idem, *Meng Shuhong wenji, vol. 4, xiandai wenxue liu ren ji*, Kunming: Yunnan daxue chubanshe, pp. 186–190.

Mitter, Rana (2016), "The War Years, 1937–1949", in: Jeffrey N. Wasserstrom (ed.), *The Oxford Illustrated History of Modern China*, Oxford: Oxford University Press, pp. 150–175.

Momose, Hiromu (1943): "Ch'iu Fêng-chia", in: Arthur W. Hummel (ed.), *Eminent Chinese of the Ch'ing Period (1644–1912)*, vol. I, Washington DC: Government Printing Office, pp. 171–172.

Morris, Andrew (2002), "The Taiwan Republic of 1895 and the Failure of the Qing Modernizing Project", in: Stéphane Corcuff (ed.), *Memories of the Future: National Identity Issues and the Search for a New Taiwan*, Armonk NY and London: M.E. Sharpe, pp. 3–24.

"Mubiao: Qiu Shuyuan huijia jiuguo (youming 'Santai yihen')" 幕表邱菽園毀家救國（又名 "三臺遺恨"） (Qiu Shuyuan Destroys His Family to Save the Nation (aka Regret of Taiwan)) 1989, in: Wang Weimin (ed.), *Zhongguo zaoqi huaju xuan*, Beijing: Zhongguo xiju chubanshe, pp. 697–700.

Müller, Wolfgang G. (1991), "Interfigurality: A Study on the Interdependence of Literary Figures", in: Heinrich F. Plett (ed.), *Intertextuality*, Berlin and New York: Walter de Gruyter, pp. 101–121.

Ouyang Yuqian 歐陽予倩 (1984), "Tan wenmingxi" 談文明戲 (On Civilised Theatre), in: *Ouyang Yuqian xiju lunwen ji* 歐陽予倩戲劇論文集 (Anthology of Ouyang Yuqian's Essays about Theatre), Shanghai: Shanghai wenyi chubanshe, pp. 175–231.

Qian, Kun (2016), *Imperial-Time-Order: Literature, Intellectual History, and China's Road to Empire*, Leiden and Boston MA: Brill.

Qian Zhonglian 錢僅聯 et al. (eds.) (2000), *Zhongguo wenxue da cidian* 中國文學大辭典 (Encyclopedia of Chinese Literature), Shanghai: Shanghai cishu chubanshe.

Qiu Shuyuan 邱菽園 (1958), "Huizhu shiyi" 揮麈拾遺 (*Gleanings of Chit-chat*), in: A Ying (ed.), *Jiawu Zhong-Ri Zhanzheng wenxue ji*, Beijing: Zhonghua shuju, pp. 546–553.

Qiu Zhuchang 邱铸昌 (2004), *Qiu Fengjia jiaowang lu* 邱逢甲交往錄 (*Record of Qiu Fengjia's Correspondences*), Wuhan: Huazhong shifan daxue chubanshe.

Rea, Christopher (2015), *The Age of Irreverence: A New History of Laughter in China*, Oakland CA: University of California Press.

San'ai 三愛 (= Chen Duxiu 陳獨秀) (1904), "Lun xiqu" 論戲曲 (*On Theatre*), *Anhui suhuabao*, 11, pp. 1–6.

Schillinger, Nicolas (2016), *The Body and Military Masculinity in Late Qing and Early Republican China: The Art of Governing Soldiers*, Lanham MD et al.: Lexington.

Shan, Patrick Fuliang (2018), *Yuan Shikai: A Reappraisal*, Vancouver and Toronto: UBC Press.

Shi Yi 石藝 (2010), "Wenmingxi dui Zhongguo chuantong xiqu de xucheng: yi mubiaoxi wei zhongxin" 文明戲對中國傳統戲曲的繼承——以幕表戲為中心 (What *wenminxi* Inherits from Chinese Traditional [Music] Theatre: Focussing on the Plot Outline), pp. 71–74.

Spakowski, Nicola (2009), "*Mit Mut an die Front': Die Militärische Beteiligung von Frauen in der Kommunistischen Revolution Chinas (1925–1949)*, Cologne et al.: Böhlau.

Strand, David (2002), "Citizens in the Audience and at the Podium", in: Merle Goldman and Elizabeth J. Perry (eds.), *Changing Meanings of Citizenship in Modern China*, Cambridge MA and London: Harvard University Press, pp. 44–69.

Taylor, Jeremy E. (n.d.), "Enemy of the People: Visual Depictions of Chiang Kai-shek", *Enemy of the People* website, Arts and Humanities Research Council, Humanities Research Institute at the University of Sheffield, https://www.dhi.ac.uk/chiangkaishek/background/ (last accessed 31 October 2018).

Tian Han (1983), "Qiusheng fu" 秋聲賦 (Rhapsody in the Sound of Autumn), in: Idem, *Tian Han wenji*, vol. 5, Beijing: Zhongguo xiju chubanshe, pp. 227–372.

Tsai, Chien-hsin (2017), *A Passage to China: Literature, Loyalism, and Colonial Taiwan*, Cambridge MA: Harvard University Asia Center, Harvard University Press.

Van Slyke, Lyman (1986), "The Chinese Communist Movement During the Sino-Japanese War 1937–1945", in: John K. Fairbank and Albert Feuerwerker, *The Cambridge History of China, vol. 13, Republican China 1912–1949, Part 2*, Cambridge et al.: Cambridge University Press, pp. 665–671.

Wagner, Rudolf G. (2007), "Joining the Global Imaginaire: The Shanghai Illustrated Newspaper Dianshizhai huabao", in: Idem (ed.), *Joining the Global Public: Word, Image, and City in Early Chinese Newspapers, 1870–1910*. Ithaca NY: State University of New York Press, pp. 105–173.

Wang Fengxia 王風霞 (2008), "Zuowei 'gongming' de wenmingxi: wenmingxi de leixing he xingtai" 作為'共名'的文明戲——文明戲的類型和型態 (*Wenmingxi* as 'Umbrella Term': Types and Forms of *wenmingxi*), *Jianghan luntan*, no. 7, pp. 112–117.

Wang Weimin 王偉民 (ed.) (1989), *Zhongguo zaoqi huaju xuan* 中國早期話劇選 (Collection of Chinese Spoken Drama of the Early Period), Beijing: Zhongguo xiju chubanshe.

Wang, Xiaojue (2013), *Modernity with a Cold War Face: Reimagining the Nation in Chinese Literature Across the 1949 Divide*, Cambridge MA and London: Harvard University Asia Center, Harvard University Press.

Wang Xiaonong 汪笑儂 (1957), "Ku zumiao" 哭祖廟 (Weeping at the Ancestral Shrine), in: *Wang Xiaonong xiqu ji* 汪笑儂戲曲集 (Anthology of Wang Xiaonong's [Music] Theatre Plays), Beijing: Zhongguo xiju chubanshe, pp. 135–149.

Wei Chi 衛琪 (2011), "Yiwei Taiwan kang-Ri: yi nüxing kang-Ri tuxiang wei yanjiu zhuti" 乙未臺灣抗日——以女性抗日圖像為研究主題 (The Taiwanese Resistance against Japan in 1895: Research on Pictures of Women Resisting Japan), *Guoli Taizhong Jishu Xueyuan tongshi jiaoyu xuebao* 4, pp. 55–72.

Wu, Yenna (1988), "The Inversion of Marital Hierarchy: Shrewish Wives and Henpecked Husbands in Seventeenth-Century Chinese Literature", *Harvard Journal of Asiatic Studies*, 48: 1, pp. 363–382.

— (1995), *The Chinese Virago: A Literary Theme*, Cambridge MA and London: Council on East Asian Studies, Harvard University and Harvard University Press.

Wu □ zai 五在 [character illegible] (1931), "Buji Qiu Shuyuan" 補記邱菽園 (Supplementary Notes on Qiu Shuyuan), *Shenbao*, 31 December 1931.

Xu Banmei 徐半梅 (1957), *Huaju chuangshiqi huiyilu* 話劇創時期回憶錄 (Reminiscences of Spoken Drama's Initial Era), Beijing: Zhongguo xiju chubanshe.

Xu Jiarui 徐嘉瑞 (1943a), "Zixu" 自序 (Author's Preface), in: Idem, *Taiwan*, Guiyang: Wentong shuju, pp. "Zixu" 1–5.

Xu Jiarui 徐嘉瑞 (1943b), "Taiwan" 臺灣 (Taiwan), in: Idem, *Taiwan*, Guiyang: Wentong shuju, pp. "Taiwan" 1–58.

"Xu Jiarui" 徐嘉瑞 (1979), in: Zhongguo Wenxuejia Cidian Bianweihui (ed.), *Zhongguo wenxuejia cidian*, Hong Kong: Wenhua ziliao gongyingshe, pp. 438–441.

Xu Jiarui 徐嘉瑞 (2008), "Paosheng xiang le" 炮聲響了 (The Sound of Canons Set In), in: Ma Yao and Xu Yan (eds.), *Xu Jiarui quanji*, vol. 4, Kunming: Yunnan chuban jituan gongsi et al., pp. 255–268.

Xu Yan 徐演 (1983), "Xu Jiarui xiaozhuan" 徐嘉瑞小傳 (Short biography of Xu Jiarui), in: Beijing Tushuguan "Wenxian" Congkan Bianjibu, Jilin Sheng Tushuguan Xuehui Huikan Bianjibu (eds.), *Zhongguo dangdai shehui kexuejia (zhuanji congshu)*, vol. 5, Beijing: Shumu wenxian chubanshe, pp. 310–319.

Xu Yan 徐演 (2008), "Xu Jiarui nianpu" 徐嘉瑞年譜 (Chronicle of Xu Jiarui's Life), in: Ma Yao and Xu Yan (eds.), *Xu Jiarui quanji*, vol. 4, Kunming: Yunnan chuban jituan gongsi et al. , pp. 641–670.

Xu Yan 徐演 (2013), *Xu Jiarui lüezhuan* 徐嘉瑞略傳 (Biographical Sketch of Xu Jiarui), Kunming: Yunnan minzu chubanshe.

Yalu 亞盧 (＝Liu Yazi 柳亞子) (1903), "Taiwan sanbai nian shi" 臺灣三百年史 (Three Hundred Years of the History of Taiwan), *Jiangsu*, 7, pp. 53–57.

— (1904), "Taiwan sanbai nian shi (xu qianqi)" 臺灣三百年史（續前期） (Three Hundred Years of the History of Taiwan (Continued)), *Jiangsu*, 8, pp. 51–55.

Yan, Haiping (2006), *Chinese Women Writers and the Feminist Imagination, 1905–1948*, London and New York: Routledge.

Yang Nancun 楊南邨 (1917), *Shijie wangguo baishi* 世界亡國稗史 (Unofficial History of the Lost Countries of the World), Shanghai: Jiaotong tushuguan.

Yang, Shu (2016), "Grafted Identities: Shrews and the New Woman Narrative in China (1910s–1960s)", Ph.D. diss., University of Oregon.

Yao Xiguang 姚錫光 (2010), *Dongfang bingshi jilüe* 東方兵事記略 (Short Record of Military Affairs in the East), arranged by Li Jikui 李吉奎, Beijing: Zhonghua shuju.

Yuan, Qinfen (2001), "Restore Schools for Girls, Optimize Personality Education, and Improve the Attributes of Females: Looking Back at the Development of the Kunming Middle School for Girls", *Chinese Education and Society*, 34: ,1, pp. 8–21.

Zhang Bilai 張畢來 (1979), "Qianyan" 前言 (Preface), in: Zeng Pu, *Niehai hua* (zeng-dingben), Shanghai: Shanghai guji chubanshe, pp. 1–12.

Zhao Ji 趙冀 (2011), *Huaju yu Shanghai shimin shehui (1907–1949)* 話劇與上海市民社會 (Modern Drama and Shanghai Civil Society (1907–1949)), Beijing: Zhongguo xiju chubanshe.

Zheng Yimei 鄭逸梅 (1931), "Gerang Taiwan shi zhi Qiu Shuyuan" 割讓臺灣時之邱菽園 (Qiu Shuyuan at the Time of the Cession of Taiwan), *Shenbao*, 27 December 1931.

Zhu Shuangyun 朱雙雲 (2014), *Xinju shi* 新劇史 (History of New Drama), Shanghai: Xinju xiaoshuo she.

Zimmer, Thomas (2001), "Vorwort", in: Zeng Pu, Thomas Zimmer (trans.), *Blumen im Meer der Sünde*, Munich: Iudicium, pp. 9–19.

Progress or Decline: China's Two Images of India during the Nineteenth Century

Zhang Ke

China and India are both old Asian civilisations, and cultural exchange between the two countries has a very long history. From the Tang dynasty 唐 (618–907) to the Song dynasty 宋 (960–1279), Buddhism had the leading role in the exchange between the two places. It reached a peak and then underwent a gradual decline. When during the Yuan 元 (1279–1368) and the Ming 明 (1368–1644) dynasties, there was no obstruction of maritime communication, the trade in goods between China and India thrived. From the Qing-dynasty 清, (1644–1911) up to the first half of the twentieth century, when Western powers, including England, penetrated into the Eastern part of Asia, the original mode of interaction between China and India was transformed and, at the same time, a new, even more complex web of relations was formed. When researching this comparatively recent period of cultural exchange, it is not possible to start from a traditional "Buddhist" or "material culture" point of view. Most scholars who do research the "Colonial Period" (the middle of the eighteenth century to the first half of the twentieth century) of the relations between China and India are ready to acknowledge this point.[1]

How did the Chinese view India in historical times? Seen from a long period perspective, the image of India in Chinese writings underwent numerous changes. Tan Chung 譚中 (born in 1929) has divided China's view of India from ancient times to the present into six phases, and, among these, has designated the period between the nineteenth and the early twentieth century as the "phase of sympathy". When speaking of "sympathy", he points out that, in facing European Colonialism, the two countries of China and India were in a situation in which they sympathised with their fellow sufferer.[2] And Ji Xianlin 季羨林 (1911–2009) also thinks that, during the nineteenth century, "the people of the two countries, especially those with a certain sensibility and a wide

---

1 For an overview of the relations between India and China during the Colonial period, cf. Madhavi Thampi, ed. (2005), *India and China in the Colonial World.*

2 Tan Zhong (2006), "Zhongguo wenhua yanjing zhong Yindu xingxiang de bianqian"p. 42, Tan Zhong, Geng Yinzeng (2016), *Yindu yu Zhongguo—liang da wenming de jiaowang he jidang,* pp. 16–18.

breadth of vision, spontaneously developed the feeling that it was necessary to help each other in times of need, and that there was a situation in which they were fellow sufferers and held a hope of understanding the other side".[3]

During the second half of the 20th century, Ji Xianlin and Tan Chung were the most famous Chinese scholars doing research into the cultural exchange between China and India, and they were both of the opinion that "sympathy" was the most important feature of the mutual image during the nineteenth century. If, however, one looks into this issue in more detail, one will discover that the emergence of this feeling of "sympathy" was by no means as "spontaneous" as they claimed, and that it actually emerged only later. In China, "sympathy" when treating India (or rather British-ruled India) only became the most important factor when the anti-colonial discourse spread from the beginning of the twentieth century. And the fact that Ji and Tan stressed "sympathy" in this way is actually also, to a great extent, due to the fact that they themselves were influenced by this "anti-colonial" discourse.

The reason for the emergence of such a complicated web of exchange and interaction between China, India and Europe lies in the substantial differences between China and India, and the fact that the processes through which the European countries penetrated these two countries were by no means similar. It was only after the Opium Wars of the mid-nineteenth century that China, as a unified Empire under the Qing-Dynasty, gradually opened its doors, and, at this time, English colonialists had been active in India for already more than two hundred years and had a very strong influence.[4] Due to the differences in space and in time, the view of the respective "other" among the intellectual strata of the two countries was varied and can by no means be generalised under the concept of "sympathy". From the angle of anti-imperialism and anti-colonialism, 20th century scholars intentionally constructed the "sympathy" narrative, and, in this way, overlooked many of the historical details embodied in it.

This chapter mainly looks into the image of India as presented in nineteenth century Chinese documents and attempts to comb them for the two leading narratives of "progress" and "decline". There have already been some scholars who have done research into the Indian image of China. Generally speaking, the knowledge of China on the part of the masses was very limited, while among intellectuals a number of different views co-existed.[5] On the Chinese side,

---

3 Ji Xianlin (2008), *Zhong Yin wenhua jiaoliu shi*, p. 126.
4 The process of the establishment of colonial rule in India has been analyzed by Metcalf (1995), *The New Cambridge History of India*.
5 For the Indian image of China see Yin Xinan (2014), *Yindu Zhongguo guan yanbian yanjiu*, Yin Xinan (2010), *Yindu de Zhongguo xingxiang*, Thampi, Madhavi (2005), *Indians in China, 1800–1949*.

because of the Western incursions into China, among those strata of the society which had some understanding of India, only a very limited number continued to view India in the old way.. Modern China's concept of "World Order" underwent the transformation from "All under Heaven" to that of the "state",[6] and, at the end of the nineteenth century, a number of Chinese began to understand that China was a normal country among the countries of the world. Their view of the countries around China also changed from the traditional view of an order with China as the centre of "All under heaven" to a concept of competition among the myriad of surrounding countries. For this reason, a process of "re-discovery" of the countries colonialised by the Western powers—including India—took place.

This chapter researches the three aspects of "China – India – England" and it discusses how Chinese documents of the nineteenth century presented the English colonial rule of India and how this rule of India was appraised and on this basis it will look into the standpoint of the nineteenth century producers of narratives (including Western missionaries writing in Chinese). The question of whether this nineteenth century image of India is correct or not, is not at the heart of this essay, we mainly want to look into the intentions and ideas of those producing the narratives. Against the backdrop of the assault of the Western powers, which the Chinese experienced in the nineteenth century, their knowledge about India later on became more and more entangled with the Chinese understanding of their own situation. Under the influence of this understanding, "India" quite often became something akin to a positive or negative symbol.

I. Early Chinese knowledge of India under English colonial rule

Since Han-times, there has been a multitude of Chinese historical records which contain accounts of India. From the time of the Six Dynasties until the Sui and Tang Dynasties, the dissemination of Buddhism in China had made mutual visits by monks a frequent occurrence. Thus, the understanding of the respective other side gradually deepened. Since Song and Yuan times, the exchange between the two countries benefited from the newly-established maritime route.[7] Chinese private navigators and people with close relations to navigators either personally witnessed the situation or heard first-hand accounts of it, and, in different ways, collected all kinds of information. There was a number of

---

6 First proposed by Levenson (1968), *Confucian China and Its Modern Fate*, chapter 7.
7 Tansen Sen (2014), "Maritime Southeast Asia Between South Asia and China to the Sixteenth Century".

narratives on the Indian area, such as, for example, the *Brief Record of the Island Barbarians (Daoyi zhilüe)* 岛夷志略 written by Wang Dayuan 汪大淵 (1311–1360) during the Yuan Dynasty, and the three books *The Overall Survey of the Ocean's Shores (Yingya shenglan* 瀛涯勝覽), *The Overall Survey of the Star Raft (Xingcha shenglan* 星槎勝覽) and The *Annals of the Foreign Counties in the Western Ocean (Xiyang fan guo zhi* 西洋番國志) compiled in the course of the voyages of Admiral Zheng He 鄭和 (1371–1433)which presented the life of the people on the Indian peninsula, as well as its products and the commercial situation.[8]

When Catholic missionaries came to China during the late Ming period, they disseminated Western knowledge, which included a large amount of geographical knowledge of the whole world. Among the explanations of the *Map of the Myriad Countries of the World (Kunyu wanguo quantu* 坤輿萬國全圖), compiled by Matteo Ricci (1552–1610), there was a column on "Ying di ya" 應帝亞, this is "India". Ricci recounted that the products of this area were abundant, so that "during all four seasons merchants from West and East come across the Seas in order to carry out trade". But he did not speak about the activities of the Jesuits and other Europeans in India, although he himself had spent some time in Goa on the coast of India.[9] Among the writings of Catholic missionaries during Ming and Qing times, it is Guido Aleni's (1582–1649) *Records of Foreign Lands (Zhifang waiji* 職方外紀), published in 1623, which contained the largest amount of information about the activities of Europeans in India. In the section entitled "Yindiya" 印第亞, he points out that "The people in the countries along the Coast, who have contact with the Westerners, all believe in Catholicism".[10] The earliest work written by Chinese who took note of the actions of Europeans in India was Chen Lunjiong's 陳倫炯 *Reports on Maritime Countries (Haiguo wenjian lu* 海國聞見錄) written in 1730. Chen Lunjiong called the area of today's Bangladesh, Minyaguo 民呀國 (Bengal) and the Eastern part of the Indian peninsula, Geshita 戈什塔 (Costa), and he also mentioned the places along the Indian coast, which were occupied by the French, the English and the Dutch, such as Pondicherry, Negapatam, Surat, Bombay, *etc*.[11]

The book entitled *Records of the Seas (Hailu* 海錄), which was published around 1820, also recorded the activities of Europeans in India and provided more detailed descriptions. The most important author of *Records of the Seas* was Xie Qinggao 謝清高 (1765–1821), who, at the end of the eighteenth century, had accompanied merchants who engaged in maritime trade. He had visited

---

8 Geng Yinzeng, (2006) "Gudai Zhongguoren yan zhong de Yindu", p. 59.

9 Ricci (2001), "Kunyu wanguo quantu", p. 212.

10 Aleni (1985), *Zhifang waiji*, p. 16.

11 Chen Lunjiong (1985), *Haiguo wenjian lu*, p. 62, for Indian place names in this book, cf. Mosca (2015), *From Frontier Policy to Foreign Policy: The Question of India and the Transformation of Geopolitics in Qing China*, p. 56.

CHINA'S TWO IMAGES OF INDIA

many places. The compiler of *Records of the Sea*, Yang Bingnan 楊炳南, had also consulted other sources in order to complement this information. Compared with the *Records of Foreign Lands*, the *Records of the Seas* offered a much clearer exposition. It clearly listed the places which were occupied by "Yingjili-country" 英吉利 (England) and introduced themselves to the English garrisons of the different places. Apart from this, *Records of the Seas* gave introductions to the opium production of the different places, and it distinguished between the different kinds of opium and their original producing regions such as "black mud" (*wutu* 烏土), "red skin" (*hongpi* 紅皮), "white skin" (*baipi* 白皮), etc. The book also predicted that the introduction of opium into China would cause ever increasing harm.[12]

The *Records of the Four Continents* (*Sizhou zhi* 四洲志), which had been compiled and translated during Lin Zexu's 林則徐 (1785–1850) incumbency in Canton in 1839 and 1840, also touched upon India, and, for the first time, employed the translated name *Yindu guo* 印度國 (Country of India). But differently from the two books mentioned above, the *Records of the Four Continents* did not aim to improve information but rather had very strong political and military goals. The compilers of the *Records of the Four Continents* were aware that Bombay (Mengmai 孟買), Bengal (Mengjiala 孟加拉) and other areas of India along the sea coast were British territory and that Britain sent officials directly in order to rule, so that these areas were by no means "vassal states" in the traditional sense.[13]

For this reason, in the presentation of the world in the *Records of the Four Continents*, the area, which today is called India, was considered as belonging to Britain. Proceeding from the perspective of resisting Britain, the *Records of Four Continents* are actually even more interested in the question of how the English occupied and ruled India, than in India as such. In a detailed way, the book describes, beginning with the arrival of the British at the Indian coast, the process of how they step, by step, occupied India, the strategies which were employed by the British as well as the question of how they exerted rule over the different regions of India. The *Records of the Four Continents* also described India's production of opium and the opium trade in much more detail than those provided in the *Records of the Seas*.

However, the narrative provided by the *Records of the Four Continents* on how the British ruled India remains within the traditional Chinese empire's perception of the peripheric areas and their management, and does not contain any "anti-colonial" consciousness. There are Chinese scholars who discuss the part on India in the *Records of the Four Continents* from an "anti-colonial perspective", claiming that the *Records of the Four Continents* in respect of India "from the be-

12 Xie Qinggao, Yang Bingnan (2001), *Hailu jiaoshe*, p. 62.
13 Lin Zexu (2002), *Sizhou zhi*, pp. 9–11.

ginning to the end focuses on the colonial exploitation of the Western powers".[14] But this was already under the influence of the "colonial" and "anti-colonial" discourse of the twentieth century and in no way corresponds to the real situation. The compilers of the *Records of the Four Continents* did not by any means have a complete knowledge of England's capitalist industrial production and her colonial system, and they even less actively put forward a critique of "colonial exploitation". If we compare the parts of the book which describe the occupation of India by the British and their rule of it with the occupation of India by Mongol tribes and their establishment of the Mughal Empire, there is no great difference in respect of the mode of expression.

When Wei Yuan 魏源 (1794–1856) compiled his *Illustrated Treatise of the Maritime Countries* (*Haiguo tuzhi* 海國圖志) in 1852, he employed the *Records of the Four Continents* as basis from the very beginning. Later on, he continuously added a large number of documents including the *Records of the Maritime Circuit* (*Yinghuan zhilüe* 瀛環志略). Many of these had quite different narrative approaches, but in respect of India, Wei Yuan continued to employ Lin Zexu's train of thought. Apart from adding excerpts from a large number of geographical records, he added numerous commentaries, making military and diplomatic suggestions. After the Opium war, the confrontation with England became one of the most important foreign affairs issues the Qing empire had to face.

In respect of geography, Wei Yuan paid a large degree of attention to the important position of the Eastern part of India with a view to the Sino-English confrontation. In the part entitled "Records on India", he began to claim that the Eastern part of India was the pivot in the Sino-British confrontation.[15] He employed the traditional diplomatic concept of "vertical and horizontal coalitions" (*Hecong liangheng* 合縱連橫) from the Warring States period and proposed the strategy of "Using the Barbarian in order to attack the Barbarians". He was of the opinion that the Qing Empire should contact the Gurkhas, who lived between India and Tibet and persuade them to dispatch troops to India in order to curb the English and destroy the production and trading of opium, so that the English living in India would suffer economic harm. He was also of the opinion that the Russians intended to conquer India. Together with the Americans and French, who were all enemies of the British, these three countries could co-operate and together attack the British forces.[16]

The *Illustrated Treatise of the Maritime Countries* was not limited to a presentation of the geography and the customs of the world, it also provided practical considerations regarding foreign and military affairs. This finds its clearest expression with regard to India. If one examines other books from the same

---

14 The last example is Wang Hongbin (2012), *Wan Qing haifang dilixue fazhanshi*, p. 5.

15 Wei Yuan (1998), *Haiguo tuzhi*, vol. 2, p. 666.

16 Ibid., vol. 2, p. 773.

period which take "overseas affairs" into account, such as, for example, Yao Ying's 姚瑩 (1785–1853) *Notes on Travels to Kang* (*Kangyou jixing* 康輶紀行), they contain a considerable number of similar discussions.[17]

In the *Illustrated Treatise of the Maritime countries*, Wei Yuan is mostly concerned with the benefits of the Qing Empire. In regard to England and India, it only rarely reveals value judgements such as virtue and vice or good and evil. In his commentary he does not express something akin to "sympathy" towards the masses of the territory of India. It is worth noting that the *Illustrated Treatise of the Maritime Countries* quotes a large number of books which had been written or compiled by Western missionaries, such as, for example, Karl F.A. Gützlaff's (1803–1851) *Complete Works on World Geography* (*Wanguo dili quantuji* 萬國地理全圖集) and the *Brief History of Foreign Countries* (*Waiguo shilüe* 外国史略) written by the Morrisons, which contained many passages criticising the cruel rule of Indian local kings and princes, the brutality and backwardness of Indian religious customs, and even praised Christianity and British rule. These narratives were not changed by Wei Yuan, but completely copied into the work. This demonstrates that, although he planned for a confrontation with England, he, in the same way as Lin Zexu, did not have any political or cultural preferences with regard to the Indian natives and the British rulers.

During the second half of the nineteenth century, most Chinese did not have a complete understanding of British rule in India. From the point of view of terminology, the terms colonise and colony, only came into wide use in Chinese newspapers after 1895.[18] Prior to this, scholars designated British rule as an "area under jurisdiction" (*xiadi* 轄地), a "dependency" (*shudi* 屬地), a "territory under one's jurisdiction" (*lingdi* 領地) or as a "vassal state" (*fanguo* 藩國). There was only a very limited number of more knowledgeable persons, such as Zou Daijun 鄒代鈞 (1854–1908), who were able to distinguish in a relative clear and correct way between the different areas of India, which ones were directly administered by England and which areas were "vassal states".[19] Basically, all nineteenth century Chinese acknowledged British rule in India, as becomes very clear when one looks into the terminology, which employed a British standpoint; for example, the English queen was designated as the Empress of India (*nüzhu* 女主) and the revolt of the Indian masses was designed as "armed rebellion".

Except for this, like Wei Yuan, most Chinese continued to employ the traditional idea that "states compete for hegemony" of the Spring-and-Autumn-period (771–476 B.C.) in order to understand the international competition of

---

17 Yao Ying (1990), *Kangyou jixingi*, especially chapter 3.

18 Pan Guangzhe (2014), "Cong 'xin mingci' dao 'guanjianci': Yi 'zhimindi' wei li".

19 Zou Daijun (2010), "Liang hu shuyuan dili jiangyi", p. 317.

the nineteenth century.[20] When speaking about the international situation and diplomacy, they lacked knowledge about the colonialism of the European states, and of their capitalist development after the industrial revolution. For this reason, the majority of Chinese observers classified the motives for British rule of India in a traditional understanding, such as "attacking a city and plundering the land" (*gongcheng lüedi* 攻城掠地), "expanding the domain" (*kuoda bantu* 擴大版圖), and "achieving hegemony" (*chengjiu baye* 成就霸業).

Wang Zhi 王芝 travelled to England in the 1870s. After his return, he noted England's favourable geographical situation and its abundance of products and resources, which made it absolutely self-sufficient. He was unable to understand why the British would strive for hegemony at a distance greater than 10.000 *li*.[21]

For most nineteenth century Chinese scholars, India had become a "middle ground" in the confrontation of the Qing Empire and the United Kingdom, and, because of traditional sinocentrism and also due to the fact that India had become British controlled territory, India was generally seen as not having an equal position to that of China. Chinese interest in the question of "how England had become so strong" and "how England had managed to occupy India" was far greater than interest in Indian society and her masses.

Related to this mentality was a kind of cultural and racial discrimination towards the Indian masses, which was widely shared among the Chinese élites and the ordinary people. In Chinese documents referring to the Indian masses, a large number of designations such as "native barbarians" (*tuyi* 土夷), "aborigines" (*turen* 土人), etc., were employed, all of which were related to a traditional superiority complex. As late as 1890, Xue Fucheng 薛福成 (1838–1894) on the way to his diplomatic mission in Europe, encountered a large number of "natives" in South-East-Asia and India and said that they "were all swarthy, small and clumsy" (*wubu mianmu youheiduanxiao cuchun* 無不面目黝黑，短小粗蠢). He was of the opinion that, culturally, Indians were inferior to the Chinese and that, in respect of their physique and appearance, they were inferior to Europeans. In the rank-system which he imagined, Indians were viewed as being one level inferior to Chinese and European people.[22]

2. Images of "progress"—Western influences

For the most part of the nineteenth century, in Chinese eyes, the Indian territory was not an independent country, and, as such, Indians independence, in the

---

20 Wang Ermin (2005), "Shijiu shiji Zhongguo guoji guannian zhi yanbian".

21 Wang Zhi (1876), *Haike ri tan*, j. 4, p. 11.

22 Xue Fucheng (1985), *Chushi Ying Fa Yi Bi siguo riji*, p. 86.

realms of politics, culture and religion, did not receive much attention. As stated above, the Chinese were concerned about the question of "How the English rule India" and what impact this had on China. While scholars of the early period, such as Lin Zexu and Wei Yuan, were all of the opinion that British rule of India constituted a menace for China, there were also some who began to realise the "positive" transformation of India brought about by British rule.

The earliest document which spoke positively of the British rule of India was Xu Jiyu's 徐繼畬 (1795–1873) *Records of the Maritime Circle*. This book was written in the 1840s, but, in contrast to the *Records of the Four Continents*, it did not simply consider the English as enemies. Xu Jiyu does not use the term "English barbarians" (*Ying yi* 英夷) but he quite often designated the Indian masses as "native barbarians" (*tuyi* 土夷). From his application of terminology, one can see that he thought that the English culture was superior. He criticises some of the original Indian states for the brutality of their rulership and their fondness for inciting wars. But, under British rule, Indian society had become stable and trade was thriving.[23] Although the *Records of the Maritime Circle* is, generally speaking, a book which presents the geography and the customs of all of the countries of the world, such statements clearly have to be considered as daring, since for the majority of the Chinese people, they challenged the "China-Barbarian" dualist concept. Zeng Guofan 曾國藩 (1811–1872) had pointed out that this description of Xu Jiyu was very dangerous since it constituted a too positive evaluation of the English.[24]

Xu Jiyu's composition of the *Records of the Maritime Circle* was closely related to Xu's contacts with Westerners during his incumbency as an Official in the Fujian-province during the 1840s. And, from the perspective of the Westerners, they were clearly very happy to discover this narrative of the progress of the British rule of India in Chinese books. This holds especially true for missionaries coming from England and the US. Because India occupied an important position in the missions in the East, many protestant missionaries loved to speak about India and they went so far as to make comparisons between China and India.

As I have pointed out above, Wei Yuan's the *Illustrated Treatise of the Maritime Countries* quoted from Gützlaff's *Complete Works on World Geography* and the Morrisons' *History of Foreign Countries*. In Gützlaff's Chinese periodical (*Dong-Xiyangkao meiyue tongjizhuan* 東西洋考每月統記傳), too, there are many introductory articles about India. As a missionary, Gützlaff's inclinations are very clear; in 1837, for example, in an article in which he presented the Bengal region, he made the criticism that the Bengal people, despite their having received an English education, still worshipped idols and were not willing to

---

23 Xu Jiyu (2001), *Yinghuan zhilüe*, p. 71.
24 Zeng Guofan (1995), *Zeng Gufan quanji. Shuxin.* p. 622.

believe in Christianity.[25] In the same year, in another article, Gützlaff praised the Englishmen for helping to restore political and social order and for beginning to develop trade in the Indian regions. He was of the opinion that, only by relying on England, would Indians receive education, change their "evil" customs and develop their own talents. Gützlaff was very optimistic about the propagation of Christianity in India, and he claimed that all active and positive transformations in the Indian regions were related to Christianity, and that, in the future, India's original religions would all decline and Christianity would take hold of the whole of India.[26]

If we look into the propagation of Christianity in nineteenth century India, we can discover that Gützlaff clearly exaggerated the achievements and the impact of Christian missions in India at the time. If we compare them with twentieth century India, it also is clear that his prediction about the future of Christianity in India was overly optimistic.[27] I think, however, that Gützlaff's narrative needs to be understood as a special strategy; he exaggerated the influence of Christianity in India and he related India's positive transformations to Christianity because he wanted to portray India as a positive "model" under British rule and, in so doing, make publicity for his mission in China and thereby push forward the dissemination of Christianity in China.[28]

Many of the journals and newspapers published by missionaries during the late Qingdynasty, such as the *Shanghae serial* (*Liuhe congtan* 六合叢談) and the *Church News* (*Jiaohui xinbao* 教會新報), had a regular column on "Developments in India", in which they regularly reported news from India.[29] After *Church News* had been changed into *The Chinese Globe Magazine* (*Wanguo gongbao* 萬國公報), the editor, Young J. Allen's (Lin Lezhi 林樂知 1837–1907) attention to India became even greater. It published many stories on politics, foreign affairs, trade, famines, folk customs, *etc.*, including some which discussed Indian Christianity. In 1874, the missionary James W. Lambuth (Lan Bo 藍柏 1830–1892) published two articles in the *Chinese Globe Magazine* (*Wanguo gongbao*) entitled "The Popularity of the Mission in India" (*Chuanjiao yu Yindu zhi sheng* 傳教於印度之盛) and "The Blooming of the Christian Church in India" (*Yindu jiaohui daxing* 印度教會大興) which gave publicity to the success of protestant missionaries in the Indian area. Lambuth pointed out that the greatest change that Christian missions had brought for the Indian masses was that Indian Christians were able to transcend the Caste boundaries and live together in equality. Moreover,

---

25 Ai Hanzhe (1997), *Dong- Xiyangkao meiyue tongjizhuan*, p. 193.

26 Ibid., p. 207.

27 There is much research on the mission in India, I consulted Frykenberg (2008), *Christianity in India*, pp.243–266.

28 On Empire propaganda by missionaries of the London Missionary Society, cf. Johnston (2003), *Missionary Writing and Empire, 1800–1860.*

29 Cf for example *Liuhe congtan* issues 1, 2, 3, 5, 7 (1857) and *Jiaohui xinbao* 1868–1873 every issue.

a part of Christian churches in India supported by their believers had already achieved economic independence and autarchy.[30] This also could offer a direction for Chinese Christian churches.

This "progress-narrative" was by no means limited to the publicity given to the successes of Christian missionaries; what was more important was that they attempted to construct a comparison between India before the arrival of missionaries, and India under British rule, using binaries such as "turmoil-peace", "ignorant-civilised", "evil-good", and upon this basis, constructed a whole "progress narrative". Let us again have a look at historical books. World history books appearing in the Chinese world in the nineteenth century were mostly compiled and translated by missionaries.[31] When they spoke about Indian history in modern times, they also employed such a "progress narrative". An example of this can be found in the *Outlines of General History* (*Wanguo tongjian* 萬國通鑒), translated by the American missionary Devello Sheffield (Xie Weilou 謝衛樓 1841–1913), which termed all of India's native religions as "heterodox" and local customs as "objectionable customs". He employed a "Christian religion saved the East"-narrative in order to recount Indian history from the seventeenth century onwards and he considered the spreading of the Christian religion and Western civilisation as India's "fortune".[32]

This progress-narrative of India under British rule, however, does not just appear in the publications of missionaries. During the nineteenth century, many Chinese had the same ideas. The Shanghai Catholic Christ Gong Zhai 龔柴 wrote a "Brief Account of India" (*Yindu kaolüe* 印度考略), whose geographical contents were to a large part copied from the *Records of the Maritime Circle* and the *Illustrated Records of the Maritime Countries*, although Gong Zhai himself also added many remarks. He thought, for example, that the original King of Bengal had wantonly committed massacres and ruled in a brutal way, and that, after the English had arrived, they had developed trade and the prosperity of Indian society. Gong Zhai not only appreciated British rule, he also considered it to be legitimate and called the uprisings of the Indian masses against British rule "armed rebellion" (*panluan* 叛亂).[33]

It is interesting that this view could even influence the Chinese who personally travelled to India. The first Chinese man who was officially dispatched to India to make on the spot observations was Huang Maocai 黃楙材. Huang went to India in 1878, his objective being to collect geographical and military information which would be of strategical use in the confrontation with Britain. But in his travel notes on India, he is still full of praise for Indian society under

---

30 Both articles in *Wanguo gongbao* 7: 301 (1874).

31 Zou Zhenhuan (2007), *Xifang zhuanjiaoshi yu wan Qing xishi dongjian*.

32 Xie Weilou (1882), *Wanguo tongjian*, p. 75.

33 Gong Zhai (1881), "Yindu kaolüe".

British rule. In his eyes, the British administrative efficiency is very high, and the society in respect of finance, jurisdiction, trade and other aspects was in a perfect order. He, moreover, used much space to describe the railways, running water, gas lamps and other new things, praising the positive effects that they had for society. What is described in his travel notes is a "modern", happy world; only rarely does he mention the negative sides of British society, and he also refrains from discussing the life of the ordinary people.[34]

Huang Maocai had an idealised and glorified image of Modern Western civilisation, but India was the model example of how this civilisation could be realised. What he wrote in his travel notes not only were merely notes on Indian society, but, at the same time, a reflection that the transformation of the Indian state brought about by the English was an experience from which the Qing Empire could draw lessons. We can find very similar narratives in articles written by British and American missionaries. They found their most systematic expression in Young J. Allens' well known article "The Twelve Advantages of India's Subordination to England" (Yindu li Ying shier yi shuo 印度隸英十二益說). This article, which was published in 1896, summarised twelve advantages which India had supposedly gained from English rule, including aspects of the judicial system, education, financial administration, transportation and culture.[35] Although, as seen from the title, the article presents England and India, actually half of it dealt with the question of whether the Indian experience could have any usefulness for China. At the end of his article, Young J. Allen even suggested that China should emulate India, and, in its South-Western region, choose two or three provinces and, in their entirety, lease them to England, and, in this way, transplant the methods of British rule in India to China. Within the "anti-imperialist" academic environment on the Chinese mainland during the second half of the twentieth century, Young J. Allen's article received severe criticism.[36]

After China's defeat in the Sino-Japanese war in 1895, the "crisis-consciousness" of Qing Empire officials and scholars suddenly increased. Many persons felt that reform on a grand scale would become increasingly necessary. Young J. Allen, Timothy Richard (1845–1919) and other missionaries in this period published a large number of articles and books hoping to introduce the experiences that the modern West had made through reforms in order to push forward reforms in China.

In actual fact, Young J. Allen himself was quite aware that the reform of Indian society had not proceeded in a very smooth way. In another article of

---

34 Huang Maocai (1886a), *Xiyou riji*, Huang Maocai (1886b), *Yindu zhaji*, Huang Maocai (1886c), *Youli zouyan*.

35 Allen (1896),"Yindu li Ying shier yi shuo".

36 Gu Changsheng (1985), *Cong Malisun dao Situ leideng*, p. 275.

1895, he compared the process of reform in the three countries of China, Japan and India, and considered the progress of the reform in India as being exceptionally difficult. Although China had started late, its prospects were much better.[37] No matter whether it was the publications of Young J. Allen or "The Records of India's Prosperity because of Reform" (*Yindu biantong xingsheng ji* 印度變通興盛記) by Timothy Richard, they all started from a colonial historical narrative or from a progress narrative.[38] At first, from a holistic point of view, they describe the prospect of the "progress" of Indian society, and then, in a second step, they attribute all this "progress" to British colonial rule. As to the question of how the original political, religious and cultural structure of the Indian regions responded to the British occupation, of how transformations took place and the complex relationship between colonialism and Indian society, all of this could not be answered by the missionaries.

However that may be, when protestant missionaries made historical comparisons between the modern history of India and China, they dragged India and China into the same "modernising" progress, and thereby challenged the concept of the "centrality of the heavenly dynasty". Reading these articles, Chinese readers became aware that China and India faced a similar environment and met with similar problems. It was through this progress that India's subjectivity obtained prominence, so that it was no longer only the "middle ground" of a confrontation of empires. What was even more important here was that Chinese began to change their own perception of their own country, as China was now only one country among a myriad of countries. Independently of whether it was facing the various Western countries or the countries of the periphery such as India, China's superiority in respect of its culture and its central position began to vanish.

III. Images of Decline: Transformations of the Chinese View

For a nineteenth century Chinese scholar, India was not a completely strange area. Because of the dominant Buddhist religion, between the late Han and the Tang and Song Dynasties, the cultural exchange between the two countries prospered. All Chinese with some historical understanding were aware of this. But from the Song Dynasty onwards, the "Buddhist factor" began to lose importance, and, during the time of the Mughal Empire, the cultural exchange between China and India was at an all-time low. For the people of the Qing

---

37 Allen (1895), "Bian zhong pian", p. 79.
38 Richard (1898), *Lieguo biantong xingsheng ji.*

Dynasty, India, this piece of land, was no longer as intimate as it had been during "Buddhist times".

Beginning with the *Records of the Sea* the *Records of the Maritime Circle* and the *Illustrated Records of the Maritime Countries*, the early geographical works all, to a certain extent, expressed surprise about how fast the British had occupied the Indian area. After the Opium wars, for quite a long time, scholars and officials interested in Indian affairs all hoped to find the reasons for the British strength. Regarding Indian political power during the later phase of the Mughal Empire, they all adopted a rather critical view. The attitude of the *Records of the Four Continents* is typical, which claims that, when the British arrived in India, the political power of the Mughal Empire was in a state of disorder. The whole Indian area had disintegrated, and a large number of states had emerged, which were constantly warring among themselves. The British made use of this situation, and crushed one state after another, and finally obtained victory.[39]

Despite this situation, there were some Chinese scholars and officials who were not satisfied by seeing the British rule of India only as a result of the success of military strategy and hoped to find more profound underlying reasons. Guo Songtao 郭嵩燾 (1818–1891) was the first Chinese envoy to Britain. While there, he often discussed the situation in India and in other British colonies with others. In Guo Songtao's eyes, the development and management of the British colonies meant that the local ethnic groups from a backward and an uncivilised condition were pushed into a condition of civilisation. The Indians were not able to utilise the natural conditions and resources of their locality fully, and the British possessed the power of civilisation. He applied the traditional Chinese "heavenly law" (*tiandao* 天道) concept and claimed that the Indians had lost their "way" and that the British understood how to employ the "way" in order to develop India as a territory.[40] This, of course, meant endowing the British colonial rule with legitimacy.

These ideas of Guo Songtao were, of course, related to the British influence upon Guo, who skilfully managed to integrate "colonialism" into the civilisation discourse of traditional Chinese sino-centrism: the reason for China's occupancy of the central position in the world lay also in the power of the "way" and its command of cultural superiority. In this way, Chinese Sino-centrism and colonialism produced an interesting alliance, in which both China and England, through complying with the "heavenly way", resided in the highest rank of civilisation, whereas India occupied a lower rank because it "did not have the way". This rank-based view of civilisation meant that the reason for Britain's occupation of India was mainly because of India's lack of "the way". When Chinese scholars identified with this concept, it was quite difficult for them to

---

39 Lin Zexu, *Sizhou zhi*, p. 9–10.
40 Guo Songtao (1984), *Lundun yu bali riji*, p. 352.

produce "sympathy" for India. Wang Tao 王韜 (1828–1897), when discussing Asian countries, directly criticised the Indians for being dissolute and not producing any resistance against the British, and for resigning themselves into being bullied.[41]

In 1881, Ma Jianzhong 馬建忠 (1845–1900) and Wu Guangpei 吳廣霈 (1855–1919) were sent to India to negotiate with the Governor-general on the regulation of opium. In his diary, Wu Guangpei offered a large number commentaries. Before he had arrived in India, the Indians of his imagination were the "dignified" Indians of the Buddhist classics. As soon as he arrived in Calcutta, he discovered that the Indians with whom he came into contact were completely different from the ones of his imagination.[42] From the very beginning, Wu Guangpei had been very surprised about the decline of Buddhism in India. He provided his own explanation, namely, that it was classical Indian culture, including Buddhism, which had caused the Indians to lose their competitiveness. Since their understanding of the external world was also very limited, a situation developed in which they were unable to adapt to the international competition of the time, so that they finally became the slaves of people who had arrived from outside their borders.[43]

Likewise, Wu Guangpei did not express any "sympathy" towards the Indians. He employed a sort of "social-Darwinist" thinking, being convinced that the law of the jungle (*ruorou qiangshi* 弱肉強食—the weak are devoured by the strong) was a perfectly normal thing, so that there was no need for any kind of sympathy. But he was already fully aware that China was similar to India, both of them being large countries in Asia, both having a long and abundant cultural tradition. For this reason the defeat of India could serve as a lesson for China. In this way, Wu Guangpei's approach was much more realistic: he did not embrace the discourse of civilisational superiority, but he did consider India and China as being placed on the same level.

After the Sino-Japanese war in 1895, the crisis of consciousness and the concept of the modern nation-state in China emerged at the same time. In this process, many persons rid themselves of the traditional Chinese sinocentric world view and began to see China and India as the same sort of classical civilisations, both facing the assault of the Western powers. For this reason, the Chinese view of India underwent a fundamental change; India was no longer a place subordinated to Britain, which had successively undergone a process of transformation from "barbarian" to "progress", but now constituted a negative example of an ancient civilisation in decline, which had lost its national autonomy.

---

41 Wang Tao (1994), "Yazhou ban shu Ouren", p. 198.
42 Wu Guangpei (1890), *Nanxing riji*, p. 15.
43 Ibid., p. 16.

The most convincing evidence for this claim is that important members of the reform-party, such as Kang Youwei 康有為 (1858 –1927), Liang Qichao 梁啟超 (1873–1929) and others were also loyal readers of newspapers which were published by missionaries, such as the *Chinese Globe Magazine*, in particular. But they did not adopt the "progress" narrative about India, which was forwarded by Young J. Allen, Timothy Richard and others. Kang Youwei mentioned India for the first time in 1895, and, together with Turkey, he saw India as a model of a large country of the past, which by now was in decline.[44] What is interesting is that he had read Timothy Richard's "Records of India's Prosperity because of Reform" and had even recommended this book to the Guangxu-Emperor.[45] But even this did not change his view of India. After he had read "Records of India's Prosperity because of Reform", Liang Qichao said that speaking about how Russia and Japan had become strong and rich because of reforms had a considerable educational significance for China, whereas India was, in contrast, the example for a "failed nation" (*wangguo* 亡國), so that it would not be possible to say that it [India] had achieved "prosperity" because of "reform".[46]

When, prior to 1900, Kang Youwei spoke about India's fate in the modern world, he did that in order to find references for his reform proposals.[47] For example, his famous 1895 petition of the Examination candidates to the Emperor (*gongche shangshu* 公車上書) claims that the reason for the decline and fall of India was that the whole nation "lacked talent", and, for this reason, was not in a position to offer resistance against the British forces. Actually, this was done to publicise his proposal to reform the traditional Chinese examination system and to change the form of training administrative personnel.[48] In 1898, he again mentioned India, this time claiming that the reason for the British attack on India and its rule over it was that the Indians were too conservative, were clinging to their ancient traditions, and unwilling to undergo reforms. This, in actual fact, was done in order to push the rulers of China into introducing reforms at the earliest possible time.[49] Both Kang Youwei's simplification of India's history and present situation, and his symbolic explanations employed a metaphor strategy which was aimed at China's reform-enterprise.

As late as 1901, Liang Qichao still exclaimed that India was such a large landmass which, surprisingly, had been destroyed by the small British East India

---

44 Kang Youwei (2007b),"Shang Qingdi di er shu", p. 42.

45 In 1898 Kang Youwei had *Lieguo biantong xingsheng ji* and *Taixi xinshi lanyao* together presented to the Guangxu-Emperor, see Kong Xiangji (1988), *Kang Youwei bianfa zouyi yanjiu*, pp. 349–350.

46 Liang Qichao (2005), "Xixue shumubiao" p. 1131

47 Only when Kang in 1901 went to India and travelled to many places, he started to develop a more complete understanding of India, cf. Kang Youwei (2007c), "Yindu youji", p. 509.

48 Kang Youwei (2007b), "Shang Qingdi di er shu", p. 42.

49 Kang Youwei (2007a), "Jingshi qiangxue hui xu", p. 89.

CHINA'S TWO IMAGES OF INDIA

481

Company. Seen from the point of view of the whole world, this seemed to be a strange fact, which was impossible to explain.[50] In nineteenth-century Chinese imagination of the world, the declined and fallen India was an extremely negative image; it was the pattern of what might happen to China in a worst case scenario. In the stories at the beginning of the twentieth 20th century, which, in great numbers, describe the "fall" of different nations, India is one of the most often cited examples.[51] Rebecca Karl has discussed how the Chinese discussions about the history of the different "weak countries" of the world, from the angle of knowledge and culture have facilitated the process of the Chinese nation to become a modern state, and, in this way, enabled it to be incorporated into world state system. There is no doubt that India in this process provided and important point of reference.[52]

But making India the typical case of decline and adding elaborations to this, did by no means imply criticism of the Western colonial powers represented by Britain. In fact, the greatest number of the authors who composed histories of the decline of India at the beginning of the twentieth century were of the opinion that the most important source of the decline of India in modern times was the chaos of the Mughal Empire during its later phase (after 1739). It was just this sort of rule which was responsible for India being reduced to becoming a "weak country" and which gave the British and other Western countries their opportunity to exploit the situation.[53] In this respect, India also can be compared with China. The triangular relationship between "Mughal Empire—Indian—Great Britain" could become the metaphor for the relationship "Manchu-Qing-Empire—Chinese (Han-Chinese)—Western countries". For this reason, the narrative of the decline of India in Chinese texts can, in fact, be explained from different angles. The crisis consciousness of national decline could point to the resistance against the Western countries, but it could also lead to resistance against the Manchu rulers.

Seen from a general point of view, the national ruin narrative caused Chinese intellectuals to relate China's and India's modern destinies with each other and to reflect on the two countries as members of the same world-system. However, during the last years of the nineteenth century and during the first few years of the twentieth century, Chinese feeling towards India at most represented "empathy", but did not reach real "sympathy". The most that Chinese intellectuals did, when speaking about India, was to exclaim that "In the future,

---

50 Liang Qichao (1901),"Mieguo xin fa lun".
51 Yu Danchu (1984), "Zongguo jinda aiguozhuyi de 'Wangguo shijian' chu kao."
52 Karl (2002),*Staging the World*, pp. 160–161.
53 Karl (1998), "Creating Asia: China in the World at the Beginning of the Twentieth Century", pp.1112–1113.

China will sink into a plight as happened to India".[54] This was pity for the situation in which it found itself at the time and being indignant about it. This means that, because of the cultural inertia of Sino-centrism, Chinese intellectuals were still not willing to admit that the Chinese and the Indians found themselves in similar conditions, and there was still a difference with regard to the understanding of the two countries.

In 1900, during the Boxer Rebellion among the British troops there was an Indian soldier named Gadhadahar Singh. He wrote a diary and recorded what he had seen and heard in China. In his diary, he noted that India and China were neighbours on the Asian continent, and that both sides had many similarities. For this reason, he thought, the people of the both countries "should help each other". He openly said that "his heart was full of sympathy for the unfortunate Chinese".[55] Behind this sort of "sympathy" was an Asian identity, which also unindentionally revealed an anti-colonialist consciousness.

Seen from the Chinese viewpoint, during the whole of the nineteenth century, it is quite difficult to find similar expressions of "sympathy" towards India. In fact, it took up to 1907, when, in Japan, Zhang Taiyan (1869–1936) edited the *Minbao* and real "resistant" nationalism was adopted, that criticism of nineteenth-century Western colonialism began. [56] Only afterwards did anti-colonialism and anti-imperialism discourse begin to become popular in China, and this provided Chinese intellectuals with a new conceptual basis for reflecting on the common fate of China and India as two countries. During the nineteenth century, the traditional feeling of cultural superiority, to a lesser or larger extent, continued to dominate the brain of the Chinese people and influenced the Chinese view of India. This is a fact which cannot be ignored by modern researchers.

(Translated by Iwo Amelung)

Bibliography

Ai Hanzhe (Karl Gützlaff) 愛漢者 (ed.), Huang Shjian 黃時鑒 (comp.) (1997), *Dong-Xiyangkao meiyue tongjizhuan*, Beijing: Zhonghua shuju.
Allen, Young J. 林樂知 (1895), "Bian zhong pian" 辨忠篇 (Distinguishing loyalities), *Wanguo gongbao*.
— (1896), "Yindu li Ying shier yi shuo" 印度隸英十二益說 (The Twelve Advantages of India's Subordination to England), *Wanguo gongbao*, No. 93, 94.

---

54 "Shijie wangguo xiaoshi" 1902, p. 24.
55 Yang (2007), "(A) Subaltern('s) Boxers, An Indian Soldier's Account of China and the World in 1900–1901."
56 Zhang Taiyan (2010), "Wu wu lun", p. 433.

Aleni, Giulio (Ai Rulüe 艾儒略) (1985), *Zhifang waiji* 職方外紀 (*Records of Foreign Lands*), Beijing: Zhonghua shuju.

Chen Lunjiong 陳倫炯 (1985), *Haiguo wenjian lu* 海國聞見錄 (Reports on maritime countries), Zhengzhou: Zhongzhou guji chubanshe.

Frykenberg, Robert Eric (2008), *Christianity in India: From Beginnings to Present.* Oxford University Press.

Geng Yinzeng 耿引曾 (2006), "Gudai Zhongguoren yan zhong de Yindu" 古代中國人眼中的印度 (India in the Eyes of the Ancient Chinese) in: Zhang Minqiu (ed.), *Kuayue Ximalaya zhangai: Zhongguo xunqiu liaojie Yindu*, Chongqing: Chongqing chubanshe.

Gong Zhai 龔柴 (1881), "Yindu kaolüe" 印度考略 (Brief account of India), *Yiwenbao*, Nos. 118, 121, 122.

Gu Changsheng 顧長聲 (1985), *Cong Malisun dao Situ leideng: Lai Hua xinjiao zhuanjiaoshi pingzhuan* 從馬禮遜到司徒雷登：來華新教傳教士評傳 (From Morrision to Leighton Steward. Critical biographies of protestant missionaries in China), Shanghai: Shanghai renmin chubanshe.

Guo Songtao 郭嵩燾 (1984), *Lundun yu Bali riji* 倫敦與巴黎日記 (Diary of London and Paris), Changsha: Yuelu shushe.

Huang Maocai 黃楙材 (1886a), *Xiyou riji* 西輶日記 (Diary of a Journey to the West).

— (1886b) *Youli zouyan* 遊歷芻言 (My Humble Opinions during Travelling for Gathering Information).

— (1886c), *Yindu zhaji* 印度札記 (Jottings on India).

Ji Xianlin 季羨林 (2008), *Zhong Yin wenhua jiaoliu shi* 中印文化交流史 (A History of Cultural Exchange between China and India), Beijing: Zhongguo shehui kexue chubanshe.

Jiaohui xinbao 教会新报

Johnston, Anna (2003), *Missionary Writing and Empire, 1800–1860*, Cambridge: Cambridge University Press.

Kang Youwei 康有為 (2007a), "Jingshi qiangxue hui xu" 京師強學會序 (Introduction to the Meeting of the Society for Strengthening through Learning in the Capital), *Kang Youwei quanji*, Beijing: Zhongghua renmin chubanshe, vol. 2, pp. 89–90.

— (2007b), "Shang Qingdi di er shu" 上清帝第二書 (Second memorial for the Qing emperor), Jiang Yihua, Zhang Ronghua 姜義華、張榮華 (eds.), *Kang Youwei quanji* 康有為全集, Beijing: Zhongguo renmin daxue chubanshe, vol. 23 pp. 32–69.

— (2007b), "Yindu youji" 印度遊記 (Travel Notes from India), in: *Kang Youwei quanji*, Beijing: Zhonghua renmin chubanshe, vol. 5, pp. 509–550.

Karl, Rebecca (1998), "Creating Asia: China in the World at the Beginning of the Twentieth Century", *The American Historical Review*, vol. 103, No.4, pp.1096–1118.

— (2002), *Staging the World, Chinese Nationalism and the Turn of the Twentieth Century*, Durham NC: Duke University Press.

Kong Xiangji 孔祥吉 (1988), *Kang Youwei bianfa zouyi yanjiu* 康有為變法奏議研究 (Researches on the reform memorials of Kang Youwei), Shenyang: Liaoning jiaoyu chubanshe.

Levenson, Joseph (1968), *Confucian China and Its Modern Fate*, Berkeley CA: University of California Press.

Liang Qichao 梁啟超 (1901),"Mieguo xin fa lun" 滅國新法論 (On a New Method for Extinguishing Countries), *Qingyibao*, 32.

- (2005), "Xixue shumubiao" 西學書目表 (Bibliography of Western Learning), *Yingbingshi heji, Jiwaiwen*, Beijing: Beijing daxue chubanshe 2005, vol 3, pp. 1121–1158.

Lin Zexu 林則徐 (2002), *Sizhou zhi* 四洲志 (Record of the Four Continents), Beijing: Huaxia chubanshe.

Liuhe congtan 六合叢談 (The Shanghai Serial)

Metcalf, Thomas (1995), *The New Cambridge History of India: Ideologies of the Raj*. Cambridge: Cambridge University Press.

Mosca, Matthew (2015), *From Frontier Policy to Foreign Policy: The Question of India and the Transformation of Geopolitics in Qing China*. Stanford CA: Stanford University Press.

Pan Guangzhe 潘光哲 (2014), "Cong 'xin mingci' dao 'guanjianci': Yi 'zhimindi' wei li" 從「新名詞」到「關鍵詞」：以「殖民地」為例 (From 'New Term' to 'Keyword': Taking 'zhimindi' (Colony) as an example), in: Sun Jiang, Chen Liwei (eds.), *Yazhou gainianshi yanjiu*, vol. 2, Beijing: Sanlian shudian, pp. 229–254.

Richard, Timothy (Liti Motai 李提摩太) (1898), *Lieguo biantong xingsheng ji* 列國變通興盛記 (Notes of Prosperity because of Reform of Different Countries), Shanghai: Guangxue hui 1898. The book consists of four chapters, which describe Russia, Japan, India and Birma and Annam respectively.

Ricci, Matteo (Li Madou 利瑪竇) (2001), "Kunyu wanguo quantu" 坤輿萬國全圖 (Map of the Myriad Countries of the World), in: Zhu Weizheng (ed), *Li Madou zhongwen zhu yi ji*, Shanghai: Fudan daxue chubanshe 2001.

Sen, Tansen (2014), "Maritime Southeast Asia Between South Asia and China to the Sixteenth Century", *Trans-Regional and -National Studies of Southeast Asia*, 2:1, pp. 31–59.

Thampi, Madhavi (ed.) (2005a), *India and China in the Colonial World*, New Delhi: Social Science Press.

"Shijie wangguo xiaoshi" 世界亡國小史 (1902)(A small history of ruined states), *Hangzhou baihua bao* 1902:2, pp. 22–24.

Tan Zhong 譚中 (2006), "Zhongguo wenhua yanjing zhong Yindu xingxiang de bianqian" 中國文化眼睛中印度形象的變遷 (Changes of the Image of India in the eyes of Chinese culture), in: Zhang Minqiu (ed.), *Kuayue Ximalaya zhangai: Zhongguo xunqiu liaojie Yindu*, Chongqing: Chongqing chubanshe, pp. 31–51.

Tan Zhong, Geng Yinzeng 譚中、耿引曾 (2016), *Yindu yu Zhongguo – liang da wenming de jiaowang he jidang* 印度與中國——兩大文明的交往和激蕩 (India and China – Interaction and Agitation between two Large Civilisations), Beiing: Shangwu yinshuguan .

Thampi, Madhavi (2005b), *Indians in China, 1800–1949*. New Delhi: Manohar.

Wanguo gongbao 萬國公報

Wang Ermin 王爾敏 (2005), "Shijiu shiji Zhongguo guoji guannian zhi yanbian" 十九世紀中國國際觀念之演變(Changes of Chinese Concepts of International Affairs during the Nineteenth Century), in: *Zhongguo jindai sixiangshi xu lunji*, Beijing: Shehui kexue wenxian chubanshe, pp. 68–138.

Wang Hongbin 王宏斌 (2012), *Wan Qing haifang dilixue fazhanshi* 晚清海防地理学发展史 (Developmental History of Maritime Defence Geography during the Late Qing), Beijing: Zhongguo shehui kexue chubanshe.

Wang Tao 王韜 (1994), "Yazhou ba shu Ouren" 亞洲半屬歐人 (Asia for a Half Belongs to the Europeans) *Taoyuan wenlu waibian*, Shenyang: Liaoning renmin chubanshe, pp. 197–199.

Wang Zhi 王芝 (1876) *Haike ri tan* 海客日譚 (Daily talk of a Maritime Guest), 1876, j. 4, p. 11.

Wei Yuan 魏源 (1998), *Haiguo tuzhi* 海國圖志 (Illustrated Treatise of the Maritime Countries), Changsha: Yuelu shushe 1998.

Wu Guangpei 吳廣霈 (1890), *Nanxing riji* 南行日記 (Diary of a Trip to the South), Taoyuan chuban.

Xie Qinggao, Yang Bingnan 謝清高, 楊炳南 (comp.) (2001), *Hailu jiaoshe* 海錄校釋 (Commented edition of Records of the Seas) commented by An Jing 安京, Beijing: Shangwu yinshuguan.

Xie Weilou (Devello Sheffield) 謝衛樓, *Wanguo tongjian* 萬國通鑒 (Outlines of General History) 1882.

Xu Jiyu 徐繼畬 (2001), *Yinghuan zhiliie* 瀛環志略 (Records of the Maritime Circle), Shanghai: Shanghai shudian chubanshe 2001.

Xue Fucheng 薛福成 (1985), *Chushi Ying Fa Yi Bi siguo riji* 出使英法義比四國日記, (Diary of a Diplomatic Mission to the Four Countries of England, France, Italy and Belgium), Changsha, Yuelu shushe.

Yang, Anand A. (2007), "(A) Subaltern('s) Boxers, An Indian Soldier's Account of China and the World in 1900–1901", in: Robert Bickers and R. G. Tiedemann (eds.)., *The Boxers, China and the World*, Lanham MD: Rowman and Littlefield Publishers, pp.43–64.

Yao Ying 姚瑩 (1990), *Kangyou jixing* 康輶紀行 (Notes on Travels to Kang), Hefei: Huangshan shushe.

Yin Xinan 尹錫南 (2010), *Yindu de Zhongguo xingxiang* 印度的中國形象 (India's image of China), Beijing: Renmin chubanshe.

– (2014), *Yindu Zhongguo guan yanbian yanjiu* 印度中國觀演變研究 (Research into the Changes of the Indian Chinese image), Beijing: Shishi chubanshe.

Yu Danchu 俞旦初 (1984), "Zongguo jindai aiguozhuyi de 'Wangguo shijian' chu kao" 中國近代愛國主義的「亡國史鑒」初考 (A First Exploration of the Book *Mirror of Ruined Countries* within the Framework of Modern Chinese Patriotism, *Shijie lishi*, 1984: 1, pp. 23–31.

Zeng Guofan 曾國藩 (1995), *Zeng Gufan quanji. Shuxin* 曾國藩全集.書信 (Complete works of Zeng Guofan, Writings and Letters), Changsha: Yuelu shushe.

Zhang Taiyan 章太炎 (2010), "Wu wu lun" 五無論 (Discourse on Five Nothings), *Zhang Taiyan quanji*, Shanghai: Shanghai renmin chubanshe, vol. 4, p. 429–443.

Zou Daijun 鄒代鈞 (2010), "Liang hu shuyuan dili jiangyi" 兩湖書院地理講義 (Lectures on Geography at the Academy of the two Hu), in: Zou Daijun, *Xizheng jicheng. Zhong E jieji*, Changsha: Yuelu shushe.

Zou Zhenhuan 鄒振環 (2007), *Xifang zhuanjiaoshi yu wan Qing xishi dongjian: yi 1815 nian zhi1900 nian xifang lishi yizhu de chuanbo yu yingxiang wei zhongxin* 西方傳教士與晚清西史東漸：以1815年至1900年西方歷史譯著的傳播與影響為中心 (Western Missionaries and the Eastern Spread of Western History during the Late Qing Dynasty: Taking the Spreading and Impact of Western Translated Works between 1815 and 1900 as Central Concern), Shanghai guji chubanshe.

Part IV:
Treating the Sick Man—Co-existence, Science and Profit

Nationalism, Human-Co-Existentialism, Pan-Asianism: The Weakness Discourse and Wang Jingwei's Intellectual Transformation

Zhiyi Yang

Wang Zhaoming 汪兆銘 (1883–1944), better known by his penname as Wang Jingwei 汪精衛, was a man of many faces. His admirers call him a true patriot, who, throughout his life, was driven by a passion to sacrifice himself for the nation. They contend that, under fairer examination, his establishing of a collaborationist regime in Japanese-occupied China during the Second World War was just another form of resistance. His critics, however, saw him as a hypocrite and career opportunist, a man whose treason was the necessary result of his cowardice and defeatism. No other figure in China's recent history has received such polarised judgment. But, as the condemnation has become the standard verdict in mainstream historiography in both China and even abroad, the defence assumes the character of a counter-narrative, breeding on its sense of correcting the historical wrongs inflicted by the victors in the name of the nation.

The criticism of Wang being a political turncoat is well documented. He had been first a nationalist revolutionary who helped to found the Republic only to recede the presidency to Yuan Shikai 袁世凱 (1859–1916), a warlord. Then, he joined the anti-Yuan force when Yuan's monarchist ambition became known. After Sun Yat-sen's (1866–1925) death, he became the leader of KMT (Chinese Nationalist Party) leftwing, and endorsed the policy of working with the Soviets and the CPC (the Communist Party of China). He then turned against the Communists and joined forces with Chiang Kai-shek 蔣介石 (1887–1975), his chief rival in the KMT. In the face of the invasion of Japan, he first championed resistance before proposing appeasement. And then he escaped Chongqing to negotiate the "peace conditions" with Japan, established a collaborationist regime in Nanjing, and died an ignominious collaborator in a Nagoya hospital in November 1944. In short, his intellectual persuasions, if there were any, appear wildly inconsistent. Yet, despite all these obvious facts, his admirers argue that the truth of a man is not determined by the world's perception of his actions, but by his genuine motivation—and in the case of Wang, it was to save China using all possible means. This view is also supported by a legion of texts, including his own poetry, speeches, writings, and oral or written memoirs by people who were close to him. The gap between institutionalised and private memories appears unbridgeable.

The case of Wang Jingwei poses a dilemma to historiography. Any effort to reach a facile verdict will be undermined by numerous complex factors which point to other possibilities. I therefore propose to follow Timothy Brook's recommendation to "hesitate before the judgment of history",[1] and aiming instead, as a first step, to examine Wang Jingwei's intellectual transformations without bias, hoping that it may ultimately help to shed light on other complicated aspects of his life. I argue that his intellectual persuasions can be summarised in three stages: Nationalism, Human-Co-Existentialism (his own term, which is, in essence, humanism), and Pan-Asianism. First, he tried to argue that only a Chinese nation dominated by the Han-ethnicity could become a genuine democratic republic, and that national unity and democracy in the form of a republic were both necessary conditions for China's self-strengthening. Then, after a period of sojourn and study in France before and during the First World War, he came to the conclusion that China should be the champion of Human-Co-Existentialism if she wanted to survive at all. Lastly, facing Japan's dominant military force, he tried to convince Japan that peace was in its best self-interest and officially adopted its rhetoric of Pan-Asianism, even though his vision was an Asia united under the principle of national equality and independence. The *leitmotif* underlying all these transformations was his concern with China's perceived national weakness in a Darwinian world dominated by the ruthless principle of the survival of the fittest. Whether the Chinese culture, of which he was the self-designated sentry, had special virtues or was at least unique, and was therefore worthy of preservation, was, for him, a question of existential resonance.

The Young Nationalist as a Hero of the Revolution

Wang Zhaoming was born in Sanshui, Guangdong Province, into an impoverished scholarly family. This coastal region had fought the two Opium Wars (First, 1839–1842; Second, 1856–1860) and had nurtured the Taiping Rebellion (1850–1864). Before the rise of Shanghai, it was here that China encountered the West and where the sense of national humiliation was felt most keenly among the educated elites. Many of China's original nationalists hailed from this region. A precocious youth, Wang braced himself through the hardship following the untimely death of both his parents. He went to study in Japan on a

---

1 Brook (2012), "Hesitating before the Judgment of History".

NATIONALISM, HUMAN-CO-EXISTENTIALISM, PAN-ASIANISM   491

Qing government fellowship. After joining the Chinese Revolutionary Alliance (Tongmenghui 同盟會) under Sun Yat-sen's leadership in Tokyo in 1905, he began to publish polemical essays in their official newspaper *Minbao* 民報 under the penname of Jingwei, the namesake of a mythological bird which carried tiny pebbles in its beak to fill up a raging ocean in order to avenge the latter's claiming its previous life as a little girl.[2] He won recognition by defending republicanism against the formidable Liang Qichao 梁啟超 (1873–1929), a democratic reformer who supported constitutional monarchy.

Handsome and eloquent, Wang Jingwei was the revolution's poster child. He became an important fundraiser among the overseas Chinese in Southeast Asia, a mission that brought him to the acquaintance of his future wife, Chen Bijun 陳璧君 (1891–1959). What really made him a national hero, however, was his failed assassination attempt at the life of the Manchu Prince Regent Zaifeng 載灃 (1883–1951), the father of the last emperor of China. His "Confession" was a powerful essay defending his beliefs. It deeply impressed the enlightened Prince Shanqi 善耆 (1866–1922), who mitigated his death sentence to life imprisonment. The four quatrains that he wrote in prison, "Orally Composed upon Being Captured" ("Beidai kouzhan" 被逮口占), which show his determination to become a martyr for the revolution, became an instant classic in modern Chinese literature.[3] He was released in November 1911 after the success of the Wuchang Uprising to broker among the Qing Government, the Nationalists, and Yuan Shikai, who had the *de facto* control of the government's Western-style modern army. The deal he reached was to change China forever.

Wang's most prominent intellectual persuasion during this period was his vehement anti-Manchu nationalism, although this common perception overshadows another side of the equation, namely, his republicanism. In 1905, the nationalists saw their most dangerous enemies not in the conservative forces that refused to change, but in the reformers who supported a constitutional monarchy. Liang Qichao, the intellectual giant of his age, was himself a wanted man in exile in Japan. Nevertheless, he regarded constitutional monarchy to be the best solution to China's problems and the most viable path to democracy. Revolution must rely on violence, he argued, and neither the Chinese people nor Chinese society was quite "ready" for democracy; a thorough and swift dissolution of the current power structures would inevitably lead to political instability, which, in turn, would give rise to plutocracy or dictatorship, or invite foreign intervention.[4] Liang did see, however, that a constitutional monarchy would eternalise the rule of the Aisin Gioro house, which belonged to an ethnic

---

2 See Yuan Ke (1980), *Shanhaijing jiaozhu*, p. 92.

3 Wang Jingwei (2012a), "Beidai kouzhan" pp. 6–7. For a translation and discussion of these poems, see Yang (2015), "Road to Lyric Martyrdom".

4 See Liang Qichao (1905 [1999]), "Kaiming zhuanzhi lun".

minority. It would be legitimised by the constitution and no longer be ordained by the "change of Heaven's Mandate," typically manifested through conquest, rebellion, or usurpation. But Liang Qichao did not feel the ethnicity of the royal house to be much of an issue. As he argued, Chineseness is not an ethnic concept, but a cultural concept; just like "barbarians" in the Spring and Autumn period had long been absorbed into the Han Chinese nation, the current distinction between the Manchu and the Han can be easily obliterated once the ban of interracial marriage is lifted and the ethnicities are treated as equal by law.[5] Liang accepted a racially-based notion of nationalism when it came to China's future in a Darwinian competition with other nations,[6] but seemed to lack the anti-Manchu racial resentment. In his view, China was weak not because of the Manchu rule, but mostly because of her national culture, custom, autocratic institutions—all of which had been formed over thousands of years. Recent historical events, for which the dynasty was responsible, also exacerbated the problem, but one primary reason for the national weakness lay precisely in the racial schism between the Manchu and the Han ethnicities.[7] In other words, the fact that aristocracy was Manchu was only a contingent factor and not the root of the problem, which was the weakness of China's native Han-ethnic culture; for China's rejuvenation, it was more urgent to eliminate the racial schism than to re-affirm it by avenging historical wrongs. Liang was not oblivious to the massacres during the Manchu conquest or to the ensuing ethnic division under its rule. But he did suggest that they bury the hatchet and just move on for the greater good.

Members of the Tongmenghui, however, generally followed the lead of Zhang Binglin 章炳麟 (1869–1936; also known as Zhang Taiyan 章太炎), who, at the time, was still in a prison in Shanghai for subversive publications. He would later be released in June 1906, go to Japan, and join the *Minbao* to take charge of its debate against Liang Qichao. Zhang did not accept the philologically shaky argument that Liang Qichao's mentor Kang Youwei 康有為 (1858–1927) advanced, namely, that the Manchu-ethnicity was historically derived from the Han. And, as he argued, even if it was so, it would not have mattered, since nations are formed through history, not at their origins; the unavenged national trauma was enough to prove their racial difference and perpetuate the racial feud. In terms of revolutionary violence, Zhang cites the examples of the Glorious Revolution in England and the Meiji Reform in Japan to argue that hoping for regime change without the backing of arms is wishful thinking.

---

5 See Liang Qichao (1896 [1999]), "Lun bianfa bi zi ping Man Han zhi jie shi", Liang Qichao (1897) [1999], *"Chunqiu Zhongguo Yi Di bian* xu"

6 See Liang Qichao (1902b [1999], "Xinmin shuo", Section 4, pp. 658–60; Liang Qichao (1902a [1999], "Lun minzu jingzheng zhi dashi".

7 See Liang Qichao (1900 [1999], "Zhongguo jiruo suyuan lun".

Moreover, if the Han could accept the Manchu rule, what prevents it from accepting another foreign conqueror's rule?[8] In other words, in order to make the Chinese gather under the banner of nationalism and patriotism, they first need to feel a sense of pride, and this starts with avenging historical humiliations.

From our point of view, both Liang Qichao and Zhang Binglin committed an anachronism in ignoring a crucial historical development, namely, that a modern state requires a different legitimising discourse from a pre-modern one. If blood ties and violence were the two dominant factors empowering a monarch before the era of nation states, nationalism, which rose at the dawn of modernity, requires an alleged "natural" community to legitimise state borders. Admittedly, a state may create an "imagined community"—to use Benedict Anderson's famous coinage[9]—by implementing a series of homogenising cultural and institutional measures. However, this process may be long and often unsuccessful, conditioned by complex historical and political factors. In the face of the actual and deep ethnic fissure running through the fabric of the late Qing society, Liang Qichao's optimism appeared somewhat naïve; while Zhang Binglin's attempt to de-legitimise the Manchu rule based upon a modern doctrine also lacked a historical perspective. Yet, as all modern nations pretend to originate from time immemorial, it seemed easier for most Chinese to imagine a nation dominated by the Han majority than one under a recent minority conqueror.

Zhang's argument in a series of passionate anti-Manchu propagandist articles had offered the emotional keynote to Wang Jingwei's *Minbao* articles, which were typically long, lucid, and well-reasoned. It was in these articles that we first gained a glimpse of Wang's intellectual talent as a propagandist with style. In "Citizens of the Nation" ("Minzu de guomin" 民族的國民), serialised in the first two issues of *Minbao* (Oct./Nov. 1905), he first defined a nation as "a historically continuous group of people sharing the same characteristics," namely, the same blood, same language and script, same region of residence, same habits, same religion(s), and the same spiritual constitutions. This static and essentialist notion of nation was prevalent in late nineteenth and early twentieth century nation-building discourse. Wang then proceeds to clarify that "citizenship" is a legal definition which has two sides: one is the legal duties and rights that define the individual's relation with the state; the other is the freedom and independence that characterise the individual citizen. Thus, only a democracy has citizens, while an autocracy has only slaves. Now, he asks himself: while a "nation" and a "citizenry" are different concepts, could their boundaries be commensurate? He regards a single-ethnicity nation-state the best scenario in

---

8 Zhang Binglin (1985), "Bo Kang Youwei lun geming shu."
9 See Anderson (1983), *Imagined Communities*.

which to realise equality and freedom among its citizens, but China clearly belongs to the league of multi-ethnicity states. In the latter case, ethnic nationalities co-existing in a state could either remain separated or integrate. If they remain separated, they could either form a union of equal nationalities or let one nationality dominate the others. The second kind spawns racial resentment and is unstable. Integration is a better scenario, and there are four possibilities: 1) equal nationalities integrate into a new nationality; 2) the majority nationality of conquerors absorbs the minority nationalities of conquered peoples; 3) a minority nationality of conquerors absorbs the majority nationality of a conquered people; 4) a minority nationality of conquerors is absorbed by the majority nationality of a conquered people. The constitutional monarchists, in his opinion, had failed to understand the case of China. He cites historical precedence of racial integration from ancient times to prove that China has always been in the second situation, namely, a majority nationality of victorious conquerors absorbing conquered ethnic minorities. Before the Manchu conquest, the only exception was the Mongols, who refused to Sinicise and were ultimately driven out of China. Under the Manchu, however, the Chinese face the danger of being absorbed by a minority nationality. Even though, as Wang admits, racial feud has relented in the recent decades and the Han has started to gain more political power, the ultimate authority is still held in the hands of a Manchu aristocracy. The so-called "constitutional monarchy" is only a trick to eternalise the ethnic hierarchy. Han reformers such as Liang Qichao fail to see it through because they have confused the nationalistic and the democratic revolutions. Racial and the political revolutions, in Wang's opinion, are different but are both necessary to attain the ultimate goal of building a democratic nation-state. With regard to Liang's question of whether the Chinese people are "ready" to become modern citizens, Wang replies optimistically that history always moves forward, so the lack of democratic institutions in the past does not prove that nation- and state-building are not possible. On the question of violence, he acknowledges that civil and military powers are at odds, but he is confident that Chinese revolutionaries, under the enlightened leadership of Sun Yat-sen, will be able to "sign a contract" with the Chinese people at the onset of the revolution in order to stipulate each other's duties and rights. Once a region is liberated, it will organise a representative body to supervise and negotiate with the military government; and, once the revolution succeeds, regional parliaments will unite to replace military rule with a civil government. If the revolutionary military government breaks its contract, the people's representatives will refuse to fulfil their duties of financial and political support, rendering the country ungovernable.[10]

---

10 Wang Jingwei (1929), "Minzu de guomin".

Despite its scientific poise, Wang's argument occasionally takes a flight into romantic passion, especially when it comes to his idealistic moral fervour or his anti-Manchu rage. The fate which he imagines of the Manchu after the success of the revolution betrays strong racial hatred. It never occurred to him to restore the Manchu to their ancestral home and make China a racially pure nation-state. Rather, in his vision, the Manchu would not be able to "escape our axes". The survivors, although deserving to be treated with humanity, are politically too dangerous to be given equal rights; instead, they should be given the legal status of "residential aliens" until they integrate or die out.[11] It should be pointed out that this paragraph comes after a long section listing the bloodbath during the Manchu conquest and the subsequent savage literary inquisitions. As modern researchers of trauma may argue, traumatic historical memory can be healed only through a long process of constructive justice, pardon, and reconciliation. The bloodbath of the Manchu conquest, however, was not only never avenged, but was actively prohibited from public commemoration throughout the Qing Dynasty. Literary inquisitions, used as a tool for intellectual control, further institutionalised aphasia, making the comeback of the counter-memory all the more vehement once the ideological control loosened and the Manchu were proven weak in front of the Western powers. The once unassailable conqueror now appeared vulnerable. A proposed re-subjugation to the Manchu monarchy, even a toothless one, stung the sense of Han racial and cultural pride, which was central to the creation of Chinese nationalism with a Han majority. After all, the monarch, even with his power stripped, remained a symbol of the state's political authority and the nation's cultural tradition, and Wang Jingwei and his comrades were not ready to concede the symbolic Chineseness to the erstwhile conqueror. Furthermore, a cynic might also point out that getting rid of the weakened Manchu house was a low hanging fruit for the revolutionaries; modernising China and defending her against colonial powers were more formidable tasks.

National pride rests upon the perception of a nation's uniqueness and strength. Late Qing intellectuals, however, generally accepted the Darwinian principle of "the survival of the fittest". If China is militarily or even culturally weak, does it deserve to live? Wang addressed this issue in another essay published in 1908. He argues that a weak nation does indeed face extinction, which is a universal principle. But the actual situation may grant it some breathing space because the stronger nations are fighting over their rights of dominance, giving it a chance to play and gain time to strengthen itself. A revolution is the best means to inspire the national spirit to seek self-strengthening. Furthermore, the Manchu proved themselves stronger than the Han through its military con-

---

11 Ibid., p. 22.

quest; he therefore repeats Zhang Binglin's argument that, if the Chinese can live with the Manchu dominance, what prevents them from accepting another foreign ruler?[12] Being a patriot, he had no choice but wishes China the best, although his vision was tinged by Han chauvinism.

It was to stimulate the nation's revolutionary spirit that Wang determined to assassinate the Prince Regent, an action apparently inspired European anarchist activism. He was not alone. Back then, the assassinations of Alexander II of Russia (31 March 1881), of Umberto I of Italy (27 June 1900), and of Alexander I of Serbia (11 June 1903) were broadly relished across progressive newspapers and journals. An article published in the *People's Journal* in 1908 even declared the time as "an Era of Regicide."[13] In the rising temperature of that parlous time, assassination was seen as a necessary means for revolution and was ardently plotted by men and women itching to add momentum to the country's course of incremental change. Intellectuals with stature no less than Cai Yuanpei 蔡元培 (1868–1940), Chen Duxiu 陳獨秀 (1879–1942), and Zhang Shizhao 章士釗 (1883–1971) had participated in one terrorist cell or another. More than fifty assassinations were attempted in the last decade of the Qing dynasty, and assassins, the martyress Qiu Jin 秋瑾 (1875–1907) included, were celebrated across progressive newspapers. Bomb-making methods were broadly shared.[14]

Wang Jingwei's attempt, though not an isolated case, was certainly the most notable in capturing the public's imagination, as it was carried by the most high-profile revolutionary. By all accounts, it was a reckless plan, ill-conceived from the start. The five young assassins had no connections in Beijing and little training in explosives, yet they planned to make a bomb undetected in Beijing, bury it underneath the path that the Prince Regent would take, and just hope that it detonated at the right moment in order to kill the Prince. As the Prince rode in a carriage drawn by two horses, the bomb had to be extra-large, too. And if everything miraculously worked out, they did not have an escape plan, as their Cantonese accent would immediately give them away to the police search force. The plan did not work out. The bomb was found and this group of Cantonese-speaking young people quickly became the suspects. Wang, however, decided to stay behind and let himself be caught, in order to realize the other, and perhaps more important, goal of his assassination plot, which was to make himself a

---

12 Wang Jingwei, "Geming keyi dujue guafen zhi shiju".

13 Jishou (1908), "Diwang ansha zhi shidai". It was ostensibly a translated article. I have yet to identity the original text.

14 On assassinations at the end of the Qing, see for instance Huang Tao (2013), "Yuansha: Qingmo gemingpai ansha yanjiu"; Luo Haoxing (2015), "1900 niandai zhongguo de zhengzhi ansha jiqi shehui xiaoying".

NATIONALISM, HUMAN-CO-EXISTENTIALISM, PAN-ASIANISM 497

martyr. His sacrifice, so he reasoned, would energise the revolutionary cause while discrediting the Qing reform as insincere.

Here, Wang betrayed the influence of the idealist moral philosophy of the Wang Yangming 王陽明 (1472–1529) School of Confucianism, an influence that he had received as a teenager through his father's instruction and which would remain with him throughout his life. In "Determination for Revolution" ("Geming zhi juexin" 革命之決心), an essay published on *Minbao* in February 1910, shortly before his assassination mission, he declared that the determination for revolution derived from one's "empathetic heart" (*ceyin zhi xin* 惻隱之心), a Mencius notion that emphasises the innate origin of moral instincts. Such moral instincts will drive an otherwise gentle soul to attempt the impossible, to perform actions of ultimate courage, in order to save the world.

Thus the most radical means can only be assumed by one with the most peaceful mind; the most steadfast integrity can only be possessed by the one with the most magnanimous temperament.

He cites Wang Yangming's famous epistle to Nie Wenwei 聶文蔚[15] to argue that, if one is absolute honest in applying one's innate "moral knowledge" (*liangzhi* 良知), one will not be deterred by thoughts of wealth, power, or even reputation, in doing the right thing. Such righteous courage will motivate one to be afraid neither of death nor of trouble. Now, the former kind of courage, namely, the courage of martyrdom, is required for the victory of the revolution; while the latter, namely, the courage of bearing the quotidian burden, is for state-building after the victory. The martyr is like firewood, while the statesman is like the pot that endures heat - both are necessary to cook the rice to feed the hungry mass.[16]

Wang Jingwei used the same set of metaphors in a private letter to Hu Hanmin 胡漢民 (1879–1936), a fellow leader of the Tongmenghui, written before he launched the mission of no return to Beijing. In this letter, he specifically wished Hu to be the pot while he would be the firewood.[17] This trope also became a recurring theme in Wang's poetry. It first appears in a poem written in 1910 in prison, allegedly upon seeing a worker chopping a worn wooden wheel into pieces; as I doubt that such a scene was likely to be spotted in a heavily guarded prison, it might be an imagined or recollected occasion for the poem. To Wang, this wooden wheel personifies the qualities of endurance and sacrifice; becoming firewood would be its final use, which is to cook newly harvested rice and feed people with warm food.[18] In 1912, after being released

---

15 See Wang Yangming (2000), *Yangming chuanxi lu*, pp. 248–52.
16 Wang Jingwei (1929b), "Geming zhi juexin".
17 Wang Jingwei (1929f), "Yu Hu Hanmin shu".
18 Wang Jingwei (2012c), "Jian ren xi chelun wei xin wei zuo ci ge", p. 22.

from prison, he decided to go to study in France. Upon crossing the Indian Ocean, Wang wrote two poems lamenting the restless journey of life; yet "if this piece of firewood can still be burnt, / I shall not regret myself becoming cold ashes" 勞薪如可爇, 未敢惜寒灰.[19] And, almost thirty years later in Nanjing, when his collaboration with the Japanese had led to his being declared a national traitor, Chen Bijun wrote a calligraphic scroll for him which bore Wang's four prison quatrains as well as the aforementioned epistle to Nie Wenwei. This scroll was possibly meant to encourage Wang not to forget his initial resolution to care solely about saving the Chinese people, and not think about his personal reputation. Wang was inspired to re-use the firewood image, reassuring in a poem that "what I expect to be is not the pot but the firewood" 不望為釜望為薪.[20]

Certainly, one's self-image does not mean the truth, nor does altruistic motivation translate into good or even wise deeds. But the consistency in Wang's rhetoric suggests a strong sense of moral subjectivity. Wang envisioned himself as being responsible to China's elite cultural tradition and to a vaguely-defined nation consisting of an anonymous mass. His moral agency is thus both temporal and spatial, set to extend an idealistic Confucian statecraft, with every practical means available, over a land populated by people whom he determined to love, but never came to personally know.

Not that the Chineseness of this anonymous people mattered. Rather, Wang, in disposition, was a man living in the abstract, and his being a Han Chinese was only contingent. His anti-Manchu rage had already appeared to dissipate when he wrote the "Confession" in the Manchu prison. There, he focuses mainly on the democratic revolution, and proposes that people of different ethnicities should all be treated equal in the future Republic of China.[21] It is possible that the heroic action of assassination was a cathartic moment that released his pent-up wrath, accumulated through reliving the nation's historical trauma in the fervent imaginations of a young revolutionary. In any case, after the victory of the 1911 Revolution, Wang shifted towards cosmopolitanism and humanism with determination.

A Humanist in France

November 1918, the First World War ended. Despite the fact that China had declared war on the Central Powers on 14 August 1917, Japan claimed its right

---

19 Wang Jingwei (2012d), "Yinduyang zhou zhong", p. 44.
20 Wang Jingwei (2012b), "Bingru shoushu Yangming xiansheng 'Da Nie Wenwei shu' [...]".
21 Cited in Zhang Jiangcai (1937), "Wang Jingwei xianshen gengxu mengnan shilu".

NATIONALISM, HUMAN-CO-EXISTENTIALISM, PAN-ASIANISM · 499

to the German colony in the Shandong Province, which it had seized in November 1914, and the Allies decided to concede to its demands. Amid the domestic protest in China, of which the most famous incident was known as the May Fourth Movement, the Treaty of Versailles was signed on 28 June 1919.

Wang Jingwei observed the ravages of the war closely from France.[22] After the foundation of the Republic, he was offered top government positions, including Governor of Guangdong. Following his anarchist persuasion, however, he declined all job offers and declared that he would continue his studies in Europe, following the steps of his senior friends and mentors Wu Zhihui 吳稚暉 (1865–1953), Cai Yuanpei 蔡元培 (1868–1940), and Li Shizeng 李石曾 (1881–1973). He wanted to become an educator and enlighten the Chinese people, improve their moral character, and make them modern citizens. Supported by a generous government stipend, he took departure in August 1912, accompanied by his loyal comrade and newly-wed wife, Chen Bijun, and by their best friend Fang Junying 方君瑛 (1884–1923) and her widowed sister-in-law Zeng Xing 曾醒 (1882–1954). The four young adults further brought with them four children: Fang Junying's sister Junbi 方君璧 (1898–1986), Zeng Xing's brother Zhongming 曾仲鳴 (1896–1939), her son Fang Xianshu 方賢俶 (1900–?), and Bijun's brother Changzu 陳昌祖 (1904–1994). Cantonese was their common tongue. This small group, bounded by blood ties, friendship, and idealism, would in later years become Wang's most faithful coterie of supporters, separable only by death. They first arrived at Montargis, a quiet small town close to Paris. After the war broke out they decided to leave Montargis, probably thinking it was too close to Paris. They moved first to Nantes and eventually to Laon. Though the town fell in September 1914, a few Chinese behind the Western Front did not seem to attract too much attention. When winter came the group migrated south. In November they made their way to Toulouse, where Cai Yuanpei and Li Shizeng already found refuge. They would eventually live in Royan and finally in Bordeaux, where some young adults of his group would study at the university.

Wang and Chen's first two children were born during this period. His plan to study, however, was frequently interrupted by China's domestic crises. He was summoned by Sun Yat-sen a few times to join the anti-Yuan movements and spent lengthy periods in China, which invariably ended with his regret for having achieved nothing and returning once again to France. Furthermore, his resolution was hobbled by his lack of talent in foreign languages. His French never reached the proficiency required for the entrance exam to any French

---

22 Wang's life in France has previously received no scholarly attention. Many crucial facts remain vague. I have reconstructed this period of his life in detail in another article: Zhiyi Yang (2018), "A Humanist in Wartime France: Wang Jingwei during the First World War."

university.[23] He did, however, manage to promote Chinese-language publishing and education in France, together with Wu, Cai, and Li. They founded and raised funds for the *Société Franco-Chinoise d'Education* (*Hua Fa jiaoyuhui* 華法教育會), promoted the Diligent Work-Frugal Study programme (*qingong jianxue* 勤工儉學), and founded the *Study in Europe* magazine (*Lü Ou zazhi* 旅歐雜誌). The *L'institut Franco-chinois de Lyon* (Li'ang Zhongfa Daxue 里昂中法大學) which he co-founded in 1921 on his return to China was to become the centre of a network of Chinese students' coming to Europe, especially France. Previously, Chinese students' primary destination for overseas education was Japan, as it was cheap, close to home, and similar in culture; those supported by fellowships or by family funds could afford to go to America. Wang and his fellow educators' endeavours would make France a popular destination for ambitious and less affluent students. These students' work-study life would further help them to forge camaraderie with labourers. They would later bring back to China not only modern science, art, and philosophy, but also Marxist idealism. Many future CPC leaders, including Zhou Enlai 周恩來 (1898–1976) and Deng Xiaoping 鄧小平 (1904–1997), participated in this programme and received their intellectual initiation in France.[24]

Wang was deeply frustrated by his lack of progress in studying European philosophy and literature. A few private epistles addressed to Wu Zhihui, now in the KMT Party Archives in Taipei, reveal his agonies. In a letter dated May 13 [1914?],[25] he expresses a wish to find out what he was to do with the rest of his life; he mentions Wu Zhihui's suggestion that, now that it was no longer possible for him to become a philosopher, perhaps he should dedicate himself to literature; Wang heartily agrees and promises to focus on reading and writing for the next few years.[26] Another letter dated to January 16 [1916] calls his negotiation in China to prevent the monarchy of Yuan Shikai "ineffective"; deeply frustrated, he vowed that he would finally commit himself to his studies and would never return to China again; even if China "should perish" (original word: *wangguo* 亡國, although its meaning remains unclear; either it means the restoration of the monarchy or foreign invasion), he would choose to commit

---

23 Many biographers mistakenly write that Wang studied sociology at the University of Lyon. My own research at Lyon Municipal Archive and Fonds Chinois Archive suggests that he might have never lived in Lyon and certainly never registered at the university. It is possible that it was the official reason of continuing to grant him the government fellowship, since if one did not register in a university in time the government would withdraw its support. But, given Wang's prestige and rank in the Party, we may not expect the rules to have been observed strictly in his case. Further research is needed to find out how the story of his studying sociology in Lyon began to circulate.

24 See Xian Yuhao (2016), *Liu Fa qingong jianxue yundong shi.*

25 Wang Jingwei's private epistles are typically dated only with month and day, but not with the year. The years provided here are my own reconstructions.

26 Wang Jingwei's letter to Wu Zhihui, Document "Zhi 稚 07595," KMT Party Archive, Taipei.

suicide facing the east, rather than returning home.[27] Another letter, dated March 21 [1916], mentions his attempt to assassinate Yuan Shikai when he was in Shanghai, but Yuan, suspecting his motive, declined to meet him. Wang even contemplated on fantastical measures to approach Yuan, such as changing one's appearance—he had read about it in detective novels, but the means he learned from a drama teacher in Paris were far less spectacular. He feels as though he is trapped in a deep existential dilemma: the purpose of his studies is, metaphorically, to melt a "hammer" (soldier) and remake it into a "saw" (educator), but, in the process of transformation, he has neither the use of a saw nor that of a hammer; even when he tries to pick up the old trade of his *Minbao* period to write polemical articles, he has no reference to rely on, as reading in Japanese (heavily peppered with Chinese characters) was easy, while reading in Western languages was beyond him. Tormented by these thoughts, he lost sleep and appetite and suffered from neurosis.[28] It was his frustration in his studies and his desire to leave a mark in history, I surmise, that finally drove Wang back to China to return to politics, relinquishing his resolutions and risking the reprimands of his friends of "losing the qualification to be a master of New China", to wit, making himself a Western-educated modern intellectual.[29]

Yet, Wang's sojourn in France did yield intellectual progress. At first, his nationalist passion weakened, and he was attracted by anarchism, of which Wu Zhihui was an adamant advocator. The outbreak of the First World War, however, shook both beliefs. Anarchism now seemed utopian, while narrow national self-interest, as represented by the viral brand of militarism developed in late nineteenth century Germany, resulted in unprecedented disasters. And, ending his French sojourn, he took the route through Siberia in early 1917 on his way back to China and saw the brewing Soviet revolution first-hand, which further helped him to look beyond China and think in terms of global challenges and world peace. In December 1918, the Guangdong Military Government elected him their representative to the appending Paris Peace Conference, to be held the following January, on the grounds that Wang was familiar with international politics and was a senior leader of the Nationalist Party (at the time still called the Chinese Revolutionary Party 中華革命黨). Wang declined the appointment, even though he did go to Paris as a private observer of the conference. The major reason he cited was his lingering attachment to anarchism. Another unstated reason, I suspect, was that as a centrist he did not want to represent a separatist regional government and therefore undermine the diplomatic effort of China's Central Government.

---

27 Wang Jingwei's letter to Wu Zhihui, Document "Zhi 09385," KMT Party Archive, Taipei.
28 Wang Jingwei's letter to Wu Zhihui, Document "Zhi 09381," KMT Party Archive, Taipei.
29 Cai Yuanpei's letter to Wu Zhihui, Document "Zhi 07810," KMT Party Archive, Taipei.

What he saw at the conference was a game of power, a reckless disregard for international justice or for China's rights. He joined the protest against the signing of the treaty, a popular demand to which the Chinese representative yielded. Two months later, in August 1919, Wang Jingwei, still in France, joined Sun Yat-sen's *Construction Monthly* (*Jianshe yuekan* 建設月刊), a journal published in Shanghai, as its chief writer. "The Co-existence of Humanity" ("Renlei zhi gongcun" 人類之共存) and "The Paris Peace Conference and the Sino-Japanese Problem" ("Bali Hehui yu Zhong Ri wenti" 巴黎和會與中日問題) were two long essays first published in this journal. Both essays were collected in an anthology entitled *China and the World after the Paris Peace Conference* (*Bali Heyi hou zhi shijie yu Zhongguo* 巴黎和議後之世界與中國), edited by Wang Jingwei and published in 1920. The title of the first article was slightly modified to become "Human-Co-Existentialism" ("Renlei gongcun zhuyi" 人類共存主義) as the preface of the anthology. The change in the title indicates a sense of its theoretical importance.

"Human-Co-Existentialism," is, in my opinion, the representative piece of Wang Jingwei's mature thoughts after the long period of his studies, observation, and thinking in France. It begins by declaring the basic principles of human co-existence, namely, that everyone should think for his or her own existence and care about the existence of others. For one's own individual existence, the most important values are independence and freedom; while, for the society, they are the divisions of labour and collaboration. Given the limit of man's existential horizon, his sense of existence expands over time. In a primitive society, it was about his individual existence; then it expanded to the existence of the family, and then to tribal existence; in the age of the nation-state, it expands to national existence; and, in a globalised world, the notion of human co-existence should arise by necessity.

Wang Jingwei then assumes the voice of a Darwinian interlocutor who challenges his vision and argues that all living creatures are dominated by the "survival of the fittest" principle, and that man should be no exception. Wang answers by distinguishing positive competition and negative competition. In the scenario of positive competition, both parties improve their skills to win a competitive edge, and, as a result, the technological level of production is improved. In the scenario of negative competition, however, the parties try to undermine each other, resulting in mutual destruction. On the societal level, negative competition would be militarism, which, in Wang Jingwei's words, is represented by the theories of "German scholars" and sees war as the necessary means of evolution. Wang Jingwei does not explicitly mention the First World War as the result of such a Social Darwinian philosophy, but readers, in 1919, would have no difficult in deducing that conclusion.

Wang then proceeds to argue that evolution postulates not only competition but also collaboration. All animals have two kinds of fundamental desires: the nutritive and the reproductive; the former leads to competition, and the latter to collaboration.[30] Even though internal collaboration may be used as a means of competition among human groups, collaboration itself also derives from a fundamental human desire and is not just a means but also an end. Moreover, there are no constant winners or losers in a negative competition for resources. So, if the social production improves to the extent that everyone will be nourished, collaboration is certainly more beneficial than negative competition.

Lastly, men are different from animals since they can make self-conscious choices. So we should be able to transcend our basest desires, abandon negative competition, and aspire for positive competition and collaboration. This, Wang Jingwei argues, establishes the theoretical foundation of his Human-Co-Existentialism.

His interlocutor then questions whether such an ideal is impractical in today's world. Wang answers that, though the League of Nations is imperfect, it is, after all, the germane point of international collaboration, a development in the right direction. As for the opinion that this ideal is too lofty for China, since China could hardly protect her own existence, let alone take care of the human co-existence, Wang replies that, it is precisely *because* of China's weakness that she should promote Human Co-Existentialism. First, in the situation of actual inequality, the weak parties could either be eliminated or be improved to attain equality. The contact of China with the rest of the world has brought both kinds of possibilities for China. If militarism and colonialism threaten to eliminate her existence, the spread of Western science gives her hope to improve herself in both material and spiritual lives.

The second point that Wang raises is of particular interest. He declares that equality should be understood not only as the equality of rights but also as equality in responsibilities. Those who claim equal rights without fulfilling their responsibilities do not deserve these rights; those who have fulfilled their responsibilities but do not receive equal rights can call it injustice. Now, China has not fulfilled its responsibilities to become equal with civilised countries in building political and social institutions or in enlightening her population. So, when countries like Italy or Japan refuse to return those rights, they could raise actual evidence to claim that China would not take care of the material equipment or social institutions in these former colonies. This sorry state of affairs should remind China how much she has degenerated from her former cultural glories. So, in order to aspire to equal rights, China should fulfil her share of

---

30 Here I fear that Wang's biological reasoning is a bit mangled, since reproductive desire can also lead to competition, as anyone who has seen a group of primates in a zoo suspects.

504   ZHIYI YANG

responsibilities towards self-improvement. This argument that the weak are complicit in their own demise will be explored below.

The enemy of Human Co-Existentialism, in Wang's opinion, is primarily militarism, represented by Germany. The First World War shows that German militarism cannot be defeated by Russia, which was a similarly militarised country, but can be defeated by democratic and liberal countries such as France and the USA, which promote justice and science among their people, who, in consequence, have something to fight for. Wang's conclusion is that human independence relies upon justice and not upon violence, and that the best defence against aggression is in promoting knowledge and learning, not in military force. In this sense, Wang regards the Paris Peace Conference as a transitive point from the era of militarism to the era of Human Co-Existentialism.

Despite China's perceived weakness and the urgent existential crisis posed by the jingoistic ambition of Japan, on which he offers a capable and comprehensive analysis in the following essay, entitled "The Paris Peace Conference and Sino-Japan Problem", Wang's optimism in this essay is quite striking. He believes that 1919 marks the end of the era of militarist Social Darwinism. As he has previously argued in an essay entitled "The Meaning of Sacrifice" ("Xisheng de yiyi" 犧牲的意義), published in August 1916 (*Lü Ou zazhi*, no.1), weakness and strength change over time, and nations develop at uneven speeds. A currently weak nation or civilisation could erupt in the future as a strong one. Social Darwinism, however, regards the process of evolution as lineal, and therefore ignores the reality of uneven development and eliminates the possibilities of catching-up. Second, a global society that develops in the Social Darwinian vision would see cultural diversity reduced, leading to the dominance of a single culture, a single race, or a single person. Thus, the "survival of the fittest" doctrine would become its own enemy, ultimately eliminating competition all together. Wang therefore regards himself to be a humanist (*rendao zhuyi zhe* 人道主義者), as Darwinian competition could exist among animals or between humans and animals, but not among men.

This period shows the evolution in Wang's ongoing reflection on the weakness of China. For the young Wang Jingwei, devoted to the anti-Manchu nationalist revolution, "weakness" was simply the declined state of the Chinese nation which was to be overcome by revolution (as shown in his earlier writings). During his stay in France, and especially since the outbreak of the First World War, however, he began to reflect more on the ethical dimension of "weakness". A poem written perhaps in late 1914, entitled "A Translation of De Florian's Fable" ("Yi Folaoliang yuyanshi" 譯佛老里昂寓言詩),[31] was inspired by the French poet Jean-Pierre Claris de Florian's (1755–1794) fable "La Brebis

---

31 Wang Jingwei (2012), *Shuangzhaolou shici gao*, p. 53. The whole poem is translated in Zhiyi Yang (2018), "A Humanist in Wartime France".

NATIONALISM, HUMAN-CO-EXISTENTIALISM, PAN-ASIANISM 505

et le Chien" ("The Lamb and the Dog"). De Florian's fable depicts a lamb and a dog lamenting their miserable fates of being enslaved or eaten by the humans; yet, as the dog argues at the end, it is better to suffer than to cause suffering.[32] De Florian's original poem is rather short and simple, Wang Jingwei's pentasyllabic ancient-style verse, however, is much longer and more elaborate. In De Florian's poem, the dog says:

> … mais crois-tu plus heureux
> Les auteurs de notre misère?
> Va, ma soeur, il vaut encore mieux
> Souffrir le mal que de le faire.

(But do you believe him to be happier—/ the authors of our misery? / Go, my sister, it is better / to suffer evil than inflict it.)

Wang creatively adapts it to:

> 弱者未云禍　Weakness leads not necessarily to misfortune,
> 強者未云福　And strength is not necessarily luck.
> 與其作刀俎　Compared to being the knife or the cutting board,
> 毋寧為魚肉　We'd rather be the fish to be gutted, the meat to be cut.

If the morale of De Florian's poem is a pious discussion of Christian happiness, a mental state that is easier to achieve when one has a clear conscience, even while being the victim of evil, Wang's adaptation shifts the focus to weakness. The first two lines relate the current discussion on weakness to Laozi's doctrine on the dialectics of misfortune and fortune ("In misfortune fortune lies; in fortune misfortune lies" 禍兮福所倚福兮禍所伏; *Laozi* 58). Thus, when saying that weakness does not necessarily lead to misfortune, he also implies that weakness could one day becomes strength. The next two lines transform the saying: "Now others are the knife and cutting board, while we are the fish and the meat" 方今人為刀俎我為魚肉, meaning a situation in which one is under total manipulation and in mortal danger.[33] Wang's adaptation is close to De Florian's in spirit, but he takes away the element of "happiness" entirely. Instead, he presents an image of the weak literally being the food for the consumption of the powerful. This image ties to his comment following the poem, in which he uses the term *ruorou qiangshi* 弱肉強食 (literally, "the meat of the weak is the fodder of the strong") which is the translation of the Darwinian doctrine of the "survival of the fittest" by Yan Fu 嚴復 (1854–1921), in order to discuss the issue between the weak and the strong:

---

32 See de Florian (1855), *Fables de Florian*, Paris: Delarue, p. 37.

33 See Sima Qian (1959), "Xiang Yu benji" 項羽本紀 (Basic annals of Xiang Yu), in *Shiji*, vol. 1, p. 314.

佛氏此詩，天下之自命為強者皆當愧死。顧吾以為弱肉強食，強者固有罪矣，即弱者亦不為無罪。罪惡之所以存於天地，以有施者即有受者也。苟無受者，將於何施？是又願天下之自承為弱者一思之也。

Reading this poem of De Florian's, all those who regard themselves as strong powers in the world should be mortally ashamed. In my opinion, in the scenario of the so-called "the meat of the weak is the fodder of the strong", though the strong have the sin, the weak share the sin too. The reason that sin and evil exist between the heaven and the earth is because there are always two parties involved, the doer and the receiver. Without a receiver, who can be the doer? This is what I would like those who admit themselves to be the weak to think about.

This colophon further complicates the relation between weakness and strength. Wang seems to say that, though the strong commit the crime of murder, the weak are complicit in this crime, a point which, as we have seen earlier, specifically refers to China's predicament. Thus, the lesson is neither to stay weak, nor to perpetuate the cycle of sin. In this poem, Wang has not offered an answer to how to break the cycle. From this poem in 1914 to the 1916 essay entitled "The Meaning of Sacrifice" and finally to the resolute proposal of a Human-Co-Existentialism in 1919, we see Wang's continuous reflection on this issue. The weak are perhaps guilty of their own victimhood, but it is also ethically more preferable than being the bully who denies others their right to exist. Ultimately, the answer lies in a humanist spirit applied to international relations. Wang wants the post-war world to share his paradigm of peaceful co-existence and positive competition. Japan's encroachment of China's territory, therefore, is not just an existential threat to China, but also a grave enemy of this emerging new global order.

Interlude: Wang Jingwei and Communism

Wang Jingwei was attracted to Communism by its promise of the liberation of the workers and world unity. Such a vision appeals to his humanist disposition. The First United Front, an alliance between the KMT and the CPC formed in 1923, was a marriage of convenience. The CPC needed a holding to survive, while KMT needed the Soviet assistance to fight the warlords who filled the power vacuum left by Yuan Shikai's untimely death. As a result, the CPC members would join the KMT while still retaining their dual-party membership; the KMT received arms, training, and military consultancy from the Soviet Union. Yet, ideologically, the later Sun Yat-sen did share many of the Communists' ideas, especially in his economic policy. In a series of speeches that he gave in 1924 towards the end of his life, to re-elaborate upon his "Three Principles of the People" (*sanmin zhuyi* 三民主義), he declared: "The Principle of the Peo-

NATIONALISM, HUMAN-CO-EXISTENTIALISM, PAN-ASIANISM   507

ple's Livelihood is simply socialism, namely, communism, or the Principle of the Great Unity" 民生主義就是社會主義，又名共產主義，即是大同主義.[34] But Sun Yat-sen's proposals differed from those of the Soviet Union's in a few important ways. First, he simultaneously emphasised nationalism and democracy, the other two principles of the triad. Second, he was against violent confiscation of land, and proposed, instead, a gentler and incremental path towards land reform, namely, the state was first to evaluate the price of land, and give the current owners a fixed price, so that, when the land price increases together with enhanced productivity, the original owner would only hold the amount of land corresponding to the original fixed value, while the land which amounted to the increased value would be confiscated and re-distributed. Clearly, no one found the proposal satisfactory: the landowners felt threatened, while the peasants, in dire destitution, could not wait.

After Sun Yat-sen's death on 12 March 1925, Wang Jingwei was broadly viewed as the successor of his political legacy. Having eventually relinquished his allegiance to anarchism, on July 3, 1925, he would be elected President of China by the Nationalist Government in Guangzhou. It was true that Wang ghost-wrote Sun's last will when the latter lay dying in Beijing. Wang's supporters elaborated the story into a myth of transmission, which evokes the "transmission of the dharma" mythology in Buddhist hagiography. Wang styled himself in this way too. In a speech given at the one-year anniversary of Sun's death, Wang summarised that Sun had left two tasks to his comrades, namely, to work together with the Soviets and to unite with various factions of the revolutionaries.[35] In another speech, he emphatically declared that, to realise nationalism and democracy, the KMT must awaken the common people, including the workers and the farmers, and must work together with "other nations that treat us as equal", namely, the Soviet Union.[36] One may suspect that Wang was eager to cast himself as Sun's successor in order to grab more power among the KMT ranks, especially against his rivals, such as Chiang Kai-shek and Hu Hanmin. Such suspicion may contain a grain of truth, but Wang's conviction as well as his friendship with leading Communists seemed genuine. More than just a working relationship, he and Chen Duxiu 陳獨秀 (1879–1942) forged a bond based upon mutual respect of each other's intellectual calibre. It was also under Wang's patronage that the young Mao Zedong's 毛澤東 (1893–1976) career took off.

In March 1927, when the Generalissimo began to purge the Communists from KMT, wary of its increasing influence, Wang took the Communists under his wing. He called Chiang an autocrat, who exploited the pretext of "putting

---

34 Sun Yat-sen (1981), "Sanmin zhuyi, minsheng zhuyi".
35 Wang Jingwei (1927), "Zenyangde jinian Zongli yanjiangci".
36 Wang Jingwei (1929e), "Xuanbu Sun Zongli shilue yanjiangci".

the Party in order" to trample upon democratic rights. The KMT regime split into two, with the leftwing gathering in Wuhan under Wang and the rightwing in Nanjing under Chiang. This serious crisis in the party history led some KMT members, including his erstwhile trusted friend Wu Zhihui, to view Wang as a traitor.

However, the Communist land confiscation and violent class-struggle policies eventually upset Wang, and he was reportedly further shocked by the Soviet secret mandate for the CPC to take over the control of the government. The nationalist and democrat in him made a swift decision to re-forge the alliance with Chiang Kai-shek. In September, the antagonism between Wuhan and Nanjing was formally over, and Wang became a resolute anti-Communist. The armed opposition between the KMT and the CPC began, and continued until the Second United Front was established in 1937, in the face of Japan's aggression.

In a speech given on 5 November 1927, a rueful Wang apologised for having created fractures within the party. He explained his change of heart by first arguing that policies are different from principles—both, he maintained, should be adjusted according to circumstances, but principles are fundamental, while policies are derivative. The policies "uniting with the Soviets, uniting with the Communists, and assisting the farmers and workers", which Sun Yat-sen advocated in the last stage of his life, were next in importance to the Three Principles of the People. Sun Yat-sen advocated these policies based upon the Soviet promise of assisting the Chinese nationalist revolution and of not promoting the Communist revolution in China. At the same time, there were three different opinions in the Soviet government concerning the United Front: the pro, the con, and Stalin's faction, which agreed to it only to manipulate the KMT from inside. When he went to Wuhan, he began to have second thoughts about the Communists' actions. The Comintern representative Manabendra Nath Roy (1887–1954), however, trusted him enough to show him a resolution from Moscow to confiscate land, reform the KMT Central Executive Committee, arm the party members, and set up "revolutionary tribunes". Wang hereby realised that the two parties were going in different directions, and decided to turn resolutely against the Communists.[37]

This, at least, was Wang's explanation for his change of heart. The mainstream narrative of mainland Chinese historiography offers another interpretation. It is believed that Wang exploited the Communists when he needed them in a power play against Chiang Kai-shek, and betrayed them once he realised that his interests were aligned with the class of the landlords and capitalists, not with the proletariat. According to this narrative, Wang was an opportunist and a

---

37 Wang Jingwei (1929d), "Wuhan fengong zhi jingguo".

traitor. In whichever case, from 1927, Wang's aversion against Communism seemed to have even outstripped that of Chiang Kai-shek's. After Chiang signed the agreement to forge a Second United Front as a result of the *coup d'état* known as the Xi'an Incident in December 1936, Wang became a strong dissenter against the union. He believed the Communists to be *provocateurs* who were trying to create friction between Japan and China, while peddling the propaganda of "united armed resistance" to exploit the public's patriotic sentiments, solely for the purpose of their own survival and expansion. (The Communists, both then and now, believe that it was all a political show to wrestle power from Chiang.) As Wang and his followers would later point out, from 1937 to 1938, Wang was the chief negotiator with Japan whenever the latter initiated a new act of aggression, but he could gain nothing on the table when the generals were not delivering on the battlefield. Wang was convinced that, barring a miracle, China could not possibly win against industrialised Japan, although Japan could not sustain a prolonged war, either. Turning to the reasonable factions on both sides, he hoped for a peaceful solution, and eventually decided to do it in his own way. His desperate solution was to work with the enemy. Whatever his motivation was, in December 1938, Wang responded to the Konoe cabinet's "Declaration of a New Order in East Asia", by fleeing from Chongqing to Hanoi to initiate a "Peace Movement", and eventually decided to collaborate with Japan and found a regime in Nanjing.

One Bed, Two Dreams: Wang Jingwei as a Pan-Asianist

The genuine intellectual persuasion of Wang Jingwei in the last ignominious period of his life is hard to determine, not least because the archives at Nanjing relating to him and his regime are closed to researchers. His official pronouncement, however, endorsed Japan's wartime propaganda of Pan-Asianism (Jp. *ajia shugi* アジア主義; Ch. *da Yazhou zhuyi* 大亞洲主義). Yet, a closer look reveals an effort to re-define his puppet-master's rhetoric in substance and in purpose.

Hannah Arendt, in her classic study on the origin of totalitarianism, argues that Pan-Movements in Europe that began in the late nineteenth century were the forerunners of totalitarianism, that "Nazism and Bolshevism owe more to Pan-Germanism and Pan-Slavism (respectively) than to any other ideology or political movement."[38] Unlike early imperialism, they were marked by lack of interest in economics and were led by the intelligentsia rather than capitalists,

---

38 Arendt (1951), *The Origins of Totalitarianism*, p.290.

held together more by a general mood than clearly-defined aims. To create that emotional center, however, the Pan-Movements needed to evoke an aura of holiness inherited from the past. "Pseudomystical nonsense, enriched by countless and arbitrary historical memories, provided an emotional appeal that seemed to transcend, in depth and breadth, the limitations of nationalism."[39]

In comparison, Pan-Asianism bore many similarities but also notable differences to its European counterparts. It was a theory that first appeared in late nineteenth century Japan to promote the regional co-operation of Asiatic peoples against Western colonial powers. Compared to the traditional Sinocentric East Asian order, it appeared to be a more modern ideology that liberally borrowed nationalistic rhetoric to serve as an integrating force, helping to fulfil the requirement for the "de-centring of China".[40] On the other hand, the Sinocentric hierarchic view of the world also encouraged some Japanese Pan-Asianists to envision a new East Asia with a new Middle Kingdom, which was to be Japan. As early as 1910, the discourse of Pan-Asianism was used by the Japanese government to legitimise Japan's annexation of Korea.[41] In the Second World War, Japan used it as propaganda to justify its aggression in Asia as liberating the Asian nations from the shackles of Western imperialism. This discursive system, however, was centred mostly on anti-colonialism by awakened Asian races, rather than on the imagined unity or holiness of a united Asian Race. And despite that it buttressed Japan's jingoistic aggressions in Asia, it never developed into the kind of full-scale, ideologically-based totalitarianism that ravaged Pan-Slavic and Pan-German circles.

But the rhetoric of equality and "co-prosperity", although a tool to disguise Japan's ambition of dominance, was important for the puppet regimes to justify themselves to their people. Wang's regime at Nanjing, formally called the Reorganised National Government (RNG), struggled to maintain an appearance of sovereignty. The RNG continued to adopt the formal trappings of the KMT national government, including using the same national flag and official insignia—much to the displeasure of Japan, as they protested that these symbols created confusion for their soldiers on the battlefield. The RNG also enhanced the aura of Sun Yat-sen as the nation's founder, and then tried to establish Wang as Sun's appointed successor. Previously, during Wang's honeymoon with the Communists, he had already portrayed it as succeeding Sun's policy of Soviet alliance. Now, he strived to establish his collaboration upon Sun's vision of Pan-Asianism.

---

39 Ibid., p. 295.
40 Saaler. Sven and Christopher W. A. Szpilman (2011), *Pan-Asianism: A Documented History*), vol. 1, p.9.
41 Ibid., vol.1, p.10.

Sun promoted this vision in a speech given at Kobe during his last trip to Japan, a mere four months before his death, with opportune timing that endorsed Wang's claim of it to be part of Sun's final legacy. In this speech, Sun Yat-sen hoped that all colonial or semi-colonial Asian countries would follow the example of Japan in strengthening themselves and abolishing unequal treaties. Japan's naval victory over Russia, furthermore, inspired all other Asian nations for their own independence. Sun suggests that the European culture adores the Despotic Way 霸道 (Ch. *badao*; Jp. *hadō*), while Asian culture is that of the Kingly Way 王道 (Ch. *Wangdao*; Jp. *ōdō*) - namely, the European way rules through force, utilitarianism, and suppression, while the Asian way rules through benevolence, justice, and morality. Such Confucian values should consequently be the basis of Pan-Asianism—a view that betrays his Sinocentric cultural perspective. So, if Asian countries learn to improve their science, industry, and weaponry from Europe, the goal is not conquest but self-defence. Japan, as the best student of Europe in building its industrial strength and military force, should unite with all other Asian countries in a struggle against the European Despotic Way. Right now, as Sun announced emphatically at the end of his speech, Japan stands at the crossroad between the Despotic Way and the Kingly Way, and it should choose very carefully.[42]

Sun's Kobe address received wide coverage in Japan at the time, though some newspapers redacted his closing note of warning. Ironically, his urging Japan to choose the Kingly Way was appropriated by Japanese chauvinism as well. In the 1930s and 1940s, Japan often proclaimed its rule in Manchukuo as the Kingly Way and further used it to legitimise an "Asian Monroe Doctrine" and a "holy war" against China.[43] According to Hiranuma Kiichirō (1867–1952), Prime Minister from January to August 1939, it was Japan's heaven-mandated duty, sparing neither "lives" nor "money", to save the de-generated China from herself.[44] Using the Confucian moralistic discourse, conquest was translated into salvation.

Sun's vision of Pan-Asianism bore significant affinity to Wang's Human-Co-Existentialism—we just need to shrink Wang's lofty vision for the whole of humanity to the scope of Asia. Yet, it takes quite a bit of rhetorical acrobatics for Wang to proclaim equality between Japan and China in their unholy alliance, a quixotic claim, he insists, much to the chagrin of domestic and international observers. The *New York Times* (31 March 1940) reports his inaugural speech when his regime was founded in Nanjing the previous day under the title "Equality is Claimed":

---

42 Sun Yat-sen (1981), "Dui Shenhu shangyehuiyisuo deng tuanti de yanshuo".

43 Saaler. Sven and Christopher W. A. Szpilman (2011), *Pan-Asianism: A Documented History*), vol. 2, pp. 77–78.

44 Ibid., vol. 2, p. 195

All policies adopted, all laws or decrees running counter to these declared policies will be abolished or amended so that our sovereign independence and territorial integrity may be safeguarded and that reciprocal, equal economic co-operation may be realised in order to lay the foundations for our co-existence and joint prosperity. With this readjustment made, China and Japan, like two brothers reconciled after an unfortunate resort to arms, will be everlastingly at peace and will jointly stabilise East Asia.

The same policy of peace by diplomacy will also be applied to all friendly powers.

The same points were stressed at a press reception after the inauguration ceremony, at which Wang further emphasised the partnership with Japan, saying:

China must maintain her independence, her sovereignty, her national freedom before she can carry out principles of good neighbourliness, a common anti-Comintern front and economic co-operation and further share the responsibility for building up a new order in East Asia. (*NYT* 31 March 1940)

Note that Wang not only calls for peaceful co-existence between China and Japan, but also with "all friendly powers" and particularly in East Asia. When the machinery of a global war among industrialised countries was wreaking havoc at an unprecedented speed and scale, such an appeal went unheeded, verging on the utopian, if not hypocritical.

Later that year, in a speech delivered on 12 November 1940, commemorating Sun Yat-sen's 74th birthday and entitled "Nationalism and Pan-Asianism" ("Minzu zhuyi yu Da Yazhou zhuyi" 民族主義與大亞洲主義), Wang weaves the three credos of his life—Nationalism, Human-Co-Existentialism, and Pan-Asianism—into a single ideological mantle. As he declares, nationalism is the means to awaken the Chinese nation's self-consciousness and to rally its solidarity, while Pan-Asianism is the means to awaken the East Asian peoples' self-consciousness and to rally their solidarity. The ultimate goal is to unite all peoples in the world who treat each other as equal in order to fight against colonialism and chauvinism, so that the Yellow Race will not suffer the same fate as the Indians in America, the Brown aboriginals in Australia, or the Blacks in Africa. In this sense, Wang's Pan-Asianism is China's nationalism writ large, or Human-Co-Existentialism writ small. Then, he further proclaims that, since, in the current world, even strong countries need to unite with others to survive, given China's weakness, she certainly needs to unite with others. Japan, being a strong country sharing the same culture and belonging to the same race, is the best candidate.[45]

What Wang fails to mention is China's cultural superiority, or even its uniqueness, which had previously driven his nationalist passion. China is now a weak nation among many, even though, culturally and racially, she bears much

---

45 Published on multiple journals funded by Wang's regime; see, e.g. Wang Jingwei 1940, "Minzuzhiyu yu da Yazhou zhuyi. for an English translation, see Saaler. Sven and Christopher W. A. Szpilman (2011), *Pan-Asianism: A Documented History*), vol. 2, pp. 213–215.

affinity to her strong neighbour, Japan, on whom her survival depends. Why she deserves to survive is hard for Wang to justify, except, perhaps, for the fact that, as a Chinese nationalist, he has no choice but to wish her the best.

Whether Wang Jingwei truly believed in Japan's good will, we cannot say. We do know that, in the previous incarnations of his life, he repeatedly denounced Japan as China's most dangerous and devious enemy. That he suddenly became naïve would defy logic. Moreover, unlike his earlier well-argued essays, his endorsement of Pan-Asianism was voiced in much shorter speeches given at formal and undoubtedly closely- watched occasions, without sophisticated reasoning. Another curious fact is that, unlike his previous intellectual persuasions, which were expounded not only in his essays and speeches, but also in his poetry—a much more intimate genre, this last incarnation of Wang as a Pan-Asianist finds no lyrical evidence. In effect, the vision of the world that he evokes in his later poetry is not an Asia happily united under a rising sun, but havoc, carnage, and universal destruction, an Armageddon to which he must sacrifice his own life, as our previous analysis of his firewood metaphor also suggests. The identification of his person with the body of the nation is most explicitly revealed in a song-lyric, "A River Full of Red" ("Manjianghong" 滿江紅),[46] written in 1940 in Nanjing. As he wrote, towards the end of the song:

邦殄更無身可贖、時危未許心能白。但一成一旅起從頭、無遺力。

When the nation extinguishes, no person is left to be ransomed;
the moment of crisis forbids me to reveal my heart.
With just one village, one brigade, I start from the beginning,
with no reserve.

The tune pattern "A River Full of Red" was associated with a patriotic song attributed to the Southern Song hero Yue Fei 岳飛 (1103–1142), which expresses his resolution to recover the lost northern territories. Wang was often compared to Qin Hui 秦檜 (1090–1155), a traitor in historical legend who schemed to kill Yue Fei—in effect, after Wang had fled Chongqing, many Chinese cities erected two statues in his and Chen Bijun's likeness to receive people's spite, evoking the kneeling statues of Qin Hui and his wife in a temple dedicated to Yue Fei.[47] Wang's decision to put words to this tune could therefore be read as a gesture of protest and self-defence. Yet, the last two couplets, as cited above, raise intriguing questions about taboo and self-revelation. He declares "the moment of crisis forbids me to reveal my heart", hinting at a possible discrepancy between his public pronouncements and his private convictions. To the future readers of his poetry, he tries to reveal his purportedly gen-

---

46 Wang Jingwei (2012), *Shuangzhaolou shicigao*, p. 310.
47 See Lin Kuo (2001), *Wang Jingwei quanzhuan*, p.400.

uine motive: although he did not defend China on the battlefield as Yue Fei did, he was defending her on another front.

Coda

In his "Autography" ("Zishu" 自述) published in *The Eastern Miscellany* (*Dong-fang zazhi* 東方雜誌) in January, 1934, Wang declares:

It is the most authentic to take one's speeches and treatises, given or written throughout one's life, as one's autobiography—there is no need for me to write another autobiography.

Yet, on his deathbed in a Nagoya hospital in November 1944, Wang reportedly announced that there would be no need to collect his essays, as his poetry alone would be his testament.[48] Indeed, an editorial committee consisting of his loyal associates duly compiled and published his poetry anthology entitled *Poetry on the Double-Shining Tower* (*Shuangzhaolou shici gao* 雙照樓詩詞薹) in 1945, just before Japan's surrender. It implies that, between 1934 and 1944, Wang changed his mind about what type of writing was one's most authentic autobiography. As Wang was considered the nation's foremost literatus-statesman, prior to 1939, his speeches and writings had been periodically collected and published, so what was left uncollected were only those after his collaboration with Japan. To sympathetic readers, it indicates that Wang considered the writings from his last stage of life to be disingenuous, perhaps a source of remorse and shame. To unsympathetic readers, it is evidence of Wang's effort to manipulate his posthumous memory. The critics do have a point: if Wang had been an steadfast believer of Wang Yangming's idealist philosophy, wishing to sacrifice his life for the ultimate good without any thought of salvaging his own reputation, then he had failed in his most lofty goal. His poetry, while trying to preserve a man's private memory of his life, betrays his lingering attachment to eternal glory, thus raising further questions about performance, self-persuasion, authenticity, and autobiographical writing. In other words, even if we accept all of Wang's self-proclamations as authentic, the literary success of his poetry was, at the same time, his moral failure.

Yet, if the reader is already so forgiving, he or she may detect, in Wang's moral failure to reconcile, with the enemy, a certain tenacity to preserve one's sense of moral subjectivity in the most unlikely situations, a paradoxical symbol of the weakness and strength of China's cultural tradition. As Wang had argued

---

48 See Jin Xiongbai (1959–65), *Wang Zhengquan de kaichang yu shouchang*, vol. 5, p,.124; Lin Kuo (2001), *Wang Jingwei quanzhuan*, p,. 750.

in his early essays promoting a nationalism based upon the Han cultural superiority, despite repeated conquests in history, the Chinese cultural community always perceived itself the ultimate victor, surviving and even expanding its influence over time. The culture's military weakness is thus its civil strength. Wang himself embodied this very feature. Arguably, he was China's last literatus-statesman. Compared to other national leaders in the Republican era or after 1949, he not only had received the full curriculum of classical education, but was also versed in traditional literati arts such as poetry, calligraphy, and painting. He also insisted on embodying the civil tradition of statecraft by refusing to build up his own military or financial powers. Rather, his cultural capital was his political capital, and his repeated retreats from politics embodied the value of eremitism in traditional Chinese political philosophy. But now he faced the futility of this cultural-political tradition in the era of military build-up powered by modern science and technology.

As a politician, Wang's idealism had a pragmatic side. The realist and cosmopolitan in him was forced to acknowledge the strengths of other civilisations, which, at the present stage of history, appeared to have left the Chinese far behind. Yet, born Chinese, he had no choice but to keep on working on the self-strengthening agenda of nation-building—but it needed time. When Japanese aggression threatened to destroy China, or, at least, throw it into domestic chaos, which might ultimately benefit a universalist doctrine, namely, Communism, Wang's only source of strength was his belief in his moral self. As Wang Yangming argued, by expanding one's moral knowledge, heeding to no reward, not even the reward of reputation, one would bring peace to All-under-Heaven. Wang responded to the doctrine by working with the enemy—wishing to convert its heart, and, if not, at least becoming a protector of the people in the occupied zone, bidding for time, and waiting for China's recovery, even if it would be a recovery without him. And in this sense, the failure of his collaborationist regime became, again, his ultimate success.

As a follower of his reported in a post-war memoir, when the news of Pearl Harbor came, Wang realised that Japan's days were numbered; he told his eldest son:

If China could still be saved, I only hope that my life and reputation be both ruined, and our family be broken and laced with tragedies. Be prepared. You should have enough courage to welcome this future fate.[49]

It implies that, only in the ruins of his regime, his life, and his reputation, could a post-war China recover under a common memory of united resistance. The mainstream historiography, even if the justice that it metes is that of the victor's, can be said to have simply fulfilled Wang's wish. His poetry, however,

---

49 Jin Xiongbai (1959–65), *Wang Zhengquan de kaichang yu shouchang*, vol. 2, p 104.

leaves a tiny refuge for a counter memory and for future redemption in a world that Wang had only dreamt of—one that is dominated not by nationalism, but by human-co-existentialism; one that is yet to come.

Bibliography

Archives

KMT-Party Archive, Taipei

Books and Articles

Anderson, Benedict (1983), *Imagined Communities: Reflections on the Origins and Spread of Nationalism.* London: Verso Books.

Arendt, Hannah (1951). *The Origins of Totalitarianism.* Penguin Classics (rpt. 2017).

Brook, Timothy (2012), "Hesitating before the Judgment of History", *The Journal of Asian Studies*, 71: 1, pp. 103–14.

Florian, Jean Pierre Claris de (1855). *Fables de Florian.* Paris: Delarue.

Huang Tao 黃濤 (2013). "Yuansha: Qingmo gemingpai ansha yanjiu" 原殺：清末革命派暗殺研究 (On the Origin of Killing: A Study of the Assassinations by Revolutionaries toward the End of the Qing), East China Normal University MA Thesis.

Jishou 尢首 trans. (1908). "Diwang ansha zhi shidai" 帝王暗殺之時代, *Minbao* 民報 (The People's Journal) , 21, pp. 80–85.

Jin Xiongbai 金雄白 (1959–1965), *Wang Zhengquan de kaichang yu shouchang* 汪政權的開場與收場 (Beginning and End of the Wang [Jingwei] Regime), Hong Kong: Chunqiu zazhishe, 1959–65.

Liang Qichao 梁啟超 (1896 [1999]), "Lun bianfa bi zi ping Man Han zhi jie shi" 論變法必自平滿漢之界始 (Reform must Start with Levelling the Differences between Manchus and Han), in: *Liang Qichao quanji*, Beijing: Beijing chubanshe, pp. 51–54.

— (1897 [1999]), "Chunqiu Zhongguo Yi Di bian xu" 春秋中國夷狄辨序 (Preface to The Distinction between the Chinese and the Barbarians in the Spring and Autumn Period), in: *Liang Qichao quanji* 梁啟超全集 (Complete Works of Liang Qichao), Beijing: Beijing chubanshe, pp., 124–25.

— (1900 [1999]), "Zhongguo jiruo suyuan lun" 中國積弱溯源論 (On the Origins of China's Accumulated Weakness), *Liang Qichao quanji*, Beijing: Beijing chubanshe, pp. 412–27.

— (1902a [1999]), "Lun minzu jingzheng zhi dashi" 論民族競爭之大勢 (On the General Situation Regarding the Competition between Nations), in: *Liang Qichao quanji*, Beijing: Beijing chubanshe, pp. 887–99.

— (1902b [1899]), "Xinmin shuo" 新民說 (On Renewing the People), in: *Liang Qichao quanji*, Beijing: Beijing chubanshe, pp. 655–735.

— (1905 [1999]), "Kaiming zhuanzhi lun" 開明專制論 (On Enlightened Autocracy), in: *Liang Qichao quanji*, Beijing: Beijing chubanshe, pp. 1470–86.

Lin Kuo 林闊 (2001), *Wang Jingwei quanzhuan* 汪精衛全傳 (Complete Biography of Wang Jingwei), Beijing: Zhongguo wenshi chubanshe.

Luo Haoxing 羅皓星 (2015), "1900 niandai zhongguo de zhengzhi ansha jiqi shehui xiaoying" 1900年代中國的政治暗殺及其社會效應 (Political Assassinations and Their Social Effects in 1900s China), *Zhengda shicui* 政大史粹, 28, pp. 153–99.

Saaler, Sven, and Christopher W.A. Szpilman (eds) (2011), *Pan-Asianism: A Documented History*, Lanham, MD: Rowman & Littlefield Publishing.

Sima Qian 司馬遷 (1959). *Shiji* 史記 (Records of the Grand Historian), Beijing: Zhonghua shuju.

Sun Yat-sen 孫中山 (1981a), "Dui Shenhu shangyehuiyisuo deng tuanti de yanshuo" 對神戶商業會議所等團體的演說 (Speeches towards Merchants, Guilds and other groups in Kobe), in *Sun Zhongshan quanji* 孫中山全集 (Complete Works of Sun Yat-sen), Beijing: Zhonghua shuju, vol.11, pp. 401–09.

- (1981b [1924]), "Sanmin zhuyi, minsheng zhuyi" 三民主義·民生主義 (The Three Principles of the People, Welfare of the People)(3 August 1924), in *Sun Zhongshan quanji*, Beijing: Zhonghua shuju, vol. 9, p. 355.

Wang Jingwei 汪精衛 (1927), "Zenyangde jinian Zongli yanjiangci" 怎樣的紀念總理演講詞 (How to Remember Our Former Prime Minister [Sun Yat-sen]), in *Wang Jingwei yanjiang lu* (Hankou: Zhongguo yinshuguan, 1927), p. 119.

- (1929a), "Geming keyi dujue guafen zhi shiju" 革命可以杜絕瓜分之實據 (Evidence that Revolution can Help to Prevent being Sliced up like a Melon), in: *Wang Jingwei ji*, Shanghai: Guangming shuju, pp. 171–96.

- (1929b), "Geming zhi juexin" 革命之決心 (Resolution for Revolution), in: *Wang Jingwei ji*, Shanghai: Guangming shuju, pp. 91–98.

- (1929c), "Minzu de guomin" 民族的國民 (National citizens), in *Wang Jingwei ji*, Shanghai: Guangming shuju, no.1: 1–30; no.2: 31–52.

- (1929d), "Wuhan fengong zhi jingguo" 武漢分共之經過 (Report on Separating from the Communists at Wuhan), in: *Wang Jingwei ji*, Shanghai: Guangming shuju, pp. 215–27.

- (1929e), "Xuanbu Sun Zongli shilue yanjiangci" 宣佈孫總理事略演講詞 (Speech on Prime Minister Sun's Deeds), in: *Wang Jingwei ji* , Shanghai: Guangming shuju, p. 121.

- (1929f), "Yu Hu Hanmin shu" 與胡漢民書 (Letter to Hu Hanmin), *Wang Jingwei ji*, Shanghai: Guangming shuju, p. 82.

- (1940), "Minzuzhuyi yu Da Yazhou zhuyi" 民族主義與大亞洲主義 (Nationalism and Pan-Asianism), *Xianzheng yuekan* 憲政月刊, 1:3: pp. 3–5.

- (2012a), "Beidai kouzhan" 被逮口占 (Orally Composed upon Being Captured), in: Wang Mengchuan 汪夢川 (ed.), *Shuangzhaolou shici gao* 雙照樓詩詞稿 (Poetry on the Double-Shining Tower), Hong Kong: Tiandi tushu chubanshe.

- (2012b), "Bingru shoushu Yangming xiansheng 'Da Nie Wenwei shu' […]" 冰如手書陽明先生答聶文蔚書 [……] (Bingru [Chen Bijun] Hand-wrote the Epistle by Wang Yangming to Nie Wenwei), in: Wang Mengchuan (ed.), *Shuangzhaolou shici gao*, Hong Kong: Tiandi tushu chubanshe, p. 285.

- (2012c), "Jian ren xi chelun wei xin wei zuo ci ge" 見人析車輪為薪為作此歌 (Song Written Upon Seeing People Chopping a Wheel into Firewood), in: Wang Mengchuan (ed.), *Shuangzhaolou shici gao*, Hong Kong: Tiandi tushu chubanshe, p. 22.

- (2012d), "Yinduyang zhou zhong" 印度洋舟中 (In a Boat Amid the Indian Ocean), Wang Mengchuan (ed.), *Shuangzhaolou shici gao*, Hong Kong: Tiandi tushu chubanshe, p. 44.

Wang Yangming 王陽明(2000), *Yangming chuanxi lu* 陽明傳習錄 (Records of Yangming's Teaching). Shanghai: Shanghai guji chubanshe.

Xian Yuhao 鮮于浩 (2016). *Liu Fa qingong jianxue yundong shi* 留法勤工儉學運動史 (History of the Diligent Work-Frugal Study Program in France). Beijing: Renmin chubanshe.

Yang, Zhiyi (2015), "Road to Lyric Martyrdom: Reading the Poetry of Wang Zhaoming (1883–1944)," *Chinese Literature: Essays, Articles, Reviews*, 37, pp. 139–40.

- (2018). "A Humanist in Wartime France: Wang Jingwei during the First World War," *Poetica*, forthcoming.

Yuan Ke 袁珂 (1980), *Shanhaijing jiaozhu* 山海經校注 (Commented Version of the *Shanhai jing*), Shanghai: Shanghai guji chubanshe.

Zhang Binglin 章炳麟 (1985), "Bo Kang Youwei lun geming shu" 駁康有為論革命書 (Refutation of Kang Youwei on Revolution), in: *Zhang Taiyan quanji* 章太炎全集 (Complete Works of Zhang Taiyan [Binglin]), Shanghai: Shanghai renmin chubanshe, 1985, vol. 4, pp. 173–84.

Zhang Jiangcai 張江裁 (1937), "Wang Jingwei xiansheng gengxu mengnan shilu" 汪精衛先生庚戌蒙難實錄 (Faithful Record on Mr. Wang Jingwei's Suffering in 1910), *Yuefeng* 越風, 2 (3), pp. 13–16.

Science and National Salvation in Early Twentieth Century China

Iwo Amelung

The assumption that China needed to be "saved" (*jiu* 救) was certainly among the most important id,eas in twentieth century China. There are numerous instances in which associations for "saving" the country (*jiuguo* 救國) were founded and became politically active. W. Callahan has shown that the idea of national salvation or "saving the country" was closely linked to the concept of national humiliation.[1] In this chapter, I will attempt to provide a related, but somehow different, trajectory. I will look into the concept of "national salvation" as being closely associating with—or even constituting—a discourse of weakness.

National salvation came in a rather bewildering multitude of forms, reaching from "saving the country by education" (*jiaoyu jiuguo* 教育救國), to "saving the country by literature" (*wenxue jiuguo* 文學救國) and "saving the country by sports" (*tiyu jiuguo* 體育救國).[2] The renowned writer Lu Xun 魯迅 (1881–1936) famously exclaimed in 1934 that:

> the call for saving the country by science can been heard for almost ten years. We all know that this is a correct attitude and that it absolutely cannot be compared to 'saving the country by dancing' or 'saving the country by worshipping Buddha'.[3]

And, indeed, the idea of saving the country by science was probably the longest-lasting concept—one which actually had a longer history than was assumed here by Lu Xun—and one may claim that it is still relevant today.

In the following, I will first trace the origins and the development of the idea of "saving the country by science", and will show that it was closely-linked to a Darwinian understanding of the rise and fall of nations and states. I will then try to explore the question of how these early origins were linked to the development of a fully-fledged discourse on the subject during the 1910s. After looking into the question of how the discourse was related to the New Culture movement and was popularised during the 1920s and 1930s, I will suggest that there was a close relationship to the idea of "national renaissance" in the early

---

1 Callahan (2004), "National Insecurities".
2 Xu Guoqi (2008), *Olympic Dreams*, pp. 61–62.
3 Lu Xun (1973), "Ou gan".

1930s. In the last part of this chapter, I will show how the discourse was related to efforts to popularise science and the "scientification movement" during the Nanjing-decade (1927–1937), and how the question of "saving the country by science" fed into the debate about "pure" and "applied" science.

I. Origins

The idea that China needed to be saved by science (*kexue jiuguo* 科學救國) is quite often related to the New Culture movement of the 1910s and the early 1920s, when science as "Mr Science" (*Sai xiansheng* 賽先生) became one of the most important calls of the young people participating in the movement. Alternatively, and at times additionally, the idea is related to the second generation of Chinese students studying abroad—in particular those who went to the US with money from the Boxer indemnity and their activities, in particular, the founding of the Science society (*kexueshe* 科學社) in 1914, and the publishing of the journal *Science* (*Kexue* 科學) in 1915.[4] However, while these assumptions are not unfounded, alternative narratives are also possible. With some justification, it can be pointed out that, shortly after the First Opium War (1839–1842), some Chinese scholars were quite aware that China was about to face an unprecedented crisis, one which required ideas and measures that were not available in the Chinese tradition. It would be necessary to apply the ideas—or. as it was called at this time, the "tricks" (*ji* 技)—of those selfsame powers which were in the process of establishing domination over China in order to be able to resist them. This anti-culturalist approach was quite widespread, and was, for example, demanded by influential scholars such as Wei Yuan 魏源 (1794–1857), Feng Guifen 馮桂芬 (1809–1874) and many others. It is clear, however, that Feng and the others could directly draw on ideas first provided by Western missionaries, such as Alexander Williamson (1829–1890), who, in 1857, in the Missionary journal *Liuhe congtan* 六合叢談 (Shanghai Serial), published an article on the "Advantages of Science" (*Gewu qiongli lun* 格物窮理論).

In my opinion, the Chinese are as clever as the Westerners. But what they produce is mediocre, it is by no means extraordinary and competitive, and the Chinese are not willing to work on it diligently. Those who are within the upper echelons of society do not use science in order to encourage those [below]. Only one-hundred years ago, we Western countries were like the Chinese, only reading the books of the ancients and not willing to use our diligence in examining the principle of things. For this reason, there were almost no extraordinary instruments. During the last hundred years, the people have engaged actively in the sciences. If they discovered a principle, they devised meth-

---

4 Wang, Zuoyue (2002), "Saving China through Science".

ods in order to prove it by experiment. And the peasants have been engaged in producing agricultural implements, the artisans have been engaged in producing instruments with which tools can be produced. It is like this, that the people have become more enlightened every day and the tools they produce have become ever more marvellous and this process has not stopped to this very day. Those who engage in studies are more numerous daily and their knowledge is ever more profound. Every month, new principles are discovered; they are published in newspapers and they circulate. In this way, their knowledge is ever improving and no end to this process is in sight. But the Chinese still use their useful ideas and bury them in the useless eight-legged essays[of the civil examination system]. Those who have a little bit of aspiration do not know anything else but to use it for poems and composing classical prose, becoming self-conceited and insolent, engaging in empty words, which are of no help. If you Chinese one day abandon this, and all people engage in the sciences, taking what the Westerners know already and use it as a guide, it will help you to improve. If it is done like this, the clear principles will emerge every day and will allow you to "invent utensils by adoring images" and we will use it to satisfy the country and strengthen the army. Who would dare to slight their benefit?[5]

Quite clearly, Western achievements, and especially Western technology, were expected to help to solve the problems which China was facing when dealing with the superior powers of the West. At the same time, however, it needs to be stressed that, in most cases, what we are dealing with is "technology", rather than science, and that there was no clear understanding of how this technology was related to "natural science", a concept which had not really been received or appropriated prior to the beginning of the twentieth century. A scholar and mathematician such as Li Shanlan 李善蘭 (1811–1882) was, however, at least *aware* that the success of the West in technology was related to practices associated with the sciences. In the preface to the translation of Whewell's *Mechanics*, which he did under the title *Zhongxue* 重學 together with Joseph Edkins (1823–1905), he writes:

Today the different countries of Europe become stronger from day to day and they cause border troubles in China. If we try to trace the reason [for this], it is because of the proficiency with which they manufacture devices. If one looks for the reasons for the proficiency of manufacturing devices, this is because their mathematics is so clear.[6]

Li relates that, for Zeng Guofan 曾國藩 (1811–1872) and Li Hongzhang 李鴻章 (1823–1901), this was the reason for insisting on the early publication of *Zhongxue*, so that, indeed, in some sense, the publication of this book can be considered as an early effort to "save the country by science". This functional approach remained popular and, to some extent, can be associated with the so-called *Self-strengthening* (*ziqiang* 自強) movement and a considerable number of "early reformers". The main goal of science—if it was mentioned at all—was to

---

5 Williamson (1857), "Gewu qiongli lun".
6 Whewell (1866), *Zhongxue*.

obtain "solid ships and efficient cannons" (*jian chuan li pao* 堅船利炮), as it was called at that time. It is widely known that the Chinese defeat in the Sino-Japanese war of 1894/95 can be considered as demonstrating the failure of the Chinese self-strengthening efforts up to that time. The consciousness of the crisis at that very moment was most clearly expressed by Yan Fu 嚴復 (1854–1921) who, from early 1895 onwards, published four articles in the Tianjin newspaper *Zhibao* 直報. In clear terms, Yan warned that the current crisis, which, in his view, had historical roots, could result in a situation in which "the country would be lost and the race extinguished (*wangguo miezhong* 亡國滅種) and [would lead to] the disintegration of the country, which cannot be controlled."[7] Yan Fu sees a comprehensive crisis which has been brought about by the fact that the Chinese strength, intelligence and morality is not as developed as it should be.[8] The reason for this dangerous situation, in his eyes, is the evil influence of the traditional Chinese examination system, or as he says:

Selecting officials by means of the eight legged essays [*i.e.,* the traditional civil examination system] results in a situation in which [everybody in the] Empire idles away his time in a useless place, one's ambition and moral fortitude degenerates into a shadowy situation, which leads to great arrogance, and darkens the minds of men. Those in the high positions do not have the ability to support the country, those in the low positions are not able to support their families. [The system] destroys talent, and the country consequently will be poor and weak![9]

Because of this argumentation, Yan Fu is quite often considered as being an early representative of the idea to "save China by education" (*jiaoyu jiuguo* 教育救國). This, of course, makes sense, but a closer look makes it quite clear that Yan Fu is not only concerned with education, but, even more so, with the question of upon *what* education needs to be based, and this, for him clearly needs to be Western science:

For what reason have we established an examination system if not for looking for talent for the state and for encouraging students to study? Looking for talent and encouraging study must all take utility as their principal aim. The efficiency of this utility will be proven by the power and wealth of the nation. The basis for wealth and power, however, are the sciences (*gezhi* 格致). If one does not base it upon the sciences, one risks having no place to go and becoming lost in vagueness.[10]

In this essay, the imagined detractor challenges him and says: "You, my dear Sir, claim that it is indispensable to employ Western science (*xixue gezhi* 西學格致) in order to save the nation. But why do we need to employ Western learning for

---

7 Yan Fu (1986), "Lun shibian zhi ji", p. 4; for a translation, see Yen Fou (1977), *Les manifestes de Yen Fou.*

8 My reading of Yan Fu is informed by Fan Hongye, (1997), "Chong du Yan Fu jiuwang pian".

9 Yan Fu (1986), "Jiuwang juelun", p. 43.

10 Ibid., pp. 42–43.

Science and National Salvation

science? Isn't *gezhi* the basis of the *Great Learning?*" But Yan Fu holds that, since the beginning of the Southern Song dynasty, Chinese learning had greatly deteriorated, and that had become completely useless, as he describes at length. And he goes one step further in order to make it clear how serious he considers the situation to be:

You, dear Sir [speaking to the imagined interlocutor], say that, at a time when the existence of China is in question, we need to look for a particular process to save ourselves. This is correct. Given the current situation, we must not only eliminate the eight-legged essay, which contributes to ruin talent, but also put Song-learning and Han-learning in the attic, as well as the genres of poetry and minor prose. We even need to postpone our quest for wealth and power, and concentrate on the means for saving our country.

In response to further doubts on the part of his imagined detractor, he finally retorts in the following way:

You, my opponents, are wrong: Western science, for us, is not a roundabout way, it is the only possible salvation for the Chinese.[11]

Yan Fu, of course, was aware that the integration of science into Chinese academia alone would not be able to solve the problems that China had. China would need a complete shift in academic thinking, of which the adaption of science and scientific thinking would be an indispensable part, and maybe even have a "driving" function.[12]

II. Early Popularisers

During the years preceding the 100 days reform of 1898, the calls to put more emphasis on science became much stronger. Translation of textbooks and the establishment of a modern education system played a very important role for reformers such as Kang Youwei 康有為 (1858–1927), Liang Qichao 梁啟超 (1873–1929), Tan Sitong 譚嗣同 (1865–1898) and others. At the same time, the publications of Chinese scholars, who were interested in the sciences, especially those of well-known, reform-minded Western missionaries such as Ernst Faber (1839–1899) and sucessively Timothy Richard (1845–1919), which were reprinted time and time again, were of great importance. Richard was quite successful in explaining how the success of Western civilisation in history was based upon science.

---

11 Ibid., p. 46.
12 Miao Chunfeng (2002), "Yan Fu de jinhua lun sixiang yu jiuwang tucun".

I here try to explain the rise and fall of the different countries by their quest for science (*gezhi*).

There is no better way to protect the people than first to strengthen the military. There is no better way to strengthen the military than first to enrich the country. When one wants to enrich the country and does not think about ordering finance, and when one wants to put finance in order without using science, then this is like chiselling jade without having any knife as an efficient instrument, or building a house without having the material for the pillars.[13]

We can, on the other hand, observe a tendency to demand a much more thorough reform in order to save the country, in which "science" would play an important, but not dominant, role.

It is of crucial importance to note that, since the last years of the nineteenth century, a Darwinist reading of the fate of China in the world, which can already be observed in Yan Fu's early essays, plays an increasingly important role. This was combined with a notion of progress, which was of considerable importance, and whose introduction into China was also closely related to the introduction of Darwinian thought. In particular, this can be seen in journals which propagated science. Already in the year 1900, Du Yaquan 杜亞泉 (1873–1933), in the preface to his *Yaquan zazhi* 亞泉雜誌, claimed "that what is called progress in political science (*zhengzhixue* 政治學), is, in actual fact, brought about by relying on the arts and the sciences".[14] The Darwinian emphasis on the struggle for existence was expressed in a very clear way by Wang Benxiang 王本祥 (1881–1938), who wrote in 1903 that:

Among the myriad countries of the World, there are hot wars and there are cold wars. They are either about industry or they are about agriculture, but none of them is not relying on "science" (*like* 理科). For this reason, "science" is an army without form, a safe projectile. [...]. The outcome of the struggle of existence can be predicted by this, the survival of the fittest can be seen by this.[15]

And the above-mentioned Du Yaquan described the reasons for which he had founded his *Yaquan zazhi*, which mainly dealt with the new chemical knowledge in the West:

I am afraid that the people of my country noisily compete with each other within our country and that they completely neglect the fact that they have to struggle for existence in the middle of myriads of countries. If one lets the specialised professions thrive and enrich society, then there is nothing to worry about. The good fortune of civilisation follows naturally from richness and strength. If this has been achieved then there is nothing under heaven which cannot be achieved, the only thing which one has to worry about is the lack of capital. This is what I wish to make clear to You, my dear Sirs

---

13 Richard (1898), "Zhongguo yi qiu gezhi zhi xue lun".
14 Du Yaquan (1900), "Yaquan zazhi xu".
15 Wang Benxiang (1903), "Lun like yu qunzhi zhi guanxi".

[addressing the readers of the magazine]. When *Yaquan zazhi*, which is published by the *Yaquan xueguan*, writes about science, mathematics, chemistry, agriculture, commerce, manufacture and arts, this is the only objective.[16]

Ma Junwu, 馬君武 (1881–1940), who would later translate Darwin into Chinese, put it in even more drastic terms:

The West uses "science" (*kexue*) in order to strengthen the country and to strengthen the race. Because of our lack of science, our country will lose its national independence and our race will be extinguished. Ah, the light of science, it has not shone for a long time. If we, today, copy the West's academic methods, we will succeed in saving our country and prevent it from sinking into chaos.[17]

It would be possible to quote a large number of similar passages, but, on a general level, we can say that these expositions had three clearly distinguishable goals:

1. The Darwinist outlook served to demonstrate the Chinese weakness as drastically as possible;
2. There was a clear dedication to the popularisation of scientific knowledge, which reflects Yan Fu's efforts to "save the country by education". Here, we can also see how authors tried to highlight the transformative power of science. A biographer of Thomas Alva Edison, for example, wrote in 1904: "I wish to demonstrate that the power of electricity has the ability to transform the world."[18] Science was thus responsible for the decline and wellbeing of nations, as the same author pointed out in another article:

The botany of Linnaeus, the mechanics of Newton, the electricity of Franklin, the study of magnetism by Faraday: their efficiency reaches so far that it is sufficient to change a society, to control the world and more. Oh, how great is the power of science and technology, how great is the value of science and technology! Around the world, there are countries which are rich and whose power is increasing, so that they are able to be counted among the great powers. It is said that this is only due to the state of the development of their technical and scientific knowledge. There are countries in which the power of the people is shrinking, and their politics and education become lifeless, so that they are on the verge of becoming extinct. This is all due to the fact that their technical and scientific knowledge is shallow and superficial.[19]

3. Most of the numerous magazines which dealt with the question at the time had some clear-cut ideas on the application of scientific ideas and the materiality of applied science, and how this could actually be employed in China. This cannot only be seen from Du Yaquan's *Yaquan zazhi* and its emphasis

---

16 Du Yaquan (1900), "Yaquan zazhi xu".

17 Ma Junwu (1903), "Xin xueshu yu qunzhi zhi guanxi".

18 Wang Benxiang (1903–1904), "Dianqi da wang Aitisen zhuan", p. 7 (in Number 5).

19 Wang Benxiang (1903), "Lun like yu qunzhi zhi guanxi".

on chemistry, but from other publications as well. *Kexue shijie* 科學世界, for example, was quite aware that, in the situation of the early twentieth century, science would be decisive for the "progress or decline of industry", but also pointed out that saving China by science at this time also meant looking at China's agricultural problems, and that China's agriculture would only thrive if it were helped by natural and applied sciences such as soil-science (*turangxue* 土壤學), husbandry (*jiachu siyangxue* 家畜飼養學), etc.[20]

III. Material Civilisation

It is possible to see here a certain transformation from Yan Fu's—in some ways—fundamental ideas, in the direction of a stronger focus on the application of science and its contribution to "material wellbeing". This is probably related to the fact that more Chinese were travelling abroad and were directly exposed to the material aspects of Western civilisation. This is at least quite clear in the case of Kang Youwei, who, after having travelled extensively in Europe and the US, began to compose his "Essay on Saving the Country by Material Civilisation" (*Wuzhi jiuguo lun* 物質救國論). This article, which, to this day, is not particularly well researched, was written in 1904 and published in 1906.[21] It provides a comparatively systematic treatment with a number of aspects which are symptomatic for the unfolding of the discourse of "Saving the Country by Science", and which are, at the same time, intimately related to Kang Youwei's convictions and idiosyncrasies. A brief look at the table of contents immediately reveals the very programmatic character of the book. The first chapter is entitled "Peter [the Great] Studies the Building of Ships", the second chapter is called "On the Fact that the Strength and Weakness of Europe and China are not Based upon Morals and Philosophy", the third chapter is clearly related to Kang's personal experience and is entitled "The Failure of all Reforms in China in the last Dozens of Years". The fourth is on "Material Civilisation as a Method for the Emergency Rescue of China", the next on "The Strength of the Europeans is Based upon Material Civilisation and this is Lacking Completely in China", the sixth chapter is entitled "England was the First to Propagate Material Civilisation and became the Strongest", and the seventh is called "Today the Strength of Countries are their Soldiers, Cannons and Arms, and These are Rooted on Material Civilisation" and so on. One chapter is even entitled, "The

---

20 Ibid.

21 My translation of the title follows Wong Young-Tsu (2008), "The Search for Material Civilization: Kang Youwei's Journey to the West".

SCIENCE AND NATIONAL SALVATION

Strength and Weakness of all the Countries of the World are Proportional to the Rise and Fall of their 'Substance' (*wuzhi*)". Kang's prescription for national salvation was at the same time related to his anti-revolutionary and anti-democratic stance, which is easily recognisable throughout the book. For him, France, in particular, is a bad example which he compares with the teachings of Bismarck. Kang writes:

Freedom, revolution, democracy, and the talk about independence, are all medicines which poison and weaken China; it is absolutely impossible to follow them.[22]

Another bad example for Kang is India, which, according to him, wanted to become independent through a revolution because its rulers and officials were not aware that a "countries weakness and strength is determined by 'material learning' (*wuzhixue* 物質學)". The result was that the 300 million Indians, who inhabit this vast land stretching over ten-thousands of *li*, all became slaves. For Kang, this was like "a blind man riding a blind horse and, in the middle of the night, approaching a pool".[23] It is interesting to see that Kang Youwei, in the "second preface" to the 1920 edition of the book, relates that he had originally hoped that his disciple, Liang Qichao, would arrange for the printing of the book directly after he had finished it, but that, according to Kang, Liang Qichao was of the opinion that "freedom, revolution and constitution" are sufficient for a state, so that he did not agree with Kang's idea and procrastinated, with the result that the text only appeared in book form 16 years after it had been finished.[24]

Kang is quite critical of religion as well, and gives the Jewish tradition and India as examples that religion was of no help at all.[25] His "material learning" basically referred to the recent progress in material civilisation, such as better ships and armaments. But it was best represented by the shrinking of the world because of trains and the telegraph.

Our compatriots are defeated by the Europeans. They have been in this situation for one or two hundred years. And there is no greater defeat than the one against the newly invented industries and weapons of the last one or two hundred years. In all cases, in which the Europeans have traversed the world during the last hundred years, there has been the supporting function of political and legal theories, but, in reality, this is all due to technology and has been brought about by weaponry and cannons. And weaponry and cannons, they are all that matter. In respect of the thorough nature of their politics and law, and the chemistry, optics, electrics, mechanics, astronomy, geography, mathematics, botany, zoology and biology, they do not all go beyond quantifiable and formable matter. But the fact that the people of our country lag behind the Europeans is a

---

22 Kang Youwei (2007), "Wuzhi jiuguo lun", p. 71.

23 Ibid., p. 64.

24 Kang Youwei (1987), "Wuzhi jiuguo lun houxu", p. 9.

25 Kang Youwei (2007), "Wuzhi jiuguo lun", p. 82.

matter of concern and this is all. Matter is the crudest physical phenomenon. The people of our country are able to speak about metaphysics, but they lack [knowledge on] physical phenomena How, then, can we save our country today? It is sufficient to deal with material.

Kang goes on:

If we throw away technology, weapons and cannons and idly talk about democracy, revolution, equal rights and freedom, then the people of the whole country will become Rousseaus, Voltaires and Montesquieus. But when a strong enemy coerces us, we are paralysed. Armoured ships will threaten the borders and land forces will invade, and they hold automatic weapons which fire 600 shots per minute; what do we do in order to defend ourselves against them?[26]

All this does not mean, however, that Kang Youwei accords superiority in "morals" (*daode* 道德) and "learning" to the states of the West. To the contrary, Kang is quite appalled by the crime rate in the US and the behaviour of the people there in general. In this respect, China has more to offer than the US or the European countries. This, for him, is again proof that, in the end, it is the "material" which decides the success of states. "Civilisation has to be seen from the outer form and cannot be talked about from inside the mind."[27] In his book, Kang gives other examples to prove his point, namely, that of England, which, for a long time, had the most advanced civilisation of the whole world, although its philosophy was much less developed than that of France or, in particular, that of Germany, with its philosopher Immanuel Kant.[28]

However, Kang's real heroes were, on the one hand, Peter the Great, whom he not only admired as a reformer, but also as somebody with great interest in material civilisation, as proven by his work on a shipyard in Holland, which he quite extensively describes in his book. On the other hand, the recent rapid rise of Germany from destitution to wealth and power, was, according to Kang Youwei, a model that China should emulate, especially for the study of technology, engineering, agriculture, commerce and navigation. There were numerous technical schools and a very strong tradition in experimental sciences. Kang also stressed Germany's excellence in building warships, and while he is aware of the excellent universities in the US, he emphasises the superiority of the German system of vocational education, which, in his view, allows the combination of science and application.

As for most of the other scholars and intellectuals quoted above, the world, for Kang Youwei, was ruled by (social-) Darwinist rules, which apply for all and which are completely independent of history or of the greatness of the past.

---

26 Ibid., p. 67.
27 Ibid., p. 66.
28 Ibid., p. 73.

SCIENCE AND NATIONAL SALVATION

In this world, which competes for the new, those who have material learning will live, while those who lack material learning will die. Small countries, such as Burma, Vietnam, Korea, do not have material science and die. The great civilised countries such as Turkey, Persia, Spain, which do not have material learning are able to slow down their death a little bit, but they are so crippled, that they will perish in the end.[29]

Interestingly, however, Kang Youwei's apprehension was that people would focus too much on democracy, and that revolution would take place in China as well. Indeed, we can see that, during the last few years of the Chinese Empire prior to the revolution of 1911, the interest of the people who wanted to save the country shifted from "material studies" and "applied science"—in the sense of Kang Youwei—to a much stronger pursuit of political solutions, in particular the organisation of political groups, mainly in Japan, or attempts to assassinate members of the ruling house of the Manchus or high officials in China. In 1911, a number of scientists who had studied abroad, such as Ren Hongjun 任鴻雋 (1886–1961), Li Siguang 李四光 (1889–1971) and others, "joined the revolution", as it was called at the time, and assumed administrative positions in the new revolutionary government. For them, it was only the failure of the "second revolution" which made them leave the country again and now fully engage in scientific activities.

IV. Students in the USA and the Science Society

The founding of the Chinese Science Society (*kexueshe* 科學社) in 1914 and the publication of the journal *Kexue* 科學 (Science), which began in 1915, are clearly of momentous importance for the development of the sciences in China. One year earlier, in 1913, Chinese students studying in the US had already founded the journal *Liu Mei xuesheng jibao* 留美學生季報 (*Periodical of Chinese Students Studying in the US*), which was actually intended to address a Chinese public in the motherland. Many authors who concurrently or successively published in the journal *Science* also published articles here, and the journal was of particular importance for the popularisation of the idea of saving China by science, not only due to two articles by Lan Zhaoqian 藍兆乾 (1891–1919), which were entitled "Kexue jiuguo lun" and "Kexue jiuguo lun er", but also due to a series of articles written by Yang Quan 楊銓 (1893–1933), Zhu Jin 朱進 (1891–?), Ren Hongjun and others. All of these essays expose the idea that science was indispensable for China on its way to modernity and national salvation. Many of these articles have a very clear Darwinian outlook. Chen Fan 陳藩, for example, argued that, basically, all the factors which would decide on the success of a

---

29 Ibid., p. 63.

given country, namely, the economy, agriculture and industry, would completely depend on the success of science within that country.

For this reason, those who want to evaluate the situation of a country in all cases use the degree of the development of the sciences as the criteria for the strength of a country.

Interestingly, in this article, which was published in 1916, Chen still uses the supposed success of Germany during World War I as evidence for the importance of science for the fate of a country.[30] And, as late as 1918, Lu Feizhi 陸費執 was able to claim that:

The Germans are really good in doing war. William [II.] is a real warrior. The reason that he achieves victories are planes, submarines, poison-gas, the necessities of life and man-made food-products. Much of this is not available for the other powers, or, if they have it, the quality is limited. Nothing of this does *not* rely on science in order to be produced.[31]

A similar view was actually put forward by Kang Youwei, who, in the second preface to his *Wuzhi jiuguo lun*, states that it had only been matter or the material (*wuzhi*) which had enabled Germany to attempt to conquer the whole of Europe. It had also been matter which had made it possible to resist the German assault for four years, and it also was matter which had made the US the richest country of the world. "All the advances of the last hundred years are due to matter, and it is these examples which make it utterly clear."[32]

Coming back to Chen and Lu's articles, we can claim that they echo the views which Ren Hongjun, one of the fathers of the *Science Society*, published in 1914 around the time of the founding of the society. They were concerned with the establishment of an "academic community" (*xuejie* 學界), which Ren Hongjun considered as something completely new and which he likened to a candle providing light in the dark night. More important, however, was that, in this article, which was filled with references to China's "utmost weakness" (*jiruo* 極弱), the dangers of "foreign aggression and encroachment" (*waiwu pingling* 外侮憑陵), *etc.*, Ren states that:

If we relate the academic community to the state, how could we only think about our imminent destiny? In reality, its present thriving and decline, its strength and weakness are directly proportional to the existence or non-existence of an academic community.

Although Ren points out that the comparatively long period of peace—which had lasted for about fifty years prior to the publication of his article—had been an important factor for the development of the sciences in Europe, he also

---

30 Chen Fan (1916), "Lun wuguo xuezhe yi huxiang lianjie yu Zhongguo kexueshe yi cujin guoshi".

31 Lu Feizhi (1918), "Zhongguo yi su zuzhi kexue xuehui".

32 Kang Youwei, *Wuzhi jiuguo lunhou xu*, p. 9.

SCIENCE AND NATIONAL SALVATION

531

stresses that war—as long as it was not a war of annihilation—could help to develop learning. According to Ren, this had happened during the period of the Warring States in China (475–221 BCE), but this could be seen from the development of Germany as well. For the purposes of our topic, it is even more important that Ren assigned an important function to a small group of persons who would be dedicated to science and who would provide something akin to the foundation of the academic community. Here, he especially points to students studying abroad, whose task it was "to deal in what the others have, in order to be of help for that which our side does not have".[33] Interestingly and somewhat self-servingly, Ren Hongjun would later on elaborate on the relationship between the number of scientists and the culture of a country. He at first quotes a certain popular science magazine, which, according to him, had stated that, "The number of scientists in a given state is an indicator for its culture", and then goes on to say:

I, however, would like to push this a little bit further and claim that the grade of neatness or confusion stands in a direct proportion to the degree of happiness or bitterness of a country as well as to the number of scientists. If this theory is correct, I have the simplest answer to the question of the survival of our country, which is, if one wants to make a country rich and strong, then one has to produce scientists first.[34]

One of Ren Hongjun's close associates was Yang Quan, who had travelled on the same ship as Ren to the US to take up his studies there. Yang would later on become one of the most important members of the Science Society. Like Ren, he had already begun to contribute to the *Periodical of Chinese Students Studying in the US* by 1914. His, for our purposes, most noteworthy contribution was an article simply called "Science and China" (*Kexue yu Zhongguo*). Here, Yang stresses the educational aspect of science, which he contrasts with the intentions of the rulers, who are always inclined to exploit the ignorance of the people. Even more important, however, is the fact that he points out that China had not valued science during the last 1400 years of her history. His deficit discourse does not stop here, and he goes one step further, by trying to identify the reasons for the non-development of science in China. Thus, he was the first Chinese to ask the question, which would later play a very important role in the discourse on Chinese traditional science and would be taken up by scholars from Ren Hongjun to Karl August Wittfogel (1896–1988), Joseph Needham (1900–1995) and beyond.[35] Yang Quan identified three factors, which, in his view, were responsible for the non-development of science in China: 1. the mentality of society; 2. the so-called tricks of the rulers; and 3. the damage self-

---

33 Ren Hongjun (1914), "Jianli xuejie lun" and "Jianli xuejie zai lun".
34 Ren Hongjun (1915), "Kexuejia renshu yu yi guo wenhua zhi guanxi", p. 84.
35 Wang Yangzong (2006), "Yang Quan yu 'Zhongguo wu kexue' wenti".

inflicted by scholars. Of particular interest, however, is his answer to the question of whether science really was of such utmost importance, given the fact that China had managed to exist without it for such a long time:

Somebody says: China does not have science, but still the country has not perished for several thousand years. If it is like this, then, what harm does it do [not to have science]?

My answer: This is not so. Learning has three major branches. One is called philosophy, one is called literature, and the third is called science. If we compare it with the human body, then philosophy constitutes the brain, literature the beard, eyebrows and hair on body and head, and science the five sense organs and the four limbs. If there is no philosophy, there is no spirit; if there is no literature, beauty will be missing; if there is no science, then everything is useless. Of these three, one cannot be abandoned, Today, China's philosophy and literature do not flourish, but at least they are there. What is necessary, however, is to perfect and develop them. If one has never even dreamt of science, then, one cannot think about stimulating it. Then, it is like this, even if the legendary Yi Yin becomes member of the cabinet, the country cannot be governed; if Yao, Shu, Yu and Tong become president, it cannot be avoided that the people will be cold and hungry.[36]

From this point of view, science is not only an indispensable factor for the development of civilisation, but also one for the development of learning as a whole.

As I have already pointed out above, the founding of the Chinese Science society was a very important event for the development of the natural sciences in China. During the earliest phase, the main purpose of the society was the publication of a journal, which was initially edited by the members of the society in the United States, but published in China. For the editors of the journal, all "civilised countries" were supposed to have scholarly associations, which, in turn, needed a journal through which scholars would be able to communicate with each other. While the "Announcement of Publication", which was most probably written by Ren Hongjun, mainly stresses the benefits of science for the development of Chinese academic thinking, a closer look reveals that, from its inception, the idea of national salvation with the help of science played an all important role. What is probably the clearest statement regarding the mission of the journal can be found in a letter from the editors to their fellow students in the US, which was published in autumn 1915:

Fellow students: Science is the special characteristic of modern culture. It is the source of the wealth and strength of the West; all the facts are available in it. It is not necessary to state this in detail. You have left home and carry your books into a foreign land in order to appropriate the useful learning of the others with the goal of saving the life of our country, which is about to die. Doing away with the plan to develop science, who could act according to this way? If we want to develop science, we cannot just rely on

---

36 Yang Quan (1914), "Kexue yu Zhongguo".

SCIENCE AND NATIONAL SALVATION

the excellence and perfectness of the individual, we have to wait for the support of the group. If we look at the development of the sciences in other countries, there is none which has not made the organisation of a scholarly society its main point.[37]

Given the importance which Ren Hongjun accorded to science, the question of why there was no science in China was unavoidable. For this reason, it was almost logical that, in the first issue of *Kexue*, Ren published an article with the title, "On the Reasons for the Lack of Science in our Country", which begins with the following words:

Today, I want to try to talk freely about the roots of the accumulated weakness and the accumulated poverty of our country. The lack of science is, without any doubt, one important reason. But what are the reasons for the lack of science in our country? I have pondered about this problem for many years and was not able to answer the question. I think, however, that, if we find an answer to this question, then this resembles a doctor searching for the roots of the sickness in order to cure it. And, in consequence, he will give injections, prescribe medicine, and provide nourishment, and it is not difficult to find a remedy quickly and drive away the illness with the result of having saved somebody from death.[38]

I hope that it has become clear that the mission of "science to save the country" was quite central to the two journals, which I have introduced here at some length. Of course, science had other functions as well, and the famous slogan of science and democracy of the May Fourth Movement, albeit in a somewhat different form, shows up in the *Science* journal as well, postulating that science has the ability to free man from the necessity to become a "slave of the need to pursue poor subsistence".[39]

Of particular influence was an article written by Lan Zhaoqian, cited above, and published in the *Periodical of Chinese Students Studying in the US* in 1915. Most probably it was this article which actually coined the phrase of *kexue jiuguo*, which, as we have seen, had implicitly been around for some time. Originally, Lan had sent his article to the *Science* magazine for publication, but apparently Ren Hongjun had considered the quality of the article to be too poor, with the consequence that he decided to have it published in the *Periodical*, instead, on the pretext that, in this way, the important article would be published and read earlier.[40] And indeed, probably due to its illustrativeness, the article caused quite a stir in China.[41] Lan was actually anything but a well-known person, and no scientist; apparently, he was a middle-school teacher from Sichuan province. As

---

37 Zhao Yuanren, Ren Hongjun, Hu Mingfu, Bing Zhi, Zhou Ren (1916), "Ben she zhi liu Mei tongxue shu".

38 Ren Hongjun (1915b), "Shuo Zhongguo wu kexue zhi yuanyin", p. 8.

39 Yang Quan (1916), "Kexue yu gonghe".

40 On this question, see: Fan Hongye (2013), "Lan Zhaoqian yu 'Kexue jiuguo lun'".

41 Zhu Hua (2006), "Lun 'Liumei xuesheng jibao' yu kexue jiuguo xuanchuan", p. 110.

is typical for Chinese discourses of weakness at the time, the article was quite alarmist in tone, not only in respect of the Chinese situation, but also of other countries as well:

Nobody who has recently seen the disaster which befell Poland, India, Korea and Vietnam, and who has vital energy (*qi* 氣) in his blood could not be aroused and indignant and think about how to save the country from its peril. For this reason, those who have will and humanity have all been speaking about "saving the country" for 20 years.

Lan then goes on to outline how the different approaches to "saving the country", such as demands for a constitution and a revolution, as well as the efforts to develop industry and improve the infrastructure, the movement for the preservation of national essence (*guocui* 國粹), the reform of education and, finally, the efforts to manage state finances better and train the army, had all failed. He points out:

The way to save the country is comparable to treating sickness. If one does not examine from whence it arises and the ramifications when treating it, even if one exhausts the power of the remedies, will this be effective? Where does the poverty and weakness of our country come from? It is its science. As a subject, it is wide-ranging and profound; all methods to enrich and strengthen the country derive from it.

Lan arrives at an almost scientistic point of view from these ideas, claiming that "science is the fundamental method for saving the country". For every one of China's weaknesses, he emphasises how science could serve as a remedy. In his view, employing science in politics would even prevent conflicts, such as the failed Second Revolution of 1913. He goes on to list a number of examples which demonstrate the power of science in Western countries, and, at the end of his essay, he lists a number of steps which are, in his view, indispensable.

For example, he thinks that the "spectacle" of the First World War could be used to arouse Chinese interest in the sciences: "How could it be a surprise that something which mankind would not have even dreamt of twenty years earlier would leave the sick man of Asia speechless."Lan is also very much in favour of translating scientific texts into Chinese. In fact, he thinks that this is of the utmost importance and he proposes an approach which distinguishes between different levels of complexity. That translated science can be employed successfully is, in his mind, proven by the example of geometry in England, Germany and France, which is practised in the respective languages of these countries and not in Greek, and also by the success of the sciences in Japan. The language of science is, in any case, a very important topic for Lan, and he suggests that textbooks which keep Western names and also include Western technical terms be employed. Interestingly enough, his main argument here constitutes a mixture of the Chinese belief in the importance of the script as the medium of the transportation of the truth and social Darwinist reasoning:

SCIENCE AND NATIONAL SALVATION

The eternal existence of a country depends on its script. A script is that which conveys the way, and which is later used to transmit it [to others]. For this reason, it is like this, that if the way is refined and practical, those who are studying [the language and script] are numerous and the country will necessarily prosper. This is the case with England, France and Germany. If it is refined but not applicable, the number of those studying it will be small. Even if the territory is lost, the soul of the country will continue to exist. This is the case for Greece and Rome. If it is inferior and not applicable, there will be nobody to study it; when the territory is lost, the soul of the nation will be lost forever. This is the case with Poland and Judea. The script of the middle territories is extraordinarily beautiful, but the way of science is definitely lacking. If material civilisation, however, is completely dependent on the art of the sciences, then people will subsequently not know how to protect the script of the middle territories, and might they not even want to do away with it completely? This is something that those who possess consciousness are deeply worried about and full of pain, and thus they promote the protection of the script. But idly chatting about protecting the script is of no use. It is necessary to make up the deficits and do away with partiality. But what is the only way for making up the deficits and doing away with partiality? It is by absorbing Western science! It is just like with the Buddhist canon during Jin and Tang times. Did it not reach its utmost glory in China? For this reason, the translation of science is also the duty of those who adhere to the old ways![42]

Lan's article attracted a high degree of attention in China, so tha some months later he published a sequel to his essay. If anything, the discourse of weakness is even more pronounced here, directly addressing the day on which China had been forced to accept Japan's infamous 21 demands.[43]

Oh, people of our country, oh people of our country, who does not still remember the Ninth of May 1915, the day of national humiliation? Several thousand *li* of our nation's soil sank into the hands of the barbarians. The sovereignty of our country was sliced in half!

Again, this was, of course, due to the lack of science in China, and if science wanted to compete with others in order to be preserved (*jingcun* 竞存) a number of conditions needed to be met, which Lan describes in the following way:

Those who want to prevent their country from perishing consider the arms industry as the only important problem. And what is most important is manufacturing airplanes, submarines, wireless telegraphy, cars and cannons [...] Those who want to strengthen the roots of the realm and stimulate the people in order to prevent them from sinking deeply into famine will do this in the first place with regard to forestry and hydraulics; mining and industry will come second [...] in respect of the arms-industry, forestry and hydraulics, they all depend on machines, and in order to drive the machines, they depend on steam power. Where, thus, is the origin of both of these? It is in the coal and iron industry! Thus, the arms-industry is the original means to guarantee survival in the

---

42 Lan Zhaoqian (1915), "Kexue jiuguo lun".

43 On this early phase of remembering "national humiliation", cf. Cohen (2002), "Remembering and Forgetting".

struggle for existence, while forestry and hydraulics are important tasks for the live-lihood of the people. Their paths differ vastly and their principles are profound. What is the road of their development? It is called science! The gentlemen among our compatriots who are willing to save our country from vanishing, they have to concentrate all their energy and join forces in order to take care of the science found in these two things![44]

V. The New Culture Movement and Beyond

As pointed out above, the titles of these essays were of great importance for the future development of the discourse on saving the country by science. At the same time, it should be acknowledged that these ideas reflect a development which was at work both in China and in other places as well. As is very well known, the calls for Mr. Science and Mr. Democracy became the war-cry of the New Culture Movement. Chen Duxiu 陳獨秀 (1879–1942), the editor of the journal *New Youth*, which became something akin to the "central organ" of the movement, from the very inception of the publication of the journal, touched upon questions related to science. In his "Call to the Youth" (*jinggao qingnian* 警告青年), which was published in 1915 in the predecessor journal of *New Youth Qingnian zazhi* 青年雜誌, he was already stressing the great importance of science for the country, a necessity which, in his view, was clearly proven by the European experience:

The fact that the Europeans today are superior to other people lies in the flourishing of science. Its effect is not subordinated to that of 'Human Rights', it is like the two wheels of a cart. Moreover, there are new things and developments every day. In all cases in which something happens, and even for the smallest things, one searches in the methods of science in order to determine its merits.

Interestingly, however, for Chen Duxiu, science was not only a resource to save the country, but, in a similar way, it was also a means to do away with danger-ous old ideas and habits which, in his view, hindered the development of the country:

Its [science's] efficiency will make the thought and the behaviour of people comply with reason and refrain from superstition, and, because of this, stupid actions will stop. The people of our country want to break away from the primitive age, they are ashamed of being an ignorant people, they thus must hotly pursue it.[45]

And, in another article, he claimed:

---

44 Lan Zhaoqian (1916), "Kexue jiuguo lun er".
45 Chen Duxiu (2008a), "Jinggao qingnian".

If we believe that science is the compass for discovering truth, then those things that go against science, such as ghosts, spirits, fortune-telling, geomancy, divination, *fengshui* and [other] mantic arts ... can all be considered pernicious and wicked lies, not to be believed in a million years.[46]

Interestingly enough, Chen goes a little bit further and tries to show how scientific ignorance does harm to different groups of people: intellectuals will engage in superstitious activities; if peasants do not know science, they will not select efficient methods to get rid of insects; if workers do not know about science, they will waste resources, so that, in times of war, the country will have to rely on other countries. If merchants do not know science, they will only think about profit and will not devise long-term plans. And if doctors do not know about science, they will not know the anatomy of the human body or about infections transmitted by bacteria, and will only apply the theory of the five phases, Yin and Yang, *etc.*[47] Quite clearly, Chen goes far beyond a narrow definition of science here, although he does not do away with it completely. He says:

In a narrow sense, science means the natural sciences; in a broader sense, it is related to the social sciences. The social sciences employ the methods of the natural sciences and employ them in all areas of research related to men and society. Disciplines such as sociology, logic, history, law, economics, *etc.*, all employ the method of natural science for their research, and this shows that they belong to the sciences. This may be the biggest effect of the sciences.

Obviously, science understood in this sense would—if used for "saving the country"—imply a complete transformation of the country.

It is quite clear that, with many of his ideas, Chen Duxiu directly referred to those students abroad who had founded the Chinese Science Society. For example, the "Announcement of publication" (*fakanci*) of the journal *Kexue* states:

In the strong countries of this world, the development of people's rights and national strength must proceed in parallel to the progress of their academic learning, while, in those countries in which learning lies wasted, there is no such good fortune. Such cases can be easily found in history.

Now, the branches of learning of the European people are numerous, but we are only interested in science. Science means making a detailed analysis in order to discover a principle, sum it up, and establish a rule, and there are patterns which one can follow.

It can be used in order to obtain virtue; it can be used in order to improve living conditions. During the last 100 years, the two continents of Europe and America have displayed an abundance in cultural and material things, which really is an unprecedented achievement. If we look for the origins, most of it is due to the sciences.[48]

---

46 Chen Duxiu (2008b), "Jinri Zhongguo zhi zhengzhi wenti".
47 Chen Duxiu (2008a), "Jinggao qingnian".
48 "Fakan ci", *Kexue* (1915).

VI. Popularisers in the 1920s

Looking back to the situation at the end of the nineteenth century, there is little doubt that the calls of Yan Fu and others played a considerable role in convincing young Chinese scholars not to pursue careers as officials, for which they had originally prepared, but to go abroad and study—and, in many cases, study the natural sciences. It is also quite clear that the experiences that these students made at universities in the West rather reinforced the conviction that it was science alone which would be able to save a weak China from perishing altogether in a world that was conceived in a Darwinian way. The next generation of young intellectuals was thus exposed to publications such as *Kexue* and *Xin qingnian* and the journals of the New Culture Movement. There is also little doubt that science as a phenomenon, a cultural practice, and maybe even as a way of leading one's life, became ever more important in early Republican China. The 1923 discussions in *Science and Metaphysics*, which were "won" by the apologists of science clearly contributed to this, and it is certainly not completely wrong, that, as Hu Shi 胡適 (1891–1962) wrote in 1923, science had acquired "an incomparable position of respect so that nobody could publicly slight it or jeer at it".[49] It is also quite clear that this visibility of science and scientists greatly helped the institutional set-up of science, as was tangible in the universities and in the establishment of research laboratories, *etc.* From the view of scientists, however, this was far from sufficient. Even if Chinese scientists considered themselves as the vanguard of the Chinese élite—a position even reinforced by the publicity of science—it was clear that science had by no means reached the critical mass which would be required to improve the situation significantly. It was thus clearly necessary to accelerate the indigenisation of science massively,[50] and, at the same time, further spread the idea of the importance of science for national salvation. This would, it was hoped, on the one hand, further increase the interest in the sciences, while, on the other, it would contribute to the development of greater patriotism, which was considered as indispensable for overcoming China's weakness. This, of course, could only be achieved if science and the message that science would save China was popularised to a wider public. While up to now there has virtually been no research into this question, we know that it was attempted, and, apparently, in many ways. One interesting example can be found in a so-called "drum song" (*dagushu* 打鼓書), which was submitted to the *Saving the Country Monthly* (*Jiuguo yuebao* 救國月報), a journal which was founded by the "Saving the Country Association" of Peking University briefly after the Shanghai shootings of 30 May 1925, when protesters were killed by the police force of the International Settlement. This

---

49 Hu Shi (1923), "Kexue yu renshengguan xu", pp. 2–3.
50 On this issue, see Amelung (2014b), "Lokalität und Lokalisierung".

SCIENCE AND NATIONAL SALVATION 539

song apparently became quite popular, and it was hailed as a major achievement by the historian Gu Jiegang 顧頡剛 (1893–1980), who relates that the essayist and critic Yu Pingbo 俞平伯 (1900–1990) also thought highly of it, since it uses both "firmness and softness". Gu says that, if a normal singer sang this song for a normal audience, he "would certainly be able to attain their sympathy for the cause of saving the nation and this would result in letting them know that China's position [in the world] also becomes their responsibility".[51]

The song is rhymed and starts with the following sentences:

Axioms have a name but they do not have substance.
A strong power easily does what it pleases and is difficult to contain.
The state is extremely weak and faces disaster. But science can still come to rescue. [...]
In the process of evolution, some men became strong.
When science appeared, it was possible to overcome disaster.
Since these white men started to deal with science,
It came like a roaring flood over the world and nobody could resist.
[...]
The happiness produced by science should be shared by all people.
[But, at the moment], we only have to bear being oppressed by science.
If it is like this, how can we use the power of science for resistance?
One method of saving the country is adding many, many schools.
[...]

The song ends with the following sentences:

In order to preserve the Chinese race, sing this song. Take care of our country, spread education and turn weakness into strength.[52]

Although it is somewhat unclear how frequently this drum-song was actually performed, it is safe to say that it was quite successful in the long run. There were at least three instances in which it was reprinted, albeit in a slightly modified form, this time mainly addressing Japan, which, at that time, had occupied Manchuria:

Please, everybody, just think about this: The battle for Shanghai on 28 January 1931 as well as the recent hostilities in the North-East. The large cannons and the aircraft which the Japanese used in order to invade with military force, are they not things manufactured with the help of science? The largest part of those goods which they used for their economic invasion, is also produced with the help of science. If we want to resist their military invasion and their economic invasion, we also have to promote science! Promoting science has this relationship to the salvation of the nation.[53]

The uncommented copy that I quoted from above appeared in the left-wing journal *Kexue shibao* 科學時報 (Scientific Times) in 1935, which was explicitly

---

51 Gu Jiegang (1925), "Kexue jiuguo dagushu xu".
52 "Kexue jiuguo dagushu" (1935).
53 Zheng Yuan (1933), "Jieshao yi pian kexue jiuguo dagushu".

540 IWO AMELUNG

dedicated to the popularisation of science. It apparently was based upon another edition from the *Beiping shishi baihua bao* 北平事實白話報 (Beiping facts vernacular newspaper).

Popularisation of the idea of "Saving the Country by Science" took other forms as well. The school-anthem of Tianjin College for Industry and Commerce (Tianjin gongshang xueyuan 天津工商學院), for example, which was composed in 1937, took the topic up. The text begins:

"Saving the country by Science: its effects are visible all over the Western ocean! Enriching the country and protecting the race, entirely relies on industry and commerce."[54] (The Chinese original, of course, rhymes). Quite tellingly, I also found a lengthy poem entitled *Saving the Country by Science*, which was published in 1934 in a magazine devoted to popular illustration and books:

It has been said that everybody has responsibility in respect of the survival or the perishing of the country. In order to make the country strong, it is first necessary to make its people strong. There are multiple methods to strengthen oneself ....

The strength of foreign countries is completely derived from science; if China wants to strengthen its country, it cannot disregard this recipe. We do not speak first about acoustics, optics, chemistry, and electricity; first, we speak about scientific hygiene and this is the first chapter [of the poem].

The poem then offers a rather lengthy description of different aspects of bodily hygiene[55]—including, of course, the insistence that people practise sports, *etc.*, and ends with the following verses:

In respect of scientific hygiene, there is evidence and proof, and there are experiments. It is not that I have just made up an article. Personal hygiene improves the body, and public hygiene makes all of us strong. Women's hygiene results in safe births and aids the nourishment of the children, and children's hygiene results in an extended life span. If the spirit of ordinary people is strong, they are able to do good scientific research in order to make the country strong. All this is only a small part of the topic of hygiene, but we come on the to question of how the country can be saved by science in the second chapter.[56]

The poem, of course, is rhymed as well, and it is possible to imagine that people memorised it. Unfortunately, I have not been able to find the second "chapter" alluded to here. It can be used as a demonstration, however, of how ideas related to national salvation through science acquired an increasingly Darwinist and eugenic subtext and permeated to the public space.

There were other ways of promoting science as well, the most important of which were performed through role models, which means drawing attention to

---

54 Hua Xiaojun (2007), "Hebei daxue".

55 On the relationship between hygiene and modernity, cf. Rogaski (2004), *Hygienic Modernity*.

56 Tianjin yishu gailiang she (1934), "Xin ciqu: Kexue jiuguo.

SCIENCE AND NATIONAL SALVATION 541

the achievements of other scientists. Writing on the achievements of scientists had been popular in China since the late nineteenth century. The names of personalities such as Galileo, Newton, Watt and Edison were familiar to many Chinese. In respect of "saving the country by science", certain tensions became apparent. Was the function of a scientist really to save his country, or was it not the function of science to discover new truths and develop universal science? And indeed the personalities alluded to did propagate the universal aspects. If they were related to their home countries, this was mainly done in order to show that their countries had sophisticated scientific institutions and that this might turn out to be a comparative advantage for the country in question. However, it was also assumed that most scientists were more dedicated to science—or maybe to their own personal glory—than to saving their country. And indeed there were scientists whose prowess would have been urgently needed in order to "save" their country, but who had clearly failed to do so. The most often cited example here is that of the Indian physicist C.V. Raman (1888–1970), who had been awarded with the Nobel prize for Physics in 1930, but whose research had not helped to save his country from continuing to constitute a British colony. But who, then, was the best role-model to be seen as the saviour of his country? The choice here became Louis Pasteur (1822–1895), who, of course, had been known in China from early on. It seems that it was a speech published by Hu Shi in 1929, who related Pasteur to his country's national salvation.[57] Hu Shi took up the example of Pasteur several times. Quoting from Thomas Henry Huxley, he pointed out that Pasteur's discoveries had earned France so much money that it was able to pay the indemnity which it had to pay to Germany after the Franco-Prussian war of 1870/71. Pasteur's ardent patriotism was highlighted in a considerable number of articles and publications,[58] and, to a certain extent, he became something of a figurehead of the campaign to "save the country by science".[59]

VII. Science and National Renaissance

At the beginning of the 1930s, the discourse of "saving the country by science" was increasingly integrated into another powerful discourse, the discourse of the "Renaissance of the Chinese Nation" (*Zhonghua minzu fuxing* 中華民族復興). This discourse had been around since about 1902 and it is not particularly difficult to understand why it was very attractive to Chinese intellectuals, since it

---

57 Hu Shizhi (1929), "Kexue jiuguo".
58 See, for example, Song Guobin (1934), "Baside Pasteur zhuan".
59 Lu Yudao (1934), "Kexue yu shehui".

likened the Chinese situation to Europe at the end of the "dark" medieval ages. A Chinese renaissance thus promised hope. In 1919, students of Peking University had already founded a journal, which they named *Xinchao* 新潮 (literal translation "New Tide") and which carried the English title *The Renaissance*.[60] In the West, the notion had become well known through Hu Shi, who had already published an English article entitled "Renaissance in China"[61] in 1926, and whose well-known Haskell lectures of 1933 had been published as a book under the title *The Chinese Renaissance*.[62] However, while science had played a certain role in the discussions from the late 1910s, it was certainly not central. However, the notion of national renaissance—in a rather broad sense—nonetheless became much more pronounced after 1931, when Japan had taken over Manchuria and was busy establishing its puppet regime there. In 1932, the discourse was integrated into the Guomindang ideological framework, and Chiang Kai-shek 蔣介石 (1887–1975) himself became the head of the "Society for the Renaissance of the Chinese Nation" (*Zhonghua minzu fuxing she* 中華民族復興社).[63]

The loss of Manchuria from the point of view of Chinese intellectuals created an atmosphere which was even more gloomy than before. China was now considered to be at a crossroads: it would either vanish or be reborn. This assumption was underlined by a very strong social Darwinian discourse, which, in contrast to the first phase of the reception of Darwinian ideas, was now driven by renowned scientists, and, in particular, biologists, such as Bing Zhi 秉志 (1886–1965). The validity of the general principles of the struggle for existence were confirmed time and time again. In a book, entitled *Brief Introduction to the Struggle for Survival*, for example, Bing Zhi claims:

In the natural world, there is the struggle for survival; it never stops. If an animal is not victorious in the brutality of the struggle for existence, its race will die out. One can also observe how they assist each other in the struggle and gradually increase in number. The human race is a zoological species as well; there is the rise and decline of national races. How could it constitute an exception? This publication first explains all the phenomena related to the competition for survival in the animal world, in order to show that it is impossible to avoid it. It then explains the brutality of the struggle that takes place in the human race, a level of brutality which is not reached by any other animal. Those who are not enthusiastic or not able to press on and unanimously resist those from the outside

---

60 On the question of renaissance, cf. Eber (1975), "Thoughts on Renaissance in Modern China: Problems of Definition", and Zhou, Gang (2006), "The Chinese Renaissance: A Transcultural Reading".

61 Hu Shih (1926), "Renaissance in China".

62 Hu Shih (1934), *The Chinese Renaissance*.

63 Yu Zhuhua，Zhao Huifeng (2015), "Minguo shiqi minzu fuxing huayu de san zhong taidu".

SCIENCE AND NATIONAL SALVATION

will be necessarily defeated by the strong enemy and will have to undergo the natural process of elimination through selection.[64]

At another place in the book, Bing Zhi points out which factors are responsible for weak "national power" (*guoli* 國力), namely:

the specificity of the environment, being shut off from information, old and rotten political customs, a too large part of the population that has not received education, the accumulation of bad societal habits, the habit of accepting wrong as right, following old routines of laziness, and, in doing so, going from bad to worse, filling the whole country with an air of unstoppable decline, the physique and the character of the people already being in an unbearable state of decline, and the mental capability deteriorating in consequence and assembling this mass of people with weak bodies and weak brains in order to form a nation.

For Bing Zhi, however, this holds true for a large number of countries. And he goes on to put forward the claim that the danger of immediate extinction will only be faced by those races, whose "brain is structured in an utterly simple way", which, even through contact with cultured races, will not be able to "enter civilisation", just as "lower orders of animals cannot be immediately transformed into human species". Bing Zhi here explicitly mentions the Australian aborigines, and other "wild men, who have been left to live in far away deep valleys".[65]

In this way, Bing Zhi, on the one hand, uses science in order to confirm the general validity of the laws of evolution, while, on the other, he stresses that, in spite of all this, there is still hope for China, because, from a scientific point of view, the Chinese do not fall into this category, they are not one of those races that will not be able to develop.

If one carefully looks into Bing Zhi's description of the manifold deficits of China and the Chinese which he observes, a clear connection to discussions on the Chinese national character can be made. As is well known today, the discussion of the supposed defects of the Chinese national character went back to Arthur Smith's *Chinese Characteristics* and remained a hotly debated issue during the first thirty or so years of the twentieth century.[66]

The first attempts to relate the Chinese national character to science in order to improve its prowess can be traced back to the the period of the May Fourth Movement. It was most clearly expressed in the *Shuguang* magazine (曙光 *Dawn*) published by students from different Peking universities, some of them close to Communist ideas. The publishing manifesto (*xuanyan*) in the first issue of the journal makes this very clear from the start by stating:

---

64 Bing Zhi（2006）, "Jingcun lüelun", p. 1.

65 Ibid., p. 46,

66 On this issue, cf. Liu, Lydia H. (1995), *Translingual Practice*, pp. 45–76.

Because we are uneasy about current life, we wish to create a new life; not being happy about modern society, we wish to create a new society. But this new life and this new society need to be built upon science. It is necessary to have developed science; only then can civilisation progress. No matter whether we are dealing with the happiness of the masses or with individual happiness, it all follows the process of civilisation.[67]

And Song Jie 宋介 (1893–?), the spiritus rector of the enterprise in an article entitled "Science and Society", even considered it necessary to defend himself against trusting science too much:

To transform a non-scientific society into a scientific society is, of course, not easy at all. It depends on the question of how enlightened humanity is, and what the current and future developments in science and its use look like. When I say these words, I know that there will be someone who says that I blindly trust science too much. Although science is not absolutely omnipotent, it is still relatively omnipotent [....] for this reason, when one speaks about reforming society, one cannot do away with science. When science progresses one degree, society will be reformed by one degree. The progress of science knows no limits, and, for this reason, the reform of society is endless as well.[68]

This idea of social engineering was later echoed by Bing Zhi in a series of articles, which included one entitled, "On the Transformation of the People's Character" (Minxing gaizao lun, 民性改造論) in which he makes a very clear statement:

The way of establishing a country cannot be reduced to one point. The character of the people, however, is most important. If the character of the people fits with the needs of the environment, the country will become stronger every day and the nation will expand. Even those who come second will not lose their will to govern the country, otherwise national strength would decline, and everybody would become lethargic and low-spirited. With regard to those who are even lower down, however, their numerous affairs of the state are in a chaotic situation and it will fall into a state of decadence. Domestic trouble and foreign invasion will occur, and the disaster of national subjugation and the extinction of the nation is unavoidable.[69]

This is an almost paradigmatic discourse of weakness, which becomes even more pronounced in a latter part of the article, in which Bing Zhi lists the "four greatest negative characteristics of our people, which are the country's mortal wounds", namely:

1. An incapability to work together;
2. Acting recklessly;
3. Not possessing persistence;
4. Being easily corrupted.

---

67 "Xuanyan" *Shuguang* (1919), p 1.
68 Song Jie (1919), "Kexue yu shehui", p. 5.
69 Bing Zhi (1936), "Mingxing gaizao lun", p. 8.

SCIENCE AND NATIONAL SALVATION

In another article, Bing Zhi especially singled out the supposed naïvety of the Chinese people. "The naïvety of the thoughts of our people is indeed the reason for the confusion that we have been in for several dozen years."[70]

Other authors supplemented the list. A certain Hua Jingfang 華景芳, for example, maybe inspired by Bing Zhi, also addressed the "mortal wounds" of the Chinese national character, which, according to him, included "deep-rooted bad traits" (*liegenxing* 劣根性) such as "procrastination", "resigning oneself to the circumstances", "corruption" and "selfishness", to which, for good measure, he later on added the following "deficits of the national character", namely, "laziness", "superstition", "hypocrisy", "messiness", "filthiness", and "conservativeness". Hua claims that these deficits all "violate the scientific spirit, so that one also could say that the deficit of our nation is the lack of scientific spirit".[71] For Hua, it is the quality of the national character that determines the pure existence of the state, although he claims that, without an "outstanding" national character, the nation "will absolutely not be able to experience a renaissance".[72]

While the deficit analysis is rather clear, the question of remedies was somewhat more difficult to answer. The most time honoured practice was the fight against so-called "superstition", which, in the eyes of critics, could be found in employing divinatory techniques, popular religion, *etc.* As is well known, the fight against these practices had already started during the late Qing period, and became a dominant feature of the Nanjing-regime of the Guomindang after 1927.[73] For Hua and other scientists, such practices originated from "primitive cultures" and resembled the people of "other backward nations" who are not able to understand natural phenomena. When such practices are still employed, they prove that "our nation is not progressive" and they "constitute a shame for the whole nation".[74]

Given this situation, quite a number of scientists and propagandists conceptionalised the conflict with Japan as something akin to a test of the character of the nation,[75] or as Zhang Yuanruo 章淵若 (1904–1996) put it:

Because the Chinese nation was conservative and even degenerate for a long time, its exposure to the present examination hall of scientific culture really exposes its weak points and its crisis. For this reason, if we want to enable the Chinese nation to free itself from its backward position and to jump to a position of equality, we first need to

---

70 *Bing Zhi wencun* (2006), vol. 3, p. 135.
71 Hua Jingfang (1941), "Kexue jingshen yu minzu fuxing" p. 41.
72 Ibid, p. 41.
73 See Rebecca Nedostup (2009), *Superstitious Regimes*.
74 Hua Jingfang (1941), "Kexue jingshen yu minzu fuxing", p. 42.
75 Ibid., p. 41.

see clearly the basic points of the movement for the renaissance of our nation and we need to create a basis of national culture and science.[76]

As we have already seen above, commentators quite often employed medical terminology and medical metaphors when dealing with the issue. Defects needed to be "cured" (*yizhi* 醫治), and, in order to do this, "efficient medicine" (*liang yao* 良藥) was required.[77] A comprehensive treatment was necessary, as "the nation is in a situation in which it is no longer possible just to treat the head because of headaches or to treat the feet because of sore feet".[78]

One common approach to the issue was to suggest the adoption of a completely new culture. Peng Guangqin 彭光欽 (1906–1991), for example, stressed that the lowest line which never could be crossed was the line of "culture":

If our culture is not able to reach that of others, we will not be able to catch up, and we will be in a position of defeat and will be eliminated in the end. For this reason, we think that the most important work in bringing about the renaissance of the nation is the renaissance of culture.[79]

Even if rarely explicitly formulated, it is clear that, here again, the relationship to the European renaissance is stressed. This culture needed to be a "scientific culture" that was necessary for the "survival of the nation", and it would be, as Zhang Yuanruo emphasised, "the real source for the development of politics, the military, economics, education and all national power". And Lu Yudao echoed this, stressing that only a developed culture would put China on the same footing as other countries.

If we want to wipe out our national shame in order to strengthen ourselves and attain a position of national renaissance, we will not be able to succeed unless we infuse science into the blood of the descendants of our old country with several thousand years of history.[80]

Thus, the renaissance of the Chinese nation, according to many scientists, hinged on the extent of its adoption of a "scientific attitude". One interesting point here is that many Chinese scientists considered the bringing about of a Chinese renaissance to be entirely possible. Given the fact that, in the past, a renaissance had taken place in an environment as hopeless as the European middle ages, working for a renaissance in twentieth century China was assumed to be much easier. Such an assessment came from Bing Zhi, who quite often provided a much gloomier picture of the Chinese situation. He stressed, however, that scientists in China were in a more favourable situation than those of

---

76 Zhang Yuanruo (1933), "Fuxing yundong zhi jidian", p. 5.
77 Hua Jingfang (1941), "Kexue jingshen yu minzu fuxing", p. 41.
78 Zhang Yuanruo (1933), "Fuxing yundong zhi jidian", p. 5.
79 Peng Guanqin (1937), "Minzu fuxing yu kexue yanjiu", p. 1.
80 Lu Yudao (1936), "Kexue de guojia yu kexue de guomin".

the European middle ages, who constantly suffered from destruction and humiliation by the ecclesiastical authorities. In the eyes of Bing Zhi, this meant that, if there were sufficient scientists in China, and they proceeded in the same fashion as the scientists in Europe did, then the effect of science would spread even faster.

If European scientists were able to transform dark Europe into a Europe with a splendid culture, why should our scientists not be able to continue the beautiful mission of former worthies and transform our old nation into a strong nation?[81]

But how would one do away with superstition and strive to attain a certain level of scientific prowess for society as a whole? Lu Yudao and others promoted a process of "scientification" in which popularisation would play an important role.

We are citizens of our Chinese nation, we hope that our country will modernise. We need to "scientify" our country. We need to add flourishing science to the richness of the things of our country. If we want to reach this goal, it is only possible by "scientifying" the citizens of our country. If we want to "scientify" the whole body of our country's citizens, we need to start with our own "scientification".[82]

As "scientification" is still a somewhat abstract notion, Lu Yudao goes back to the *Great Learning* of the Confucian canon pointing out that those who want to put their country (*zhi guo* 治國) in order, first need to put their family in order. And this, Lu acknowledged, was a serious demand for action.

Cleanliness, hygiene, basic medical and pharmaceutical knowledge, as well as knowledge on nourishment, all belong to the realm of habit. And, for all of them, scientific knowledge is required.

He then comes up with a list of improvements, which was appropriated from the New Life Movement and which went from brushing one's teeth regularly to using one's own cup and one's own towel. He then—quite typical—links this to the very high rate of infant mortality in China, which is "the highest in the world".

Just think about the harm which is brought about by not applying science! It leads to the reduction of the number of our people! Isn't that enough to scare you?

According to the *Great Learning*, however, the process of ordering the state must begin with the individual, and, according to this logic, the process of "scientification" also needs to begin here.

Every citizen must have scientific knowledge, only then will there be scientific families and only then will there be a scientific state.

---

81 Bing Zhi (1934), "Kexue yu minzu fuxing", p. 322.
82 Lu Yudao (1936)," Kexue de guojia yu kexue de guomin".

And Lu points out that this was the mission of the journal that he edited, *Illustrated Science*, when addressing its more than 20,000 readers.[83] In an article entitled "Science and National Renaissance", Bing Zhi's remedies started with "the knowledge of the people, which needs to follow the development of science and become stronger daily", technological capability, the lives of the people, "the physique of the people, which needs to become stronger", the argument being here, that it is the lack of science which is responsible for starvation, epidemics, *etc.*, the "thought of the people, which, because of this, can become more progressive", and finally the "morality of the people, which, because of this, can be renewed". Bing Zhi's ideas on science and national renaissance enjoyed a high degree of popularity, and he also presented them as a speech in a somewhat simplified way, which was distributed as an article in several journals.[84]

It is not surprising that some participants in the discussion on science and national character imbued the debate with biologic traits. The question thus became one of whether the Chinese "race" was, in an anthropological and biological sense, inferior to other races. And, indeed, it seems as if the participants in the debate who had a biological or medical science background were very familiar with race theories, which were popular in the West at this time, and thus were deeply concerned about the biological and environmental limitations which, supposedly, might hinder the development of the Chinese national character. The person who was probably most influenced by this was Lu Yudao, an American trained anatomist and neurologist:

Our Chinese nation in the past had Genghis Khan, who threatened and shocked Europe and Asia, and was responsible for the terror that the members of the White Race viewed as the Yellow Peril. Today, it has gained the very bad reputation of being an inferior nation because it is frail, dirty, poor, Opium-smoking, and spreading stink throughout the world. De Gobineau claimed that the Yellow Race was weak in desire and passion, stubborn, and of no power. "Mediocre" [English in the original text] in every respect and unable to penetrate deeply into problems. Unfortunately, today, the Chinese nation's politics, economy, learning, thought, morals and physique all meet de Gobineau's claim. Who of the determined members of the Chinese race, regardless of those who are wealthy, or have an excellent academic reputation or are cherished as leaders, can bear these insinuations and abuse and still look for momentary ease?"[85]

While the appropriation of Genghis Khan into the Chinese race was, of course, somewhat far-fetched, it is not surprising that Lu Yudao and other Chinese scientists were especially irked by the attempts of Western scientists to employ supposedly scientific insights to prove the backwardness of the Chinese race.

---

83 Ibid.

84 Cf. for example Huang Xiying (1936), "Kexue yu minzu fuxing".

85 Lu Yadao (1934a), "Kexue de minzu fuxing".

SCIENCE AND NATIONAL SALVATION

This had been attempted, for example, by E. Kurz, who had pointed out the supposed primitiveness of the brain of the "Yellow Race", going so far as to doubt that the Chinese really had been able to invent the compass, paper and other things.[86] Lu Yudao had also been annoyed by the work of other Western anthropologists, who had done research on the size of the Chinese brain, and who concluded that it was smaller than the brain of Europeans and less developed. Lu and many others were equally critical of assumptions of environmental determinism, which had been forwarded by Ellsworth Huntington and others from the 1910s and had a certain influence in China, especially in the work of important scientists such as the meteorologist Zhu Kezhen.[87] It was here that Chinese scientists began to waver: How ought they deal with science when it was apparently directed against Chinese interests? What ought they to do with science when it was used to justify a Western "civilising mission"? Quite a number of Chinese scientists started to try to refute such ideas with the help of scientific arguments. This, apparently, was the background for the publication of a book in 1937, which was closely related to the efforts of the *Science Society*, and was entitled *A Scientific Renaissance of the Nation* (*Kexue de minzu fuxing* 科學的民族復興) and edited by Zhu Kezhen and other members of the *Science Society*. The preface pointed out that, of those countries which are usually considered as "old countries", such as Ancient Greece, Egypt and Rome, only China had survived. In recent years, however, developments in the realm of science and efficient technology had resulted in a stronger threat from the outside world. It was for this reason that leading Chinese citizens had embarked on a path of national renaissance, although some doubts remained, which not only originated from the political situation but also stemmed from scientific assessments:

Isn't the nature of others assertive and strong and our own one weak and old? How, then, can bad habits all of a sudden be changed, a withered away life prolonged, in order to engage in resistance in a fiercely competing world?[88]

The mission of the book was thus to prove by the means of science that China was able to do this. The book provided information on different aspects of China, such as history, the geographical situation, the relationship between the climate and the Chinese nation, the intelligence of the Chinese nation, as well as on the "question of how to reform the Chinese race". In the chapter on climate,

---

86 Cf. for example, E. Kurz (1924), "Das Chinesengehirn, ein Beitrag zur Morphologie und Stammesgeschichte der gelben Rassen". On the question in general, see Michael Keevak (2011), *Becoming Yellow. A Short History of Racial Thinking*.

87 A brief treatment of Huntington's influence in Zhu Kezhen, see Chen Zhihong (2012), "Climate's Moral Economy".

88 Zhu Kezhen (1937), "Xu".

for example, Lü Jiong 呂炯 (1902–1985) directly challenged Huntington and provided the following argument:

The places where other cultures emerged first, such as the Babylonians of Egypt (sic!), or the Inca-Empire of South America, have already been extinguished, and if we look to India, it, too, is facing the pitiful fate of becoming a "conquered nation". Among the old countries of the world, only China still exists. The fact that it alone has survived for a period of several thousand years in this world, is, in my opinion, thanks to the climate.

According to the author, this was because China has a temperate as well as a tropical climate. This brings a number of problems, but, in the end, it provides the Chinese nation with a unique "flexibility" (*tanxing* 彈性). The greatness of the Chinese nation also becomes clear through its ability to assimilate other people, such as the Mongols and the Manchu.[89]

In respect of the size of the brain, Lu Yudao was able to show that there was no significant difference between Western [in this case Dutch] brains and Chinese brains. Lu even recorded the result of intelligence tests, in which, interestingly, he did not question the whole issue of racial differences, but showed that the average IQ-quotient of the Chinese is similar to that of members of the "White Race", and—incidentally—significantly higher than that of peoples from Mexico or Latin America.[90]

In its conclusion the book asserted that the Chinese nation was well endowed for future greatness. The "problems" to be addressed mainly existed in the realms of nourishment and health ("There is no nation which is not healthy and whose culture at the same time is exceptional"). The authors consequently suggested that physical education be extended, and eugenics, hygiene and the economic ability of the nation all be improved.[91]

And, indeed, using eugenics in order to cure China's ills echoed a discourse which, at that time, was quite widespread, not only among eugenicists, such as Pan Guangdan 潘光旦 (1898–1967), but also among quite a number of scientists as well. Most prominent, in this respect, was Bing Zhi, who was unhappy with the commonly used term *yousheng* 優生 ("excellent birth") and preferred the term *jinzhong* 進種 (literally, "improving the race"). Bing Zhi suggested using methods of scientific education in order to improve the environment. The government was then expected to encourage those families who had chosen an orderly and "scientific" environment in which to produce many children, which would "improve the human force of the country and foster its vitality".[92] For Bing Zhi, the question of eugenics was closely linked to the question of mar-

---

89 Lü Jiong (1937), "Zhonghua minzu yu qihou de guanxi", p. 136.

90 Lu Yudao (1937), "Zhongguo rennao ji zhili", p. 204–205. On the issue, see, also, Yen Hsiao-pei (2006), "Formation of Race and Racial Identity in China in the 1930s".

91 Zhu Kezhen, Lü Yudao, Li Zhenjiang (1937), "Jielun".

92 Bing Zhi (1946), *Kexue husheng*, p. 19.

riage. If every person had some knowledge of Mendel's theory and Galton's ideas for racial improvement, humans suffering from chronic illness would not be able to find partners and thus would be extinguished, while the persons who were better able to reflect on this, would consciously look out for extraordinary, well-suited partners.[93] Interestingly, Bing Zhi linked his ideas about marriage to another problem, which was considered as one of China's ills, namely, the question of early marriage, which had been rather intensively discussed from the beginning of the century. Most intellectuals considered this mainly to be a social problem. They looked into the marriage age in "civilised" countries and observed that it was much higher than in China. Even a country which had begun its reforms recently, such as Japan, had quickly changed its habits. For Bing Zhi, however, the question was quite central for the Chinese renaissance, since, in his eyes, early marriage "violated scientific principles". According to him, every peasant was aware that, in order to grow pumpkins, one only used the seeds of the ripest pumpkins, whereas if one used the seeds of pumkins which had not completely ripened, the harvest would be inferior. Although this principle was "extremely easy to understand", the people in the interior provinces of China often disregarded it and let their offsprings marry while they still were children.

Regarding the age of humans, the development of the body of humans is still not completed when aged twenty. When using seeds which are not ripe in order to sow seeds [sic!], then the body of the male and the female [who procreate] must be affected and the natural endowment of the male and female offspring naturally must be poor [...] if this habit continues for a long time, I do not even dare to think about the physique of the citizens. The bodies of the people all over the world become stronger and stronger, and, in our country, they tend to become shorter.[94]

However, on the whole, and in spite of the complicated situation, Bing Zhi was nonetheless quite optimistic about bringing about a "national renaissance". At the same time, however it is possible to read his work as proof of how thin the line between pseudo-science and real science could become. In his article on "Science and the National Renaissance" of 1934, he mentions the Russian surgeon Serge Veronoff, who became famous in the 1920s and 1930s for grafting monkey testicles onto older human males, claiming that they would be greatly rejuvenated by this. While Bing Zhi is careful enough to state that it is too early to trust this story completely, he points out that history has left a great deal of proof that science is able to transform a nation. He goes on to say:

If the testicles of a small gorilla are able to transform an old man back into a child, then how could it be impossible for the young people of our nation to be able to transform

---

93 Bing Zhi (2006c), "Shengwuxue yu minzu fuxing", p. 178.
94 Bing Zhi (1946) *Kexue husheng*, p. 36.

our weak and old nation back into a youthful one? Moreover, our country still has a culture of 5,000 years, which can serve as the background for the national renaissance [...] if we are diligent in studying for science, it will really not be difficult to bring about a renaissance for our weak and old Chinese nation.[95]

VIII. Scientification

We should take care to note here that the science of the China of the 1920s and 1930s did not just consist of mere rhetoric. In fact, given the fact that China's first university had only been established in 1898, and that no specialised research institutions existed at all, the institutionalisation of scientific research progressed surprisingly fast. Academia Sinica as a government financed national academy was founded in 1928, the biology laboratory of the *Science Society* had been founded in 1922, and the huge Fan Memorial Institute of Biology was launched in Beijing in 1928. Many of the personalities mentioned in this essay worked in these or other scientific institutions. Establishing and developing these institutions would not have been possible without the support of a modernising government. However, as we have just seen, the Japanese aggression in Manchuria and Shanghai put the issue of "science as the saviour" of the now physically threatened China high on the agenda again. In order to reach an even larger number of people, new methods were necessary. From the beginning of the 1930s, a large number of new journals dedicated to the popularisation of science were published. The trend was also noted by the members of the Chinese *Science Society*, which, in 1933, began to publish its *Kexue huabao* 科學畫報 (Illustrated Science), edited, among others, by the above-mentioned Lu Yudao, which specifically addressed both children and the Chinese masses, including the peasants, noting that, in the event of a disaster, the latter could do nothing but "prostrate themselves in front of Buddha and pray to the gods", so that science was urgently necessary as a better remedy and should be brought to them by employing "simple words and clear and interesting illustrations and photographs".[96]

The founding of this journal (which still exists today) can be seen as a reaction to the massive government sponsored "scientification movement" (*kexuehua yundong* 科學化運動), which had begun the year before.

This movement published a journal, which was optimistically called *Kexue de Zhongguo* 科學的中國 (Scientific China), which, in its first issue, contained a

---

95 Bing Zhi (1934), "Kexue yu minzu fuxing", p. 322.
96 "Fakan ci" *Kexue huabao* 1:1 (1933), p. 1.

SCIENCE AND NATIONAL SALVATION

programmatic article entitled "On the Purpose of Initiating the China 'Scientification Movement'".

We have assembled a considerable number of men who do research or apply the natural sciences, and we aim to distribute scientific knowledge to the people, in order to make it a wisdom shared by the common people. We even more hope that this kind of knowledge, once it has been spread among the people, will be able to produce an enormous power which will help us to extend the life of our nation, which has already reached the point of life and death, and that it will revive our Chinese culture, which is deteriorating daily. It is in this way that we daringly announce to [Chinese] society the beginning of our work on the scientification of China.[97]

The plan of operations for the second phase of the movement, which was published in 1935, makes some of the goals even clearer:

The scientification movement does not have the goal of moving science itself forward. Its importance lies in helping to build up the nation state. It also does not aim to satisfy the interests of a small number of men, but its importance lies in improving the life of a large number of people. Thus, the motivation for our work is the rescuing of the nation and rescuing of the state.[98]

This document on the purpose of the movement makes a number of interesting points regarding the basic assumptions underlying its mission:

We firmly believe that science occupies a very important position in today's society. In particular, we acknowledge that science has a position of utmost importance in present day Chinese society. Knowledge is capacity, and science is systematic knowledge. For this reason, science, too, is organisational ability. Only if a society enters [the stage] of organisational capacity, can spiritual and material power directly operate on the whole society and indirectly operate on the individual elements of the society. Only then is it possible to avoid all kinds of calamities and obtain all kinds of benefits. Moreover, it is only in this way that poverty and ignorance can be eradicated and stupidity can be driven away. So, simply stated, our goal only consists of ten Chinese characters: "The socialisation of science and the scientification of the society" (*kexue de shehuihua, shehui de kexuehua* 科學的社會化，社會的科學話).[99]

It should be noted here, however, that the scientification movement was, in some respects, markedly different from earlier approaches to "saving China with science". This becomes particularly clear when one looks into the publicly-proclaimed attitude of the movement regarding the past, the present and the future:

All past material should be organised by using the scientific method: its essence should be preserved, the waste should be removed. In respect of all forms which are related to

---

97 "Zhongguo kexuehua yundong xiehui faqi zhiqu shu" (1933), p. 1.
98 "Zhongguo kexuehua yundong xiehui dier qi gongzuo jihua dagang (1935), p. 3.
99 "Zhongguo kexuehua yundong xiehui faqi zhiqu shu" (1933), p. 2.

modern life, these should be scrutinised with the help of scientific principles, and their superstitious and self-centred aspects should be removed. Their rational and public intention should be made clear in order to be able to determine a rational philosophy of life based upon truth. In respect of the future, we will entice normal people to progress on the road of scientific development in order to make efforts to fulfil the wish to create happiness for mankind and to produce things for the human race and not use things in order to kill people.[100]

Since the scientification movement was supported by the Guomindang and actually run by members of the CC clique of Chen Lifu 陳立夫 (1900–2001) and Chen Guofu 陳果夫 (1892–1951) we can already discern a more conservative tone in these brief quotations. What is particularly interesting is the movement's attempt to link modern science with the Chinese tradition. This claim was also made by Chiang Kai-shek, when he stated that "science" (*kexue*) was nothing other than the "investigation of things and extension of knowledge" (*gezhi* 格致) already mentioned in the *Great Learning* (*Daxue* 大學)[101]—and was based upon a rather peculiar distinction between "civilisation" (*wenming* 文明) and "culture" (*wenhua* 文化). *Wenming* was presented here as the capacity of a nation to control material and spiritual resources in such a way that it would be able to guarantee its existence against the challenges of the environment. *Wenhua*, however, and here the character *hua*, "to change", was employed in a literal way, is the ability to transform the environment and, by extension, other nations. All this was framed in a Darwinian way. There had been nations whose *wenming* had declined, so that they were eliminated by natural selection (*taotai* 淘汰). This had happened, for example, to the Indians in the Americas. In the 1930s, China was in a similar situation, but it was not too late to stop this process and for China not only to regain its "civilisational" position, but also to strengthen its transformative power—that is to say, its culture—again. The precondition for all of this, however, was the scientification of its people.[102]

While the initiators of the "scientification movement" were, first and foremost, leading GMD politicians, a large number of scientists actively took part in the movement as well. The theorist of the movement was Gu Yuxiu 顧毓琇 (1902–2002), an American-trained electrical engineer, who had had Alfred North Whitehead (1861–1947) among his teachers. In 1936, he published a monograph on the question of scientification, which, in a rather systematic way, detailed his thoughts on how science could help to save China. Probably his most important contribution here was that he made it clear that there was no necessary relationship between science and the idea of saving China by science.

---

100 Chen Lifu (1933), "Zhongguo kexuehua yundong yu wenhua fuxing de guanxi".
101 Amelung (2014), "Historiography of Science and Technology in China. The First Phase", see also, Chen Shou (2007), "Xin wenhua yundong yu kexuehua yundong zhong de 'kexue'".
102 Chen Lifu (1933), "Zhongguo kexuehua yundong yu wenhua fuxing de guanxi".

SCIENCE AND NATIONAL SALVATION

This means that this relationship needed to be forged by a number of conscious efforts, as only then would it be able to do what was expected:

If we say that relativity or the quantum hypothesis is not able to save China, and scientists hear that they will naturally ridicule [this thought]. Who would not try to protect relativity and the quantum analysis or say that they did not have a function in saving China? For this reason, if we want to understand science or if we want to value science, we calmly have to admit: science is science and China is China.[103]

For Gu Yuxiu, it was only the concept of "scientification" which established the relationship between science and the nation, or, even more clearly, between the single parts of the nation:

In all cases in which we use science in order to combine science with culture, society or mankind, we call this scientification. Or, to put it the other way around: if science is separated from such partners as culture, society or mankind, then the stage of scientification has not been reached.

Gu, however, goes one step further and demands that there be a process of "socialisation" (*shehuihua* 社会化), which must be bi-directional:

Society needs to welcome "scientification", while, at the same time, science needs to adopt to the expectations of society.

In order to make this point even clearer, Gu introduces two further terms, namely, "scientific humanism" (*kexue shang de renbenzhuyi* 科學上的人本主義) and "scientific statism" (*kexue shang de guobenzhuyi* 科學上的國本主義), the former in order to stress that there must be a direct relationship between science and individual life, and the latter in order to stress that science needs to adapt itself to the requirements of the country.

The problem here is quite clearly the question of applied science, which, to some extent, was always lurking in the background of the whole discussion of "saving the country by science", and which increasingly moved to the core of the issue. Gu Yuxiu makes a number of quite interesting statements here, to wit, that, in the last instance, this has to be decided by the scientists themselves. Thus, it is not science that saves the country, but it is "scientists who save the country". While Gu does not wish to rule out that a scientist who continues to engage in pure science with this work might lay the foundation of the renaissance of the nation (*minzu fuxing* 民族復興), he, at the same time, warns of the futility of such a hope, pointing to the case of India, which had, as cited above, been awarded a Nobel Prize, but was still an British colony, and which he contrasts with the situation of Japan, which he did not consider as particularly

---

103 Gu Yuxiu (1936), *Zhongguo kexuehua de wenti*, p. 14.

strong in physics and chemistry, although it was still able to bring other countries to the brink of being enslaved (*wangguonu* 亡國奴).[104]

Gu Yuxiu ends his plea with the following words:

1. Science does not necessarily want to save China, but China needs science.
2. Only when science is willing to save China, will science save China.
3. The answer to the question of how science can save China does not reside with science itself, but with the scientists.[105]

But Gu Yuxiu's ideas were, by no means, shared by everybody. As we have seen, Bing Zhi was a firm believer in the ability of science to save the country, and time and time again, he stressed the need for scientific education in order to overcome the problems of the country. On the other hand, however, he repeatedly defended the importance of pure science:

There are those who doubt the importance of pure science, since much of it does not have any application. Even if research is carried out, they hold that it is not possible to establish theories, or they hold that it does not directly profit the urgent need of the state and the people. And it is not true that only those who are not scientists consider this to be correct, as many who engage in the sciences consider this to correct as well. For this reason, they say that a certain area or piece of research is useless, or a certain area or piece of research is completely empty. These people apparently do not have any relationship with real science and have never been enlightened by the history of science. The only goal of science is to discover the truth. And, in all cases, the truth has a relationship with the application. Once the truth has been discovered, an application follows and manifests itself. This is one of the great wonders of science![106]

While it is not clear whether Bing Zhi criticism directly targeted the scientification movement or even Gu Yuxiu personally, there is no doubt that Gu's ideas met with stiff and persistent resistance from quite a number of scientists who did not question the idea of "Saving the country by science", but who were genuinely concerned about the consequences of such proposals for the scientific development of the state, and, by implication, for the scientific freedom of the country.[107]

---

104 Ibid., p. 50
105 Ibid., p. 58.
106 Bing Zhi (1932), "Kexue yu guoli".
107 Cf. Sun Yi (1933), "Du Gu Yuxiu 'Women xuyao zenyang de kexue' hou", and Wang Jingxi (1933), "Women xuyao zenyang de kexue taolun".

IX. As a Conclusion

The idea of "saving China by science" is closely related to a discourse of weakness. At the same time, the salvation discourse becomes a discourse of weakness in itself. It is only necessary to save somebody if he or she is in trouble or in a weak and helpless situation. For this reason, many statements which fed into the "saving the country discourse" make more or less explicit references to the unbearable state of Chinese weakness (*jiruo* 極弱–utterly weak). From the end of the nineteenth century, starting with Yan Fu, the Darwinian reasoning was made increasingly explicit and became ever more visible over time. This, on the one hand, was due to the perceived hopeless situation of China—especially with regard to external enemies, such as Japan. On the other hand, however, it was due to the fact that the number of scientists who were concerned about the situation in China increased considerable. Given the fact that the increase in the number of scientists was—at least partially—the result of the shifting of resources into the realm of science, this outcome appears to be somewhat ironical. There is no doubt at all that Chinese biologists, in particular, were greatly influenced by Darwinian arguments.

The discourse of "saving the country by science", however, went far beyond the rather narrow scientific realm. Given that one of its most important goals was mobilisation, many of the most active participants made great efforts to popularise it. There is little doubt that this goal was dramatically attained. Not only were semi-independent organisations, such as the *Science Society*, totally dedicated to the cause of "saving the country by science", government-sponsored organisations, such as the "scientification" movement and the "Society for the Renaissance of the Chinese Nation", were too. It seems that these campaigns were directly related to the success of the "scientification" movement during its first phase—that is, prior to the founding of the Nanjing government in 1927.

While it should not be ruled out that members of the *Science Society*, who, at least during the earlier period, were the foremost promoters of the idea of "saving the country by science", aimed at supporting an emerging civil society, as Wang Zuoyue suggested, we can certainly say that the discourse in which they played such an important role contributed to a gradual change of the system of distributing those resources within whose framework the science society had to operate. It is no accident that Ren Hongjun—a founder of the Science Society—became a high functionary in the China Foundation for the Promotion of Education and Culture, or that Yang Xingfo (Quan), also co-founder, became an executive director of the Academia Sinica, or that Hu Shi, also among the founders of the society, at a later point of his career, would become president the Academia Sinica, which had moved to Taiwan. Thus, the calls for "saving

China by science" had contributed to the production of a whole generation of very knowledgeable and efficient scientists and functionaries of science, who would shape the development of science in China almost up to the present day. And, of course, these personalities were closely related to the institutional build-up of the scientific enterprise from the 1920s, although it is more difficult to draw direct lines of relationship here. It also becomes clear that science deeply penetrated into other realms, such as linguistics and history, which were established within the Academia Sinica on a completely new "scientific" footing by Fu Sinian 傅斯年 (1896–1950).[108] Another positive result of the discourse was certainly the importance accorded to the language of science and scientific terms, which was of great benefit for the "localisation" of natural sciences not only during the Republican era, but also beyond.

But notwithstanding all this, the Chinese road to science was not free from misunderstandings and irritation. While a large number of Chinese scientists did not have any problems in accepting the supposed implication of Darwinism, namely, that the Chinese race was on the brink of perishing, they clearly and understandable found Western attempts to relate the Chinese deficits to the environment or to "scientifically observed" racial traits to be highly objectionable. This, quite clearly, was the "flip side" of "science", and it needed to be contested by better scientific research. As the examples of Lu Yudao and Bing Zhi demonstrate, the goal was not to show that there was no scientific basis for distinguishing between races, but rather to postulate that the Chinese were equal to the Caucasian race. This could be considered to be a somewhat depressing outcome of the development of science in China during the first half of the twentieth century. However, it can also be seen as proof that science in China continued to be seen as highly utilitarian—independently of the question of "applied sciences".

We should finally note that the history of the *Kexue jiuguo* discourse did not end with the founding of the People's Republic. In 1976, during the last phase of the Cultural Revolution, the discourse was branded as capitulationist and as betraying the country, an accusation mainly directed against Liu Shaoqi 劉少奇 (1898–1969, already dead at that time) and Deng Xiaoping 鄧小平 (1904–1997) and his "Four modernisations" (*sig e xiandahui* 四個現代化), who, in this way, were put together with persons such as Kang Youwei and other *bourgeois* traitors.[109] In 1992, the Chinese Communist Party under the leadership of Jiang Zemin 江澤民 officially promulgated the formula of *Kejiao xingguo* 科教興國 (Reviving the country by scientific education), which can clearly be considered as an echo of the discourses of the Republican era, including the discourse on renaissance. Gu Yuxiu, who—as we have seen above—was one of the most

---

108 Cf. Wang Fan-sen (2000), *Fu Ssu-nien*, pp. 73–81.
109 Hai Cheng (1976), "Kexue jiuguo lun jiushi toujiang maiguo lun".

SCIENCE AND NATIONAL SALVATION

important promoters of the scientification movement, after 1945 worked at Shanghai Jiaotong University, where he was one of the most important teachers of Jiang Zemin, as Jiang stressed time and time again. Jiang even visited Gu Yuxiu in the US in 1997, which resulted in a very high degree of popularity for Gu Yuxiu, who, at that time, was already 95-years old and would only die in 2002, at the age of 100. During the 1970s and 1980s, Gu had also met with Zhou Enlai and Deng Xiaoping. It thus seems possible that Gu Yuxiu's ideas on scientification had a direct impact on the political line of Deng Xiaoping and Jiang Zemin with regard to science. This, however, has never been officially acknowledged.

Bibliography

Amelung, Iwo (2014a), "Historiography of Science and Technology in China. The First Phase", in: Jing Tsu, Benjamin Elman (eds.), *Science and Technology in Modern China, 1880s–1940s*, Leiden, Boston: Brill, pp. 39–65.

— (2014b), "Lokalität und Lokalisierung—zur Entwicklung der Wissenschaften im China des späten 19. und frühen 20. Jahrhunderts", *Jahrbuch zur Überseegeschichte*, 14, pp. 193–214.

Bing Zhi 秉志 (1932), "Kexue yu guoli" 科學與國力 (Science and National Strength), *Kexue*, 16:7, pp. 1013–1020.

— (1934), "Kexue yu minzu fuxing" 科學與民族復興 (Science and National Renaissance), *Kexue*, 19:3, pp. 317–322.

— (1936), "Minxing gaizao lun" 民性改造論 (On Reforming the Nature of the People), *Guofeng yuekan*, 8:1, pp. 8–11.

— (1946), *Kexue husheng* 科學呼聲 (A Voice for Science), Nanjing: Zhongguo kexue tushuyiqi gongsi.

— (2006a), *Bing Zhi wencun* 秉志文存 (Works of Bing Zhi), Beijing: Beijing daxue chubanshe 2006.

— (2006b), "Jingcun lüelun" 競存略論 (Brief Introduction to the Competition for Survival), in: Qu Qihui, Hu Zonggang (ed.), *Bing Zhi wencun*, Beijing: Xinhua shudian, vol. 2, pp. 1–48.

— (2006c), "Shengwuxue yu minzu fuxing" 生物學與民族復興 (Biology and national renaissance), in: Qu Qihui, Hu Zonggang (ed.), *Bing Zhi wencun*, Beijing: Xinhua shudian, vol. 2, pp. 135–200.

Callahan, William A. (2004). "National Insecurities: Humiliation, Salvation, and Chinese Nationalism", *Alternatives*, 29, pp. 199–218.

Chen Duxiu 陳獨秀 (2008a), "Jinggao qingnian" 警告青年 (Alarming the Young), in: Ren Jianshu (ed.), *Chen Duxiu zhuzuo xuanbian*, Shanghai: Shanghai renmin chubanshe, vol. 1, pp. 158–163.

— (2008b), "Jinri Zhongguo zhi zhengzhi wenti" 今日中國之政治問題 (The Political Problems of China Today), in: Ren Jianshu (ed.), *Chen Duxiu zhuzuo xuanbian*, Shanghai: Shanghai renmin chubanshe, vol. 1, pp. 417–419.

Chen Fan 陳藩 (1916), "Lun wuguo xuezhe yi huxang lianjie yu Zhongguo kexueshe yi cujin guoshi" 論吾國學者宜互相連結於中國科學社以促進國勢 (The Scholars of our Country should Unite within the Chinese Science Society in Order to Promote National Strength), *Liu Mei xuesheng jibao*, 3:2, pp. 77–82.

Chen Lifu 陳立夫 (1933), "Zhongguo kexuehua yundong yu wenhua fuxing de guanxi" 中國科學化運動與文化復興的關係 (The Chinese Scientification Movement and its Relation to the Renaissance of Culture), *Kexue de Zhongguo*, 2:4, pp. 129–132.

Chen Shou 陳首 (2007), "Xin wenhua yundong yu kexuehua yundong zhong de 'kexue'" 新文化運動與科學化運動中的科學, *Ershiyi shiji*, 12, pp. 57–66.

Chen Zhihong (2012), "Climate's Moral Economy. Geography, Race, and the Hand in Early Republican China", in: Thomas S. Mullaney, James Leibold, Stéphane Gros, Eric Vanden Bussche (eds.), *Critical Han Studies. The History, Representation, and Identity of China's Majority*. Berkeley CA: University of California Press, pp. 73–91.

Cohen, Paul A. (2002), "Remembering and Forgetting. National Humiliation in Twentieth-Century China", *Twentieth Century China*, 27:2, pp. 1–40.

Du Yaquan 杜亞泉 (1900), "Yaquan zazhi xu" 亞泉雜誌序 (Preface to the Yaquan magazine), *Yaquan zazhi*, 11, p. 1.

Eber, Irene (1975), "Thoughts on Renaissance in Modern China: Problems of Definition", in: *Laurence E. Thompson* (ed.), *Studia Asiatica: Essays in Asian Studies in Felicitation of the Seventy-fifth Anniversary of Prof. Chen Shou-yi*, (Occasional Series 29), San Francisco CA: Chinese Materials Center, pp. 189–218.

"Fakan ci" 發刊詞 (1915) (Announcement of Publication), *Kexue*, 1:1, pp. 3–4.

"Fakan ci" 發刊詞 (1933) (Announcement of Publication), *Kexue huabao*, 1:1, p. 1.

Fan Hongye 樊洪業 (1997), "Chong du Yan Fu jiuwang pian" 重讀嚴復救亡篇, (Rereading Yan Fu's "On our salvation) *Minzhu yu kexue*, 6, pp. 18–20.

— (2013), "Lan Zhaoqian yu 'Kexue jiuguo lun'" 藍兆乾與《學救國說》 (Lan Zhaoqian and his Saving the Country by Science), *Baicaoyuan*, 65:1, pp. 1–2.

Gu Jiegang 顧頡剛 (1925), "Kexue jiuguo dagushu xu" 科學救國大鼓書序 (Preface to the Drum song "Saving the Country by Science"), *Jingbao fukan*, 315, pp. 4–6.

Gu Yuxiu 顧毓琇 (1936), *Zhongguo kexuehua de* wenti 中國科學化的問題 (The Question of the Scientification of China), Zhongguo kexuehua yundong xiehui Beiping fenhui.

Hai Cheng 海成 (1976), "Kexue jiuguo lun jiushi toujiang maiguo lun" 科學救國論就是投降賣國論 (The Discourse on Saving the Country by Science is a Theory, which is Capitulationist and Betraying the Country), *Wen shi zhe*, 3, pp. 41–43.

Hu Shi 胡適 (1923), "Kexue yu renshengguan xu" 科學與人生觀序 (Preface to Science and Philosophy of Science), in: Wang Mengzou 汪孟鄒 (eds.), *Kexue yu renshengguan* 科學與人生觀, Shanghai: Yadong tushuguan, pp.1–32.

— (1926), "Renaissance in China", *Journal of the Royal Institute of International Affairs*, 5: 6, pp. 265–283.

— (1934), *The Chinese Renaissance*, Chicago IL: University of Chicago Press.

Hu Shizhi 胡適之 [i.e. Hu Shi](1929), "Kexue jiuguo" 科學就國 (Saving the Country with Science) , *Guohuo pinglun kan*, 2:9, pp. 20–24.

Hua Jingfang 華景芳 (1941), "Kexue jingshen yu minzu fuxing" 科學精神與民族復興 (Scientific Spirit and National Renaissance), *Qingnian zhenglun*, 3:1–2, pp. 39–43.

Huang Sixing 黃似馨 (1936), "Kexue yu minzu fuxing" 科學與民族復興 (Science and National Renaissance), *Kexue shijie*, 6:6, pp. 429–433.

Kang Youwei 康有為 (1987), "Wuzhi jiuguo lun houxu" 物質救國論后序 (Postface for Saving the Country by Material Civilisation), in: Jiang Guilin (ed.), *Kang Nanhai xiansheng yizhu huikan*, Taibei: Hongye shuju, vol. 15, pp. 8–9.

– (2007), "Wuzhi jiuguo lun" 物質救國論 (Essay on Saving the Country by Material Civilisation), in: Jiang Yihua, Zhang Ronghua (eds.), *Kang Youwei quanji*, Beijing: Zhongguo renmin daxue chubanshe, vol. 8, pp. 61–101.

Keevak, Michael (2011), *Becoming Yellow: A Short History of Racial Thinking*. Princeton NJ: Princeton University Press.

"Kexue jiuguo dagushu" 科學救國大鼓書 (1935), (Drum Song for Saving the Country by Science), *Kexue shibao*, 3, pp. 81–83.

Kurz, E. (1924), "Das Chinesengehirn, ein Beitrag zur Morphologie und Stammesgeschichte der gelben Rassen", *Zeitschrift für Anatomie und Entwicklungsgeschichte*, 72, pp. 199–382.

Lan Zhaoqian 藍兆乾 (1915), "Kexue jiuguo lun" 科學救國論 (On the Idea of Saving the Country by Science), *Liumei xuesheng jibao*, 2:2 (1915), pp. 63–73.

– (1916), "Kexue jiuguo lun er" 科學救國論二, (On the Idea of Saving the Country by Science Two) *Liumei xuesheng jibao*, 3:2 , pp. 1–7.

Liu, Lydia (1995), *Translingual Practice. Literature, National Culture, and Translated Modernity – China, 1900–1937*, Stanford CA. Stanford University Press.

Lu Feizhi 陸費執 (1918), "Zhongguo yi su zuzhi kexue xuehui" 中國宜速組織科學學會 (China should Quickly Organise Scientific Societies), *Liu Mei xuesheng jibao*, 5:1, pp. 93–96.

Lü Jiong 呂炯 (1937), "Zhonghua minzu yu qihou de guanxi" 中華民族與氣候的關係 (The Chinese Nation and its Relationship to Climate), in: Zhu Kezhen, Lu Yudao, Li Zhenjiang (eds.), *Kexue de minzu fuxing*, Shanghai: Zhongguo kexue she, pp. 113–141.

Lu Xun 魯迅 (1973), "Ou gan" 偶感 (Random Thoughts) in: Lu Xun, *Huabian wenxue* (Lu Xun quanji 5), Bejing: Renmin wenxue chubanshe, pp. 533–534.

Lu Yudao 盧于道(1934a), "Kexue de minzu fuxing" 科學的民族復興 (A Scientific Renaissance of the Nation), *Kexue huabao*, 1:23 (1934), p 1.

– (1934b), "Kexue yu shehui" 科學與社會 (Science and Society), *Kexue huabao*, 2:5, n.p.

– (1936), "Kexue de guojia yu kexue de guomin" 科學的國家與科學的國民 (Scientific State and Scientific Citizens), *Kexue huabao*, 3:12, p.1.

– (1937), "Zhongguo rennao ji zhili" 中國人腦及智利 (The Chinese Brain and Intelligence), in: Zhu Kezhen, Lu Yudao, Li Zhenjiang (eds.), *Kexue de minzu fuxing*, Shanghai: Zhongguo kexue she, pp. 170–210.

Ma Junwu 馬君武 (1903), "Xin xueshu yu qunzhi zhi guanxi" 新學術與群治之關係 (The New Academic Learning and the Governing of the Masses), *Zhengfa xuebao*, 1903:9 and 1903:13.

Miao Chunfeng 苗春風 (2002). "Yan Fu de jinhua lun sixiang yu jiuwang tucun" 嚴復的進化論思想與救亡圖存 (Yan Fu's Thoughts about Progress and his Places for Rescourcing the Country), *Dali xueyuan xuebao*, 1:1, pp. 59–62.

Nedostup, Rebecca (2009), *Superstitious Regimes: Religion and the Politics of Chinese Modernity* (Harvard East Asian monographs 322), Cambridge MA: Harvard University Press.

Peng Guangqin 彭光欽 (1937), "Minzu fuxing yu kexue yanjiu" 民族復興與科學研究 (The National Renaissance and Scientific Research), *Beifang qingnian*, 1:2, pp. 1–2.

Ren Hongjun 任鴻雋 (1914), "Jianli xuejie lun", 建立學界論 (On the Establishment of an Academic Community), *Liumei xuesheng jibao*, 1:2, pp. 43–50 and "Jianli xuejie zai lun" 建立學界再論 (More on the Establishment of an Academic Community), *Liumei xuesheng jibao*, 1:3, pp. 27–33.

— (1915a), "Kexuejia renshu yu yi guo wenhua zhi guanxi" 科學家人數與一國文化之關係 (On the Relationship between the Number of Scientists and the Culture of a State), *Kexue*, 1:5, pp. 484–489.

— (1915b), "Shuo Zhongguo wu kexue zhi yuanyin" 說中國無科學之原因 (On the Reason that China does not have Science), *Kexue*, 1:1, pp. 8–13.

Richard, Timothy 李提摩太, (1898), "Zhongguo yi qiu gezhi zhi xue lun" 中國宜求格致之學論 (China should Strive to Employ the Sciences), in: Chen Zhongyi 陳忠倚 (ed.), *Huangchao jingshi wen sanbian* 皇朝經世文三編, Shanghai: Shanghai shuju, J. 10, p. 36a.

Rogaski, Ruth (2004), *Hygienic Modernity. Meanings of Health and Disease in Treaty Port China* (Asia Local Studies/Global Themes), Berkeley CA: University of California Press.

Song Guobin 宋國賓 (1934), "Baside Pasteur zhuan" 巴斯德 Pasteur 傳 (Biography of Pasteur)", *Yiyao pinglun*, 111, pp.77–78.

Song Jie 宋介 (1919), "Kexue xu shehui" 科學與社會 (Science and Society), *Shuguang* 1:1, pp. 3–10.

Sun Yi 孫逸 (1933), "Du Gu Yuxiu 'Women xuyao zenyang de kexue' hou" 讀顧毓琇《我們需要怎樣的科學》後 (Having read Gu Yuxiu's 'What Kind of Science do we Need?'), *Duli pinglun*, 36, pp. 14–18.

Tianjin yishu gailiang she 天津藝術改良社 (1934), "Xin ciqu: Kexue jiuguo" 新詞曲：科學救國 (A New Piece of Poetry: Saving the Country by Science) *Tianjin shi shili tongshu tushu yuekan*, 4–6, pp. 50–51.

Wang Benxiang 王本祥 (1903), "Lun like yu qunzhi zhi guanxi" 論理科與群治之關係 (On the Relationship between Science and Governing the Masses), *Kexue shijie* 7.

— (1903–1904), "Dianqi da wang Aitisen zhuan" 電氣大王愛提森傳 (Biography of the King of Electricity Edison), *Kexue shijie*, 5, 6, 7, 8.

Wang Fan-sen (2000), *Fu Ssu-nien. A Life in Chinese History and Politics* (Cambridge Studies in Chinese History and Politics), Cambridge MA: Harvard University Press.

Wang Yangzong 王揚宗 (2006), "Yang Quan yu 'Zhongguo wu kexue' wenti" 楊銓與"中國無科學"問題 (Yang Quan and the Problem why China does not have Science), *Guangxi minzu xueyuan xuebao (ziran kexue ban)*, 12:3, pp. 34–36.

Wang Jingxi 汪敬熙 (1933), "Women xuyao zenyang de kexue de taolun" 我們需要怎樣的科學的討論 (Discussion on "What kind of Science do we Need"), *Duli pinglun*, 38, pp. 16–17.

Wang, Zuoyue (2002), "Saving China through Science. The Science Society, Scientific Nationalism, and Civil Society in Republican China", *Osiris*, 17, pp. 291–322.

Whewell, William (Hu Weili 胡威立) (1866), *Zhongxue* 重學 (An Elementary Treatise on Mechanics), transl. by Joseph Edkins (Ai Yuese 艾約瑟) and Li Shanlan 李善蘭.

Williamson, Alexander 韋廉臣 (1857), "Gewu qiongli lun" 格物窮理論 (On the sciences), *Liuhe congtan*, 6.

Yan Fu 嚴復 (1986), "Jiu wang jue lun" 救亡決論 (Decisive Words on our Salvation) in: Wang Shi 王栻 (ed), *Yan Fu ji* 嚴復集, Beijing: Zhonghua shuju, vol. 1, pp. 40–53.

— (1986). "Lun shibian zhi ji" 論世變之亟 (On the rapid change of the world), in: Wang Shi 王栻 (ed.), *Yan Fu ji* 嚴復集, vol. I, Beijing: Zhonghua shuju, pp. 1–4.

SCIENCE AND NATIONAL SALVATION

Wong Young-Tsu (2008), "The Search for Material Civilization: Kang Youwei's Journey to the West", *Taiwan Journal of East Asian Studies*, 5:1, pp. 33–59.

Xu Guoqi, *Olympic Dreams. China and Sports 1895–2008*, Cambridge MA: Harvard University Press, 2008.

Yang Quan 楊銓 (1914), "Kexue yu Zhongguo" 科學與中國 (Science and China), *Liumei xuesheng jibao*, 1:4 , pp. 65–69.

– (1916), "Kexue yu gonghe" 科學與共和 (Science and the Republic), *Kexue*, 2:2 , pp. 143–158.

Yen Fou (1977), *Les manifestes de Yen Fou. Traduit et présenté par François Houang*, Paris: Fayard.

Yen Hsiao-pei (2006), "Formation of Race and Racial Identity in China in the 1930s: Eugenic and Scientific Racial Revival and the China-based Cultural Reconstruction Debate", in: Zhongguo shehuikexueyuan jindaishi yanjiusuo (ed.), *1930niandaide Zhongguo* (China in the 1930s), (Beijing: Shehuikexue wenxuan chubanshe, pp. 704–719.

Yu Zuhua, Zhao Huifeng 俞祖華, 趙慧峰 (2015), "Minguo shiqi minzu fuxing huayu de san zhong taidu" 民國時期民族復興話語的三種態度 (Three Different Attitudes Reflected in the Discourse on National Renaissance during the Republican Era), *Zhongguo wenhua yanjiu*, pp. 59–73.

Zhang Yuanruo 章淵若 (1933), "Fuxing yundong zhi jidian" 復興運動之基點 (The Basic Points of the Renaissance Movement) in: *Fuxing yuekan*, 2:1, pp. 1–5.

Zhao Yuanren, Ren Hongjun, Hu Mingfu, Bing Zhi, Zhou Ren 趙元任, 任鴻雋, 胡明復, 秉志, 周仁 (1916), "Ben she zhi liu Mei tongxue shu" 本社致留美同學書 (Letter of our Society to the Chinese Students in America), *Kexue*, 2:10, pp. 1177–1178.

Zheng Yuan 鄭垣 (1933), "Jieshao yi pian kexue jiuguo dagushu" 介紹一篇科學救國大鼓書 (Introducing a Drum Song for Saving the Country with Science), *Jiaoyu zhoukan*, 150.

"Zhongguo kexuehua yundong xiehui dier qi gongzuo jihua dagang", 中國科學化運動協會第二期工作計劃大綱 (Outline of the working plan of the association for the Chinese scientification movement), *Kexue de Zhongguo* 5:5 (1935), pp. 3–6.

"Zhongguo kexuehua yundong xiehui faqi zhiqu shu" 中國科學化運動協會發起旨趣書 (On the purpose of initiating the China scientification movemen), *Kexue de Zhongguo*, 1:1 (1933), pp. 1–3.

Zhou, Gang (2006), "The Chinese Renaissance: A Transcultural Reading", in: Brenda Deen Schildgen, Gang Zhou and Sander L. Gilman, (eds.), *Other Renaissances: A New Approach to World Literature*, London: Palgrave MacMillan, pp. 113–132.

Zhu Hua 朱華 (2006), "Lun 'Liumei xuesheng jibao' yu kexue jiuguo xuanchuan" 論《留美學生季報》與科學救國宣傳, *Tianzhong xuekan*, 21:6, pp. 108–111.

Zhu Kezhen 竺可楨 (1937), "Xu" 序 (Preface) in: Zhu Kezhen, Lu Yudao, Li Zhenjiang (eds.), *Kexue de minzu fuxing*, Shanghai: Zhongguo kexue she, pp. I–II.

Zhu Kezhen, Lü Yudao, Li Zhenjiang 竺可楨，盧于道，李振翩 (1937), "Jielun" 結論 (Conclusion) in: Zhu Kezhen, Lu Yudao, Li Zhenjiang (eds.), *Kexue de minzu fuxing*, Shanghai: Zhongguo kexue she, pp. 281–284.

Capitalising on Crisis: The Expansion of the Late Qing Newspaper Market

Tze-ki Hon

In recent years, the significance of the late Qing newspaper market has been well documented. From the writings of Joan Judge, Barbara Mittler and Weipin Tsai, we learn that the late Qing newspaper market not only expanded by leaps and bounds after the Sino-Japanese War (1894–95), but also that it became part of a public forum to share information and ideas.[1] Along with other printed items (such as novels and textbooks), newspapers were instrumental in connecting different sectors of Chinese society and creating a collective identity among the Chinese people. As shown in the current scholarship, the growth of the newspaper market was partly due to the expansion of the late Qing infrastructure, particularly the postal, railway and shipping networks. At the same time, newspaper publishers were creative in using these communication networks to attract large numbers of readers and thereby making an impact on public opinion.

In this chapter, I will examine one commonly used strategy to increase readership—national disaster (*guonan* 國難). As the late Qing government was in the process of confronting a series of crises (including the palace *coup d'état* of 1898, the Boxer Rising of 1900, the death of Empress Dowager in 1908, *etc.*), newspaper publishers presented these crises as a continuing saga that revealed China's doomed fate at the turn of the twentieth century. To show the effectiveness of this strategy, I focus on *Zhengyi tongbao* 政藝通報 (Penetrative Reports on Political Thought and Technological Skills, 1902–1908). Edited and published by Deng Shi 鄧實 (1877–1951), *Zhengyi tongbao* was a hotchpotch of government documents, cable news, political commentaries, technological newsletters, and literary writings. This hybrid form, known as *baokan* 報刊 or *shubao* 書報, made *Zhengyi tongbao* partly a newspaper and partly a journal. By providing news, political analyses and technical information, *Zhengyi tongbao* linked the events unfolding in China to the developments of the Eurocentric global order.

In what follows, I will show that Deng Shi was effective in using various strategies to attract the attention of the readers. By focusing on national crises

---

1 See Judge (1996), *Print and Politics,* Mittler (2004), *A Newspaper for China?,* Tsai (2010), *Reading Shenbao.*

in particular, Deng Shi was able to expand the readership of *Zhengyi tongbao* to such an extent that, for six years, he could finance the publication of the newspaper-journal based solely upon subscription. To a great extent, the success of *Zhengyi tongbao* demonstrates the expansion of what Joan Judge calls "the middle realm", which became a hallmark of the New Policies period (1901–1911).[2]

Print Market and Time-Space Compression

Like many of the newspapers published in China in the early 1900s, *Zhengyi tongbao* was published in a treaty port, which, in turn, was linked to the global system of trade and transport. When the first issue of *Zhengyi tongbao* appeared in 1902, sixty years had passed since China had opened its ports and cities to Westerners. Now ocean-going ships travelled directly from London to Shanghai, ending the centuries-long separation of three discrete regions—the Atlantic, the Indian Ocean, and the South China Sea. Inside China, steamships had replaced sailing junks to carry passengers and goods from one end of the Yangzi River to the other, greatly reducing travel time from weeks to days, and from days to hours.[3] Although China was still behind other countries in the building of railways, thousands of miles of rail track had been laid by the end of the nineteenth century crisscrossing northern, central, and southern China.[4] The combined speed of land, river, and sea transportation gave rise to what David Harvey calls the "time-space compression" in which distance was shortened and travellers and goods could reach their destinations faster.[5]

In 1896, the veteran newspaper columnist Liang Qichao (梁啟超, 1873–1929) described the impact of this time-space compression in his usual crisp and vivid language. "In the present day," he wrote, "we have nations co-existing like next-door neighbours and continents linked together like friends in the same room."[6] In the early 1900s, in addition to Liang's striking metaphors of "next-door neighbours" (*bilin* 比鄰) and "sharing the same room" (*tongshi* 同

---

2 Joan Judge argues that the publishing industry (especially newspapers) became "the middle realm" in late Qing China that linked the state and society. See Judge (1996), *Print and Culture*, pp. 17–31.

3 For the changes in China's domestic and international shipping industry after 1842, see Chen Zhengshu (2002), "Yanjiang chengshi jiaotong".

4 For railway construction in late nineteenth-century China, see Chen Zhengshu (2002), "Yanjiang chengshi jiaotong".

5 For the concept of "space-time compression" (or "spacetime"), see Harvey (2009), *Cosmopolitanism and Geographies of Freedom*, pp. 133–165.

6 Liang Qichao (1896), "Lun baoguan youyi yu guoship. 100". The original line is: 今夫萬國並立，猶比鄰也。齊州以內，猶同室也。

室), the sense of proximity to lands far away was also conveyed in a variety of ways, such as "the ten thousand countries on the globe" (*diqiu wanguo* 地球萬國), "the world" (*shijie* 世界), and "the stage of the five continents" (*wuzhou zhi wutai* 五洲之舞臺).[7] The metaphor of the stage (*wutai* 舞臺) was particularly poignant in highlighting the proximity of far-flung lands when they were connected through intricate networks of cables, canals, railways, roads, shipping lines, telegraphs, and waterways. It evoked an image of people from different places sharing the same spot and at the same time.[8]

In the early 1900s, this sense of proximity and simultaneity was greatly enhanced by mechanised print technology that allowed the presses to produce large numbers of books, leaflets, magazines, newspapers and pamphlets quickly. Chinese "print capitalism", as Christopher Reed has suggested, triggered a rapid expansion of the print market, which combined traditional print culture with the efficiency of modern machines.[9] With the convenience of modern transportation and communication, many of these printed products were distributed rapidly and widely from the coast (where most of the presses were located) to various parts of the country. For the majority of the Chinese who could not afford to travel, their sense of proximity and simultaneity developed mainly from reading newspapers. In news reports, events that happened hundreds of miles away were rendered as though they had happened locally. For instance, Ma Xulun (馬敍倫, 1885–1970), a writer of *Zhengyi tongbao*, told us that, in 1900, residents in Hangzhou (杭州) learned about the foreign occupation of Beijing from three Shanghai newspapers: *Shenbao* (申報), *Xinwen bao* (新聞報), and *Zhongwai ribao* (中外日報). The newspaper reports brought home an event that took place hundreds of miles away.[10]

More importantly, in reading the same stories in the same newspapers, readers in different parts of China could participate in what Benedict Anderson calls "homogeneous empty time".[11] As a veteran newspaper columnist, Liang Qichao once described homogeneous empty time as "connectivity" (*tong* 通)—the same character that was used in *Zhengyi Tongbao*. Drawing on Chinese traditional medicine, Liang compared homogeneous empty time to the invisible nervous system within a human body that connects and energises limbs, organs, and the brain. When "connected" by newspapers, Liang told us, one could reach the world while still staying at home.[12]

---

7 For an example of how these three terms were used, see Deng Shi (1902d), "Xianfa".

8 For a detailed discussion of the implications of the metaphor of "the stage" (*wutai*) in China at the turn of the twentieth century, see Karl (2002), *Staging the World*, pp. 1–52.

9 Christopher A. Reed (2004), *Gutenberg in Shanghai*, pp. 1–9.

10 Ma Xulun (1947), *Wo zai liushi sui yiqian*, p. 11.

11 For the concept of homogeneous empty time, see Anderson (1991), *Imagined Communities*, pp. 22–36.

12 Liang Qichao (1896), "Lun baoguan youyi yu guoshi", p. 101.

Print Capitalism and Cultural Entrepreneurship

In many respects, *Zhengyi tongbao* was a product of the twentieth-century global trade. The bimonthly newspaper-journal was published by the Association for Preservation of National Learning (Guoxue Baocunhui 國學保存會) located on the Fourth Avenue (Simalu 四馬路) in the Anglo-American concessions in Shanghai. By the end of the nineteenth century, Shanghai had become the hub of domestic and foreign trade. It was the terminus of the trade and transport along the Yangzi River as well as the centre of international commerce and communication between China and the world. Despite perpetual conflicts among the residents of different races, the foreign concessions in Shanghai provided a lively environment where advanced foreign technology was introduced, corporate finance was readily available, and skilled workers were abundant.[13] With these advantages, Shanghai quickly became the capital of the burgeoning Chinese print capitalism. By Xiong Yuezhi's 熊月之 counting, there were 514 newspapers published in Shanghai from 1850 to 1911, almost one-third of the total number of newspapers published in the entire country.[14] Among the newspapers published in Shanghai was the foreign-owned *Wanguo gongbao* 萬國公報 (Globe magazine), which, at its height in 1898, enjoyed a circulation of 38,400 copies.[15]

As cultural producers based in Shanghai, the editors of *Zhengyi tongbao* were keenly aware of both the benefits and perils of print capitalism. Although they did not use the term *capitalism* in their writings, they knew they were dealing with a system that was designed for production, circulation, appropriation, and dispossession. They also understood that the capitalist system promoted cut-throat competition around the world in order to maximise profits and eliminate ineffective producers. More importantly, they realised that the capitalist system was full of contradictions and that the best way to understand it was to come to grips with its many paradoxes. Together, these insights allowed the writers of *Zhengyi tongbao* to see both the strengths and weaknesses of China as a player in global competition. The insights also gave them reasons to believe that, although China was slow in catching up with the West in the early twentieth century, it could someday "surpass Europe and America" (*ling'ou jiamei* 凌歐駕美) after it had mastered modern technological and production skills.[16]

---

13 For a discussion of the significance of Shanghai at the turn of the twentieth century, see Xiong Yuezhi (2002), "Yanjiang chengshi yu xixue zhuanbo".

14 Ibid., p. 683.

15 Ibid. pp. 685–686.

16 The phrase "surpass Europe and America" (*ling'ou jiamei*) appeared in Deng Shi (1903), "Shanghai zhengyi tongbao she bianji zhengyi congshu yuanqi", p. 1a.

The Double Meaning of "Opening to the Ocean"

Despite the convenience of travel and the benefit of reaching the world from one's home through reading newspapers, many Chinese had mixed feelings about the global system of trade and transport. After all, the system was imposed upon them by foreigners who used superior military power to force them to accept the terms and conditions of the system. Although often presented as being fair and open, the system was designed to advance the interests of Western powers, particularly those Britain. Worse still, in joining the system, the Chinese discovered that they needed to change many of their traditional practices in order to adapt to the global requirements.

To express these mixed feelings about joining the global system, the term *opening to the ocean* (*haitong* 海通) carried a double meaning. When used in a certain context, *opening to the ocean* could mean *literally* the opening of ports and cities along the coast. It described China's integration into the global system of trade and transport after the First Opium War (1839–1842). It also underscored the fact that the time when China dominated East Asia was long gone.[17] But when used in other context, *opening to the ocean* could mean the pains and sufferings that the country had endured since the First Opium War The term referred to a series of defeats and humiliations that had humbled the country. It registered the fact that Westerners had succeeded in expanding their influence into the heartland of China, drastically altering the everyday life of many Chinese.[18]

These two sides of *opening to the ocean* were particularly clear to people who lived in Shanghai. On the one hand, the foreign concessions in the treaty ports provided a dynamic environment where advanced technology was introduced and international finance was available. This dynamic environment spurred economic production and private entrepreneurship that made Shanghai the leading metropolis of China. On the other hand, under what Xiong Yuezhi calls "one city, three governments" (the Chinese, the French, and the Anglo-American), foreigners and Chinese lived in the same city, but were segregated in different neighbourhoods and spheres of activity.[19] When conflicts arose, foreigners always gained the upper hand by either exercising the rights of extra-territoriality through foreign diplomats in the city, or by appealing to imperial officials in Beijing.[20]

---

17 For the literal meaning of *haitong*, see Deng Shi (1902), "Zhengyi tongbao xu shang 政藝通報序上 (Preface to Zhengyi tongbao, part 1)", in *Zhengyi congshu* 1902, "Xuli 序例": 1a.

18 For the contemptuous meaning of *haitong*, see Deng Shi (1902a), "Diguozhuyi".

19 Xiong Yuezhi (2002), "Yanjiang chengshi yu xixue zhuanbo", pp. 334–347.

20 For some of the conflicts between local and foreign residents in Shanghai, see ibid., pp. 307–397.

Nevertheless, in the print industry, the two sides of *opening to the ocean* could be a lucrative market gambit. In 1902, Deng Shi began publishing *Zhengyi tong-bao*, which combined traditional imperial bulletins (*dibao* 邸報), news reports, political analyses, technological newsletters, and literary writing. Published bimonthly, the hybrid newspaper-journal was aimed at a wide variety of readers (see Figure 1). To maximise profits, it provided an array of information about politics, the economy, foreign policy, society, and technology. What made the bimonthly publication a sensation in its first few years of publication was Deng Shi's market-savvy move to highlight the paradox of *opening to the ocean*.

In two articles published in 1902 that explained the purpose of publishing *Zhengyi tongbao*, Deng Shi skilfully discussed China's perils and prospects in global competition. In one article, he focused on the sorrow of *opening to the ocean* by reminding readers of China's defeats and humiliation since 1842. To make his point, he described the Chinese loss of territories and prestige as "unprecedented in Chinese history" (*gu wei you ye* 古未有也) and called on his readers to contribute to the rebuilding of the country by learning political philosophy (*zheng* 政) and acquiring technological expertise (*yi* 藝).[21] By contrast, in the second article, Deng emphasised the benefits of *opening to the ocean*. Using *The Thames* in Britain and *Osaka News* in Japan as examples, he gave an upbeat account of a globally-connected world based upon print technology, the mass media, and journalism. In particular, he promoted journalism as a rewarding career for gifted writers who served as the liaison between the government and the people. Calling journalism "a study of interconnections" (*ertong zhixue* 二通之學), he highlighted the contribution that journalists made in linking the ruler and the ruled *vertically* and the different groups of people in society *horizontally*. Although Deng did not explicitly link journalism to the spread of print capitalism, he was confident that, when there were more newspapers in China, the "people's intelligence" (*minzhi* 民智) would be improved.[22]

This theme of a China which both benefited from and was humbled by "*opening to the ocean*" made *Zhengyi tongbao* an exciting newspaper-journal. The theme connected the manifold government documents, news reports, political analyses, and technical information into a riveting drama in which the Chinese were struggling to make sense of a perplexing situation. Like all drama, the excitement in reading about the Chinese saga came from having no immediate solution. Readers must read on to discover the next episode, which promised—but never delivered—a closure or solution. Although seemingly disjointed and purely factual, the reprinting of government documents (*shangyu* 上諭) and the

---

21 Deng Shi (1902e), "Zhengyi tongbao xu shang", p. 1a.
22 Deng Shi (1902f), "Zhengyi tongbao xu xia", pp. 1b–2a. Liang Qichao had made similar argument earlier in his famous essay on historical writing, cf. Liang Qichao (1902) "Xin shixue".

summary of national and international news in *Zhengyi tongbao* were important because they provided a glimpse of the complexity and fluidity of national and international events. Even though the news was reported bimonthly, rather than daily, the news accounts reminded readers that China was facing challenges that were not only multifaceted but also rapidly changing.

For Deng Shi, the government documents and the news reports were only the starting-point of a critical reflection on China's problems. While the government documents and the news reports conveyed the complexity and fluidity of national and international events, Deng argued that readers must put the information in the context of China's struggle to find its role in the twentieth-century global order. For this reason, Deng decided to publish *Zhengyi tongbao* bimonthly, so that the "monthly narratives based upon daily reports" (*riji yueshu* 日紀月書) would allow readers to develop their own opinions on China's fate. By connecting daily events to the broader picture, Deng suggested that the hybrid form of newspaper-journal would help readers, particularly government officials and educated élites, to find solutions for China's problems.[23]

To help readers "connect the dots", Deng Shi published an annual version of *Zhengyi tongbao*. Known as *Zhengyi congkan* 政藝叢刊 (Collection of [Writings on] Political Thought and Technological Skills), the annual version not only provided another source of revenue to the publishers by reprinting the bimonthly-journal one more time, it also offered (in Deng's words) "a reliable historical account" (*xinshi* 信史) that included a systematic arrangement of daily events and monthly reflections. The format of the annual version was slightly different from that of the bimonthly version. Rather than reprinting the twenty-four issues of *Zhengyi tongbao* as they had first appeared, Deng grouped the news accounts, the political analyses, and the featured articles according to themes, so that readers could follow an event, an issue, or an argument, from beginning to end. In such manner, Deng turned the twenty-four issues of the newspaper-journal into a book with a coherent theme, a clear argument, and an illuminating message. More significantly, through this double process of publishing news and analyses first bimonthly and then annually (*yuechu weibao nianding weishu* 月出為報，年訂為書), Deng highlighted both the fluidity and the underlying pattern of national and international events.[24]

---

23 Deng Shi (1903), "Shanghai zhengyi tongbao she bianji zhengyi congshu yuanqi".
24 Deng Shi (1903), "Shanghai zhengyi tongbao she bianji zhengyi congshu yuanqi."

Two Views of Natural Selection

A successful marketing gambit notwithstanding, the two sides of *opening to the ocean* pointed to a deeper issue: the conflict between the "scientistic" and the "humanistic" views of natural selection. By the early 1900s, the Chinese educated elites had learned about the universal law of evolution from Yan Fu's (嚴復, 1853–1921) translation of T.H. Huxley's *Evolution and Ethics*. Entitled *Tianyan lun* 天演論 (On Natural Evolution, 1898), Yan Fu's translation made two major concepts of social evolution popular: natural selection based upon competition (*wujing tianze* 物競天擇) and the survival of the fittest (*shizhe shencun* 適者生存).[25] The two concepts were popular because they explained China's defeats and humiliation based upon its backwardness in political, social, and technological development. More importantly, the two concepts provided justification for launching aggressive reforms to save China from being eliminated through natural selection. For many Chinese, particularly the educated élite, the occupation of Beijing by eight foreign powers in the year 1900 renewed their fear of China being eliminated from the globe.[26]

While the law of evolution helped to explain China's defeats and humiliation, it did not offer a clear solution to China's predicament. Looking at the *opening to the ocean* from the law of natural selection, China's defeats were inevitable as the world weeded out the weak and the unfit. From the standpoint of the collective good of humankind, the *opening to the ocean* benefited all peoples around the globe (including the Chinese) by pushing them to reach a higher stage of development through fierce competition. For those who adopted this perspective, they focused on the progress in technological transfer and economic growth in China after the First Opium War. Some went a step further by explaining the schema by which to measure social evolution. Invariably, they put China one or two stages behind Europe and the United States, showing that the Chinese must endure what was unendurable in order to catch up with the Westerners. As one author noted in *Zhengyi tongbao*, the law of evolution was like "a circle without a beginning or an end" (*ruhuan wuduan* 如環無端) that was open and fair to everyone. Being behind in evolution, the author argued, the Chinese should blame themselves for their defeats and humiliation.[27]

---

25 On the impact of *Tianyan lun* on Chinese intellectuals in cities such as Shanghai, see Xiong Yuezhi (1994), *Xixue dongjian yu wanqing shehui*, pp. 681–686. On the intellectual background of Yan Fu's translation, see Max Ko-Wu Huang (2008), *The Meaning of Freedom: Yan Fu and the Origins of Chinese Liberalism*, pp. 65–114.

26 Deng Shi frequently used the 1900 occupation of Beijing as an example of China's danger of being eliminated in global competition. See, for instance, Deng Shi (1903), "Shanghai zhengyi tongbao she bianji zhengyi congshu yuanqi", p. 1a.

27 He Tingmo (1903), "Tianyan lun shuhou", p. 6a.

Capitalising on Crisis

However, when viewing the *opening to the ocean* from the perspective of the victims or the losers, the event looked tragic and distasteful. For those who adopted this perspective, they focused on the savage killings in battles, the creation of treaty ports, the unfair treatment of local residents in foreign concessions, and, above all, the loss of China's prestige among its neighbouring states. They questioned why the law of natural selection was so brutal and merciless, and resulted in the killing of many innocent people and the destruction of properties and lands. They questioned the intent of global competition when it was conducted so ferociously with the winners showing no mercy for their fellow human beings.

In *Zhengyi tongbao*, Deng Shi was a vocal supporter of the humanistic view of natural selection. In an article in 1902 written to celebrate the dawn of the new century, he began with what seemed to be an affirmation of the scientistic view of perpetual progress:

With the Eastern and Western hemispheres connected by transportation networks and the new and old cultures united in marriage, we will enjoy the fortunes of the golden world and the happiness of tea and cotton production. This is our time. Indeed, this is the time of our twentieth century.[28]

Following this glorification of the global system of trade and transport, Deng immediately changed tone and turned to the humanists' view of natural selection. He drew attention to Chinese suffering during the second half of the nineteenth century. He wrote:

However, as people in the East and the West welcome the new century with fragrant flowers and honour it with bells and songs, we should not forget the nineteenth century because it gave birth to the twentieth century. Without the nineteenth century, there would not have been the twentieth century. The nineteenth century was the stage where [nations in] the whole world competed [with one another].[29]

In bringing up the theme of nineteenth-century competition, Deng skilfully reminded his readers of the defeats, humiliation, and suffering that global competition had brought to China. Particularly revealing was the "stage" metaphor that he used to describe the global competition of power. Similar to the *opening to the ocean*, the "stage" (*wutai* 舞臺) had a double meaning. In addition to the usual meaning of "the stage of the five continents" that referred to the intricate networks of roads, railways, waterways, rivers, and shipping routes, the "world

---

28 Deng Shi (1902c), "Shijiu shiji mo shijie zhi zhengzhi lun ", pp 37a–37b. The original is: 通東西半球之郵，結新舊兩文化之婚，享黃金世界之幸福，食茶棉生涯之樂利。今豈非二十周新世紀之景象乎！

29 Ibid., p. 37b. The original is: 雖然東西人莫不香花以歡迎此世紀，鐘鼓以歌舞此世紀矣，然吾腦中所不能忘情者，則十九世紀也。蓋十九世紀者，二十世紀之母也。無十九世紀不能生二十世紀。十九世紀世界一大競爭之舞臺。

stage" also evoked a sinister image of brutality and mercilessness in the global completion of national power. In addition to being a platform for actors or performers to express their artistic talents, the "world stage" was also a Colosseum in which the strong hunted down the weak, and the powerful exterminated the powerless.

Because of the brutality and mercilessness of global competition, Deng Shi was both hopeful and fearful about the future of China. He argued that, whereas the nineteenth century was "the age of nationalism", the twentieth century would be "the age of nationalist imperialism".[30] As global competition became more intense in the twentieth century, when it expanded its scope from military confrontation to economic rivalry, it would become even more brutal and hostile. The site of competition would move from the battlefields to the everyday lives of ordinary people. Hence, competition would involve people from every sector of society, extending from the cities to the countryside and from the coast to the hinterlands. When the scope and scale of competition expanded exponentially, he predicted that China would face more challenges in global competition. And yet, even though the future of China was not promising, he rallied his countrymen to do whatever they could to participate in global competition. He urged his readers to work hard to expel foreign imperialists and to dominate the Pacific Ocean region.[31]

Capitalising on National Crises

In the early 1900s, this conflict between the scientistic and humanistic views of natural selection was not just idle talk among writers who wanted to sell newspapers. The conflict had direct repercussions on the direction of the New Policies of the Qing government. One of the contentions among the New Policies reformers was the type of political structure that the Qing government would build in order to catch up with the world. Should it be a constitutional monarchy like Meiji Japan or the republican system in France and the United States?

In *Zhengyi tongbao*, there was no consensus on this issue. Worst still, even the supporters of the "scientistic" view of natural selection could not come to an agreement on the specific stage that China had reached in evolution. As a result, both constitutional monarchy and republicanism seemed to be acceptable,

---

30 Deng Shi (1902c), "Shijiu shiji mo shijie zhi zhengzhi lun", p. 37b. The original is: 十九世紀為民族主義之時代，二十世紀為民族帝國之時代。

31 Deng Shi (1902c), "Shijiu shiji mo shijie zhi zhengzhi lun", p. 40a. The original statement is: 吾願吾同胞之青年血性男子，普天下造時勢之英雄，揮洒其熱血，犧牲其赤心，以橫衝於世界經濟競爭、驚濤駭浪之大劇場，而摯我國旗之大光輝，雪亞洲白人殖民之奇辱。

depending on one's perspective.[32] Another contentious issue among the New Policies reformers was the status of the *literati* (*shi* 士) when the Qing government prepared to abolish the civil service examinations. As journalists and essayists, some *Zhengyi tongbao* writers saw their writings as fulfilling some of the work previously assigned to the *literati*, such as connecting the government and the people. On this score, the supporters of the "scientistic" view of natural selection appeared to triumph over the supporters of the "humanistic" view of natural selection. Showing the inevitability of linear progression, the supporters of the "scientistic" view of natural selection emphasised the growth of print technology, the expansion of the print market, and the impact of reaching millions of people through journals, magazines and newspapers.[33] And yet, despite their optimism about the post-examination society, none of the *Zhengyi tongbao* writers directly challenged the traditional system of the "four groups of people" (*si min* 四民)—scholars, farmers, artisans, and merchants. As cultural workers who made a living from the print market, the *Zhengyi tongbao* writers found themselves in an awkward situation in which they were partly *literati* and partly merchants, but they could not claim to be either one of them.[34]

One may argue that this lack of consensus in *Zhengyi tongbao* is precisely its success, being what Joan Judge calls "the middle realm" between the state and society. The communication between the rulers and the ruled did not need to be uniform or scripted because the key point was to convey opinions and views between the two parties. One may also argue that the polyphony in *Zhengyi tongbao* exemplified the "fin-de-siècle splendour" that David Der-wei Wang identifies as the "repressed modernity" in China at the turn of the twentieth century.[35] The confusion and the competing voices in *Zhengyi tongbao* brought forth liveliness in a debate in which new ideas and concepts emerged out of disagreement.

Showing his gift as a cultural entrepreneur, in 1903 Deng Shi took advantage of this polyphony of *Zhengyi tongbao* by offering discount coupons to readers who would buy the combined set of the first twenty-four issues of the newspaper-journal (see the top half of Figure 2). Now in its third printing after

---

32 Deng Shi appeared to be of two minds regarding constitutional monarchy and republicanism. When he discussed the stages of political evolution, he supported constitutional monarchy due to China being behind in political development. See Deng Shi (1902g), "Zhengzhi xueshu". But when he discussed the power of the people, he supported republicanism. See Deng Shi (1902c),"Shi renquan.

33 Li Zhenduo (1902), "Junquan zhi jieshuo", Kato Hiroyuki (1903), "Xinwen zhi yu zazhi zhi guanxi".

34 This confusion of not being able to fit journalists, writers, and publishers into the traditional system of *simin* is clearly shown in Li Zhenduo [See above note]. In the article, Li tried to explain the new roles that *simin* would play in a modern nation-state. But he had a hard time discussing the role of the *literati* (*shi* 士).

35 Wang (1997), *Fin-de-siècle*, pp. 13–52.

thousands of copies had been sold, the combined set of the newspaper-journal was sold at the reduced price of three silver dollars rather than the original four silver dollars. At a lower price, Deng Shi said, readers would receive "a useable and practical book" because of its faithful reports of events in the country since "the national disaster of 1900" (*gengzi guonan* 庚子國難). By referring to the combined set as "a book" (*shu* 書), Deng highlighted the cohesion of what appeared to be a hotchpotch of official documents, news columns, and political commentaries. And by reminding readers of the recent occupation of Beijing by foreign powers and the reforms that the Qing court had launched to strengthen the country, Deng underscored the urgency and utility of reading the newspaper-journal. For readers who were eager to learn more about China's fate, Deng Shi suggested that they buy the combined set, which showed China's predicament in the global age. If they had a bit more money in their pockets, he urged them to subscribe immediately to the 1904 *Zhengyi tongbao* at a deep discount price with another coupon (see the lower bottom of Figure 3). Indeed, as a skilful cultural entrepreneur, Deng knew how to sell products.

Conclusion

In reviewing the development of print capitalism in China in the early twentieth century, it is clear that print, profit, and perception took turn to influence the publishing industry. While print technology gave impetus to the growth of the print market, the rapid increase in the number of readers reinforced the need for efficient print machines. Also fuelling the expansion of the reader market were the national crises of China's failures in global competition, and the drastic political and social reforms undertaken by the Qing government to turn imperial subjects into citizens. For the editors of newspapers and journals, national crises and national projects were lucrative assets because they drew the immediate attention of their readers. Yet, while it is clear that print, profit, and perception each played a role in changing the Chinese publishing industry, it is also clear that, at any given moment, it was always a combination of factors— cultural, economic, political, or technological—that shaped the players' decisions. For players in the newspapers industry, making the right decision was not easy, because it involved risks, calculations, and betting on the political wind.

One difficult decision was the readership. In the 1900s, the editors of *Zhengyi tongbao* found themselves in an awkward situation in which they were neither "global" enough to be part of the transnational enterprises (such as the Commercial Press) that controlled the lion's share of readership, nor "local" enough to specialise in serving the wealthy clients of specialised interests. This conundrum forced the writers of *Zhengyi tongbao* to ponder the different options. As the "middle realm" between the government and the people, should they serve the government by joining the propaganda regime, or should they continue to preserve their independence as "the voice of the people" in the print market? When the nation was under threat, should they focus on making a profit by providing the readers with what they wanted to read, or should they save the nation by writing about what the readers should know. Eventually, the editors of *Zhengyi tongbao* settled on targeting a small group of educated élites, namely, government officials, provincial leaders, and cultural élites. They believed that the political and cultural élites would be the leaders of the new Chinese nation because of their deep knowledge of China's past and their self-sacrificing mission. Although the political and cultural élites were small in number in terms of the national print market, the editors of *Zhengyi tongbao* believed that it was worthwhile to trade its market share for a bigger impact on future national leaders.

Another difficult decision was how to present national crises in a way which would boost the sale of newspapers. As Weipin Tsai points out, reporting on wars and national disasters were always an effective way to attract reader attention. As shown in her detailed study of the reports on the Sino-Japanese War (1894–95), Tsai concludes that:

[t]he Chinese public was extremely eager to read any news that could be gathered about the war, and newspaper proprietors grasped this opportunity to promote their businesses, competing to provide the latest information using wartime reporting practices already established in Britain and the United States.[36]

Nevertheless, once wars were over or national crises were under control, newspapers proprietors had difficulty in continuing to maintain reader interest when they turned their attention to normal life. In this regard, the editors of *Zhengyi tongbao* were unique because they did not put emphasis on national disasters *per se*, but on how national disasters might trigger a rethinking of the political and social orders. By adopting the hybrid format of newspaper-journal, the editors of *Zhengyi tongbao* were able to use the foreign occupation of Beijing in 1900 as the starting-point to chronicle and assess the New Policies. Consequently, by providing "a monthly narrative based upon daily news", they were able to keep their readers' attention focused on the big picture of China's changing role in the global system.

Certainly, the influence of the newspaper-journal format was limited. It was only targeted at a special group of readers who looked for informed discussion of national events. For the vast majority of readers, they would find the news-

---

36 Weipin Tsai (2014), "The First Casualty: Truth, Lies and Commercial Opportunism in Chinese Newspapers during the First Sino-Japanese War".

paper-journal format too slow and too detached to capture the emotions and tension of the events unfolding. And yet, notwithstanding their small number,[37] the readers of *Zhengyi tongbao* would probably have a bigger impact on the nation's reforms because they were keenly interested in the debate over the Qing government's "New Policies". They were, in Deng Shi's terms, the practitioners of "the study of interconnections" (*ertong zhixue*) that linked the ruler and the ruled *vertically*, and the different groups of people in society *horizontally*.

Illustrations

Figure 1: The cover of the 1907 Zhengyi tongbao. On the right-hand side of the cover, the editors announced that the newspaper-journal was going to be printed with new printing technology.

---

37 There is no accurate number of copies of *Zhengyi tongbao* and *Zhengyi congshu* published from 1902 to 1908. But in the 1903 advertisement that offered discount rates to readers or distributors who bought stack of *Zhengyi congshu*, the expected readership of *Zhengyi congshu* in that year should have been in the hundreds. The biggest discount was 50% cut of the listed price for distributors who sold 100 copies.

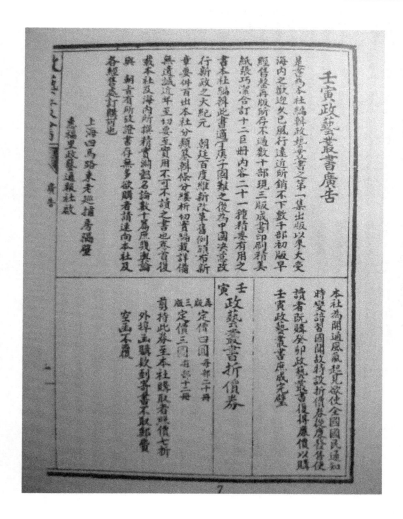

Figure 2: The advertisement page in the 1903 Zhengyi congshu. At the bottom left corner was the discount coupon for ordering 1903 Zhengyi tongbao.

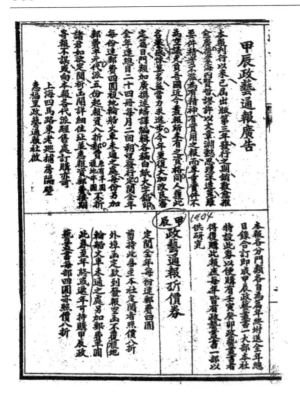

Figure 3: The advertisement for 1904 Zhengyi tongbao. In the lower bottom is a discount coupon for 1904 Zhengyi tongbao readers.

Bibliography

Anderson, Benedict (1991), *Imagined Communities: Reflections on the Origin and Spread of Nationalism*, revised edition. London: Verso Books.

Chen Zhengshu 陈正书 (2002),"Yanjiang chengshi jiaotong jiegou jindaihua 沿江城市交通結構近代化 (The Modernisation of the Structure of Transportation in Cities along the Yangzi River)", in: Zhang Zhongli, Xiong Yuezhi, and Shen Zuwei (eds.), *Changjiang yuanjiang chengshi yu Zhongguo jindaihua*. Shanghai: Shanghai renmin chubanshe, pp. 272–315.

Deng Shi 鄧實 (1902a), "Diguo zhuyi 帝國主義 (Imperialism), *Zhengyi congshu*, 1902, (Zhengyi tonglun waipian 政藝通論外篇), pp. 9a–9b.

— (1902b), "Shi renquan" 釋人權 (On People's Rights), *Zhengyi congshu* (Zhengxue wenpian), pp. 23b–24a.

- (1902c), "Shijiu shiji mo shijie zhi zhengzhi lun 十九世紀末之政治論 (The Political Theories at the End of the Nineteenth Century", *Zhengyi congshu* (Zhengxue wenpian 政學文篇), pp. 37a–40a.
- (1902d), "Xianfa 憲法 (On Constitution)", *Zhengyi congshu* (Zhengxue tonglun 政藝通論), pp. 10a–10b.
- (1902e), "Zhengyi tongbao xu shang 政藝通報序上 (Preface to Zhengyi tongbao, Part 1)", *Zhengyi congshu*, 1902, Xuli 序例, 1a.
- (1902f), "Zhengyi tongbao xu xia 政藝通報序下 (Preface to Zhengyi tongbao, Part 2)", *Zhengyi congshu*, 1902, *Xuli* 序例: pp. 1b–2a.
- (1902g). "Zhengzhi xueshu 政治學述 (A Discussion of Political Theories)", *Zhengyi congshu 1902, Zhengxue wenpian* 政學文篇, pp. 27b–32b.
- (1903), "Shanghai zhengyi tongbao she bianji zhengyi congshu yuanqi 上海政藝通報社編輯政藝叢書緣起 (The Reasons for Publishing Zhengyi congshu by the Editors of Zhengyi tongbao in Shanghai), *Zhengyi congshu* 1903, p. 1a.

Harvey, David (2009), *Cosmopolitanism and Geographies of Freedom*, New York: Columbia University Press, 2009.

He Tingmo 賀廷謨 (1903) "Tianyan lun shuhou 天演論書後 (After Reading Tianyan lun)", *Zhengyi congshu* (Zhengxue wenpian), p. 6a.

Huang, Max Ko-Wu (2008), *The Meaning of Freedom: Yan Fu and the Origins of Chinese Liberalism*, Hong Kong: The Chinese University of Hong Kong..

Judge, Joan (1996), *Print and Culture: 'Shibao' and the Culture of Reform in Late Qing China*, Stanford CA: Stanford University Press.

Karl, Rebecca E. (2002), *Staging the World: Chinese Nationalism at the Turn of the Twentieth Century*, Durham NC: Duke University Press.

Kato Hiroyuki 加籐弘之 (1903). "Xinwen zhi yu zazhi zhi guanxi" 新聞紙與雜誌的關係 (The Relationship between Newspapers and Journals)", *Zhengyi congshu* (Zhengxue wenpian 政學文篇), p. 20b.

Li Zhenduo 李振鐸 (1902), "Junquan zhi jieshuo" 君權之界説 (On the Limits of the Power of the Emperor), *Zhengyi congshu* 1902, (Zhengxue wenpian 政學文篇), pp. 24a–27b.

Liang Qichao 梁啓超 (1896 [1989]), "Lun baoguan youyi yu guoshi 論報館有益於國事 (The Benefits of Newspapers on National Affairs)", in: Liang Qichao, *Yinbingshi quanji, wenji*, vol. 1 (*Bianfa tongyi* 變法通議), Beijing: Zhonghua shuju, pp. 100–103.
- (1902 [1989]), "Xin shixue 新史學 (New Historiography)" ,in Liang Qichao, *Yinbingshi quanji. Wenji* (The Collected Works from the Studio of Ice-drinker: Articles), vol. 1. Beijing: Zhonghua shuju.

Ma Xulun 馬敍倫 (1947), *Wo zai liushi sui yiqian* 我在六十歳以前 (My First Sixty Years). Shanghai: Shenghuo shudian.

Mittler, Barbara (2004), *A Newspaper for China? Power, Identity, and Change in Shanghai's News Media, 1872–1912*, Cambridge MA: Harvard University Press.

Reed, Christopher A (2004), *Gutenberg in Shanghai: Chinese Print Capitalism, 1876–1937*. Honolulu: University of Hawaii Press.

Tsai, Weipin (2010), *Reading Shenbao. Nationalism, Consumerism and Individuality in China 1919–37*, London: Palgrave Macmillan.
- (2014), "The First Casualty: Truth, Lies and Commercial Opportunism in Chinese Newspapers during the First Sino-Japanese War", in: Lin, Pei-yin, Tsai Weipin (eds.),

Print, Profit, and Perception: Ideas, Information and Knowledge in Chinese Societies, 1895–1949, Leiden: Brill, pp. 216–240.

Wang, David Der-wei (1997), *Fin-de-siècle Splendor: Repressed Modernities of Late Qing Fiction, 1849–1911*, Stanford CA: Stanford University Press.

Xiong Yuezhi 熊月之 (1994). *Xixue dongjian yu wanqing shehui* 西學東漸與晚清社會 (Western Learning and Late Qing Society). Shanghai: Shanghai renmin chubanshe.

— (2002), "Yanjiang chengshi yu xixue zhuanbo" 沿江城市與西學轉播 (Cities along the Yangzi River and the Dissemination of Western Learning), in: Zhang Zhongli, Xiong Yuezhi and Shen Zuwei (eds.), *Changjiang yuanjiang chengshi yu Zhongguo jin-daihua*, Shanghai: Shanghai renmin chubanshe, pp. 653–70.

Acknowledgements

This volume is the result of an international conference organised at Goethe-University, Frankfurt am Main in December 2015 within the framework of the Collaborative Research Cluster "Discourses of Weakness and Resource-Regimes" funded by the Deutsche Forschungsgemeinschaft. Special thanks go to the members and the staff of the research cluster, especially Mi Anh Duong. The conference organisation was in the hands of Sebastian Riebold, who also supported the compilation of this book. Parts of the translations were done by Mei Chen, for which we express our gratitude. I would like to thank Benjamin Steiner (Gotha) for important suggestions. Special thanks go to Chris Engert in Florence for the language revision and copy-editing of this book.

Iwo Amelung

Frankfurt am Main, April 2020

Authors

Iwo Amelung is professor of Chinese studies at Goethe-University, Frankfurt am Main. His main research is on intellectual and scientific contact between China and the West in the late 19th century and the history of science in 19th and 20th century China.

Clemens Büttner is lecturer at the Department of Chinese Studies at Goethe-University, Frankfurt am Main. His main research areas are the history of modernisation of China from the late Qing period up to the present day, with a particular focus on the military and Chinese nationalism.

Daniel Hausmann is a post-doctoral fellow at the International Consortium for Research in the Humanities at University of Erlangen-Nuremberg. His main research area is the history of the Qing dynasty with a focus on natural disasters and official discourses.

Tze-ki Hon 韓子奇 is professor at the Department of Chinese and History of City University of Hong Kong. His main research focus is the social and intellectual history of modern China and topics related to the Book of Changes (*Yijing*).

Huang Xingtao 黃興濤 is professor and dean of the School of History at Renmin University in Beijing. He is researching modern Chinese history with a special focus on intellectual and cultural exchanges.

Li Fan 李帆 is professor at the school of history of Beijing Normal University. His research mainly covers issues of intellectual history during the late Qing and early Republican era, as well as questions related to history textbooks, in a broad sense.

Li Lifeng 李里峰 is professor of political science at the School of Government at Nanjing University. His research covers Chinese politics in the 20th century, history of political thought, as well as issues of conceptual history.

Sebastian Riebold is a fellow at Goethe-University, Frankfurt am Main. His main research areas are the intellectual sphere of late nineteenth and early twentieth century China, as well as the history and exegetical techniques of commentaries on the Chinese Classics.

Sun Qing 孫青 is associate professor at the Department of History, Fudan University in Shanghai. Her research interests include modern Chinese history and the history of cross-cultural interactions.

Mirjam Tröster is lecturer at the Department of Chinese Studies at Goethe-University, Frankfurt am Main. Her key research areas are modern Chinese-language performing arts and literature.

Jui-sung Yang 楊瑞松 is professor at the Department of History of National Chengchi University in Taipeh. He specialises in Chinese intellectual and cultural history, and is also researching the realm of psychohistory.

Zhiyi Yang 楊治宜 is professor of Chinese studies at Goethe-University, Frankfurt am Main. She has written extensively on traditional Chinese literary and aesthetics and now focuses her research on historical memory as well as the question of modern nationalism.

Zhang Ke 章可 is associate professor in the Department of History and International Center for Studies of Chinese Civilisation at Fudan University. His research interests include modern Chinese intellectual history, comparative intellectual history and the global history of cultural exchange.

Zhang Qing 章清 is professor of history at Fudan-University, Shanghai. He has published widely on intellectual and cultural history in late 19th and early 20th century China with a special focus on Chinese-foreign interaction.

Zou Zhenhuan 鄒振環 is professor of history at Fudan University, Shanghai. He is the author of numerous books and articles related to the translation of Western geographical and historical knowledge into Chinese during the Qing-dynasty.